BRITISH ACADEMY CENTENARY

1902-2002

ARCHAEOLOGY

THE WIDENING DEBATE

ARCHAEOLOGY

The Widening Debate

EDITED BY
Barry Cunliffe
Wendy Davies
Colin Renfrew

Published for THE BRITISH ACADEMY
by OXFORD UNIVERSITY PRESS

Oxford University Press, Great Clarendon Street, Oxford OX2 6DP

Oxford New York

Athens Auckland Bangkok Bogotá Buenos Aires Cape Town
Chennai Dar es Salaam Delhi Florence Hong Kong Istanbul Karachi
Kolkata Kuala Lumpur Madrid Melbourne Mexico City Mumbai Nairobi
Paris São Paulo Shanghai Singapore Taipei Tokyo Toronto Warsaw
and associated companies in
Berlin Ibadan

British Library Cataloguing in Publication Data
Data available

ISBN 0–19–726255–4

Typeset in Palatino
by J&L Composition Ltd., Filey, North Yorkshire
Printed in Great Britain
on acid-free paper by
Bookcraft Ltd
Midsomer Norton, Somerset

Contents

List of Contributors

PETER BELLWOOD
School of Archaeology and Anthropology, Australian National University, Canberra, ACT 0200, Australia

ANNA MARIA BIETTI SESTIERI
Soprintendenza Archeologica per l'Abruzzo, Palazzo Zambra – via degli Agostiniani 14, 66100 Chieti, Italy

ROBIN BOAST
Museum of Archaeology and Anthropology, Downing Street, Cambridge, CB2 3DZ

MARTIN CARVER
Department of Archaeology, University of York, The King's Manor, York, YO1 7EP

ALBERTO CAZZELLA
Cattedra di Paletnologia, Università di Roma "La Sapienza", Rome, Italy

GEORGE L. COWGILL
Department of Anthropology, Arizona State University, Tempe, AZ 85287, USA

BARRY CUNLIFFE
Institute of Archaeology, 36 Beaumont Street, Oxford, OX1 2PG

WILLIAM W. FITZHUGH
Director, Arctic Studies Center, National Museum of Natural History, Smithsonian Institution, Washington DC 20560, USA

ROBERT FOLEY
Leverhulme Centre for Human Evolutionary Studies, Department of Biological Anthropology, Downing Street, Cambridge, CB2 3DZ

MARTIN HALL
Centre for African Studies, University of Cape Town, Private Bag, Rondebosch 7700, South Africa

A.F. HARDING
Department of Archaeology, University of Durham, South Road, Durham, DH1 3LE

MICHELLE HEGMON
Department of Anthropology, Arizona State University, Tempe, AZ 85287, USA

C.F.W. HIGHAM
Department of Anthropology, University of Otago, PO Box 56, Dunedin, New Zealand

IAN HODDER
Department of Cultural and Social Anthropology, Stanford University, Stanford, CA 94305, USA

RHYS JONES
The Research School of Pacific and Asian Studies, Australian National University, Canberra, ACT 0200, Australia

VINCENT M. LAMOTTA
Department of Anthropology, University of Arizona, Tucson, Arizona 85721, USA

WILLIAM A. LONGACRE
Department of Anthropology, University of Arizona, Tucson, Arizona 85721, USA

NICK MERRIMAN
Institute of Archaeology, University College London, 31–34 Gordon Square, London, WC1H 0PY

GEORGE R. MILNER
Department of Anthropology, Pennsylvania State University, State College, PA 16802, USA

K. PADDAYYA
Department of Archaeology, Deccan College, Pune 411 006, India

GUSTAVO G. POLITIS
CONICET-Facultad de Ciencias Sociales, Universidad Nacional del Centro de la Pcia. de Buenos Aires, Argentina

NICHOLAS POSTGATE
Trinity College, Cambridge, CB2 1TQ

WILLIAM L. RATHJE
Archaeology Center, Stanford University, Stanford, CA 94305, USA

COLIN RENFREW
The McDonald Institute for Archaeological Research, Downing Street, Cambridge, CB2 3ER

ALAIN SCHNAPP
Professeur d'Archéologie, Université Paris 1, Sorbonne, Paris, France

MATTHEW SPRIGGS
School of Archaeology and Anthropology, A.D. Hope Building, Australian National University, Canberra, ACT 0200, Australia

Preface

The idea for this book was developed by a small working party set up by the Archaeology Section of the British Academy. The working party determined that the scope would be world-wide and the mood celebratory. The guide-lines were set down and a list of possible contributors drawn up. The three editors were then entrusted to see the volume through to completion. The work has taken a little longer to bring together than we originally anticipated not least because our contributors all have heavy commitments but we are grateful to them for accepting to take part in the first place and bearing, with such good grace, our gentle reminders.

The volume has been coordinated at the Institute of Archaeology, University of Oxford, the project being managed with exemplary efficiency and skill by Lynda Smithson to whom we are deeply indebted not only for keeping us all at work but also for her considerable editorial input. That the volume appears in the centenary year is entirely due to her.

The Academy's editorial team under James Rivington has been responsible for the design of the book and for guiding it through the press.

Barry Cunliffe
Oxford
21.vi.01

It is with great sadness that we have to record the death of Rhys Jones while this book was in press.

Archaeology and the British Academy

BARRY CUNLIFFE

This book is a celebration by archaeologists world-wide of the strengths, the energies and the sheer intellectual excitement of their discipline. It sets out unashamedly to proclaim what we all believe, that over the last hundred years archaeology has transformed itself from a genteel antiquarian pursuit, deeply rooted in the classical tradition, to a rigorous and demanding discipline, spanning the humanities and the sciences, yet at the same time one widely accessible to the public at large.

The occasion to compile this work was provided by the impending centenary of the British Academy. Wishing to mark the occasion the Council of the Academy invited the different sections to suggest ways in which their aims and aspirations might best be recorded. The Archaeology Section chose to produce a book written by archaeologists from around the world, who were asked, within the constraints of a short essay focused on their own region or studies, to give their personal views on what archaeology has achieved and where they believe it to be heading. The result is *Archaeology: The Widening Debate*.

The British Academy has long been an active supporter of the pursuit of archaeology throughout the world. In the first 50 years of its existence, it must be admitted that, despite the best efforts of such key figures as Sir Frederic Kenyon, comparatively little was achieved, for want of funds to back good intentions; but when, in 1949, Sir Mortimer Wheeler became Secretary to the Academy (a post which he held for 20 years) all this changed — though arguably to the detriment of other subjects. Wheeler had a broad vision and proceeded to implement it with his customary energy, coupled with persuasive skills practised on the nation's financial custodians. One of the first beneficiaries were the Schools and Institutes abroad.

Britain, like other West European countries, had begun in the late nineteenth century to establish Schools abroad to facilitate a variety of academic studies, most particularly archaeology. The British School in Athens was founded in 1885 and that in Rome in 1901. Others were to follow, Jerusalem in 1919, Iraq in 1932 and Ankara in 1948. These, together with the Egyptian Exploration Society, were variously, and usually precariously, funded and were constantly looking to Government to provide for financial support. Reviewing the situation in 1950 Wheeler saw that 'some measure of tidying up in the administration of these partially similar but also partially disparate institutions . . . had become inevitable and indeed urgent'. Focusing his energies on the problem he soon secured a reasonable level of government funding for the Schools which thereafter was administered through the Academy. This done, the Academy, inspired by Wheeler's vision, went on to establish the British Institute in East Africa in 1960, the British Institute in Iran in 1961 and the British School in Amman in 1978.

In parallel with this activity the Academy administers research funds from a variety of sources a percentage of which supports archaeological fieldwork and associated research. In 1994, before the creation of the Humanities Research Board, it was contributing £350,000 towards excavations and field projects around the world. Other funds were sending British scholars on academic visits abroad while providing for foreign scholars to visit Britain. In more recent years the Archaeology Section, through the Academy, has been able to organize a series of international conferences which have led to major research publications.

The last half century has seen not only an increase in archaeological activity on the part of the Academy, but also an extension in its geographical range. Fifty years ago the focus was very much European, Mediterranean and Near Eastern: now it is world-wide as the spread of Corresponding Fellows shows.

In planning this book we have invited contributions from archaeologists throughout the world. Our intention has been to provide a comprehensive geographical cover to which we have added a few more general themes. The brief we gave to our authors was summary — the purpose of the book was to celebrate the achievements of archaeology world-wide and to look to the future. We wanted to show archaeology as a fast-changing, forward-looking discipline, ever expanding our understanding of human achievement. Given the constraints of space we accepted that each contribution would have to be highly selective but in what the individual author chose to focus on would lie the fascination. This, and the theme title, were all the guidance that the contributors were given. Our intention was to offer freedom, not to circumscribe or constrain. The result is, as we had hoped, not a sterile textbook but a brightly coloured kaleidoscope of archaeological endeavour. Here is the discipline laid bare, its successes and aspirations, its social consciousness and concerns, robust in its infinite variety. We are immeasurably indebted to our colleagues from across the world for joining us in our celebration.

Parallel tracks in time: Human evolution and archaeology

ROBERT FOLEY

Introduction

At first sight, human evolution and archaeology are intimately linked. In the public mind discoveries of new fossils are largely referred to as archaeological finds, and seen as part of the body of archaeological knowledge, along with such glories as Schleimann's tomb and Sutton Hoo. The discoveries of the Leakeys at Olduvai Gorge in Tanzania were the fundamental starting point for the African hominids origins paradigm that dominated the second half of the twentieth century, and the techniques and approaches that they used were classically archaeological. The excavations at Klasies River Mouth in South Africa have been pivotal in the 'out of Africa' model of modern human origins, for the first time in many decades bringing together issues related to the origins of the species with the evolution of modern human behaviour.

Historically it is certainly the case that what is now called palaeoanthropology grew up with archaeology, part of the same tradition of enquiry and method, and moreover for many periods of human evolution, especially the most recent, discoveries relating to human biological evolution occur almost exclusively in the context of archaeological excavations.

And yet institutionally and intellectually the study of human evolution is nowadays quite divided from that of archaeology as a whole. Few archaeologists are either trained in biology, let alone human biology, or are concerned with the biological or morphological characteristics of the people they study. Modern archaeology has moved on beyond the reconstruction of evolutionary narrative, and has developed a view of human behaviour in the past that is largely independent of any biological considerations. Where archaeology became the study of the cultural history of mankind, human evolution became the preserve of anatomists for whom behaviour, the essence of humanity, was soft speculation about things that could not be verified scientifically. For the most each discipline has been content to 'live and let live'; the archaeologists were

there to provide the key specimens for the biological anthropologist, while the archaeologists in turn used those fossils as a passive backdrop for the more interesting questions of behavioural adaptation.

This, of course, is a caricature of a much more diverse and active field, but nonetheless it contains more than an element of truth. In the United States the idea of a single
field of anthropology is under assault, as the subfields of archaeology and anthropology have staked out their intellectual territories. In the United Kingdom the traditions
have never been closely aligned except in a few institutions. In Europe the connections
are stronger, largely as a function of the richness of the Palaeolithic sequences in areas
such as south-west France.

This state of affairs is very historically contingent, and a comparison at other times
would reveal a different story. Over the last century archaeology and the study of
human evolution have in fact converged and diverged in response to a number of factors, from the chances of discovery to the shifts in intellectual environment. In the nineteenth century evolutionary ideas gave the stimulus to the uncovering of the deep
antiquity of man, and in turn provided the main interpretive framework. Early archaeology was essentially evolutionary archaeology. The demise of evolutionary
approaches in the social sciences during most of the twentieth century was also
reflected in a shift in archaeology. As archaeology became more focused on the reconstruction of cultural and behavioural rather than physical history, so its practitioners
turned more and more to cultural and sociological ideas to provide the explanatory
framework for the patterns they were revealing.

Thus for much of the latter half of the twentieth century the two branches of
palaeoanthropology can be described as pursuing parallel paths into the human past.
However, the resurgence of evolutionary ideas in the last two decades of the twentieth
century, the growth of sociobiology, behavioural ecology, and evolutionary psychology
have resurrected an interest in human behaviour from a Darwinian perspective, and the
ripples of this change have been felt in archaeology (Boone and Smith 1998). Perhaps
more importantly, the growth of powerful new techniques in biology, particularly
molecular genetics, which have the ability to reconstruct population histories in ways
that archaeologists have done for many years, has brought the two disciplines closer
together than for many decades.

The widening debate for archaeology at the millennium, posed by the title of this
book, will differ for each part of the discipline. In considering human evolution we
should certainly examine what has been learnt, what are the achievements of the last
century, and what the future has to offer. But perhaps for human evolution more than
other aspects of archaeology, there is a broader set of issues. In looking at later prehistory, the central role of archaeology remains unchallenged, and these parts of the discipline have forged their own ideas, models and syntheses. When it comes to prehistory
beyond our own species the centrality of archaeology becomes more debatable, and

there is a case for seeing Palaeolithic studies as being a branch of evolutionary biology rather than archaeology. This is not to say that the role of archaeology is lessened, but that its theoretical development is strongly constrained by the ideas developed by evolutionists. It is this theme that I shall pursue in this essay, by exploring how human evolution both needs a strong archaeological input, but also goes beyond that, and that when looking at a world before our own species, the assumptions of biology and culture break down. I shall discuss five central themes in current human evolutionary studies, and explore how archaeological ideas and data relate to a broader evolutionary approach. These issues are: 1) the patterns of hominid evolution over the last five million years; 2) the adaptive approach, and the question of how the evolution of behaviour is rooted in biology; 3) the relationship between phylogeny and technological change; 4) the evolution of modern humans; 5) the evidence for the evolution of cognition and behaviour that can be approached from beyond the ethnographic record and archaeological inference. In the concluding section I shall then discuss how an evolutionary approach may have implications beyond the deep and remote past.

The pattern of hominin evolution

The establishment of a chronology of human evolution has been one of the greatest challenges — and triumphs — of archaeology. Darwin himself worked very much in a chronological vacuum. He recognized the fundamental importance of long periods of time for his theory — gradual evolution required long stretches of time — but the absolute resolution of that timescale was not available to him. Stratigraphy and educated guesswork provided some estimates, but it was only the gradual introduction of radiometric techniques in the second half of the twentieth century that allowed these to be confirmed or rejected. Here is not the place to review this achievement in detail (see Reader 1988 for an excellent discussion of the history of palaeoanthropology), but two key points can be made. The first is that for both theoretical and empirical reasons the expectation was that the chronology of human evolution would be a long one (Foley 1995). The primary reason for this was the belief that humans were so different and special that they must have taken longer to evolve than other taxa. The hominid lineage was therefore assumed to stretch back deep into the geological past, and it was not unusual for this to be placed in such remote periods as the Oligocene — now considered to be more than 30 million years ago. Some estimates were even longer. Nevertheless, in making such a statement it must be taken into account that the 'educated guesses' concerning the calibration of the geological record were generally very conservative, and the Oligocene itself was not considered to be more than a few million years ago. However, whether in absolute time or in relative time, a long chronology was the dominant model. This was perhaps at its apogee in the 1970s, when absolute dating techniques had established the ages of the major geological epochs, and when fossils such as *Ramapithecus* were taken as evidence for hominids being present from at least the early Miocene (more than 20 million years ago) (Pilbeam 1968).

The second factor in this longer chronology was perhaps a more understandable human one — the desire of archaeologists and palaeontologists to find earlier and earlier evidence for things that could be labelled as 'human' or on the road to humanity. In this sense there was perhaps an element of wish fulfilment in the interpretations of early fossils such as *Ramapithecus*. Perhaps the best illustration of this is the fate of the Leakeys' earliest discovery at Olduvai Gorge, what they called *Zinjanthropus boisei* (now called *Australopithecus boisei*). This fossil is a classic form of the robust australopithecine radiation (see below), with certain hominid features such as bipedalism, but essentially a specialized form of ape. However, Louis Leakey extracted every anatomical detail he could in support of its claims to be very human-like (Leakey 1961). It was only when an earlier and more human-like form, *Homo habilis*, was discovered at Olduvai that the predominant non-human features of this creature were allowed to be emphasized (Leakey *et al.* 1961).

The net effect of these conceptual biases was to push back the origins of hominids as far as was possible. Certainly that achievement was considerable, and the presence of hominids in the Pliocene is now beyond dispute. However, it was not archaeology, but the first discoveries of evolutionary genetics that brought this search for a longer chronology to an end. From the 1960s onwards various biological markers have been used to reconstruct evolutionary relationships.

Molecular biology has had only a small impact on archaeology more generally, primarily through ancient DNA (Krings *et al.* 1997) and discussions relating to Indo-European origins and the spread of agriculture (see Renfrew, this volume). Across evolutionary studies the impact has been very significant (Avise 1994). This is not the place to discuss the assumptions and techniques; in essence, analysing genes drawn from living populations and species can be used to infer three things — phylogeny (evolutionary relationships), the timing of evolutionary events (the molecular clock), and ancient demography. There are many problems associated with all of these, but results are more and more robust, and have led to major revisions in much of evolutionary biology (see Goodman *et al.* 1990 for a review of these revisions with respect to primates). This is certainly the case for human evolution.

The key finding is that chimpanzees and gorillas are more closely related to humans than to orang utans, and that chimpanzees are more closely related to humans than to gorillas (Fig. 1) (see Gagneux *et al.* 1999 for a recent summary of hominoid genetics). Furthermore, this relationship is remarkably close, both genetically and chronologically. Conventionally, if somewhat arbitrarily, the origin of the branch leading to humans is taken to be the split from our closest living relatives. The chimpanzee fills this role, and the split most probably occurred between 7 and 5 million years ago, perhaps a little later or earlier. This is remarkably recent in geological terms, and has overturned the long-held assumption of a deep origin to the human line. The findings of molecular biology have ruled out the possibility that the majority of Miocene fossil apes can be uniquely related to the human line. Instead, it is only with the beginnings of the Pliocene that we are likely to find the first unique ancestors. There is in fact now a remarkable — given the limitations of the fossil record — concordance between the fossil and molecular evidence, showing that the trend towards human features occurred in Africa somewhere between 6 and 4.5 million years ago. This can be considered a major achievement of twentieth-century palaeoanthropology, and provides a sound framework for going beyond chronology and considering the pattern of hominin evolution.

What is this pattern? At this stage, parenthetically, it may be useful to define briefly some terms. Under the traditional taxonomy, the hominoids (i.e. the Hominoidea, that group including humans and all the apes) were considered to have three families — the hylobatids or gibbons or lesser apes; the pongids, the great apes (chimpanzee, bonobo, gorilla, and orang utan); and the hominids (humans and their ancestral forms). Molecular systematics has thrown this into confusion. Chimpanzees and gorillas should be placed with humans rather than orang utans, and humans do not really deserve a separate family — the Hominidae. The term 'hominid', which has become widely used to refer to all fossils relating to the evolution of humanity, should really include at least the chimpanzee and bonobo, and most probably the gorilla as well. Although such a change is confusing, it is increasingly being accepted, and so the many fossil discoveries are now generally referred to as 'hominins' — a lower taxonomic rank. Thus in the discussion presented here, I shall be referring to a suite of extinct species, more closely related to us than the chimpanzee/bonobo clade, as hominins. These include the ardipithecines, the australopithecines and members of our own genus, *Homo*.

To return to the question, what is the evolutionary pattern they display, the answer is, a complex and in some ways surprising one. Again, I will not pay a great deal of attention to the many biological and morphological details, but will focus on what the overall pattern implies for archaeologists interested in the evolutionary context of prehistory.

The major expectation of earlier palaeoanthropologists was that hominin evolution should consist of a single trend, towards bipedalism, larger brains and more complex technology and behaviour (see Lewin 1990 for a discussion of this theme). In terms of the new chronology, this would occur over five million years. The reality is very different. There are two components to this difference. The first is that rather than there being a single evolving lineage, there are a multiplicity of species now known. Many of these species are contemporary with each other, and this is true right the way through to and beyond the appearance of modern humans in the last 200,000 years. Hominin evolution is therefore not a single line or trend, but an adaptive radiation, a diversification of forms (Foley 1987a). This can be seen clearly in Figure 2, which compares a hominin

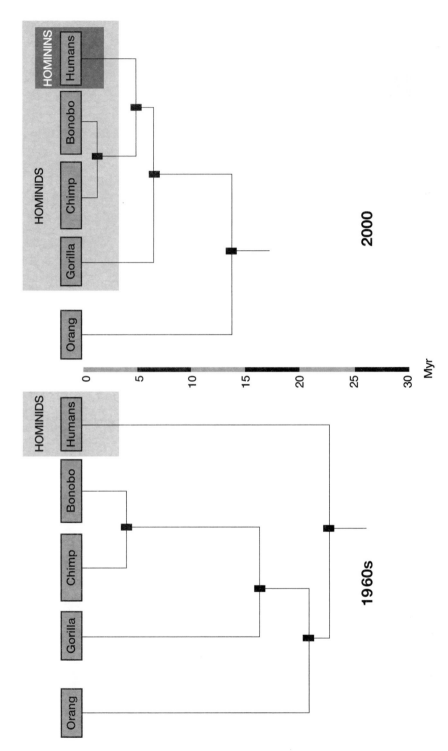

Figure 1. Hominoid evolutionary relationships: the 1960s version shows humans as well separated from the great apes, and in their own family, the Hominidae. Molecular genetic and other studies have shown this to be wrong, and in fact humans and chimpanzees/bonobos are the most closely related. The term hominid now best refers to all the African apes and humans, and the lower taxonomic rank — hominin — is used for humans and their ancestors.

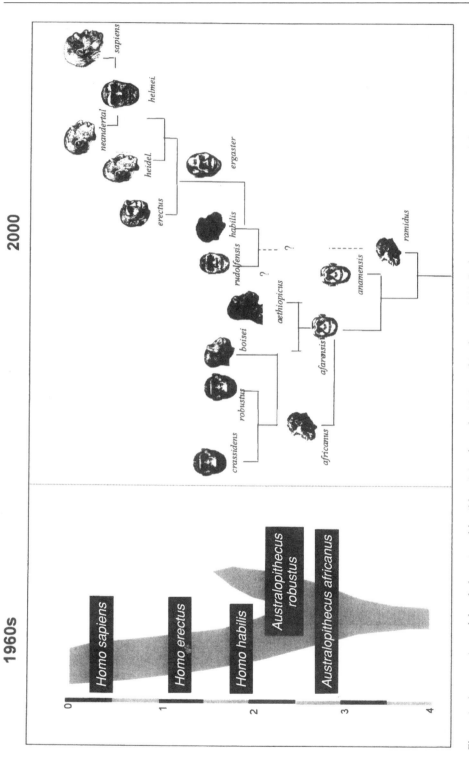

Figure 2. A comparison of the phylogenies of fossil hominins from the 1960s and in the year 2000. Both are representative, and there is no consensus yet, but the 1960s schemes tend to have very few branches and several ancestor–descendant relationships. More recent phylogenies emphasize branching events and diversity. (Cartoons courtesy of Jonathan Kingdon.)

phylogeny from the 1960s, to one representing today's consensus. The earlier one has few if any branching events, and places virtually all species in an ancestor–descendant relationship. The modern one shows many branching events, many extinct forms, and few ancestral forms. While a hypothetical line of direct descent from the earliest hominin to *Homo sapiens* can be followed, it is but one among a number of such lines linking fossil hominins.

The second component is that these multiple forms of hominin do not show a simple trend away from conservative apes' characters towards human ones. To explore this, it is necessary to give a brief description of the hominin fossil record (see Table 1 and Fig. 3 for summary) (and see also postscript on p. 39). The earliest known fossil hominin is from Aramis in the Middle Awash in Ethiopia dated to 4.5 Myr (White *et al.* 1994). Published remains are fragmentary, and its hominin status is not settled, but it shows a mixture of ape-like and more human-like traits, particularly a smaller canine. If a hominin, both its date and its morphology place it very close to the origins of the clade. This is known as *Ardipithecus ramidus*. At 4.2 Myr there is a second species, *Australopithecus anamensis*, from northern Kenya (Leakey *et al.* 1995). This has more hominin features, and in particular shows some evidence for bipedal adaptations (Ward *et al.* 1999). From close to this date also comes the earliest *Australopithecus afarensis*. This is far better known, and includes the famous 'Lucy', a partial skeleton which shows clear bipedal adaptations (Johanson *et al.* 1982; Johanson and White 1979). The morphology of the skull is significant for much of what is understood about the australopithecines more generally and their place in hominin evolution. The face is less prognathic than an ape, but still protrudes forward; the anterior dentition is smaller than a chimpanzee's, and the posterior dentition is larger. The brain size is not significantly larger than that of an extant ape.

A. afarensis is known only from eastern Africa, but over approximately the same chronological span there also exists in South Africa another species, *A. africanus*. This is morphologically quite similar to *A. afarensis*, differing in some dental and facial characters. Both species are known to have existed to less than 3 million years ago.

Between 3 and 2 million years ago other forms of hominin come into existence, and display greater diversity of characteristics. These include *A. aethiopicus* (Walker *et al.* 1986), known from eastern Africa between 2.7 and 2.3 Myr, which has a very small brain, a prognathic face, very large molar teeth, and a pronounced sagittal crest along its skull — a precursor of forms that are more widespread later and are known broadly as the 'robust australopithecines'; *A. gahri*, a recently discovered species from Ethiopia, which has again very large molar teeth, but also a larger brain and some features that link it to later specimens of *Homo* (Asfaw *et al.* 1999); and early forms that have been assigned to the genus *Homo* itself, with smaller teeth and some signs of larger brains. The other forms that appear shortly before 2 million years ago are the more widely known robust australopithecines (sometimes placed into their own genus *Paranthropus*).

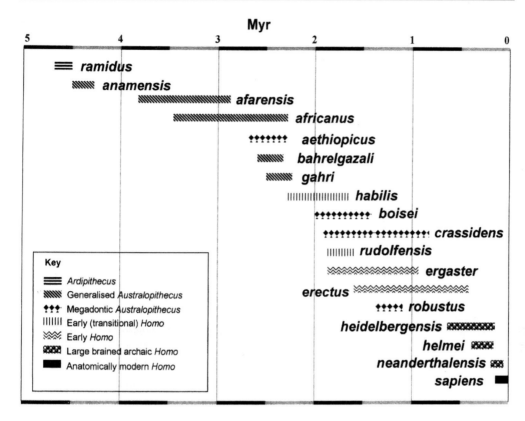

Figure 3. Distribution of fossil hominin taxa through time, grouped into major categories discussed in the text.

These consist of two major species, *A. robustus* in South Africa, and *A. boisei* in East Africa (see Grine 1989 for a review of the issues involved in the evolution and diversity of this group). These are characterized by what is referred to as megadonty, with associated specialized musculature of the skull and jaw, and a wide but flat face. They show little sign of further encephalization.

For this period prior to two million years there are therefore a range of species of hominin. Beyond the diversity described here, there is probably yet more of which we have only a small understanding. There may be a further early species of australopithecine in South Africa, as yet unnamed (Clarke 1985), as well as a species closely related to *A. afarensis* from Chad (*A. bahrelgazali*) (Brunet *et al.* 1995), and perhaps a second later robust australopithecine from South Africa, known as *A. crassidens* (Grine 1989).

These species, mostly australopithecine in form, dominate the period from 5 to 2 million years ago. After 1.5 Myr, they become increasingly rare, although they may have persisted until close to a million years ago in parts of Africa. Instead, the second major genus of hominin becomes predominant, *Homo*. While this shows less diversity

Table 1. Adaptive grades or super-species of hominids. There is considerable controversy as to what the species of hominin evolution are. This table gives a summary of the main species groups — that is species which show similar adaptations — and the species or possibly sub-species that would belong to them. These species groups may represent 'adaptive grades'. A thumbnail sketch outlining the basic characteristics for each is provided (from Foley 1999).

Last common ancestor/ earliest hominids	Early Savanna Bipedal apes	Later Savanna Bipedal apes
SUPER-SPECIES *Ardipithecus ramidus*	SUPER-SPECIES *Australopithecus africanus*	SUPER-SPECIES *Australopithecus (Paranthropus) robustus*
SPECIES/SUB-SPECIES *A. ramidus*	SPECIES/SUB-SPECIES *A. anamensis* *A. afarensis* *A. africanus* *A. bahrelgazali*	SPECIES/SUB-SPECIES *A. robustus* *A. crassidens* *A. aethiopicus* *A. boisei*

General characteristics

This taxon is generally considered to be very close to the point of divergence from the LCA with *Pan*. Poorly known, but probably in the size range of a large chimpanzee (35–45 kg), it may or may not be bipedal. Small canines, thin dental enamel and projecting face all indicate its very mixed character. Overall it is probably a frugivorous/ omnivorous ape. Brain size and sexual dimorphism are unknown, but probably similar to *Pan*. Perhaps indicates geographical origin of Hominidae in north-eastern Africa.

Variation

Not known.

General characteristics

These are the early australopithecines. Although often described as gracile, these taxa are larger than chimpanzees, and mostly fall within the range 45–60 kg. In absolute terms brain size is between 400 and 550 cm^3. In relative terms EQ is slightly above that of a chimpanzee (2.1), approximately 2.3 to 2.6. Facultatively bipedal; in general terms these australopithecines have relatively long arms, short legs, large guts and chests, suggesting a mixed locomotion/positional behaviour involving terrestrial and arboreal activities. Generally show a trend towards larger posterior teeth, with some anterior reduction. *Africanus* is often heavily megadontic. Tooth enamel is thick. On the basis of tooth morphology and wear, most of these would have been frugivores, with elements of both coarser lower quality food and meat in the diet. Growth rates are ape-like and rapid, with age of first reproduction probably similar to *Pan*. Probably highly sexually dimorphic these species are best considered geographical and time transgressive variants on the theme of bipedal African apes, less specialized than the later australopithecines.

Variation

A. anamensis and A. *afarensis* represent the earlier eastern forms, while *A. africanus* and A. *bahrelgazali* are slightly later southern and north-western extensions of range and thus allopatric species. They exhibit considerable body size variation within and between species (*anamensis* (47–55 kg), *afarensis* (27–45 kg), *africanus* (30–43 kg)). Posterior tooth size and wear in *africanus* overlaps with that of some later australopithecines.

General characteristics

These are the so-called robust australo-pithecines or paranthropines. Their robustness is largely cranial, although they do tend to be slightly larger than the earlier forms. Overall body size ranges from around 40 kg to over 80 kg, with an average around 50. Some increase in brain size compared to other australopithecines, with an EQ between 2.2 and close to 3. Bipedal, but still with relatively long forelimbs and shorter hindlimbs, and broad thoraxes. Megadontic posterior dentition, with thick tooth enamel, highly reduced anterior dentition. All teeth show the effects of heavy wear and chewing, and have flat occlusal surfaces. Tooth wear and morphology indicate very coarse, small object foods, probably high in grit and fibre. Mostly plant foods, but likely to be eclectic on basis of hominoid ancestry and includes some meat. Highly sexually dimorphic across all taxa where known.

Variation

The robust australopithecines are all variants on a theme. *Boisei* is the most extreme in its megadonty, while the older *aethiopicus* possesses the smallest brain (410 cc) and a projecting face. They may represent convergent evolutionary trends.

Early intelligent and opportunistic omnivores	Later intelligent and opportunistic omnivores	Technological colonizers and dominant herbivores
SUPER-SPECIES *Homo habilis*	SUPER-SPECIES *Homo erectus*	SUPER-SPECIES *Homo sapiens*
SPECIES/SUB-SPECIES *H. habilis* *H. rudolfensis*	SPECIES/SUB-SPECIES *H. ergaster* *H. erectus* *H. heidelbergensis* *H. antecessor*	SPECIES/SUB-SPECIES *H. helmei* *H. neanderthalensis* *H. sapiens*

General characteristics

Early *Homo* taxa show mixed features, in some ways similar to australopithecines but exhibiting larger brains and dental/facial reduction. Body size is very variable, but probably around 45–50 kg. Brain size exceeds 600 g, and the EQ estimates are close to 3.0. Early *Homo* is poorly known post-cranially, but some specimens indicate a body structure similar to australopithecines. Problems of taxonomic assignment make estimates of sexual dimorphism problematic, but it is likely to have been considerably dimorphic. *Homo* is associated with the first stone tools, and may have been increasingly omnivorous. Growth patterns would be closer to apes than humans.

Variation

There are basically two forms — a smaller and more gracile australopithecine type (*habilis*), showing some brain enlargement and facial reduction, and a larger, more megadontic form with larger brain (*rudolfensis*).

General characteristics

Pleistocene *Homo* is generally larger than the Pliocene australopithecines and *Homo*, with brain sizes between 800 and 1200 cc. EQs are greater than 3.0. Full bipedalism and linear body form are established, but with developed muscularity. Teeth are smaller, and technology extensive. Substantial hunting/meat-eating may have been in place. Sexual dimorphism where known remains substantial. Growth patterns shifted towards the human condition.

Variation

Pleistocene *Homo* is very variable. There is a general temporal trend towards greater brain size especially in African and European forms (*heidelbergensis*); increased robusticity in African lineage of *heidelbergensis*. The early African forms are much taller and more linear, with body mass above 50 kg. Later *erectus* are larger and more robust (>60 kg) than *H. ergaster* (52–65 kg). *H. heidelbergensis* (55–80 kg) is often very large and robust (Bodo, Petralona). Other differences may be local geographical ones (*antecessor* in Europe, *erectus* in Asia).

General characteristics

All these forms are generally large, often greater than 60 kg, with larger cranial capacities well within the range of living humans. EQ is in excess of 5. There is full bipedalism, and a general loss of extreme cranial superstructures, facial and dental reduction. Technology is much more complex (Mode 3). Sexual dimorphism is reduced, and life history parameters are likely to be close to or largely within the range of modern humans. Extreme habitat tolerance appears to be characteristic, possibly associated with high levels of omnivory (hunting).

Variation

Variability in this form is quite marked across time. *Helmei* is the early common ancestor to the later form, and so retains more primitive characters and is robust. *Neanderthalensis* is the most derived, with cold climate adaptation in terms of face size, body proportion, body mass (55–70 kg) and posture/locomotion. Early *sapiens* are large and robust, but become increasingly variable, gracile (35–70 kg) and widespread, with the most cultural and technological complexity. Sexual dimorphism is high in early forms of all taxa, but reduced in later *sapiens*.

than the australopithecines, nonetheless it is still a far from simple story. The earliest forms, known mostly from East Africa, are very primitive, and some would consider them to be australopithecines (Wood and Collard 1999a; Wood and Collard 1999b). Two forms are known, *H. habilis*, a small-bodied but larger-brained species, possibly with a primitive post-cranium, and *H. rudolfensis*, a larger form, with larger teeth, as well as a larger brain. The key point with the emergence of *Homo* is that there is a reversal of evolutionary direction. Where the australopithecines exhibited relatively little change in brain size, but major expansion of tooth size, *Homo* showed the reverse — declining tooth size and expanding brains. This is seen clearly with the appearance of *Homo ergaster* in Africa some 1.8 million years ago. This creature is much more human-like, with a brain size of up to 900 cc, a relatively flat face, and human-sized teeth, and an essentially modern skeletal form (Walker and Leakey 1993). In addition to being present in Kenya, Tanzania and Eritrea, it has also been found in Georgia, dated to 1.6 Myr (Gabunia *et al.* 2000).

Derivatives of *H. ergaster* are the first to appear outside Africa, a theme that will be discussed below. There is considerable controversy as to what they should all be called, and the extent to which they form separate species, as well as the phylogenetic relationships among them. These details are not really relevant here, but the primary groups that have been suggested, and which form the basis for understanding later hominin evolution are: *H. erectus*, known from Java and China, and perhaps from East Africa (OH9), from North Africa, and from Europe (a recently discovered skull from Ceprano in Italy), and which persists from over a million years to around a quarter of a million years ago; *H. heidelbergensis*, a more robust and larger-brained form, known from Africa and Europe from about 600,000 years ago (Rightmire 1998); *H. antecessor*, recently described from Atapuerca in Spain, dated to approximately 800,000 years ago, which has a number of more derived and modern-looking features (deCastro *et al.* 1997); *H. helmei*, from Africa, a larger-brained and more modern-looking form which may be ancestral to the two later Pleistocene species of hominin (Lahr and Foley 1998), *H. neanderthalensis* and *H. sapiens*.

These last two species are essentially contemporaries during the later Pleistocene; both appear around 150,000 years ago, Neanderthals in Europe and modern humans in Africa (Hublin 1996; Stringer 1992). They are both large brained, capable of making complex technology, and share many traits. They differ in that Neanderthals exhibit a number of morphological specializations, particularly large faces and noses, robust and short limbs, and heavy brow ridges, whereas modern humans (*H. sapiens*) have smaller faces, high rounded skulls, and long gracile limbs. They also differ, of course, in that modern humans have persisted and expanded dramatically in the last 30,000 years, whereas Neanderthals have become extinct. These different evolutionary trajectories will be discussed later. In addition, it should be added that there are further specimens, such as those from China (at Mapa and Dali) during the later Pleistocene, which do not fit easily into any of these groups, and thus there may yet be more complexity to be unravelled in the next few years.

The reason for describing briefly the diversity of the hominin fossil record is to identify the trends that make up the pattern of hominin evolution (Fig. 4). We have already seen that there is a basic pattern of diversification and radiation. However, this is not a single event, but rather a number of events, each exhibiting a different evolutionary trend.

The earliest of these is very poorly known, and is basically speculation. The very primitive and ape-like nature of *Ardipithecus*, and the possibility that it may not have been bipedal, probably place this taxon as part of the diversification of the African apes.

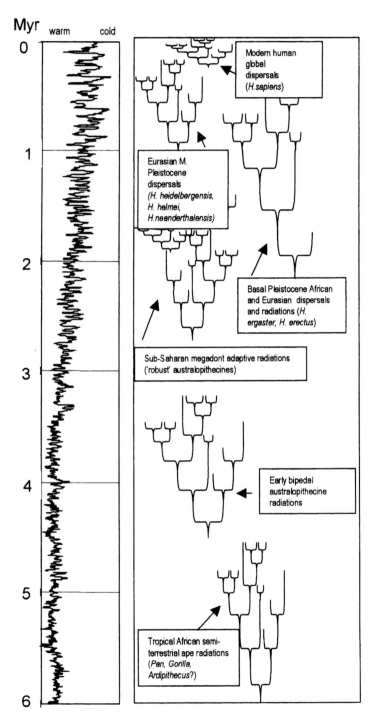

Figure 4. The main pattern of hominin evolution. On the left is shown the pattern of climatic change, a shift to colder environments, but also marked by considerable instability. On the right are shown the main radiations discussed in the text.

The period from 7 to 4.5 million years ago may, it has recently been suggested (Stewart and Disotell 1998), have seen the dispersal into Africa of the ancestors of the African ape/human clade, and that during this period they spread across Africa, becoming in the process chimpanzees, gorillas and ardipithecines. The latter may have been the most terrestrial and the most eastern, and thus the clade from which later hominins arose.

The second event is the australopithecine radiation, occurring from perhaps as much as 4.0 Myr. This is the radiation of bipedal apes, for while australopithecines show little sign of technology or brain enlargement, they are all clearly bipedal to some extent. The suggestion would be that this is an adaptation to the increasingly dry and open environments that emerged on the eastern side of Africa during the Pliocene. However, and this is the key point, the trend developed by these bipedal apes over two or three million years was not in a 'human direction' but towards dental specialization. All australopithecines, and especially the later ones, have large molars, with flat, worn surfaces. The musculature associated with mastication is extreme. This is a long way from modern humans, with very small teeth and larger brains; indeed, in terms of molar dentition, modern humans are closer to chimpanzees than to the robust australopithecines. The early part of hominin evolution is thus primarily the evolution of bipedal, megadontic apes, not humans.

Thus, although the hominin clade has been in existence for as much as five million years, the first three million years of these are not related to the evolution of the features that have made humans so special — larger brains, culture, technology and language. The trend in that direction can only be said to have started in the last two million years, and in practice it is really only since one million years ago that we can genuinely say that we see this trend clearly. Hominin evolution is really two distinct events, an australopithecine radiation, and a *Homo* one.

Even within the evolution of *Homo* there are some complexities to any trend. The first of these is that brain size actually remains relatively stable for the early part of the period (Fig. 5), and it is only in the last half million years that there is a clearly accelerated trend (Mithen 1996; Ruff *et al.* 1997). The second is that rather than brain size increase being the predominant trend of the whole period, increased body mass and robusticity seem to have been more important. The early *Homo* were relatively lightly built, but later specimens of, for example *H. heidelbergensis*, were massive by comparison, and clearly very strong (Ruff *et al.* 1997). That trend dominated the bulk of the Pleistocene. Only in the last 100,000 years, and in practice even more recently, did the shift to the lighter skeletal frame we associate with modern humans occur (Foley 1989; Stringer and Gamble 1993; Stringer 1992).

In summary, then, the pattern of human evolution consists of a series of adaptive radiations, in which key features emerge and give rise to a diverse group of hominins. While these radiations do build on each other, they do not constitute a simple linear

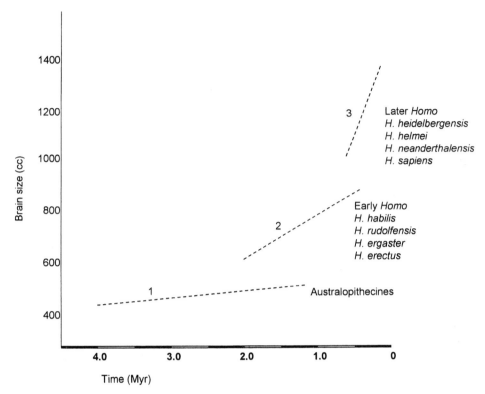

Figure 5. Pattern of brain size evolution. During the australopithecine phase brain size stayed relatively stable and close to living ape levels. Brain size increases during the course of the evolution of *Homo,* particularly after 0.5 Myr. Pattern extrapolated from data in Ruff *et al.* 1997.

trend from ape to human. Understanding the pattern of australopithecine evolution is going to require a very different framework from that of human evolution. To return to the theme of the long chronology that was expected by the first evolutionary anthropologists, this now seems illusory. Not only does human evolution occur over a relatively short geological period, the last five million years, but it is also only in the last two million years that *Homo* itself takes on its characteristic form; furthermore, it is only in the last quarter of a million years that human evolution starts to come into a modern form.

What are the implications of this for the archaeologist? I would suggest that there are two important lessons to be learnt. The first is that fossil discoveries of the last century have shown that there were many different species of hominid, each with its distinctive characteristics. Prehistory is populated not by amorphous 'fossil hominids' or 'archaic peoples', terms often found in the archaeological literature, but by specific biological populations and species. Archaeological reconstructions must relate to these more specifically, for they are not merely the backdrop of prehistory, but the actual creators of it. The diversity we see is not just the product of anatomists' obsessions, but reflects the evolutionary process.

The second implication is that for the archaeologist, interested primarily in the roots of human behaviour through the material record, much of the overall time-span of hominin evolution will be invisible. This alone supports the view that the australopithecines were really very different from us.

The hominin adaptive complex: biology and behaviour

The argument set out in the previous section essentially says that the complexities of the hominin fossil record, and the pattern of human evolution overall, should be taken into account more fully by prehistorians working with the archaeological record of the Pleistocene. One response to this proposal might be that such complexities are only of relevance for biologists, and that human behaviour, mediated by the flexibility of the human mind and its cultural outputs, can be studied independently of the who's who approach beloved of palaeoanthropologists. However, while such a response might be appropriate for some aspects of recent human history — and even there is highly debatable — this certainly cannot be claimed for the long stretches of prehistory in which the behavioural and biological are deeply intertwined. In considering the relevance of an understanding of human evolution to archaeology, and how this will become increasingly important in the coming decades, I will use this section to explore the question of how the human behaviour we can see emerging during the course of the Pleistocene is embedded in the evolutionary biology of the hominins.

Three examples can be used to make the point, each relating to a major aspect of human behavioural evolution. The first of these relates to patterns of growth. It is a well-known fact that humans display a delayed growth pattern. Although human gestation is not significantly longer than that of other hominoids, age of maturity and first reproduction are, and furthermore human longevity is greatly extended (Schultz 1969). This has long been an accepted part of discussions of human behaviour and cultural capacity. The form this most often takes is the argument that the human social and cultural environment is so complex that a functioning individual requires a prolonged period of learning to acquire sufficient understanding, hence the prolonged period of growth. In this sense the human developmental make-up is an essential setting for human cultural and social performance. Evolutionary biology allows this proposition to be considered in more detail through two approaches. The first is that of life history theory. Life history theory is concerned with explaining how and why different organisms partition their lives in different ways, why some grow fast and die young, and others grow more slowly and live longer (Charnov and Berigan 1993).

Comparative analyses of many organisms have shown that these traits are highly correlated with each other. The most significant of the relationships, from the point of view of human evolution, is that slow growth is directly related to brain size. The larger the brain, the slower the growth, and the more delayed adulthood; it is also the case that larger-brained animals also live longer. These relationships have been the subject of many detailed quantitative analyses, and they show that where there is selection for larger brains, growth rates will be delayed at predictable rates. Although humans lie at an extreme end of such relationships, nonetheless the pattern we see in living humans, where we have both large brains and prolonged life history strategies, is simply an extension of what is found for mammals and primates more generally. More importantly, perhaps, what is expected to occur theoretically with these changes — a later age of reproduction, a greater length between offspring, and an overall longer lifespan — is also found in the human species (Smith 1989).

Evolutionary biology thus offers insights into why the unique behavioural flexibility of humans is dependent upon a pattern of developmental biology that is common to all species, and indeed is found in rudimentary form among the primates. However, while these theoretical insights help to explain the interaction between biology and culture, they do little to help with the specifics of human evolution, and it is here that the second approach comes in. The key question to ask is 'when during the course of hominin evolution does the pattern of growth change from an ape-like one to a human-like one?' Only recently have the techniques to answer this question become available.

Teeth have long been used to provide the age of death of a specimen. This has normally been based on the pattern of eruption; using human models it is possible to estimate the age of a child on the basis of which teeth have erupted. However, this assumes that the actual growth rates are known, which is clearly not true for extinct hominin taxa. Calibration can be provided through analysis of the enamel that caps teeth (Bromage and Dean 1985). All enamel grows at a very regular rate, formed by the secretion of prisms as the enamel extends over the tooth surface. Again, the details need not concern us here, but by counting the prisms and other regular structures within the tooth enamel, it is possible to gain an absolute, rather than relative, estimate of the age of a fossil specimen. This actual age can then be compared with the state of eruption of a tooth, and an estimate of the pattern of maturation — the key biological factor — can be made.

This approach has now been applied to fossil hominins, with revealing results (Beynon and Dean 1988; Beynon and Wood 1987; Bromage and Dean 1985). Where it has been possible to assess the maturation patterns of australopithecines, they have been shown to grow in ways very similar to that of the apes, thus confirming the insights discussed above, that the australopithecines are essentially ape-like, not just in their behaviour, but also in their biology. In contrast, early *Homo* shows some shift towards more human growth patterns. However, this is not a sudden shift. Early *H.*

ergaster, at 1.6 Myr, has a more rapid rate of growth than a modern human; the Nariokotome skeleton, which in terms of biological maturation would have been considered to be a 13 year old child, was most probably between 9 and 11 when he died (Smith 1993). Only in the last half million years or so, and probably less, were fully modern growth rates achieved (Foley and Lee 1989) (Fig. 6).

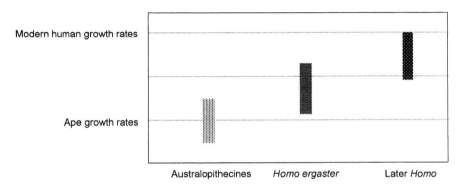

Figure 6. Pattern of changes of growth rates among hominins. See text for discussion.

Why should this matter to the archaeologist? For the simple reason that if the aim of the archaeologist is to reconstruct the behaviour of the early hominins, then any reconstruction must be consistent with the biological potential of each species. *H. ergaster* may have done many things that modern humans did, but if so, it did them in the context of a different pattern of biological, and presumably social, development, and any model must take this into account. In this light, biology and behaviour cannot be separated. We can see this even more clearly with the second example, which extends this interest in brain size and its behavioural connections. Archaeologists have debated extensively the scale and nature of meat-eating among early hominins (Binford 1981; Binford 1984; Bunn and Kroll 1986; Isaac 1981; Potts 1984). Views have ranged from the extreme position held by Ardrey (Ardrey 1961) and others that early hominins were intensive hunters, to equally extreme views posed initially by Binford (Binford 1981), that in fact such hominins were at most terminal scavengers, getting little more than the marrow from an animal. In the middle are views relating to the role of hunting versus scavenging, and the differences between modern human abilities and those of other hominin taxa. Furthermore, hunting has also been proposed as playing an important part in human behavioural evolution more generally, either in terms of providing a basis for food sharing (Isaac 1978), for technological development, or for changes in social behaviour. For example, hunting has been seen as a promoter of language and communication skills, foresight and planning, and changes in group size (Laughlin 1968).

There is, however, an important dimension associated with carnivory that is more directly related to evolutionary biology, and provides an essential context for archaeological discussions of meat-eating. To understand this, it is necessary to return to the issue of brain evolution. There is little doubt that having a large brain provides a species with a number of advantages — increased processing of information, improved memory, planning of strategies, etc. However, it is necessary to set against these advantages the costs, which are primarily related to the fact that the growth and maintenance of neural tissue is metabolically very expensive (Martin 1983). The human body is made up of many different tissues, but they vary considerably in the energetic costs they impose. Some tissues, such as skin and muscle, are relatively inexpensive, in that they require little to be maintained. Others, such as the brain, the guts, the kidneys, etc. are very expensive (Aiello and Wheeler 1995).

In discussing life history theory and growth above, it was noted that animals with larger brains tend to grow more slowly. One of the reasons for this is that a slower rate of growth allows for the additional energetic expenditure, and in particular places less of a metabolic burden on the mother, upon whom most of the energetic costs fall as brain growth occurs primarily during gestation and immediately after birth (Martin 1983). In sum, energy is a major constraint on the size of an animal's brain, and is probably responsible for the observation that most animals do in fact have relatively small brains compared to primates and humans — the costs are simply greater than the benefits. This biological dimension is essential for understanding the development of meat-eating among hominins; the hunting–scavenging debate cannot make sense except in the light of the biological and evolutionary requirements of the hominins. If brains are becoming larger during the course of later hominin evolution, then it is not simply because of the cognitive advantages, but also because there has been a change in energetics, and meat is likely to be crucial in this (Foley and Lee 1989).

Meat is what can be termed a high quality resource — that is, it is high in protein, fats and energy, compared to say, leaves or most fruits. For an animal with high nutritional demands, and ones that must be maintained regularly, meat is an important resource, and for hominins able to acquire meat this would be a major advantage. Furthermore, meat requires relatively little by way of digestive processing — the guts of carnivores are relatively short, and as noted above, guts themselves are expensive tissues (Aiello and Wheeler 1995). There is thus a pay-off of energy being released from the guts to the brain as the proportion of meat in the diet increases. When we look at the hominin fossil record we can see evidence in support of this relationship between brain size, gut size and meat-eating. The earliest evidence for meat-eating comes from the period between 2 and 2.5 million years ago, which coincides with the emergence of the genus *Homo* and the development of a stone tool technology (de Heinzelin *et al.* 1999). More consistent and conclusive evidence for larger-scale meat-eating can be found with the appearance of *H. ergaster*, some time after 2 million years ago. While this is a correlative association, it is striking that the expansion of the brain in hominins is related to the evidence for more meat-eating. Furthermore, the appearance of *H. ergaster* also shows a change in body shape among early hominins. Great apes and australopithecines all have large guts, and this is evidenced in the shape of their rib-cage, which expands close to the stomach to support the gut. However, modern humans have greatly reduced guts, and this is reflected in the shape of the rib cage, which is more cylindrical, and this feature is also found in the Nariokotome skeleton, one of the earliest representatives of *H. ergaster* (Aiello and Wheeler 1995).

There is thus a concordance between what is seen in the archaeological record in terms of the appearance of stone tool technology and evidence for significant meat-eating, and the biological record in terms of increased brain size and reduced guts, as well as delayed growth patterns. This underscores the central point of much of this essay, that it is impossible to look at the archaeological record and the hominin fossil record independently; behaviour and biology evolve in an integrated manner, and the adaptive complex cannot be partitioned into two components.

This point can be extended by considering a third example, again related to meat-eating. Evolution proceeds by a process of divergence — populations disperse across landscapes, become isolated and under novel selective pressures, and thus diverge to form separate species. There are some patterns in this process of divergence. Not all lineages speciate at the same rate. For example small-bodied creatures are more likely to speciate as they spread across a landscape than large ones, as geographical barriers are more likely to occur. A small river or stream may act as a barrier to a rodent, but not to an elephant. In addition to body size — and all hominins are essentially large-bodied creatures — there are other factors that influence the rate of speciation. Diet is one of these. On the whole, herbivores speciate more than carnivores. This can be observed in two dimensions; first, there are many more herbivore species than carnivores, and second, each herbivore species will have a relatively limited distribution. In contrast carnivore species can be found over very large areas — the lion, for example, was historically known over the whole of Africa and much of western and southern Asia, and the leopard had a distribution over both the old and new worlds.

As herbivores, primates basically fit the pattern of small ranges and relatively high diversity. The diversity of australopithecines in the fossil record also shows a very similar pattern, and this indicates that they were speciating in much the same way as other primates (Foley 1991). However, this pattern shifts with the appearance of *H. ergaster*. All known *Homo* have broadly continental distributions — *H. ergaster* occurs over much of Africa and parts of Asia; *H. erectus* is distributed in eastern and southern Asia, and possibly Africa and Europe as well; *H. heidelbergensis* is known in Africa and Europe. There is thus a contrasting evolutionary signature among early (australopithecine) hominins and later (*Homo*) hominins; the former conform to the primate and herbivore pattern, the latter to a more carnivorous one (Foley 1991) (Fig. 7). Although other

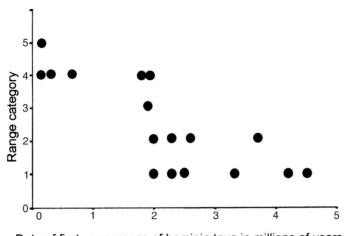

Figure 7. This graph shows the changing distribution of hominin taxa against time. The horizontal axis shows the date of first appearance of the major taxa; the vertical axis shows whether they had 1, local (e.g. a single area of East Africa); 2, regional (e.g. eastern Africa); 3, continental (e.g. Africa); 4, transcontinental (present on more than one continent); and 5, global. Only *Homo sapiens* is fully global.

factors, including social behaviour, may be responsible for this shift, in the context of the evidence for a change to a more meat-based diet discussed above, it can be strongly suggested that a change in the foraging behaviour of the hominins has led not just to a change in their morphology, but also in the way the evolutionary process has occurred.

This consideration of the relationship between a classic topic in biologically-based human evolution — encephalization — and a classic topic in archaeology — the development of hunting and scavenging — demonstrates the importance of not partitioning early prehistory into biological and cultural or behavioural components. The adaptive process is seamless, and behaviour is strongly rooted in biology. Furthermore this is no one way street, from biology to behaviour, but changes in behaviour lead to broader evolutionary changes. Indeed, it can be argued that a shift in behaviour will be the starting point for most evolutionary changes (Bateson 1988). Meat-eating will start as a simple opportunistic change in what an individual and then a population will do. This in turn will lead perhaps to a relaxation on the selective pressure favouring large guts, which will in turn release energy which can be allocated for brain growth, and thus the selection for larger brains will be transformed into an observable evolutionary trend, and as this new adaptive complex emerges it in turn changes the probability of populations becoming isolated, and hence likely to speciate in response to wider geographical distributions.

Apart from the insights this provides into both the evolutionary process and the relationship between archaeology and human evolutionary biology, it also throws light on what actually happened in prehistory. There is ample evidence here that there was a significant gradual shift that occurred with the emergence of *H. ergaster*, and increased meat-eating may, along with a new technological capacity, have been responsible for this, with major consequences for the subsequent pattern of human evolution.

Technology and phylogeny

If there is a basis for the historical separation of archaeology from the biological study of human evolution, it can be typified in terms of 'stones' and 'bones'. Although often coming from the same archaeological excavations, these two relics of the past were subject to different analytical procedures and sent to different specialists. Over the years the questions asked by each of these became very different. Anatomists could use the hominin bones to look for similarities and differences to reconstruct phylogenetic history, to draw the family tree of the hominins. While the archaeologists of the early part of the twentieth century, typified by practitioners such as François Bordes (Bordes 1961) and Charles McBurney, also used stone tool typology to make phylogenetic inferences, in general the last 40 years have seen a withdrawal from this approach. Strongly influenced by the new archaeologists, especially Binford (Binford and Binford 1966), the emphasis shifted towards the interpretation of stone tools in terms of their function. This indeed was the basis for the so-called 'Mousterian debate'. On the one hand, Bordes saw the differences in Mousterian assemblages (La Quina, Mousterian of Acheulean tradition, La Ferrassie, Denticulate and Typical) as being the product of different cultural or ethnic groups; Binford argued that they were merely functional facies, reflecting different activities carried out at different sites and at different seasons by the same hominins and cultural groups. Binford's functional model has generally been seen to be the winner in this debate (although it is worth pointing out that the greatest empirical support is probably for Mellars' long-held view that the differences also represent chronological patterns (Mellars 1970)). The triumph of the functional model in the Mousterian debate, however, had a major effect on Palaeolithic studies more generally. Stone tool assemblages were seen largely as adaptive systems, produced by largely anonymous hominins in response to the demands of their environment and subsistence needs. 'Cometh the environment, cometh the stone tool' was the basic message of late twentieth-century Anglo-American Palaeolithic archaeology.

Underlying this shift was a general disinterest in the question of either the relationship between the artefacts and their biological makers, or of how the lithic record could be used to explore phylogenetic patterns in prehistory. Once again, terms like 'the early hominids' or 'ancient peoples' were sufficient to capture the biological basis for the production of stone tool variability. In 1987 I published a paper suggesting that this was a misplaced change of direction, and that the lithic record as much as the hominid fossil record could be used to reconstruct, or at least supplement, reconstructions of hominin phylogeny (Foley 1987b). Although subject to severe criticism (Clark 1989), there seemed to me to have been four reasons why there should be renewed interest in the classic, population tradition approach to lithics. The first of these was the emerging debate on modern human origins, which emphasized the differences between groups such as Neanderthals and modern humans, between which differences in stone tool technology could be observed. The second was that since the Mousterian debate there had been a shift in hominin taxonomy, and a massive growth in the diversity seen in the hominin fossil record (as shown above); as it was no longer possible to sweep all Pleistocene hominins into *H. erectus* and *H. sapiens*, it seemed appropriate to consider how a more diverse set of hominins could be matched to the technological record. Thirdly, cladistics seemed to offer a way of looking at stone tool variability in a phylogenetic light. And fourthly, there was the question of scale. Functional models of variability were basically drawn from the ethnographic record, and reflected small-scale differences within closely related groups, or seasonal differences within a group. Fluctuations in assemblage should therefore be expected to track small-scale local differences, or intra- and inter-annual variations in resources. While this might apply to the recent parts of prehistory, where such differences could be observed, the scale of variation in the greater time depth of the Pleistocene did not match this ethnographic pattern. Lithic assemblages were stable over tens and hundreds of thousands of years, and showed relatively invariant distributions over whole continents. There seemed to be no concordance between the observed scale of variation and the factors proposed to account for it. Rather, the scale of lithic variation is not significantly different from that of morphological variation. A further, if somewhat pragmatic, reason is that if there is a phylogenetic signal in stone tool assemblages, then it would be an enormous advantage to human evolutionary biologists, as the archaeological record is so much richer than the hominin fossil one.

How can the lithic record be used to reconstruct phylogeny? Ironically the answer lies in returning to many of the older and more traditional methods of typology as used by archaeologists in the first half of the twentieth century. These methods were based on the idea of type fossils or type artefacts, distinctive signatures of particular archaeological assemblages or technocomplexes. While functional studies have put more and more attention on debitage and the less distinctive end of technology (the democratization of lithic studies, as it were), phylogenetic studies are more concerned with unique differences among a few tools or techniques, rather than what all assemblages share. Within this approach little has changed since the basic structure of the Palaeolithic was outlined by Breuil, Burkitt, Movius and many others. The clearest and most useful system for this approach is that of Grahame Clark (Clark 1968). He grouped all the various archaeological cultures based on stone tool typology under five modes: Mode 1, which was simple choppers, chopping tools and flakes, including the Oldowan and the Far Eastern chopping tool tradition; Mode 2, which was the production of bifaces or handaxes, based on the production of large flakes or the bifacial modification of cores (the Acheulean and its variants); Mode 3, which covered prepared core technologies (for example Levallois), such as those found in the Middle Palaeolithic of Europe and the Middle Stone Age of Asia and Africa; Mode 4, which represented the production of blades with reduced platforms, primarily those of the Upper Palaeolithic of Eurasia, but also found to some extent in Africa and the Indian sub-continent; and Mode 5, which referred to microliths such as are found in the African Later Stone Age and the Mesolithic of Eurasia.

Clark's intention was to cut through the plethora of local cultural terms, mostly, I suspect, to arrive at a better system for studying function and economics. However, his system also represents by coincidence a cladistic approach to the archaeological record (Fig. 8). Each of the traits defining modes represents a unique development in technique, building on previous techniques. While a Mode 5 industry may contain tools made using Mode 1, the presence of the most derived technological mode is what defines the assemblage, and provides the evolutionary information. The key question is — what is the pattern of modes across the Pleistocene, and how do they relate to the fossil record?

A discursive essay such as this is not the place to provide the full details of the analyses (but see Foley and Lahr 1997). Perhaps the key point to make is that there is a remarkably good fit between the two (Fig. 9). Firstly, the scale of variation is much the same, in that both the modes and the recognized hominin taxa have much the same distribution through time and space. The Acheulean or Mode 2, for example, is known across Africa and Eurasia, and the early part of it coincides with the known distribution of *H. ergaster*, and the later with *H. heidelbergensis*. The absence of Mode 2 in eastern Asia (the so-called Movius Line), although often disputed, is not dissimilar to the distribution of *H. erectus*, arguably an Asian lineage. Although this approach is controversial, nonetheless it would perhaps be surprising if such a fit did not exist, and the stones and the bones should be telling the same story. That they do also underpins the idea that technology among early hominins was a part of their basic biology, not a culturally flexible system as is the case with recent prehistory and history.

If this broad pattern can be used as a basis for exploring the events of hominin evolution, we can use it to provide a synthesis for the broad pattern of hominin evolution. Mode 1 technology appears with the early *Homo*, and persists through into early *H. ergaster*. This taxon, still making Mode 1 tools, was the first to disperse beyond Africa, most probably into the Middle East, in the Caucasus, and across into South Asia. This South East Asian population developed in isolation into *H. erectus*, but retained throughout its existence the Mode 1 technologies. There is some indication in the presence of specimens such as Ceprano in Italy and the existence of early Mode 1 industries in Europe, that it was, for at least part of its time, also present more broadly in the north-

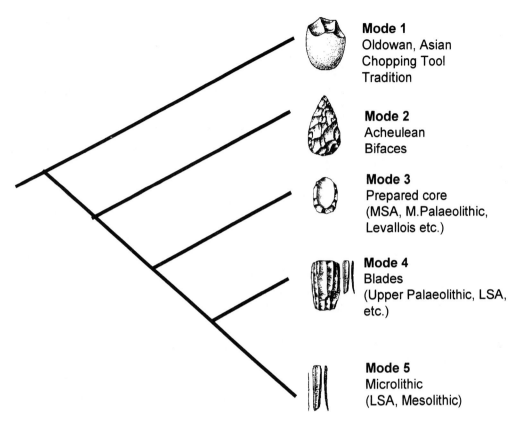

Mode 1
Oldowan, Asian
Chopping Tool
Tradition

Mode 2
Acheulean
Bifaces

Mode 3
Prepared core
(MSA, M.Palaeolithic,
Levallois etc.)

Mode 4
Blades
(Upper Palaeolithic, LSA,
etc.)

Mode 5
Microlithic
(LSA, Mesolithic)

Figure 8. Cladogram of stone tool technology, using Clark's modes. See Foley and Lahr 1997 for a full discussion.

ern parts of Eurasia, and indeed possibly in parts of Africa. Mode 2 technologies appear around 1.4 Myr, in association with *H. ergaster* in Africa. They remain, as far as current evidence goes, an essentially African phenomenon (with the probable exception of the Middle East) until after 700,000 years ago. At about this time *H. heidelbergensis* evolved in Africa, and it was this species that dispersed, with the Mode 2 technologies, into parts of Europe and Asia, giving rise to the European Acheulean.

The pattern after this becomes more complex, but also more interesting, for it is here that a focus on the lithic traditions can throw light on later human phylogeny. The current consensus, supported by both fossil and genetic evidence, is that modern humans evolved in Africa and dispersed from there (Lahr and Foley 1998). According to this model their ancestors diverged from the ancestors of Neanderthals with the first dispersals of *H. heidelbergensis* into Europe, some 600,000 years or more ago, after which there was no contact until the appearance of anatomically modern humans and the Aurignacian in Europe around 40,000 years ago. However, from an archaeological

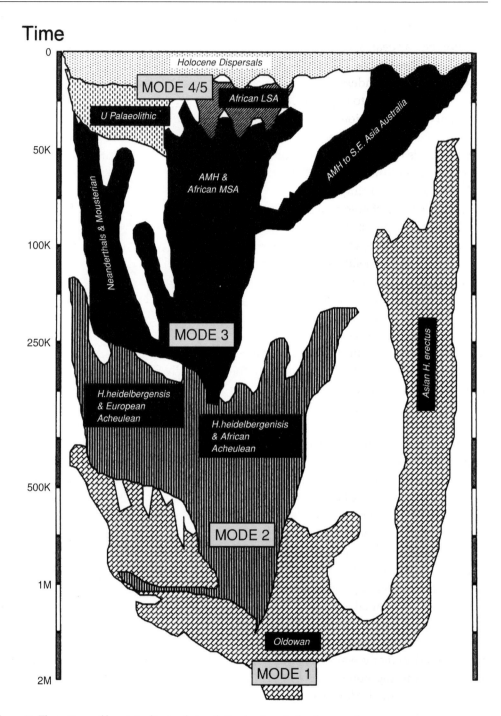

Figure 9. The pattern of hominin dispersals in relation to stone technology modes.

perspective this model raises a number of problems. About 250,000 years ago Mode 3 technologies appear, and they are found in both Africa and among the Neanderthals of Europe and the Middle East. Indeed, across the period from 150,000 years ago to 50,000 years ago both Neanderthals and modern humans were employing Mode 3 technologies. This may seem to support the idea of either contact (and presumably gene flow) between the populations, or else independent evolution. This former possibility seems to be precluded by what is known from genetics, including ancient DNA from Neanderthals (Krings *et al.* 1997). The latter possibility is consistent with the functional perspective on lithics of most archaeologists. However, the chances of two lineages independently acquiring the same technology at approximately the same time, after a million years of technological stability, seem remote. The alternative explanation is that rather than the ancestor Neanderthals and modern humans independently inventing Mode 3 technologies, they both possessed the technology because of a common ancestor. In other words, using a phylogenetic perspective, the shared Mode 3 technologies of modern humans and Neanderthals should be taken as evidence of them having a common ancestor after the development of these technologies — not over half a million years ago, but rather less than 300,000.

Such a perspective solves a number of problems; it explains why the Neanderthals and modern humans in the Mount Carmel area were both using a Middle Palaeolithic (Mode 3) technology; it is consistent with the genetically estimated date of the last common ancestor of Neanderthals, not more than 0.5 Myr; and most importantly, it helps to account for the fact that Neanderthals seem in so many ways to be very similar to modern humans — in their hunting abilities, in their use of fire, in their technology, in their increased large cranial capacity, and in the probability that they possessed language (Fig. 10). Although several problems remain, for example the question of tracking the morphological evolution of the Neanderthals, this explanation, based on integrating archaeological and fossil evidence in phylogenetic reconstruction, seems the most parsimonious. To accommodate this model, it has therefore been suggested that there is an African species of hominin, around 300,000 years ago, that was derived from the African branch of *H. heidelbergensis*, and which gave rise to both Neanderthals (by dispersing into Europe), and to *Homo sapiens*. This species has been tentatively identified as *H. helmei*, the type specimen of which is from Florisbad, and which possesses a number of derived cranial features that make it a potential generalized ancestor of the larger-brained later forms (Fig. 11).

This way of looking at the archaeological record and attempting to link it in to the fossil record in many ways harks back to an earlier form of archaeology. To some this may seem a retrograde step, more suitable for the first part of the twentieth century than the twenty-first. However, it is in no sense proposed that this should replace functional studies, but that cladistics offers a way of extracting further information out of the archaeological record, and, more specifically, bringing the story of human evolution,

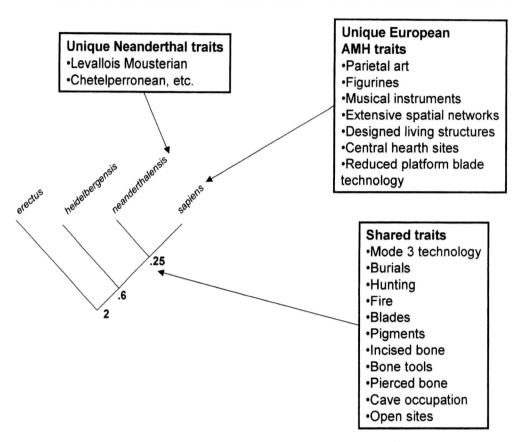

Figure 10. Cladogram of later hominins showing the proposed unique and close relationship between humans and Neanderthals, and a list of traits that are unique to each of them, and shared.

as told by the stone tools, into line with the approaches used in the biological sciences. In this case it also has implications for understanding the role of the Upper Palaeolithic and the problem of the emergence of modern humans, the next issue to be addressed here.

The evolution of modern humans

Among the various insights that can be derived from the attempt to look at the overall pattern of hominin evolution in terms of phylogeny are two that give a flavour of recent interpretations of the processes involved. The first is that there is a strong geographical element to human evolution (Foley 1999; Lahr and Foley 1998). In the past evolution was seen largely in terms of time and chronology — hominin species passed through

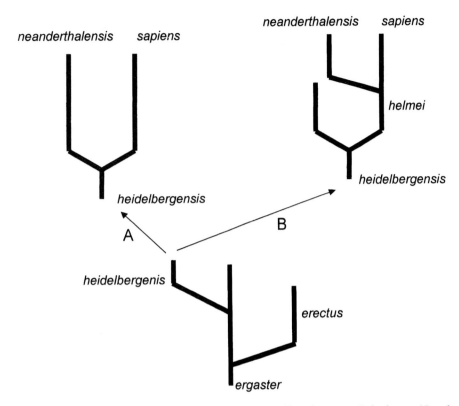

Figure 11. Alternative models of the evolutionary relationships of later hominins. In both cases Neanderthals and modern humans are derived from *H. heidelbergensis*, but in one case (A) they have a distant common ancestor, and in the other (B) they have a more recent common ancestor in *H. helmei*.

stages on their way to being modern humans, but in which part of the world they did this was largely irrelevant. Now geography is seen as of major significance. In current models it is clear that what is happening in Europe is different from what is happening in Africa, and that Asia presents yet a different pattern. This is far more complex than had previously been expected, but it is also consistent with the way evolution works. Since Darwin and Wallace, who wrote a book on the geographical distribution of species in an evolutionary light, it has been recognized that spatial patterns play a large role in evolution. The reason for this is that evolutionary changes require some degree of isolation, and geographical separation provides the primary basis for this. Evolution is a geographical process before it is a temporal one.

The second flavour that emerges, and which is related to the geographical emphasis, is that a key event in evolution is that of dispersal. Archaeological thought about migrations and dispersals has shifted considerably over the years. Under the influence of people such as Haddon and Elliott Smith extreme migrationist theories were predominant in the early part of the twentieth century. Later thinkers, such as Renfrew (Renfrew 1970), rejected these models, and for most of the second half of the twentieth century, autochthonous and local models of change predominated. People in the past became increasingly stationary and immobile. However, evolutionary thinking has always placed a greater emphasis on dispersals, and seen it as a major element of any model. For human evolution this is perhaps inevitable, given that the story of human evolution is one of a shift from a small local African population to a global one.

Geography and dispersals are thus the key elements in current models of the evolution of modern humans. Although this issue is usually considered in terms of a multiregional model, essentially an autochthonous, local process distributed across the world (Wolpoff 1989) and an 'out of Africa' model (Stringer 1989), virtually all the evidence supports the latter, and it is variants of these that are debated. For the purposes of this essay, a brief description of the evidence relating to the emergence of modern humans will suffice (for recent reviews and papers on which this description is based see Harpending 1994; Harpending *et al.* 1993; Klein 1999; Lahr and Foley 1998; Relethford and Harpending 1995; Sherry *et al.* 1994; Stringer 1995).

Studies of modern human genetics have shown that despite the size of the current human population, the amount of genetic diversity is very small. Diversity accumulates over time as a function of mutation, and so low levels of diversity are evidence for a recent and small ancestral population. In effect, this shows a bottleneck in our past, perhaps as small as 10,000 people. Current estimates suggest that this occurred between 200,000 and 150,000 years ago. In effect this genetic evidence, which now comes from several gene systems (mitochondrial DNA, Y chromosome, and microsatellites on the X chromosome) rules out any long-term global model for the evolution of modern humans. Our species must have had a small local origin, from which they spread.

The second finding is that the genetic variation among African populations is far greater than that of any other part of humanity, and, indeed, non-African diversity is a subset of African diversity. This is best interpreted as evidence for the origin being in Africa; this African population then grew, and parts of it dispersed across the world. The genetic evidence shows that this is not a single event, but involved a series of fragmentations and dispersals, with possibly an earlier southern Asian one (including Melanesia and Australia), and a later northern Eurasian one (Fig. 12).

The fossil evidence broadly supports this. The first anatomically modern form of human is found in Ethiopia at 140 Kyr (at Omo Kibbish), and earlier African hominin fossils indicate some morphological continuity. By 100,000 years these modern forms are present at both the southern and northern extremes of the continent. There is archaeological evidence for the presence of humans in Australia by between 50,000 and 60,000 years ago, and in Europe by 40,000 years. In non-African parts of the world there is no morphological continuity. The only area for which there is good fossil evidence on archaic populations, Europe, shows the persistence of Neanderthals until after 30,000

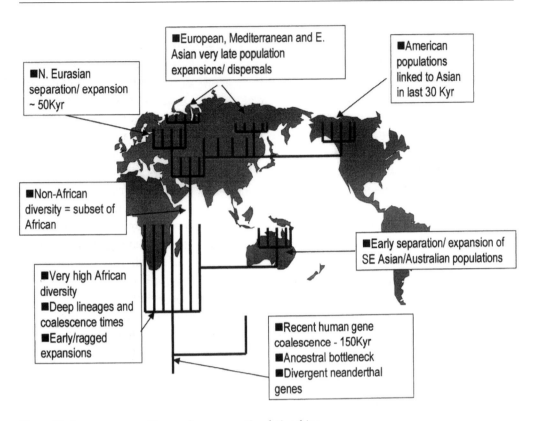

Figure 12. Summary map of known human genetic relationships.

years ago, with no trend towards modern forms, and no evidence for significant admixture.

A synthesis of modern human evolution would thus consist of a background of widely dispersed and geographically separated non-modern forms — basically the descendants of earlier dispersals out of Africa — *H. erectus* in Asia, *H. heidelbergensis* and *H. helmei* in Europe and Africa. During the extreme cold phase of the penultimate glaciation, around 150,000 years ago (Stage 6 according to the marine isotope record), African populations became greatly reduced and fragmented, and one of these developed modern human features. As the climate warmed from 125,000 years ago (Isotope Stage 5), these African populations underwent an initial set of dispersals, across Africa and into the Middle East. However, these dispersals were brought to an end by the onset of the cold conditions of the last glaciation. There was at this stage further fragmentation of the modern human population, and isolation during which time diversity accumulated, diversity that would later be spread across the world. In some parts the modern human populations would have become extinct, as perhaps occurred in the Levant, where Neanderthals replaced the modern forms. After 60,000 years, populations again began to disperse out of Africa; first, by a southern route across the Indian Ocean rim, and into South East Asia and Australia; and second, after 50,000 years, through the Middle East into Europe (the Upper Palaeolithic expansions, bringing the Neanderthals to an end), and ultimately across northern Eurasia and into the Americas. However, these dispersals were by no means a continuous and even process. The period between 25,000 and 15,000 years ago saw a major reduction in global temperatures and the onset of the last glacial maximum, during which time human populations again crashed and fragmented, and it was only after 15,000 years ago that many parts of the world were either occupied or reoccupied by humans as they dispersed widely and densely, both as hunter-gatherers such as in the African Later Stone Age or the European Mesolithic, or as agriculturalists from the Middle East.

What are the implications of this emerging synthesis for archaeology? Perhaps the most obvious is the increasing potential of molecular genetics to be used as a tool for prehistoric investigations, a theme discussed by Renfrew in this volume in relation to later prehistory. Molecular genetics can provide insights into the timing of evolutionary events, the movements of populations, and give estimates of past demography. The techniques are still being developed, but there is little doubt that much of the palaeoanthropology of the twenty-first century will involve the integration of such data with both fossil and archaeological information.

Beyond this, the evidence for modern human evolution shows a number of things that are a challenge to archaeological thought. First, that there is clear evidence that there is a disjunction in the Palaeolithic between modern populations and archaic ones. The Pleistocene cannot be reduced to a gradual and seamless global evolution of humanity; rather, it is a pattern of discontinuity and geographical and chronological complexity, one that continues through into the diversification of human populations more recently. This means that archaeologists have to be much more specific in the relationships they seek to find between populations and their environments, or reconstructions of their social lives, for each population and species has a particular context and particular characteristics. The hominin diversity discussed here is more than just a backdrop, it is the reality of early human prehistory.

A second implication is the complexity of the last 150,000 years. The 'out of Africa' model is often reduced to the idea of a small population in Africa evolving modern human features and behaviour, and dispersing across the world immediately — the so-called Upper Palaeolithic or cultural or symbolic revolution. In fact this 'event' is actually multiple events spread over more than one hundred thousand years (Lahr and Foley 1994). The evolution of human behaviour, perhaps the key concern of archaeologists, cannot be compressed into a single step. How it might have occurred will be the next theme discussed here.

Evolution of modern human behaviour and cognition

In the second half of the twentieth century there have essentially been two archaeological models for the evolution of human behaviour. The first of these is a gradualist one, seeing human behaviour as having evolved gradually in all its components from a very early date, with most elements being in place in rudimentary form from the origins of *Homo*. Manifestations and elements of this model can be seen in Isaac's food sharing model (Isaac 1978), in Richard Lee's statement that 99 per cent of all human prehistory was that of the hunter-gatherer (Lee and DeVore 1968), and in Tobias' interpretation of the endocasts of *Homo habilis* showing evidence for language (Tobias 1991). At the other extreme is a late revolutionary model, one that sees human behaviour being radically contrasted with that of earlier hominins, and evolving only late and relatively quickly. The origins of this model probably lie with Binford's reinterpretation of the evidence for meat-eating among early hominins discussed earlier (Binford 1984), but are more fully developed in Mellars' interpretation of the French Middle to Upper Palaeolithic transition (Mellars 1991), and Klein's ideas concerning the explosive transition of the Upper Palaeolithic and its evidence for a new mode of thought (Klein 1992). It is also elaborated by Mithen (Mithen 1996) and Noble and Davidson (Noble and Davidson 1991) in terms of the origins of language.

If there is one point that is clear from this paper, it is that the answer to which of these models, or some intermediate one, is correct cannot come solely from either archaeology or biology, for the behaviour must be based on broader evolutionary biology. Language, for example, is rooted in biological structures in the brain and the rest of the body, and to consider art as a manifestation of language without considering its biological context would be misleading. Equally it is clear that the biological appearance of new species, including *Homo sapiens* itself, does not necessarily coincide with any evidence for major behavioural change. In this case the archaeological evidence for the significance of modern humans relative to other hominins is at least 50,000, if not 100,000, years after the morphological and genetic changes.

In the light of the evidence discussed here, a number of generalizations about the emergence of modern behaviour can be made. First, for the first three million years of hominin evolution there is little evidence for any behaviours that would fall outside the range of living ape behaviour. Second, that with the emergence of *Homo ergaster* we can see a number of components of behaviour that are closer to the human than ape form, but still intermediate; these include more meat-eating and probably hunting, a slower rate of growth and so presumably more pronounced parental care and complex sociality. However, there are also a number of very clear differences between the archaic *Homo* — *H. ergaster*, *H. erectus*, *H. heidelbergensis* — and later forms. These can principally be seen in the technology. The phylogenetic tracking of technology shown above is essentially evidence for a very conservative and inflexible approach to technology, suggesting that the cognition of the hominins was limited in terms of innovation and the production of novel variants. This can be taken as evidence for either a radically different process of cultural transmission among early hominins, or else strong cognitive constraints on production. While these constraints did not place very marked ecological limits on the spread of hominins, they clearly affected their potential for the accumulation of denser and more complex populations.

Thirdly, this pattern is contrasted with the later representatives of *Homo* — *H. neanderthalensis* and *H. sapiens*. Despite the efforts that have been made to emphasize marked differences between these two species, they in fact share many advanced characteristics, and Neanderthals are in many ways more similar to modern humans than they are to earlier *Homo*. Both species were capable of hunting with projectiles, using fire extensively, producing regionally variable technologies, perhaps making some form of art, and burying their dead. They were also both able, unlike earlier species, to survive extreme cold environments. It can further be argued that Neanderthals as well as modern humans possessed some linguistic capabilities, for they show evidence for the fine control of the diaphragm musculature that is a central part of speech (McLarnon 1996). Using the ideas developed above (see pp. 27–9), the evolution of *H. helmei* brought this about. Finally, the evolution of modern humans morphologically did not lead to an immediate flourishing of culture and population expansion, for the primary evidence for these is the Upper Palaeolithic, which is essentially a Eurasian rather than global phenomenon, and does not occur until after 40,000 years ago (Fig. 13).

How can these findings be pulled together? Perhaps the most important point is that it is not possible to lump together all archaic *Homo* in contrast to modern humans, for they show very different cognitive and behavioural characteristics. Equally, there are clearly significant changes that occur after the appearance of modern humans (Foley 1988). Genetic evidence precludes these from being simply biological, for it would mean that different human populations would have very different cognitive traits, given that many of them diverged from each other more than 40,000 years ago. All humans seem to have the same cultural and linguistic potential.

There is thus a paradox emerging. All the evidence points to the emergence of modern humans being a biologically significant event, and yet the detailed archaeological chronology suggests that it cannot be solely biological. The solution to this paradox will, I would argue, be the greatest challenge to archaeology and palaeoanthropology over the next decade. There are a number of pointers to a solution. One is that specific ecological, demographic and social conditions determine how the cultural and cognitive potential of humans is developed and expressed. For the early success of the human species one possibility is that of the greater use of marine resources and the ability to move around the aquatic environment. This gave them enormous potential for dispersal, and to some extent for social elaboration. However, the real key lies in

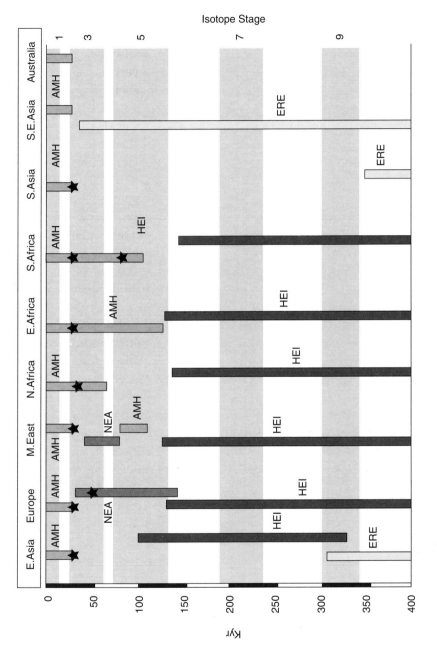

Figure 13. The relationship between modern human fossils and blade technology (often associated with the Upper Palaeolithic). As can be seen, in Africa there is a long period of anatomical modernity with no blades, and this pattern is found elsewhere.

population density; it is only when populations are densely packed, either in naturally rich environments, or when agriculture develops, and human mobility is limited, that what we think of as the innate cultural and social complexity of humans emerges. In other words, human evolution did not 'stop' 150,000 years ago with the evolution of our own species, but was a continuous process throughout the later parts of the Pleistocene and into the Holocene.

Evolutionary archaeology

The history of prehistoric archaeology and biological approaches to human evolution during the twentieth century is essentially one of divergence. The achievements of both are massive in terms of establishing a firm chronological and geographical framework for the history of our species and its predecessors, and this framework is largely concordant. However, conceptually the two disciplines have grown apart. Most archaeologists have paid little heed to the increasing power of evolutionary ideas or the power of techniques such as cladistics and molecular genetics to throw light on the past. Social, cultural and post-modernist ideas have dominated debates in archaeological theory, at the expense of evolutionary ones. By and large these have had little or no impact on evolutionary biology, and that is likely to continue to be the case. Instead evolutionary biology has extended its concepts and models to incorporate more and more of human life — evolutionary psychology, social evolution, behavioural ecology and life history theory are but a few of these. If there is to be a widening debate in archaeology, it is likely to incorporate more and more of these ideas, and the methods and approaches of biology. If the twentieth century was the century of social theory, the twenty-first is equally likely to be that of evolutionary theory. The impact of this is likely to be greatest on Palaeolithic archaeology, which more and more will be carried out in the broader context of evolutionary ideas. The divide between the 'stones' and the 'bones' will be seen as increasingly archaic and arbitrary. It is already the case that the term 'palaeoanthropology' is increasingly used to describe both archaeologists and biological anthropologists specializing in human evolution. It will be as important for archaeologists to know the details of molecular genetics as they do of Quaternary geology. Whether this will occur within archaeology, or by archaeologists migrating into other disciplines, remains to be seen.

However, it is not merely a case of learning new techniques and using new datasets. The central point of this essay has been that evolution is not merely a way of referring to what happened in the deep past, but of thinking about archaeological problems in particular ways. Evolutionary theory, and especially its Darwinian components, is a way of explaining how populations change and adapt. Such changes occur at all timescales and in all populations, and although at the moment it is the earlier phases of prehistory that are most susceptible to this approach, it is likely that all of archaeology will eventually feel the effects of the growth of human evolutionary studies. If this is the case, then ironically the archaeologists of the twenty-first century will share much of their concerns and approaches with those of the nineteenth-century pioneers who first started to track the evolutionary history of our species, and so created modern archaeology in the first place.

Postscript

Since this was written there have been two new discoveries that add further to the diversity of fossil hominin forms described here. The first of these is from the Baringo basin of Kenya, dated to around six million years ago. Known as *Orrorin tugenensis*, this find is subject to considerable controversy, but perhaps indicates the presence of bipedal hominin forms at an earlier date than other known specimens. The second, referred to as *Kenyanthropus platyiops* is dated to around 3.5 million years, and adds considerably to the known diversity of hominins around the time of *Australopithecus afarensis*.

References

AIELLO, L.C. and WHEELER, P. 1995: The Expensive Tissue Hypothesis. *Current Anthropol.* 36, 199–222.

ARDREY, R. 1961: *African Genesis* (London).

ASFAW, B., WHITE, T., LOVEJOY, O., LATIMER, B., SIMPSON, S. and SUWA, G. 1999: *Australopithecus garhi*: A New Species of Early Hominid from Ethiopia. *Science* 284, 629–35.

AVISE, J.C. 1994: *Molecular Markers, Natural History and Evolution* (New York).

BATESON, P.P.G. 1988: The Active Role of Behaviour in Evolution. In Ho, M.W. and Fox, S.W. (eds.), *Evolutionary Processes and Metaphors* (New York), 191–207.

BEYNON, A.D. and DEAN, M.C. 1988: Distinct Dental Development Patterns in Early Fossil Hominids. *Nature* 335, 509–14.

BEYNON, A.D. and WOOD, B.A. 1987: Patterns and Rates of Molar Crown Formation Times in East African Hominids. *Nature* 326, 493–6.

BINFORD, L.R. 1981: *Bones: Ancient Men and Modern Myths* (New York and London).

BINFORD, L.R. 1984: *Faunal Remains from Klasies River Mouth* (New York and London).

BINFORD, L.R. and BINFORD, S.R. 1966: A Preliminary Analysis of Functional Variability in the Mousterian of Levallois Facies. *American Anthropologist* 68, 238–95.

BOONE, J.L. and SMITH, E.A. 1998: Is It Evolution Yet? A Critique of Evolutionary Archaeology. *Current Anthropol.* 39, S141–S173.

BORDES, F. 1961: *Typologie Du Paleolithique Ancien Et Modern* (Bordeaux).

BROMAGE, T.G. and DEAN, M.C. 1985: Re-Evaluation of the Age at Death of Plio-Pleistocene Fossil Hominids. *Nature* 317, 525–8.

BRUNET, M., BEAUVILAIN, A., COPPENS, Y., HEINTZ, E., MOUTAYE, A.H.E. and PILBEAM, D. 1995: The First Australopithecine 2,500 Kilometers West of the Rift-Valley (Chad). *Nature* 378, 273–5.

BUNN, H.T. and KROLL, E.M. 1986: Systematic Butchery by Plio/Pleistocene Hominids at Olduvai Gorge, Tanzania. *Current Anthropol.* 27, 431–52.

CHARNOV, E. and BERIGAN, D. 1993: Why Do Female Primates Have Such Long Lifespans and So Few Babies? Or Life in the Slow Lane. *Evolutionary Anthropol.* 1, 191–4.

CLARK, G.A. 1989: Alternative Models of Pleistocene Biocultural Evolution — a Response. *Antiquity* 63, 153–9.

CLARK, J.G.D. 1968: *World Prehistory: A New Outline* (Cambridge).

CLARKE, R.J. 1985: Australopithecus and Early Homo in Southern Africa. In Delson, E. (ed.), *Ancestors: The Hard Evidence* (New York), 171–7.

DE HEINZELIN, J., CLARK, J.D., WHITE, T. *et al.* 1999: Environment and Behavior of 2.5-Million-Year-Old Bouri Hominids. *Science* 284, 625–9.

DECASTRO, J.M.B., ARSUAGA, J.L., CARBONELL, E., ROSAS, A., MARTINEZ, I. and MOSQUERA, M. 1997: A Hominid from the Lower Pleistocene of Atapuerca, Spain: Possible Ancestor to Neanderthals and Modern Humans. *Science* 276, 1392–5.

FOLEY, R.A. 1987a: *Another Unique Species: Patterns of Human Evolutionary Ecology* (Harlow).

FOLEY, R.A. 1987b: Hominid Species and Stone Tools Assemblages: How Are They Related? *Antiquity* 61, 380–92.

FOLEY, R.A. 1988: Hominids, Humans & Hunter-Gatherers: An Evolutionary Perspective. In Ingold, T., Riches, D. and Woodburn, J. (eds.), *Hunters and Gatherers 1: History, Evolution and Social Change* (Oxford), 207–21.

FOLEY, R.A. 1989: The Ecological Conditions of Speciation: A Comparative Approach to the Origins of Anatomically Modern Humans. In Mellars, P. and Stringer, C.B. (eds.), *The Human Revolution* (Edinburgh), 298–320.

FOLEY, R.A. 1991: How Many Species of Hominid Should There Be. *J. Human Evolution* 20, 413–27.

FOLEY, R.A. 1995: *Humans before Humanity: An Evolutionary Perspective* (Oxford).

FOLEY, R.A. 1999: The Evolutionary Geography of Pliocene Hominids. In Bromage, T. and Schrenk, F. (eds.), *African Biogeography, Climatic Change, and Hominid Evolution* (Oxford).

FOLEY, R.A. and LAHR, M.M. 1997: Mode 3 Technologies and the Evolution of Modern Humans. *Cambridge Archaeol. J.* 7, 3–36.

FOLEY, R. and LEE, P.C. 1989: Finite Social Space, Evolutionary Pathways, and Reconstructing Hominid Behavior. *Science* 243, 901–6.

GABUNIA, L., VEKUA, A., LORDKIPANIDZE, D. *et al.* 2000: Earliest Pleistocene Hominid Cranial Remains from Dmanisi, Republic of Georgia: Taxonomy, Geological Setting, and Age. *Science* 288, 1019–25.

GAGNEUX, P., WILLS, C., GERLOFF, U. *et al.* 1999: Mitochondrial Sequences Show Diverse Evolutionary Histories of African Hominoids. *Proc. Nat. Acad. Sciences United States of America* 96, 5077–82.

GOODMAN, M., TAGLE, D.A., FITCH, D.H.A. *et al.* 1990: Primate Evolution at the DNA Level and a Classification of Hominoids. *J. Molecular Evolution* 30, 260–6.

GRINE, F.E. 1989: *The Evolutionary History of the 'Robust' Australopithecines* (Chicago).

HARPENDING, H. 1994: Signature of Ancient Population Growth in a low Resolution Mitochondrial DNA Mismatch Distribution. *Human Biol.* 66, 591–600.

HARPENDING, H., SHERRY, S.T., ROGERS, A.R. and STONEKING, M. 1993: The Genetic Structure of Ancient Human Populations. *Current Anthropol.* 34, 483–96.

HUBLIN, J.J. 1996: The First Europeans. *Archaeology* 49, 36–44.

ISAAC, G. 1978: The Food-Sharing Behaviour of Protohuman Hominids. *Scientific American* 238, 90–108.

ISAAC, G. 1981: Bones in Contention: Competing Explanations for the Juxtaposition of Artefacts and Faunal Remains. In Clutton-Brock, J. and Grigson, C. (eds.), *Animals and Archaeology: 1. Hunters and Their Prey* (Oxford, BAR 163).

JOHANSON, D.C., TAIEB, M. and COPPENS, Y. 1982: Pliocene Hominids from the Hadar Formation, Ethiopia (1973–1977): Stratigraphic, Chronologic and Palaeoenvironmental Contexts. *American J. Physical Anthropol.* 22, 373–402.

JOHANSON, D.C. and WHITE, T.D. 1979: A Systematic Assessment of Early African Hominids. *Science* 203, 321–30.

KLEIN, R.G. 1992: The Archaeology of Modern Human Origins. *Evolutionary Anthropol.* 1, 5–14.

KLEIN, R.G. 1999: *The Human Career* (Chicago, 2nd edition).

KRINGS, M., STONE, A., SCHMITZ, R.W., KRAINITZKI, H., STONEKING, M. and PAABO, S. 1997: Neandertal DNA Sequences and the Origin of Modern Humans. *Cell* 90, 19–30.

LAHR, M.M. and FOLEY, R.A. 1994: Multiple Dispersals and Modern Human Origins. *Evolutionary Anthropol.* 3, 48–60.

LAHR, M.M. and FOLEY, R.A. 1998: Towards a Theory of Modern Human Origins: Geography, Demography, and Diversity in Recent Human Evolution. *Yearbook of Physical Anthropology* 41, 137–76.

LAUGHLIN, W.S. 1968: Hunting: An Integrating Biobehavior System and Its Evolutionary Importance. In Lee, R.B. and DeVore, I. (eds.), *Man the Hunter* (Chicago), 304–20.

LEAKEY, L.S.B. 1961: New Finds at Olduvai Gorge. *Nature* 189, 649–50.

LEAKEY, L.S.B., TOBIAS, P.V. and NAPIER, J.R. 1961: A New Species of the Genus *Homo* from Olduvai Gorge, Tanganyika. *Nature* 202, 308–12.

LEAKEY, M.G., FEIBEL, C.S., MCDOUGALL, I. and WALKER, A. 1995: New 4-Million-Year-Old Hominid Species from Kanapoi and Allia Bay, Kenya. *Nature* 376, 565–71.

LEE, R.B. and DEVORE, I. 1968: Problems in the Study of Hunters and Gatherers. In Lee, R.B. and DeVore, I. (eds.), *Man the Hunter* (Chicago), 3–12.

LEWIN, R. 1990: *Bones of Contention* (New York).

MARTIN, R.D. 1983: *Human Brain Evolution in an Ecological Context* (New York, American Museum of Natural History).

MCLARNON, A. 1996: The Evolution of the Spinal Cord in Primates: Evidence from the Foramen Magnum and the Vertebral Canal. *J. Human Evolution* 30, 121–38.

MELLARS, P.A. 1970: The Chronology of Mousterian Industries in the Perigord Region of South-Western France. *Proc. Prehist. Soc.* 35, 134–57.

MELLARS, P. 1991: Cognitive Changes and the Emergence of Modern Humans in Europe. *Cambridge Archaeol. J.* 1, 63–76.

MITHEN, S. 1996: *The Prehistory of the Mind* (London).

NOBLE, W. and DAVIDSON, I. 1991: The Evolutionary Emergence of Modern Human-Behavior — Language and Its Archaeology. *Man* 26, 223–53.

PILBEAM, D. 1968: The Earliest Hominids. *Nature* 219, 1335.

POTTS, R. 1984: Hominid Hunters? Problems of Identifying the Earliest Hunter/Gatherers. In Foley, R. (ed.), *Hominid Evolution and Community Ecology: Prehistoric Human Adaptation in Biological Perspective* (London), 129–66.

READER, J. 1988: *Missing Links* (London, 2nd edition).

RELETHFORD, J.H. and HARPENDING, H. 1995: Ancient Differences in Population Size Can Mimic a Recent African Origin of Modern Humans. *Current Anthropol.* 36, 667–74.

RENFREW, A.C. 1970: New Configurations in Old World Archaeology. *World Prehist.* 2, 199–211.

RIGHTMIRE, G.P. 1998: Human Evolution in the Middle Pleistocene: The Role of *Homo heidelbergensis*. *Evolutionary Anthropol.* 6, 218–27.

RUFF, C.B., TRINKAUS, E. and HOLLIDAY, T.W. 1997: Body Mass and Encephalization in Pleistocene Homo. *Nature* 387, 173–6.

SCHULTZ, A.H. 1969: *The Life of Primates* (New York).

SHERRY, S.T., ROGERS, A.R., HARPENDING, H., SOODYALL, H., JENKINS, T. and STONEKING, M. 1994: Mismatch Distributions of MtDNA Reveal Recent Human Population Expansions. *Human Biol.* 66, 761–75.

SMITH, B.H. 1989: Dental Development as a Measure of Life History in Primates. *Evolution* 43, 683–8.

SMITH, B.H. 1993: The Physiological Age of Wt15000. In Walker A.C. and Leakey R.E. (eds.) 1993, 195–220.

STEWART, C.B. and DISOTELL, T.R. 1998: Primate Evolution — in and out of Africa. *Current Biol.* 8, R582–R588.

STRINGER, C.B. 1989: Documenting the Origin of Modern Humans. In Trinkaus E. (ed.), *The Emergence of Modern Humans* (Cambridge), 67–96.

STRINGER, C.B. 1992: Reconstructing Recent Human Evolution. *Phil. Trans. Roy. Soc. London, Series B337*, 217–24.

STRINGER, C.B. 1995: The Evolution and Distribution of Later Pleistocene Human Populations. In Vrba, E.S., Denton, G.H., Partridge, T.C. and Burckle, L.H. (eds.), *Paleoclimate and Evolution with Emphasis on Human Origins* (New Haven), 524–31.

STRINGER, C. and GAMBLE, C. 1993: *In Search of the Neanderthals* (London).

TOBIAS, P.V. 1991: *Olduvai Gorge Volume 4: The Skulls, Teeth, and Endocasts of Homo Habilis* (Cambridge).

WALKER, A.C. and LEAKEY, R.E. (eds.) 1993: *The Nariokotome Skeleton* (Cambridge, MA).

WALKER, A., LEAKEY, R.E., HARRIS, J.M. and BROWN, F.H. 1986: 2.5 Myr *Australopithecus boisei* from West of Lake Turkana, Kenya. *Nature* 322, 517–22.

WARD, C., LEAKEY, M. and WALKER, A. 1999: The New Hominid Species *Australopithecus anamensis*. *Evolutionary Anthropol.* 7, 197–205.

WHITE, T.D., SUWA, G. and ASFAW, B. 1994: *Australopithecus ramidus*, a New Species of Early Hominid from Aramis, Ethiopia. *Nature* 366, 261–5.

WOLPOFF, M.H. 1989: Multiregional Evolution: The Fossil Alternative to Eden. In Mellars, P. and Stringer, C.B. (eds.), *The Human Revolution* (Edinburgh), 62–108.

WOOD, B. and COLLARD, M. 1999a: Anthropology — the Human Genus. *Science* 284, 65–71.

WOOD, B. and COLLARD, M. 1999b: The Changing Face of Genus *Homo*. *Evolutionary Anthropol.* 8, 195–207.

Genetics and language in contemporary archaeology

COLIN RENFREW

At the turn of the century and of the millennium the impact of molecular genetics is only now beginning to be felt in contemporary archaeology.[1] The delay comes partly from the extreme difficulty in recovering usable data from Ancient DNA. With a few notable exceptions the most important results have come from the examination of samples taken from living populations. These results have been reported in technical journals, such as the *American Journal of Human Genetics*: they are little known yet in archaeological circles. Already it is clear that a whole new field of information is opening up which will be of particular use in giving insights into demographic processes during the Upper Palaeolithic period and subsequently. There remain many interpretive difficulties, and it is not yet clear how numerous or how reliable will be the insights offered into events and processes over the past four or five millennia. What is clear is the pace and scale of the flow of new information. This is a dynamic, expanding area and every year there are new insights. I predict that over the next decade this will be one of the fastest moving fields in archaeological research — even if it carries with it the paradox (for the archaeologist) that much of the new information comes from the genes of living populations.

With the insights to be gained from the study of languages the situation is very different. This is a field which for over a century has had a well-established overlap with archaeology. There is a distinct feeling of *déjà vu* about many discussions of archaeology and language, which have been well established since before the days of Childe (1926) and *The Aryans*. Yet historical linguistics too is now on the move. The earlier, simplistic notions about prehistoric migrations are giving way to much more sophisticated analyses of language change (e.g. Thomason and Kaufman 1988).

Some years ago I suggested, perhaps rather boldly (Renfrew 1991), that a 'new synthesis' now seemed possible between the three adjacent disciplines of prehistoric

---

[1] This article draws upon three earlier reviews: Renfrew 1992b; 1998a and 1998c.

archaeology, historical linguistics and molecular genetics. That claim was indeed perhaps a shade premature and the new synthesis may be still a little way off. But since an initial attempt at rethinking the issues (with particular reference to the Indo-European language family), *Archaeology and Language,* was first published (Renfrew 1987) there has been a steady flow of volumes devoted to the same or related topics at a world-wide level (Blench and Spriggs 1997, 1998, 1999a, 1999b; McConvell and Evans 1997), where the areas of intersection between the two disciplines are given systematic consideration. Ultimately perhaps of even greater significance are the developments within the discipline of historical linguistics itself, giving more systematic scrutiny to themes such as linguistic diversity (Nettle 1999a), convergence and creole languages (Thomason and Kaufman 1988), general processes of language change (Dixon 1997), morphological and structural aspects considered in great time depth (Nichols 1992) and contact-induced language change (Ehret 1988; Ross 1996, 1997; also Tryon 1999). Convincing synthesis may not yet be available, but the ground is certainly being prepared.

The overlap areas between the three disciplines may be illustrated in the following diagram.

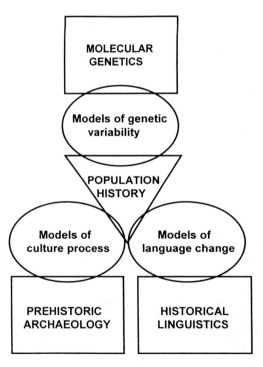

Figure 1. The relationship between molecular genetics, historical linguistics and prehistoric archaeology. Each is an autonomous discipline, and inference from one to another involves conceptual difficulties. (From Renfrew 1998a, 175.)

There are real conceptual and methodological difficulties in moving from one field to the other. For instance there are no genes controlling individual languages. Molecular genetics and historical linguistics are related primarily through the field of human population history. So that although there have been pioneering attempts to establish relationships between molecular genetics and historical linguistics (e.g. Cavalli-Sforza, Piazza, Menozzi and Mountain 1988) these have been robustly criticized as being both premature and methodologically flawed (Bateman *et al.* 1990; McMahon and McMahon 1995; Sims-Williams 1998a).

Archaeology and genetics

Classical genetic markers

In recent years the general emphasis has shifted away from the traditional use of metrical parameters derived from bones and teeth towards biochemical methods. Many of these are now well established: together they constitute what may be termed the 'classical' approach. The procedures of craniometry, supported by multivariant statistical methods, are still useful for the study of human evolution, but seem of relatively little value for studies within the species of fully modern *Homo sapiens*.

Long before the development of molecular biology, indeed before the determining role of DNA in inheritance was understood, Mendelian genetics and cell biochemistry had together made very significant strides in the investigation of human genetic variability. It is now well understood that a whole series of biochemical systems, for instance, blood groups, blood sera, proteins, antigens, etc., are under close genetic determination. The genes are located principally along the chain-like chromosomes within the nucleus of the human cell. Within a given system (for instance, a specific blood group system) phenotypic differences, such as between Rhesus positive and Rhesus negative, are determined by genetic differences of a specific nature. *Polymorphism*, the condition that within a population there exist such differences, implies the presence of two or more *alleles*: alternative genes, similar but not identical, located at a particular position or locus on a chromosome.

The now-classical biochemical approach (Cavalli-Sforza, Menozzi and Piazza 1994) consists in taking samples, usually blood samples, from a well-defined human population and testing these to determine for each individual the presence or absence of the alleles of the given polymorphisms under investigation, for instance, specific blood groups. The number of individuals within the given sample of the population who possess a particular blood group, or immune reaction, or whatever, is expressed as a frequency. The matter becomes interesting when these frequencies, often termed *gene frequencies*, are compared for the different sample populations. Initially, this is done in

tabular form, with a matrix of frequencies for the different alleles of the various different blood or immune systems considered, as seen in the various human populations
sampled.

In general there are two approaches towards the analysis of such data. The first
approach is *spatial*, with the production of *gene frequency maps* (e.g. Mourant *et al.* 1976;
Cavalli-Sforza 1988, 1991). Statistical methods, including principal components analysis, are available to allow the pooling of all the data and the production of a single map,
or of a series of maps, which gives an accurate picture of the spatial variation in the data
(e.g. Menozzi *et al.* 1978). In this case the first principal component could be compared
plausibly with the effect to be anticipated from the spread of farming across Europe by
demic diffusion, assuming that the genetic contribution of the first farmers from
Anatolia was increasingly attenuated as the farming population spread and as time
passed (see Sokal *et al.* 1991).

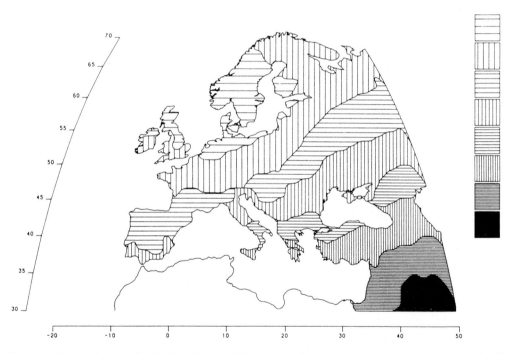

Figure 2. Geographic map for the First Principal Component from the analysis of gene frequencies for 95
genes measured for different sampling locations in Europe. (From Cavalli-Sforza, Menozzi and Piazza 1994,
292.)

Sophisticated techniques exist to put together and evaluate the information contained in a whole series of such maps. One technique, known as 'wombling', makes it
possible to define the localized parts of the map where the genetic frequencies change

most rapidly, the *clines* (Barbujani *et al.* 1989). Work by Barbujani and Sokal (1990), for instance, indicates that the area corresponding to modern Hungary is separated by clines of genetic variability from its neighbours, and it is, of course, tempting to link this with the circumstance that a Finno-Ugrian language is spoken in Hungary which is radically different from those of its Indo-European-speaking neighbours.

There are, however, several problems surrounding the use of gene frequency maps in this way in the correlation of long-term population history, and hence possibly of linguistic history (Slatkin 1987; Barbujani 1991). The first is the obvious and well-known phenomenon of *genetic drift*. Just how stable through time are such spatial structures in gene frequencies, even when the populations are relatively isolated? The second problem is that some of these genes and their phenotypes may not be adaptively neutral — that they will be actively selected for (or against) over time, so that some of the variation is to be associated with environmental — including climatic — variables. And above all, the gene frequency map is a map of now. It is the product of millennia of historical events, many of them minor, but cumulatively difficult to predict in their effects. We may well be willing to admit that early demographic processes may have had a determining impact on both genetic and linguistic distributions. But how do we know which gene frequencies are pertinent to the question without independent evidence for the gene frequencies of earlier populations? This will always be difficult to obtain, since even if the necessary genetic information could be extracted from ancient human remains, the limited availability of material (i.e. the scarcity of preserved remains of individuals) will always make it difficult to achieve results that are statistically significant using Ancient DNA.

A different approach is to use the genetic data to create a *phenetic dendrogram*, a tree based on the computation of similarities and differences among the populations sampled. A good example is offered by the work of Excoffier and his colleagues on a range of African populations (Excoffier *et al.* 1987, 170). The frequencies of the various *haplotypes* (i.e. varieties) of Gamma-globulin in the blood of various African populations (sampled on the basis of language families) were determined and a phenetic dendrogram constructed. A notable correspondence was observed between the grouping of the populations as seen on the tree, derived entirely from genetic data, and the language families to which these populations belonged.

The same logical approach has been applied at a world level (aggregating numerous genetic markers), achieving a structure in which the populations of sub-Saharan Africa differ from those of the rest of the world. Here a family tree is produced which correlates very neatly with the 'out-of-Africa' model of the palaeontologists. Cavalli-Sforza and his colleagues have produced a similar tree using frequency studies of DNA polymorphisms (Cavalli-Sforza 1991, 75). But we should note that only a few years earlier Cavalli-Sforza and Edwards (1965) were suggesting a tree of different form, as indeed subsequently were Excoffier and his colleagues (Excoffier *et al.* 1987,

180), where the big split came not between Africa and the rest, but between Occidentals and Orientals, with a secondary split between Caucasoids and Black Africans. Given the frailness of the 'constant divergence' assumption, we should not yet regard the interpretive problems in the construction and interpretation of such trees as resolved. The appropriate manner of constructing a phylogenetic tree from contemporary data has been much discussed in recent years, with emphasis laid upon the maximum parsimony tree (Maddison 1991; Templeton 1992). It is not, however, clear that the maximum parsimony tree is an entirely safe approximation towards the goal of a real *phylogenetic tree*. To the extent that these two trees coincide, the nodes in the diagram will represent actual fission events, and the ancestral forms which precede them. These ancestral forms will actually have lived at some specific time in the past. In favourable cases evidence for them (in the shape of records of extinct languages, or ancestral fossils, or DNA recovered from ancient tissue or bone) may be recovered and examined.

About DNA: the molecular genetic background

A *gene* may be defined as the smallest unit of heredity encoding a molecular cell product. Neither Darwin nor Mendel, the early fathers of what we today call 'genetics', had the possibility of understanding the molecular basis which emerged as the result of developments in the field of biochemistry in the middle of this century. It came to be understood that the essential genetic information is contained within the nucleus of the cell. More specifically it is contained within the *chromosomes* which are small, thread-like bodies within the cell. In the human case there are 22 pairs of chromosomes plus 2 sex chromosomes within the nucleus. In 1953 (half a century after the chromosome theory of heredity was formulated) James Watson and Francis Crick, working in Cambridge, put forward a structural model for the stuff that genes are made of: *deoxyribonucleic acid* (DNA). They suggested that the molecule consists of two chains of *nucleotides* wound about each other to form a double helix. The structure can be thought of as a twisted ladder, with a sugar-phosphate backbone, and projecting inward from each sugar, to form the horizontal rungs, are pairs of bases. Four different bases occur in DNA: adenine (A), guanine (G), thyamine (T) and cytosine (C). Each rung of the ladder consists either of an A-T or a C-G link. The essential genetic information is contained in the sequence of bases along the DNA molecule. The amount of information is huge: the genetic information coded in the nucleotide sequence of the DNA strands in humans amounts to some 3000 million base pairs.

Various techniques of DNA analysis allow the determination of the nucleotide sequence (or *base pair* sequence) along the length of the DNA chain in the specific region of the particular chromosome in which one may be interested, but it is not feasible to deal here with the laboratory techniques.

If one is interested in human diversity then it is the specific and often minor differences (*alleles*) in the nucleotide sequence between one human and another which concern us. When there are variations between individuals at a particular locus in the sequence of bases then we may speak of *polymorphisms* in the population, and the specific combination of the sites is referred to as a *haplotype*.

Nuclear DNA has been used in several interesting studies. In one of these, workers at the MRC Haematology Unit in Oxford (Wainscoat *et al.* 1986, 1989) studied DNA polymorphisms (haplotypes) in the β-globin gene cluster of chromosomes of 601 individuals from eight different populations. The two African populations studied had a common haplotype which was absent from all the non-African populations sampled. From this study they were able to produce the phenetic dendrogram shown in Figure 3. In this case there are arguments for regarding it also as a phylogenetic tree, since there is some underlying understanding of the specific structures involved.

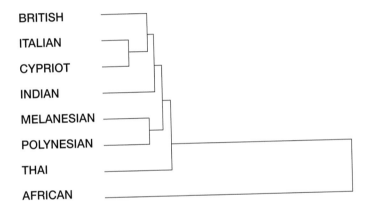

Figure 3. Phenetic dendrogram based on human nuclear DNA utilizing the frequencies of haplotypes in the ß-globin gene cluster of chromosomes of 601 individuals from eight different populations: the first basic division into African versus non-African supports the 'out-of-Africa' hypothesis for human origins. (From Renfrew 1992b, 467, after Wainscoat *et al.* 1989.)

This diagram carries significant implications for the question of human origins. Physical anthropologists have discussed the question as to whether our own species, *Homo sapiens sapiens*, which is generally assumed to have evolved from our earlier predecessor *Homo erectus*, did so in Africa, or in Western Asia, or indeed in Southeast Asia, or whether all three areas might have been in some kind of contact with significant gene flow between, so that some multi-regional origin hypothesis might be involved (Stringer 1999). The theory most favoured at the moment by human biologists is the 'out-of-Africa' theory, whereby the transition from *H. erectus* to *H. sapiens sapiens* would have taken place in Africa, and only in Africa, around 150,000 years ago. Our species would subsequently have populated the rest of the earth in a series of radiations or migrations.

The first and basic division based on the study of DNA from the beta-globin gene cluster is that between Africa and the rest. This is what would be predicted if the 'out-of-Africa' hypothesis were correct, and gives significant support towards it. It should clearly be realised that this is based entirely on genetic material derived from living populations. But despite this it can be used to add to our understanding of events occurring in remote antiquity. For if we accept that the population which differs most from the others is the African population, then it may be that this has been in isolation from the others for the longest period of time. The most likely explanation for that is that it separated first through the migration of part of the population out of Africa, before it too underwent processes of divergence and fragmented into smaller units, which themselves became different through genetic drift.

Lineage methods: mitochondrial DNA and Y-chromosome DNA

With the development of DNA sequencing came the possibility of utilizing DNA analysis of human lineages, both in the female line (using mitochondrial DNA) and in the male line (using the non-recombining portion of the Y-chromosome). This has been an area of very rapid development in research, with immediate and significant developments for archaeology. Indeed it has been possible to identify a new research field: *archaeogenetics*, defined as 'the study of the human past using the techniques of molecular genetics' (Renfrew and Boyle 2000, 3).

Undoubtedly the most intriguing of recent approaches comes from the study of *mitochondrial DNA* (abbreviated *mtDNA*), that is to say, DNA from the mitochondria, small organelles within the cell. Mitochondrial DNA has a circular structure and represents some 16,000 base pairs as compared with the more than 3000 million for the DNA of the nucleus. But the most remarkable thing about mtDNA is that it is inherited exclusively in the female line. Thus, unless some mutation has occurred, your mtDNA is identical to that of your mother, your maternal grandmother, her mother, and so on. Moreover, there are some grounds for thinking that the rate of mutation may be regarded as approximately constant, and that this rate is several times faster for mtDNA than it is for nuclear DNA. Comparison between the mtDNA of humans and other apes has led to one estimate for the rate of mutation of mtDNA, although several estimates are available.

In an interesting study, Cann, Stoneking and Wilson compared the mtDNA of 147 human individuals (Cann *et al.* 1987). The tree which they produced (Fig. 4) presents the similarities and differences of those 147 individuals in terms of their mtDNA. It should be noted that if we had grounds for thinking that the mutation rate was faster in one part of the world or under one climatic regime than another, the shape of the tree (although not all its detail) might be very different. Thus the analysis once again depends on a regularity assumption, for which there may be no more theoretical basis

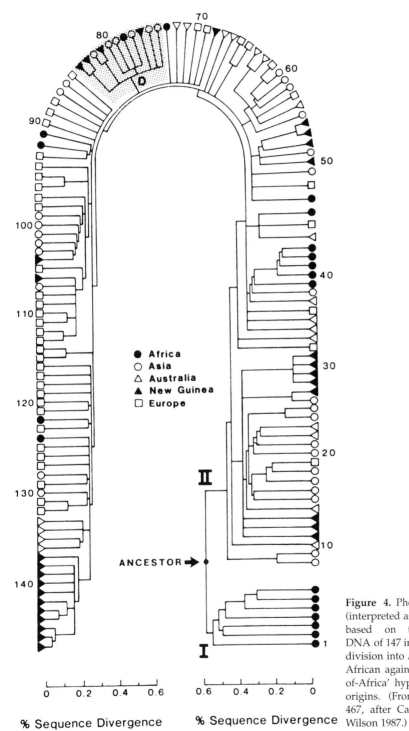

Figure 4. Phenetic dendrogram (interpreted as phylogenetic tree) based on the mitochondrial DNA of 147 individuals. The first division into African versus non-African again supports the 'out-of-Africa' hypothesis for human origins. (From Renfrew 1992b, 467, after Cann, Stoneking and Wilson 1987.)

% Sequence Divergence

Legend: Africa (●), Asia (○), Australia (△), New Guinea (▲), Europe (□)

or empirical justification than there is for the analogous assumption underlying the language dating technique known as 'glottochronology', which relies on a supposedly constant rate of decay.

What makes this tree so interesting is that it shows relationships between 147 living individuals. The tree produced by Cavalli-Sforza and his colleagues, using classic biomolecular markers, was again derived from samples of living populations, but the similarities were computed in terms of gene frequencies within the populations. Here, however, it is human individuals which are being compared with each other, and in some respects the interpretation is that much easier. Two other points are of note. First, mtDNA is able to give a magnificent view of the diversity present in the human gene pool, because mutations accumulate in the mtDNA several times faster than in the nucleus (Cann *et al.* 1987, 31). And secondly, because mtDNA is inherited maternally, the *recombination* which takes place in the case of nuclear DNA (which is inherited from both parents) does not occur, so that we are studying evidence derived from maternal lineages which are invariant over very long periods (and whose variation comes about through mutation, rather than through a process of recombination with each generation).

The mtDNA work so far supports a very clear distinction between sub-Saharan Africans and the rest, thus confirming the basic division noted above from studies based on the classic genetic markers and from nuclear DNA. It is this division that gives such significant support to the 'out-of-Africa' hypothesis for human origins since, by inference, it appears to reflect the original human dispersal from the more localized area of origin (Stoneking and Cann 1989). And the inheritance of mtDNA in the female line inevitably leads us back towards the hypothetical 'African Eve', the 'mitochondrial mother' who is ancestral to us all — although population geneticists prefer to think in terms of a group of mitochondrial mothers rather than a single, solitary individual. As we noted, however, the quantitative basis for the interpretation offered by Wilson, Stoneking and Cann, resting as it does on the construction of maximum parsimony trees, has been questioned (Maddison 1991; Templeton 1992). This need not invalidate the 'out-of-Africa' hypothesis (Vigilant *et al.* 1991; Hedges *et al.* 1992). But it does serve to re-emphasize the point that the path from contemporary phenetic data to the construction of a valid phylogenetic tree is not without its pitfalls.

More recently work has been undertaken on the non-recombining part of the *Y-chromosome*, opening a whole new field, since in this case the genetic material is specific to the human male. It is thus possible to investigate male lineages in a manner in some ways analogous to the work with mtDNA on female lineages. Once again the highest diversity is seen in Africa, and the arguments support the out-of-Africa hypothesis for our own species *Homo sapiens sapiens* (Underhill *et al.* 2000; Semino *et al.* 2000).

Network methods

Over the past few years considerable advances have been made in the analysis and interpretation of DNA lineage data (from both mtDNA and Y-chromosome DNA) using network methods. Here the data are no longer presented in the form of dendrograms compiled upon the basis of the overall similarities and differences between individuals, in terms of their mtDNA. Instead the evolutionary or mutational pathways between and within the different haplogroups are considered. For instance, Martin Richards, Bryan Sykes and their colleagues in Oxford studying the sequence variation in mtDNA from some 757 individuals in Europe compiled a diagram seen in Figure 5 (Richards *et al.* 1996). The sequence variation in question under study was contained in some 350 base pairs from the control region of mtDNA.

The data are shown in network form, representing the phylogeny of the haplotypes. Each haplotype which occurred more than once in the sample is shown, and the sizes of the circles are proportional to the number of occurrences of that specific haplotype in the sample.

One advantage of this method is that it offers the possibility of dating the haplogroup clusters. Using certain assumptions it is possible to suggest which specific haplotype may be regarded as the cluster founder. The average number of mutations which have accumulated from the cluster ancestor is measured, and using the mutation rate for the relevant mtDNA control region (of 1 mutation per 20,000 years) it is possible to calculate the approximate age of the cluster.

This represents a considerable conceptual breakthrough, since it offers the remarkable possibility of a DNA chronology which is effectively independent of directly archaeological considerations. Of course the method is not precise, and it makes a number of assumptions, not least that there is a constant mutation rate which is known. That is a matter for argument, but it does not depend upon archaeological considerations.

The peopling of Europe

Richards and his colleagues put these arguments to very good use, suggesting that the ages of the different haplogroups could be used to suggest a number of population events in European prehistory. Their results, as revised (Sykes 1999), are seen in Table 1.

Table 1. Summary of the three main waves in the human colonization of Europe from Anatolia, based on the network analysis of mitochondrial DNA of 82 individuals seen in Figure 5. (From Sykes 1999, 137.)

Component	dates (BP)	main associated clusters	contribution to modern gene pool
Neanderthal	300 000	unclassified	0%
Early Upper Palaeolithic	50 000	U5	10%
Late Upper Palaeolithic	11 000–14 000	H, V, I, W, T, K	70%
Neolithic	8500	J (+ more of H, T, K?)	20%

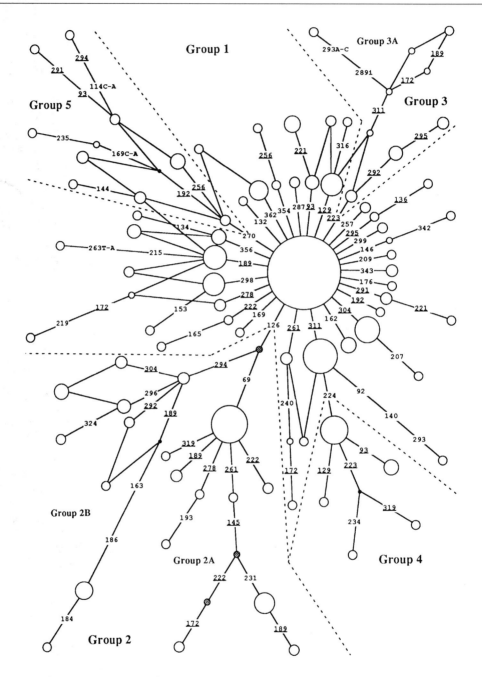

Figure 5. The network approach to the interpretation of data from human mitochondrial DNA from 821 European and Near Eastern individuals: showing the mtDNA phylogeny obtained using the control region sequence haplotypes occurring more than once in the sample. The size of circle shows the number of individuals assigned to the specific haplotype. Dotted lines separate the different groups identified, of which Group 2a (later renamed haplogroup J) reflects the Neolithic population event. (From Sykes 1999, 134.)

We see now their central claim, that the greater part of the diversity is the result not of the demic diffusion of the first farmers to Europe at the onset of the Neolithic period, as Cavalli-Sforza and his colleagues (Menozzi *et al.* 1978) had suggested — see their First Principal Component in Figure 2 — but largely of population expansions in the Upper Palaeolithic period. Richards and his colleagues did indeed recognize one haplogroup, haplogroup J, whose arrival in Europe, presumably from Anatolia, could by its date — around 8500 BP — be associated with the coming of farming. But this would represent a contribution of only some 20 per cent to the modern gene pool. These observations have given rise to lively controversy (Cavalli-Sforza and Minch 1997; Barbujani, Bertorelle and Chikhi 1998; Richards *et al.* 1997; Richards and Sykes 1998). But the differences between the two camps — i.e. those ascribing much of the variability (with Cavalli-Sforza) to the Neolithic period, and those (with Sykes and Richards) regarding it as in the main established already in the Upper Palaeolithic — may not be as great as it at first seemed since both agree that the variability to be assigned to the Early Neolithic period and the coming of farming lies between 20 per cent and 30 per cent of the total.

Comparable data, using analogous internal chronological methods, are now available also from Y-chromosome data for Europe (Malaspina *et al.* 1998), and the field is expanding rapidly.

Moreover it has been possible to suggest some correlations or relationships between the lineage data from mtDNA and Y-chromosome DNA and the climatic data bearing upon the human population history of the Upper Palaeolithic (Housley *et al.* 1997). For it now seems well established that during the Late Glacial Maximum of *c.*20,000 BP the climate in Europe was so cold that the human population retreated to refugia in Iberia and east-central Europe (Housley *et al.* 1997; van Andel 2000) and expanded from these at the onset of warmer climatic conditions. Torroni and his colleagues (1998; also Torroni *et al.* 1996) have suggested on the basis of mtDNA analysis that the modern distribution of haplogroup V (apparently a haplogroup originating in Europe through mutation), which has high frequencies not only in Iberia but in western Europe as far as Scandinavia, is due to the expansion of population from the Iberian refugium at the end of the cold period and the recolonization of northern Europe.

These are exciting conclusions because they suggest, whatever the outcome of the controversy in the present case, that methods such as these, using DNA from modern populations, will be able to reconstruct much of the world's population history of the Upper Palaeolithic period and subsequently. It should be noted that the present conclusion of this work is that Neanderthal hominids made no contribution to the later gene pool of Europe. This implies that Europe was repopulated from about 40,000 BP by our own species, to which earlier fossil hominids found in Europe would not be ancestral.

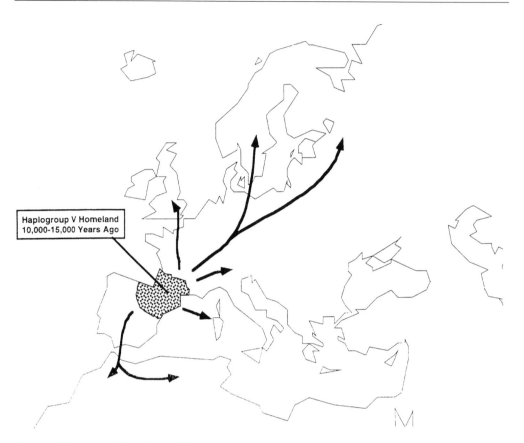

Figure 6. The proposed homeland of haplogroup V, indicating the expansion of population after the end of the Late Glacial Maximum *c.*15,000 BP, as suggested by the study of the mitochondrial DNA of 419 contemporary individuals. This illustrates the extent to which molecular genetic studies are now elucidating demographic events in the late Pleistocene period. (From Torroni *et al.* 1998.)

Polynesia

Comparable analyses are now being carried out in many parts of the world. For instance the population history of Africa is now being clarified by very recent work (Scozzari *et al.* 1999). In Polynesia the issues are particularly clear since this was a relatively recent population episode. A number of scholars, including Peter Bellwood (1989), have argued on linguistic grounds that much of the island Pacific was peopled from Taiwan by speakers of an early Austronesian language. Moreover there is good archaeological evidence suggesting that the spread of the Lapita culture in Polynesia is associated with the dispersal of a food-producing population which might have spoken a Proto-Polynesian language (Kirch 1997). Genetic aspects of the population dispersal are being investigated using mitochondrial DNA (Sykes *et al.* 1995; Hagelberg *et al.*

1999) and by Y-chromosome studies (Hurles *et al.* 1998). The matter has been complicated by the analysis of Ancient DNA supposedly associated with Lapita ware
(Hagelberg and Clegg 1993) and there are several problems still to resolve. One may
confidently expect that the molecular genetic evidence will within the next few years
give a reasonably coherent picture of the first population of Polynesia. Whether or not
that will resolve the linguistic problems is another matter.

DNA and the peoples and languages of the Americas

One of the most controversial and interesting areas where mtDNA studies have been
applied is the question of the peopling of the Americas, and the origins of the languages
of the native Americans (Renfrew 2000b). Some years ago the distinguished American
linguist Joseph Greenberg proposed a classification of the languages of the Americas
into just three large families or macrofamilies (Greenberg 1987), a proposal that has not
been accepted by the majority of linguists. The first of these, Eskimo-Aleut, is spoken
by the Eskimo of the extreme north. The second, the Na-Dene family, is spoken by several tribes of the North American northwest, including the Haidu and the Tlingit, and
includes also the Athabascan language family of the North American southwest
(including the Navajo and Apache). His third macrofamily, which he termed 'Amerind',
includes all the other language families of the Americas, North, Central and South.
Greenberg postulated that these three linguistic groupings were the result of three
episodes of migration across the Bering Strait. He felt able to give approximate dates for
these episodes on the basis of 'glottochronology', a controversial method based upon
the degree of similarity or difference among the vocabularies of the various languages
within each family. The first, Amerind migration would have taken place as much as
10–20,000 years ago, the second (Na-Dene) some 9000 years ago, and the third (Eskimo-
Aleut) some 4000 years ago. In fact there is nothing very controversial about the second
and third of these suggestions (although the archaeological evidence might lead to
some adjustment in the dates). But the first, his view that all the other languages might
belong to one great 'Amerind' macrofamily, has produced a storm of criticism among
American linguists. Greenberg's methods are the subject of considerable controversy,
but it is only fair to note that his classification of the languages of Africa (Greenberg
1963), using the same method of multilateral comparison, has met with almost universal acceptance.

It is important to realise that molecular genetic studies cannot throw direct light on
questions of early languages. There are no specific genes that are indicators of specific
languages, and the relationships between molecular genetics and historical linguistics
must always be indirect. There is, however, as noted earlier, an overlap area, namely
population history. Language change is often in part the result of demographic effects:
of population increase, of human dispersals, of disease and population collapse, of

migrations and population replacements. Human genetics (including population genetics as well as molecular studies) is very well placed to investigate such phenomena.

The application of mtDNA studies by Douglas Wallace, Antonio Torroni and their colleagues (e.g. Torroni *et al.* 1992; Renfrew 2000b) does seem, however, to have lent at least initial support to some of Greenberg's findings. By analysing divergences in the sequence variation in mtDNA of a number of native American groups they have suggested that the first Amerind-speakers entered the Americas between about 42,000 and 21,000 years ago, while a population ancestral to the present-day Na-Dene arrived between 16,000 and 5500 years ago. More recent studies, however, have given somewhat different conclusions (e.g. Saillard *et al.* 2000). (It is notable that the date for the Amerind migrations of some 20,000 years ago or more is earlier than that attested by the widespread distribution of Clovis points in North America some 14,000 years ago, often regarded as the first clear evidence of human occupation, and thus re-opens long-standing questions about the first population of the Americas.)

Further studies have shown that some tribes speaking particular Amerind languages show characteristic mtDNA varieties in high frequency: these have been termed 'population private polymorphisms' (i.e. polymorphisms which occur in high frequency only among members of a specific tribe or population group). This might suggest that the process of tribalization may have begun early in the history of the Amerind-speakers with relatively little intertribal genetic interchange occurring subsequently. These are however preliminary results, and it will be interesting to see whether comparable patterns are found when there has been more comprehensive study of male lineages through Y-chromosomal DNA. There is clearly scope here for well-focused and detailed studies on a regional basis of the DNA of ethnic groups (which are, of course, generally defined mainly on the basis of the languages which they speak).

In particular, one study (Torroni *et al.* 1994) examined mtDNA in 60 individuals (Mixtecs from the Alta, Mixtecs from the Baja, Valley Zapotecs and Highland Mixe) from southern Mexico. In general four groups of mtDNA haplotypes (referred to as haplotypes A, B, C and D) were found to characterize native American populations, but only three were observed in these Mexican populations. The comparison of their mtDNA variation with that observed in other populations from Mexico and Central America permitted a clear distinction among the different Middle American tribes, and raised questions about some of their linguistic affiliations. It was possible to produce alternative phylogenetic trees based on these mtDNA data — the difference in the trees being dependent upon the quantitative procedures used for handling the data (which gives, incidentally, a good illustration of the way the results obtained depend upon the assumptions which are used in the treatment of the data).

These are early days yet in the study of DNA, and interpretive procedures are still being worked out (see Ward 1999). Moreover Ancient DNA is beginning to make contributions to our understanding of American population history (Stone and Stoneking

1998, 1999). But the presence of what appear to be population private polymorphisms among ethnic or linguistic groups offers the promise that further studies will prove fruitful.

More recently, however, the 'four founder lineage' hypothesis has been questioned. It has been suggested that the picture is more complex and that further haplogroups can be recognized, and Merriwether (1999) has argued that 'It is much more parsimonious with a single wave of migration containing all these types, followed by linguistic and cultural diversification after or during entry.' At the moment it would seem wise to take a cautious view, and to recognize that these studies are still at an early stage. Moreover in the Americas the archaeologists themselves cannot yet decide definitively between a date of c.30,000 BP and one of c.14,000 BP for the first settlement (see also Nettle 1999b). Certainly, until the population history is more reliably established it would be premature to try to correlate it with the broad outlines of linguistic history, whether as envisaged by Greenberg or by other linguists who take a view very different from his.

Population specific polymorphisms

So far much of the discussion surrounding population genetics has been concerned with the early history of populations. Such populations are frequently regarded as ethnic groups. But this raises a real problem. For while it may be reasonable to regard a population unit in South America, defined primarily by the language spoken by members of the group, as a tribal or ethnic unit, it is not at all clear that it is appropriate to project such an idea back to prehistoric times (Renfrew 2000b). It is widely realised today that 'ethnicity' is a difficult concept, referring to what those individuals who choose to belong to a group believe about their own group identity (Jones 1997; Sims-Williams 1998b). It is not necessarily based upon enduring and observable criteria which we could safely project back to a remote past. This therefore is a conceptual difficulty for those who think in terms of group origins.

One of the remarkable features about DNA studies, however, is that they are very well adapted to speak about individuals and relationships between individuals. For indeed DNA studies normally do indeed start with samples taken from a good number of individuals, and then go on to consider the relationships between them.

One very remarkable example is offered by the study undertaken by David Goldstein and his colleagues (Thomas *et al.* 1998) of individuals bearing the name Cohen. It is well established in the Jewish faith that those bearing the name Cohen are frequently priests, and that this role is passed on in the male line. Were this convention strictly followed, and were the historical documentation correct that the first such Cohen was consecrated during the Temple period around the seventh century BC one might hope to show a family relationship between those bearing the name Cohen today. On the other hand a sceptic might argue that paternity is not always infallibly implied by the family name, and that in some societies individuals are not obliged to retain their name at birth. The results of the Y-chromosome-based study showed that the Y-chromosomes of Cohenim could be distinguished in both Ashkenazic and Sephardic populations. Moreover, using network analysis it was possible to estimate the time at which Cohen Y-chromosomes were derived from a common ancestral chromosome (coalescence time): the calculation suggested a date of approximately 2650 BP (assuming a generation time of 25 years), which would equate well with the suggested historical date when the lineages may first have diverged. This pioneering study illustrates well how molecular DNA techniques may be used to study descent lineages over relatively recent time spans, a point made even more graphically by the use of mitochondrial DNA analysis to identify the fragmentary skeletal remains of the last Tsar of Russia, Nicholas II, and his family, known to have been shot at Ekaterinburg in 1918. The identity of the bones was unequivocally established using samples from surviving relatives whose maternal lineage could be traced back to the same maternal ancestor (Gill *et al.* 1994; Gibbon 1998).

Ancient DNA

One of the most promising fields for further research is the study of DNA not from the blood, hair and tissue of living populations (as in the cases discussed above) but from ancient human remains, where the conditions of preservation are favourable. This may be the case when quantities of human tissue are preserved, as for instance in frozen bodies (such as the Alpine Ice Man), or with desiccated remains, including Egyptian mummies. There has indeed been some success with such cases (e.g. Handt *et al.* 1994) and mtDNA has been successfully recovered. Often, however, the outcome is simply to demonstrate a very early origin for a specific lineage which can then be shown to be still represented among living populations in the same area, which is not a very surprising result.

One very interesting piece of work with Ancient DNA has, however, given highly significant results. DNA (once again mtDNA) has been successfully extracted from a Neanderthal skeleton (discovered in Germany over a century ago) which must be of the order of 40,000 years old. The relationship between the Neanderthalers (*Homo sapiens neanderthalensis*) and our own species (*Homo sapiens sapiens*) has for long been a matter of controversy. Both are generally believed to be descendants of the earlier hominid *Homo erectus*, but the closeness of the relationship has been a matter for discussion — in simple terms, it has been uncertain whether the Neanderthalers were close cousins of our own species, or more distant cousins with a much earlier branching point of separation from our own sapiens lineage.

The recent success in reconstructing a DNA sequence of 379 base pairs of Neanderthal mtDNA (Krings *et al.* 1997; Ward and Stringer 1997) has led to important

results. Human mtDNA lineages along the same stretch of DNA do show some variation among themselves (up to 8 substitutions on average), but they differ from the
Neanderthal DNA much more, by some 27 substitutions. This means that the overall difference between the Neanderthal sequence and that of humans was about three
times the average difference among humans. The difference between humans and
chimpanzees (our closest relatives among the apes) is naturally very much greater,
but even so it turns out to be only about twice the difference between humans and
Neanderthalers.

The important conclusion that has been drawn from these results is that the
Neanderthal/sapiens divergence is of very great antiquity, dating to as much as
600,000 years ago and very much earlier than the age of the common ancestor of modern human mtDNA which is c.150,000 years. So the Neanderthalers turn out to be more
distant cousins than had been thought, and it is unlikely that they made a direct genetic
contribution to modern humans.

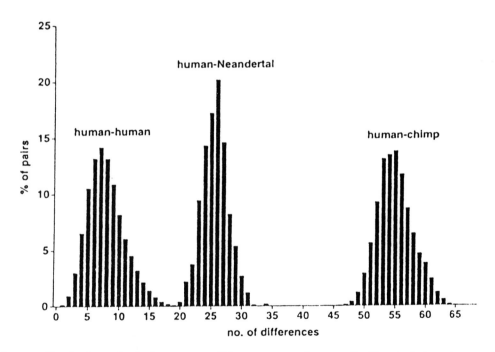

Figure 7. Distributions of pairwise sequence differences among humans, the Neanderthal specimen and
chimpanzees, using ancient mitochondrial DNA obtained from the fossil hominid found in 1856 near
Neanderthal in Germany. The pairwise sequence difference distributions show that the Neanderthal
hominid was more different from modern humans than had previously been realised, suggesting a date
of c.600,000 years before the present for the divergence of the Neanderthal mtDNA and contemporary
human mtDNA (using an estimated divergence date between humans and chimpanzees of 4–5 million
years ago). (From Krings *et al.* 1997, 5.)

This is the first major contribution to archaeological knowledge that has come to us from the study of Ancient DNA (see Pääbo 1999), to be set alongside the numerous important findings of archaeological significance that have been contributed by the study of living populations. We can expect many more, both ancient and modern, in the years to come.

Plants and animals

Naturally the techniques of molecular genetics are not restricted to the study of humans and hominids. On the contrary they are now being applied to the elucidation of the histories of plant and animal populations, and in particular to episodes of domestication of plant and animal domesticates, which, since these involve selection for particular phenotypes and therefore genotypes, are particularly susceptible to study by such means.

Once again the most striking successes to date have been based upon the study of living populations, although work with Ancient DNA from early plant remains is making increasing progress (Renfrew 1998b; Brown 1998). In particular the study of einkorn in Turkey and nearby areas of the Near East and of the Balkans has proved outstandingly successful (Heun *et al.* 1997). This project examined 1362 samples in all of modern einkorn wheat (*Triticum monococcum boeticum*) from this region, of a different form occurring in the Balkans (*T. m. aegilopoides*) and of domesticated einkorn (*T. m. monococcum*), using amplified fragment length polymorphism fingerprinting of nuclear DNA. Their phylogenetic study of the 388 lines studied of cultivated einkorn suggested that cultivated einkorn is monophyletic (i.e. descends from a single original lineage) which they were able to situate in the Karacadağ mountains area in the Diyarbakir region of southern Turkey. They drew attention to the proximity of such very early farming sites as Çayönü and Abu Hureyra. This is an interesting result which at first sight appeared to run counter to conventional wisdom that the wheats were first domesticated in the southern Levant, but which now seems supported by further palaeobotanical evidence (Nesbitt 1998; Nesbitt and Samuel 1998). It is to be expected that comparable studies will be undertaken for emmer and for the hexaploid wheats and for barley.

So far the most successful work on domesticated animals has been focused upon cattle (Bailey *et al.* 1996; Bradley *et al.* 1996), and it is to be expected that similar work applied to sheep and goat will give interesting results, since these seem to have been the earliest domesticates of importance for food.

Clearly the techniques are of relevance for farming origins in any part of the world. Comparable work is under way for rice, maize, sorghum and other domesticates using contemporary samples, as well as Ancient DNA in some cases. Once again our understanding of the processes of domestication and of their locations is likely to be significantly clarified in the next few years.

Archaeology and language

The origins of language as an inherently human capacity are widely discussed (Noble and Davidson 1996). It is generally argued that modern speech capacity is closely associated with the emergence of our own species *Homo sapiens sapiens* but the extent to which earlier hominids, such as *Homo erectus* or *Homo ergaster*, had significant linguistic abilities is unclear, just as the linguistic capacities of Neanderthal hominids, *Homo sapiens neanderthalensis*, are a matter of lively controversy sustained by very limited concrete evidence.

Already however molecular genetics has thrown some useful, if indirect, light upon the matter. The Ancient DNA work by Krings and his colleagues (1997), discussed above, showed the Neanderthal hominids to be much further removed genetically from modern humans than had been widely believed. The analysis also suggested that it was necessary to go very much further back before finding the common ancestor of both forms than had been thought — perhaps 600,000 years. This finding would certainly weaken the argument that the Neanderthal hominids, as very close relatives of *Homo sapiens sapiens*, might share some of the latter's speech abilities. To the extent that this argument depends upon the close relationship between the two species it is weakened by the molecular genetic work showing this affinity to be more remote than had been thought. Of course this analysis of Ancient DNA tells us nothing directly about the linguistic abilities of the Neanderthalers. The genes governing linguistic abilities, if they exist at all, have not yet been identified, and mitochondrial DNA is probably not the best place to look for them. But to the extent that the analysis shows the two species to have been very remote cousins, it reduces the force of the assumption that linguistic behaviour in the one might imply something similar in the other.

It is widely assumed that, when the ancestors of our species radiated from Africa around 60,000 years ago, they already were in possession of fully modern speech abilities. That is in effect an assumption, but it is sustained by the observation that all known living human communities are in possession of such abilities. That they should be so endowed is thought to be a result of their shared descent from the common ancestor. For were this not so, it would imply that the linguistic ability, and the mutations which produced the genotype responsible, arose separately on different occasions. That of course would appear to run counter to the out-of-Africa theory, itself well supported by molecular genetics, where our species is regarded as fully developed prior to the dispersal.

Turning to the patterns of linguistic diversity seen today, it is generally thought that there are some 6500 different languages in the modern world, although their number is fast falling through processes of linguistic extinction.

Since the time more than two centuries ago of Sir William Jones, the great pioneer of Indo-European studies, it has been recognized that many of the languages of the world may be grouped together in language families. The languages in each family have similarities in phonology, morphology and lexicon which are usually explained in terms of community of origin — as Sir William Jones put it 'sprung from some common source'. That this need not be so in every case has been argued by R.W. Dixon (1997) for the Pama-Nyungan language 'family' in Australia. Although still regarded by some scholars as a true 'family', with an ancestral proto-language from which the daughter languages would have developed, Pama-Nyungan has been seen by Dixon as a product of linguistic convergence — that is to say of the increasing similarity, through interaction, of a number of languages occupying adjacent territories which may have been previously unrelated.

As any textbook in historical linguistics will show (e.g. Antilla 1989; Campbell 1998), the classical approach in historical linguistics is to compare systematically languages within the family, with a view to reconstructing the rules for sound changes that led the daughter languages to evolve from the ancestral proto-language. It is the procedure of historical linguistics to reconstruct that hypothetical proto-language as well as to study and document the rules for language change from it.

The remarkable thing is that some of these language families have very wide geographical distributions — the area covered by speakers of Indo-European languages was vast, even before the colonial expansions of the past five centuries. Sino-Tibetan is another family with many millions of speakers today. For the archaeologist there is the obvious problem of explaining these very wide distributions.

Problems in correlating archaeology with historical linguistics

As noted earlier the problem of correlating the archaeological record with the data provided by historical linguistics is an old one. In earlier days the explanations offered were almost invariably in migrationist mode. If several languages could be recognized as belonging to the same linguistic family, then their current distribution was to be explained in terms of a series of migrations from the hypothetical 'homeland' where the reconstructed proto-language was first spoken.

At first the techniques of archaeology seemed to offer some sort of methodology to allow the construction of a narrative which could serve as an explanation. In the words of Gordon Childe (1929, vi):

> We find certain types of remains — pots, implements, ornaments, burial sites, house forms — constantly recurring together. Such a complex of regularly associated traits we shall term a 'cultural group' or just a 'culture'. We assume that such a complex is the material expression of what today would be called a 'people'. . . The same complex may be found with relatively negligible diminutions or additions over a wide area. In such cases of the total and bodily transference of a complete culture from one place to another we think ourselves justified in assuming a 'movement of people'.

It was easy, in such a framework, to equate 'peoples' with languages, and to imagine that the archaeological map of cultures and their supposed movements could be equated with a notional one of languages and their migrations. Today, however, archaeologists have realised that archaeological cultures are not readily to be equated with ethnic groups or peoples, nor indeed with languages. This entire mode of thought has fallen into disfavour among archaeologists, although not all historical linguists have abandoned what might be termed a migrationist mode of argument.

It is accepted however that among the general models for language change in a given area (which include initial colonization, divergence processes and convergence processes), one of particular interest to the archaeologist is that of language replacement. But rather than subsuming episodes of replacement under the rubric of 'migration' it is often felt appropriate to analyse more carefully and consider a range of models for language replacement (Renfrew 1989) which include:

(a) élite dominance

(b) the demographic effects of new technology, including subsistence technology

(c) the effects of system collapse

(d) the consequences of the formation of a *lingua franca*

(e) contact-induced language change.

The traditional migrationist model, often involving an incoming warrior group achieving ascendancy by force of arms, generally fell within the category of élite dominance. But for such a model to make sense there has indeed to be an 'élite', which implies the existence of what the social anthropologist might term a stratified society or at least a ranked society. The existence of ranking or social stratification can generally be recognized in the archaeological record, and it makes little sense to speak of 'élite dominance' in cases where the archaeological evidence shows that the societies in question may be considered to have been egalitarian communities. In practice it may not be at all easy to detect episodes of language replacement from the archaeological record, although there are cases, such as the formation by conquest of the Roman empire with the subsequent development of the Romance languages, where the causal linkage is clear enough. One serious problem in seeking to relate language replacement events to the archaeological record is the difficulty of finding an approximate date for the linguistic event. Recent studies have shown (e.g. Renfrew, McMahon and Trask 2000) that estimates for the ages of language families are difficult to establish, and that in the past such estimates of time depth have sometimes been too small.

Approaches to linguistic diversity

The American linguist Joanna Nichols, one of the pioneers of the population typology approach to linguistic diversity (Nichols 1992), has made a useful distinction between regions of the world where the pattern of language distribution may lead to the identification of 'spread zones', and others where a different distribution pattern may lead to the designation of 'retention zones' for which the term 'mosaic zones' has also been proposed (Renfrew 2000a, 25, fig. 7). In a spread zone the languages comprising just one or two language families (or linguistic 'stocks') are widely distributed in space, and the time depth seems relatively shallow. The density of language families per unit area is low, and the ratio of languages per family is high. The converse is the case for the retention zone (or mosaic zone) where the density of families per unit area is high (but with fewer languages per family) and where the time depth seems greater. The underlying thought is that in a spread zone, the language distribution is often suggestive of a rather recent dispersal (or replacement) process, whereas in a retention zone there has been a long and uninterrupted period of *in situ* linguistic development.

R.W. Dixon has recently given consideration to the social and economic mechanisms which might underlie such distributions. He contrasts periods of equilibrium with episodes of change which, following Stephen Jay Gould, he terms punctuations (Dixon 1997, 3):

> Over most of human history there has been an equilibrium situation. In a given geographical area there would have been a number of political groups, of similar size and organisation, with no one group having undue prestige over the others. Each would have spoken its own language or dialect. They would have constituted a long-term linguistic area, with the languages existing in a state of relative equilibrium. Nothing is ever static — there would be ebbs and flows, changes and shiftings around, but in a relatively minor way. Then the equilibrium would be punctuated, and drastic changes occur. The punctuation may be due to natural causes such as drought or flooding; or to the invention of a new tool or weapon; or to the development of agriculture; or of boats, with movements into new territories; or to the development of secular or religious imperialism. These punctuations to the state of equilibrium are likely to trigger dramatic changes within languages and between languages. They give rise to expansion and split of peoples and of languages. It is during a period of punctuation — which will be brief in comparison with the eras of equilibrium that precede and follow — that the family tree model applies.

Dixon is here clearly describing the sort of circumstances which would lead to a spread zone effect, as formulated by Nichols. The archaeological implications of such a view are very different from those outlined above by Gordon Childe. Of course it is not necessary to follow every detail of Dixon's analysis, which has already proved controversial among linguists. No doubt the sort of convergence processes which he describes for his episodes of equilibrium are always at work. But he is surely correct in emphasizing that an episode of language dispersal, such as would give rise to a 'family tree' of daughter languages, must have some concrete cause in the real world, whether climatic or ecological or cultural. Both the causative phenomenon and its effects should, in the face of such radical change, be evident in the archaeological record.

We have already discussed in passing several such 'punctuation' cases. The Glacial Maximum in Europe during the Upper Palaeolithic period was followed by a milder phase which allowed the recolonization of northern Europe — a clear case of such a punctuation. The colonization of Polynesia by farmers, accompanied by their characteristic Lapita ware, is another case in point. The spread of the Bantu (i.e. Niger-Congo) languages of Africa can also be discussed in such terms (Ehret 1999), linked both to yam cultivation and the spread of iron technology. The conquest of much of Europe by the Roman armies with the consequent adoption of Latin speech is another obvious instance, this time of élite dominance. Each of these was an episode of decisive change, over a wide area, not the minor ebbs and flows also cited by Dixon. Each can be well documented archaeologically. It may be inferred that each episode marked the inception of a new language family or sub-family, not just a single language. And it is appropriate, as we shall discuss below, to consider whether each would have left clear effects in the molecular genetic record also.

The most rigorous consideration yet available of world linguistic diversity has been offered by Daniel Nettle (1999a). He is influenced by the ideas of Nichols and of Dixon, but takes on board also such ecological considerations as the length of the growing season in different parts of the world, and its apparent effects on the density distribution of languages and language families (stocks) on a world-wide basis. His concern is also with population density, and he is led by this to make a clear distinction between hunter-gatherer societies and their language densities, and those of agrarian societies. Indeed he goes so far as to see the colonial expansion of the fifteenth to nineteenth centuries AD as a delayed secondary effect of the primary punctuation or dispersal associated with the origins of the farming economies of Europe seven or eight millennia earlier.

These ideas harmonize well with the thrust of the farming/language dispersal model which I formulated some time ago for the Indo-European language family (Renfrew 1973, 1987) and then more widely (Renfrew 1992a, 1996) and which Peter Bellwood (1991) developed independently for the Polynesian and then the Austronesian languages, and then also developed as a more general model (Bellwood 1997a, 1997b). The Indo-European case is in some respects a special one which is being addressed elsewhere (Renfrew 1999a, 1999b; see also Zvelebil 1995; Zvelebil and Zvelebil 1990). A similar case can be made for the Afroasiatic language family (Renfrew 1991), recently supported by a linguistic analysis by Diakonoff (1998). It should be recognized, however, that many, perhaps most, historical linguists currently prefer the classical view developed by Childe and Gimbutas as reformulated by Mallory (1989) and the Indo-European case will not be addressed further here except in respect of molecular genetics, mentioned below. The point here, however, is that aspects of the older Childean approach, with emphasis upon individual cultures and specific migrations, do now seem to be giving way to a view which lays more emphasis upon processes of change and their underlying causes. At the same time, however, it should be recognized that many linguists regard the generalizing approach of Dixon or Nichols or Nettle with some suspicion, and prefer to focus upon one language family at a time, in a much more fine-grained analysis.

Problems with macrofamilies

One of the most intriguing and controversial problems in current historical linguistics is the reality or otherwise of 'macrofamilies', taxonomic entities which unite a number of recognized language families into a larger taxonomic unit. 'Reality' in this sense may be an odd word to use when speaking of taxonomic concepts. But the existence of a macrofamily, such as Nostratic, would imply the earlier existence of a Proto-Nostratic language ancestral to the proto-languages of the constituent families. Genetic relationships are being proposed which it would be desirable to test. These are of course genetic relationships in the linguistic sense, but the question may legitimately be raised as to whether there might be a corresponding relationship in the molecular genetic sense also.

The best known and longest debated macrofamily is Nostratic, regarded by its principal exponents Ilich-Svitych and Dolgopolsky as containing the Indo-European, Afroasiatic, Uralic, Dravidian, Kartvelian and Altaic families (Dolgopolsky 1998). The concept of Eurasiatic, proposed by Joseph Greenberg (see Ruhlen 1991) overlaps with, but does not equate with, Nostratic.

Greenberg had earlier (1963) proposed a classification of the languages of Africa into just four linguistic phyla or macrofamilies, and in this he has been widely followed (although he finds no place in the bibliography or indeed of the work by Ehret (1999) mentioned above). But his division (Greenberg 1987) of the languages of America, as noted above, into just three macrofamilies (Eskimo-Aleut, Na-Dene and Amerind) met with the disapproval of most Americanist linguists, who felt that the case had not been made with sufficient attention to linguistic reconstruction, and that it laid too much emphasis upon lexical similarities which might be due to chance. The debate is a lively one (Ringe 1999).

For the archaeologist these issues may hold a certain fascination, since if the macrofamily hypotheses, which have been developed also for the hypothetical Austric macrofamily in the Pacific (Blust 1996), were to be accepted, there might be very significant archaeological implications. These have been developed for Nostratic (Renfrew and Nettle 1999) and for Austric (Glover and Higham 1996). These questions have also attracted the attention of molecular geneticists and statisticians (Barbujani *et al.* 1994, 1998), but in a review article such as this it may be appropriate to sound a somewhat cautionary note. The task of bringing data together from the fields of archaeology, historical linguistics and molecular genetics is already difficult enough when the discussion is restricted to concepts such as that of the language family which have a well-established status within their own specific discipline. Until some procedures can be agreed for doing so, it may be premature to discuss at length the possible archaeological or molecular genetic implications of linguistic macrofamilies. It should nonetheless be borne in mind that the implications would indeed be wide-ranging if such linguistic phyla or macrofamilies received wide recognition and support within their own field of historical linguistics.

Language and genetics

The foregoing discussions should have made clear not only that there are areas where the three disciplines of archaeology, historical linguistics and molecular genetics intersect, but that there are also very considerable methodological difficulties in relating and reconciling them. For that reason suggestions of equations and equivalencies should be regarded with caution. Just such a case was made several years ago by Cavalli-Sforza and his colleagues (Cavalli-Sforza *et al.* 1988). It did indeed receive severe initial criticisms (Bateman *et al.* 1990), some of which did not always distinguish with sufficient clarity between what did make sense, at least potentially, and what was altogether too sweeping. Indeed it has been well shown by statistical methods that there are often very significant correlations (e.g. Barbujani, Oden and Sokal 1989; Barbujani and Sokal 1990) although the underlying causes of these are not always easy to interpret.

It should be recognized in the first place that linguistic change is certainly faster than genetic change. Even if the formulations of glottochronology be viewed with disfavour, it must be conceded that the common lexicon shared between two related languages will be very much attenuated, to a low percentage indeed, after 10,000 years (Renfrew, McMahon and Trask 2000). Yet so short a time span will produce very few molecular genetic changes through mutation in two lineages both deriving from a single ancestor. Attention should therefore be drawn to two useful surveys (McMahon and McMahon 1995; Sims-Williams 1998a) which sound a cautious note in this area.

It is, of course, perfectly clear that there is no direct correlation between specific languages and specific genes. As we have seen, language replacement can occur in a population with only very minor genetic effects precisely because a language can be learnt and need not be inherited. Such may often be the case when language replacement occurs through élite dominance (although we might expect the incoming élite to leave some molecular genetic trace, if only a minor one). And such may also be the case when contact-induced language change occurs.

We saw earlier that Cavalli-Sforza and his colleagues explained the marked clines seen in the First Principal Component of their genetic analysis for Europe as the result of the spread of farming by a process which they called 'demic diffusion' (Ammerman and Cavalli-Sforza 1984), implying that the spread of farming was to a significant extent carried by the local movement of farmers, who will therefore have had a strong genetic input to the European population. In such a case the coming of farming may well have been accompanied by a change of language. Indeed in 1973 I suggested that the language in question was Proto-Indo-European, although this view was not then taken up by Cavalli-Sforza and his colleagues and is still treated rather cautiously by them. That may be because at an early stage, influenced by the theories of Marija Gimbutas (1997, see also Gimbutas 1989, 1991, 1999), they associated their Third (east–west) Principal Component with her hypothetical 'Kurgan' invasions. The interesting point, however, is that more recent work, as noted above, based upon mtDNA suggests that the clines of their Principal Component 1 are in the main to be explained by the demographic episodes of the Upper Palaeolithic period, with only some 20 per cent attributable to the allegedly Neolithic haplogroup J.

The African case has not yet been studied in comparable detail using mtDNA, but we have already seen that the pattern attained by Excoffier and his colleagues using the classical genetic marker gamma-globulin seemed a very clear one, with the Niger-Kordofanian language-speakers readily distinguishable. That however is an early result which now needs revisiting (see Watson *et al.* 1997). Similarly, as we saw earlier, the situation in the Americas seems more complex than at first appeared to be the case (Renfrew 2000b).

It seems to me that we can now reach some preliminary conclusions. The first is that molecular genetics and historical linguistics are not easy to correlate (but see also Barbujani 1997; Poloni *et al.* 1997). As noted at the outset the mediating concept is that of population history. That implies that instances of demic diffusion will always show up more clearly in the molecular genetic record than those of élite dominance or contact-induced language change. In every case it will be preferable to have a good understanding of the relevant archaeology in order to have a clear insight into the mechanism of change.

The second point, however, is that these are early days yet, so far as applications of molecular genetics are concerned. The 'broad sweep' explanations of five or ten years ago are being rectified by studies undertaken with a finer grain. For instance we are now beginning to learn that in many cases the strongest signals, as it were, which we receive from the molecular genetic data (including those based upon data from living populations) are Palaeolithic signals. We shall have to understand and measure these first before we can understand how they have been modulated by more recent signals of lesser amplitude. Yet the strength of our position is the vast quantities of data that could in principle be available. Different genetic markers can be taken in association. The mtDNA and the Y-chromosome data for each individual can be considered together, and statistical means developed to consider both when large numbers of individuals are being compared. And then there is the possible future development of the study of Ancient DNA, which we have only briefly mentioned in the foregoing (see Renfrew 1998b). No one can doubt that in some cases Ancient DNA will be in a position to adjudicate over current hypotheses, and to present also some new interpretive problems. I remain optimistic therefore (Renfrew 2000a) that our three disciplines are indeed capable of proving mutually informative and look forward to the lessons which we shall learn in the early years of the new century and of the new millennium.

References

AMMERMAN, A.J. and CAVALLI-SFORZA, L.L. 1984: *The neolithic transition and the genetics of populations in Europe* (Princeton).

ANTILLA, R. 1989: *An Introduction to Historical and Comparative Linguistics* (Amsterdam, 2nd edition).

BAILEY, J.F., RICHARDS, M.B., MACAULAY, V.A., COLSON, I.B. *et al.* 1996: Ancient DNA suggests a recent expansion of European cattle from a diverse wild progenitor species. *Phil. Trans. Roy. Soc., Ser. B* 263, 1467–73.

BARBUJANI, B. 1991: What do languages tell us about human microevolution? *Trends in Ecology and Evolution* 6, 151–6.

BARBUJANI, G. 1997: DNA variation and language affinities. *American J. Human Genetics* 61, 1011–14.

BARBUJANI, G., BERTORELLE, G. and CHIKHI, L. 1998: Evidence for palaeolithic and neolithic gene flow in Europe. *American J. Human Genetics* 62, 488–91.

BARBUJANI, G., ODEN, N.L. and SOKAL, R.R. 1989: Detecting regions of abrupt change in maps of biological variables. *Systematic Zoology* 38, 376–89.

BARBUJANI, G., PILASTRO, A., DE DOMENICO, S. and RENFREW, C. 1994: Genetic variation in North Africa and Eurasia: neolithic demic diffusion v. palaeolithic colonisation. *American J. Physical Anthropol.* 95, 137–54.

BARBUJANI, G. and SOKAL, R.R. 1990: Zones of sharp genetic change in Europe are also linguistic boundaries. *Proc. Nat. Acad. Sci. USA* 87, 1816–19.

BATEMAN, R., GODDARD, I., O'GRADY, R., FUNK, V.A., MOOI, R., KRESS, W.J. and CANNELL, P. 1990: Speaking with forked tongues: the feasibility of reconciling human phylogeny and the history of language. *Curr. Anthropol.* 31, 1–24.

BELLWOOD, P. 1989: The colonisation of the Pacific: some current hypotheses. In Hill, A.V.S. and Serjeantson, W. (eds.), *The Colonisation of the Pacific: a Genetic Trail* (Oxford), 1–59.

BELLWOOD, P. 1991: The Austronesian dispersal and the origin of languages. *Scientific American* 265 (1), 88–93.

BELLWOOD, P. 1997a: The origins and spread of agriculture in the Indo-Pacific region: gradualism and diffusion or revolution and colonization? In Harris, D.R. (ed.), *The Origins and Spread of Agriculture and Pastoralism in Eurasia* (London), 465–98.

BELLWOOD, P. 1997b: Prehistoric cultural explanations for the existence of widespread language families. In McConvell, P. and Evans, N. (eds.) 1997, 123–34.

BLENCH, R. and SPRIGGS, M. (eds.) 1997: *Archaeology and Language I, Theoretical and Methodological Orientations* (London).

BLENCH, R. and SPRIGGS, M. (eds.) 1998: *Archaeology and Language II, Archaeological Data and Linguistic Hypotheses* (London).

BLENCH, R. and SPRIGGS, M. (eds.) 1999a: *Archaeology and Language III, Artefacts, Language and Texts* (London).

BLENCH, R. and SPRIGGS, M. (eds.) 1999b: *Archaeology and Language IV, Language Change and Cultural Transformation* (London).

BLUST, R. 1996: Beyond the Austronesian homeland: the Austric hypothesis and its implications for archaeology. In Goodenough, W.H. (ed.), *Prehistoric Settlement of the Pacific* (Philadelphia, Transactions of the American Philosophical Society 26(5)), 117–40.

BRADLEY, D.G., MacHUGH, D.E., CUNNINGHAM, P. and LOFTUS, R.T. 1996: Mitochondrial diversity and the origins of African and European cattle. *Proc. Nat. Acad. Sci. USA* 93, 5131–5.

BROWN, T.A. 1998: How ancient DNA may help in understanding the origins and spread of agriculture. *Phil. Trans. Roy. Soc., Ser. B* 354, 88–98.

CAMPBELL, L. 1998: *Historical Linguistics, an Introduction* (Edinburgh).

CANN, R.L.M., STONEKING, M. and WILSON, A.C. 1987: Mitochondrial DNA and human evolution. *Nature* 325, 31–6.

CAVALLI-SFORZA, L.L. 1988: The Basque population and ancient migrations in Europe. *Munibe Antrop. Arqueol. (Supl.)* 6 (San Sebastian), 129–37.

CAVALLI-SFORZA, L.L. 1991: Genes, people and languages. *Scientific American* 265 (5), 72–8.

CAVALLI-SFORZA, L.L. and EDWARDS, A.W.F. 1965: Analysis of human evolution. In Geerts, S.P. (ed.), *Genetics today: Proceedings of the Eleventh International Congress of Genetics, The Hague, Sept. 1963*, Vol. 3 (New York).

CAVALLI-SFORZA, L.L., MENOZZI, P. and PIAZZA, A. 1994: *The History and Geography of Human Genes* (Princeton).

CAVALLI-SFORZA, L.L. and MINCH, E. 1997: Palaeolithic and neolithic lineages in the European gene pool. *American J. Human Genetics* 61, 247–51.

CAVALLI-SFORZA, L.L., PIAZZA, A., MENOZZI, P. and MOUNTAIN, J. 1988: Reconstruction of human evolution: bringing together genetic, archaeological and linguistic data. *Proc. Nat. Acad. Sci. USA* 85, 6002–6.

CHILDE, V.G. 1926: *The Aryans, a Study of Indo-European Origins* (London).

CHILDE, V.G. 1929: *The Danube in Prehistory* (Oxford).

DIAKONOFF, I. 1998: The earliest Semitic society. *J. Semitic Stud.* 43, 209–17.

DIXON, R.M.W. 1997: *The Rise and Fall of Languages* (Cambridge).

DOLGOPOLSKY, A.B. 1998: *The Nostratic Macrofamily and Linguistic Palaeontology* (Cambridge, McDonald Institute).

EHRET, C. 1988: Language change and the material correlates of languages and ethnic shift. *Antiquity* 62, 564–74.

EHRET, C. 1999: *An African Classical Age* (Charlottesville).

EXCOFFIER, L.B., PELLEGRINI, B., SANCHEZ-MASAS, A., SIMON, C. and LANGANEY, L. 1987: Genetics and the History of Sub-Saharan Africa. *Yearbook of Physical Anthropol.* 30, 151–94.

GIBBON, A. 1998: Calibrating the mitochondrial clock. *Science* 279, 28–9.

GILL, P., IVANOV, P.L., KIMPTON, K., PIERCY, L. *et al.* 1994: Identification of the remains of the Romanov family by DNA analysis. *Nature Genetics* 6, 130–5.

GIMBUTAS, M. 1989: *The Language of the Goddess* (San Francisco).

GIMBUTAS, M. 1991: *The Civilization of the Goddess: the World of Old Europe* (San Francisco).

GIMBUTAS, M. 1997: *The Kurgan Culture and the Indo-Europeanization of Europe* (Washington D.C., Institute for the Study of Man).

GIMBUTAS, M. 1999: *The Living Goddesses* (Berkeley, California).

GLOVER, I.C. and HIGHAM, C.F.W. 1996: New evidence for early rice cultivation in South, Southeast and East Asia. In Harris, D.R. (ed.),*The Origins and Spread of Agriculture and Pastoralism in Eurasia* (London), 413–42.

GREENBERG, J.H. 1963: *The Languages of Africa* (Stanford).

GREENBERG, J.H. 1987: *Languages in the Americas* (Stanford).

HAGELBERG, E. and CLEGG, J.B. 1993: Genetic polymorphisms in prehistoric Pacific islanders determined by analysis of ancient bone DNA. *Proc. Roy. Soc. London, Ser. B* 244, 45–50.

HAGELBERG, E., KAYSER, M., NAGY, M., ROEWER, L. *et al.* 1999: Molecular genetic evidence for the human settlement of the Pacific: analysis of mitochondrial DNA, Y chromosome and HLA markers. *Phil. Trans. Roy. Soc., Biological Sciences* 354, 141–52.

HANDT, O., RICHARDS, M., TROMMSDORFF, M., KILGER, C. *et al.* 1994: Molecular Genetic Analysis of the Tyrolean Ice Man. *Science* 264, 1775–8.

HEDGES, S.B., KUMAR, S., TAMURA, K. and STONEKING, M. 1992: Human origins and analysis of mitochondrial DNA sequences. *Science* 255, 737–9.

HEUN, M., SCHÄFER-PREGL, R., KLAWAN, D., CASTAGNA, R. *et al.* 1997: Site of einkorn wheat domestication identified by DNA fingerprinting. *Science* 278, 1312–14.

HOUSLEY, R.A., GAMBLE, C.S., STREET, M. and PETTITT, P. 1997: Radiocarbon evidence for the late glacial human recolonisation of northern Europe. *Proc. Prehist. Soc.* 63, 25–54.

HURLES, M.E., IRVEN, C., TAYLOR, P.G., SANTOS, F.R., LOUGHLIN, J., JOBLING, M. and SYKES, B.C. 1998: European Y-chromosomal lineages in Polynesia: a contrast to the population structure revealed by mitochondrial DNA. *American J. Human Genetics* 63, 1793–1806.

JONES, S. 1997: *The archaeology of ethnicity: constructing identities in the past and present* (London).

KIRCH, P.V. 1997: *The Lapita Peoples: Ancestors of the Oceanic World* (Oxford).

KRINGS, M., STONE, A., SCHMITZ, R.-W., KRAINITZKI, H., STONEKING, M. and PÄÄBO, S. 1997: Neanderthal DNA sequences and the origin of modern humans. *Cell* 90, 19–30.

MADDISON, D.R. 1991: African origin of human mitochondrial DNA re-examined. *Systematic Zoology* 40, 355–63.

MALASPINA, P., CRUCIANI, F., CIMINELLI, B.M., TERRENATO, L. *et al.* 1998: Network analyses of Y-chromosomal types in Europe, Northern Africa and Western Asia reveal specific patterns of geographic distribution. *American J. Human Genetics* 63, 847–60.

MALLORY, J.P. 1989: *In Search of the Indo-Europeans: Language, Archaeology and Myth* (London).

McCONVELL, P. and EVANS, N. (eds.) 1997: *Archaeology and Linguistics, Aboriginal Australia in Global Perspective* (Oxford).

McMAHON, A.M.S. and McMAHON, R. 1995: Linguistics, genetics and archaeology: internal and external evidence in the Amerind controversy. *Trans. Philological Soc.* 93, 125–225.

MENOZZI, P., PIAZZA, A. and CAVALLI-SFORZA, L.L. 1978: Synthetic map of human gene frequencies in Europe. *Science* 210, 786–92.

MERRIWETHER, D.A. 1999: Freezer anthropology: new uses for old blood. *Phil. Trans. Roy. Soc., Biological Sciences* 354, 121–9.

MOURANT, A.E, KOPEC, A.C. and DOMANIEWSKA-SOBCZAK, K. 1976: *The Distribution of the Human Blood Groups* (Oxford).

NESBITT, M. 1998: Where was einkorn wheat domesticated? *Trends in Plant Science* 3, 82–3.

NESBITT, M. and SAMUEL, D. 1998: Wheat domestication: archaeobotanical evidence. *Science* 279, 1433.

NETTLE, D. 1999a: *Linguistic Diversity* (Oxford).

NETTLE, D. 1999b: Linguistic diversity of the Americas can be reconciled with a recent colonization. *Proc. Nat. Acad. Sci. USA* 96, 3325–9.

NICHOLS, J. 1992: *Linguistic Diversity in Space and Time* (Chicago).

NOBLE, W. and DAVIDSON, I. 1996: *Human Evolution, Language and Mind* (Cambridge).

PÄÄBO, S. 1999: Ancient DNA. In Sykes, B. (ed.), *The Human Inheritance* (Oxford), 119–34.

POLONI, E.S., SEMINO, O., PASSARINO, G., SANTACHIARA-BENERECETTI, A.S., DUPANLOUP, I., LANGANEY, A. and EXCOFFIER, L. 1997: Human genetic affinities for Y-chromosome P49,f /*Taq*I haplotypes show strong correspondence with linguistics. *American J. Human Genetics* 61, 1015–35.

RENFREW, C. 1973: Problems in the general correlation of archaeological and linguistic strata in prehistoric Greece: the model of autochthonous origin. In Crossland, R.A. and Birchall, A. (eds.), *Bronze Age Migrations in the Aegean* (London), 263–76.

RENFREW, C. 1987: *Archaeology and language, the Puzzle of Indo-European Origins* (London).

RENFREW, C. 1989: Models of change in language and archaeology. *Trans. Philological Soc.* 87, 103–55.

RENFREW, C. 1991: Before Babel, speculations on the origins of linguistic diversity. *Cambridge Archaeol. J.* 1, 3–23.

RENFREW, C. 1992a: World languages and human dispersals, a minimalist view. In Hall, J.H. and Jarvie, I.C. (eds.), *Transition to Modernity* (Cambridge), 11–68.

RENFREW, C. 1992b: Archaeology, genetics and linguistic diversity. *Man* 27, 445–78.

RENFREW, C. 1996: Language families and the spread of farming. In Harris, D.R. (ed.), *The Origins and Spread of Agriculture and Pastoralism* (London), 70–92.

RENFREW, C. 1998a: The origins of world linguistic diversity: an archaeological perspective. In Jablonski, N.G. and Aiello, L.C. (eds.), *The Origin and Diversification of Language* (San Francisco, California Academy of Sciences), 171–92.

RENFREW, C. 1998b: Applications of DNA in archaeology: a review of the DNA studies of the Ancient Biomolecules Initiative. *Ancient Biomolecules* 2, 107–16.

RENFREW, C. 1998c: La arqueologia y el ADN. *Arqueologia* (Mexico City) 19, 3–23.

RENFREW, C. 1999a: Reflections on the origins of linguistic diversity. In Sykes, B. (ed.), *The Human Inheritance* (Oxford), 1–31.

RENFREW, C. 1999b: Time depth, convergence theory and innovation in Proto-Indo-European: 'Old Europe' as a PIE linguistic area. *J. Indo-European Stud.* 27, 257–93.

RENFREW, C. 2000a: At the edge of knowability, towards a prehistory of languages. *Cambridge Archaeol. J.* 10, 7–34.

RENFREW, C. (ed.) 2000b: *America Past, America Present: Genes and Languages in the Americas and Beyond* (Cambridge, McDonald Institute).

RENFREW, C. and BOYLE, K. (eds.) 2000: *Archaeogenetics: DNA and the Population Prehistory of Europe* (Cambridge, McDonald Institute).

RENFREW, C., McMAHON, A. and TRASK, L. (eds.) 2000: *Time Depth in Historical Linguistics* (2 vols.) (Cambridge, McDonald Institute).

RENFREW, C. and NETTLE, D. 1999: *Nostratic — Examining a Linguistic Macrofamily* (Cambridge, McDonald Institute).

RICHARDS, M.R., CORTE-REAL, H., FORSTER, P., MACAULAY, V. *et al.* 1996: Palaeolithic and neolithic lineages in the European mitochondrial gene pool. *American J. Human Genetics* 59, 185–203.

RICHARDS, M.R., MACAULAY, V., SYKES, B., PETTIT, P. *et al.* 1997: Reply to Cavalli-Sforza and Minch. *American J. Human Genetics* 61, 251–4.

RICHARDS, M. and SYKES, B. 1998: Reply to Barbujani *et al. American J. Human Genetics* 62, 491–2.

RINGE, D. 1999: Language classification: scientific and unscientific methods. In Sykes, B. (ed.), *The Human Inheritance* (Oxford), 45–74.

ROSS, M. 1996: Contact-induced change and the comparative method: cases from Papua New Guinea. In Durie, M. and Ross, M. (eds.), *The Comparative Method Reviewed* (Oxford), 180–217.

ROSS, M. 1997: Social networks and kinds of speech-community event. In Blench, R. and Spriggs, M. (eds.) 1997, 209–61.

RUHLEN, M. 1991: *A Guide to the World's Languages I* (Stanford) (with postscript).

SAILLARD, J., FORSTER, P., LYNNERUP, N., BANDELT, H.-J. and NØRBY, S. 2000: mt DNA variation among Greenland Eskimos: the edge of the Beringian expansion. *American J. Human Genetics* 67, 718–26.

SCOZZARI, R., CRUCIANI, F., SANTOLAMAZZA, P., MALASPINA, P. *et al.* 1999: Combined use of biallelic and microsatellite Y-chromosome polymorphisms to infer affinities among African populations. *American J. Human Genetics* 65, 829–46.

SEMINO, O., PASSARINO, G., OEFNER, P.J., LIN, A.A., ABRUZOVA, S., BECKMAN, L.E. *et al.* 2000: The genetic legacy of palaeolithic *Homo sapiens sapiens* in extant Europeans: a Y chromosome perspective. *Science* 290, 1155–9.

SIMS-WILLIAMS, P. 1998a: Genetics, linguistics and prehistory: thinking big and thinking straight. *Antiquity* 72, 505–27.

SIMS-WILLIAMS, P. 1998b: Celtomania and Celtoscepticism. *Cambrian Medieval Celtic Stud.* 36, 1–35.

SLATKIN, M. 1987: Gene flow and the geographic structure of natural populations. *Science* 236, 787–92.

SOKAL, R.R., ODEN, N.L. and WILSON, A.C. 1991: New genetic evidence supports the origin of agriculture in Europe by demic diffusion. *Nature* 351, 143–4.

STONE, A.C. and STONEKING, M. 1998: mtDNA analysis of a prehistoric Oneota population: implications for the peopling of the New World. *American J. Human Genetics* 62, 1153–70.

STONE, A.C. and STONEKING, M. 1999: Analysis of ancient DNA from a prehistoric Amerindian cemetery. *Phil. Trans. Roy. Soc., Biological Sciences* 354, 153–9.

STONEKING, M. and CANN, R.L. 1989: African origin of human mitochondrial DNA. In Mellars, P. and Stringer, C.B. (eds.), *The human revolution: behavioural and biological perspectives on the origins of modern humans, vol. 1* (Edinburgh), 17–30.

STRINGER, C. 1999: The fossil record of the evolution of *Homo sapiens* in Europe and Australasia. In Sykes, B. (ed.), *The Human Inheritance* (Oxford), 33–44.

SYKES, B. 1999: The molecular genetics of European ancestry. *Phil. Trans. Roy. Soc., Biological Sciences* 354, 131–40.

SYKES, B., LEIBOFF, A., LOW-BEER, J., TETZNER, S. and RICHARDS, M. 1995: The origins of the Polynesians: an interpretation from mitochondrial DNA lineage analysis. *American J. Human Genetics* 57, 1463–75.

TEMPLETON, A.R. 1992: Human origins and analysis of mitochondrial DNA sequences. *Science* 255, 737.

THOMAS, M.G., SKORECKI, K., BEN-AMI, H., PARFITT, T., BRADMAN, N. and GOLDSTEIN, D.B. 1998: Origins of Old Testament priests. *Nature* 394, 138–40.

THOMASON, S.G. and KAUFMAN, T. 1988: *Language contact, creolization and linguistics* (Berkeley, California).

TORRONI, A., BANDELT, H.-J., D'URBANO, L., LAHERMO, P. *et al.* 1998: mtDNA analysis reveals a major palaeolithic population expansion from southwestern to northeastern Europe. *American J. Human Genetics* 62, 1137–52.

TORRONI, A., CHEN, Y.-S., SEMINO, O., SANTACHIARA-BENECERETTI, S. *et al.* 1994: Mitochondrial DNA and Y-chromosome polymorphisms in four native American populations from southern Mexico. *American J. Human Genetics* 54, 1–15.

TORRONI, A., HUOPONEN, K., FRANCALACCI, P., PETROZZI, M. *et al.* 1996: Classification of European mtDNAs from an analysis of three European populations. *Genetics* 44, 1835–50.

TORRONI, A., SCHURR, T.G., CABELL, M.F., BROWN, M.D. *et al.* 1992: Native American mitochondrial DNA analysis indicates that the Amerind and Nadene populations were founded by two independent migrations. *Genetics* 130, 153–62.

TRYON, D. 1999: Language, culture and archaeology in Vanuatu. In Blench, R. and Spriggs, M. (eds.) 1999a, 109–26.

UNDERHILL, P.A., SHEN, P., LIN, A.A., JIN, L., PASSARINO, G., YANG, W.H. *et al.* 2000: Y-chromosome sequence variations and the history of human population. *Nature Genetics* 26, 358–61.

VAN ANDEL, T.H. 2000: When received wisdom fails — mid-Palaeolithic and Early Neolithic climates. In Renfrew, C. and Boyle, K. (eds.), *Archaeogenetics: DNA and the Population Prehistory of Europe* (Cambridge, McDonald Institute), 31–40.

VIGILANT, L., STONEKING, M., HARPENDING, H., HAWKES, N. and WILSON, A.C. 1991: African populations and the evolution of human mitochondrial DNA. *Science* 253, 1503–7.

WAINSCOAT, J.S., HILL, A.V.S., BOYCE, A.L., FLINT, J., HERNANDEZ, M., THEIN, S.L., OLD, J.M., LYNCH, J.R., FALUSI, A.G., WEATHERALL, D.J. and CLEGG, J.B. 1986: Evolutionary relationships of human populations from an analysis of nuclear DNA polymorphisms. *Nature* 319, 491–3.

WAINSCOAT, J.S., HILL, A.V.S., THEIN, L., FLINT, J., CHAPMAN, J.C., WEATHERALL, D.J., CLEGG, J.B. and HIGGS, D.R. 1989: Geographic Distribution of alpha- and beta-globin gene cluster polymorphisms. In Mellars, P. and Stringer, C.B. (eds.), *The human revolution: behavioural and biological perspectives on the origins of modern humans, vol. 1* (Edinburgh), 31–8.

WARD, R. 1999: Languages and genes in the Americas. In Sykes, B. (ed.), *The Human Inheritance* (Oxford), 135–58.

WARD, R. and STRINGER, C. 1997: A molecular handle on the Neanderthalers. *Nature* 388, 225–6.

WATSON, E., FORSTER, P., RICHARDS, M. and BANDELT, H.-G. 1997: Mitochondrial footprints of human expansions in Africa. *American J. Human Genetics* 61, 691–704.

ZVELEBIL, M. 1995: Indo-European origins and the agricultural transition in Europe. *J. European Archaeol.* 3 (1), 33–70.

ZVELEBIL, M. and ZVELEBIL, K.V. 1990: Agricultural transition, 'Indo-European origins' and the spread of farming. In Markey, T.L. and Greppin, J.A.C. (eds.), *When Worlds Collide: the Indo-Europeans and the Pre-Indoeuropeans* (Ann Arbor), 237–66.

Archaeological theory

IAN HODDER

Looking back over the last century of archaeological theory, there are sound reasons to be optimistic as the new millennium begins. In comparison with the period around 1900, there is in the years around 2000 an undoubted diversity of archaeological theory, and an undoubted vigour in theoretical debates. Certainly most archaeologists today would flinch from describing themselves as primarily theoretical. The discipline remains absorbed with cultural sequence and with data recovery and analysis. And yet there is sufficient evidence from books, conferences and dissertations that archaeologists are more than ever aware of the theoretical underpinnings of all data recovery, description and sequencing, and that they are more than ever aware of the diversity of theoretical approaches being explored.

So this is an exciting time for archaeological theory, a time in which theoretical debate has clearly widened. I will discuss later the causes of this increased theoretical diversity, but for the moment it may be helpful to identify some of the main dimensions of the diversity itself. As well as the widely recognized shifts in the twentieth century from culture-historical to processual to postprocessual archaeology, other directions and divisions have recently been identified, such as cognitive-processual archaeology (Renfrew 1994), behavioural archaeology (Schiffer 1995), neo-Darwinian archaeology (Dunnell 1989), feminist archaeology (Gero and Conkey 1991). This internal diversity is partly the product of closer ties between archaeology and other sciences and humanities. One of the distinctive characteristics of archaeological theory towards the end of the twentieth century is that it has 'caught up with' and entered into debate with other disciplines. This is a sign of greater maturity in the discipline, but these closer interconnections have opened up a wider world in which disciplinary canons are everywhere being flouted and transgressed. The diversity in archaeological theory is a component of the diversity evident across many sciences and humanities. In archaeology, the result is sometimes faddish and short-term copying, such as in the borrowing of Central Place Theory (Hodder 1972), Chaos Theory (van der Leeuw and Torrence 1989), Catastrophe

Theory (Renfrew and Cooke 1979), or Derrida's version of poststructuralism (Bapty and Yates 1990). But in other cases the interconnections have led to sustained impact and novel directions.

Wider debates in the arts, humanities and social sciences in the twentieth century have often been given impetus by interactions with the world outside Europe and North America. In particular, the emergence of a postcolonial context for 'western' theoretical debate has led both to internal and to external critique. 'Other' voices have increasingly been incorporated. Archaeology emerged as a discipline in the eighteenth and nineteenth centuries within the context of the nation state. At the end of the twentieth century there has been much talk of the decline of the nation state and the emergence of thoroughly global economic, social and cultural relations. Archaeology is having to define itself differently in this new context: one impact has been the recognition that the western theoretical debate in archaeology needs to be situated within a wider discourse (e.g. Ucko 1995).

Describing the theoretical debate

There have been a number of recent attempts to capture the current theoretical diversity in archaeology (e.g. Johnson 1999; Whitley 1998; Ucko 1995; Preucel and Hodder 1996). For example, one approach is to identify differing epistemological frameworks. Preucel (1995) argues that contemporary archaeological theory consists of analytic, hermeneutic and critical epistemologies. Analytic approaches seek to explain systemic relationships in terms of cause and effect. The main struts have been systems theory and positivism. Although the deductive positivism embraced by Fritz and Plog (1970) and Watson, Redman and Leblanc (1971) was later dropped or softened (e.g. Flannery 1973), some archaeologists, especially in the United States, have held to the view that archaeology should be like a natural science. This attachment to the natural sciences was linked to a questionable assumption that natural scientists tested hypotheses against independent and objective data using positivist methods, even though a positivist view of the natural sciences had long been contested (e.g. Kuhn 1962; Feyerabend 1975).

Recent analytic approaches have attempted to move beyond the notion that archaeologists can only discuss and test hypotheses about the observable world. Some forms of positivism had become linked to a general archaeological feeling that we can only talk about past economies and technologies because these leave a direct material trace. Less can be said about past societies and ideologies (Hawkes 1954). But a shift from positivism to realism has allowed some archaeologists to claim that an analytic framework can be used to explore the social and cognitive dimensions of past societies (Wylie 1989;

Renfrew 1982). Such a view, however, has to retain the notion that there are objective, universal and deterministic links between mind, society and material residues.

For those espousing a hermeneutic epistemology, on the other hand, there is an arbitrariness and creativity to culture that cannot be tamed within an analytical framework. The focus is placed on the interpretation of meaning, both from the actor's point of view and from that of the archaeologist interpreting the actor's point of view. The approach recognizes that different people at different times and places will make different interpretations of events around them or in the past (Hodder 1999), but that systematic attempts can be made to accommodate past and present meanings. Rather than theories being 'tested' against data, a hermeneutic approach tries to 'fit' theory and data as best as possible, but always provisionally, given a particular historical context of research.

A third, critical epistemology would go further than either the analytical or hermeneutic approaches by asking whose interests are served by a particular interpretation of the past. Deriving from Marxism and a continental tradition of philosophies, these approaches aim to situate knowledge claims within the context of the production of knowledge (e.g. Leone, Potter and Shackel 1987; Shanks and Tilley 1987). Statements about the past are seen as ideological, either supporting the interests of the dominant, or underpinning the resistance of subordinate groups. The relationships between archaeological knowledge and power are examined, and processes of legitimation exposed. In some versions, emancipation from ideological distortion can ultimately be achieved; in others, archaeologists can only engage in a continual process of critique.

Another way of describing theoretical diversity in archaeology is in terms of levels or scales (e.g. Raab and Goodyear 1984). At the lower levels are 'basic' descriptions and observations of what was often called 'primary' data. Theories concerning these lower levels have not been well developed in archaeology. Certainly there has been much codification and systematization of the recording of excavations and the finds from them, but the degree of theorization at these levels is limited. There are, however, important areas of theoretical advance, as in the recording of stratigraphical relationships (Harris 1989) and micromorphological characteristics of deposits (Matthews et al. 1996), and in the understanding of the postdepositional processes that have affected material traces of past activities (Schiffer 1987).

Middle level theories link the observations made of the archaeological record to behavioural dynamics; they link things to what people did in the past. One source of middle-range theory linking statics and dynamics is ethnoarchaeology. Here modern ethnographic observation is used to develop theories about the relationships between behaviour and material residues, using either an analytic (Binford 1978) or a hermeneutic (Hodder 1982a) perspective. Another source of middle-range theories is experimental archaeology. The aim here is to replicate past processes (pot making, house building, tool manufacture, etc.) in a controlled setting in order to understand the factors which may have led to particular material traces (e.g. Keeley 1980).

High level theories are general theories which integrate low level theories into broad explanations or interpretations. There are various kinds of such theory in archaeology, including ecological, anthropological, evolutionary, structuralist, Marxist, phenomeno-logical, and so on. As Trigger points out (1989, 22), all high level theories found in archaeology are also found in other social sciences and humanities. Across the human sciences, there is no widely accepted unifying theory or synthesis. As noted before, it is increasing intercommunication between archaeology and other disciplines which has encouraged the diversity of theoretical debate in the discipline. However, intercommu-nications are equally prevalent at other theoretical 'levels'.

In practice it is difficult to hold to these different attempts at categorization of the theoretical diversity in archaeology. At least for hermeneutic and critical perspectives, high level theory intrudes into the lowest levels. So observation is linked to generaliza-tion at high theoretical levels, and links between statics and dynamics are described from within specific theoretical frameworks. And from a hermeneutic point of view, the attempt to describe archaeology in analytic terms is false consciousness, since all archaeology is interpretation, whatever practitioners claim. Any scheme of archaeolog-ical theory that might be presented is itself subject to theoretical critique.

Archaeological theory in the twentieth century

Perhaps the most widely accepted scheme, at least the one most commonly used in textbooks, is developmental: culture-historical to processual to postprocessual archae-ology from the beginning to the end of the twentieth century. Certainly there is more agreement about the earlier parts of this sequence as the passing of time creates a his-torical distance. For the more recent developments most claims remain contested. However the most recent developments in archaeological theory are described, it will be helpful for the purpose of this paper briefly to describe the overall sequence of development of archaeological theory in the twentieth century, paying particular attention to the conditions of production of the different types of archaeological knowledge. It is in this way that an attempt can be made to interpret the recent widening of theoretical debate.

Much archaeology today remains culture-historical in that it is concerned with establishing chronologies and sequences of types within specific regions. Stylistic change in pot or settlement types is examined so that sites and artefacts can be dated, so that influences between regions can be documented, and so that regional traditions and the movements of people between them can be identified. The conditions for the production of this type of knowledge are partly pragmatic. Faced with a new region about which little is known, archaeologists have first to understand the cultural sequence, and before the development of radiocarbon dating, this had largely to be achieved by typological and stratigraphical comparison. Certainly, in the early development of archaeology, the systematic analysis of cultural sequence played an important role in countering Biblical schemes and in establishing a long-term process of human activity.

But the establishment of regional traditions also played its part in the emerging nation states in Europe in the nineteenth century. Archaeology grew as a discipline in the context of the construction of national museums and national antiquities legislation. In a European world dominated in the nineteenth and twentieth centuries by the struggles of nation states and ethnic groups, the 'description' of culture-historical sequences always had wider political significance. Whether one was concerned, as Childe, with the origins of European identity, with the origins of the Aryans (Arnold 1990), or more recently with ethnic identities in Europe (e.g. Olsen 1991), there is a tendency for a 'simple' culture-historical sequence to become embroiled in the definition of and claims for national and ethnic rights. At times in the twentieth century, archaeological knowledge has been used to justify genocide and ethnic cleansing at an appalling scale.

One of the results of the use of archaeology to legitimate atrocities in Europe was a withdrawal by archaeologists from interpretative debates. While there is nothing inherently untheoretical about a culture-historical approach (see, for example, the theoretical discussions of Pitt Rivers (1896) or Flinders Petrie (1904)), especially in parts of Europe which had been dominated by the Germanic tradition, after the Second World War there was an understandable reluctance to engage in theoretical debate. Much the same can be said for those countries in Europe in which a Marxist perspective had been imposed as part of Soviet domination (Hodder 1991).

Outside Europe, too, there are countries in which nationalism has provided a sufficient framework for a limited and untheorized emphasis on cultural sequence. Japan, Hispanic South America and Indonesia provide examples (Tsude 1995; Politis 1995; Tanudirjo 1995). In all these cases there was little impetus for developing an open theoretical debate; nationalism and identity provided a self-evident context for the study of cultural sequence.

Processual archaeology developed in the 1960s and 1970s. It reacted against the presumed authoritarian and unsystematic claims to knowledge of previous generations of archaeologists. Personal and political manipulation of the past was to be subverted by an embrace of scientific and objective methods. Anthropology was embraced as providing the research questions archaeologists should explore, and positivism was seen as providing the methods such as careful sampling and testing of hypotheses against data. The initial concern was with ecology and systemic adaptation, but later, social and cognitive factors were included.

David Clarke (1973) recognized that this 'New' or processual approach involved a 'loss of innocence'. By this he meant that archaeologists could no longer remain uncritical or unreflexive about their claims to knowledge. Prior to processual archaeology, archaeologists had asserted their scientific credentials, but the procedures by which they came to conclusions often seemed murky and unspecified. Membership of the academy had sometimes seemed as important as demonstrations of proof. But within the processual phase, it became necessary to open inference to greater scrutiny, examination and test. From here on, theoretical debate became an integral part of the archaeological process. One institutional product was the series of conferences in the United Kingdom called 'Theoretical Archaeology Group'.

However, in examining why processual archaeology continued to seek a unified and non-diverse theory, it is important to identify its site of production. Its main source and impact were, and are, in the United States. Its influence was always viewed with some suspicion in Europe, although there was an avid take-up in Britain and Scandinavia. In other parts of the world, the impact has been varied (e.g. Ucko 1995). In the United States, claims for a scientific status made sense in terms of gaining access to major sources of funding. Claims for objectivity and neutrality supported the view that archaeology could provide secure knowledge about the past and could thus help in planning a better future. A clear social value and relevance for archaeology could be identified. In such a context the insistence on unitary scientific theory can be understood. To be of social value archaeologists had to speak with a single, secure, and hence scientific voice.

Trigger (1984) is amongst the many that have pointed out how this objective, scientific, unitary, processual perspective excluded, dominated and marginalized others. With particular reference to processual archaeological accounts of native Americans, Trigger showed how indigenous peoples were treated only as examples of general processes, not as specific groups with particular histories and their own cultural meanings. The increasingly successful attempts by native Americans to confront archaeologists in their treatment of skeletal remains undermined claims to objectivity, neutrality and universality in the very heartlands of processual archaeology. Outside the United States, processual archaeology was readily identifiable as colonial and the proliferation of alternative voices, from Australia to Africa or the Sami of Norway, began to be heard most clearly in the 1980s and 1990s.

I will examine more fully below the causes for the recent rise in theoretical diversity in archaeology. For the moment I have wanted only to point to the link between processual archaeology and a concern with unified theory. But already, at least by the 1970s, alternative theoretical perspectives were being championed on the edges of the processual core. In historical North American archaeology, Deetz (1977) had embraced structuralism. In Canada, Trigger (e.g. 1978) maintained a sustained critique of the rejection of history by processual archaeology. In Britain, a strong structural-Marxism had emerged (Freidman and Rowlands 1978).

But in the 1980s and 1990s various self-styled postprocessual directions were taken. The term 'postprocessual' can be used either to describe a British-based embrace of social theory, or to describe all the theoretical directions that have been taken in reaction to the processual archaeology of the 1960s and 1970s. As regards the first definition, postprocessual archaeology derives its ideas from the various derivatives of structuralism (e.g. poststructuralism) and Marxism (critical theory, neo-Marxism, and agency theory), and from the critique of positivism leading to the discussion of relativism, hermeneutics and realism. Postprocessual archaeology was initially defined in opposition to processual archaeology (e.g. Hodder 1982b) but it later developed an 'interpretative' programme of its own (e.g. Tilley 1991). Some of the main themes of the interpretative programme are that the past is meaningfully constituted from different perspectives, that human agency is active, not passive, and that cultural change is historical and contingent.

As regards the second definition of postprocessual archaeology, there have been many recent reactions both to processual archaeology and to postprocessual archaeology as narrowly defined above. For example, especially in Britain, there has been a strong move towards a phenomenological position. While accepting many of the critical points made by interpretative archaeologists, these authors often deny the possibility of getting at meanings 'in the heads of' people in the past. Instead the emphasis is placed on how meanings were controlled and reproduced (Barrett 1994). In particular, emphasis is placed on how landscapes and monuments can be structured to control bodily movements such that a hegemonic reading of the world is inculcated and passed on. This approach can be critiqued for its attempt to separate bodily from other meanings, but it has led to fruitful discussions of different theoretical perspectives, particularly those of Heidegger (Thomas 1996; Gosden 1994) and Merleau-Ponty (Kus 1992).

Perhaps the major contribution to postprocessual debate has been from feminist and gender archaeology, strongly influenced by developments in other disciplines. Feminist archaeology has a strong political focus, aimed at the androcentrism in the discipline, especially Western assumptions about the division of labour as in the 'Man the Hunter/Women the Gatherer' model. The main concern was initially to redress androcentric bias and 'find' women in the archaeological record. Gender archaeology has developed theories of gender relations and gender ideologies in relation to societal change (Gero and Conkey 1991), the use of space and material culture (e.g. Moore 1985). In its focus on power and its representation, on active social agency and on the critique of ideology, feminist and gender approaches have close parallels with other postprocessual archaeologies. More recently, debate within feminism outside and inside the discipline has critiqued the way in which gender studies have tended to focus on women only, has questioned the opposition between biological sex and cultural gender, and has opened up a radical discussion of 'difference' — in particular the ways in which dimensions of sex interact with class, age, occupation, race, ethnicity, etc. In this commitment to difference the role of individuals has come to the fore (Meskell 1999).

While cognitive-processual archaeology accommodates many of the critiques of processual archaeology made by postprocessualists (see above and Renfrew 1994), other critiques of processual archaeology have emerged from within the North American tradition (e.g. Schiffer's 1995 redefined behavioural approach tradition). One of the most distinctive groups of developments is towards various forms of evolutionary archaeology, often strongly influenced by neo-Darwinian debates. For example, Dunnell (1989) has tried to develop a theory of cultural evolution that conforms to Darwinian principles. Highly critical of the processual view that adaptation offers an adequate causal explanation for changes in human history, he draws direct parallels between biological and cultural evolution. He suggests that artefacts can be considered as part of the human phenotype in much the same way that nests are part of the phenotype of birds. Human intention and meaning are of little interest to this approach since what is ultimately of importance is whether human products (whatever the intention behind them) are subject to selective pressures which affect reproductive fitness. For an example of this approach the reader is referred to O'Brien and Holland (1992) and for an alternative and less reductionist evolutionary perspective to Shennan (1989).

The above description of theoretical diversity in archaeology has been largely confined to Anglo-American archaeology. Inhibition of theoretical debate elsewhere in Europe has been described above, but nevertheless distinctive traditions have emerged in most countries (Hodder 1991). For example, some French prehistoric studies are characterized by an interdisciplinary focus, derived from Mauss and Leroi-Gourhan, on the history and ethnography of techniques, culminating in the study of operational chains within sequences of technical acts. This work in prehistory has had considerable impact beyond the borders of France (Dobres 1999).

Outside Europe it is again possible to identify strongly divergent theoretical traditions. For example, there has been a distinctive Marxist perspective in several countries in South America. This has been characterized as a 'Latin American Social Archaeology School' (Politis 1995; Funari 1995).

Paddayya (1995) notes that there is a rich and very long tradition of philosophical thought in India. Some of the key ideas and concepts deal with time, space and causality. He argues that these perspectives have had little impact in transforming archaeological thought, either in India or elsewhere. In related disciplines, successful attempts have been made to compare and contrast Western theoretical concepts with philosophical themes from Indian scholarship (e.g. Paranjpe 1990).

In contrasting Western and other theoretical frameworks in archaeology it often appears helpful to distinguish between a Western objectified, distanced perspective and one in which artefacts and monuments have direct meaning in guiding everyday life. For example, Langford (1983) contrasts a dead past of archaeological science with a lived past of contemporary aboriginal people in Australia. Mamani Condori (1989) describes a similar contrast for the Bolivian Aymara. He also discusses specific theoretical ideas which have no direct translation within Western language and archaeology. For example, *pacha* is similar to but different from concepts used in space-time geography (e.g. Barrett 1994), and the Aymara idea of *nagra*, that 'the future is behind our backs', seems to confront Western notions of time.

Interpreting the widening theoretical debate

Above, I situated culture-historical and processual archaeology within a variety of contexts including nationalism, colonialism and the functional desire to make Western archaeology into a relevant science. All these factors also contributed to a unification of theoretical perspective. What are the conditions for a more diverse production of archaeological theories in the 1980s and 1990s?

There has certainly been an internal process of critique, debate and development in Western archaeology. This has partly involved shifts in position as processual archaeologists respond to postprocessual critique, or as postprocessual archaeology responds to feminist archaeology, and so on. But many of the internal developments have occurred because of interactions with other disciplines. In particular, many disciplines have been influenced by a variety of perspectives from neo-Darwinian thought to post-modern debate. As regards the latter the archaeological theoretical diversity is linked to wider concerns with fluidity, fragmentation, and pastiche. Another strong intellectual influence from outside has been feminism. It is often difficult to separate internal theoretical debate from external intellectual influence.

But beyond the intellectual debates, other factors have changed the conditions of knowledge production for archaeological theory. For example, there has been a major increase in the importance of various forms of 'popular' archaeologies. There has been a massive rise in the number of museums, heritage and interpretative centres in developed countries. There has also been an increase in the 'fringe', such as Goddess and New Age groups, ley line hunters or metal detector users. At the same time, central government funding for archaeology has in many countries decreased; alternative sources have often been sought from corporate and private sectors. For all these reasons there has been a need to broaden interpretations, and to make them more accessible and inclusive. A greater availability of and involvement with the archaeological past has been enhanced by new information technologies. In particular, the various forms of the Internet have encouraged a proliferation of 'e-sites' at which the past can be explored, at many different levels of engagement.

The impact of the Internet has been strongest in developed countries, but there are many global processes which have led to widening engagement with the past. These involve changes in global markets, global environmental concerns, and global scales of production. Cultural heritage is increasingly defined on a global scale. International agencies such as UNESCO or the World Monuments Fund (New York) define certain sites as significant for world heritage. Global involvement also occurs as tourism is attracted to sites and is exploited for commercial gain. But global processes of heritage definition and popular consumption of archaeological sites are often resisted locally. Indigenous groups may claim universal rights in relation to heritage issues. But in a postcolonial world, they may also wish to strengthen local identities and to reclaim ownership of local pasts.

All these processes, from popularization and dissemination of the past to the rise in claims made about the past by indigenous groups, give an authority to voices outside the Western archaeological establishment. It has become 'pc' to be multivocal. Theoretical archaeology has seen a wider debate as the conditions around it have changed. It is difficult to argue today, as was argued by processual archaeologists, that there is only one way to do archaeology. Most claims made about the past are open to critique from one quarter or another.

Conclusion

I have argued in this chapter that the widening debate in archaeological theory can be situated within a specific context of knowledge production. In particular, in information-based global economics in a postcolonial era, there is a need for a diversification of perspectives about the past. It is often argued that hierarchies of knowledge are shifting to networks of information flow (e.g. Castells 1996). Rather than being centralized and controlled by the academy, archaeological theoretical knowledge is becoming dispersed and contested at many different nodes.

Certainly this dispersal of archaeological knowledge into networks has encouraged a new diversity of perspectives. Alternative constructions of the past proliferate in developed countries, and indigenous groups around the world forge new and varied links with their pasts. But these new forms of archaeological knowledge pose challenges for the ideas of authority and canon within the discipline. How is the archaeologist to speak with authority within this new and more fluid environment? Many of the theoretical debates described above attempt to grapple with this question. Within much feminist or postprocessual archaeology there is a dual commitment to dialogue and science. By this I mean there is a recognition of the need both to incorporate other voices, and to argue that the archaeologist as intellectual can provide specialized in-depth knowledge which can contribute to debates about the past, however social or political those debates might be (Hodder 1999).

Perhaps a final trend that can be recognized as archaeologists face a widening debate in a new global context concerns the embedding of theory in practice. It is widely recognized that as archaeology moved through culture-historical to processual to postprocessual phases, archaeological theory became more and more rarified and divorced from practice. This resulted from the incorporation into the discipline of ideas from elsewhere, and from specialization so that it became possible for archaeologists to make careers largely as 'theory specialists'. Much theorization concentrated on the 'textualization' of the discipline — that is on the reading and writing of archaeological texts rather than on excavation or fieldwork (e.g. Tilley 1991). Postprocessual archaeology seemed increasingly to be moving into an ivory tower, or alternatively into a theoretical ghetto.

But the dispersal and popularization of archaeological knowledge into networks, and the taking up of the past by local and indigenous groups, make the separation of archaeological theory increasingly untenable. Feminists have argued for putting 'people back in the past' (Gero and Conkey 1991). As noted above, phenomenologists have tried to understand how people in the past experienced monuments. Different theoretical directions have sought to reconstruct the lives of specific individuals (Hodder 1999; Meskell 1999). There has been much study of archaeology in the media, and much archaeological theory is concerned with the presentation of the past, and how it gives meaning to the lives of people today (e.g. Layton 1989).

It may be fitting, as new global contexts emerge for archaeology at the turn of the millennium, to talk of the 'untheorizing' of archaeological theory. I do not mean by this the demise of archaeological theory. If anything, theory has established itself as a necessary component of a mature, reflexive archaeological discipline. But archaeological theory may gradually lose its abstract character, separate from practice. A necessary part of a self-critical and self-aware discipline, theory may in archaeology increasingly come close to ethics as issues of individual and group rights are brought to the fore in practice. As the canon is challenged and as specialist knowledge is dispersed, professional archaeologists retain a role in the gathering and dissemination of information. But they also become involved in ethical issues dealing with the use of information. Self-critical evaluation of assumptions and knowledge thus constitutes a necessary function for archaeological theory. But it is a theory embedded in rights and social issues; that is in ethics. It is theory made concrete, contextualized, an element of practice.

References

ARNOLD, B. 1990: The past as propaganda: totalitarian archaeology in Nazi Germany. *Antiquity* 64, 464–78.

BAPTY, I. and YATES, T. 1990: *Archaeology after structuralism* (London).

BARRETT, J. 1994: *Fragments from Antiquity* (Oxford).

BINFORD, L.R. 1978: *Nunamiut ethnoarchaeology* (New York).

CASTELLS, E. 1996: *The rise of the network society* (Oxford).

CLARKE, D.L. 1973: Archaeology: the loss of innocence. *Antiquity* 47, 6–18.

DEETZ, J. 1977: *In small things forgotten* (New York).

DOBRES, M.-A. 1999: *Technology and social agency* (Oxford).

DUNNELL, R.C. 1989: Aspects of the application of evolutionary theory in archaeology. In Lamberg-Karlovsky, C.C. (ed.), *Archaeological thought in America* (Cambridge), 35–49.

FEYERABEND, P. 1975: *Against method* (London).

FLANNERY, K. 1973: Archaeology with a capital S. In Redman, C. (ed.), *Research and theory in current archaeology* (New York), 47–58.

FRIEDMAN, J. and ROWLANDS, M. 1978: *The evolution of Social Systems* (London).

FRITZ, J. and PLOG, F. 1970: The nature of archaeological explanation. *American Antiquity* 35, 405–12.

FUNARI, P. 1995: Mixed features of archaeological theory in Brazil. In Ucko, P. (ed.) 1995, 236–50.

GERO, J. and CONKEY, M. 1991: *Engendering archaeology* (Oxford).

GOSDEN, C. 1994: *Social being and time* (Oxford).

HARRIS, E.C. 1989: *Principles of archaeological stratigraphy* (London, 2nd edition).

HAWKES, C. 1954: Archaeological theory and method: some suggestions from the old world. *American Anthropologist* 56, 155–68.

HODDER, I. 1972: Locational models and the study of Romano-British settlement. In Clarke, D.L. (ed.), *Models in archaeology* (London).

HODDER, I. 1982a: *Symbols in action* (Cambridge).

HODDER, I. 1982b: *Symbolic and structural archaeology* (Cambridge).

HODDER, I. 1991: *Archaeological theory in Europe: the last three decades* (London).

HODDER, I. 1999: *The archaeological process* (Oxford).

JOHNSON, M. 1999: *Archaeological theory. An introduction* (Oxford).

KEELEY, L. 1980: *Experimental determination of stone tool uses: a microwear analysis* (Chicago).

KUHN, T. 1962: *The structure of Scientific revolutions* (Chicago).

KUS, S. 1992: Toward an archaeology of body and soul. In Gardin, J.-C. and Pebbles, C.S. (eds.), *Representations in archaeology* (Bloomington), 168–77.

LANGFORD, R.F. 1983: Our heritage — your playground. *Australian Archaeol.* 16, 1–6.

LAYTON, R. 1989: *Conflict in the archaeology of living traditions* (London).

LEONE, M., POTTER, P. and SHACKEL, P. 1987: Toward a critical archaeology. *Current Anthropol.* 28, 283–302.

MAMANI CONDORI, C. 1989: History and prehistory in Bolivia: What about the Indians? In Layton, R. 1989, 46–59.

MATTHEWS, W., FRENCH, C., LAWRENCE, T. and CUTLER, D. 1996: Multiple Surfaces: the micromorphology. In Hodder, I. (ed.), *On the surface* (McDonald Archaeological Institute and British Institute of Archaeology at Ankara), 301–42.

MESKELL, L. 1999: *Archaeologies of social life* (Oxford).

MOORE, H.L. 1985: *Space, text and gender* (Cambridge).

O'BRIEN, M.J. and HOLLAND, T.D. 1992: The role of adaptation in archaeological explanation. *American Antiquity* 57, 36–59.

OLSEN, B. 1991: Metropolises and satellites in archaeology. In Preucel, R. (ed.), *Processual and postprocessual archaeology* (Southern Illinois University, Centre for Archaeological Investigations, Occasional Paper 10), 211–24.

PADDAYYA, K. 1995: Theoretical perspectives in Indian archaeology. In Ucko, P. (ed.) 1995, 110–49.

PARANJPE, M. 1990: The invasion of 'theory': an Indian response. *New Quest* 81, 151–61.

PETRIE, F. 1904: *Methods and aims in archaeology* (London).

PITT RIVERS, A.H.L.F. 1896: *The evolution of culture and other essays* (Oxford).

POLITIS, G. 1995: The socio-politics of the development of archaeology in Hispanic South America. In Ucko, P. (ed.) 1995, 197–235.

PREUCEL, R. 1995: The postprocessual condition. *J. Archaeol. Res.* 3, 147–75.

PREUCEL, R. and HODDER, I. 1996: *Contemporary archaeology in theory: a reader* (Oxford).

RAAB, L.M. and GOODYEAR, A.C. 1984: Middle range theory in archaeology. *American Antiquity* 49, 255–68.

RENFREW, C. 1982: *Towards an archaeology of mind* (Cambridge).

RENFREW, C. 1994: Toward a cognitive archaeology. In Renfrew, C. and Zubrow, E. (eds.), *The ancient mind* (Cambridge), 3–12.

RENFREW, C. and COOKE, K. 1979: *Transformations: mathematical approaches to culture change* (London).

SCHIFFER, M.B. 1987: *Formation processes of the archaeological record* (Albuquerque).

SCHIFFER, M.B. 1995: *Behavioural Archaeology: first principles* (Salt Lake City).

SHANKS, M. and TILLEY, C. 1987: *Re-constructing archaeology* (Cambridge).

SHENNAN, S. 1989: Cultural transmission and cultural change. In van der Leeuw, S.E. and Torrence, R. (eds.) 1989, 330–46.

TANUDIRJO, D.A. 1995: Theoretical trends in Indonesian archaeology. In Ucko, P. (ed.) 1995, 61–75.

THOMAS, J. 1996: *Time, culture and identity* (London).

TILLEY, C. 1991: *The art of ambiguity: material culture and text* (London).

TRIGGER, B. 1978: *Time and traditions* (New York).

TRIGGER, B. 1984: Alternative archaeologies: nationalist, colonialist, imperialist. *Man* 19, 355–70.

TRIGGER, B. 1989: *A history of archaeological thought* (Cambridge).

TSUDE, H. 1995: Archaeological theory in Japan. In Ucko, P. (ed.) 1995, 298–311.

UCKO, P. (ed.) 1995: *Theory in archaeology. A world perspective* (London).

VAN DER LEEUW, S.E. and TORRENCE, R. (eds.) 1989: *What's new?* (London).

WATSON, P.J., REDMAN, C. and LEBLANC, S. 1971: *Explanation in archaeology: an explicitly scientific approach* (New York).

WHITLEY, D. 1998: *Reader in archaeological theory: postprocessual and cognitive approaches* (London).

WYLIE, A. 1989: Archaeological cables and tacking: the implications of practice for Bernstein's 'Options beyond objectivism and relativism'. *Philosophy of the Social Sciences* 19, 1–18.

Yamal to Greenland: Global connections in circumpolar archaeology

WILLIAM W. FITZHUGH

The early history of mankind is usually thought of as a tropical story and that of the past 70,000 years of human biological and cultural development as a period in which humans pioneered new environments and opportunities in the temperate zones. In fact, the course of human history has been strongly influenced by human adaptations to climates and environments of Late Pleistocene northern Eurasia where during the past hundred thousand years Neanderthals and early *Homo sapiens* lived under arctic and subarctic conditions similar to those of today's Eskimos and other northern indigenous peoples. Learning to survive as hunters of mammoth, reindeer, and other Late Pleistocene fauna on the Eurasian tundra and in northern boreal settings challenged early humans to develop new technologies, warm dwellings, tailored clothing, and spiritual beliefs that later became important in the formation of Holocene cultures in Eurasia and the Americas. Even after temperate climates replaced arctic and subarctic conditions over much of the northern hemisphere 12,000 years ago, and after food-producing economies began to dominate human subsistence, ancient hunting adaptations continued to sustain northern peoples until the end of the twentieth century. For this reason, in addition to illuminating the history of modern and prehistoric northern cultures, circumpolar studies contribute to understanding the broader history of human origins and adaptations by providing insight into a part of the human past that has been lost elsewhere due to massive cultural and environmental change.

Since it is impossible to summarize circumpolar archaeology in the space available here, I have chosen to discuss several key themes and issues. These include common misconceptions about the 'hostile' arctic and its 'remote' peoples; geographic and environmental features that make the circumpolar region unique; a brief history of circumpolar culture theory; and selected cases illustrating advances in studies of transitions and processes of northern culture change. These examples follow the west-to-east chronology of arctic settlement: Early Holocene adaptations in the Siberian High Arctic; the movement into America; development of northern maritime cultures in the North

Pacific; the Asian reindeer breeding revolution and spread of metal; the origin and dispersion of Eskimo cultures; human–environmental interactions at the forest–tundra boundary in Labrador; and Norse response to climate and environmental change in the North Atlantic. These case studies reveal that human history in the circumpolar north has been influenced by developments throughout the northern hemisphere for the past 10,000 years, whereas cultural histories in southern regions of Eurasia and the Americas have developed independently from one another.

In this discussion I use the term 'arctic' rather loosely to include the Arctic, Subarctic, and adjacent seas; 'circumpolar' to refer to both true polar and boreal regions; and the badly compromised but irreplaceable collective term 'Eskimo' to refer to the composite of those cultures and ethnic peoples known more precisely as Kaaladlit in Greenland, Inuit in Canada, Inupiat in North Alaska, Yupik in the Bering Strait areas, Yup'ik in south-east Alaska, and Alutiiq in Pacific Coast Alaska, as well as to their prehistoric Thule ancestors and their predecessors — Okvik, Old Bering Sea, Punuk, Dorset, and Pre-Dorset cultures — who may in fact not be linguistically or biologically 'Eskimo' at all. I also include as 'Eskimo' the Aleut (known today as Unangan), who are culturally and linguistically related to Eskimo in the distant past. Such 'Eskimo' terms are used by archaeologists to designate cultural traditions and do not signify biological affinity, for while it is known that Thule tradition people were biologically and linguistically ancestral to modern Inuit, the language and biological relationships of Pre-Dorset and Dorset 'paleoeskimos' are problematic (Schindler 1985), although the few Dorset skeletons known appear Asian. All ages are expressed in uncorrected radiocarbon years.

Arctic stereotypes: from cultural refugium to global 'conveyor belt'

Emerging from the convergence of ethnography and 'Palaeolithic' archaeology in the Eastern Canadian Arctic and Greenland in the late nineteenth century (Collins 1984), the study of circumpolar peoples was essentially synonymous with 'Eskimology' as practised by Danish anthropologists from the 1880s until the 1940s, when modern archaeology began to provide an historical framework. Circumpolar archaeology developed in close co-operation with anthropologists, historians, and natural scientists. Integrated approaches utilizing ethnography, human biology, linguistics, mythology and folklore have been especially important in reconstructing the recent history of northern peoples. Natural sciences like botany, palaeoecology, geology, climatology, and others have been especially important for understanding the early history of northern peoples, but they have also made important contributions to recent circumpolar history. Such events as the first peopling of the Americas from Asia prior to 12,000 years ago, the eastward movement of Siberian 'Neolithic' peoples into Alaska and northern Canada c.6–4000 years ago, the eastern expansion of Thule whale hunters from Alaska into Canada and Greenland some 1000 years ago, and the contemporaneous westward expansion of Norse from northern Europe across the North Atlantic to Greenland and North America all are linked with times of climatic warming. Conversely, the effects of climatic cooling have often produced starvation, extinction, retreat from marginal territories, loss of crops and animals, and social and economic distress. The abandonment of the Greenland colonies by the Norse at the beginning of the 'Little Ice Age' in the fourteenth to fifteenth centuries is only one of many examples that demonstrates the tenuous nature of human enterprise in northern regions. These and other arctic examples are some of the strongest archaeological evidence of human responses to climatic and environmental change known from Holocene times.

Most of the Arctic has been inaccessible to visitors from southern lands until very recently. Although Vikings first met Canadian Inuit in the twelfth to thirteenth century, and Martin Frobisher and John Davis met Inuit in Baffin Island and Labrador in the late sixteenth century, detailed descriptions of Inuit culture were not written down until the nineteenth century, and many Inuit continued to live as subsistence hunters until the mid-twentieth century. In the North Pacific European contacts with Native peoples were not common until after 1800 in Russian America and until the 1840–50s north of Bering Strait. In Eurasia, the chronology of European contact inclined in the other direction, beginning first among the Sami in the Viking Age and trending upward in time across the northern coast of Siberia to Bering Strait, where Chukchi came under some Russian influence in the seventeenth and eighteenth centuries. Thus Sami reindeer herders were paying tribute to Vikings one thousand years before the Chukchi first met Russian Cossacks. Such clines in 'connectivity' occurred at earlier times as well. Paleoeskimo cultures of Canada developed largely in isolation from external contacts for three thousand years (4000–1000 BP), while cultures in Beringia and Scandinavia have been exposed to cultural exchange and innovation constantly for the past ten thousand years.

Therefore, contrary to the views of early anthropologists, the Arctic is not a refuge where cultures and peoples existed — isolated, marginalized, and unchanging — through millennia. Although some adaptations persisted for long periods and some areas, like the Central Canadian Arctic, have been more isolated than others, northern peoples, when challenged, have not hesitated to accept useful ideas from outsiders or to change their way of life. Indeed, they frequently found unique ways to adapt and utilize innovation: trade metal replaced chipped and ground stone tools; European hardwoods and textiles were eagerly sought out; glass beads substituted brilliantly for less fashionable (to Eskimos) ivory decorations; and Christianity rapidly replaced shamanism when dealings with Europeans became important. Ingenuity in the face of adversity produced novelties like frozen fish substituting for sled runners when wood was not available, or using a single hair from one's parka ruff to indicate the presence of an exhaling seal rising into its breathing hole.

Conversely, innovations produced by arctic peoples have also had a major influence in the wider world. Consider the European whaler's toggling harpoon, which was responsible for launching one of the world's earliest energy booms — whale oil for the lamps of Europe and America (Tuck and Grenier 1992). This classic implement developed from a Canadian or Greenlandic Inuit form of toggling harpoon first seen and copied by European explorers in the sixteenth or seventeenth century, when it replaced the barbed but non-toggling Basque harpoon. Its function is as simple as it is elegant: a point with a hole for attaching a line and having a bevelled or spurred base that causes the point to turn sideways and toggle under the skin of the animal, making a fast connection (Fig. 1). Archaeological evidence suggests, however, that the toggling harpoon may not have been Eskimo originally. It probably was first developed by Maritime Archaic Indians in Labrador 7500 years ago and was adopted by the first Paleoeskimos to arrive in Labrador from the north c.4000 years ago (Tuck 1976, 121; McGhee 1978, 45). The latter, in turn, modified its form and passed it back across the North American Arctic to Bering Strait, where it evolved further before reappearing in Arctic Canada again when Thule whale hunters migrated east from Alaska about AD 1100. An alternate theory suggests that an early toggling harpoon existed in Jomon culture 6000 years ago (Yamaura 1980), and some have suggested an origin in American Paleoindian culture of the northern plains (Dennis Stanford, pers. comm.) or in the late Paleoindian

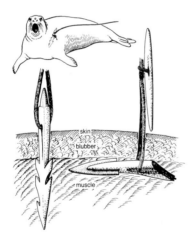

maritime adaptation in the Champlain Sea and Canadian Maritimes (Tuck 1977; Loring 1980).

The toggling harpoon is only one of many inventions developed by northern peoples. The engraved ivory art of the Old Bering Sea culture dating to the first few centuries AD in Western Alaska and Chukotka is one of the most highly-valued styles of tribal art (Wardwell 1986). Eskimos also invented the kayak, umiak (open skin boat), snow-goggles, and igloo. Other northern inventions include parkas, mukluks (skin boots); dog-sleds, reindeer transport, oil lamps, toboggans and snowshoes (Subarctic American Indians); skis (Finland, 6000 BP); ice crampons (Old Bering Sea Eskimos, 1500 BP). Explorer Martin Sauer expressed his astonishment at the beauty and complexity of Aleut culture in these words: 'the capacity of the

Figure 1. Harpoons are crucial to human survival in arctic and northern seas. Efficient hunting of marine mammals requires use of toggling (right) and non-toggling (left) harpoons. The simpler non-toggling forms appear in the archaeological record as early as 70,000 years ago in Africa, while toggling forms first appeared along the North Pacific and north-western Atlantic coasts about 7000 years ago. (Illustr. Arctic Studies Center.)

natives of these islands infinitely surpasses every idea that I had formed of the abilities of savages . . . Their behavior . . . is not rude or barbarous, but mild, polite, and hospitable. At the same time, the beauty proportion, and art with which they make their boats, instruments, and apparel evince that they by no means deserve to be termed stupid; an epithet so liberally bestowed upon those whom Europeans call savages' (Sauer 1802, 273–4). Most other European explorers were not so observant and often died because they failed to learn from northern peoples.

Northern peoples have also had their share of crisis and failure. Archaeological evidence documents many local extinctions and cultural disasters. Some of these problems resulted from the human propensity to over-exploit resources and fail to adapt to changing conditions, as seen in the case of the Greenland Norse. But mostly, northern peoples deserve admiration for having developed remarkable cultures that survived tens of thousands of years in one of the earth's most challenging environments.

The circumpolar world

The shared, common features of the north are best expressed in the concept of circumpolarity — the notion that many features of the northern environment, such as plants, animals, weather, and climates, have zonal similarities from one region of the arctic to another (Fig. 2). In temperate and tropical regions, geography and time have resulted in divergent historical and evolutionary trends. Even though tropical climates are similar around the globe, history and geographic separation have produced different life forms in different regions. The opposite of this process governs life in northern latitudes; here plants, animals, habitats, and ecozones become more unified, and in many cases very similar geographic, climatic, and environmental conditions encircle the pole, producing ecological conditions that allowed identical species of caribou, moose, beaver, porcupine, wolf, wolverine, and many others to be found throughout the circumpolar region. These conditions have been even more effective in producing global distributions of marine life like seals, walrus, whales, as well as very closely-related species of birds, waterfowl, fish, and marine organisms (Young 1989). As we shall see, these processes have also been important determinants in the rapid spread of artefact types (like harpoons), cultural themes (like whaling, reindeer herding, and shamanism), peoples and cultures (like Thule) over huge regions of the north.

These conditions have produced an environment whose maritime, tundra, and boreal zones and climates are latitudinally continuous. The southern boundary of the arctic has been defined variously as the northern limit of the forest, the presence of permanently-frozen ground (permafrost), the 10-degree Celsius isotherm, or others, depending on one's purpose or academic discipline. Cold ocean waters — some ice-covered throughout the year, others having seasonal pack-ice, and still others defined

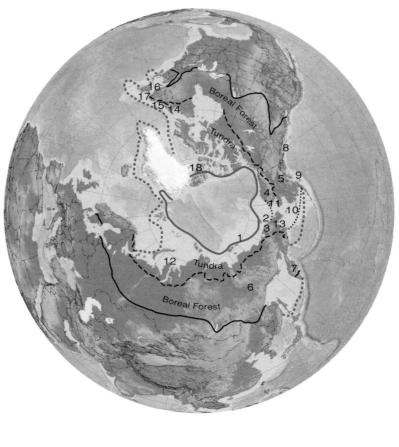

1. Zhokov Island
2. Wrangel Island/Chertov Ovrag
3. Pegtymel
4. Utukok
5. Nenana
6. Dyuktai/ Sakha
7. Ushki/Kamchatka
8. On Your Knees Cave
9. Kodiak

10. St. Lawrence Island
11. Ipiutak
12. Yamal Peninsula
13. Chukotka
14. Nulliak, Labrador
15. Rattler's Bight
16. Port au Choix
17. L'Anse aux Meadows
18. Skraeling Island

...... Bering Land Bridge13-14,000 yrs
− − − northern treeline
⎯⎯ southern limit of boreal forest
⎯⎯ northern (summer) limit of pack ice
▪▪▪▪▪ southern (winter) limit of pack ice

Figure 2. Map of the circumpolar region showing boreal forest and tundra zones, Bering Land Bridge, northern and southern limit of pack ice, and major sites discussed in text.

by temperature, salinity, or both — bathe the arctic coasts and extend south along the continental margins, providing similar ecological conditions and identical or closely related species of fish, sea mammals, and sea birds. On land, wide expanses of tundra with caribou/reindeer, grizzly bear, geese, and with lakes teeming with whitefish, occur throughout the circumpolar region, reaching hundreds of miles into the continental masses. South of the tundra, northern birch and coniferous forests with a fauna dominated by moose, black bear, small fur-bearers, ptarmigan, salmon, and other fish are found from Scandinavia eastward to Newfoundland.

The cause of this condition is only partly climatic, for it has been strongly influenced by the geography of lands which encircle the Arctic Ocean. This is dramatically revealed in a circumpolar map projection or satellite image. With eastern Eurasia and north-western North America separated by only 90 km at Bering Strait, this body of water hardly constitutes a biotic or cultural barrier. Today and in the recent past Eskimo people maintained contact across Bering Strait by boat in summer and over the ice in winter, and in Pleistocene times the emerged Bering Land Bridge created a broad land bridge 500–1000 km wide connecting Asia and North America. At this time Alaska west of the Cordilleran glacier was geographically and biologically more connected to Asia than to North America. The wider geographic separation in the North Atlantic was a more formidable geographic barrier, but its open water crossings between islands and land masses are mostly under 500 km.

At the same time that the arctic and subarctic zones provided channels for the rapid latitudinal spread of ideas, materials, and peoples from Scandinavia to Greenland, north-trending coastlines connected and north-flowing rivers, especially numerous in Eurasia, facilitated communication between temperate zones and arctic regions. Rivers filled with fish and bird life provided natural north–south transport routes, brought masses of driftwood annually from the southern forests to woodless arctic river banks, ocean coasts, and islands, and when frozen in winter could be travelled upstream as easily as downstream in summer. In similar fashion, reindeer, whose annual migrations took them from the forest edge to the northern tundra and back each year, provided stimulus and sustenance for human movements from temperate regions into the north. Such geographic lanes facilitated contacts in which southern peoples exchanged materials like metal, cloth, weapons, and other items for precious northern ivory, hides, furs, falcons, and feathers. Southern biota and southern peoples and concepts, including animal domestication and metal-use, revolutionized northern cultures, and once integrated into northern life spread rapidly across the east–west interaction networks. Both east–west zonal contacts and north–south 'cross-economy' transfers (Moberg 1975) produced the unique dynamism that stimulated circumpolar prehistory. Some of these transfers were simply incorporated into northern or southern life; others had to be rationalized by social or ideological systems. Some aspects of Neolithic economy, like pottery and domesticated animals, were readily adopted by arctic cultures while others, like religious beliefs linked to agricultural production, were not. Shamanism and belief in the spirits of nature remained dominant in arctic regions from Palaeolithic times to the modern day.

These geographic features created conditions that influenced the development of northern peoples in special ways. South of the circumpolar zone Eurasian and American cultures developed in near, if not total, isolation from each other for most of the past 10,000 years. Although a number of theories of mid-latitude trans-oceanic contact have been proposed (Meggers, Evans and Estrada 1965), none has been confirmed as having left a major imprint on Native cultures of the Americas, leaving the arctic and subarctic regions of the North Pacific and possibly the North Atlantic (see below) as the only area where contacts between Eurasia and America probably took place throughout the entire history of New World peoples. Such contacts may also have occurred in the North Atlantic from the Viking period *c.*AD 1000 to the present. What effect, if any, did the existence of this global circumpolar interaction sphere have on the development of Eurasian and American cultures? Are its cultures more or less similar to each other than cultures in southern regions? Did technological developments pass more quickly from one region to another because of the greater human mobility and transport systems in northern regions? Or did the existence of different circumpolar ethnic cultures block the spread of cultural developments that originated in southern cultures or other regions of the arctic? Finally, what effect has climate and environmental change had on northern culture history? Although studies of these cross-cultural inquiries have barely begun, research reveals Arctic culture history was dynamic and influential beyond the confines of the Arctic region itself.

Circumpolar theory

In the mid-1800s, archaeologists excavating well-preserved European Palaeolithic cave sites were at first perplexed by the implements they were finding. Some of the artefacts, like antler tines with holes through them, had no obvious function (Fig. 3). But when European explorers began returning from the Canadian Arctic and Alaska, they brought home Eskimo barbed harpoons, oil lamps, and spear-throwers (atlatls) that were nearly identical to Palaeolithic tools and even included similar objects that the Eskimos used as wrenches to straighten bent arrow and spear shafts. More curious were aspects of Palaeolithic art and mysterious ritual objects that had close parallels with Eskimo art and shamanistic objects. Although some of the relationships implied by these similarities have been discounted, particularly in graphic arts (Fig. 4; De Laguna 1932–3), other aspects of ritual and shamanistic art continue to inspire confidence as part of an ancient cultural tradition (Schuster and Carpenter 1986–8, 1996; Carpenter 2001). In either case — whether by history or analogy — ethnography and material culture studies of Eskimos and other northern groups brought new insight to the study of European Palaeolithic and Mesolithic cultures.

These similarities inspired theories that Eskimos and other northern peoples were direct descendants of Palaeolithic peoples who migrated north following the retreat of glacial ice and tundra animals at the end of the Ice Age. This theory, first promoted by William Boyd Dawkins (1874) and elaborated by W.J. Sollas (1911), benefited from an absence of arctic archaeological evidence from the intervening 10–15,000 years but nevertheless seemed to make sense intuitively. It did not seem out of the question that

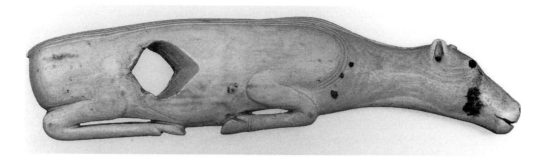

Figure 3. Wrenches to straighten arrow shafts appeared first in the European Upper Palaeolithic. Remarkably similar forms remained in use by historic Alaskan Eskimos, who decorated them with carvings like this foetal caribou that enhanced a hunter's ability to capture this animal. (SI-NMNH; photo ASC.)

Figure 4. The tooth motif was one of the designs common to Palaeolithic and Eskimo art that was once thought to indicate an unbroken historical tradition between the two. This example is seen on a nineteenth-century Yupik Eskimo fungus ash box from Western Alaska. (SI-NMNH 38472; photo ASC.)

somehow in northern Europe, Siberia, or North America Early Palaeolithic and Mesolithic traditions survived to some degree in Eskimo technology, art, shamanism, and spiritual beliefs.

A number of interesting questions arise from similarities between Palaeolithic and Eskimo art. Why are so many forms of Palaeolithic art found in Eskimo culture and its antecedents and not in later temperate zone cultures? Are Palaeolithic and Eskimo cultures historically related or are their similarities due to similar function or chance? Do similar forms imply similar meaning? Is it a coincidence that recent studies of Eskimo and other tribal arts appear to inform Palaeolithic and Mesolithic art? We know from ethnography that many prehistoric objects must have had a ritualistic or shamanistic function. Alaskan Eskimo ethnography helps explain why so-called 'x-ray' skeletal patterns and joint-marks signify power centres in art representing animals and humans (Fig. 5); why Palaeolithic and Eskimo female figurines were made to hang upside-down

Figure 5. Life-lines and skeleton motifs represented the sources of power in animals to many Eskimo and other ethnographic peoples. Similar ideas probably motivated their use in Palaeolithic and Mesolithic art. (SI-NMNH 43528, 49014; photo ASC.)

(Carpenter 2001); how animal masks and images of deities were employed by shamans to manipulate the spirit world (Nelson 1899; Fitzhugh and Kaplan 1982; Fienup-Riordan 1996); how ancient Ipuitak burial equipment functioned as shamanistic equipment; how plugging the body orifices of ancient Eskimo dead with jet or ivory ornaments made it difficult for malevolent spirits to re-animate the deceased. In some cases we have been able to link these ethnographic traditions with ancient archaeological manifestations by tracing continuities in forms and contexts into the past, revealing, for instance, 1500 years of historical development of specific images like the wolf-like hunter's spirit helper and the *tunghak* deity that controlled animal movements (Figs. 6 and 7; Fitzhugh and Kaplan 1982; Fitzhugh 1988a, 1993). Were these concepts

Figure 6. Spirit-helpers in the form of wolf-like predators helped nineteenth-century Alaskan Eskimos capture their prey. This form of harpoon embellishment can be traced back for 2000 years into ancient Old Bering Sea Eskimo Culture. (SI-NMNH 37746; Photo ASC.)

Figure 7. *Tunghak*, the spirit-keeper of the animals in Yupik Eskimo cosmology, is depicted in this nineteenth-century ceremonial mask collected from near the mouth of the Yukon River. The spirit's prey animals are depicted on his forehead. (SI-NMNH 33118; photo ASC.)

and even specific material forms and art transmitted across Siberia from the Upper Palaeolithic to modern times? Were there a series of cultures, still unknown, in northern Europe and Siberia through which these concepts were maintained and elaborated? Were these similarities simply the result of independent invention by later Eskimo societies who faced similar problems hunting northern game animals? Or were they part of a basic cultural 'boiler-plate' built into the behaviour of northern peoples? Here we have the crux of the circumpolar culture dilemma.

The problem is an interesting one, for no other societies except Eskimos and north-ern Indians exist today in which a northern hunting tradition that began deep in the Pleistocene has survived into the present. All others, including even recent Siberian Native peoples, most of whom gave up big game hunting for reindeer breeding, have undergone material and spiritual transformation as various social and technological revolutions allowed humans to take control of their destiny from the gods. Among Eskimo groups, as among Palaeolithic peoples (if most rock art has been interpreted correctly), it was the gods and the animal spirits — not solely the hunter — who deter-mined the outcome of the hunt. Eskimos and Indians of the Subarctic forests (Nelson 1973) still follow technological and spiritual traditions that appear to be based on the same core beliefs that motivated Old World Palaeolithic peoples.

In 1929 the Palaeolithic continuity hypothesis was reformulated by Waldemar Bogoras, one of two Russian ethnologists who participated in the famous Jesup North Pacific Expedition of 1897–1902, led by Franz Boas (Krupnik 2000). Bogoras saw many similar features among cultures, past and present, that had lived in the polar region, and proposed they belonged to a circumpolar culture 'type' whose common elements included tailored fur clothing, skin boats, dog or reindeer trans-port, shamanism, certain types of folklore, and other elements. Bogoras was not so naive as to believe there was only one arctic culture; rather he believed that Eskimo culture was the 'true' circumpolar culture type and saw its absence in Scandinavia and Eurasia as a result of an intrusive historical event. In his view the adoption of reindeer and population movements like the expansion of Turkic-speaking peoples into north-eastern Asia had disrupted the original Eskimo circumpolar culture type that had occupied this area before the Eskimo. Bogoras had not come to these con-clusions independently; he had been strongly influenced by the Danish ethnologist, Gudmund Hatt, who was the first systematically to inventory cultural similarities and differences among northern peoples. Hatt's conclusions suggested that the cir-cumpolar distribution of skin clothing, snowshoes, and folklore/mythology held important clues about historical connections between what he considered to be an older coastal Eskimo and a younger inland Indian people (Hatt 1914, 1934, 1949; Collins 1984).

Bogoras' circumpolar culture was a static ethnographic reconstruction that in his day lacked historical and archaeological grounding. His ideas were later refined by the Norwegian anthropologist, Gutorm Gjessing, who proposed the existence of a 'Circumpolar Stone Age' as a prehistorical equivalent to Bogoras' circumpolar ethno-graphic culture (Gjessing 1944). Built upon new archaeological finds from Younger Stone Age and Iron Age sites in northern Scandinavia that seemed similar to prehis-toric cultures in north-eastern North America (which in turn were considered as pro-totypes of ethnographic Eskimo culture), Gjessing proposed a Circumpolar Stone Age culture that contained stone lamps, ground slate tools, toggling harpoons, skin boats, semilunar (ulu) knives, and other artefacts that he believed had developed in response to adaptation to arctic conditions. Following the same reasoning as Dawkins and Sollas, he further proposed that these circumpolar elements had developed in Scandinavian Stone Age cultures from earlier European Palaeolithic and Mesolithic prototypes and later spread along the Siberian arctic coast and into North America, eventually appearing in the Eskimo and Archaic Indian cultures of the Northeast.

A few years later Albert Spaulding (1946) argued, after reviewing the available Russian evidence, that the conduit for the spread of these ideas could not have been — as Gjessing had proposed — along the Siberian arctic coast, where archaeological evidence in any case was lacking, but rather through the boreal/taiga forest zone, a view amplified further by Alan Bryan (1957), Frank Ridley (1960), and James B. Griffin (1960). Later, other variants of the circumpolar diffusion model were advanced. Simonsen (1975) argued for a refinement of Gjessing's model by introducing trade and occupational specialization as features of prehistorical northern cultures; Chernetsov (1935, 1970) refined archaeological details concerning links between the Yamal Iron Age Ust-Poluj cultures and early Alaskan Eskimo complexes; Moberg (1960, 1975) introduced the concept of cross-economy transformations between groups of northern hunters and southern Neolithic, metal-using, or reindeer-breeding societies; Chard (1960) presented archaeological evidence supporting the idea that instead of being a cultural wedge blocking exchange across Bering Strait, Eskimos formed a crucial connecting link between Siberia and America; and Fitzhugh (1975a and b) proposed that circumpolar cultures might be divided into three more-or-less independent regional developmental sequences centred in the richest areas of maritime resources: northern Scandinavia, the North Pacific/Bering Straits, and the Eastern Canadian Arctic and Subarctic, and Greenland. Since there was little evidence of contact between these centres, such similarities as ground slate tools, skin boats, oil lamps, toggling harpoons, and others probably arose from convergent adaptation in similar environments rather than by historical contact or diffusion (Fitzhugh 1974). In recent years the study of circumpolar culture history and theory has been less active, although some researchers have tested concepts of convergent evolution in southern South America, Tasmania, the Chatham Islands, and in north-eastern and north-western North America (McCartney 1975; Yesner 1980; Sutton 1982; Nash 1983). New syntheses (Khlobystin 1998), overviews (Pitulko 1999b) and field work (Feodorova *et al.* 1998) being conducted in the Eurasian arctic prehistory are stimulating anew the old studies of circumpolar issues in the large, relatively unknown Russian Arctic. Finally, although not in the archaeological domain, recent years have also seen an increase in circumpolar comparisons of ethnographic material culture, folklore, and art (e.g. Collins *et al.* 1973; Fitzhugh and Crowell 1988; Oakes and Riewe 1996; Oakes 1998).

Circumpolar links

One of the major problems complicating circumpolar archaeology results from regional disparity in site preservation. Unlike artefact preservation, which is often excellent even for organic remains, the preservation of sites has depended on dynamic relationships between sea-level and tectonic activity (Andrews 1975). In areas where glaciers did not develop in the Pleistocene and where isostatic uplift has not occurred — as in most of the Russian Arctic from the White Sea to Bering Strait (Velichko *et al.* 1984), in Alaska, and in Greenland, East Baffin and northern Labrador — rising Holocene sea-levels have flooded coastal regions, destroying most sites of the past 10,000 years. On the other hand, in areas where post-glacial land uplift has outpaced sea-level rise, as in northern Scandinavia, the Central Canadian Arctic and Eastern Canadian Subarctic, long sequences of archaeological sites have been preserved on former beachlines and marine terraces. In some areas relationships between sea-level changes, uplift, and local tectonics have been more complicated, for instance on the Northwest Coast, in the Aleutian Islands, around Bering Strait, and along Chukchi Sea coast of Alaska (Giddings 1965; Giddings and Anderson 1986), where sites have been preserved for the past 2–3000 years but where earlier sites have been lost to sea-level rise. In some areas of the Russian Arctic where the continental shelf and coastal plain have almost no topographic relief, submergence, permafrost melting, and erosion have resulted in hundreds of kilometres of coastal retreat between Early Holocene times and the present. Similar processes have inundated Bering Land Bridge sites and those of early maritime cultures along much of the North Pacific rim (Mann *et al.* 1998). Site destruction more than any other factor is responsible for the gaps in knowledge that plague archaeological reconstructions in the circumpolar region and have eliminated the archaeological record of Pleistocene and Early Holocene maritime adaptations throughout the world.

Since little could be done about the huge data gap in the Eurasian arctic record, researchers until recently concentrated their efforts in areas of the north where the record was better preserved. Consequently, detailed information has become available about culture and environmental history in Scandinavia and the Eastern Canadian Arctic and Subarctic, where isostatic uplift has protected archaeological sites from erosion (Andrews *et al.* 1971), and in interior regions of the Russian Arctic. However, occasionally sites have been found in areas where geology suggested they could not occur. One such site has been found on Zhokhov, a tiny island in the northern Laptev Sea currently being excavated by Vladimir Pitulko with a team of Russian and American scientists.

Zhokhov: Early Holocene coastal hunters of the Russian High Arctic

The Zhokhov site (Pitulko 1993, 1999a, 2001; Fig. 8) is remarkable for its 7800 year age (*c*.8408–8175 BP calibrated), its extreme northern location, and its unusual faunal com-

Figure 8. Excavations in progress during the summer of 2000 at Zhokhov, an 8000 year old Mesolithic site in the high arctic region of northern Siberia, where the tundra today is almost devoid of plant life. The masses of wood preserved in the site must have been obtained from driftwood that floated down the Lena River. (Photo: Adelaide de Menil.)

plex (Pitulko and Kasparov 1996). At present Zhokhov is the earliest archaeological site known in the High Arctic and lies on a small 8 km long volcanic island south of the De Long Chain in the northern Laptev Sea at 76 degrees North, 425 km from the nearest Siberian mainland and 300 km south-west of the continental shelf. The depth of the surrounding waters, *c*.50 m, suggests that this portion of the Laptev basin was flooded by rising sea-level some time between 7–9000 years ago, providing two possible palaeogeographic scenarios: the existence of the site on a prominent cape on the 8000 BP High Arctic coast or as part of an island archipelago becoming inundated and isolated from the retreating mainland coast.

Zhokhov's early environmental setting is crucial to the interpretation of its archaeological finds. The latter are surprisingly simple in terms of lithic assemblage and include prismatic (rather than wedge-shaped) microblade cores, microblades, scrapers, chipped axes with ground bits, and abrading tools (Giria and Pitulko 1994). This assemblage (Fig. 9) fits loosely within the Mesolithic Sumnagin culture of the Lena River basin (Mochanov 1973; Pitulko 2001) and would be unexceptional but for preservation of its bone, ivory, and wood industries, which are almost never preserved in sites of this age

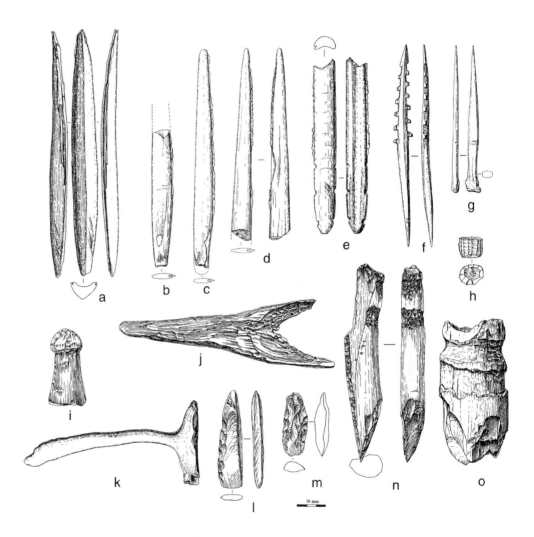

Figure 9. Bone, antler, wood, and stone tools recovered from the 8000 year old Zhokhov site. Many of the points are armed with flint side-blades. (Illustr. V. Pitulko, M. Bakry.)

in northern Russia. In this case Zhokhov's arctic climate has preserved metre-thick deposits that contain, in addition to stone tools, such organic implements as antler and mammoth ivory spear points and knives whose edges have been slotted and contain microblade insets; mammoth ivory axes and picks; antler adze handles; wood handles for stone-bladed tools; bone needles; wood scoops and bowls; wood sled runners; and mysterious knobbed objects. Originally tested in 1989 and 1990, new excavations in 2000 produced additional finds including a large fragment of a woven grass basket (the earliest example of weaving known in the Arctic), a wood paddle-like object, a possible net-weaving shuttle, and an engraved mammoth ivory ornament. The 8000-sq m site seems to contain the remains of several houses and associated middens which are currently being eroded by a small stream during the brief period of summer melt. The deposits contain huge quantities of frost-shattered wood that must have arrived on Zhokhov as driftwood, for their roots and branches are ice-battered and no bark is present. Charred ends indicate that some of the wood was used for fuel, but the majority seems to have been used for house construction and tool-making. No other site has provided such quantities and diversity of organic remains representing Siberian Mesolithic culture.

Equally important are the Zhokhov faunal remains, which include large numbers of reindeer and polar bear (mostly female), many of whose skulls were crushed to extract the brain. These two species account for almost the entire faunal assemblage, with small additions of wolf, fox, walrus, seal, dog, swan, goose, and sea-gull (Pitulko and Kasparov 1996). This peculiar faunal assemblage with its equal dominance of reindeer and polar bear has resulted in endless discussion and speculation. Sites occupied in interior regions of the Eurasian or North American Arctic usually contain wild reindeer/caribou (both belonging to the single species, *Rangifer tarandus*). Coastal sites, on the other hand, especially as typified by Eskimo sites, often contain caribou and a few polar bear bones, but always in small numbers compared with the more common remains of seal and walrus. The combination of equal numbers of individuals of polar bear and reindeer, the absence of harpoon technology, and barely a trace of seal and walrus bone suggests that the Zhokhov people were primarily land hunters who supplemented reindeer catches made during their annual northern migration to the arctic coast in summer with a nearly equal diet of polar bear.

The presence of polar bear remains indicates that Zhokhov people must have been living at or near the coast where they probably hunted bears in their dens in early spring or when they emerged, using dogs to bring them to bay. Summer kills are indicated by the tooth eruption data from reindeer bones and by presence of geese and other summer coastal migrants in the faunal assemblage. On the other hand, the large size of the site, deep midden deposits, and huge amounts of wood indicate that Zhokhov was hardly a simple summer camp; it probably functioned as a home base and winter settlement for 30–40 people for at least several years.

Preliminary results from Zhokhov provide a fascinating glimpse of a High Arctic coast variant of Sumnagin culture (Pitulko 2001) which has been known previously only from sites located in the forested portion of the Lena River basin hundreds of

kilometres to the south (Mochanov 1973). The Zhokhov people utilized a similar Late
Mesolithic technology and were also accomplished reindeer hunters. For at least a few
years they occupied the far northern fringe of the Siberian mainland, perhaps as far east
as Eastern Chukotka (Pitulko 2001), where they hunted reindeer and polar bear, and
lived, possibly year-round, in a very unforgiving environment far from the forest edge
without oil lamps or other technology normally associated with life on the arctic coast.
Their economy and technology clearly indicate that they were not 'Eskimos'; at least
they had not yet become culturally 'Eskimo' as defined by early sites in the Bering Strait
region (see below). Furthermore, judging from the Siberian nature of the Zhokhov tool
industry, the inhabitants were not cultural 'survivors' of the European Palaeolithic or
Mesolithic. Whether or not Zhokhov people were part of the historical sequence that
led to Eskimo culture, the model they present of interior reindeer hunters just beginning to utilize arctic maritime resources fits well with the early theory promoted by
Boas, Steensby, and Birket-Smith of incipient arctic maritime adaptations leading to
classic Eskimo culture (Boas 1902; Birket-Smith 1929).

It is also noteworthy that Zhokhov people moved north to the arctic coast one thousand years after the peak period of East Siberian Holocene climatic warmth, which
occurred in this part of Siberia about 9000 years ago. The forest edge reached its northernmost limit somewhat north of the current southern coast of the Laptev Sea about
9000–11,000 BP, and the assemblage of arctic plants that existed on Zhokhov at that time
was significantly more complex than that present today and approximated the current
vegetation of the modern Lena River delta 300 km south of Zhokhov. Trees never grew
on the emerged shelf near Zhokhov, but they were present in abundance as driftwood,
which is another indicator that Zhokhov must have been an arctic coastal or river delta
site. It was undoubtedly the availability of wood as much as reindeer and polar bear
that made it possible for Zhokhov people to occupy for an extended seasonal period,
and perhaps year-round for several years, a coastal village on the shores of the Arctic
Ocean. Whether this was one site as part of a broad pioneering adaptation to the Early
Holocene coast of Siberia or a unique experiment by a particular Mesolithic group may
never be known; but at least in this one instance, such a site has been preserved. At
Zhokhov this way of life was short-lived, for within a few years the site was abandoned, perhaps because it had become an island or because Zhokhov people had
exhausted its polar bear, driftwood, or reindeer resources. Six thousand years would
pass before the earliest Eskimo sites in Bering Strait would provide as detailed a view
of a more developed form of arctic coastal adaptation.

Dwarf mammoths and 'mushroom people'

A second recent Siberian breakthrough, although not directly archaeological, is the discovery that a small population of woolly mammoth (*Mammuthus primigenius*) existed as

an isolated and dwarfed species on Wrangel Island until 4000 years ago (Vartanyan, Garutt, and Sher 1993). Discovered originally by Sergei Vartanyan on the Russian Wrangel Island biological reserve or *zapovednik*, this relic population must have become trapped on this 180 km long island 100 km north of the Chukotka coast by sea-level rise about 10,000 years ago. Isolation and poor habitat resulting from the warm Holocene climate on their small island refuge resulted in the population becoming increasingly dwarfed through time such that by 4000 years ago a 30 per cent reduction in tooth size had occurred and may have been smaller, as dental changes often lag behind changes in body size. Ironically, their survival 6000 years longer than anywhere else on earth resulted from the same condition that caused dwarfing — isolation from wolf and human predators on the Siberian mainland, where their biological relatives went extinct 4000 years earlier from a combination of environmental change and increased human hunting prowess. Their disappearance is thought to have been natural, but it seems to have occurred only a few hundred years before the earliest archaeological site known on Wrangel Island at Chertov Ovrag (Tein 1979; Dikov 1988) dated at *c*.3300 BP. Although one wonders if these people killed off the last mammoths on earth (Martin and Stuart 1995), a slight gap in dating and absence of freshly-butchered mammoth remains on the site suggest people arrived on Wrangel after the extinction. It is also interesting that the artefacts recovered are unlike any found elsewhere in Chukotka and closely resemble tools found in 3500 BP Old Whaling culture sites in north-western Alaska (Ackerman 1984; Dumond and Bland 1996).

There is interesting folklore that may be connected with the Wrangel mammoths. Alaskan Yup'ik and Siberian Natives tell stories about long-tusked creatures, known in Russian as *mamont* and in Yup'ik as *kogukhpuk,* that once trod the earth (Fig. 10; Nelson 1899, 443). Later they disappeared underground, where they continued to burrow under the earth. They are said to be seen on the surface only on moonlit nights once a year when they roam the earth; otherwise if so much as the tip of their nose appears above ground and breathes the air, they die, for they belong to the underworld and the air of the outer world is fatal to them. For this reason they are only encountered as bones in eroded riverbanks and sea cliffs. It has always seemed surprising that such stories could be retained as an active part of Native oral tradition throughout the entire Holocene. One suspects that knowledge of the living Wrangel mammoths was known to Siberians if not also Alaskan Natives as recently as 4500 years ago.

A more graphic view of the Siberian past became known in 1967 when Nikolai Dikov investigated a series of petroglyphs that had been reported on the banks of the Pegtymel' River between Cape Schmidt and Pevek west of Wrangel Island (Dikov 1971). Among the images are reindeer being hunted with dogs, men in boats spearing swimming reindeer, a man hunting a bear, sea mammals including seal, beluga, and orca, and a dramatic illustration of a large whale being hunted from an open boat (Fig. 11a). The latter is similar to the Eskimo umiak or baidar, having several paddlers and a

Figure 10. Bentwood bowl with illustration of elephant-like tusked beast known in Yupik mythology as *kogukhpuk*. (SI-NMNH 38642.)

Figure 11a. Petroglyph from Pegtymel', Chukotka, depicting 'mushroom' people, boat, kayak, and harpooned whale and reindeer. (Illustr. N. Dikov.)

harpooner in the bow with his harpoon line attached to the whale. Other boat types include a large high-prowed vessel and skin boats resembling Eskimo kayaks. To date, these images are the only petroglyphs known in the Siberian Arctic, and while less detailed than rock art from Scandinavia, the Siberian Subarctic (e.g. Kochmar 1994), and the North Pacific (Fig. 12), they nevertheless provide a tantalizing glimpse of ancient arctic life. Dikov has interpreted the images as ritual hunting art intended to increase the hunter's mastery of his prey. A special class of images included thirty-four illustrations of people, many of whom are seen with mushroom forms on or floating above their heads and are thought by Dikov to be 'dancing amanitas'. The form of the mushrooms identifies them as *Amanitas muscaria*, an hallucinogenic mushroom that can be found sporadically in Arctic Chukotka. The early Siberian ethnologist Waldemar Bogoras wrote about 'mushroom people' described in Chukchi mythology as being members of a 'special tribe' of intoxicating amanitas: 'Amanitas appear to people in a strange humanlike form. So, for example, one amanita is in the form of a one-armed man, while another resembles a stump. These are not spirits. They are precisely amanitas as such. The number seen by a person corresponds to how many he has eaten . . . Amanitas take a man by the hand and lead him to the afterworld, showing him everything that is there, doing the most improbable things with him' (Bogoras 1904–9, cited in Dikov 1999, 25). Some images of figures holding hands may be representations of amanitas leading living people to the people of the 'upper world'. Based on associated archaeological evidence, images of whale hunting (which began in Chukotka *c.*AD 0–500), an absence of images of domesticated reindeer, and modern graffiti, Dikov believes Pegtymel' petroglyphs date from the first millennium BC to modern times and were largely executed by Chukchi people under varying degrees of Eskimo influence; however Eskimos may also have been involved, since they once occupied these coastal regions.

Beringia: Arctic gateway to the Americas

The peopling of the Americas has been the 'holy grail' of archaeologists in North America and north-east Siberia ever since it became clear that most — if not all — American Indian and Eskimo biology was of Asian origin. Most linguists also believe that Native American languages were originally Asian but have been unable to prove this (except for closely-related modern Yupik languages found among Eskimos on both sides of Bering Strait; see Fortescue 1998) because the historical markers shared by any two related languages tend to become obscure after 5000 years of separation. Earlier theories about westward American culture migrations into north-east Asia — the so-called 'Americanoid' theory promoted by Franz Boas in 1903 (Ousley 2000) — are no longer considered valid. Nor are the theories of so-called Palaeoasiatic language ties, or even ancient Ainu language ties, to Alaskan or Northwest Coast Indians supportable today. This is not to say that there were no prehistoric migrations or exchanges across Bering Strait during the past 10,000 years. Quite the contrary, archaeological evidence suggests that the Americas were never isolated from Asia, even though few Asian roots are still discernible in American Indian languages (Dumond and Bland 1996).

The most recent ideas about the entry of humans into the New World result from new dates for the submergence of the Bering Land Bridge, the diversity of the earliest archaeological cultures known in north-western North America, and the growing realization that American sites older than the widespread Clovis culture (11,600–10,500 BP) do not date earlier than 13–14,000 years ago.

Until 1992 the best estimate for the submergence of the Land Bridge was thought to be c.14,000 years (McManus and Creager 1984). Since then, submerged terrestrial peat from the Chukchi Sea floor 55 m below sea-level has been dated to 11,000 BP and contains both terrestrial insects and fresh- and brackish-water ostracods (Elias 1996). At this time the Bering Land Bridge was still 500–800 km wide, and was being inundated rapidly. The new dates are important because they mean that the explosion of archaeological sites that occurs at this time in Alaska and in North America south of the ice sheets occurred simultaneously with the flooding of the Bering Land Bridge, rather than 3000 years *after* it submerged.

During the past decade consensus has emerged on the earliest sites in Alaska. Clovis is known so far in Alaska only as an undated, scattered distribution of distinctive bifacial Clovis-like fluted projectile points found mostly in north-western Alaska (Fig. 11b). Their location in the north-eastern part of the Bering Land Bridge has led archaeologists to speculate that the Clovis point must have had an Asian origin. But to date no Clovis points nor any convincing prototype has been found in Asia (Hoffecker *et al.* 1993). The earliest well-dated complexes in Alaska — Nenana, Mesa, and Denali — all date to c.10–9000 BP (West 1996). Mesa points are bifacial and of Agate Basin Paleoindian type but lack fluting and other features of the Clovis complex; Nenana has bifaces and burins but lacks microblades (Powers and Hoffecker 1989); and Denali has wedge-shaped cores, microblades, burins, and bifaces (West 1967) similar to those in Siberian Dyuktai culture, whose dates span 35–11,000 BP. Despite the presence of suitable elements like blades, wedge-shaped cores, and bifaces, the technique of fluting a thin, finished biface has not yet been demonstrated in Asia, and its continued absence has recently stirred interest in a radical new hypothesis proposed by Dennis Stanford and Bruce Bradley based on the dating and concentration of Clovis sites in south-eastern North America and technological similarities between Clovis and Late Solutrean culture of south-western Europe. Solutrean has similar biface technology but lacks Clovis' basal fluting and ends 4000 years

Figure 11b. A Clovis-like fluted point from the Utukok River, north-west Alaska. (SI-NMNH 391806.)

before Clovis culture begins in eastern North America. This bold and speculative hypothesis, like the voyage it requires, has yet to be proven and has strong critics (Straus 2000). By contrast, the similarities between the early post-Clovis Denali horizon in Alaska, in the Yukon, and in coastal British Columbia, and Late Pleistocene/Early Holocene sites in north-east Siberia are so great that they are now included in a single complex called variously the American Paleo-Arctic (Anderson 1968, 1970), the Siberian–American Paleoarctic (Arutiunov and Fitzhugh 1988), or the Beringian (West 1981, 1996) tradition. The upward-sloping date cline shows this second wave of early Americans emerged from a Dyuktai culture base in north-east Siberia (Mochanov and Fedoseeva 1996; Dikov 1968; Dikov and Titov 1984; Dumond and Bland 1996).

It is interesting, however, that the diversity of these early sites in Alaska — some with microblades, others with bifaces; some with plano-style points, others with leaf-shaped points — and the fact that their dates cluster in the 10–11,000 period, may best be explained by having originated from multiple migrations from different Siberian homeland regions, where regional artefact diversity between Dyuktai, Ushki Lake, and Sakhalin sites, for instance, is also evident at this time. Siberian cultural diversity, huge geographical areas, and rapidly changing Late Pleistocene/Holocene sea-levels, climate, geography and environment (Hopkins *et al.* 1982) must have placed a premium on human innovation, adaptation, and migration.

The coastal migration hypothesis

Until recently archaeologists felt justified in considering the peopling of the New World and the development of maritime adaptations as two distinct topics, and even today many archaeologists are still most comfortable with the concept of entry into North America across the interior of the Bering Land Bridge (West 1996, 549). Most of the early sites in Alaska are found in the interior and contain the remains of mammoth, moose, reindeer, musk-ox, bison and other interior species. But the continued absence of early sites from the 'ice-free' corridor route between the Laurentide and Cordilleran ice sheets (Bobrowsky *et al.* 1990; Carlson 1991; Mandryk 1990; West 1996), which was open throughout the past glaciation except possibly for a period of closure between 15–13,500 years ago, suggests that this route was either environmentally unsuitable or was transited so rapidly that the traces of a pre-Clovis, Clovis, or Denali migration have remained undetected.

In fact, the much more realistic possibility of a migration route along the coast of Alaska and British Columbia has gained favour in recent years. Growing numbers of Paleoarctic tradition sites containing microblades and marine fauna dated to 9–11,000 are being found in coastal sites from the Eastern Aleutians to southern British Columbia. Previously it had been thought that the coastal route was blocked by a wall of Cordilleran ice at the Pacific Coast edge, but new terrestrial and underwater research

(Josenhans *et al.* 1997; Mann and Hamilton 1995) has shown that ice-free enclaves existed, and in any case coastal glaciers may not have been a serious impediment for people with watercraft and thousands of years of maritime skills. While the Beringian interior may also have been an entry route, its southern coast and the emerged shelf of the North Pacific would have been much warmer, with diverse plant and animal communities and a rich marine fauna. The Late Pleistocene salmon-based Ushki site (Dikov 1968) and numerous Siberian and Japanese coastal sites suggest that north-east Asian peoples were well-adapted to maritime life at least by 18,000–14,000 years ago; these groups would have been the most likely people to move east along the southern edge of the Land Bridge and south along the coast of British Columbia, as William S. Laughlin (1963) and Knut Fladmark (1979) hypothesized many years ago. Unfortunately much of the proof of this logical supposition is covered by 50–100 m of water.

New data from more than a dozen sites, including Ground Hog Bay, Hidden Falls, Chuck Lake, Anangula, Namu, Thorne River, and several on the Queen Charlotte Islands (Dumond and Bland 1996; West 1996), indicate an early version of the Beringian tradition adapting to life along the ecologically productive Northwest Coast of North America. Finding early sites in this inundated, heavily-forested region is more difficult than in the open tundra or broken forest, but recent work by E. James Dixon and others has shown promise in opening up this relatively unexplored area, which has been found to have, in addition to other types of sites, seaside caves that contain Early Holocene human remains and artefacts associated with brown bears and seal remains (Dixon *et al.* 1997; Dixon 2001). The problem here, as in early hominid sites in Africa, is to determine who was doing the eating.

In addition to documenting a likely coastal route into North America, these sites also help explain the apparent sudden appearance about 6000 years ago of fully-adapted maritime fishing and hunting societies that have been known archaeologically for years along the Northwest Coast, in South Alaska, and in the Eastern Aleutians. Beginning with such maritime-based sites as Anangula in the Eastern Aleutians and Tanganak and Ocean Bay on Kodiak Island, these societies developed productive economies based on fishing and harpoon hunting of seals, sea lions, and small whales; occupied village sites with large houses and deep middens; used similar forms of human-face rock art (Fig. 12) and began to engage in complex ceremonialism, extensive inter-regional trade and warfare, and hierarchical social development (Clark 1984; Jordan 1984; B. Fitzhugh 1996, in press). Excavations at hundreds of sites from the Aleutians to the Columbia River document the extraordinary cultural elaboration that occurs in the eastern North Pacific and culminates in a series of ethnographic cultures that are among the most complex settled hunter-gatherers anywhere in the world (Fitzhugh and Crowell 1988; McCartney *et al.* 1998). Today this long, detailed archaeological record is providing the basis for new theory about pre-agricultural social evolution and development (Matson 1983; Arnold 1996; Coupland 1996; Crowell 1997; Ames

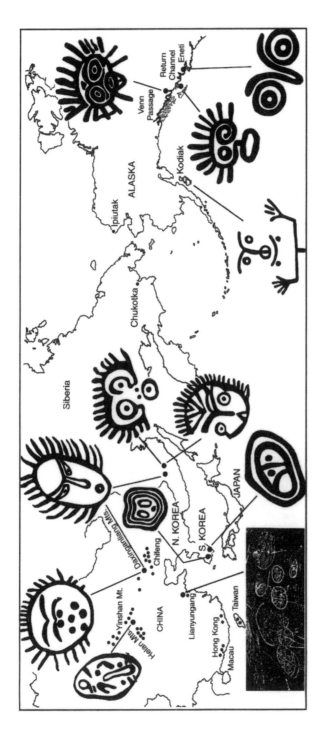

Figure 12. Map of North Pacific with human-face petroglyphs. (ASC Newsletter Supplement 1998; illustr. Y. Song, M. Bakry.)

and Maschner 1999; Fitzhugh and Habu in press). Such intensive northern maritime adaptations provide opportunities for societies to develop levels of socio-cultural and political complexity once thought attainable only in agrarian state-level societies.

Eskimo origins

One hundred years ago the question of Eskimo origins was the only really 'hot' issue in arctic anthropology. By 1930, scores of different theories had been proposed, including ones that brought Eskimos into the Eastern Arctic across the North Atlantic from Western Siberia (Rink 1875), from central Canada (Boas 1910; Steensby 1917; Birket-Smith 1929, 1930), or from Eastern Siberia. But it was not until Henry Collins excavated large stratified frozen sites on St Lawrence Island and defined a 2000-year sequence of Eskimo development that a long Bering Sea/Bering Strait history was finally established (Collins 1937; Fig. 13). Collins also demonstrated that mid-way through this sequence one of these cultures, Punuk and its North Alaskan counterpart known as Birnirk (Ford 1959; Taylor 1963; Stanford 1976), both of which became proficient at hunting large baleen whales with float gear and toggling harpoons, expanded east along the north coast of Alaska into Canada shortly after AD 1000, forming the basis for Thule and later Canadian and Greenland Inuit cultures. This migration was facilitated by climatic warming that allowed bowhead whales, and their Thule pursuers, to expand rapidly into areas that whales had previously been blocked from by ice (McGhee 1969/70). The rapid spread of this new whale-hunting adaptation, together with new technology like the dog-sled, the sinew-backed bow, pottery, and organized warfare helped Thule people establish dominance over the previous inhabitants of the Western Arctic and the Dorset peoples of the

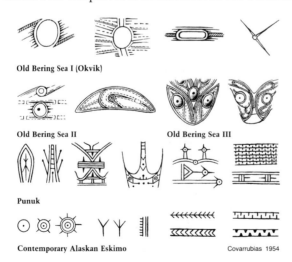

Old Bering Sea I (Okvik)

Old Bering Sea II   Old Bering Sea III

Punuk

Contemporary Alaskan Eskimo   Covarrubias 1954

Figure 13. Style elements in Okvik, Old Bering Sea, and Punuk art from Bering Strait. (Illustr. ASC.)

Eastern Arctic. The rapid spread of Thule people from Western Alaska (Taylor 1963; Morrison 1989) also set the clock at 'zero' for cultural, linguistic, and biological diversification leading to modern Eskimo groups from Bering Strait to Greenland and Labrador. Unlike the Eastern Arctic and Greenland, where the Thule culture largely replaced the existing Dorset people and culture, along the coasts of the Bering Sea and South Alaska occupied by large populations of Yup'ik Eskimos,

Thule culture influenced but did not replace earlier traditions, and the earlier roots of these cultures can be traced into modern times.

Some of these Yup'ik traditions in art, iconography, and ceremonialism — seen especially in spiritual aspects of material culture — can be traced back for 2000 years into the earliest Eskimo cultures of Bering Strait: the Okvik and Old Bering Sea cultures, and the Ipiutak culture of north-western Alaska (Fitzhugh 1984a; Arutiunov and Fitzhugh 1988; Fig. 14). Their art is rooted in hunting magic used to propitiate the spirits of animals and the spirit-controllers that govern animals and human affairs and

Figure 14. Ancient Old Bering Sea harpoon socket piece and hat ornament (lower) illustrating a hunter's predator-like helping spirits. Compare with nineteenth-century specimen seen in Figure 6, indicating continuity in Eskimo art and spiritual traditions for 2000 years. (SI-NMNH 344674, 378054; photo ASC.)

is expressed in personal rituals including the decoration of one's hunting equipment and clothing, and in communal rituals, masked ceremonies, and elaborate burial ritual (Fitzhugh 1993). In addition to exhibiting a distinct regional art style, the famous Ipiutak cemetery at Point Hope contained burial masks that show Chinese influence (Collins 1971), and its intricate antler carvings document the spread across Bering Strait of a type of shamanism still practised by Siberian ethnographic cultures. Other features of Ipiutak art suggested ties to the West Siberian Bronze Age and were interpreted as evidence of circumpolar influence in the development of a pan-arctic Eskimo-like culture (Larsen and Rainey 1948; Chernetsov 1970). Today, with better knowledge about East Siberian and East Asian prehistory, there is little need to invoke West Siberian ties to explain the art and shamanistic elements of early Alaskan Eskimo cultures (Zykov *et al.* 1994; Fitzhugh and Golovnev 1998). Chinese and Scytho-Siberian influences appear more likely sources of artistic innovation, transmitted through north-east Asian cultures that were beginning to be transformed by bronze and iron production (Schuster 1951; Arutiunov and Fitzhugh 1988). Both of these materials were also traded into the Old Bering Sea cultures. Nor were Asian influences limited to the Bering Sea region; the introduction of iron, armour, sinew-backed bows, institutionalized warfare, use of military forts, and other elements of Asian military culture spread as far into North America as southern British Columbia (Fig. 15). Such cultural interaction made the North Pacific rim a crossroads of continents for thousands of years (Dumond 1977; Fitzhugh and Crowell 1988; Fitzhugh and Chaussonnet 1984; Dumond and Bland 1996).

Collins and others did indeed prove that Eskimos had a long development in the Bering Strait region, but since the earliest 'Eskimo' cultures (Okvik, Old Bering Sea) appeared in the archaeological record already fully formed, their origins still remain a mystery seventy years later. Some archaeologists argue for local origins from earlier Bering Strait cultures like Denbigh, Old Whaling, Choris, Norton, and their Chukotkan counterparts (Giddings and Anderson 1986); some see its formation from the long sequence of early maritime cultures of South Alaska, Kodiak Island, and the Aleutians (Dumond and Bland 1996, 443); and still others, mostly Russians, see Eskimo origins in the Neolithic cultures of the Okhotsk Sea or Lena River Basin (Rudenko 1961; Vasil'evskii 1987; Orekhov 1987; Lebedintsev 1990). Each theory has its strengths, but the origins of the Eskimo tradition still remain to be revealed in detail. The basic problem lies with cultural identity and geology. On one hand, what characteristics — technology, adaptation, biology, art, language reconstructions, or others — are we to use to recognize proto-'Eskimo' ethnicity in the crucial period c.3500–2000 years ago? And when and how do they emerge as the ethnic entity known as 'Eskimo' in Bering Strait? On the other hand, how is this problem to be solved when the North Pacific and Bering/Chukchi Sea sites of this period and region have been lost to sea-level rise and erosion?

Figure 15. Mannikin of Chukchi warrior dressed in walrus-hide armour from the *Crossroads of Continents* exhibition. (SI-NMNH, AMNH; photo ASC.)

Hunters and herders: the Neolithic revolution reaches the Arctic

By the time that Eskimo culture had developed its characteristic features in the Bering Strait 1500 years ago an economic and cultural revolution was under way in Siberia. Reindeer breeding had begun and was spreading throughout the Eurasian taiga and tundra regions (Fig. 16). Like most social or economic revolutions, its consequences were both destructive and pro-

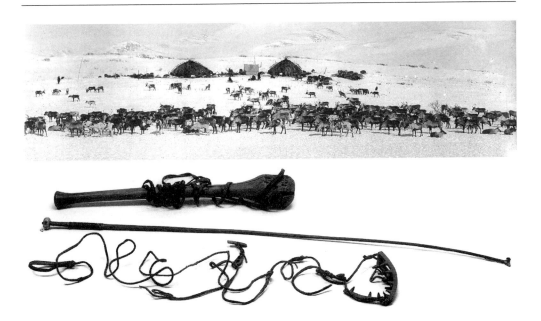

Figure 16. Reindeer herders of Chukotka photographed by V. Jochelson for the Jesup North Pacific Expedition, *c.*1900, with reindeer bit, hobble, and drive stick. (AMNH 4619.)

gressive. The origins of reindeer domestication and breeding are unknown and after more than one hundred years of debate are still a subject of debate and speculation. Two theories have received most attention: one based on the use of captured reindeer for use as hunting decoys and another based on the transfer of knowledge of domesticating horses and other livestock in southern Siberia (Vainstein 1980, 1981; Ingold 1980; Shnirelman 1980; Krupnik 1993; Paine 1994). The date of this 'event,' which was in reality probably a long discontinuous process, is also unknown. Harness swivels indicating animal traction for sleds are known from a number of Siberian Arctic sites, such as Ust-Poluj in Yamal (Chernetsov and Moshinskaya 1974, 294; Pitulko 1999c), but from these alone one cannot determine whether the animal harnessed was a dog or a reindeer. Dog traction probably appeared in Western Siberia *c.*2000 BP and more than one thousand years later in Alaska. But it is only with the appearance of bridle parts such as found at Ust-Poluj and the sixth- to ninth-century AD site of Tiutey Sale in Yamal (Feodorova 1996; Fitzhugh and Golovnev 1998; Feodorova *et al.* 1998) that one can be certain that reindeer were being kept for decoy hunting and possibly being bred for riding and sled transport (Fig. 17).

    One of the principal reasons that reindeer cannot be fully domesticated is because their food sources — lichens and mosses — cannot be stored, so the animals cannot be corralled and fed on fodder. Thus even in southern Siberia where some reindeer migrate relatively short distances between summer pastures in the mountains and

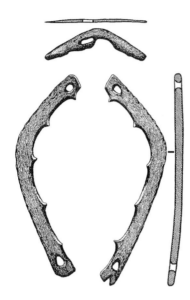

Figure 17. Reindeer antler training or hobble harness found at the Iron Age Tiutey-Sale site in western Yamal, c.AD 800. (Illustr. N. Feodorova.)

winter pastures in the forests below, or remain year-round exclusively in a forest habitat, domestication was no more effective than in the arctic regions where reindeer must migrate long distances between their summer and winter pastures (Burch 1972; Spiess 1979; Ingold 1980; Paine 1988). For this reason the human–reindeer association is actually only a 'pay-as-you-go' contract between man and beast — reindeer agreed to carry loads and pull sleds, and men agreed to travel with them and act as protectors and shepherds. But absolute human control has always been tenuous, for at any moment a herd might become spooked and run off to join wild reindeer. The history of Siberian reindeer herding is replete with stories of proud owners of huge reindeer herds (sometimes numbering 5000 or more animals) who found themselves princes one day and paupers the next. Zoonotic diseases, icing of winter pastures, over-grazing, and theft were threats that were always just over the horizon (Krupnik 1993). The successful herder tended his herd closely at all times; and many, like the Yamal Nenets, who practised one of the most intensive styles of reindeer herding, travelled as many as 300–600 miles annually between the forest edge winter pastures and the tundra summer ranges during the yearly migration cycle (Golovnev and Osherenko 1999).

At first the stimulus for domesticating reindeer may have been for travel, as a way to extend a hunter's territory and carry or drag the camp. But through time more intensive herding practices were developed, and when this happened it was always accompanied by a reduction in the number of local wild reindeer. Whether this occurred as a purposeful strategy or was a side-effect of intensified herding is uncertain, but the loss of wild herds preserved pasture for domestic animals and removed the distracting influence of wild reindeer on the domestic herd. The result was an economy that grew increasingly focused on maximizing herd size and on eliminating wolves and wild reindeer competition.

In terms of ecology, intensive reindeer herding was highly aggressive, destructive of tundra habitat, and was predatory in the sense that it quickly replaced any other form of local livelihood that existed in open tundra areas. Providing both transport and food, it quickly spread throughout northern Eurasia until it became entrenched from Scandinavia to Chukotka. In the process, it transformed the peoples of the north from hunters and fishermen into animal-keepers, substituting a Neolithic economy for a hunting way of life that had been practised for tens of thousands of years. The combined study of archaeological and ethnological data from north-eastern Asia suggests that everything about these ancient hunting cultures changed, including their technology, settlement patterns, and housing styles, as well as their gods, rituals, art, and beliefs (Fitzhugh 1988a, 1988b, 1993).

The use of transport reindeer replacing the earlier use of dogs for hauling sleds seems to have spread first, probably reaching Scandinavia and Chukotka about 1000 years ago, whereas intensive herding as practised by the Sami, Nenets, and Chukchi is thought to be only a few hundreds of years old, originating around AD 1600. As use of domestic reindeer spread, hunters who could not or chose not to adopt herding found their game — especially the wild reindeer crucial to their survival — disappearing, killed or driven off by the herders to reduce competition for grazing grounds and avoid distraction for their own domestic herds. The Yukagir, a hunting people living in north-eastern Siberia, may have suffered this fate. Since efficient herders tended to multiply, the only hunters who were spared the loss of their wild game were those, like the Siberian Eskimos, who hunted marine mammals or others, like the Yukagir or Nganasan in Taimyr, who occupied mountainous regions or poor tundra unsuited for intensive herding. Such groups often entered into trade or exchange relationships with the herders, finding a symbiotic existence that benefited both. In similar fashion, many ethnic groups like the Scandinavian Sami and north-east Siberian Koryak and Chukchi adopted a dual economic strategy in which half of their population specialized in migratory reindeer herding on the interior while the other half practised fishing and sea mammal hunting from sedentary coastal villages, each group trading with the other for necessities of life required from both regions, principally reindeer meat and skins, and sea mammal oil (Paine 1957; Krupnik 1993). Later, even before the appearance of Europeans in Bering Strait, foreign products were added to this internal exchange, and Chukchi and Asian Eskimo middlemen were able to make a fine business of trading Chinese and Russian tea, beads, iron, and tobacco across Bering Strait for Alaskan Eskimo fur, jade, and ivory.

Despite its rapid spread across Siberia, reindeer herding did not cross Bering Strait and had not been implemented even on St Lawrence Island, close to the Chukotka mainland, by the time Europeans first arrived in the eighteenth century. The reason this indigenous introduction failed to occur may have been because of the treacherous ice conditions and the absence of a strong motive for Chukchi or Siberian Eskimo herders to chance a hazardous crossing over ice or water with a restive herd of reindeer. Or it may have been because intensive reindeer herding had reached Bering Strait only in relatively recent times. Because techniques for successful reindeer herding cannot be acquired as easily as the animals themselves can be purchased, the herding system would have to be implemented as a full-scale population movement by trained Siberian herders. Herding, like hunting, is a way of life that takes a lifetime to learn. The presence of Eskimos as the dominant group on both sides of Bering Strait and who were only marginally involved in reindeer herding in Chukotka may have been a deterrent to Chukchi expansion across Bering Strait as well. For whatever reason, this new technology did not enter North America until it was introduced as a US Government experiment to alleviate starvation after rifle-hunting and climate changes decimated the Western Alaskan caribou herds in the late 1800s. But even then the business of herding reindeer did not inspire Alaskan Eskimos. Lacking close supervision the animals soon wandered off or were shot for food. Only those managed by white enterprises — often assisted by imported Sami (Lapp) or Chukchi herders — continued to be maintained, and these only for a short period, until over-grazing and market collapse doomed the enterprise in the late 1930s (Spencer 1984; Ray 1992). Most Alaska Natives, as their lives, art, and beliefs clearly demonstrate, remained hunters at heart, and their way of relating to animals, as consensual partners rather than as chattel to be owned, was literally a world apart from the mind of the Siberian reindeer herder. It still is. The fact that reindeer herding did not cross Bering Strait like so many other elements of Asian culture had momentous implications for the culture history of the North American Arctic and Subarctic, which might otherwise have undergone the same transformation that revolutionized Eurasia's northern peoples. As a result many of the ancient cultural patterns, beliefs, and art styles that disappeared in the wake of Neolithic and Metal Age changes in the Old World were maintained into modern times among the hunting and fishing peoples of northern North America.

Culture, climate, and environmental change: Canadian Arctic and Labrador

The final part of our story is reserved for the last area of the circumpolar region to be colonized by humans: the Eastern Canadian Arctic, Greenland, and Labrador. The earliest people to appear in these regions were the descendants of Paleoindians who moved into the coastal fringe of southern Labrador about 9000 years ago when an ice sheet covered all but the southern fringe of Labrador. The origin of these early Labradorians, known as the Maritime Archaic culture, remains obscure but appears to have developed as Paleoindians adapted to the marine mammal hunting along the shores of the Late Glacial Champlain Sea and north-east coast moved north into Newfoundland and Labrador as glacial ice retreated and rising sea-levels flooded the Gulf of St Lawrence basin (Tuck 1977; Loring 1980). During the next several thousand years Maritime Archaic Indians colonized a coastal strip of shrub tundra that extended north from Newfoundland into central Labrador, hunting caribou and sea mammals (Fitzhugh 1978). These Indian groups never developed the capabilities for living permanently beyond the forest or shrub–tundra boundary. To the north, the Central Canadian Arctic remained covered in glacial ice, and much of the interior of Labrador as well, until about 5000 years ago (McGhee 1978; Maxwell 1985; Clark and Fitzhugh 1990, 1991). When the Central Canadian Arctic ice sheet melted, and caribou, musk-ox, and seals, walrus, and polar bear moved in between 5000–4500 years ago, it was not the Indian peoples of Labrador, Quebec, or Keewatin who colonized these arctic lands as Boas, Steensby, Birket-Smith and others had theorized, but a population from north-east Asia and Bering Strait which had already learned to live in treeless arctic regions. Archaeologists call these people the Denbigh Flint Complex or the Arctic Small Tool tradition because of its characteristic microlithic technology (Irving 1969–70, 1962; McGhee 1996). This tradition appears to have originated among the Neolithic cultures of Siberia about 6000 years ago and spread across Bering Strait 4500 years ago. Emerging from north-east Siberian Sumnagin and Ymyiakhtak Mesolithic cultures, Neolithic groups who were primarily interior reindeer hunters had retained the use of earlier technologies like microblades and burins but had acquired new technologies, including bows and arrows with finely-flaked bifacial points, and ceramics. As these technologies, and probably north-east Asian peoples themselves, spread into the Bering Sea region, they became acquainted with local residents who had already developed capabilities for hunting sea mammals in the open waters of the North Pacific and southern Bering Sea, and their resource base expanded to take in the rich maritime resources available in these regions, resulting in the development of Alaska's Denbigh culture (Giddings 1964; Powers and Jordan 1990; Dumond and Bland 1996).

At the same time that Denbigh people expanded into the coastal regions of Western Alaska, Kodiak and Eastern Aleutians, a North Alaskan branch of the Siberian Neolithic moved east along the northern coast of Alaska into the Western Canadian Arctic. Here, known as Pre-Dorset (or Early Paleoeskimo) culture (Maxwell 1984), they initially hunted land game but were ill-equipped for taking sea mammals, having inefficient barbed harpoons that did not toggle fully. Pre-Dorset people followed the coast south into Labrador where they met Maritime Archaic Indians, and although the two groups seem to have maintained strict territorial boundaries, the early Canadian Pre-Dorset harpoon was rapidly replaced by one similar to that used by Maritime Archaic Indians (McGhee 1978; Tuck 1976), as related earlier. This implement soon became the major instrument for the intensified seal, walrus, and whaling hunting economy that characterized all later 'Paleoeskimo' and subsequent whale-hunting Neoeskimo (Thule tradition) cultures in Greenland, Canada, and Alaska (McGhee 1984; Maxwell 1985).

The Maritime Archaic Indian culture these early Paleoeskimos encountered in Labrador had developed its own complex maritime adaptation following the retreat of glacial ice from the Labrador coast. Between 8000–4000 years ago, this pioneering Indian culture expanded its settlements from isolated small house sites to large coastal villages with multiple-room houses. Most of these houses were 30–40 m long, with 8–10 dwelling units per house; but some structures have been found to be 100 m long and to contain as many as 15–20 separate family dwelling spaces (Fig. 18; Fitzhugh 1984c). The large numbers of these long-houses at sites near the northernmost extent of the Maritime Archaic culture area in northern Labrador, together with the presence of elaborately-furnished burials (Fig. 19), and trade in exotic materials — especially the distinctive translucent stone, Ramah chert, found in prominent geological beds in northern Labrador — distributed as far south as New England, make Late Maritime Archaic the most complex prehistoric Indian culture in north-eastern North America (Tuck 1976; Fitzhugh 1975b, 1975c, 1978, 1984c). In many ways their life and technology resembled ethnographic Northwest Coast Indian culture, and it is therefore all the more remarkable that this elaborating tradition reached its peak expression in the Middle Holocene, whereas Northwest Coast culture did not reach its maximum complexity until the Late Holocene. The Maritime Archaic development climaxed during the warm, stable climatic period c.6–3500 BP and came to a close with cooling climates that followed the Hypsithermal, coincident with the appearance of the Pre-Dorset Paleoeskimo peoples who arrived in northern Labrador c.4000 BP (Fitzhugh and Lamb 1985).

Pre-Dorset culture also spread into Greenland, where it lasted, as in Canada, for 1500 years until it evolved into Dorset culture about 2500 years ago (Fitzhugh 1984b; Grønnow 1996). The Pre-Dorset/Dorset transition (Nagy 1997) coincided with the cool 'sub-boreal' period experienced in most areas of the northern hemisphere c.2500–2000 years ago. During this period Pre-Dorset settlements at inner island locations shifted to Dorset locations at more maritime outer island sites that were prime areas for winter and spring sea mammal hunting; house types changed from Pre-Dorset tent-houses to insulated semi-subterranean Dorset sod and earth houses; middens began to accumulate as seasonal site tenure increased to encompass the entire winter season; marine mammal hunting became more specialized and the hunting of caribou, musk-ox and other land game declined; and the appearance of intricate, naturalistic carvings of animals, carved face masks, and shamanistic objects indicate increased attention to spiritual expression in art, ritual, and shamanistic religion (Figs. 20 and 21).

The Eastern Arctic Paleoeskimo tradition developed for more than 3000 years (4000–600 BP) with little stimulation from other cultures or regions. Although some Alaskan Norton and Choris influences may have helped stimulate the transition from Pre-Dorset to Dorset, the more dominant force was probably the effect of climatic cooling that gave advantage to those who lived in warmer, more substantial and more sedentary winter villages fuelled and fed by marine mammals than to those following the migratory life of the earlier Pre-Dorset caribou and musk-ox hunters. As Dorset culture became firmly established in the Eastern Arctic and Greenland and subsequently spread south into the forested coastal regions of Newfoundland and the eastern Gulf of St Lawrence, it seems not to have been influenced either by early Eskimo cultures in

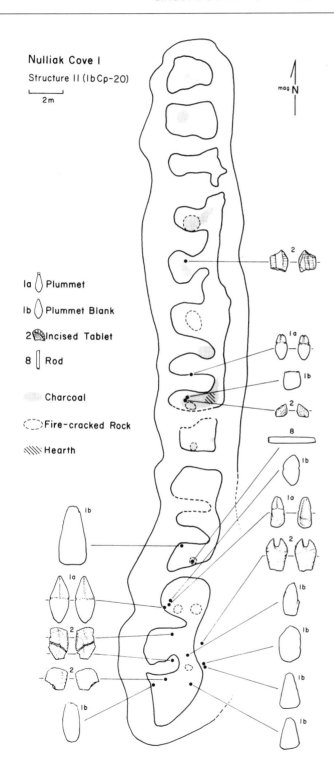

Nulliak Cove I

Structure II (IbCp-20)

2m

mag N

Ia ⬭ Plummet

Ib ⬭ Plummet Blank

2 ◨ Incised Tablet

8 ▯ Rod

⬭ Charcoal

⬭ Fire-cracked Rock

⬭ Hearth

Figure 18. Plan of Nulliak Cove 1, Structure 11 longhouse on northern Labrador coast, c.4200 BP, illustrating family dwelling spaces and unusual carved soapstone pendants. (Illustr. M. Bakry.)

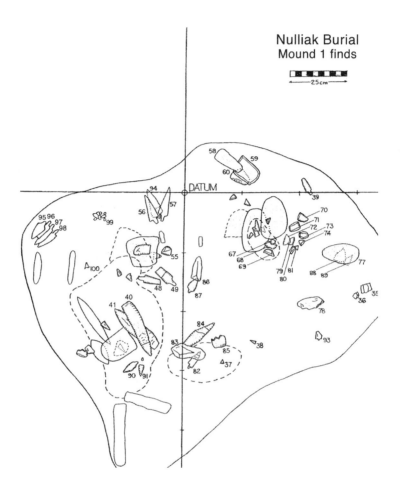

Figure 19. Extensive burial deposit of Ramah chert, slate, mica and red ochre at base of stone mound at Nulliak Cove 1, northern Labrador, *c.*4200 BP. (Newfoundland Museum; illustr. S. Wraussman.)

Alaska or by Indian groups to the south. Then, after more than one thousand years of rather steady-state stylistic elaboration, Dorset people discovered Neoeskimo Thule culture people moving into their territory from the west. Hunting bowhead whales, driving dog-teams, and using powerful Asian-style sinew-backed bows, the more highly organized and aggressive Thule people overwhelmed and out-competed the smaller, spiritually oriented Dorset societies and inaugurated the Inuit Neoeskimo tradition that continued until historical times.

As in the case of Dorset origins, the Thule migration from Alaska also seems to have been stimulated by climatic change, although in this case it was warming rather than cooling that set the stage. Beginning about AD 900, a strong climatic warming trend

Figure 20. Soapstone carving of Dorset figure in high-collared garment from Shuldham Island, Saglek, Labrador. (Newfoundland Museum; photo: V. Krantz.)

Figure 21. Dorset wood maskette from Avayalik site, northern Labrador. (Newfoundland Museum; photo: V. Krantz.)

began in most regions of the north, and for the next several centuries the pack ice cover that had blocked the North Alaska coast and the Canadian Arctic islands in summer retreated and seasonal open water passages began to appear (McGhee 1969/70). Taking advantage of new feeding grounds, bowhead whales which previously had been restricted to the waters of the Chukchi and Beaufort Seas and Davis Strait and Baffin Bay expanded their range into the Central Canadian Arctic and soon were able to pass freely from the Pacific to the Atlantic Ocean, reconnecting breeding stocks that may have been isolated since the Mid-Holocene. Alaskan Punuk and Thule culture, which had pioneered the hunting of large whales with harpoons and floats in Bering Strait during the preceding 500 years, immediately took advantage of this opportunity to follow their quarry and began settling along the whale migration routes among the Canadian Arctic islands (Savelle and McCartney 1991; McCartney and Savelle 1993), replacing, displacing, and in some cases probably absorbing local Dorset people and borrowing some of their ideas, like snow-houses, snow-knives, harpoon types, and soapstone vessels, that proved useful in this new and climatically harsher environment. When the warming phase ended in the late 1300s bowheads once again withdrew from the Central Arctic and Canadian and Greenlandic Thule cultures were forced to reorient their economy and settlement system to something more like that of the previous Dorset culture, specializing in seal, walrus, caribou and other game, except in areas like Labrador, eastern Baffin, and south-west Greenland where open water allowed whaling to continue until European whaling decimated the bowhead stock in the eighteenth to nineteenth centuries.

Compared with the more tumultuous Western Arctic history, the 3000-year development of Paleoeskimo culture in Canada and Greenland was relatively slow-paced and has been described as a 'steady-state' system that responded to climate and environmental forces more than to external social pressures and radical innovation (Nash 1976). Gradual changes in tool typology and house forms were the prime expressions of culture change seen in the archaeological record. Its chief competitor was 'mother nature', as shown by the frequent occupational cycles in which local populations colonized and abandoned new territories, only to colonize and abandon them again (Maxwell 1976; McGhee 1976; Fitzhugh 1997). These cycles seem best explained by climatic and human biogeographic models and predator–prey cycle behaviour in which humans are constantly adjusting to boom-and-bust economies by over-hunting pristine regions until they are forced to abandon them until they are replenished. Only along the south-eastern forest–tundra fringe where arctic peoples came into contact with northern Indian groups, do external factors seem to have played an important role. However, here, unlike in Western Alaska where new ideas from Pacific Coast Alaska and Siberia periodically introduced or stimulated changes in local cultures, in Labrador, contacts with Indian groups did not produce changes in culture so much as changes in cultural territory (Fitzhugh 1977, 1987). The lack of any evidence of inter-ethnic contact or trade, at least as seen in Labrador's predominantly lithic assemblages, suggests that along this culture boundary, hostility and avoidance was the norm, probably because neither side had much economic interest in the other's way of life. Indians continued to find the northern forest and its resources the economic and spiritual centre of their lives and utilized coastal resources only for short periods during the summer; Eskimo groups on the other hand found the forest confining and had little interest in straying from the rich resource base of the coast. Without the strong technological gradient that existed between Asian and North American cultures in the North Pacific region, where for the past 3000 years new materials like bronze and iron, new weapon technologies, and exotic trade goods stimulated inter-cultural exchange, Labrador Indian and Eskimo people traded territory rather than new technology or goods.

Further, when we look back over the longer chronological record of 4000 years, there is a strong correlation of northward Indian movements with climatic warming events, and of southern movements of Eskimo groups with climatic cooling (Fig. 22; Fitzhugh 1972, 1977). Cooling events that produced expansion of storminess and pack ice made Indian life on the coast more difficult at the same time that it expanded the niche available to Eskimo sea mammal hunters. On the other hand, warming events which produced less ice-cover, quiet summer seas, and northward forest expansion, favoured Indian coastal hunting and travel at the expense of Eskimo ice-edge resources. Even in

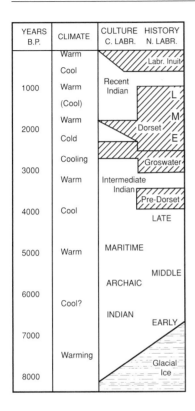

YEARS B.P.	CLIMATE	CULTURE HISTORY C. LABR. N. LABR.

Figure 22. Climate and culture change in Labrador prehistory. Indian cultures shown in white; Eskimo cultures hatched. (Illustr. M. Bakry.)

the eighteenth century climate and environmental change continued to have a significant impact on Labrador Inuit culture (Kaplan and Woollett 2000).

The circumpolar world reconnects

The final stage in our circumpolar odyssey is reserved for the Vikings, since it was they who completed the final portion of the circumpolar voyage and brought humanity 'full circle'. The details of this story are especially interesting because of their contextualization with historical, archaeological, and palaeoenvironmental data (McGhee 1984; McAleese 2000; Fitzhugh and Ward 2000).

Although it is generally thought that regular contacts across the North Atlantic did not begin until the Viking expansion to Iceland and Greenland in the tenth century, Irish monks or other northern seafarers may have travelled these routes as early as the sixth century, and theories of possible Late Ice Age or Early Holocene crossings have been raised sporadically to explain similarities between north European and north-east North American archaeological complexes and artefacts (Greenman 1960, 1963; Kehoe 1962, 1971; Fitzhugh 1975a and b). The discovery of a small, highly distinctive wedge-shape microblade core resembling cores from Eastern Siberia and Alaska *c.*12–9000 years ago, found below the floor of a Viking site in Iceland (Smith 1997), adds further intrigue to the possibility of earlier crossings in a region that most archaeologists believe was not bridged by intentional human voyaging until *c.*AD 1000.

Sailing westward from Norway and the British Isles in the early 800s, Viking farmers settled Faroe and Iceland about 870, and the Icelandic sagas tell us that Erik the Red settled south-western Greenland about 985, finding signs of former inhabitants but no living people. Shortly thereafter, Leif Eriksson set out to explore lands seen by storm-driven Bjarni Herjolfsson and named the lands he found Helluland (stone land/Baffin Island), Markland (forest land/Labrador), and Vinland (grape land/Newfoundland and the Maritimes). He and a group of Norse remained in Vinland a few years, exploring to the south, and returned to Greenland, where they maintained settlements until the mid-fifteenth century.

The Vinland voyages mark an epic in humanity's quest of northern frontiers. Although these voyages did not result in permanent settlement of the shores of North America, they produced the first descriptions by Europeans of these lands and its Native peoples. The tales they tell may not all be historically accurate, but they are invaluable as self-described impressions of the experiences of an early people expanding the limits of their known world. These lands were apparently as bountiful as the local inhabitants, who Vikings called 'skraelings,' were feisty, and after a number of battles that made them feel in constant danger, the Norse withdrew to the safety of their farms in Greenland. In what is the North American equivalent of Schliemann's discovery of Troy, Helge Ingstad and his wife, Anne Stine, basing their search on the Vinland sagas and cartographic clues alone, found and excavated in the 1960s the probable site of Leif's camp at L'Anse aux Meadows in northern Newfoundland (Ingstad 1977, 1985; Ingstad and Ingstad 2000; Fig. 23). The excavations were later completed by a Parks Canada team directed by Bent Schoenbaek and Birgitta Wallace (Wallace 1991).

Although the greatest attention has been given to the discovery of the L'Anse aux Meadows site and its probable role in events described in the Vinland sagas, it appears that the Norse contacts in Labrador, Newfoundland, and the Gulf of St Lawrence were only an early, brief episode in the continuing Norse involvement with North America. Except for a Norse penny dating to the reign of Norwegian king Olaf Kyrhe in 1065–80, found in a Woodland period archaeological site on the coast of Maine and thought to have been traded through Indian hands south from its original acquisition location in Labrador or Newfoundland (Bourque and Cox 1981; Skaare 1979), all other traces of Norse remains in North America come from Dorset and Thule sites in Hudson Bay, the Central and High Canadian Arctic, and northernmost Greenland (Odess *et al.* 2000; Sutherland 2000; Schledermann 1980). These are not the temperate regions that Vikings sought for farms and grapes, so it seems that after a brief and unsuccessful period of southern exploration the Greenland and Icelandic Norse turned to areas closer to home for trade and profit in ivory. Among these northern finds are a Dorset pendant made from Norse copper found on the east coast of Hudson Bay, iron fragments from north-western Hudson Bay, a Thule carving of a cloaked Norseman from southern Baffin, a bronze trade balance arm, fragments of wool, and a bronze pot fragment from the Canadian High Arctic (Sutherland 2000). From Thule houses at Skraeling Island in Ellesmere came a host of Viking materials including cloth, iron chain mail, a carpenter's plane, and many other finds, and from north-west Greenland, iron, bronze, and other Norse goods (Schledermann 1980, 1996, 2000). These finds, coming from both Dorset and Thule culture sites dating from the twelfth to fourteenth centuries, suggest that Norse explorers and traders, and perhaps shipwreck victims, met Native Americans over a wide area of the Eastern Arctic for more than two centuries. It seems likely that Norse activity in the Central and High Canadian Arctic was prompted by something more important than geographic exploration and sheep farming — the themes identified as responsible for

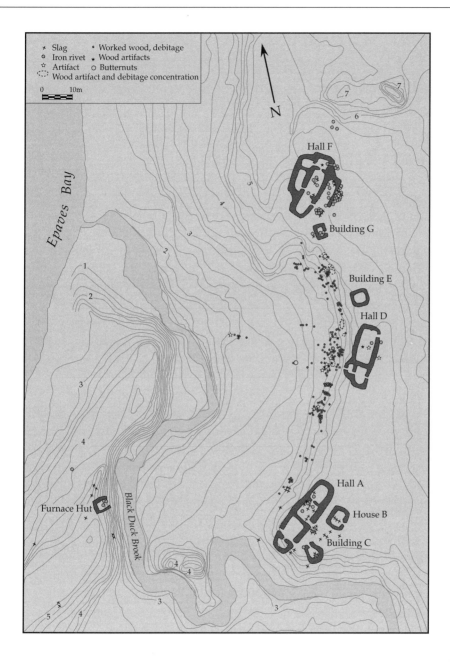

Figure 23. L'Anse aux Meadows Viking site in northern Newfoundland, showing longhouses, outbuildings, smithy, and primary finds. (Illustr. M. Bakry after B. Wallace.)

launching the Vinland voyages. The appearance of Norse remains in large numbers of Native sites probably reflects a more practical goal: the Norse need to acquire ivory to help pay Greenland's bills to Iceland and Europe. The fact that most finds date to the thir-teenth to fourteenth century when Norse ivory hunting in the Greenland Nordsetur was declining due to difficulties with increased ice, Native incursions, and local walrus stock depletion suggests that enterprising (or desperate) hunters chanced voyages farther afield where they might acquire ivory from Eskimo peoples who were the most accomplished walrus hunters in the world (Arneborg 2000; Gulløv 2000; McGovern 2000; Seaver 2000).

The Viking story is also a fitting way to conclude this review of circumpolar archae-ology. Not only does it mark the closing of the last open link in the distribution of humanity around the northern part of the globe, it also exemplifies what modern sci-ence can bring to the understanding of the Vikings and their northern world. The Viking expansion is not only evident in artefacts and house-sites excavated from Orkney to Newfoundland. It is also seen in the cattle, insect fauna, bits of wool sail, pieces of European wood, and other remains that have been preserved in archaeologi-cal sites. Studies of these, and of peat bogs and ice cores, of sea ice and weather, are revealing answers to many intriguing questions about North Atlantic lifeways and cli-mate. With co-operation between social and natural scientists, and with knowledge obtained from modern residents of these northern lands, the old theories about Norse extinction in Greenland are starting to fade away. Rather than emphasizing attacks by Eskimos, inbreeding, or disease, two factors have become central to this discussion: (1) the gradual cooling of the North Atlantic climate which led to livestock losses and physical and economic isolation from Iceland and Europe, and (2) the overly successful achievements of the initial three centuries of Norse settlement that resulted in the over-growth of a farming community that soon outstripped its capacity to sustain a Norse population of nearly 5000 people and their herds (Ogilvie and McGovern 2000). What-ever the final blows (climate? pirates? European trade foreclosure? religious crisis?) that led to the abandonment of the Greenland Western Settlement about 1350 and the East-ern Settlement about a hundred years later, a combination of short-sighted human prac-tices, climatic change, and environmental losses led to problems that were also experienced by Iceland and other Norse societies in the North Atlantic in the fourteenth to fifteenth centuries (Seaver 1996; Arneborg 2000). Ironically, these very conditions produced a great expansion of Inuit peoples into southern Greenland and Labrador, demonstrating once again whether cultures succeed or fail in arctic regions — as else-where — is a highly individualistic phenomenon. The common feature of most of these disasters is human hubris and the tragedy of self over community interest.

Conclusion

Archaeological research has brought an awareness that the prehistory of the Arctic and Subarctic has also made important contributions to the rest of the world. The bow and arrow almost certainly arrived in the New World with the Siberian Neolithic complex known as the Arctic Small Tool tradition about 5000 years ago, which also brought some of the earliest pottery to appear in the Americas. While this pottery tradition did not contribute to the history of ceramics south of Alaska, other Asian imports like the sinew-backed bow spread throughout the North American Arctic, and slat armour and other military concepts like fortresses and refuge sites became common features of life among the warring tribes of northern regions of British Columbia and south-east Alaska more than one thousand years ago. In like manner interaction with the rich arctic and subarctic maritime environment of the 'Far Northeast' was a crucial ingredient in the development of one of North America's most complex early hunting and fishing cultures, the Maritime Archaic, which was distributed for over a thousand miles from Labrador to southern Maine; its burial ceremonialism, extensive trading networks, and northern long-house villages is perhaps the most surprising and spectacular cultural development ever to occur in a region of North America long considered more as a marginal backwater than a centre of cultural development.

Speaking more broadly, the peopling of the New World has a special arctic legacy in that all cultural developments in the Americas other than those attributed to Vikings or post-Columbian times had to survive the passage through a Beringian arctic 'cultural filter' which no doubt influenced the types of cultural behaviours and technologies that were carried or transmitted into southern portions of the continent. It is remarkable therefore that American cultures should have developed the diverse and elaborate systems known from archaeological and ethnographic evidence in so short a time period as 10,000 years. Surely the coherence of Native American religion, folklore, and mythology, diverse as they are, reflects this special arctic legacy which has been preserved in many cultures in the Americas, where state-level societies were restricted in scope and did not impose 'imperial' dogma everywhere (Fitzhugh 1996). If so, some of this ancient Asian–Arctic legacy may also be found in Olmec art, which Covarrubias (1954) suspected had an Asian connection. That connection seems far more likely to be a circum-North Pacific littoral one than a trans-Pacific one, considering the similarity of spirit-masking and human–animal transformation concepts in the intervening regions of the North Pacific, especially in ethnographic Northwest Coast and Yup'ik Eskimo traditions and its 1500-year old Old Bering Sea and Ipiutak antecedents (Fitzhugh in press). Similar arguments can be made concerning arctic contributions to non-arctic Eurasian societies; but for that we need another article and can only note here the important role that arctic resources like walrus ivory and thong, fur, feathers, falcons, and northern minerals like amber played in Eurasian prestige and ecclesiastical systems. It also seems possible that even the Viking boat owes part of its history to the sewn skin and plank boats of northern Scandinavian cultures. At least we are now beginning to see that arctic cultural developments have not taken place in an isolated, frigid vacuum. Rather Arctic–Temperate interaction and exchanges have enriched cultures on both sides of the treeline around the globe for thousands of years.

As the above discussion illustrates, arctic archaeology has moved forward rapidly in recent years, and the interpretations being achieved now with the assistance of natural scientists, historians, and Native peoples are helping archaeologists produce a picture of vibrant societies which were constantly exploring the possibilities and boundaries of their northern world. For 30,000 years northern peoples have learned new ways to exploit and adapt to their lands, inventing new technology, adopting ideas from others, occasionally failing and trying again. Episodes of population expansion, rapid spread of new technologies like the microblade-inset spear, the toggling harpoon, harpoon float gear, reindeer domestication, and the persistence of ancient spiritual connections between people and animals that is an especially strong Palaeolithic legacy among arctic peoples in North America, all give pause for reflection on the remarkable achievements and the expressive art and spirituality of prehistoric circumpolar peoples.

Finally, the last decade has produced a new social environment for archaeology and other sciences in the north. After decades when scientists failed to develop meaningful and productive relationships with northern Natives and arctic residents, a new era of collaboration between scientists and northern Native peoples has begun (Nicholas and Andrews 1997; Loring 2001). Scientists working in the north in any capacity should do everything within their power to engage northern residents in their work. The future of northern peoples, their cultures, and archaeology depends on it.

Postscript

As this book goes to press a series of new discoveries from the circumpolar region has just been announced: The Zhokhov Project has announced the recovery of more baskets and organic finds, including possible human remains and the discovery of a Palaeolithic site dating to 25–27,000 years ago near the mouth of the Yama River east of the Lena Delta containing stone artefacts, bone tools, and faunal remains (Pitulko, pers. comm.). An article in *Nature* reports results of excavations at the Mamontovaya Kurya site on the Usa River north of the Arctic Circle and west of the northern Urals, containing stone tools and worked mammoth tusks, raising questions of whether the inhabitants were Neanderthal or *Homo sapiens* (Pavlov *et al.* 2001). And in a second year of excavation at the Zeleny Yar site near Salekhard at the mouth of the Ob River, among many graves recovered from an Iron Age cemetery were five mummies, many with well-preserved fur clothing and one individual with red hair (Feodorova, pers. comm.), making this one of the most important cemeteries with human remains known in the Eurasian Arctic.

Acknowledgements

This paper is based on a lecture given at the American Association for the Advancement of Science in San Francisco in February 2001, organized by Rolf Sinclair with assistance from the Office of Polar Programs, National Science Foundation. I would like to thank the following for assistance of various kinds: Adelaide de Menil, Edmund Carpenter, Marcia Bakry, Natalia Feodorova, Igor Krupnik, Stephen Loring, Daniel Odess, Andrei Golovnev, Vladimir Pitulko, James Quiggle, Edmund Searles for research and inspiration, without prejudice; and Amoco Eurasia Corporation, Nadym Gasprom, Smithsonian Institution, Rock Foundation, and Salekhard Museum for funding and material assistance.

References

ACKERMAN, R.E. 1984: Prehistory of the Asian Eskimo Zone. In Damas, D. (ed.), *Handbook of North American Anthropology. Volume 5. Arctic* (Washington, D.C., Smithsonian Institution), 106–18.

AMES, K.M. and MASCHNER, H.D.G. (eds.) 1999: *Peoples of the Northwest Coast: Their Archaeology and Prehistory* (New York).

ANDERSON, D.D. 1968: A Stone Age Campsite at the Gateway to America. *Scientific American* 188, 24–33.

ANDERSON, D.D. 1970: Akmak: an Early Archaeological Assemblage from Onion Portage, Northwest Alaska. *Acta Arctica* 16 (Copenhagen, Arctic Institute).

ANDREWS, J.T. 1975: *Glacial systems: an approach to glaciers and their environments* (North Scituate, Mass.).

ANDREWS, J.T., MCGHEE, R. and MCKENZIE-POLLOCK, L. 1971: Comparison of elevations of archaeological sites and calculated sea levels in Arctic Canada. *Arctic* 24(3), 210–28.

ARNEBORG, J. 2000: Greenland and Europe. In Fitzhugh, W.W. and Ward, E.I. (eds.) 2000, 304–17.

ARNOLD, J.E. 1996: The archaeology of complex hunter-gatherers. *J. Archaeol. Method and Theory* 3, 77–126.

ARUTIUNOV, S.A. and FITZHUGH, W.W. 1988: Prehistory of Siberia and the Bering Sea. In Fitzhugh, W.W. and Crowell, A. (eds.) 1988, 117–29.

BIRKET-SMITH, K. 1929: The Caribou Eskimos: material and social life and their cultural position. *Report of the Fifth Thule Expedition 1921–1924*. Vol. 5(1–2) (Copenhagen).

BIRKET-SMITH, K. 1930: The question of the origin of Eskimo culture: a rejoinder. *American Anthropologist* 32(4), 608–24.

BOAS, F. 1902: Some problems in North American archaeology. *American J. Archaeol.* (2nd Ser.) 6, 1–6. [Reprinted 1940 in Boas, F., *Race, Language, and Culture* (New York), 525–9.]

BOAS, F. 1903: The Jesup North Pacific Expedition. *American Mus. J.* 3(5), 73–119.

BOAS, F. 1910: Ethnological problems in Canada. *J. Roy. Anthropol. Inst. Great Britain and Ireland* 40, 529–39.

BOBROWSKY, P.T., CATTO, N.R., BRINK, J.W., SPURLING, B.E., GIBSON, T.H. and RUTTER, N.W. 1990: Archaeology geology of sites in western and northwestern Canada. In Lasca, N.P. and Donahue, J. (eds.), *Archaeological geology of North America* (Boulder, Geological Society of America), 87–122.

BOGORAS, W. 1904–9: The Chukchi. *The Jesup North Pacific Expedition 7. Memoirs of the American Museum of Natural History* (Leiden/New York). [Reprinted 1975, New York.]

BOGORAS, W. 1929: Elements of the culture of the circumpolar zone. *American Anthropologist* 31(4), 579–601.

BOURQUE, B.J. and COX, S.L. 1981: Maine State Museum Investigation of the Goddard Site. *Man In the Northeast* 22, 3–27.

BRYAN, A.L. 1957: Results and interpretations of recent archaeological research in western Washington with circum-boreal implications. *Davidson J. Anthropol.* 3, 1–16.

BURCH, E.S., Jr. 1972: The Caribou — Wild Reindeer as a Human Resource. *American Antiquity* 37, 339–68.

CARLSON, R.L. 1991: Clovis from the perspective of the ice-free corridor. In Bonnichson, R. and Turnmire, K. (eds.), *Clovis origins and adaptations* (Corvallis, Center for the Study of the First Americans, Oregon State University), 81–90.

CARPENTER, E. 2001: Tradition and Continuity in Eskimo Art. In Fitzhugh, W.W., Loring, S. and Odess, D. (eds.), *The Elders Conference on the History of Archaeology in the Eastern Arctic* (Washington, Arctic Studies Center, Smithsonian Contributions to Circumpolar Anthropology, 1).

CHARD, C.S. 1958: The western roots of Eskimo culture. In *Actas del XXXII Congresso Internacional de Americanistas, San Jose, Costa Rica* 2 (Costa Rica), 20–7.

CHARD, C.S. 1960: Northwest Coast — Northeast Asiatic similarities: a new hypothesis. In Wallace, A.F.S. (ed.), *Selected Papers of the Fifth International Congress of Anthropological and Ethnological Sciences* (Philadelphia), 236–40.

CHARD, C.S. 1974: *Northeast Asia in Prehistory* (Madison).

CHERNETSOV, V.N. 1935: An early maritime culture on the Yamal Peninsula. *Sovietskaya Etnografiia* 4–5, 109–33. [English translation on file at Arctic Studies Center, National Museum of Natural History. Smithsonian Institution. Washington, D.C.]

CHERNETSOV, V.N. 1970: On the problem of ancient substratum in the cultures of the circumpolar region. In *Seventh International Congress of Anthropological and Ethnological Sciences*, Vol. 10 (Moscow), 260–7.

CHERNETSOV, V.N. and MOSHINSKAYA, W. 1974: *Prehistory of Western Siberia* (edited by H.N. Michael) (Montreal and London, Arctic Institute of North America, Anthropology of the North: Translations from Russian Sources, 9).

CLARK, D.W. 1984: Pacific Eskimo: historical ethnography. In Damas, D. (ed.), *Handbook of North American Indians. Volume 5. Arctic* (Washington, D.C., Smithsonian Institution), 185–97.

CLARK, P.U. and FITZHUGH, W.W. 1990: Late deglaciation of the central Labrador coast and its implications for the age of glacial Lakes Naskaupi and McLean and for prehistory. *Quat. Res.* 34, 296–305.

CLARK, P.U. and FITZHUGH, W.W. 1991: Shorelines and prehistory: an investigation of method. Chapter 9 in Johnson, L. (ed.), *Shorelines and Prehistory* (Telford), 189–213.

COLLINS, H.B. 1937: Archaeology of St. Lawrence Island, Alaska. *Smithsonian Miscellaneous Collections* 96(1) (Washington, Smithsonian Institution).

COLLINS, H.B. 1971: Composite masks: Chinese and Eskimo. *Anthropologica* n.s. 13(102), 271–8.

COLLINS, H.B. 1984: History of Research Before 1945. In Damas, D. (ed.), *Handbook of North American Indians. Volume 5. Arctic* (Washington, D.C., Smithsonian Institution), 8–16.

COLLINS, H.B., DE LAGUNA, F., CARPENTER, E. and STONE, P. 1973: *The Far North. 2,000 years of American Eskimo and Indian art* (Washington, D.C., National Gallery of Art).

COUPLAND, G. 1996: This old house: cultural complexity and household stability on the northern Northwest Coast of North America. In Arnold, J.E. (ed.), *Emergent complexity: the evolution to intermediate societies* (Ann Arbor, International monographs in prehistory, archaeological series, 9), 74–90.

COVARRUBIAS, M. 1954: *The Eagle, the Jaguar, and the Serpent. Indian Art of the Americas; North America, Alaska, Canada, and the United States* (New York).

CROWELL, A.L. 1997: *Archaeology and the Capitalist World System. A study from Russian America* (New York and London).

DAWKINS, W.B. 1874: *Cave Hunting: Researches on the Evidence of Caves Respecting the Early Inhabitants of Europe* (London). [Reprinted 1973, with foreword by D.C. Mellor.]

DE LAGUNA, F. 1932–3: A comparison of Eskimo and Paleolithic art. *American J. Archaeol.* 36(4), 477–511; 37(1), 77–107.

DIKOV, N.N. 1968: The discovery of the Paleolithic in Kamchatka and the problem of the initial occupation of America. *Arctic Anthropol.* 5(1), 191–203. [Summary in West 1996.]

DIKOV, N.N. 1971: *Naskal'nye zagadki drevnei Chukotki (petroglify Pegtymelia)* [*Cliff-face enigmas of ancient Chukotka (The Pegtymel petroglyphs)*] (Moscow, Nauka).

DIKOV, N.N. 1988: The earliest sea mammal hunters of Wrangell Island. *Curr. Anthropol.* 25(1), 80–93.

DIKOV, N.N. 1999: *Mysteries in the rocks of ancient Chukotka. Petroglyphs of Pegtymel'* (translated from Russian by R. Bland) (Anchorage, National Park Service, Department of Interior). [Originally published in 1971 as *Naskal'nye Sagadki Drevnei Chukotki (Petroglify Pegtymelia)* (Moscow, Nauk).]

DIKOV, N.N. and TITOV, E.E. 1984: Problems of the stratification and periodization of the Ushki sites. *Arctic Anthropol.* 21(2), 69–80. [Summary in West 1996.]

DIXON, E.J. 2001: Human colonization of the Americas: timing, technology and process. In Elias, S.A. and Brigham-Grette, J. (eds.), *Beringian Paleoenvironments: Festschrift in Honor of David M. Hopkins. Quat. Sci. Rev.* 20(1–3), 277–99.

DIXON, J.E., HEATON, T.H., FIFIELD, T.E., HAMILTON, T.D., PUTNAM, D.E. and GRADY, F. 1997: Late Quaternary Regional Geoarchaeology of Southeast Alaska Karst: A Progress Report. Geoarchaeology of Caves and Cave Sediments. Special Issue. *Geoarchaeology: An International Journal* 12(6), 689–712.

DUMOND, D.E. 1977: *The Eskimos and Aleuts* (London).

DUMOND, D.E. and BLAND, R.L. 1996: Holocene prehistory of the Northernmost North Pacific. *J. World Prehist.* 9(4), 401–51.

ELIAS, S. 1996: Insect fossil evidence on late Wisconsin environments of the Bering Land Bridge. In West, F.H. (ed.), *American Beginnings: the prehistory and paleoecology of Beringia* (Chicago), 110–19.

FEODOROVA, N.V. 1996: Tiutey Sale, a site in northern Yamal: on the issue of the circumpolar maritime adaptation (45 pp.) (Manuscript in Russian on file at the Arctic Studies Center, National Museum of Natural History, Smithsonian Institution).

FEODOROVA, N.V., KOSINTSEV, P.A. and FITZHUGH, W.W. 1998: *'Gone into the Hills': Culture of the Northwestern Yamal Coast Population in the Iron Age* (Russian Academy of Sciences; Institute of Plant and Animal Ecology; and Arctic Studies Center, Smithsonian Institution) [in Russian].

FIENUP-RIORDAN, A. 1996: *Ugayuliyararput: Our Way of Making Prayer. The Living Tradition of Yup'ik Masks* (Washington, Anchorage Museum of History and Art).

FITZHUGH, B. 1996: *The evolution of complex hunter-gatherers on the North Pacific: a case study from Kodiak Island, Alaska* (Ph.D. dissertation, Department of Anthropology, University of Michigan) (Ann Arbor, University Microfilms).

FITZHUGH, B. in press: The evolution of complex hunter-gatherers on the Kodiak Archipelago. In Habu, J. and Koyama, S. (eds.), *Hunter-Gatherers of the North Pacific Rim* (Osaka, National Museum of Ethnology, Senri Ethnological Reports).

FITZHUGH, B. and HABU, J. (eds.) in press: Beyond foraging and collecting: evolutionary change in hunter-gatherer settlement systems (Kluwer Academic/Plenum Press).

FITZHUGH, W.W. 1972: *Environmental archaeology and cultural systems in Hamilton Inlet, Labrador* (Washington, Smithsonian Contributions to Anthropology, 16).

FITZHUGH, W.W. 1974: Ground slates in the Scandinavian Younger Stone Age with reference to circumpolar maritime adaptations. *Proc. Prehist. Soc.* 40, 45–58.

FITZHUGH, W.W. (ed.) 1975a: *Prehistoric Maritime Adaptations of the Circumpolar Zone* (The Hague, World Anthropology).

FITZHUGH, W.W. 1975b: A comparative approach to northern maritime adaptations. In Fitzhugh, W.W. (ed.) 1975a, 339–86.

FITZHUGH, W.W. 1975c: A Maritime Archaic sequence from Hamilton Inlet, Labrador. *Arctic Anthropol.* 12(2), 117–38.

FITZHUGH, W.W. 1977: Population movement and culture change on the central Labrador coast. *Annals of the New York Academy of Sciences* 288, 481–97.

FITZHUGH, W.W. 1978: Maritime Archaic cultures of the central and northern Labrador Coast. *Arctic Anthropol.* 15(2), 61–95.

FITZHUGH, W.W. 1984a: Images from the past: thoughts on Bering Sea Eskimo art and culture. *Expedition* 26(2), 24–39.

FITZHUGH, W.W. 1984b: Paleo-Eskimo cultures of Greenland. In Damas, D. (ed.), *Handbook of North American Indians. Volume 5: Arctic* (Washington, D.C., Smithsonian Institution), 528–39.

FITZHUGH, W.W. 1984c: Residence pattern development in the Labrador Maritime Archaic: longhouse models and 1983 surveys. In Sproull Thomson, J. and Thomson, C. (eds.), *Archaeology in Newfoundland and Labrador 1983* (Historic Resources Division, Government of Newfoundland and Labrador, Annual Report no. 4), 6–47.

FITZHUGH, W.W. 1987: Archaeological ethnicity and the prehistory of Labrador. In Auger, A., Glass, M.F., MacEachern, S. and McCartney, P. (eds.), *Ethnicity and culture* (Calgary, Chacmool Archaeological Association, University of Calgary), 141–53.

FITZHUGH, W.W. 1988a: Persistence and change in art and ideology in Western Alaskan cultures. In *The Late Prehistoric Development of Alaska's Native Peoples* (Alaska Anthropological Association Monograph 4), 81–105.

FITZHUGH, W.W. 1988b: Comparative art of the North Pacific Rim. In Fitzhugh, W.W. and Crowell, A. (eds.) 1988, 294–312.

FITZHUGH, W.W. 1993: Art and iconography in the hunting ritual of North Pacific peoples. In *Proceedings of the 7th International Abashiri Symposium* (Abashiri, Abashiri Museum of Northern Peoples), 1–13.

FITZHUGH, W.W. 1996: Early contact and acculturation in the north: Native America and the global system. In Turgeon, L., Delage, D. and Ouellet, R. (eds.), *Cultural Transfer, America and Europe: 500 years of Interculturation* (Laval), 94–104.

FITZHUGH, W.W. 1997: Biogeographical Archeology in the Eastern North American Arctic. *Human Ecology* 25(3), 385–418.

FITZHUGH, W.W. in press: Art, Artifacts, and Boundaries: Exploring Pattern and Explanation in North Pacific Art. In King, J. and Taylor, P. (eds.), *Boundaries in the Art of the Northwest Coast of America* (Papers from a Conference at the British Museum, 18–20 May, 2000) (London).

FITZHUGH, W.W. and CHAUSSONNET, V. (eds.) 1984: *Anthropology of the North Pacific Rim* (Washington).

FITZHUGH, W.W. and CROWELL, A. (eds.) 1988: *Crossroads of continents: cultures of Siberia and Alaska* (Washington).

FITZHUGH, W.W. and GOLOVNEV, A.V. 1998: Searching for the grail: virtual archaeology in Yamal and circumpolar theory. In Gilberg, R. and Gulløv, H.-C. (eds.), *Fifty years of Arctic research. Anthropological studies from Greenland to Siberia* (Copenhagen, National Museum of Denmark, Publications of the National Museum Ethnographical Series, 18), 99–118.

FITZHUGH, W.W. and KAPLAN, S.A. (eds.) 1982: *Inua: spirit world of the Bering Sea Eskimo* (Washington).

FITZHUGH, W.W. and LAMB, H. 1985: Vegetation history and culture change in Labrador prehistory. *J. Arctic and Alpine Res.* 17(4), 357–70.

FITZHUGH, W.W. and WARD, E.I. (eds.) 2000: *Vikings: The North Atlantic Saga* (Washington, National Museum of Natural History).

FLADMARK, K.R. 1979: Routes: alternative migration corridors for Early Man in North America. *American Antiquity* 44(1), 55–69.

FORD, J.A. 1959: Eskimo prehistory in the vicinity of Point Barrow, Alaska. *Anthropol. Pap. American Mus. Nat. Hist.* 47(1) (New York).

FORTESCUE, M. 1998: *Language relations across Bering Strait: Re-appraising the archaeological and linguistic evidence* (London and New York, Open Linguistics Series).

GIDDINGS, J.L. 1964: *The archaeology of Cape Denbigh* (Providence).

GIDDINGS, J.L. 1965: Cross-Dating the Archaeology of Northwestern Alaska. *Science* 153(3732), 127–35.

GIDDINGS, J.L. 1967: *Ancient Men of the Arctic* (New York).

GIDDINGS, J.L. and ANDERSON, D.D. 1986: *Beachridge Archeology of Cape Krusenstern* (Washington, U.S. Department of the Interior, National Park Service Publications in Archeology, 20).

GIRIA, E.Yu. and PITULKO, V.V. 1994: High Arctic Mesolithic culture of Zhokhov Island: inset tools and knapping technology. *Arctic Anthropol.* 31(2), 17–29.

GJESSING, G. 1944: The Circumpolar Stone Age. *Acta Arctica* 9(2), 1–70.

GOLOVNOV, A.V. and OSHERENKO, G. 1999: *Siberian Survival: the Nenets and Their Story* (Ithaca).

GREENMAN, E. 1960: The North Atlantic and Early Man in the New World. *Michigan Archaeologist* 6(2), 19–39.

GREENMAN, E. 1963: The Upper Paleolithic and the New World. *Curr. Anthropol.* 4, 41–66.

GRIFFIN, J.B. 1960: Some prehistoric connections between Siberia and America. *Science* 131(3403), 801–12.

GRØNNOW, B. (ed.) 1996: *The Paleo-Eskimo Cultures of Greenland. New Perspectives in Greenlandic Archaeology* (Papers from a Symposium at the Institute of Archaeology and Ethnology, University of Copenhagen, 1992) (Copenhagen, Danish Polar Center).

GULLØV, H.C. 2000: Natives and Norse in Greenland. In Fitzhugh, W.W. and Ward, E.I. (eds.) 2000, 318–26.

HATT, G. 1914: *Arktiske skinddragter i Eurasien og Amerika: en etnografisk studie* (Copenhagen). [Translated and republished as Arctic skin clothing in Eurasia and America: an ethnographic study. *Arctic Anthropol.* 5(2), 3–132.]

HATT, G. 1934: North American and Eurasian culture connections. *Proceedings of the Fifth Pacific Science Conference.*

HATT, G. 1949: Asiatic influences in American folklore. *Det Konlige Danske Videnskabernes Selskab (Historisk-Filologiske Meddelelser)* 31(6), 1–122 (Copenhagen).

HOFFECKER, J.F., POWERS, W.R. and GOEBEL, T. 1993: The colonization of Beringia and the peopling of the New World. *Science* 259, 46–53.

HOPKINS, D.M., MATTHEWS, J.V., Jr., SCHWEGER, C.E. and YOUNG, S.B. (eds.) 1982: *The Paleoecology of Beringia* (New York).

INGOLD, T. 1980: *Hunters, Pastoralists, and Ranchers* (Cambridge, Cambridge Studies in Social Anthropology).

INGSTAD, A.S. 1977: *The Discovery of a Norse Settlement in North America* (Oslo).

INGSTAD, A.S. 1985: *The Norse Discovery of America* (Oslo).

INGSTAD, H. and INGSTAD, A.S. 2000: *The Viking Discovery of North America. The Excavation of a Norse Settlement in L'Anse aux Meadows, Newfoundland* (St. John's, Newfoundland).

IRVING, W.N. 1962: A Provisional Comparison of some Alaskan and Asian Stone Industries. In Campbell, J.M. (ed.), *Prehistoric Relations Between the Arctic and Temperate Zones of North America* (Montreal, Arctic Institute of North American Technical Paper 11), 55–68.

IRVING, W.N. 1969–70: The Arctic Small Tool tradition. In *Proceedings of the 8th International Congress of Anthropological and Ethnological Sciences*, Vol. 3 (Tokyo and Kyoto), 340–2.

JORDAN, R.H. 1984: *Qasqiluteng*: feasting and ceremonialism among the traditional Koniag of Kodiak Island, Alaska. In Fitzhugh, W.W. and Chaussonnet, V. (eds.) 1984, 147–73.

JOSENHANS, H., FEDJU, D., PIENITZ, R. and SOUTHON, J. 1997: Early humans and rapidly changing Holocene sea levels in the Queen Charlotte Islands — Hecate Strait, British Columbia. *Science* 277, 71–4.

KAPLAN, S.A. and WOOLLETT, J.M. 2000: Challenges and Choices: Exploring the Interplay of Climate, History, and Culture on Canada's Labrador Coast. *Arctic, Antarctic, and Alpine Res.* 32(3), 351–9.

KEHOE, A.B. 1962: A hypothesis on the origin of northeastern American pottery. *Southwestern J. Anthropol.* 18(1), 20–9.

KEHOE, A.B. 1971: Small boats upon the North Atlantic. In Riley, C. (ed.), *Man Across the Sea* (Austin), 275–92.

KHLOBYSTIN, L.P. 1998: Taimyr: archaeology of northernmost Eurasia (Manuscript being edited for Contributions to Circumpolar Archaeology series, Arctic Studies Center, National Museum of Natural History, Smithsonian Institution. Translated from Russian).

KOCHMAR, N. 1994: *Rock-drawings of Yukutia* (edited by V. Ye. Larichev) (Novosibirsk, Yakut State University. Russian Academy of Sciences, Siberian Division. Institute of Archaeology and Ethnology).

KRUPNIK, I. 1993: *Arctic Adaptations: Native Whalers and Reindeer Hunters of Northern Eurasia* (Dartmouth, Dartmouth College).

KRUPNIK, I. 2000: Jesup-2: the precious legacy and a centennial perspective. *European Rev. Native American Stud.* 14(2), 1–3.

LARSEN, H.E. and RAINEY, F.G. 1948: Ipiutak and the Arctic whale hunting culture. *Anthropol. Pap. American Mus. Nat. Hist.* 42 (New York).

LAUGHLIN, W.S. 1963: Eskimos and Aleuts: their origin and evolution. *Science* 142(3593), 633–45.

LEBEDINTSEV, A.I. 1990: *Drevnie Primorskie kul'tury severo-zapadnogo Prikhot'ya [Early coastal cultures of northwestern Priokhot'e]* (Moscow, Nauka).

LORING, S. 1980: Paleoindian hunters and the Champlain Sea: a presumed association. *Man in the Northeast* 19, 15–41.

LORING, S. 2001: Repatriation and Community Anthropology: The Smithsonian Institution's Arctic Studies Center. In Bray, T.L. (ed.), *The Future of the Past. Archaeologists, Native Americans, and Repatriation* (New York and London), 185–98.

MCALEESE, K. 2000: *Full circle: first contact. Vikings and Skraelings in Newfoundland and Labrador* (St. John's, Newfoundland Museum, Government of Newfoundland and Labrador).

MCCARTNEY, A.P. 1975: Maritime adaptations in cold archipelagoes: an analysis of environment and culture in the Aleutian and other island chains. In Fitzhugh, W.W. (ed.) 1975a, 281–338.

MCCARTNEY, A.P., OKADA, H., OKADA, A. and WORKMAN, W. (eds.) 1998: North Pacific and Bering Sea Maritime Societies: the Archaeology of prehistoric and early historic coastal peoples. Papers from a symposium, Tokai University, Honolulu. *Arctic Anthropol.* 35(1).

MCCARTNEY, A.P. and SAVELLE, J.M. 1993: Bowhead whale bone and Thule Eskimo subsistence patterns in the Central Canadian Arctic. *Polar Record* 29, 1–12.

MCGHEE, R. 1969/70: Speculations on climatic change and Thule culture development. *Folk* 11–12, 173–84 (Copenhagen).

MCGHEE, R. 1976: Paleoeskimo occupations of Central and High Arctic Canada. In Maxwell, M.S. (ed.), *Eastern Arctic Prehistory: Paleoeskimo problems* (Memoirs of the Society for American Archaeology, 31), 15–39.

MCGHEE, R. 1978: *Canadian Arctic Prehistory* (Toronto, New York).

MCGHEE, R. 1984: Thule Prehistory of Canada. In Damas, D. (ed.), *Handbook of North American Indians. Volume 5. Arctic* (Washington, D.C., Smithsonian Institution), 369–76.

MCGHEE, R. 1996: *Ancient people of the Arctic* (Vancouver, BC).

MCGOVERN, T.H. 2000: The Demise of Norse Greenland. In Fitzhugh, W.W. and Ward, E.I. (eds.) 2000, 327–39.

MCMANUS, D.A. and CREAGER, J.S. 1984: Sea-level data for parts of the Bering-Chukchi shelves of Beringia from 19,000 to 10,000 14C yr B. P. *Quat. Res.* 21, 317–25.

MANDRYK, C.A. 1990: Could humans survive the ice free corridor? Late-glacial vegetation and climate in West Central Alberta. In Agenbroad, L.D., Mead, J.I. and Nelson, L.W. (eds.), *Megafauna and man: discovery of America's heartland* (Hot Springs, The Mammoth Site of Hot Springs, South Dakota, Inc. Scientific Papers, Vol. 1), 67–79.

MANN, D.H., CROWELL, A.L., HAMILTON, T.D. and FINNEY, B.P. 1998: Holocene geologic and climatic history around the Gulf of Alaska. *Arctic Anthropol.* 35(1), 112–31.

MANN, D.H. and HAMILTON, T.D. 1995: Late Pleistocene and Holocene paleoenvironments of the north Pacific coast. *Quat. Sci. Rev.* 14, 449–71.

MARTIN, P.S. and STUART, A.J. 1995: Mammoth Extinction: Two Continents and Wrangel Island. *Radiocarbon* 37(1), 7–10.

MATSON, R.G. 1983: Intensification and the Development of Cultural Complexity: the Northwest versus the Northeast Coast. In Nash, R.J. (ed.) 1983, 125–48.

MAXWELL, M.S. 1976: Introduction. In Maxwell, M.S. (ed.), *Eastern Arctic prehistory: Paleoeskimo problems* (Memoirs of the Society for American Archaeology, 31), 1–5.

MAXWELL, M.S. 1984: Pre-Dorset and Dorset Prehistory of Canada. In Damas, D. (ed.), *Handbook of North American Indians. Volume 5. Arctic* (Washington, D.C., Smithsonian Institution), 359–68.

MAXWELL, M.S. 1985: *Prehistory of the Eastern Arctic* (Orlando).

MEGGERS, B.J., EVANS, C. and ESTRADA, E. 1965: *Early Formative Period of Coastal Ecuador: the Valdivia and Machalilla Phases* (Washington, Smithsonian Contributions to Anthropology, 1).

MOBERG, C.-A. 1960: On some circumpolar and arctic problems. *Acta Arctica* 12, 67–74.

MOBERG, C.-A. 1975: Circumpolar adaptation zones east–west and cross-economy contacts north–south: an outsider's query, especially on Ust'-Poluj. In Fitzhugh, W.W. (ed.) 1975a, 101–10.

MOCHANOV, Y.A. 1973: Northeastern Asia 9,000–5,000 Years BC (the Sumnagin Culture). In *Problems of Archaeology of the Urals and Siberia* (Moscow), 29–44 [in Russian].

MOCHANOV, Y.A. and FEDOSEEVA, S.A. 1996: Dyuktai Cave. In West, F.H. (ed.), *American Beginnings: the prehistory and paleoecology of Beringia* (Chicago), 164–74. [Summary in West 1996.]

MORRISON, D. 1989: Radiocarbon dating Thule culture. *Arctic Anthropol.* 26(2), 48–77.

NAGY, M.I. 1997: *Palaeoeskimo Cultural Transition: a Case Study from Ivujivik, Eastern Arctic* (Montreal, Avataq Cultural Institute, Nunavik Archaeology Monograph Series 1).

NASH, R.J. 1976: Cultural systems and cultural change in the Central Arctic. In Maxwell, M.S. (ed.), *Eastern Arctic Prehistory: Paleoeskimo problems* (Memoirs of the Society for American Archaeology, 31), 150–5.

NASH, R.J. (ed.) 1983: *The evolution of maritime cultures on the northeast and the northwest coasts of America* (Vancouver, Department of Archaeology, Simon Fraser University, Department of Archaeology Publication 11).

NELSON, R.K. 1973: *Hunters of the northern forest. Designs for survival among the Alaska Kutchin* (Chicago).

NELSON, W.E. 1899: The Eskimos About Bering Strait. *Bureau of American Ethnology Annual Report* 18, 1–518 (Washington, D.C., Smithsonian Institution). [Reprinted 1983 with introduction by William W. Fitzhugh, Classics of Smithsonian Anthropology Series.]

NICHOLAS, G.P. and ANDREWS, T.D. (eds.) 1997: *At a crossroads: archaeology and First Peoples in Canada* (Burnaby, B.C., Department of Archaeology, Simon Fraser University, Publication 24).

OAKES, J.E. and RIEWE, R. 1996: *Our boots: an Inuit women's art* (Vancouver and Toronto).

OAKES, J.E. 1998: *Spirit of Survival: traditional native life, clothing, and footwear* (Washington).

ODESS, D., LORING, S. and FITZHUGH, W.W. 2000: *Skraeling*: First Peoples of Helluland, Markland, and Vinland. In Fitzhugh, W.W. and Ward, E.I. (eds.) 2000, 193–206.

OGILVIE, A.E.J. and MCGOVERN, T.H. 2000: Sagas and Science: Climate and Human Impacts in the North Atlantic. In Fitzhugh, W.W. and Ward, E.I. (eds.) 2000, 385–93.

OREKHOV, A.A. 1987: *An early culture of the Northwest Bering Sea* (Moscow, Nauka). [English translation by R.L. Bland published by National Park Service, Anchorage, Alaska, 1999.]

OUSLEY, S.D. 2000: Boas, Brinton, and the Jesup North Pacific Expedition: the return of the Americanoids. *Native American Stud.* 14(2), 11–17.

PAINE, R. 1957: *Coast Lapp Society: a study of neighbourhood* (Tromso).

PAINE, R. 1988: Reindeer and Caribou *Rangifer tarandus* in the Wild and Under Pastoralism. *Polar Record* 24(148), 31–42.

PAINE, R. 1994: *Herds of the Tundra. A Portrait of Saami Reindeer Pastoralism* (Washington).

PAVLOV, P., SVENDSEN, J.I. and INDRELID, S. 2001: Human presence in the European Arctic nearly 40,000 years ago. *Nature* 413, 64–7.

PITULKO, V.V. 1993: An Early Holocene site in the Siberian High Arctic. *Arctic Anthropol.* 30(1), 13–21.

PITULKO, V.V. 1999a: *The Zhokhov site* (St Petersburg).

PITULKO, V.V. 1999b: Ancient humans in Eurasian Arctic ecosystems: environmental dynamics and changing subsistence. *World Archaeol.* 30(3), 421–36.

PITULKO, V.V. 1999c: Archaeological Survey in Central Taymyr. In Kassens, H., Bauch, H.A., Dmitrenko, I., Eichen, H., Hubberten, H.-W., Melles, M., Thiede, J. and Timokhov, L. (eds.), *Land–ocean systems in the Siberian Arctic: dynamics and history* (Berlin), 457–67.

PITULKO, V.V. 2001: Terminal Pleistocene–Early Holocene occupation in northeast Asia and the Zhokhov assemblage. *Quat. Sci. Rev.* 20, 267–75.

PITULKO, V.V. and KASPAROV, A.K. 1996: Ancient arctic hunters: material culture and survival strategy. *Arctic Anthropol.* 33(1), 1–31.

POWERS, W.R. and HOFFECKER, J. 1989: Late Pleistocene settlement in the Nenana Valley, Central Alaska. *American Antiquity* 54(2), 263–87. [See also West 1996.]

POWERS, W.R. and JORDAN, R.H. 1990: Human Biogeography and Climatic Change in Siberia and Arctic North America in the Fourth and Fifth Millennia BP. *Phil. Trans. Roy. Soc. London A* 330, 665–70.

RAY, D.J. 1992: *The Eskimos of Bering Strait, 1650–1898* (Seattle).

RIDLEY, F. 1960: Transatlantic contacts of primitive man: Eastern Canada and Northwestern Russia. *Pennsylvania Archaeologist* 30(2), 46–57.

RINK, H.J. 1875: *Tales and traditions of the Eskimo: with a sketch of their habits, religion, language and other peculiarities* (edited by R. Brown) (Edinburgh and London; Copenhagen).

RUDENKO, S.I. 1961: *The Ancient Culture of the Bering Sea and the Eskimo Problem* (translated by P. Tolstoy) (Toronto, Arctic Institute of North America, Anthropology of the North: Translations from Russian Sources, 1).

SAUER, M. 1802: *An account of a geographical and astronomical expedition to the northern parts of Russia . . . in the years 1785, etc. to 1794* (London).

SAVELLE, J.M. and MCCARTNEY, A.P. 1991: Thule Eskimo subsistence and bowhead whale procurement. In Stiner, M.C. (ed.), *Human predators and prey mortality* (Boulder), 201–16.

SCHINDLER, D.L. 1985: Anthropology in the arctic. A critique of racial typology and normative theory. *Curr. Anthropol.* 26(4), 475–99.

SCHLEDERMANN, P. 1980: Notes on Norse Finds from the East Coast of Ellesmere Island, N.W.T. *Arctic* 33(3), 454–63.

SCHLEDERMANN, P. 1996: *Voices in Stone: a Personal Journey into the Arctic Past* (Calgary, Arctic Institute of North America, University of Calgary, Komatik Series 5).

SCHLEDERMANN, P. 2000: Ellesmere: Vikings in the Far North. In Fitzhugh, W.W. and Ward, E.I. (eds.) 2000, 248–56.

SCHUSTER, C. 1951: A survival of the Eurasiatic animal style in modern Alaskan Eskimo art. In Tax, S. (ed.), *Selected Papers of the 29th Congress of Americanists, New York, 1949* (Chicago), 35–45.

SCHUSTER, C. and CARPENTER, E. 1986–8: *Materials for the Study of Social Symbolism in Ancient and Tribal Art* (New York, Rock Foundation).

SCHUSTER, C. and CARPENTER, E. 1996: *Patterns that Connect: Social Symbolism in Ancient and Tribal Art* (New York).

SEAVER, K. 1996: *The Frozen Echo: Greenland and the Exploration of North America ca. A.D. 1000–1500* (Stanford).

SEAVER, K. 2000: Unanswered Questions. In Fitzhugh, W.W. and Ward, E.I. (eds.) 2000, 268–79.

SHNIRELMAN, V. 1980: *The Origin of Animal Husbandry (A Cultural and Historical Issue)* (Moscow, Nauk).

SIMONSEN, P. 1975: When and why did occupational specialization begin at the Scandinavian north coast? In Fitzhugh, W.W. (ed.) 1975a, 75–86.

SKAARE, K. 1979: An Eleventh-Century Norwegian Penny Found on the Coast of Maine. *Norwegian Numis. J.* 2, 4–17.

SMITH, K. 1997: A microblade core from western Iceland: possibilities and implications (Paper presented at the North Atlantic Biocultural Organization's NABO '97 conference, St. John's, Newfoundland, 5 September, 1997).

SOLLAS, W.J. 1911: *Ancient Hunters and Their Modern Representatives* (London).

SPAULDING, A.C. 1946: Northeastern archaeology and general trends in the northern forest zone. In Johnson, F. (ed.), *Man in Northeastern North America* (Amherst, Papers of the Robert S. Peabody Foundation, 3), 143–67.

SPENCER, R. 1984: The North Alaskan Eskimo: Introduction. In Damas, D. (ed.), *Handbook of North American Indians. Volume 5. Arctic* (Washington, D.C., Smithsonian Institution), 278–84.

SPIESS, A.E. 1979: *Reindeer and Caribou Hunters. An Archaeological Study* (New York).

STANFORD, D.J. 1976: *The Walakpa Site, Alaska: Its Place in the Birnirk and Thule Cultures* (Washington, Smithsonian Contributions to Anthropology, 20).

STANFORD, D.J. and BRADLEY, B. 2001: The Solutrean Solution: Did Some Ancient Americans Come from Europe? *Discovering Archaeology* 2(1), 54–5.

STEENSBY, H.P. 1917: An anthropogeographical study of the origin of the Eskimo culture. *Meddelelser om Grønland* 53(2) (Copenhagen).

STRAUS, L.G. 2000: Solutrean settlement of North America? A review of reality. *American Antiquity* 65(2).

SUTHERLAND, P. 2000: The Norse and Native North Americans. In Fitzhugh, W.W. and Ward, E.I. (eds.) 2000, 238–47.

SUTTON, D.G. 1982: Towards the recognition of convergent cultural adaptation in the subantarctic zone. *Curr. Anthropol.* 23(1), 77–97.

TAYLOR, W.E., Jr. 1963: Hypotheses on the origin of Canadian Thule culture. *American Antiquity* 28(4), 456–64.

TEIN, T.S. 1979: Archaeological investigations on Wrangel Island [in Russian]. In *Novye Arkheologicheskie Pamiatniki Severa Dal'nego Vostoka [New Archaeological Monuments of the Northern Far East]* (Magadan, Akademia Nauk SSR).

TUCK, J.A. 1976: *Ancient People of Port au Choix* (St. John's, Institute of Social and Economic Research, Memorial University of Newfoundland, Newfoundland Social and Economic Studies, 17).

TUCK, J.A. 1977: Early cultures on the Strait of Belle Isle, Labrador. In Newman, W.S. and Salwen, B. (eds.), Amerinds and their paleoenvironments in northeastern North America. *Annals of the New York Academy of Sciences* 288, 472–80.

TUCK, J.A., Jr. and GRENIER, R. 1992: *Red Bay, Labrador: World Whaling Capitol, 1550–1600* (St. John's, Atlantic Archaeology).

VAINSTEIN, S.I. 1980: *Nomads of South Siberia* (Cambridge) (translated from Russian original 1972).

VAINSTEIN, S.I. 1981: On the Distribution of the Reindeer Economy among the Samoyed Peoples. In *Congressus Quintus Internationalis Finno-Ugristarum* 8 (Turku, Finland), 118–23 [in Russian].

VARTANYAN, S.L., GARUTT, V.E. and SHER, A.V. 1993: Holocene dwarf mammoths from Wrangel Island in the Siberian Arctic. *Nature* 362, 337–40.

VASIL'EVSKII, R.S. 1987: The Development of a Maritime System of Economy in the Northern Part of the Pacific Ocean Basin. *Etudes/Inuit/Studies* 11, 73–90.

VELICHKO, A.A. (ed.) 1984: *Late Quaternary environments of the Soviet Union* (H.E. Wright, Jr. and C.S. Barnosky, editors of the English-language edition) (Minneapolis).

WALLACE, B. 1991: L'Anse aux Meadows: Gateway to Vinland. *Acta Arctica* 61, 166–98.

WARDWELL, A. 1986: *Ancient Ivories of the Bering Strait* (New York, American Federation of Arts).

WEST, F.H. 1967: The Donnelly Ridge site and the definition of an early core and blade complex in Central Alaska. *American Antiquity* 32(2), 360–82. [See also West 1996.]

WEST, F.H. 1981: *The Archaeology of Beringia* (New York).

WEST, F.H. 1996: Beringia and New World Origins. In West, F.H. (ed.), *American Beginnings: the prehistory and paleoecology of Beringia* (Chicago), 537–59.

YAMAURA, K. 1980: On the Relationships of the Toggle Harpoon Heads Discovered on the Northwestern Shore of the Pacific. *Material Culture* 35, 1–19.

YESNER, D.R. 1980: Maritime hunter-gatherers: ecology and prehistory. *Curr. Anthropol.* 21, 727–50.

YOUNG, S.B. 1989: *To the Arctic. An Introduction to the Far Northern World* (New York).

ZYKOV, A.P., KOKSHAROV, S.F., TEREKHOVA, L.M. and FEODOROVA, N.V. 1994: *Ugrian heritage: West Siberian antiquities from the collection of the Urals University* (Ekaterinburg, History and Archaeology Institute, Russian Academy of Sciences with 'Tyumentransgaz').

North America and Mesoamerica

GEORGE L. COWGILL, MICHELLE HEGMON AND
GEORGE R. MILNER

Introduction

We were invited to cover all of northern and Central America. We concluded, however, that it was better to concentrate on those areas we know best, rather than try to do justice to such a vast and varied expanse. This introduction is a joint effort. Thereafter Cowgill discusses Mesoamerica, Hegmon deals with the 'Greater Southwest' (the south-western US and parts of northern Mexico), and Milner covers eastern North America. Within these regions, our treatment is necessarily selective. We do not attempt to cover north-western North America, nor southern Central America (the parts of Honduras, Nicaragua, and Costa Rica that are outside Mesoamerica). This is assuredly not because there are no important developments in these regions, but is only because we are not competent to deal with them.

A number of generalizations apply to all or many of the regions we discuss. Throughout the US and Canada changes in our views of prehistoric life are driven largely by the stream of new data generated by contract archaeology, although this is less so in Mesoamerica. The amount of fieldwork conducted as part of contract archaeology far surpasses work funded through other sources (i.e. granting agencies and field schools). An impressive number of sites have been excavated and large regions surveyed, often with the most up-to-date field techniques and broad arrays of specialists. Although the locations of such projects are dictated by construction and management needs, data from a few projects have been used as a basis for important synthetic contributions (e.g. Bareis and Porter 1984; Jenkins and Krause 1986; Mabry 1998; Plog 1986; Schlanger 1988; Whittlesey *et al.* 1997). Many projects establish internally consistent databases but it is often difficult for outside researchers to use these data for comparative purposes because of inconsistent sampling, data collection, and information presentation (problems by no means unique to contract archaeology). In addition, most contract reports (known as the grey literature) are poorly disseminated and only local specialists know of the existence of a particular project and its results. We expect that in the next century data generated by contract archaeology will continue to increase in both quality and quantity. Ongoing efforts (discussed below) to develop sophisticated databases and knowledge repositories should make these important data more usable.

In Mesoamerica, 'rescue' projects are important but they are probably a smaller proportion of the total investment in archaeology. Sometimes disproportionate emphasis is given to projects driven by tourism. However, there are similar problems of inconsistent data collection and presentation and poorly disseminated findings.

Throughout the regions we discuss there is great need for electronic knowledge bases. It is unrealistic and perhaps undesirable to try to impose uniform systems of recording and description, yet we need far more than mere accumulations of disparate electronic files. Large projects are proposed, if not already under way, to create knowledge bases that will include search engines and the kinds of data about data ('metadata') that are needed to make good use of information from numerous independent projects. Because of the volatility of electronic media and rapid changes in technology and quick obsolescence of hardware and software, it is not enough simply to create these knowledge bases; strong institutional support is needed to maintain them and 'migrate' them to new platforms. Effective implementation of such knowledge bases will greatly expand the possibilities for archaeology in the twenty-first century.

Everywhere in the regions we discuss, sites are being rapidly damaged and destroyed. In Mesoamerica, at least, resources to protect sites from modern development and looting are woefully inadequate, and we are in a race against time to conserve irreplaceable archaeological resources. Political and social contexts often further complicate research. One example is legislation intended to protect the interests of indigenous people, such as the Native American Graves Protection and Repatriation Act (NAGPRA) in the US. In parts of Mesoamerica, political and social troubles sometimes render fieldwork hazardous or impracticable. Archaeologists in the twenty-first century will continue to face such issues, and it is important to find creative solutions that recognize the legitimacy of other interests and at the same time enable us to pursue the questions most meaningful to us as archaeologists. We have not done well in overcoming public misperceptions of archaeology and replacing them with more accurate understandings. Political sophistication and effective public outreach will become increasingly necessary, and an important aspect of professional training.

A number of features are shared by pre-Columbian societies of North America and Mesoamerica. There was almost no use of metal other than for rare ritual objects except in Mesoamerica, where copper and bronze working reached west Mexico from South America by AD 600–900 and was widespread by the 1400s (Hosler 1988; Hosler and Macfarlane 1996). Dogs were important from very early times, and used in some places for food and/or transport, but otherwise there were no beasts of burden; in itself a good reason for not developing wheeled vehicles (though wheels were known and used on animal figurines in Mesoamerica). The only other domesticated animals of importance were some birds, especially turkeys. Maize became a staple in all agricultural areas, though it was both preceded and supplemented by numerous other domesticated plants, particularly in the eastern US. Socially complex societies with marked difference in rank among members were developing in parts of Mesoamerica as early as 1500 bc (uncalibrated; about 1800 BC in calendar years) and by the last centuries BC there were societies organized as states. Ranked societies also existed in parts of North America, although none should be called states. In any case, labels such as 'chiefdom' and 'state' do not do justice to the range of variation in how societies were organized and how and why they changed over time. A vast amount remains to be learned and understood regarding changes in social complexity.

The antiquity of humans in the New World is still hotly contested. A Clovis horizon *c.*9500 bc (uncalibrated) is well established in North America and Mesoamerica. Wide acceptance of a date around 10,500 bc for the human occupation of Monte Verde in southern Chile (Dillehay 1996; Meltzer *et al.* 1997) is leading archaeologists throughout the Americas to re-examine early but equivocal sites and to renew the search for truly ancient sites. Many (including Cowgill) doubt whether sites that are much earlier will be found, but the question will not be resolved without considerably more exploration in all parts of the New World. At present there are two plausible routes for the earliest migrations; along the Pacific coast (using boats to move rapidly from north-eastern Asia to southern South America) and overland down the so-called ice-free corridor. Cowgill favours the former because he thinks it makes sense of the Monte Verde date; the others of us are more neutral.

Mesoamerica

General issues

Mesoamerica extends from central and south-eastern Mexico through northern Central America, including Guatemala, Belize, El Salvador, western parts of Honduras and Nicaragua, and north-western Costa Rica (Fig. 1). Although the extent of Mesoamerica varied somewhat over time the spatial definition given by Kirchhoff (1943) remains valid. This region is characterized by great linguistic diversity and considerable diversity in culture, but a recognizable 'family resemblance' distinguishes Mesoamerican cultures from those of northern Mexico and southern Central America. It includes traditions such as 'Aztec', 'Maya', 'Olmec', 'Toltec'; and many others.

Environments range from coastal lowlands that are narrow in places but quite broad elsewhere (especially in the Yucatán peninsula) to upland plateaux (up to around 2700 m) and areas of canyons and high rugged mountains. The lowlands are hot but the highlands are generally cool. Rainfall is extremely varied, in places averaging over 2000 mm per year (especially in parts of the lowlands) but as little as 300 mm elsewhere.

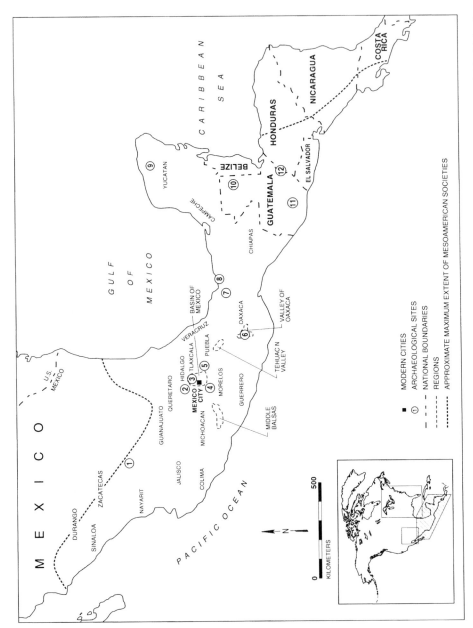

Figure 1. Mesoamerica. Numbered sites are 1, La Quemada; 2, Tula; 3, Teotihuacan; 4, Xochicalco; 5, Cacaxtla-Xochitécatl; 6, Monte Albán; 7, San Lorenzo; 8, La Venta; 9, Chichén Itzá; 10, Tikal; 11, Kaminaljuyú; 12, Copán. Many, but not all, states of Mexico are indicated.

Much of Mesoamerica, especially in the uplands, is semi-arid; dry during much of the year and quite rainy for a few months in the summer. In drier parts irrigation greatly improves reliability and sizes of harvests.

A few sites have been subjects of multiple large archaeological projects, such as Teotihuacan (in the Basin of Mexico); Monte Albán (in the Valley of Oaxaca); and Tikal, Copán, and Chichén Itzá (all in the Maya area) (Fig. 1), and important work has been carried out at many other sites. Nevertheless, much remains to be learned from even the most intensively studied sites, and their further exploration, using new techniques and with reference to newly-formulated problems, will be a major task for the twenty-first century. Furthermore, large parts of Mesoamerica are still almost unknown archaeologically. This is especially true outside focal regions listed above. Sheer exploration remains an important task in much of Mesoamerica.

Survey is an important aspect of exploration. Beyond exploration, systematic studies of settlement patterns were stimulated by the seminal work of Gordon Willey (1956). Area surveys have been conducted in several regions, especially in the highlands, including the Basin of Mexico (Sanders et al. 1979), other parts of central Mexico (e.g. García Cook 1981; Mastache and Cobean 1989; Hirth and Angulo Villaseñor 1981), parts of Oaxaca (Marcus and Flannery 1996; Blanton et al. 1999), and parts of the Gulf Lowlands (Stark and Arnold 1997). It is important to emphasize, however, that survey techniques and intensities have varied greatly. Many surveys, even when labelled 'full coverage' (Fish and Kowalewski 1990) have only recorded sites visible to workers walking 20 to 50 metres apart. Many archaeological occurrences that would be considered important data in some other regions, such as the US Southwest and Eastern Woodlands, are surely being missed. It is unlikely that truly intensive surveys will ever be feasible for most of Mesoamerica. A combination of full coverage of large areas (hundreds or thousands of square kilometres) at low intensity and high intensity surveys of selected smaller areas is likely to be the best realistic compromise.

Even in the more-studied areas chronologies usually have a resolution of no better than two centuries, and minimal time units are often three centuries or more. Such coarse-grained chronologies are woefully inadequate for studies of culture process (M. Smith 1992). We urgently need finer relative chronologies based on ceramics and other materials, many more radiocarbon dates firmly connected to relevant contexts, and the application of sophisticated statistical methods for combining multiple radiocarbon dates with stratigraphy and other kinds of chronological information (Buck et al. 1996). Results from other methods for estimating absolute dates, such as obsidian hydration, have been controversial but further research may improve this situation.

In short, vastly more remains to be done by way of establishing accurate time-space frameworks and tracing stylistic and technological continuities and discontinuities, however unfashionable these tasks may be in some quarters. By no means should there be a moratorium on proposing interpretations and explanations. However, such work will remain needlessly speculative and prone to demonstrable error if it is not anchored in vastly better knowledge of what, when, and where. Research on how, why, and who should proceed concomitantly.

Artefact typology is important for both description and interpretation. In North America in the 1930s and 1940s there was explicit discussion of systematics, culminating by the late 1950s in a fairly well-developed paradigm, often expressed in 'type-variety' terminology (Lyman *et al.* 1997). This approach has been widely adopted in the Maya area but has not been so well received in many other parts of Mesoamerica. It serves fairly well for the broad outlines of time-space systematics but lends itself less well to finer-grained chronologies and to investigation of processes reflected by partial resemblances in time and across space. Such resemblances used to be interpreted in terms of migrations and diffusion. Over-reliance on purported migrations provoked a tendency to be sceptical of *all* proposed migrations, but in Mesoamerica there is abundant evidence for many migrations, based on languages and indigenous traditions, as well as strictly archaeological data. Major problems remain in determining *who* migrated, *from* where and *to* where, and *when*, as well as *why*.

Diffusion is a hopelessly vague and abstract way to characterize interactions, which we now think about in terms of phenomena such as gift exchange (especially among élites), commercial trade, willing emulation/imitation, forcibly imposed changes, and active signalling of belongingness and otherness. Archaeological practice often produces typological units and concepts that are inappropriate for all these topics, yet criticisms (e.g. Dunnell 1971; Cowgill 1990) have not led to widely accepted new practices. Studies that go beyond traditional typological methods tend to be *ad hoc* innovations. Both processualists and postprocessualists have been surprisingly neglectful of problems with typology. Methods more attuned to questions that go beyond coarse time-space systematics are increasingly desirable in Mesoamerica as elsewhere, and this should become an area of active innovation, supported by the information storage and processing capabilities of electronic media.

Specific topics

Most archaeological attention in Mesoamerica has been concentrated on sites with ceramics, or at least with evidence bearing on plant domestication. Adequately funded searches will undoubtedly reveal far more evidence of early hunters and the time-space distribution of their varied adaptations.

Mesoamerica was an independent centre of domestication of many plants, including maize and several species of beans, cucurbits (squash, pumpkins, gourds), amaranths, *chiles*, avocados, and others. Manioc may have been important also in early times. Work in the 1960s, especially by MacNeish and others in the Tehuacán Valley (MacNeish 1981) and by Flannery and his colleagues in the Valley of Oaxaca (Flannery

1986; Marcus and Flannery 1996), seemed to have filled in the broad outlines of the story of domestication in Mesoamerica — so much so that their achievements probably discouraged others from what was seen as merely filling in details. In the past few years the topic has come alive again. AMS radiocarbon dates are unexpectedly early for some domesticates (e.g. cucurbits, as early as 6–8000 BC) (B. Smith 1997a, 1997b). Plant genetic studies have confirmed teosinte as the wild ancestor of maize and suggest a plausible centre of its domestication in the low altitude middle Río Balsas region of the Mexican state of Guerrero (Doebley 1990). Recognition is growing that the pioneering studies, crucial as they were, left many uncertainties (Hardy 1996, 1999; Flannery 1973; Flannery and MacNeish 1997; Buckler *et al.* 1998; Fritz 1994). The time is ripe for a new wave of research on this topic, and the early twenty-first century is likely to produce important changes in our ideas about regions, dates, and tempos of domestication, and in our explanations for this major transition.

Agriculture and the earliest use of ceramics clearly do not go hand-in-hand. Unexpectedly, some of the earliest pottery in Mesoamerica, from the Pacific lowlands of Chiapas and Guatemala, around 1550 bc, is not crude or utilitarian, but consists of very finely made serving vessels, often modelled after gourds. Styles are distinctively local, but the technology was probably acquired from Central or South America, where pottery-making began earlier. Clark and Blake (1994) and Clark and Gosser (1994) argue that pottery was adopted for competitive feasting by individuals bent on gaining prestige and the political advantages associated with prestige. Persons with access to this surprising new material could out-compete those who still relied on decorated gourds for beverages (most likely maize beer) at feasts they hosted. Perhaps this interpretation will not be supported in all details, but it has usefully shaken up comfortable assumptions that innovations such as ceramics were adopted in order to solve utilitarian problems. It is contrary to what adaptationist models would suggest, but it fits well with practice theory and notions of social agency, which are likely to be increasingly used in explanations of the Mesoamerican archaeological record.

By 2000 BC farming villages were well established in many parts of Mesoamerica. Before 1200 bc (1500 BC calibrated) some showed notable internal differences in richness of grave goods and quality of residences. Most famed of these is the 'Olmec' phenomenon of the southern Gulf Lowlands *c.*1200–400 bc, with spectacular sites such as San Lorenzo and La Venta, celebrated for colossal stone heads, other multi-ton monuments, and large earthworks. These were societies in which a few élite individuals enjoyed a considerable degree of dominance over sizeable populations. There has been a rather tedious debate over whether these societies should be labelled 'chiefdoms' or 'states', hampered by abstract and simplistic concepts about types of political systems inherited from the 1970s and earlier. Advances will come partly from improvements in theory. More data are also badly needed from more excavations at the major sites and from far more regional surveys. Happily, some surveys have been carried out (Grove 1997).

Miguel Covarrubias (1946) called Olmec the 'mother culture' from which all other Mesoamerican great traditions derived. Debate over this view persists (e.g. Sharer and Grove 1989; Grove 1997). Some argue for Gulf Lowlands pre-eminence and priority, while others call attention to numerous developments at about the same time elsewhere in Mesoamerica and suggest that 'sister culture' would be a better term. This debate will be settled partly by more data from diverse regions and better chronological control. We will also profit from sharper conceptualization of just what is, and is not, being claimed by various proponents. Kin metaphors, useful in their time, no longer seem productive because they tend to conflate several issues. One is determining the regions in which the earliest strong ranking occurred, where some individuals acquired great wealth, influence, and authority. Another is the extent to which there were regionally developed early 'great traditions' that owed little or nothing to innovations in the Olmec heartland. To what extent did elements of the 'Olmec style' originate outside this heartland (e.g. in Guerrero, Oaxaca, and/or the Pacific lowlands of Chiapas and Guatemala)? Some important elements may have originated elsewhere, but on present evidence they were integrated into more complex expressions in the heartland by a society that could mobilize unprecedented resources for monumental ceremonial structures and great art. Another issue is whether interactions with the Olmec heartland stimulated increases in social complexity elsewhere that, without such interactions, would have occurred significantly later or possibly not at all. Finally, there is the question of the extent to which (if at all) heartland Olmec centres ever had any degree of economic or political domination over other regions and, if so, when.

Pre-Columbian Mesoamerica was long described in terms of rises and falls of 'empires', movements of peoples, and their periods of ascendancy and decline. Beginning with Armillas (1948), and strongly influenced by Steward (1949, 1955), developmental stages were proposed as organizing concepts. Following early hunters and archaic foragers and incipient food-producers, these stages were Preclassic or Formative, Classic, and Postclassic (Fig. 2). Supposedly the Preclassic saw the development of agricultural villages, leading up to the glories of the Classic era (c.AD 200/300–900), when 'theocratic' priest-led and generally peaceable societies built ceremonial centres and splendid pyramids. This was thought to be followed by more secular and 'militaristic' leadership in the Postclassic, and probably by increased importance of a merchant class. The terms Preclassic, Classic, and Postclassic were also deemed to have chronological significance although different authors cheerfully assign absolute dates to these periods that sometimes differ by several centuries.

As descriptions of types of societies and their changes, these stages and their subdivisions are now hopelessly inadequate. Another characterization is in terms of 'horizons' of relative stylistic uniformity, separated by intermediate periods of greater regional diversity (e.g. Sanders et al. 1979). The horizon concept was extremely useful for chronology before many radiocarbon dates were available but it has become prob-

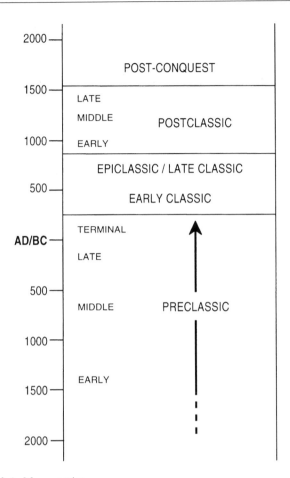

Figure 2. Major periods in Mesoamerica.

lematic as an interpretive concept and many Mesoamericanists feel a need to replace both stages and horizons with other concepts (e.g. most of the contributors in Rice 1993). One difficulty is that the old stages no longer characterize the various eras as they are now understood. For example, already by the Middle Preclassic many Mesoamerican societies were far from simple villages, and by the Late Preclassic (by anyone's definition), very complex and stratified societies with monumental civic-ceremonial architectural groups were widespread in Mesoamerica.

Another notable difficulty is that the Classic period no longer seems especially peaceable. There is abundant evidence for concern with war in Maya inscriptions and iconography, as well as at highland sites in Oaxaca (e.g. Marcus and Flannery 1996; Spencer and Redmond 1997) and central Mexico. At Teotihuacan there is good evidence for mass sacrifice, soon after AD 200, of about 200 individuals, many (though not all) dressed as soldiers (Cabrera *et al.* 1991; Sugiyama 1993, 1995). This is not to say that religion was unimportant or that agricultural fertility and general social and individual well-being were not also of great importance. Religiosity is not at all inconsistent with militarism. By the same token, the importance of war and conquest in the Postclassic era (well attested by historical records) does not mean that religion had declined in significance.

This dissatisfaction with evolutionary stage terminology and schemes of alternating horizons and eras of greater regional diversity has not yet been met by any widely accepted new set of concepts. There have been attempts to apply notions such as 'world systems', derived from Wallerstein (1976), but their applicability in Mesoamerica is probably limited. Concepts borrowed from Braudel (1972) such as *longue durée* and *conjoncture* are probably useful in a very general way, but they need to be filled with a fairly specific content that is still lacking. Creation and/or borrowing of better concepts for characterizing periods of the Mesoamerican past is badly needed and is a challenge for the twenty-first century.

For the Classic period, it is unclear whether many generalizations apply to societies as apparently diverse as those of the Lowland Maya and the highland city of Teotihuacan. There have been dramatic advances in decipherment of Maya inscriptions in the past few decades and there is every reason to think these will continue. Epigraphers can now read an impressive proportion of the inscriptions with considerable security. They are generally terse and sanctified, pertaining overwhelmingly to accounts of élite achievements and pedigrees. Business, legal and administrative documents, extended chronicles, and literature are absent and very unlikely to be found (although many survive from Postclassic and Colonial times). Nevertheless, the Maya inscriptions provide a wealth of data lacking for other Classic period societies. Debate seems to be less over what the inscriptions say than how they are to be interpreted. Undoubtedly there is a large element of self-serving propaganda, but the texts are surely not wholly unrelated to actual events and situations. Discovery of new texts, further decipherments, and fuller integration of epigraphic and archaeological data will continue to be very active and productive. To some extent epigraphers and field archaeologists have tended to see themselves in opposition to one another, but it seems obvious that the various sources of information are complementary.

A great deal remains to be learned about Classic Maya societies, but clearly there were a number of political centres and dynastic lineages, legitimizing their rule through descent as much as through personal achievements. It is also clear that armed conflict among centres was common and no one centre was overwhelmingly the most powerful. Debate continues over whether there were many autonomous statelets or a few paramount centres that exercised political dominance over lesser centres. The situation doubtless changed considerably over time.

In sharp contrast, the highland city of Teotihuacan, which covered about 20 square kilometres with an estimated population of around 100,000, overwhelmingly dominated the Basin of Mexico and adjoining parts of central Mexico. Inscriptions at Teotihuacan are far more limited than in the Maya area and use a different system of standardized notation (Langley 1986, 1992). So far they have provided little solid information, and interpretations are based largely on archaeology and iconography. Given the extent of the city, surface survey followed by problem-oriented excavations in selected places has been emphasized. Comprehensive mapping and surface survey directed by René Millon in the 1960s provides a baseline for all further work (Millon 1973; Millon *et al.* 1973). The collections and data files of this mapping project are a resource for new methods of spatial and statistical analysis (e.g. Robertson 1999).

The iconographic 'low profile' of Teotihuacan rulers suggests that there may have been relatively little emphasis on inheritance of office within a single dynastic lineage, and it is possible that rulers were selected from among a number of élite lineages by some sort of election process (Cowgill 1997). Further research may test this conjecture. The spatial extent of Teotihuacan political control beyond central Mexico is unclear and was perhaps not large, but Teotihuacan 'presences' or 'influences' of diverse and generally still poorly understood kinds were widespread in Mesoamerica, reaching over 1100 km to the Maya area. After a period of scepticism about the significance of these influences (Schele and Freidel 1990; Demarest and Foias 1993) mounting evidence (much still unpublished) suggests that Teotihuacan-related persons actively intervened in local politics and even assumed rulership at lowland sites such as Tikal and Copán and at the highland site of Kaminaljuyú (Kidder *et al.* 1946; Sanders and Michels 1977). This by no means implies that any part of the Maya area was ever administered from Teotihuacan.

Models of Teotihuacan commerce proposed by Santley (1983, 1984) were based on little evidence and overdrawn (Clark 1986), but Teotihuacan commerce was not negligible. The nature and extent of Teotihuacan commercial activity remain highly unclear. Evidence for military symbolism at Teotihuacan is abundant, and it is very unlikely that the Teotihuacan state could have risen to dominance in central Mexico (in the Terminal Preclassic and the beginning of the Early Classic) without having been militarily effective, but the scale and practical significance of war may have declined thereafter. Military symbolism was only one aspect of Teotihuacan public religion, which also focused on agricultural fertility and other concerns.

In Oaxaca, a Zapotec-speaking state centred on Monte Albán was already expanding in Late Preclassic times (Marcus and Flannery 1996; Blanton *et al.* 1999). Expansion ended during the Classic but Monte Albán successfully resisted Teotihuacan. Oaxacan inscriptions are considerably more extensive and more deciphered than those of Teotihuacan, but less so than Maya inscriptions, and in a notational system different from both (Marcus and Flannery 1996).

The interval between the decline and collapse of the Teotihuacan state (and the burning and abandonment of the principal civic-ceremonial structures of the city) and the rise of the 'Toltec' state centred on the site of Tula is called 'Epiclassic' in central Mexico. This seems to have been a watershed in Mesoamerica, perhaps the initiation of a new Braudelian cycle. New ceramic styles appear in central Mexico that are related to apparently earlier developments to the north-west, in and around the state of Guanajuato. It is possible, though still not demonstrated beyond reasonable doubt, that the first sizeable influx of Nahua-speakers arrived in central Mexico at this time. (Nahuatl, the language of the Aztec empire, is a member of the Uto-Aztecan family, whose heartland is well north-west of central Mexico.) Elsewhere in central Mexico, at about this time (chronological imprecision is especially irksome here), new centres arose that often combined local traditions with stylistic and symbolic elements of Maya derivation (cf. chapters by Nagao and Baird in Diehl and Berlo 1989). Principal examples are Xochicalco in the state of Morelos and Cacaxtla-Xochitécatl in Tlaxcala. There are numerous debates and unsolved problems, and the Epiclassic period is a subject of very active research.

This period appears also to be poorly understood in Oaxaca. In the Maya Lowlands the early part of this interval (especially in the 700s) saw a Late Classic climax, followed by decline in the 800s. Though the lowlands were never totally abandoned, population declined drastically in a large part of the Southern Lowlands (Culbert and Rice 1990), and remained low until late in the twentieth century. This localized demographic collapse is still not satisfactorily explained. In the Northern Lowlands, especially in the states of Yucatán and Campeche, there was no such decline, and sites of the 'Puuc' and other regional styles flourished.

During the Early Postclassic, Tula, in Hidalgo, became a pre-eminent centre in central Mexico. It exhibits a number of traits derived from central and north-western Mexico, but a number of very specific features are shared with the Northern Lowland Maya site of Chichén Itzá. Tozzer (1957) and others postulated an invasion of the Northern Maya Lowlands from central Mexico. His scenario has been widely criticized, and some scholars (e.g. Kubler 1961) have gone so far as to propose that innovations went in the opposite direction, from Chichén to Tula. Probably few Mayanists would go that far, but many still minimize the influence of Tula to an extent that seems ill-informed from a central Mexican perspective. Here, again, chronological imprecisions contribute to the murk.

The dominating event of the Late Postclassic was the rise of the Aztec Empire, centred on the Basin of Mexico, which conquered most of what is now central and southern Mexico. In west Mexico the Purépecha ('Tarascan') state fought the Aztecs to a standstill. This period is marked by an abundance of ethnohistoric sources, including surviving indigenous documents and oral traditions, ethnographic works by Spaniards, and Spanish and indigenous legal and administrative records. The very richness of these resources, plus the extent to which Late Postclassic settlements are often underneath present-day settlements, has discouraged Late Postclassic archaeology in central Mexico. Happily, this situation is changing; considerably more archaeology is being done and it is better integrated with the ethnohistoric and iconographic data (e.g. Berdan *et al.* 1996; Hodge 1984, 1998; Hodge and Smith 1994; Matos Moctezuma 1988; Charlton *et al.* 1991; Otis Charlton *et al.* 1993; Evans 1988; M. Smith 1996; Brumfiel 1996). Modes of interpreting ethnohistoric sources are also improving; there is less effort to 'winnow' grains of 'historic truth' from confused or legendary chaff, and far more awareness of the contexts in which the materials were produced, and the presuppositions, perceived interests, and intended audiences of the producers (e.g. Gillespie 1989; Lockhart 1992; Mónaco 1998). These newer interpretations are sometimes controversial and do not always pay enough attention to archaeological data, but further work integrating archaeological and ethnohistorical knowledge will be extremely productive.

Western and north-western Mexico have been unjustly neglected by many Mesoamericanists. It is useful to distinguish a southerly western area, roughly including Querétaro, Guanajuato, Michoacán, Guerrero, Colima, southern and central Jalisco, and Nayarit. Relatively elaborate developments, including fine ceramics and shaft tombs, begin in the Early to Middle Preclassic in western parts of this area. There were connections with the west coast of South America, including some stylistic resemblances in pottery, figurines, textiles, use of shaft tombs, and eventually the introduction of metal-working (Hosler 1988; Hosler and Macfarlane 1996). By middle Classic times there were large centres with elaborate ceramics in Colima and northward along the Sinaloa coast. Inland in Zacatecas, Durango, and northern Jalisco there is as yet no evidence for strong chiefdoms or small states much before the Epiclassic, and by Early Postclassic times these seem to have declined inland (Nelson 1997), although they lasted longer in Colima, Nayarit, and Sinaloa.

Still further to the north-west the Greater US Southwest begins. It is culturally very distinct, but it was never wholly isolated from Mesoamerica. Maize and some other domesticates came from Mesoamerica. Some motifs on Hohokam ceramics in southern Arizona, *c.*AD 550–900, resemble some of those in Epiclassic Zacatecas and Durango and, given chronological uncertainties in both areas, derivation from north-western Mesoamerica does not seem implausible. A little later, copper bells and other metal objects in the US Southwest undoubtedly came from far western Mesoamerica (Vargas 1994). Macaws, parrots, and other birds important in Southwestern rituals were obtained from Mesoamerica, although in Late Postclassic times the Southwestern site of Paquimé (in northern Chihuahua) appears to have bred scarlet macaws, partly for local ritual use but probably also for distribution to other sites (Rizo 1998). There is no clear evidence that Mesoamericans were obtaining much from the US Southwest before the Epiclassic, but after that Mesoamericans used a significant amount of turquoise from Southwestern US sources (Weigand and Harbottle 1993).

Other supposed ties are more problematic. Features in some Southwestern sites interpreted as ballcourts bear a vague resemblance to the ballcourts widespread and important in Mesoamerica, and possibly derive from Mesoamerica (Scarborough and Wilcox 1991). Some symbols associated with Katsina ritual clearly have ties to Mesoamerica but most researchers (e.g. Adams 1991; Crown 1994) see the religious developments as a Southwestern phenomenon. Numerous other ideational aspects, such as colour and directional symbolism, are shared in a general way but are found widely elsewhere in the New World, and may derive from a very early common heritage.

Some US Southwesternists emphasize the cultural autonomy of the region they study and minimize Mesoamerican connections. Others have been curiously eager to argue for much stronger connections, often to the point of offering interpretations now shown to be clearly incorrect in some cases and at least doubtful in others (e.g. Di Peso 1974; Kelley and Kelley 1975). These interpretations will probably dwindle with time. The degree to which beliefs about the extent and nature of connections between Mesoamerica and the US Southwest have been driven by considerations other than 'raw' archaeological data poses fascinating problems in the history of archaeological thought. Mesoamerican connections to the south-eastern US were once thought to have been instrumental in the origins of late prehistoric Mississippian societies, but Milner notes that such ideas have all but disappeared from the literature due to a complete lack of evidence for them.

The Greater US Southwest

Background and perspectives

The Southwest culture area, which includes the US Southwest and northern Mexico (Fig. 3), is traditionally distinguished by the practice of agriculture in an arid environment. An exceptional diversity of non-state social forms (both ethnographic and archaeological) that defy categorization as 'tribes' or 'chiefdoms' also characterize the Southwest and are the focus of much research. Cordell (1997) provides an excellent overview of Southwest archaeology.

Most research has focused, and probably will continue to focus, on three major archaeological areas, distinguished environmentally and materially. The Hohokam area has irrigable rivers and encompasses the biotically rich and very hot (frequently over 38° C) Sonoran desert. The diverse and mountainous Mogollon area is fairly well watered but has patchy arable land. The Ancestral Pueblo (formerly called Anasazi) area encompasses the northern Southwest; it has much arable land, but freezes and the scarcity of water limit productivity. In general, except in some parts of the southern Southwest, surplus crop production was limited prehistorically by the paucity and unpredictability of precipitation.

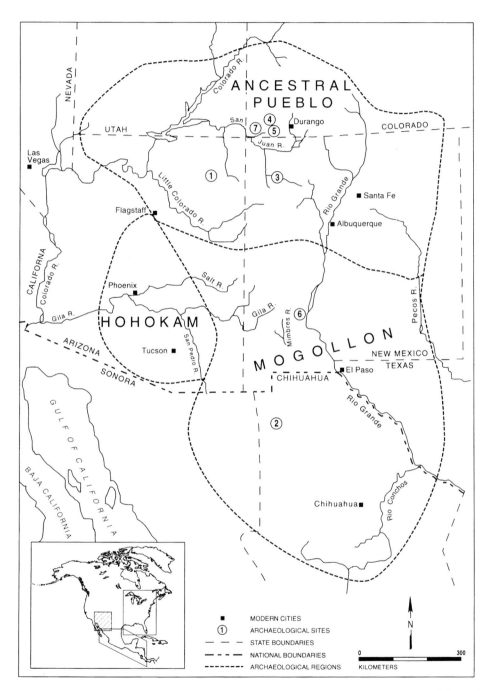

Figure 3. Map of the Greater Southwest. Archaeological sites and areas are indicated by encircled numbers as follows: 1, Black Mesa; 2, Paquimé (Casas Grandes); 3, Chaco Canyon; 4, Dolores; 5, Mesa Verde; 6, Ronnie Pueblo; 7, Sand Canyon Pueblo.

Borders and boundaries will be important in the future of Southwest archaeology. The immense amount of archaeological work done in the Southwest makes it necessary for many researchers to focus on one area, and this is unlikely to change. However, work that crosses the areal boundaries (e.g. Adler 1996; Gumerman 1994; Lekson 1999) or that compares developments in the Southwest with other areas of the world (e.g. Kolb and Snead 1997; Neitzel 1999) will also become increasingly common, both because researchers are recognizing the need to understand pan-Southwestern phenomena and because electronic data (if they are available in usable form) will facilitate syntheses and comparisons. In addition, areal boundaries themselves are likely to be an important topic of research, involving issues such as technological style (Hegmon 1998) and the transfer of technology (Reid and Montgomery 1998; Zedeño 1995). Finally, northern Mexico, although long considered to be part of the Southwest, has only recently received much attention by US and Mexican scholars (e.g. Kelley and Villalpando 1996; B. Nelson 1999; though some important earlier work is summarized in Riley and Hedrick 1978), and we look forward to new insights gained as a result of multi-national collaboration. We hope the border will also be crossed in the other direction, and that more Mexican archaeologists will work in the US.

Many native peoples in the Southwest today are descendants of the prehistoric residents. Some links, such as those between contemporary Pueblo peoples and many Ancestral Pueblo sites, are unambiguous, while others are more complex. Given that NAGPRA requires the determination of the cultural affiliation of human remains and other sacred objects, we expect continued focus on the relationship between native groups and the prehistoric record. Such research has the potential to be enormously frustrating, since many of today's tribal distinctions have little antiquity. However, such research may also lead to new kinds of theoretical and cultural insights — involving issues such as ethnicity and methods of interpreting oral tradition as history — particularly if native scholars are fully involved (see Dongoske *et al.* 1997).

The arid environment, masonry construction, and relatively limited re-use of sites all contribute to exceptional preservation of the archaeological record in the Southwest. Precise chronologies involving 50–100 year phases are common, and in some areas sequences of site construction and occupation can be dated to the year with dendrochronology (e.g. Dean 1969; Lightfoot 1994). Dendroclimatology and other techniques also provide a wealth of palaeoenvironmental information (e.g. Dean 1988; Petersen 1988). As a result, the Southwest had been called a 'laboratory' for archaeological research (Longacre 1970, 1–3) particularly in the heyday of the New Archaeology. The archaeological record is indeed an exceptional resource, but it is a laboratory only to the extent that researchers ask good questions of it. We expect that archaeologists studying the Southwest in the next millennium will continue work on time-space systematics and topics of long-standing interest (such as the relation between cultural processes, demography, and environmental changes), and that these archaeologists will also address more recently defined issues, such as the nature of power. In addition, we hope that future researchers will pursue topics unfathomable at the end of the twentieth century, and that those of us active today will be open to the questions of the next generation.

Chronological developments

Most research in the Southwest has focused, and will probably continue to focus, on the agricultural periods, although more research on the earlier periods would certainly be fruitful (Table 1). The major cultigens (maize, beans, squash, and gourds) were domesticated in Mesoamerica, but maize in the Southwest probably does not pre-date 2000 BC

Table 1. Chronology of major developments in the Southwest.

Date	Major Developments
AD 1539	First Spanish contact
AD 1300	Begin spread of new ceramic and religious traditions, extensive trade networks, new social and architectural organization, population concentrates and many areas are abandoned
AD 1280–1300	Depopulation of northern San Juan region; migrations southward
AD 1200s	Major developments at Paquimé (Casas Grandes); aggregation in many areas
AD 1150–1450	Hohokam Classic
AD 1150	Decline of Chaco and Hohokam regional systems; Mimbres reorganization
AD 975–1150	Height of Hohokam regional system
Early AD 1100s	Height of Chaco regional system
AD 1000–1130	Classic Mimbres Period
AD 700	Above-ground Pueblo architecture
300–500 BC	First domestic beans in SW
1000 BC	Established agricultural villages in southern SW
2000–1500 BC	Earliest maize in SW

(Smiley 1994). Squash and gourds were roughly contemporary with corn, but domestic beans may not have been present until 300–500 BC. Local native plants were also domesticated but probably not used as extensively as their counterparts in eastern North America. The domesticates seem to have spread rapidly, as early maize is found in all three areas/environments (Smiley 1994). Early cultivation in the Mogollon and Pueblo areas seems to have been incorporated into a mostly gathering and hunting lifestyle (Wills and Huckell 1994). In contrast, some of the most interesting research in the past decade is demonstrating that the earliest crops in the southern Southwest were grown by people who relied heavily on farming, who (by *c*.1000 BC) established some of the earliest villages in the Southwest (Fish *et al.* 1992; Huckell 1995), and who even constructed massive terraced sites (Hard and Roney 1998). Continued work at sites with early domesticates, combined with increasingly detailed genetic and nutritional analyses of the domestic and wild resources and the palaeoenvironment, will add to our understanding of these processes. We also hope that future research will address the various social and subsistence strategies involved; for example, understanding how and why early domesticates were important as sources of basic nutrition in some contexts, as portable and storable resources in others (Wills 1988), and as prestige goods in others (see Hayden 1998).

Pithouses and shallow houses-in-pits were the earliest forms of residential architecture in the Southwest. Pithouse settlements are traditionally labelled 'villages', but this category is extremely variable. Early pithouses sites in the southern Southwest seem to have been true villages housing settled cultivators, while pithouse sites in other areas were associated with more mobile adaptations until more than a millennium later (Wills and Windes 1989). Above-ground architecture, including pueblos, was first constructed *c*.AD 700, although pithouses continue well after that date in many areas. The pithouse-to-pueblo transition was once thought to signal a switch to a sedentary lifestyle, but this assumption has been questioned (Gilman 1987). In general, the nature of mobility is likely to be an important topic in future work. New multi-dimensional concepts of mobility do away with the simple dichotomy between 'sedentism' (i.e. living year-round in one place) and 'mobility' (changing residences) (Rocek 1996; Varien 1999). Instead, focus is on issues such as the interrelation of community permanence and household movement (Varien 1999), or different forms of residential mobility (Gilman 1997; M. Nelson 1999). Future research should build on these theoretical insights and continue to develop methods for recognizing relevant variables, such as site use life (Varien and Mills 1997).

From approximately AD 900 to 1150 elaborate cultural developments characterized much of the Southwest. In the Mogollon area, the Classic Mimbres period (AD 1000–1130 in south-west New Mexico) is associated with aggregated sites concentrated along major drainages and elaborate pottery with naturalistic designs (LeBlanc 1983; Fig. 4). The Chaco regional system (Crown and Judge 1991; Lekson *et al.* 1988), centred in Chaco Canyon, covered much of the Puebloan Southwest (*c*.65,000 km^2) by the early 1100s. It is recognized by the distribution of Chaco-style ritual architecture at 'outlier' sites. Large quantities of goods (including pottery and timber) were moved into Chaco Canyon (which may have been a locus of ritual pilgrimages (Judge 1989)), but few goods seem to have been moved to or among the outliers. The Hohokam regional system (Crown and Judge 1991; Gumerman 1991) stretched across much of southern Arizona, reaching its maximum extent between *c*.AD 975–1150. It is similarly recognized by ritual architecture (ballcourts) and by the distribution of other forms of material culture, but it lacks a single nucleus. Large quantities of goods — including shell, ground stone, ceramics, and probably agricultural and forest products — were distributed throughout the system, possi-

CM

Figure 4. Classic Mimbres Black-on-white bowl from Ronnie Pueblo in the Mimbres region of south-west New Mexico, AD 1100s (Nelson, M.C. 1999).

bly by means of traders and trade fairs as well as kin networks (Doyel 1991; McGuire and Howard 1982). Much remains to be learned about these developments: Did these regional systems involve some sort of political or social control? To what extent were they linked economically? What was the role of ritual in these processes?

Ongoing and future research in the non-core areas such as the Chacoan outliers (Kantner and Mahoney 2000) and the eastern Mimbres area (Hegmon *et al.* 1998; M. Nelson 1999), as well as large-scale synthetic work (Crown and Judge 1991; Doyel 1992; Lekson n.d.; Neitzel 1999) will make important contributions to our understandings of these regional phenomena.

Enormous efforts devoted to chemical and mineralogical sourcing are contributing to a detailed understanding of where goods (especially pottery) were made and distributed, as part of the Chaco and Hohokam systems and in other contexts (e.g. Abbott and Walsh-Adouze 1995; Harry 1997; Glowacki and Neff in press; Miksa 1998; Simon and Burton 1998). These data should set the stage for two avenues of future research. First, Southwest archaeologists (e.g. Mills and Crown 1995) are recognizing the need to expand Costin's (1991) multi-dimensional model of production and specialization to encompass the kinds of variables that are important in societies less politically complex than those discussed by Costin. Second, much research is still needed to better understand the mechanisms by which goods were moved, the extent to which such movement should be assumed to be the result of 'exchange', and the organization of exchange (e.g. Doyel 1991; papers in Hegmon 1999). Such research will profit from the sourcing data and from increasing attention to the varying distributions of different classes of artefacts in order to distinguish the movement of material from the movement of people (Zedeño 1994). In addition, insights gained from ethnographic and theoretical research on production and exchange (e.g. Healey 1990; Weiner 1992; Wiessner and Tumu 1998) may provide Southwestern researchers with new perspectives and models.

The centuries between AD 1100 and 1300 saw major changes in large-scale organizations and prehistoric land use. Major developments at Paquimé (Casas Grandes) are now dated to the 1200s (Dean and Ravesloot 1993) and are linked to a complicated economic system that may have affected much of the southern Southwest (Minnis 1988; Schaafsma and Riley 1999). AD 1150 marks the end of both the Chaco and Hohokam regional systems and the Mimbres Classic period. In the Hohokam area this date marks a shift from an expansive system to a more intensive and concentrated occupation — centred around Phoenix and Tucson — known as the Hohokam Classic (c.AD 1150–1450), and researchers have long recognized both continuity and change in the Hohokam area. Recent research is recognizing such continuity and change in the other areas as well. Chacoan ideational concepts continued to be important after 1150, as represented in pottery forms, architecture, and settlement location (Bradley 1996; Kintigh *et al.* 1996; Fowler and Stein 1992; Lekson 1999). Interpretation of post-1150 Mimbres developments as regional reorganization (Hegmon *et al.* 1998) similarly emphasizes both continuity and change. These findings suggest that future research needs to reconceptualize ideas such as 'collapse', at least for non-state societies such as those seen in the Southwest. Such research will also benefit by considering the concept of archaization (see *World Archaeology* 1998), that is, how the societies we study used their own past. This process has long been recognized in the Southwest (e.g. the link between early pithouses and later ritual structures known as kivas) but rarely examined systematically or theoretically.

The archaeological record of the Southwest documents many population movements into, and especially out of, areas such as the Dolores (Schlanger and Wilshusen 1993) and Mimbres (M. Nelson 1999) River Valleys or northern Black Mesa (Plog 1986). By the 1200s, people who had lived in small settlements across the northern Southwest aggregated in a series of large villages and towns such as Sand Canyon Pueblo (Fig. 5).

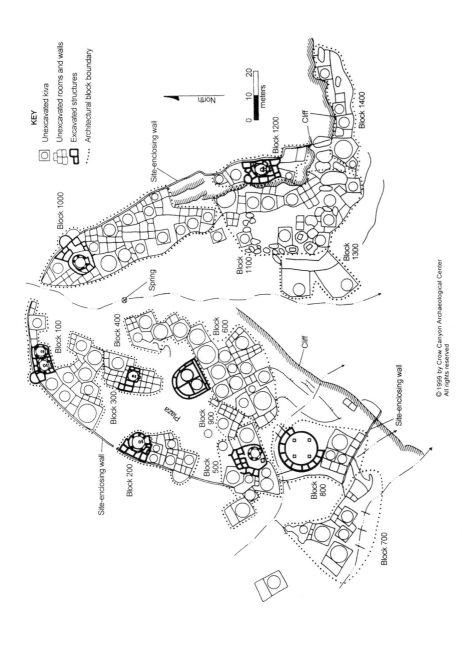

Figure 5. Sand Canyon Pueblo, an aggregated town site in the northern San Juan region, occupied c.AD 1250–1280 (reproduced from Varien and Kuckelman 1999, fig. 1.5).

But by the end of the century, these aggregated sites were abandoned, and *c.*10,000–30,000 people left the northern San Juan or Mesa Verde region of south-west Colorado and moved south (see Cameron 1995), many to the area around the northern Rio Grande in New Mexico. Such population movements have been, and will continue to be, topics of intense research interest. Future research will involve a re-evaluation of the concept of 'abandonment' (Fish *et al.* 1994; M. Nelson 2000), both because it is objectionable to Native peoples (Ferguson 1996b) and because many so-called abandonments are better viewed as changes in settlement and mobility strategies, as discussed above. Detailed data regarding palaeoenvironmental conditions and patterns of variation, and GIS-based reconstructions of agricultural productivity (e.g. Brady 1999; Dean *et al.* 1994; Tainter and Tainter 1996; Van West 1994), will continue to be important in this research and should be interpreted in relation to information on the social and cultural landscape (e.g. Lipe 1995). A related issue also likely to receive increasing attention is human environmental impact (Redman 1999), including evidence of environmental degradation (e.g. Kohler and Matthews 1988; Minnis 1985) and research into the sustainability of strategies such as high residential mobility (Nelson and Anyon 1996; M. Nelson 1999).

AD 1300 represents a major turning point in Southwest prehistory. Changes in ceramic and architectural traditions indicate shifts in the nature of community and the organization of religion (see Lipe 1989; Spielmann 1998a). Beginning with the depopulation of the northern San Juan, populations continued to concentrate in smaller and smaller portions of the Southwest (Fish *et al.* 1994), leaving many areas devoid of residential occupation at the time of Spanish contact in 1539. The post-1300 period is characterized by many pan-Southwestern developments such as the spread of iconography and new religious systems (Adams 1991; Crown 1994), exchange systems that spanned much of the Southwest and beyond (Spielmann 1991), and the eventual decline of Paquimé. These issues should continue to receive considerable attention and may benefit from perspectives that consider the interrelationships among religion, production and exchange, and social power (e.g. Spielmann 1998b; see discussion of power below). Migration is today receiving considerable attention (e.g. Herr 1999; papers in Spielmann 1998a), and we hope that future research will continue to gain insights from geography (see Anthony 1990) while at the same time building models that are applicable to non-urban societies with long traditions of residential mobility (see Herr and Clark 1997). Finally, research on the post-1300 period will continue to investigate processes of community formation and organization (e.g. Mills 1998), often involving disparate groups with distinct traditions. Communities or groups of settlements are sometimes described as 'multi-ethnic', and we hope future research will carefully consider the concept of ethnicity, including whether and how it is applicable to pre-state societies (see Shennan 1990).

General issues

Although women have long made major contributions to the anthropology and archaeology of the Southwest, and considerable attention has focused on their contributions
(e.g. Bishop and Lange 1991; Parezo 1993), the Southwest has been a latecomer to the
tremendous recent growth in feminist archaeology and the archaeology of gender.
Recent work (e.g. Crown and Fish 1996; Spielmann 1995) suggests that the Southwest
has much to offer to these approaches. In the Southwest, it is quite often possible to
identify the activities of women and men prehistorically, both through the analysis of
skeletal morphology (Martin 2000) and archaeological evidence such as the distribution
of grinding features (Mobley-Tanaka 1997; Ortman 1998). However, efforts to engender
our understanding of prehistory must do more than simply engender activity analyses,
they must also incorporate insights from feminist theory and address issues such as
relations between genders and their varying degrees of autonomy, power, and status
(Conkey and Gero 1991; Ortner 1996). For example, we know prehistoric Pueblo
women spent hours every day grinding corn; should we interpret their labour as a
source of economic empowerment or as oppressive drudgery? Important insights can
be gained by comparing different contexts and assessing how activities changed in relation to other social and cultural changes. This kind of comparative perspective is taken
in a recent volume (Crown 2000), which we expect will direct much productive research
on gender in Southwest prehistory.

     Puebloan peoples have long been characterized as relatively peaceful and egalitarian
— perhaps harking back to Benedict's (1934) depiction of them as Apollonian — and
archaeologists had often assumed the same for the prehistoric Southwest. Recent
research is changing our perspectives in both respects. The existence and nature of prehistoric violence is the focus of much recent research involving both skeletal studies
(e.g. Martin 1997; Turner and Turner 1999) and analyses of settlement location and
structure (Bernardini 1998; Haas and Creamer 1993; Le Blanc 1999; Rice 1998b) and
iconography (Plog and Solometo 1997). Evidence of violence in various forms spans
much of the past two millennia and includes cases of what appear to be institutionalized abuse of women (Martin 1997); mutilation and processing of human bone that is
sometimes (controversially) interpreted as cannibalism (Turner and Turner 1999; but
see Darling 1998; also Walker 1998); and injuries/deaths that result from raiding
(Lightfoot and Kuckelman 1995). Unfortunately, many of the human remains cannot be
restudied because they have been or will soon be reburied, but future research will
likely focus on understanding the contexts of the various kinds of violence. For example, more work is needed (perhaps involving more collaboration between physical
anthropologists and archaeologists) on understanding the distribution of violence with
regard to social and cultural developments. Analyses of site distributions and other
logistical variables, in addition to cross-cultural comparisons (e.g. Keeley 1996) may

also facilitate a better understanding of the apparent raiding; did it involve endemic intra-village conflict or raiding by outsiders?

New theoretical developments have recently directed Southwestern researchers away from debates about whether prehistoric societies were egalitarian *or* hierarchical and towards sophisticated understandings of myriad forms of power and complexity (e.g. B. Nelson 1995; McGuire and Saitta 1996; Potter 1997a). Although this work is certainly influenced by Foucault as well as Wolf (1990; see also 1999), it draws most heavily on several other sets of ideas. One involves ethnographic evidence regarding Pueblo secrecy and ritual control (especially Brandt 1994; Whiteley 1988). That is, Pueblo leadership, although sometimes hierarchical, is linked to esoteric and ritual knowledge and has few material or economic manifestations (recall the Southwest's limited potential for surplus production). Second, researchers working in other areas of the world have explored diverse organizational forms such as heterarchy (Ehrenreich *et al.* 1995) and the distinction between corporate and network strategies (Blanton *et al.* 1996), and researchers have begun to apply these concepts to the prehistoric Southwest (Mills 2000). Finally, Southwest researchers have been strongly influenced by theoretical and historical work by Giddens (1984), Bourdieu (1990) and Mann (1986) that develops concepts regarding symbolic power and authoritative resources. This (non-material) topic is obviously not an easy one for archaeologists, but future work in the Southwest is likely to make significant advances in our understanding of these kinds of power, particularly through analyses of ritual spaces and ritually significant materials (Graves 1996; Potter 1997b, 1998), and by focus on the results of leadership (such as labour mobilization) rather than the identification of leaders (Plog 1990; Sebastian 1992). These analyses will also be advanced by comparing Puebloan developments to those in the Hohokam area where large-scale irrigation (involving more than 800 km of canals, some 20 m wide) facilitated surplus production and where élite leadership (i.e. residences and stores of preciosities on platform mounds) have more obvious material manifestations (Rice 1998a; Wilcox 1991), as well as by comparisons between the Southwest and other areas of the world (Neitzel 1999).

Approaches based on practice theory (Bourdieu 1990), or structure and agency perspectives (Giddens 1984), have great potential in the Southwest, although they are only recently gaining much popularity. Just as gender research involves more than the identification of women, practice-based perspectives must involve much more than the identification of individuals. At the same time, practice approaches are facilitated by a record in which it is possible to identify details such as the movement of a specific group of people (e.g. Haury 1958). For example, the detailed record of settlement and ritual change in south-west Colorado in the ninth century AD allowed Schachner (2001) to identify contexts in which agents tried (and in the long-term apparently failed) to institute ritual changes. One of the most important directions for future research involving practice theory is development of the relationship between agency *and* structure, or between practice *and* habitus. Varien (1999) has demonstrated this kind of approach by considering how the construction of a site contributes to the structure of the social landscape and thus influences future construction. Numerous other issues might benefit from these approaches. For example, the mobility of an individual in relation to the development of a migration stream and subsequent social change could be conceptualized in terms of agency and structure. The fairly rapid development and dissolution of the Chacoan network might be examined from the perspective of the time-space distanciation of an institution. Or reproduction, variability, and change in domestic architecture could be investigated from the perspective of habitus and the potential of practice to bring about change.

Finally, new approaches to architecture, as well as new conceptions of space and place are likely to be important in future research in the Southwest. Space syntax analysis is becoming increasingly popular as a means of analysing site layout (e.g. Bustard 1996; Fangmeier 1998; Ferguson 1996a; Potter 1998; Shapiro 1997) and its use should continue to provide important information. Architectural and engineering studies will provide data regarding labour and building requirements relevant to issues such as communal labour and leadership. In addition, architectural training (and contributions from archaeologically informed architects) should continue to give archaeologists new insights into issues such as the construction of features (such as berms) with unknown function (Thompson *et al.* 1997) and use of the landscape (Fowler and Stein 1992). Geographers, social theorists, and cultural anthropologists are increasingly developing theoretical understandings of place, in contrast and in relation to space. Although this terminology is rarely used in Southwest archaeology today, we expect that conceptions of place will become increasingly important in the future. A sense of place is clearly vital to Southwestern peoples today (e.g. Basso 1996; Swentzell 1988), and the concept is important to research closely tied to issues such as community (Varien 1999), mobility, and connections to residentially 'abandoned' areas (M. Nelson 2000).

Eastern North America

The Eastern Woodlands stretches from the Atlantic Coast westward to the states bordering the Mississippi River, and from the Gulf Coast northward into Canada (Fig. 6). Forest composition varied throughout this broad region according to temperature and moisture gradients (warmer to the south and drier to the west), as well as elevation (the Appalachian Mountains). Lying to the west of what was once virtually a continuous forest were extensive prairies, broken up by long fingers of woodlands flanking major rivers. Modern vegetation patterns were for the most part established during the early Holocene, and by the mid-Holocene the sea-level had risen to its current position, which in many places involved a considerable landward movement of the coastline.

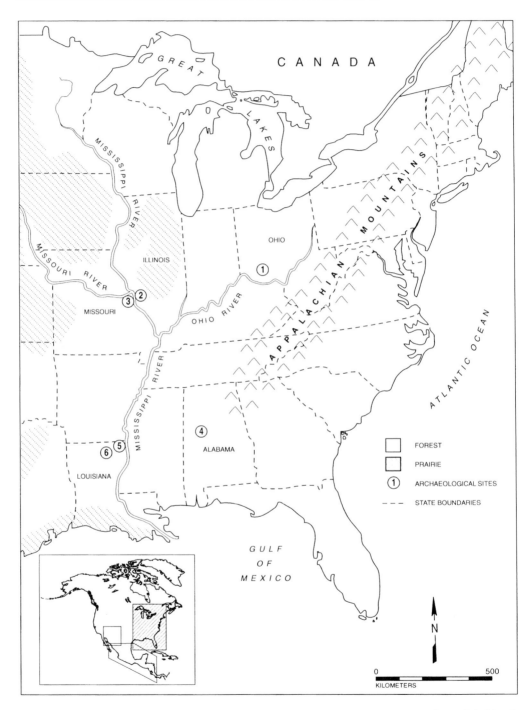

Figure 6. Eastern North America showing sites mentioned in the text: 1, Hopewell; 2, Cahokia; 3, Kimmswick; 4, Moundville; 5, Poverty Point; 6, Watson Brake.

The current understanding of eastern North American prehistory is a pastiche of solid archaeological data, field lore, and extrapolations from historical and ethnographic materials (Fig. 7). Much like other parts of the Americas, research emphases over the past several decades have shifted from artefact description and chronology building, to settlement patterns and subsistence, to the social, political, economic, and ritual lives of ancient peoples. Yet it is precisely the emphasis on local concerns, such as the refinement of chronological sequences, that makes it possible to address more broadly applicable research topics. Theoretical issues current in anthropology and allied disciplines certainly influence eastern North American archaeology, but too often studies go no further than the use of jargon to mark positions staked out in scholarly debates. Better linkages are needed between theoretically based arguments and appropriately sampled and analysed data.

Early dates from Monte Verde — the human occupation of Chile about 12,500 radiocarbon years ago (Dillehay 1996; Meltzer *et al.* 1997) — will undoubtedly trigger additional interest in the peopling of eastern North America. But for now, Paleoindians known primarily for their lanceolate, mostly fluted, points are the earliest reasonably well-documented inhabitants of eastern North America.

The Paleoindian occupation of the East was uneven, at least as viewed from the distribution of projectile points (Anderson 1996). For example, the distributions of different Paleoindian points vary across geologically distinct parts of Illinois, much of which was once covered by glaciers (Wiant 1993). As with other efforts to deal with artefacts and sites scattered across broad geographical areas, any inferences drawn from observed patterns are confounded by collector, recording, preservation, and site visibility biases.

The nature of Paleoindian subsistence strategies continues to be debated, although increasingly these peoples are characterized more as generalized foragers than as specialized hunters (Anderson 1996; Meltzer 1988; Meltzer and Smith 1986). There is little direct evidence for big-game hunting — once thought to epitomize Paleoindian subsistence practices — although stone tools have been found associated with the bones of extinct megafauna at sites such as Kimmswick in eastern Missouri (Graham *et al.* 1981; for a few other sites see Anderson 1996 and Meltzer 1988).

The following seven millennia — the Early, Middle, and Late Archaic periods — spanned changes in hunter-gatherer sedentism, interregional exchange, intercommunity conflict, and subsistence strategies. All such topics deserve further work, building on the solid foundation of research undertaken over the past few decades (Anderson and Sassaman 1996; Brown 1985a; Phillips and Brown 1983; Sassaman and Anderson 1996). The largest of the sites were deep middens or shell heaps in especially resource-rich places that date from the late Middle Archaic to Late Archaic periods (Dye 1996; Jefferies and Butler 1982; Russo 1996b). Change over time in settlements, however, was not a simple shift in one direction towards larger size, longer

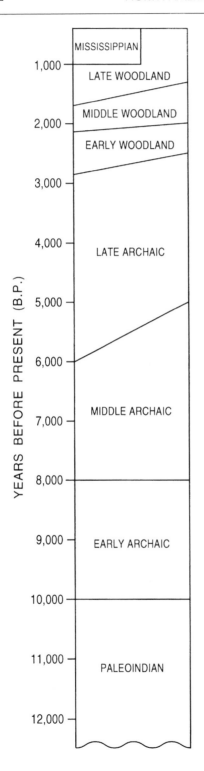

Figure 7. Major culture periods in Eastern Woodlands prehistory. The dating of periods varies across this large region, and much of that variation is indicated by diagonal lines. Societies labelled Mississippian were present in the southern Eastern Woodlands, whereas elsewhere Late Woodland societies persisted to the time of contact.

duration, and reduced seasonal mobility. Settlement size, configuration, and longevity varied from one time and place to another, topics that deserve more attention (Sassaman 1995).

Work on the geographical distribution of stylistically distinctive Middle Archaic and later objects, such as bone pins and some large projectile points, is beginning to delineate groups of widely separated hunter-gatherers who maintained some form of regular interaction with one another (Jefferies 1996, 1997; Johnson and Brookes 1989). Such studies are being conducted on the spatial scale needed to understand interactions among hunter-gatherers.

A person's status in Archaic societies, in addition to being dictated by age and sex, was heavily influenced in at least some places by that individual's productive and reproductive capacity. Disabled people were differentially treated (Buikstra 1981), and old people had fewer artefacts than those who died in the prime of life (Milner and Jefferies 1998). Such conclusions are best derived from large samples of skeletons, the majority of which come from midcontinental sites excavated during the Great Depression of the 1930s. These collections must be reanalysed because age and sex estimates made many decades ago are often erroneous, important skeletal characteristics such as trauma from intergroup conflict were not always recognized, and the original field notes contain unpublished information essential for systematic analyses of artefacts and the spatial arrangements of burials and other features. The need for such work underscores the continuing importance of museum collections, although many skeletal samples are unfortunately threatened with reburial.

The earliest steps to agriculture were deeply embedded in the Archaic, as was the early production of food storage or preparation containers fashioned from steatite, pottery, and cucurbits (Sassaman 1993; Smith 1986, 1989). The transition to agriculture in the Eastern Woodlands has been a topic of great interest since the early twentieth century. But knowledge about this process derives mostly from studies following the widespread adoption of flotation, a field procedure first used in the Midwest during the 1960s, and analyses of the stable carbon isotope composition of human bone.

Eastern North America is now regarded as an independent centre for the origin of agriculture (Smith 1989, 1995). Several plants that yield starchy or oily seeds were grown along with cucurbits, collectively known as the Eastern Agricultural Complex, long before maize and beans were introduced, ultimately from Mesoamerica. The most heavily used native plants varied from one place to another, presumably according to human subsistence needs and plant habitat requirements.

Both native cultigens and maize were in use in the midcontinent long before they became important, indeed essential, parts of diets. The first domesticated forms of several native cultigens date as far back as 1000 to 2000 BC (Smith 1989, 1995). But people widely scattered across the southern Midwest and northern Southeast did not rely heavily upon these plants until about AD 1, during the Middle Woodland period. Maize first appeared at about AD 200, but only around AD 1000 did it become an important element of the diets of many Late Woodland and Mississippian peoples (Fritz 1995; Smith 1989, 1995).

Stable carbon isotope signatures of human skeletons and plant remains from habitation sites indicate that the transition to a heavy reliance on maize occurred within just a few centuries across much of the Eastern Woodlands (Buikstra 1992; Katzenberg *et al.* 1995; Smith 1989). It is only now becoming apparent that this relatively sudden shift in subsistence strategies was not the first rapid transformation in food procurement strategies. During the Middle Woodland period, several native cultigens rather abruptly became a major component of diets in many parts of the midcontinent. People elsewhere, however, continued to rely mostly on wild plants, especially hickory nuts and acorns (Fritz 1995).

It therefore appears that the transition from a fully hunting-and-gathering way of life to one based largely on agriculture was indeed long, but it was far from gradual. The overall pattern is best characterized by long periods of near stasis punctuated by episodes of rapid change spanning only a few centuries that resulted in more productive subsistence strategies in many places. It seems that incremental changes in existing ways of life had only a limited capacity to accommodate new circumstances. Research should focus on identifying the particular conditions that led to step-like shifts in subsistence strategies, particularly the selective advantage conferred by new food procurement practices and attendant changes in ways of life. This is just one example of a situation where the pace of change at different times, not only its overall direction, demands our attention.

Earthen mounds were built in some places as early as late Middle to Late Archaic times, usually small ones for burial purposes but also large complexes of unknown function such as Watson Brake and Poverty Point in Louisiana (Gibson 1996; Russo 1996a; Saunders *et al.* 1997). However, mounds did not become common in many areas until the Middle Woodland period (Brose and Greber 1978; Pacheco 1996). They were accompanied by large geometric earthworks in some places, particularly in the middle Ohio River Valley. Middle Woodland societies also are known for elaborate mortuary-related artefacts, many of which were fashioned from non-local materials. While some people in many of these societies were differentiated from everyone else in how they were buried, similarly sharp distinctions have not been found in habitation sites (Smith 1992). In addition to a mortuary function, the geometric earthwork enclosures were places where poorly understood socially and ritually significant activities were conducted, including feasting and the fashioning of exotic, symbol-laden artefacts (Smith 1992). More research should be directed towards the role of mound and earthwork complexes in the social integration of the local populations responsible for these impressive sites.

The nature of Middle Woodland exchange systems, at least those encompassing the middle Ohio River Valley, remains to be explained. Large hoards of valued materials from distant places, such as copper, mica, and obsidian, have been found in mortuary contexts at a few sites. The overall distribution of some of these items and the presence of a few huge caches of them — including obsidian from Wyoming, most of which was found at the Hopewell site in Ohio (Greber and Ruhl 1989) — indicate that something other than simple down-the-line exchange was occasionally at work. Social boundaries must have been permeable enough to allow at least a few people, perhaps on rare occasions, to travel unhindered across long distances for as yet unexplained reasons.

Late prehistoric societies, especially those referred to as Mississippian, have received disproportionate attention over the past two decades. Mississippian chiefdoms, which date from the eleventh century AD to early contact with European explorers, had their roots in the smaller and organizationally simpler societies of the terminal Late Woodland (or Emergent Mississippian) period (Smith 1990). These chiefdoms, regardless of their size, seem to have been organized along similar lines (Milner 1998; Muller 1997). They ranged from simple chiefdoms with one administrative level above the local community to complex chiefdoms. The latter seem to have been serially homologous groups of large and small sites where one centre, accompanied by its own closely affiliated subordinate communities, was dominant over the others. Each segment of a complex chiefdom was politically quasi-autonomous and economically self-sufficient, at least in the goods needed for survival.

Existing linkages among chiefs — probably more political than economic in nature — permitted the rather rapid emergence of large regional chiefdoms. Just such a process seems to have taken place near Cahokia in Illinois and Moundville in Alabama, two of the most impressive Mississippian sites (Milner 1998; Knight and Steponaitis 1998; Pauketat 1994, 1997; Steponaitis 1991). Yet complex chiefdoms appear to have been riven by factional competition (Anderson 1994a, 1994b). Paramount chiefs found it difficult to control their principal subordinates, subchiefs who enjoyed the backing of their own supporters. At Cahokia, for example, it eventually became necessary to erect a strong palisade, probably for protection from ostensibly subordinate chiefs elsewhere in the region (Milner 1998).

Mississippian chiefdoms were different from earlier societies, such as those responsible for the impressive Middle Woodland mounds, by having both mortuary and habitation contexts indicating the existence of people who enjoyed a higher social position than the bulk of the population. But despite distinctions in architecture and artefacts separating people of high and low rank, there is no clear-cut and consistent skeletal evidence demonstrating that important members of these societies either ate better or were healthier than everybody else (Powell 1998; Schoeninger and Schurr 1998).

Archaeologists have different opinions about the roles of chiefs in Mississippian societies, but it seems that prestigious positions often were associated with success in war (Anderson 1994a, 1994b; Brown 1985b). Impressive artefacts, including finely engraved marine shells, have been found that depict elaborately costumed warriors wielding weapons and holding severed heads. Such an emphasis is consistent with the development of organizationally similar societies in many places over a period spanning no more than a few centuries. This process probably was related to the necessity of matching the warrior mobilization potential of antagonistic neighbours in increasingly competitive social settings.

The origin and organization of these societies have been attributed to the self-serving activities of far-seeing and highly efficient leaders who utterly enthralled their social inferiors with a newly created ideology and its attendant symbols (Pauketat 1994, 1997). Emphasis is placed on the supposed control of chiefs over their subordinates. Other archaeologists adopt a more bottom to top perspective, with the ordinary needs of lowly households having a much greater effect on changes in basic ways of life and the fundamental character of Mississippian chiefdoms (Milner 1998; Muller 1997). Here agency is moved from a few to many people; i.e. from the chiefs and their principal henchmen to all members of society regardless of their rank. The trajectory of chiefdom development is only likely to be understood by delineating the complex and ever-changing interactions among environmental settings, population pressure on resources, risk minimization strategies, conflicting interests of variously constituted sociopolitical groups within these societies, and both cooperative and antagonistic contacts among separate societies.

There is also disagreement over the extent to which chiefs in the most powerful Mississippian societies exerted control over distant peoples. The largest of the Mississippian societies, centred on Cahokia, has been cast as a giant that controlled a vast area, even to the extent of shipping bulk commodities on a regular basis across hundreds of kilometres to feed a valley teeming with hungry people (Dincauze and Hasenstab 1989). It is certainly true that non-local materials, such as marine shell, copper, and particular kinds of pottery, are found scattered thinly across broad areas. But because of poor sampling, such items loom disproportionately large in our vision of prehistory. The places traditionally targeted for excavation — large sites, mounds, and cemeteries — are precisely those most likely to yield the most artefacts and the fanciest ones. Once analysed quantitatively, the distributions of chert hoes and shell gorgets conform closely to what would be expected in down-the-line exchanges encompassing many people from widely distributed communities (Brown et al. 1990; Muller 1995, 1997). Speculation about models inappropriately borrowed from elsewhere, such as World Systems Theory (even gutted forms of the original concept), far outstrips attempts to support such notions with convincing data. Much of the movement of highly prized non-local materials and artefacts was undoubtedly conducted under the aegis of chiefs and their close kinfolk. But non-local materials also passed through net-works that linked common villagers, and these transactions occurred simultaneously with those between chiefs and other important people (Milner 1998). Thus the needs and interests of common folk deserve as much attention as those of their social superiors.

Work is already under way that will produce a more balanced view of Mississippian societies — from the largest to the smallest settlements. In some places, such as around Cahokia, small settlements and what went on in them are better understood than the large mound centres, even though the latter are disproportionately repre-sented in the earlier literature (Milner 1998). Elsewhere the situation is reversed, such as in the Moundville area where much more is known about the composition and configuration of large centres than small settlements (Steponaitis and Knight 1998; Welch 1991).

Individual households in large and small sites have received considerable attention over the past quarter century (Mehrer 1995; Milner 1998; Muller 1997; Rogers and Smith 1995). We are still far from an adequate understanding of the range of variation in domestic architecture and artefacts, and what such variation might mean in terms of household composition, activities, and social standing. But with more information comes the realization, which should have been obvious at the outset, that most people most of the time were muddling along, doing what they could in their own short-term self interest with widely shared but imperfect knowledge about their natural and social environments.

Despite a widespread reluctance to acknowledge evidence of prehistoric warfare, the subject has begun to attract increasing interest during recent years (Anderson 1994a; DePratter 1991; Dye 1990; Milner 1999). It is now clear that warfare practices — from frequent ambushes to occasional massacres — closely approximated conflicts described in the ethnographic and historical literature (Milner *et al.* 1991). In addition, casualties were at times as high as those in better-documented, conflict-prone societies from more recent times (Keeley 1996).

But the interesting issue is not whether people in prehistory fought one another. There can be no doubt that conflicts occurred, despite the curious persistence of overly romantic notions about distant times (Sale 1990). The question that needs to be asked is much more difficult to answer: why did conflicts break out more often and were more severe in some times and places than in others? The late prehistoric period, in particular, was a time of worsening intergroup relations in many parts of the Eastern Woodlands (Milner 1999). Conflict-related trauma increased late in the first millen-nium AD, about the time the bow-and-arrow, an admirable stealth-attack weapon, was widely adopted (Blitz 1988; Seeman 1992; Shott 1996). A few centuries later pal-isades began to be a common feature of settlements in Mississippian chiefdoms as well as the more northerly tribal-scale societies referred to as Late Woodland or Upper Mississippian.

Palisaded sites, particularly major centres, became common in the southern Eastern Woodlands from the eleventh century AD onward, coincident with the development of Mississippian chiefdoms (Milner 1999). In the northern Eastern Woodlands, an area for the most part dominated by weakly integrated constellations of villages, the numbers of sites with palisades increased in the eleventh century and then yet again in the fifteenth century. The later increase coincided with the onset of the Little Ice Age when times got harder and the hazards of living in suboptimal areas became greater. Various strategies for coping in places with a high likelihood of resource shortfalls deserve more attention than they have received (O'Shea 1989). Incidentally, this topic is also applicable in the Mississippian area. In at least one river valley, chiefdom success, or lack of it, was related to the frequency of stretches of bad years that exceeded storage capabilities (Anderson *et al.* 1995).

Studies of warfare and exchange systems are not the only investigations that will benefit from the systematic organization of archaeological data from broadly defined geographical areas. Throughout the Eastern Woodlands, better temporal controls and broader survey coverages, both largely a result of contract archaeology, have shown that even the best land — primarily river valleys — was spottily occupied by late prehistoric tribal to chiefdom-scale societies. Pockets of population were separated by unoccupied zones, some of which were quite large and included both uplands and resource-rich rivers and shorelines (Anderson 1991, 1994b; Milanich 1998; Snow 1995a). Clusters of settlements tended to be several tens of kilometres long, with the largest being somewhat in excess of a hundred kilometres (Hally 1993; Milner 1998; Snow 1995a). Most of the settlements were occupied by several tens of people to a few hundred of them, but the largest had up to a few thousand inhabitants (Milner 1998; Muller 1997; Snow 1995a; Steponaitis 1998). Frequently cited population figures in the low tens of thousands for Cahokia, the biggest site in the Eastern Woodlands, are based on questionable assumptions and biased data. Large population estimates have the unfortunate effect of bolstering correspondingly exaggerated notions of sociopolitical complexity and economic interdependence, including the existence of exploitative cores and farflung impoverished peripheries.

Throughout the Eastern Woodlands, an ever-changing distribution of people and fluctuating regional population histories characterized the late prehistoric period. While the details have yet to be fully worked out, archaeologists must come to grips with sociopolitical and demographic landscapes that were more dynamic than previously recognized. A number of areas have been identified that underwent marked population increase or abandonment over a few centuries or less (Anderson 1994b; Butler 1991; Milner 1998; Snow 1995a). This realization should encourage more research on population expansion and decline, including migration and the displacement of earlier peoples (Snow 1995b). Some communities on the advancing front of population movements suffered numerous casualties in violent confrontations with their enemies

(Milner *et al.* 1991; Santure *et al.* 1990). Once again, the need to compile information from numerous projects in many places makes data access, organization, and comparability some of the most critical problems facing archaeologists today.

Acknowledgements

Cowgill thanks Ben A. Nelson and Barbara L. Stark for providing helpful comments and information and correcting some errors. Hegmon thanks Cathy Cameron, Bill Doelle, Kelley Hays-Gilpin, Steve Lekson, Barbara Mills, Peggy Nelson, Kate Spielmann, and Chip Wills for providing helpful comments and references. Several people graciously provided comments that strengthened the eastern North American section: David G. Anderson, Richard W. Jefferies, Claire McHale Milner, Sissel Schroeder, Dean R. Snow, and David Webster. Linda Countryman prepared Figures 1, 2, 3, 6, and 7. Figure 5 is courtesy of Crow Canyon Archaeological Center, Cortez, Colorado.

References

ABBOTT, D.R. and WALSH-ADOUZE, M.E. 1995: Temporal Patterns without Temporal Variation: The Paradox of Hohokam Red Ware Ceramics. In Mills, B.J. and Crown, P.L. (eds.) 1995, 88–114.

ADAMS, E.C. 1991: *The Origins and Development of the Pueblo Katsina Cult* (Tucson, AZ).

ADLER, M.A. (ed.) 1996: *The Prehistoric Pueblo III World: A.D. 1150–1350* (Tucson, AZ).

ANDERSON, D.G. 1991: Examining prehistoric settlement distribution in eastern North America. *Archaeology of Eastern North America* 19, 1–22.

ANDERSON, D.G. 1994a: Factional competition and the political evolution of Mississippian chiefdoms in the southeastern United States. In Brumfiel, E.M. and Fox, J.W. (eds.), *Factional Competition and Political Development in the New World* (Cambridge), 61–76.

ANDERSON, D.G. 1994b: *The Savannah River Chiefdoms: Political Change in the Late Prehistoric Southeast* (Tuscaloosa, AL).

ANDERSON, D.G. 1996: Models of Paleoindian and Early Archaic settlement in the lower Southeast. In Anderson, D.G. and Sassaman, K.E. (eds.) 1996, 29–57.

ANDERSON, D.G. and SASSAMAN, K.E. (eds.) 1996: *The Paleoindian and Early Archaic Southeast* (Tuscaloosa, AL).

ANDERSON, D.G., STAHLE, D.W. and CLEAVELAND, M.K. 1995: Paleoclimate and the potential food reserves of Mississippian societies: A case study from the Savannah River valley. *American Antiquity* 60, 258–86.

ANTHONY, D.W. 1990: Migration in Archaeology: The Baby and the Bathwater. *American Anthropologist* 92, 895–914.

ARMILLAS, P. 1948: A Sequence of Cultural Development in Mesoamerica. In Bennett, W.C. (ed.), *A Reappraisal of Peruvian Archaeology* (Society for American Archaeology, Memoir 4), 105–11.

BAREIS, C.J. and PORTER, J.W. (eds.) 1984: *American Bottom Archaeology* (Urbana, IL).

BASSO, K. 1996: Wisdom Sits in Places: Notes on a Western Apache Landscape. In Feld, S. and Basso, K.H. (eds.), *Senses of Place* (Santa Fe), 53–90.

BENEDICT, R. 1934: *Patterns of Culture* (Boston).

BERDAN, F.F., BLANTON, R.E., BOONE, E.H., HODGE, M.G., SMITH, M.E. and UMBERGER, E. 1996: *Aztec Imperial Strategies* (Washington, D.C., Dumbarton Oaks).

BERNARDINI, W. 1998: Conflict, Migration, and the Social Environment: Interpreting Architectural Change in Early and Late Pueblo IV Aggregations. In Spielmann, K.A. (ed.) 1998a, 91–114.

BISHOP, R.L. and LANGE, F.W. (eds.) 1991: *The Ceramic Legacy of Anna O. Shepard* (Niwot, CO).

BLANTON, R.E., FEINMAN, G.M., KOWALEWSKI, S.A. and NICHOLAS, L.M. 1999: *Ancient Oaxaca* (Cambridge).

BLANTON, R.E., FEINMAN, G.M., KOWALEWSKI, S.A. and PEREGRINE, P.N. 1996: A Dual-Processual Theory for the Evolution of Mesoamerican Civilization. *Current Anthropol.* 37, 1–14.

BLITZ, J.H. 1988: Adoption of the bow in prehistoric North America. *North American Archaeologist* 9, 123–45.

BOURDIEU, P. 1990: *The Logic of Practice* (translated by R. Nice) (Cambridge).

BRADLEY, B.A. 1996: Pitchers to Mugs: Chacoan Revival at Sand Canyon Pueblo. *Kiva* 61, 241–57.

BRADY, J.A. 1999: Agricultural Productivity in the Eastern Mimbres Area: A GIS Approach (Poster presented at the 64th Annual Meeting of the Society for American Archaeology, Chicago).

BRANDT, E.A. 1994: Egalitarianism, Hierarchy, and Centralization in the Pueblos. In Wills, W.H. and Leonard, R.D. (eds.), *The Ancient Southwestern Community* (Albuquerque), 9–23.

BRAUDEL, F. 1972: *The Mediterranean and the Mediterranean World in the Age of Philip II* (New York).

BROSE, D.S. and GREBER, N.B. (eds.) 1978: *Hopewell Archaeology* (Kent, OH).

BROWN, J.A. 1985a: Long-Term Trends to Sedentism and the Emergence of Complexity in the American Midwest. In Price, T.D. and Brown, J.A. (eds.), *Prehistoric Hunter-Gatherers: The Emergence of Cultural Complexity* (Orlando, FL), 201–31.

BROWN, J.A. 1985b: The Mississippian period. In *Ancient Art of the American Woodland Indians* (New York), 93–145.

BROWN, J.A., KERBER, R.A. and WINTERS, H.D. 1990: Trade and the evolution of exchange relations at the beginning of the Mississippian period. In Smith, B.D. (ed.) 1990, 251–80.

BRUMFIEL, E.M. 1996: Figurines and the Aztec State: Testing the Effectiveness of Ideological Domination. In Wright, R.P. (ed.), *Gender and Archaeology* (Philadelphia), 143–66.

BUCK, C.E., CAVANAGH, W.G. and LITTON, C.D. 1996: *Bayesian Approach to Interpreting Archaeological Data* (Chichester and New York).

BUCKLER IV, E.S., PEARSALL, D.M. and HOLTSFORD, T.P. 1998: Climate, Plant Ecology, and Central Mexican Archaic Subsistence. *Current Anthropol.* 39, 152–64.

BUIKSTRA, J.E. 1981: Mortuary practices, palaeodemography and palaeopathology: A case study from the Koster site (Illinois). In Chapman, R., Kinnes, I. and Randsborg, K. (eds.), *The Archaeology of Death* (Cambridge), 123–32.

BUIKSTRA, J.E. 1992: Diet and disease in late prehistory. In Verano, J.W. and Ubelaker, D.H. (eds.), *Disease and Demography in the Americas* (Washington, D.C.), 87–101.

BUSTARD, W.J. 1996: *Space as Place: Small and Great House Spatial Organization in Chaco Canyon, New Mexico, A.D. 1000–1150* (Ph.D. dissertation, Department of Anthropology, University of New Mexico) (Ann Arbor, University Microfilms).

BUTLER, B.M. 1991: Kincaid revisited: The Mississippian sequence in the lower Ohio valley. In Emerson, T.E. and Lewis, R.B. (eds.), *Cahokia and the Hinterlands: Middle Mississippian Cultures in the Midwest* (Urbana, IL), 264–73.

CABRERA, R., SUGIYAMA, S. and COWGILL, G.L. 1991: The Templo de Quetzalcóatl Project at Teotihuacan. *Ancient Mesoamerica* 2, 77–92.

CAMERON, C.M. (ed.) 1995: Special Issue: Migration and the Movement of Southwestern Peoples. *J. Anthropol. Archaeol.* 14(2).

CHARLTON, T.H., NICHOLS, D.H. and OTIS CHARLTON, C. 1991: Aztec Craft Production and Specialization: Archaeological Evidence from the City-State of Otumba, Mexico. *World Archaeol.* 23, 98–114.

CLARK, J.E. 1986: From Mountains to Molehills: A Critical Review of Teotihuacan's Obsidian Industry. In Isaac, B.L. (ed.), *Economic Aspects of Prehispanic Highland Mexico* (Greenwich, CT), 23–74.

CLARK, J.E. and BLAKE, M. 1994: The Power of Prestige: Competitive Generosity and the Emergence of Rank Societies in Lowland Mesoamerica. In Brumfiel, E.M. and Fox, J.W. (eds.), *Factional Competition and Political Development in the New World* (Cambridge), 17–30.

CLARK, J.E. and GOSSER, D. 1994: Reinventing Mesoamerica's First Pottery. In Barnett, W.K. and Hoopes, J.W. (eds.), *The Emergence of Pottery* (Washington, D.C.), 209–22.

CONKEY, M.W. and GERO, J.M. 1991: Tensions, Pluralities, and Engendering Archaeology: An Introduction to Women and Prehistory. In Gero, J.M. and Conkey, M.W. (eds.), *Engendering Archaeology: Women and Prehistory* (Oxford), 3–30.

CORDELL, L.S. 1997: *Archaeology of the Southwest* (New York, 2nd edition).

COSTIN, C.L. 1991: Craft Specialization: Issues in Defining, Documenting, and Explaining the Organization of Production. *Archaeological Method and Theory* 3, 1–56.

COVARRUBIAS, M. 1946: *Mexico South* (New York).

COWGILL, G.L. 1990: Artifact Classification and Archaeological Purposes. In Voorrips, B. (ed.), *Mathematics and Information Science in Archaeology: A Flexible Framework* (Bonn), 61–78.

COWGILL, G.L. 1997: State and Society at Teotihuacan, Mexico. *Ann. Rev. Anthropol.* 26, 129–61.

CROWN, P.L. 1994: *Ceramics and Ideology: Salado Polychrome Pottery* (Albuquerque).

CROWN, P.L. (ed.) 2000: *Women and Men in the Prehispanic Southwest* (Santa Fe).

CROWN, P.L. and FISH, S.K. 1996: Gender and Status in the Hohokam Pre-Classic to Classic Transition. *American Anthropologist* 98, 803–17.

CROWN, P.L. and JUDGE, W.J. (eds.) 1991: *Chaco and Hohokam: Prehistoric Regional Systems in the American Southwest* (Santa Fe, School of American Research).

CULBERT, T.P. and RICE, D.W. (eds.) 1990: *Precolumbian Population History in the Maya Lowlands* (Albuquerque).

DARLING, J.A. 1998: Mass Inhumation and the Execution of Witches in the American Southwest. *American Anthropologist* 100, 732–52.

DEAN, J.S. 1969: Chronological Analysis of Tsegi Phase Sites in Northeastern Arizona (Tucson, AZ, Papers of the Laboratory of Tree-Ring Research 3).

DEAN, J.S. 1988: Dendrochronology and Paleoenvironmental Reconstruction on the Colorado Plateaus. In Gumerman, G.J. (ed.), *The Anasazi in a Changing Environment* (Cambridge), 119–67.

DEAN, J.S., DOELLE, W.H. and ORCUTT, J.D. 1994: Adaptive Stress: Environment and Demography. In Gumerman, G.J. (ed.) 1994, 53–86.

DEAN, J.S. and RAVESLOOT, J.C. 1993: The Chronology of Cultural Interaction in the Gran Chichimeca. In Woosley, A.I. and Ravesloot, J.C. (eds.), *Culture and Contact: Charles C. DiPeso's Gran Chichimeca* (Albuquerque), 83–103.

DEMAREST, A.A. and FOIAS, A.E. 1993: Mesoamerican Horizons and the Cultural Transformations of Maya Civilization. In Rice, D.S. (ed.) 1993, 147–91.

DEPRATTER, C.B. 1991: *Late Prehistoric and Early Historic Chiefdoms in the Southeastern United States* (New York).

DIEHL, R.A. and BERLO, J.C. (eds.) 1989: *Mesoamerica After the Decline of Teotihuacan, A.D. 700–900* (Washington, D.C., Dumbarton Oaks).

DILLEHAY, T. 1996: *Monte Verde: A Late Pleistocene Settlement in Chile*, Vol. 2 (Washington, D.C.).

DINCAUZE, D.F. and HASENSTAB, R.J. 1989: Explaining the Iroquois: Tribalization on a prehistoric periphery. In Champion, T.C. (ed.), *Centre and Periphery* (London), 67–87.

DI PESO, C.C. 1974: *Casas Grandes: A Fallen Trading Center of the Gran Chichimeca* (Dragoon, AZ, Amerind Foundation).

DOEBLEY, J. 1990: Molecular Evidence and the Evolution of Maize. *Economic Botany* 44 (supplement), 6–27.

DONGOSKE, K.E., YEATTS, M., ANYON, R. and FERGUSON, T.J. 1997: Archaeological Cultures and Cultural Affiliation: Hopi and Zuni Perspectives in the American Southwest. *American Antiquity* 62, 600–8.

DOYEL, D.E. 1991: Hohokam Exchange and Interaction. In Crown, P.L. and Judge, W.J. (eds.) 1991, 225–52.

DOYEL, D.E. (ed.) 1992: *Anasazi Regional Organization and the Chaco System* (Albuquerque, Maxwell Museum of Anthropology, Anthropological Papers No. 5).

DUNNELL, R.C. 1971: *Systematics in Prehistory* (Riverside, NJ).

DYE, D.H. 1990: Warfare in the sixteenth-century Southeast: The De Soto Expedition in the Interior. In Thomas, D.H. (ed.), *Columbian Consequences*, Vol. 2 (Washington, D.C.), 211–22.

DYE, D.H. 1996: Riverine adaptation in the Midsouth. In Carstens, K.C. and Watson, P.J. (eds.), *Of Caves and Shell Mounds* (Tuscaloosa, AL), 140–58.

EHRENREICH, C.L., CRUMLEY, C.L. and LEVY, J.E. (eds.) 1995: *Heterarchy and the Analysis of Complex Societies* (Arlington, VA, Anthropological Papers of the American Anthropological Association, No. 6).

EVANS, S.T. 1988: *Excavations at Cihuatecpan: An Aztec Village in the Teotihuacan Valley* (Nashville, TN, Vanderbilt University Publications in Anthropology).

FANGMEIER, K.L. 1998: *A Pattern Recognition Analysis of Household Space and Activities in Two Pueblo Communities: Issues in Theory, Method, and Interpretation* (M.A. paper, Department of Anthropology, Arizona State University, Tempe).

FERGUSON, T.J. 1996a: *Historic Zuni Architecture and Society: An Archaeological Application of Space Syntax* (Tucson, University of Arizona, Anthropological Papers No. 60).

FERGUSON, T.J. 1996b: Native Americans and the Practice of Archaeology. *Ann. Rev. Anthropol.* 25, 63–80.

FISH, P.R., FISH, S.K., GUMERMAN, G.J. and REID, J.J. 1994: Toward an Explanation for Southwestern abandonments. In Gumerman, G.J. (ed.) 1994, 135–63.

FISH, S.K., FISH, P.R. and MADSEN, J.H. 1992: Early Sedentism and Agriculture in the Northern Tucson Basin. In Fish, S.K., Fish, P.R. and Madsen, J.H. (eds.), *The Marana Community in the Hohokam World* (Tucson, University of Arizona, Anthropological Papers No. 56), 11–19.

FISH, S.K. and KOWALEWSKI, S.A. (eds.) 1990: *The Archaeology of Regions: A Case for Full-coverage Survey* (Washington, D.C.).

FLANNERY, K.V. 1973: The Origins of Agriculture. *Ann. Rev. Anthropol.* 2, 271–310.

FLANNERY, K.V. 1986: *Guilá Naquitz: Archaic Foraging and Early Agriculture in Oaxaca, Mexico* (Orlando, FL).

FLANNERY, K.V. and MACNEISH, R.S. 1997: In Defense of the Tehuacán Project. *Current Anthropol.* 38, 660–70.

FOWLER, A.P. and STEIN, J.R. 1992: The Anasazi Great House in Space, Time, and Paradigm. In Doyel, D.E. (ed.) 1992, 101–22.

FRITZ, G. 1994: Are the First American Farmers Getting Younger? *Current Anthropol.* 35, 305–9.

FRITZ, G.J. 1995: New dates and data on early agriculture: The legacy of complex hunter-gatherers. *Annals of the Missouri Botanical Garden* 82, 3–15.

GARCÍA COOK, A. 1981: The Historical Importance of Tlaxcala in the Cultural Development of the Central Highlands. In Sabloff, J.A. (ed.), *Supplement to the Handbook of Middle American Indians. Volume One: Archaeology* (Austin, TX), 244–76.

GIBSON, J.L. 1996: Poverty Point and greater southeastern prehistory: The culture that did not fit. In Sassaman, K.E. and Anderson, D.G. (eds.) 1996, 288–305.

GIDDENS, A. 1984: *The Constitution of Society* (Berkeley, CA).

GILLESPIE, S. 1989: *The Aztec Kings: The Construction of Rulership in Mexican History* (Tucson, AZ).

GILMAN, P.A. 1987: Architecture as Artifact: Pit Structures and Pueblos in the American Southwest. *American Antiquity* 52, 538–64.

GILMAN, P.A. 1997: *Wandering Villagers: Pit Structures, Mobility and Agriculture in Southeastern Arizona* (Tempe, Arizona State University, Anthropological Research Papers No. 49).

GLOWACKI, D. and NEFF, H. (eds.) in press: *Chemical Sourcing in the Southwest* (Los Angeles).

GRAHAM, R.W., HAYNES, C.V., JOHNSON, D.L. and KAY, M. 1981: Kimmswick: A Clovis-Mastodon association in eastern Missouri. *Science* 213, 1115–17.

GRAVES, W.M. 1996: Social Power and Prestige Enhancement Among the Protohistoric Salinas Pueblos, Rio Grande Valley, New Mexico (Unpublished M.A. thesis, Department of Anthropology, Arizona State University, Tempe).

GREBER, N.B. and RUHL, K.C. 1989: *The Hopewell Site: A Contemporary Analysis Based on the Work of Charles C. Willoughby* (Boulder, CO).

GROVE, D.C. 1997: Olmec Archaeology: A Half Century of Research and Its Accomplishments. *J. World Prehist.* 11, 51–101.

GUMERMAN, G.J. (ed.) 1991: *Exploring the Hohokam: Prehistoric Desert Dwellers of the Southwest* (Albuquerque).

GUMERMAN, G.J. (ed.) 1994: *Themes in Southwest Prehistory* (Santa Fe, School of American Research).

HAAS, J. and CREAMER, W. 1993: *Stress and Warfare Among the Kayenta Anasazi of the Thirteenth Century AD* (Chicago, Field Museum of Natural History, Fieldiana: Anthropology N.S. 21).

HALLY, D.J. 1993: The territorial size of Mississippian chiefdoms. In Stoltman, J.B. (ed.), *Archaeology of Eastern North America: Papers in Honor of Stephen Williams* (Jackson, Mississippi Department of Archives and History, Archaeological Report 25), 143–68.

HARD, R.J. and RONEY, J.R. 1998: A Massive Terraced Village Complex in Chihuahua, Mexico, 3000 Years Before Present. *Science* 279, 1661–4.

HARDY, K. 1996: The Preceramic Sequence from the Tehuacán Valley: A Reevaluation. *Current Anthropol.* 37, 700–16.

HARDY, K. 1999: On the Tehuacán Project: Reply to Flannery and MacNeish. *Current Anthropol.* 40, 63–9.

HARRY, K.G. 1997: *Ceramic Production, Distribution, and Consumption in Two Classic Period Hohokam Communities* (Ph.D. dissertation, University of Arizona).

HAURY, E.W. 1958: Evidence at Point of Pines for Prehistoric Migration from Northern Arizona. In Thompson, R.H. (ed.), *Migrations in New World Culture History* (Tucson, University of Arizona Bulletin 29, Social Science Bulletin 27), 1–6.

HAYDEN, B. 1998: Practical and Prestige Technologies: The Evolution of Material Systems. *J. Archaeol. Method and Theory* 5, 1–55.

HEALEY, C.J. 1990: *Maring Hunters and Traders: Production and Exchange in the Papua New Guinea Highlands* (Berkeley, CA).

HEGMON, M. 1998: Technology, Style, and Social Practices: Archaeological Approaches. In Stark, M.T. (ed.), *The Archaeology of Social Boundaries* (Washington, D.C.), 232–80.

HEGMON, M. (ed.) 1999: *The Archaeology of Regional Interaction: Religion, Warfare, and Exchange Across the Southwest and Beyond* (Niwot, CO).

HEGMON, M., NELSON, M.C. and RUTH, S.M. 1998: Abandonment and Reorganization in the Mimbres Region of the American Southwest. *American Anthropologist* 100, 148–62.

HERR, S.A. 1999: *Organization of Migrant Communities on a Pueblo Frontier* (Ph.D. dissertation, Department of Anthropology, University of Arizona) (University Microfilms, Ann Arbor).

HERR, S. and CLARK, J.J. 1997: Patterns in the Pathways: Early Historic Migrations in the Rio Grande Pueblos. *Kiva* 62, 365–89.

HIRTH, K.G. and ANGULO VILLASEÑOR, J.V. 1981: Early State Expansion in Central Mexico: Teotihuacan in Morelos. *J. Field Archaeol.* 8, 135–50.

HODGE, M.G. 1984: *Aztec City States* (Ann Arbor, University of Michigan Museum of Anthropology).

HODGE, M.G. 1998: Archaeological Views of Aztec Culture. *J. Archaeol. Res.* 6, 197–238.

HODGE, M.G. and SMITH, M.E. (eds.) 1994: *Economies and Polities in the Aztec Realm* (Albany, Institute for Mesoamerican Studies, The University at Albany, State University of New York).

HOSLER, D. 1988: Ancient West Mexican Metallurgy: South and Central American Origins and West Mexican Transformations. *American Anthropologist* 90, 832–55.

HOSLER, D. and MACFARLANE, A. 1996: Copper Sources, Metal Production, and Metals Trade in Late Postclassic Mesoamerica. *Science* 273, 1819–24.

HUCKELL, B.B. 1995: *Of Marshes and Maize: Preceramic Agricultural Settlements in the Cienega Valley, Southeastern Arizona* (Tucson, University of Arizona, Anthropological Papers No. 59).

JEFFERIES, R.W. 1996: The emergence of long-distance exchange networks in the southeastern United States. In Sassaman, K.E. and Anderson, D.G. (eds.) 1996, 222–34.

JEFFERIES, R.W. 1997: Middle Archaic bone pins: Evidence of mid-Holocene regional-scale social groups in the southern Midwest. *American Antiquity* 62, 464–87.

JEFFERIES, R.W. and BUTLER, B.M. (eds.) 1982: *The Carrier Mills Archaeological Project: Human Adaptation in the Saline Valley, Illinois* (Carbondale, Center for Archaeological Investigations, Southern Illinois University, Research Paper 33).

JENKINS, N.J. and KRAUSE, R.A. 1986: *The Tombigbee Watershed in Southeastern Prehistory* (University, AL).

JOHNSON, J.K. and BROOKES, S.O. 1989: Benton points, Turkey Tails, and cache blades: Middle Archaic exchange in the Midsouth. *Southeastern Archaeol.* 8, 134–45.

JUDGE, W.J. 1989: Chaco Canyon — San Juan Basin. In Cordell, L.S. and Gumerman, G.J. (eds.), *Dynamics of Southwest Prehistory* (Washington, D.C.), 209–61.

KANTNER, J. and MAHONEY, N. (eds.) 2000: *Great House Communities Across the Chacoan Land-scape* (Tucson, Anthropological Papers of the University of Arizona, No. 64).

KATZENBERG, M.A., SCHWARCZ, H.P., KNYF, M. and MELBYE, F.J. 1995: Stable isotope evidence for maize horticulture and paleodiet in southern Ontario. *American Antiquity* 60, 335–50.

KEELEY, L.H. 1996: *War Before Civilization* (New York).

KELLEY, J.C. and KELLEY, E.A. 1975: An Alternative Hypothesis for the Explanation of Anasazi Culture History. In Frisbie, T.F. (ed.), *Collected Papers in Honor of Florence Hawley Ellis* 2 (Norman, OK, Papers of the Archaeological Society of New Mexico), 178–223.

KELLEY, J.H. and VILLALPANDO, M.E. 1996: An Overview of the Mexican Northwest. In Fish, P.R. and Reid, J.J. (eds.), *Interpreting Southwestern Diversity, Underlying Principles and Overarching Patterns* (Tempe, Arizona State University, Anthropological Research Papers No. 48), 69–77.

KIDDER, A.V., JENNINGS, J.D. and SHOOK, E.M. 1946: *Excavations at Kaminaljuyu, Guatemala* (Washington, D.C., Carnegie Institution of Washington).

KINTIGH, K.W., HOWELL, T.L. and DUFF, A.I. 1996: Post-Chacoan Social Integration at the Hinkson Site. *Kiva* 61, 257–74.

KIRCHHOFF, P. 1943: Mesoamerica. *Acta Americana* 1, 92–107.

KNIGHT, V.J. and STEPONAITIS, V.P. 1998: A new history of Moundville. In Steponaitis, V.P. and Knight, V.J. (eds.) 1998, 1–25.

KOHLER, T.A. and MATTHEWS, M.H. 1988: Long-Term Anasazi Land Use and Forest Reduction: a Case Study from Southwest Colorado. *American Antiquity* 53, 537–64.

KOLB, M.J. and SNEAD, J.E. 1997: It's a Small World After All: Comparative Analyses of Community Organization in Archaeology. *American Antiquity* 62, 609–28.

KUBLER, G. 1961: Chichén Itzá y Tula. *Estudios de Cultura Maya* 1, 47–80.

LANGLEY, J.C. 1986: *Symbolic Notation of Teotihuacan* (Oxford, BAR Int. Ser. 313).

LANGLEY, J.C. 1992: Teotihuacan Sign Clusters: Emblem or Articulation? In Berlo, J.C. (ed.), *Art, Ideology, and the City of Teotihuacan* (Washington, D.C., Dumbarton Oaks), 247–80.

LeBLANC, S.A. 1983: *Mimbres People* (New York).

LeBLANC, S.A. 1999: *Prehistoric Warfare in the American Southwest* (Salt Lake City).

LEKSON, S.H. 1999: *The Chaco Meridian: Centers of Political Power in the Ancient Southwest* (Walnut Creek, CA).

LEKSON, S.H. n.d. (organizer): *The Chaco Synthesis Conference Series* (Boulder, University of Colorado).

LEKSON, S.H., WINDES, T.C., STEIN, J.R. and JUDGE, W.J. 1988: The Chaco Canyon Community. *Scientific American* 259(1), 100–9.

LIGHTFOOT, R.R. 1994: *The Duckfoot Site, Volume 2: Archaeology of the House and Household* (Cortez, CO, Crow Canyon Archaeological Center, Occasional Papers No. 3).

LIGHTFOOT, R.R. and KUCKELMAN, K.A. 1995: Ancestral Pueblo Violence in the Northern Southwest (Paper presented at the 60th Annual Meeting of the Society for American Archaeology, Minneapolis).

LIPE, W.D. 1989: Social Scale of Mesa Verde Anasazi Kivas. In Lipe, W.D. and Hegmon, M. (eds.), *The Architecture of Social Integration in Prehistoric Pueblos* (Cortez, CO, Crow Canyon Archaeological Center, Occasional Papers No. 1), 53–71.

LIPE, W.D. 1995: The Depopulation of the Northern San Juan: Conditions in the Turbulent 1200's. *J. Anthropol. Archaeol.* 14, 143–69.

LOCKHART, J. 1992: *The Nahuas After the Conquest* (Stanford, CA).

LONGACRE, W.A. 1970: *Archaeology as Anthropology: A Case Study* (Tucson, Anthropological Papers of the University of Arizona, No. 17).

LYMAN, R.L., O'BRIEN, M.J. and DUNNELL, R.C. 1997: *The Rise and Fall of Culture History* (New York and London).

MABRY, J.B. 1998: *Archaeological Investigations of Early Village Sites in the Middle Santa Cruz Valley: Analyses and Synthesis* (Tucson, AZ, Center for Desert Archaeology).

MACNEISH, R.S. 1981: Tehuacan's Accomplishments. In Sabloff, J.A. (ed.), *Supplement to the Handbook of Middle American Indians. Volume One: Archaeology* (Austin, TX), 31–47.

MANN, M. 1986: *The Sources of Social Power* (New York).

MARCUS, J. and FLANNERY, K.V. 1996: *Zapotec Civilization* (London).

MARTIN, D.L. 1997: Violence Against Women in the La Plata River Valley (A.D. 1000–1300). In Martin, D.L. and Frayer, D.W. (eds.), *Troubled Times: Violence and Warfare in the Past* (Amsterdam), 45–75.

MARTIN, D.L. 2000: Women's Bodies, Women's Lives: Biological Indicators of Gender Differentiation and Inequality in the Southwest. In Crown, P.L. (ed.) 2000, 267–300.

MASTACHE, A.G. and COBEAN, R.H. 1989: The Coyotlatelco Culture and the Origins of the Toltec State. In Diehl, R.A. and Berlo, J.C. (eds.) 1989, 49–67.

MATOS MOCTEZUMA, E. 1988: *The Great Temple of the Aztecs* (London).

McGUIRE, R.H. and HOWARD, A.V. 1982: The Structure and Organization of Hohokam Shell Exchange. *Kiva* 52, 113–46.

McGUIRE, R.H. and SAITTA, D. 1996: Although They Have Petty Captains, They Obey Them Badly: The Dialectics of Prehispanic Western Pueblo Social Organization. *American Antiquity* 61, 197–216.

MEHRER, M.W. 1995: *Cahokia's Countryside: Household Archaeology, Settlement Patterns, and Social Power* (DeKalb, IL).

MELTZER, D.J. 1988: Late Pleistocene human adaptations in eastern North America. *J. World Prehist.* 2, 1–51.

MELTZER, D.J., GRAYSON, D.K., ARDILA, G., BARKER, A.W., DINCAUZE, D.F., HAYNES, C.V., MENA, F., NÚÑEZ, L. and STANFORD, D.J. 1997: On the Pleistocene antiquity of Monte Verde, southern Chile. *American Antiquity* 62, 659–63.

MELTZER, D.J. and SMITH, B.D. 1986: Paleoindian and Early Archaic subsistence strategies in eastern North America. In Neusius, S.W. (ed.), *Foraging, Collecting, and Harvesting: Archaic Period Subsistence and Settlement in the Eastern Woodlands* (Carbondale, Center for Archaeological Investigations, Southern Illinois University, Occasional Paper 6), 3–31.

MIKSA, E.J. 1998: *A Model for Assigning Temper Provenance to Archaeological Ceramics with Case Studies from the American Southwest* (Ph.D. dissertation, Tucson, University of Arizona).

MILANICH, J.T. 1998: Native chiefdoms and the exercise of complexity in sixteenth-century Florida. In Redmond, E.M. (ed.), *Chiefdoms and Chieftaincy in the Americas* (Gainesville, FL), 245–64.

MILLON, R. 1973: *The Teotihuacan Map. Part One: Text* (Austin, TX).

MILLON, R., DREWITT, R.B. and COWGILL, G.L. 1973: *The Teotihuacan Map. Part Two: Maps* (Austin, TX).

MILLS, B.J. 1998: Migration and Pueblo IV Community Reorganization in the Silver Creek Area, East-Central Arizona. In Spielmann, K.A. (ed.) 1998a, 65–80.

MILLS, B.J. (ed.) 2000: *Alternative Leadership Strategies in the Prehispanic Southwest* (Tucson, AZ).

MILLS, B.J. and CROWN, P.L. (eds.) 1995: *Ceramic Production in the American Southwest* (Tucson, AZ).

MILNER, G.R. 1998: *The Cahokia Chiefdom: The Archaeology of a Mississippian Society* (Washington, D.C.).

MILNER, G.R. 1999: Warfare in prehistoric and early historic eastern North America. *J. Archaeol. Res.* 7, 105–51.

MILNER, G.R., ANDERSON, E. and SMITH, V.G. 1991: Warfare in Late Prehistoric West-Central Illinois. *American Antiquity* 56, 581–603.

MILNER, G.R. and JEFFERIES, R.W. 1998: The Read Archaic shell midden in Kentucky. *Southeastern Archaeol.* 17, 119–32.

MINNIS, P.E. 1985: *Social Adaptation to Food Stress: A Prehistoric Southwestern Example* (Chicago).

MINNIS, P.E. 1988: Four Examples of Specialized Production at Casas Grandes, Northwest Chihuahua. *Kiva* 53, 181–93.

MOBLEY-TANAKA, J.L. 1997: Gender and Ritual Space During the Pithouse to Pueblo Transition: Subterranean Mealing Rooms in the North American Southwest. *American Antiquity* 62, 437–48.

MÓNACO, E. 1998: Quetzalcóatl de Tollan. *Arqueología* 19, 119–55.

MULLER, J. 1995: Regional interaction in the later Southeast. In Nassaney, M.S. and Sassaman, K.E. (eds.), *Native American Interactions: Multiscalar Analyses and Interpretations in the Eastern Woodlands* (Knoxville, TN), 317–40.

MULLER, J. 1997: *Mississippian Political Economy* (New York).

NEITZEL, J.E. 1999: *Great Towns and Regional Polities in the Prehistoric American Southwest and Southeast* (Dragoon, AZ, Amerind Foundation, and Albuquerque).

NELSON, B.A. 1995: Complexity, Hierarchy, and Scale: A Controlled Comparison between Chaco Canyon, New Mexico, and La Quemada, Zacatecas. *American Antiquity* 60, 597–618.

NELSON, B.A. 1997: Chronology and Stratigraphy at La Quemada, Zacatecas, Mexico. *J. Field Archaeol.* 24, 85–109.

NELSON, B.A. 1999: Aggregation, Warfare, and the Spread of the Mesoamerican Tradition. In Hegmon, M. (ed.) 1999, 316–36.

NELSON, B.A. and ANYON, R. 1996: Fallow Valleys: Asynchronous Occupations in Southwestern New Mexico. *Kiva* 61, 241–56.

NELSON, M.C. 1999: *Mimbres During the Twelfth Century: Abandonment, Continuity, and Reorganization* (Tucson, AZ).

NELSON, M.C. 2000: Abandonment: Conceptualization, Representation, and Social Change. In Schiffer, M.B. (ed.), *Explorations in Social Theory* (Salt Lake City), 52–62.

ORTMAN, S.G. 1998: Corn Grinding and Community Organization in the Pueblo Southwest, A.D. 1150–1550. In Spielmann, K.A. (ed.) 1998a, 165–92.

ORTNER, S.B. 1996: *Making Gender: The Politics and Erotics of Culture* (Boston).

O'SHEA, J.M. 1989: The role of wild resources in small-scale agricultural systems: Tales from the lakes and the plains. In Halstead, P. and O'Shea, J.M. (eds.), *Bad Year Economics: Cultural Responses to Risk and Uncertainty* (Cambridge), 57–67.

OTIS CHARLTON, C., CHARLTON, T.H. and NICHOLS, D.L. 1993: Aztec Household-Based Craft Production: Archaeological Evidence from the City-State of Otumba, Mexico. In Santley, R.S. and Hirth, K.G. (eds.), *Prehispanic Domestic Units in Western Mesoamerica* (Boca Raton, FL), 147–71.

PACHECO, P.J. (ed.) 1996: *A View From the Core: A Synthesis of Ohio Hopewell Archaeology* (Columbus, Ohio Archaeological Council).

PAREZO, N.J. (ed.) 1993: *Hidden Scholars: Women Anthropologists and the Native American Southwest* (Albuquerque).

PAUKETAT, T.R. 1994: *The Ascent of Chiefs: Cahokia and Mississippian Politics in Native North America* (Tuscaloosa, AL).

PAUKETAT, T.R. 1997: Cahokian political economy. In Pauketat, T.R. and Emerson, T.E. (eds.), *Cahokia: Domination and Ideology in the Mississippian World* (Lincoln, NE), 30–51.

PETERSEN, K.L. 1988: *Climate and the Dolores River Anasazi* (Salt Lake City, University of Utah Anthropological Papers 113).

PHILLIPS, J.L. and BROWN, J.A. (eds.) 1983: *Archaic Hunters and Gatherers in the American Midwest* (New York).

PLOG, S. (ed.) 1986: *Spatial Organization and Exchange: Archaeological Survey on Northern Black Mesa* (Carbondale, IL).

PLOG, S. 1990: Agriculture, Sedentism, and Environment in the Evolution of Political Systems. In Upham, S. (ed.), *The Evolution of Political Systems: Sociopolitics in Small-Scale Sedentary Societies* (Cambridge), 177–99.

PLOG, S. and SOLOMETO, J. 1997: The Never-Changing and the Ever-Changing: The Evolution of Western Pueblo Ritual. *Cambridge Archaeol. J.* 7, 161–82.

POTTER, J.M. 1998: The Structure of Open Space in Late Prehistoric Settlements in the Southwest. In Spielmann, K.A. (ed.) 1998a, 137–64.

POTTER, J.M. 1997a: *Communal Ritual, Feasting, and Social Differentiation in Late Prehistoric Zuni Communities* (Ph.D. dissertation, Department of Anthropology, Arizona State University) (University Microfilms, Ann Arbor).

POTTER, J.M. 1997b: Communal Ritual and Faunal Remains: An Example from the Dolores Anasazi. *J. Field Archaeol.* 24, 353–64.

POWELL, M.L. 1998: Of time and the river: Perspectives on health during the Moundville chiefdom. In Steponaitis, V.P. and Knight, V.J. (eds.) 1998, 102–19.

REDMAN, C.L. 1999: *Human Impact on Ancient Environments* (Tucson, AZ).

REID, J.J. and MONTGOMERY, B.K. 1998: The Brown and the Gray: Pots and Population Movement in East-Central Arizona. *J. Anthropol. Res.* 54, 447–60.

RICE, D.S. (ed.) 1993: *Latin American Horizons* (Washington, D.C., Dumbarton Oaks).

RICE, G.E. (ed.) 1998a: *Synthesis of Tonto Basin Prehistory: The Roosevelt Archaeology Studies, 1989 to 1998* (Tempe, Office of Cultural Resource Management, Department of Anthropology, Arizona State University, Roosevelt Monograph Series 12, Anthropological Field Studies 41).

RICE, G. 1998b: War and Water: An Ecological Perspective on Hohokam Irrigation. *Kiva* 63, 263–301.

RILEY, C.L. and Hedrick, B.C. (eds.) 1978: *Across the Chichimec Sea: Papers in Honor of J. Charles Kelley* (Carbondale, IL).

RIZO, M.J. 1998: *Scarlet Macaw Production and Trade at Paquimé, Chihuahua* (Tempe, Master's thesis, Department of Anthropology, Arizona State University).

ROBERTSON, I. 1999: Spatial and Multivariate Analysis, Random Sampling Error, and Analytical Noise: Empirical Bayesian Methods at Teotihuacan, Mexico. *American Antiquity* 64, 137–52.

ROCEK, T.R. 1996: Sedentism and Mobility in the Southwest. In Fish, P.R. and Reid, J.J. (eds.), *Interpreting Southwestern Diversity: Underlying Principles and Overarching Patterns* (Tempe, Arizona State University, Anthropological Research Papers No. 48), 17–22.

ROGERS, J.D. and SMITH, B.D. (eds.) 1995: *Mississippian Communities and Households* (Tuscaloosa, AL).

RUSSO, M. 1996a: Southeastern Archaic mounds. In Sassaman, K.E. and Anderson, D.G. (eds.) 1996, 259–87.

RUSSO, M. 1996b: Southeastern mid-Holocene coastal settlements. In Sassaman, K.E. and Anderson, D.G. (eds.) 1996, 177–99.

SALE, K. 1990: *The Conquest of Paradise: Christopher Columbus and the Columbian Legacy* (New York).

SANDERS, W.T. and MICHELS, J.W. (eds.) 1977: *Teotihuacan and Kaminaljuyu: A Study in Prehistoric Culture Contact* (University Park, PA).

SANDERS, W.T., PARSONS, J.R. and SANTLEY, R.S. 1979: *The Basin of Mexico: Ecological Processes in the Evolution of a Civilization* (New York).

SANTLEY, R.S. 1983: Obsidian Trade and Teotihuacan Influence in Mesoamerica. In Miller, A.G. (ed.), *Highland-Lowland Interaction in Mesoamerica* (Washington, D.C., Dumbarton Oaks), 69–124.

SANTLEY, R.S. 1984: Obsidian Exchange, Economic Stratification, and the Evolution of Complex Society in the Basin of Mexico. In Hirth, K. (ed.), *Trade and Exchange in Early Mesoamerica* (Albuquerque), 43–86.

SANTURE, S.K., HARN, A.D. and ESAREY, D. (eds.) 1990: *Archaeological Investigations at the Morton Village and Norris Farms 36 Cemetery* (Springfield, Illinois State Museum, Reports of Investigations 45).

SASSAMAN, K.E. 1993: *Early Pottery in the Southeast* (Tuscaloosa, AL).

SASSAMAN, K.E. 1995: The cultural diversity of interactions among mid-Holocene societies of the American Southeast. In Nassaney, M.S. and Sassaman, K.E. (eds.), *Native American Interactions: Multiscalar Analyses and Interpretations in the Eastern Woodlands* (Knoxville, TN), 174–204.

SASSAMAN, K.E. and ANDERSON, D.G. (eds.) 1996: *Archaeology of the Mid-Holocene Southeast* (Gainesville, FL).

SAUNDERS, J.W., MANDEL, R.D., SAUCIER, R.T., ALLEN, E.T., HALLMARK, C.T., JOHNSON, J.K., JACKSON, H.E., ALLEN, C.M., STRINGER, G.L., FRINK, D.S., FEATHERS, J.K., WILLIAMS, S., GREMILLION, K.J., VIDRINE, M.F. and JONES, R. 1997: A mound complex in Louisiana at 5400–5000 years before present. *Science* 277, 1796–9.

SCARBOROUGH, V.L. and WILCOX, D.R. (eds.) 1991: *The Mesoamerican Ballgame* (Tucson, AZ).

SCHAAFSMA, C. and RILEY, C. (eds.) 1999: *The Casas Grandes World* (Salt Lake City).

SCHACHNER, G. 2001: Ritual Control and Transformation in Middle-Range Societies: An Example from the American Southwest. *J. Anthropol. Archaeol.* 20, 168–94.

SCHELE, L. and FREIDEL, D. 1990: *A Forest of Kings* (New York).

SCHLANGER, S.H. 1988: Patterns of Population Movement and Long-Term Population Growth in Southwestern Colorado. *American Antiquity* 53, 773–93.

SCHLANGER, S.H. and WILSHUSEN, R.H. 1993: Local Abandonments and Regional Considerations in the North American Southwest. In Cameron, C.A. and Tomka, S.A. (eds.), *Abandonments of Settlements and Regions* (Cambridge), 85–98.

SCHOENINGER, M.J. and SCHURR, M.R. 1998: Human subsistence at Moundville: The stable-isotope data. In Steponaitis, V.P. and Knight, V.J. (eds.) 1998, 120–32.

SEBASTIAN, L. 1992: *The Chaco Anasazi: Sociopolitical Evolution in the Prehistoric Southwest* (Cambridge).

SEEMAN, M.F. 1992: The bow and arrow, the intrusive mound complex, and a Late Woodland Jack's Reef horizon in the mid-Ohio valley. In Seeman, M.F. (ed.), *Cultural Variability in Context: Woodland Settlements in the Mid-Ohio Valley* (Kent, OH, Kent State University, MCJA Special Paper 7), 41–51.

SHAPIRO, J.S. 1997: *Fingerprints on the Landscape: Space Syntax Analysis and Cultural Evolution in the Northern Rio Grande* (Ph.D. dissertation, Department of Anthropology, Pennsylvania State University) (University Microfilms, Ann Arbor).

SHARER, R.J. and GROVE, D.C. (eds.) 1989: *Regional Perspectives on the Olmec* (Cambridge).

SHENNAN, S.J. 1990: Introduction: Archaeological Approaches to Cultural Identity. In Shennan, S.J. (ed.), *Archaeological Approaches to Cultural Identity* (London), 1–32.

SHOTT, M.J. 1996: Innovation and selection in prehistory: A case study from the American Bottom. In Odell, G.H. (ed.), *Stone Tools: Theoretical Insights into Human Prehistory* (New York), 279–309.

SIMON, A.W. and BURTON, J.H. (eds.) 1998: Anthropological Interpretations from Archaeological Ceramic Studies in the U.S. Southwest. *J. Anthropol. Res.* 54(4).

SMILEY, F.E. 1994: The Agricultural Transition in the Northern Southwest: Patterns in Current Chronometric Data. *Kiva* 60, 165–90.

SMITH, B.D. 1986: The archaeology of the southeastern United States: From Dalton to De Soto, 10,500–500 B.P. In Wendorf, F. and Close, A. (eds.), *Advances in World Archaeology*, Vol. 5 (Orlando, FL), 1–92.

SMITH, B.D. 1989: Origins of agriculture in eastern North America. *Science* 246, 1566–71.

SMITH, B.D. (ed.) 1990: *The Mississippian Emergence* (Washington, D.C.).

SMITH, B.D. 1992: Hopewellian farmers of eastern North America. In *Rivers of Change: Essays on Early Agriculture in Eastern North America* (Washington, D.C.), 201–48.

SMITH, B.D. 1995: *The Emergence of Agriculture* (New York, Scientific American Library).

SMITH, B.D. 1997a: The Initial Domestication of Cucurbita pepo in the Americas 10,000 Years Ago. *Science* 276, 932–4.

SMITH, B.D. 1997b: Reconsidering the Ocampo Caves and the Era of Incipient Cultivation in Mesoamerica. *Latin American Antiquity* 8, 342–83.

SMITH, M.E. 1992: Braudel's temporal rhythms and chronology theory in archaeology. In Knapp, A.B. (ed.), *Archaeology,* Annales, *and ethnohistory* (Cambridge), 23–34.

SMITH, M.E. 1996: *The Aztecs* (Oxford).

SNOW, D.R. 1995a: Microchronology and demographic evidence relating to the size of pre-Columbian North American Indian populations. *Science* 268, 1601–4.

SNOW, D.R. 1995b: Migration in prehistory: The northern Iroquoian case. *American Antiquity* 60, 59–79.

SPENCER, C.S. and REDMOND, E.M. 1997: *Archaeology of the Cañada de Cuicatlan, Oaxaca* (New York, American Museum of Natural History).

SPIELMANN, K.A. (ed.) 1991: *Farmers, Hunters, and Colonists: Interaction Between the Southwest and the Southern Plains* (Tucson, AZ).

SPIELMANN, K.A. (ed.) 1995: The Archaeology of Gender in the American Southwest. *J. Anthropol. Res.* 51(2).

SPIELMANN, K.A. (ed.) 1998a: *Migration and Reorganization: The Pueblo IV Period in the American Southwest* (Tempe, Arizona State University, Anthropological Research Papers No. 51).

SPIELMANN, K.A. 1998b: Ritual Craft Specialists in Middle Range Societies. In Costin, C.L. and Wright, R.P. (eds.), *Craft and Social Identity* (Washington, D.C., American Anthropological Association, Archaeological Paper No. 8), 153–9.

STARK, B.L. and ARNOLD, P. (eds.) 1997: *Olmec to Aztec* (Tucson, AZ).

STEPONAITIS, V.P. 1991: Contrasting patterns of Mississippian development. In Earle, T. (ed.), *Chiefdoms: Power, Economy, and Ideology* (Cambridge), 193–228.

STEPONAITIS, V.P. 1998: Population trends at Moundville. In Steponaitis, V.P. and Knight, V.J. (eds.) 1998, 26–43.

STEPONAITIS, V.P. and KNIGHT, V.J. (eds.) 1998: *Archaeology of the Moundville Chiefdom* (Washington, D.C.).

STEWARD, J.H. 1949: Cultural Causality and Law: A Trial Formulation of the Development of Early Civilizations. *American Anthropologist* 51, 1–27.

STEWARD, J.H. 1955: *Theory of Culture Change: The Methodology of Multilinear Evolution* (Urbana, IL).

SUGIYAMA, S. 1993: Worldview Materialized in Teotihuacan, Mexico. *Latin American Antiquity* 4, 103–29.

SUGIYAMA, S. 1995: *Mass Human Sacrifice and Symbolism of the Feathered Serpent Pyramid in Teotihuacan, Mexico* (Tempe, Doctoral dissertation, Arizona State University).

SWENTZELL, R. 1988: Remembering Tewa Pueblo Houses and Spaces. *Native Peoples* 3(2), 6–12.

TAINTER, J.A. and TAINTER, B.B. (eds.) 1996: *Evolving Complexity and Environmental Risk in the Prehistoric Southwest* (Reading, MA).

THOMPSON, I., VARIEN, M., KENZLE, S. and SWENTZELL, R. 1997: Prehistoric Architecture with Unknown Function. In Morrow, B.H. and Price, V.B. (eds.), *Anasazi Architecture and American Design* (Albuquerque), 149–58.

TOZZER, A.M. 1957: *Chichen Itza and its Cenote of Sacrifice: A Comparative Study of Contemporaneous Maya and Toltec* (Cambridge, MA, Peabody Museum of American Archaeology and Ethnology).

TURNER II, C.G. and TURNER, J.A. 1999: *Man Corn: Cannibalism and Violence in the Prehistoric American Southwest* (Salt Lake City).

VAN WEST, C.R. 1994: *Modeling Prehistoric Agricultural Productivity in Southwestern Colorado: a GIS Approach* (Pullman, Washington State University and Cortez, CO, Crow Canyon Archaeological Center).

VARGAS, V.D. 1994: *Copper Bell Trade Patterns in the Prehistoric Greater American Southwest* (Norman, Master's thesis, University of Oklahoma).

VARIEN, M.D. 1999: *Sedentism and Mobility in a Social Landscape: Mesa Verde and Beyond* (Tucson, AZ).

VARIEN, M.D. and KUCKELMAN, K.A. 1999: Introduction. In Varien, M.D. (ed.), *The Sand Canyon Archaeological Project: Site Testing, CD-ROM version 1.0* (Cortez, CO, Crow Canyon Archaeological Center).

VARIEN, M.D. and MILLS, B.J. 1997: Accumulations Research: Problems and Prospects for Estimating Site Occupation Span. *J. Archaeol. Method and Theory* 4, 141–91.

WALKER, W.A. 1998: Where are the Witches of Prehistory? *J. Archaeol. Method and Theory* 5, 245–308.

WALLERSTEIN, I. 1976: *The Modern World-System* (New York).

WEIGAND, P. and HARBOTTLE, G. 1993: The Role of Turquoises in the Ancient Mesoamerican Trade Structure. In Ericson, J. and Baugh, T. (eds.), *The American Southwest and Mesoamerica: Systems of Prehistoric Exchange* (New York).

WEINER, A.B. 1992: *Inalienable Possessions: The Paradox of Keeping-While-Giving* (Berkeley, CA).

WELCH, P.D. 1991: Moundville's Economy (Tuscaloosa, AL).

WHITELEY, P.M. 1988: *Deliberate Acts: Changing Hopi culture Through the Oraibi Split* (Tucson, AZ).

WHITTLESEY, S.M., CIOLEK-TORRELO, R. and ALTSCHUL, J.H. (eds.) 1997: *Vanishing River: Landscapes and Lives of the Lower Verde Valley* (Tucson, AZ).

WIANT, M.D. 1993: Exploring Paleoindian site distribution in Illinois. *Illinois Archaeol.* 5, 108–18.

WIESSNER, P. and TUMU, A. 1998: *Historical Vines: Enga Networks of Exchange, Ritual, and Warfare in Papua New Guinea* (Washington, D.C.).

WILCOX, D.E. 1991: Hohokam Social Complexity. In Crown, P.L. and Judge, W.J. (eds.) 1991, 253–76.

WILLEY, G.R. (ed.) 1956: *Prehistoric Settlement Patterns in the New World* (New York, Wenner-Gren Foundation for Anthropological Research).

WILLS, W.H. 1988: *Early Prehistoric Agriculture in the American Southwest* (Santa Fe, School of American Research).

WILLS, W.H. and HUCKELL, B. 1994: Economic Implications of Changing Land-Use Patterns in the Late Archaic. In Gumerman, G.J. (ed.) 1994, 33–52.

WILLS, W.H. and WINDES, T.C. 1989: Evidence for Aggregation and Dispersal During the Basketmaker III Period in Chaco Canyon, New Mexico. *American Antiquity* 347–69.

WOLF, E.R. 1990: Distinguished Lecture: Facing Power — Old Insights, New Questions. *American Anthropologist* 92, 586–96.

WOLF, E.R. 1999: *Envisioning Power: Ideologies of Dominance and Crisis* (Berkeley, CA).

WORLD ARCHAEOLOGY 1998: *The Past in the Past* 30(1).

ZEDEÑO, M.N. 1994: *Sourcing Prehistoric Ceramics at Chodistaas Pueblo, Arizona: The Circulation of People and Pots in the Grasshopper Region, Arizona* (Tucson, Anthropological Papers No. 58).

ZEDEÑO, M.N. 1995: The Role of Population Movement and Technology Transfer in the Manufacture of Prehistoric Southwestern Ceramics. In Mills, B.J. and Crown, P.L. (eds.) 1995, 115–41.

South America: In the Garden of Forking Paths

GUSTAVO G. POLITIS

Introduction

In 1941, the Argentinian writer Jorge Luis Borges published his famous story *In the Garden of Forking Paths*. From the mouths of the principal protagonists, Dr. Yu Tsun and Stephen Albert, as well as throughout the piece, Borges expounded his almost obsessive reflections on time; about parallel futures and present pasts. In this chapter I will use the ideas and reflections expressed in the tale metaphorically because I believe they will help us to understand some of the contemporary issues and future developments I envision for the archaeology of South America.

The subject areas and problems tackled in South American archaeology are innumerable and diverse (see for example the recent overviews in volumes by Bruhns 1996; Lavallée 1995; Politis and Alberti 1999; Salomon and Schwartz 1999; Wilson 1999), but a perennial interest has been maintained in some in particular. Amongst the latter, the following will be examined in the current article: the early colonization of the subcontinent; the adaptation of humans to the Amazon rainforest; and the emergence of complex societies and the production of food in the Andes. In addition, in recent decades several research projects have been orientated towards the development of sub-disciplines of archaeology which have had an original trajectory in the region, among which taphonomy and ethnoarchaeology stand out.

Particular themes in the region have expanded the boundaries of archaeological practice and have given an ethical and moral dimension to the discipline. Archaeology in South America has been considerably disconnected from social critique, and with the exception of its involvement in the indigenous movements in the mid-twentieth century, the discipline has been constituted as a scientific practice with little impact on social transformation in the region. Nonetheless, some original developments in South American archaeology have played a transformative role in praxis in recent years. Some of the best examples of these developments are forensic anthropology and historical archaeology, which focus on the oppressed classes who have been made invisible by official history.

In this article, I will run quickly through some subjects of recurrent interest, as well as theoretical and methodological developments in the discipline and its new frontiers of application. This examination of the contemporary archaeology of South America is necessarily incomplete and the selection of topics is essentially a personal choice. Nonetheless, I believe they reflect two key characteristics of the archaeology of the region: diversity and vitality.

Finally, I will also discuss some of the many possible futures I envision for archaeology in (not of) South America, since it appears that, at the beginning of this millennium, the discipline finds itself in a labyrinth like that created by Ts'ui Pen in Borges' tale, with '. . . diverse futures, diverse times which themselves also proliferate and fork'.

How did the discipline come into being? Or *How the road descended and forked among the now confused meadows* (Borges 1941)

Archaeology in South America is the result of national and regional developments; in no way can it be considered an homogeneous process, nor a compact set of related concepts and theories. Investigations in the region have been framed by two main streams of research, one conducted by local archaeologists, the other by foreign scholars. Both groups have contributed to the generation of knowledge of the South American past, but in different ways.

South American archaeology is diverse and heterogeneous, as is to be expected of a region with such cultural diversity. In spite of the fact that most countries share a Spanish or Portuguese colonial background, the divergence in their historical developments and socio-political contexts has led to distinct regional and national (not nationalistic) archaeologies. Recent scholarship has highlighted how regional archaeological traditions in other parts of the world have developed, and how such traditions are deeply influenced by their socio-political contexts (Trigger 1992; Ucko 1995).

In the case of South America, few attempts have been made to understand the regional processes of growth and development of the discipline (for exceptions, see Oyuela-Caycedo 1994; Politis 1995), although histories of national archaeologies have proliferated in the past two decades, often written from very different perspectives (see, for example, Barreto 1998; Berenguer Rodríguez 1995; Burger 1989; Cabrera Pérez 1988; Collier 1982; Crivelli Montero 1990; Fernández 1982; Funari 1992; Gnecco 1995; Mendonça de Souza 1991; Orellana Rodríguez 1996; Politis 1992; Salazar 1995). The growth in interest in the systematic study of the development of national archaeologies is one consequence of the perceived necessity for reflection on, and analysis of, how knowledge of the past is constructed — of realizing that social and political factors mould the practice and theory of archaeology, and of the distancing of archaeology from supposed positivist objectivity (Gathercole and Lowenthal 1990; Kohl and Fawcett 1997; Ucko 1995).

The heterogeneity of South American archaeology is partly a consequence of the non-concurrent organization of professional courses in archaeology in each country. This also implies that the social legitimization of the discipline and its entry into academic life occurred at different times. Although scientists with an interest in archaeology — some of whom were of notable importance (e.g. Florentino Ameghino and Juan B. Ambrosseti in Argentina, José Toribio Medina in Chile, Julio Tello in Peru, J.H. Figueira in Uruguay) — have been in evidence since the end of the last century, the creation of departments of archaeology in South American universities and the systematization of the teaching of the discipline have only occurred since the middle of the twentieth century. Peru was one of the first, where a degree course in archaeology was established in the Universidad Mayor de San Marco in the second half of the 1950s (Lumbreras and Cisneros 1986). Almost simultaneously, the two principal universities in Argentina (in La Plata and Buenos Aires) inaugurated courses in anthropology with an archaeological orientation (in 1957 and 1958 respectively). Uruguay and Ecuador, where archaeology only achieved academic status in the late 1970s and early 1980s (Cabrera Pérez 1988; Salazar 1995), are at the other extreme.

Another source of significant variation in the different types of archaeology that have developed is the diversity and number of indigenous peoples in each country. In countries such as Peru (and Mexico in Central America), with its large indigenous population, the discipline was connected to the indigenous movements during various stages in its development and has had an explicitly political content. In other countries, in which the indigenous populations are far smaller (such as Argentina, Chile or Venezuela), or almost non-existent (such as Uruguay), archaeology has never had the potential to be considered an instrument of social change or a tool with which to re-establish the dignity and legitimate the rights of Native Americans.

In spite of the extent of such diversity, the archaeology of South America has some common characteristics. First, South American archaeology is largely empiricist. Although there are a few original theoretical approaches, such as the Marxist-orientated Latin American social archaeology (Bate 1977, 1998; Lorenzo *et al.* 1976; Lumbreras 1974; Vargas Arenas and Sanoja 1992, 1999; for a critical view see Oyuela-Caycedo *et al.* 1997 and Lanata and Borrero 1999), and serious attempts have been made to incorporate and develop some North American and European methodological and theoretical perspectives, the practice of archaeology within the region remains heavily grounded in empiricism. Interpretation and the placement of finds into the context of past 'cultures', or into archaeological units (such as 'phases', 'traditions' or 'industries') are frequently the final goal of research. Secondly, South American archaeology is basically culture–history orientated. Culture–history has been the dominant paradigm in the region as a result of what has been defined as the 'Classificatory–Historical Period' (Willey and Sabloff 1980), an era when the main objective of (North) American archaeologists was the cultural synthesis of the various regions of America. Culture–history was predominant in the greater part of the world, although with different variations (see summary in Trigger 1992) but South American archaeology basically (although not exclusively) followed the North American line. This was especially the case after World War II, when the United States consolidated its hegemony in the area which had fallen within its political and economic sphere of influence (or domination, as some would say).

The North American culture–historical approach had a direct impact on the archaeology practised in several countries in South America. Archaeological finds were organized into a framework of cultures and periods; ceramics were compartmentalized into styles, and artefacts into complexes (see, for example, Bennett *et al.* 1948 in the case of north-west Argentina; Cruxent and Rouse 1958 for Venezuela; Meggers and Evans 1957 for the Amazon; Bennett and Bird 1949 for Peru; and Willey 1958 for a comparative synthesis). The framework for the reconstruction of the past in the region has been, and still is, a complex mosaic in which regional sequences, sites, and some units of integration such as traditions and horizons, are articulated within a culture–history-dominated lineage. Most local archaeologists followed the trend established by the popularization of North American culture–history, although the influence of British culture–history, mainly through the work of Gordon Childe, has been felt in some areas (see discussion in Perez Gollán 1981). Childe was also a central influence on the theoretical foundations of the Latin American social archaeology (Vargas and Sanoja 1999). The Austro-German *Kulturkreise* school and a variety of French trends (i.e. structuralism) were also influential (see discussions in Barreto 1998; Funari 1999b; Gnecco 1995; López Mazz 1999; Politis 1995), although in a thematically and geographically restricted manner.

The processual trend in archaeology first appeared in South America in the 1970s and, consequently, focus shifted to problem-orientated research. As a result, South America became a kind of laboratory for the testing of hypotheses and models developed elsewhere. Processualism, in its ecological functionalism orientation, was initially evident in the work of North American archaeologists conducting research in the region (e.g. Rick 1980; Stuart 1977) and later it can be more clearly recognized in a generation of South American archaeologists who embarked on their careers in the 1970s and 1980s (e.g. Borrero 1986; Mena 1991; Mengoni Goñalons 1988; Olivera 1988; Salazar 1995). The principal concepts and the subjects that were approached from this trend were mainly concentrated in the study of hunter-gatherers (see review in Lanata and Borrero 1999). In certain countries, such as Argentina, the work of Binford was the principal source for those archaeologists who were exploring the possibilities of a processual archaeology.

In other countries, such as Chile and Uruguay, Schiffer's 'behavioural archaeology' had a greater impact. However, in some cases the adoption of a processual approach was more cosmetic than real, and, in an attempt to modernize scientific discourse, some processual concepts were pegged onto a clearly culture–historical interpretative nucleus, which did not bring about substantial changes in the interpretation and explanation of social processes.

Due to its empirical roots and culture–historical focus, it is not unusual that post-processualism has had only a modest impact on South American archaeology where current change is actually directed more towards processualism. Moreover, few South American archaeologists (e.g. Gnecco 1999; Haber 1997; Zarankin and Acuto 1999) explicitly recognize that they are working with some of the multiple variants that can be clustered within the increasingly loosely-defined label 'postprocessual'. In addition, it is important to recognize that several themes of the postprocessual agenda have been present for a long time in the work of many South American archaeologists, although they have not formally been developed as such. For example, the interest in ideology (not as an adaptive system) of the pre-Hispanic population and its central role in social processes has been a continuous preoccupation in the archaeological study of Andean societies. Moreover, in Latin America, the explicit political and social involvement of academia in some countries (such as Peru, Mexico and Cuba) produced the kind of critique of a politically responsible archaeology that has occurred relatively more recently in North America and Great Britain (McGuire and Navarrete 1999). Because of the existence of large indigenous populations and popular social movements in several South American countries, some aspects of a postprocessual critique — for example, issues concerned with ethnicity, indigenous rights or multivocality — appear to be much more immediately relevant than other issues, such as the study of gender or the role of the individual. Gender archaeology is poorly represented in South America when compared to North America or Western Europe; of the little work accomplished, the majority has been carried out by foreigners (e.g. Hastorf 1991; Gero 1991, 1992). Moreover, the Latin American social archaeologists, probably the best known theoreticians in the region, claimed to be 'the first postprocessualists' (Manuel Gándara, pers. comm. 1990) since they early on reacted against the Anglo-Saxon processualists (McGuire and Navarrete 1999).

Nonetheless, it would be unjust to consider Latin American archaeology as a passive reflection of foreign, essentially North American, influence. Of course, local archaeologists have developed original methods and generated their own conceptual frameworks, although their contributions have obviously been sustained by foreign theories and methods, since, as with any researcher in the western world, South American archaeologists practise within open scientific communities and are exposed to intellectual movements generated in other countries. The reverse process is far less notable, and other than the scarce exceptions (for example, the case of the Latin American social archaeology and its repercussions in Spain) the theoretical product of the archaeologists of the region, although of course fairly limited, has not entered the theoretical debate at a world level.

Finally, in order to offer an accurate picture of the development of archaeology in South America during recent decades, it is important to recognize the impact of military coups on scientific development in specific countries. Lamentably, this is a very particular characteristic of the region, and in every case the *coup d'état* has resulted in the persecution and, in many cases, murder of scientists orientated towards the political left, several of whom were archaeologists. During the 1960s, the crystallization of socialist leftist movements in general occurred throughout the region. Some of these chose guerrilla warfare as their way to fight (e.g. in Colombia, Uruguay and Argentina) and others gained power through free elections (e.g. the governments of Allende in Chile and Cámpora in Argentina). Many archaeologists took part in this process bearing aloft the indigenous flame carried to the discipline in the hands of Julio Tello in Peru and Manuel Gamio in Mexico. However, the reaction from conservative sectors was quick and decisive. Consequently, during the 1970s the majority of countries in the region fell under the brutal control of military regimes; the socialist dream was buried beneath wide-scale repression which had its bloodiest expression in Argentina, leaving more than 15,000 *desaparecidos* ('disappeared'). Several professional archaeologists and an indeterminate number of students, from Argentina, Chile and Uruguay, had to flee their countries and go into exile in other, more tolerant and democratic societies. Mexico was the preferred refuge, and the freedom that prevailed there, plus the strong Spanish republican tradition, fostered a fruitful debate that resulted in new lines of research for archaeology. With all these traditions of investigation, the archaeology of South America was nurtured by various theoretical approaches and crystallized in diverse academic and political contexts.

The human colonization of South America or *In the invisible labyrinth of time* (Borges 1941)

The issue of the human colonization of South America has been at the centre of archaeological debate since the end of the last century. In 1880 Florentino Ameghino postulated a South American — actually, an Argentinian Pampean — origin for humankind, based on a series of controversial finds which were later successfully refuted by Ales Hrdlička (1912). From Hrdlička onwards, the tendency has been towards the confirmation of the Mongoloid/Sinodont nature of the Amerindian population (Turner 1983), although the age and characteristics of the early human population of America have always been the subject of an intense and somewhat peculiar debate. Furthermore, physical anthropologists have recently challenged the Three Migrations Model formulated by Greenberg *et al.* (1986), proposing, through cranial morphology of the earlier human remains from the Americas, that such remains cannot be classified as typically Mongoloid and that they actually closely resemble modern Pacific and African populations (Neves and Pucciarelli 1989, 1991; Neves *et al.* 1999). Consequently, it has been proposed that the Americas were first colonized by proto- or pre-Mongoloid people, different from North Asian Mongoloids (Lahr 1997; Neves *et al.* 1999; Steele and Powell 1992). The classical populations model has also been challenged by the recent finding of the so-called Kennewick Man in Washington state, USA, with supposedly Caucasoid characteristics (Chatters 1997; Morell 1998). Recent multivariate analysis of this controversial skeleton dismisses the hypothesis that the Kennewick Man may represent an Early Holocene European immigrant; on the contrary it features a morphology closely related to Polynesian (Chatters *et al.* in press).

Paleoindian research since the late nineteenth century has been polarized into two camps, distinguishable by their attitude towards claims for a Pleistocene human occupation of the Americas. The 1927 Folsom site visit by a 'blue ribbon panel' of scientists who confirmed the association of human artefacts with Pleistocene fauna was a landmark in the evolution of a consensus concerning the date of human entry into the Americas south of the ice sheets. Subsequently, however, the extension of the duration of Paleoindian occupation of the Americas backwards into the Pleistocene has been limited by the 'Clovis barrier'. Radiocarbon dates with clear cultural associations from Clovis sites indicate a range between 11,570 ± 70 BP (the Aubrey site) and 10,890 ± 50 BP (the Murray Springs site) (Taylor *et al.* 1996). Reports of radiocarbon dates from both North and South American sites pre-dating this age-range, or even dating from within this age-range, have been subjected to widely-disseminated critiques (among many others Dinkauze 1984, 1991; Lynch 1990; West 1993).

From my point of view, the structure of the debate has been deeply influenced by academic politics and personal quarrels, in a scenario where it appears that professional standing is linked inseparably to a cluster of early radiocarbon dates. In this context, professional strategic alliances between proponents or detractors play a major role, and the contesting of evidence and standards of acceptance are subject to these alliances. The debate has had more than one judicial proceeding that has produced a scientific argument and one can easily see the role that each participant plays (or is forced to play): judge, the accused, public prosecutor and defence lawyer. The evidence is therefore presented and argued, not in supposedly objective scientific terms, but rather in order to win the case, to escape free of accusations and to gain (or conserve) professional prestige. Although the same could be said of any other subject in archaeological debate, in no other case is it so clear-cut.

Several potential pre-Clovis sites in South America have been at the centre of the discussion because they provide earlier dates than the Aubrey site and reflect distinctive adaptive patterns. After an intense debate in the 1970s (see, amongst many others,

Bryan 1973, 1975; Haynes 1974; Lynch 1974; Martin 1973; Morlan and Cinq-Mars 1982) few of the proposed pre-Clovis sites remain as candidates. The sites studied during the last two decades, Monte Verde, Pedra Furada and, even more recently, Monte Alegre (also known as Pedra Pintada), were the prime candidates to challenge the pre-Clovis barrier for the peopling of the Americas (Fig. 1). Other sites with pre-11,500 dates occupy a peripheral position in the debate for a number of reasons: because they have not been appropriately published; the finds are not so spectacular; the evidence is still weak; or simply because they have not entered into the mainstream of the debate for reasons that are difficult to understand (Ardila 1992). Among these sites are, for example, Taima-Taima (Bryan *et al.* 1978; Ochsenius and Gruhn 1979), Tibitó (Correal Urrego 1981), Piedra Museo (Miotti and Cattáneo 1997; Miotti *et al.* 1999) and several rockshelters from eastern Brazil (Kipnis 1998; Prous 1991, 1992–3).

The site which has currently most successfully challenged the 'Clovis-first' model is Monte Verde. This site is located in southern Chile on the banks of Chinchihuapi Creek, a small tributary of the Maullín River (Fig. 2). In the MV-6 strata, dated between 12,300 and 12,800 BP Dillehay and his associates (1989, 1997) recovered wooden foundations of dwellings, a variety of botanical remains, thousands of artefacts made from local cobbles brought from the creek, wooden artefacts, and animal bones from both extinct and extant taxa. For this component, named Monte Verde 2, Dillehay suggested a forest-adapted economy, based primarily on the collection of wild plant foods and, secondarily, on the scavenging and/or hunting of large and small preys. This is the better-known component of the site. In the deeper sandy level three potential cultural features containing charcoal were found in association with several fractured stones. Two radiocarbon dates gave ages of more than 33,000 BP. The context remains ambiguous and Dillehay prefers not to consider it as securely anthropogenic.

The site has been criticized by some North American archaeologists (Dincauze 1991; Lynch 1990; Roosevelt *et al.* 1996, 383; West 1993). Criticisms vary from the potential non-human origin of the artefacts, to their actual association with the dated material. The second volume on Monte Verde (Dillehay 1997) and some recently published articles (i.e. Taylor *et al.* 1999) appear to have satisfactorily answered most of these criticisms.

Recent publicity in both the media in general and scientific journals claims that the visit of several (mainly North American) scholars to Monte Verde confirmed the pre-Clovis age and human origin of the material and features, and that the barrier had been finally broken. Besides ample coverage in newspapers and on TV in the US and the rest of the world, the popular *National Geographic Magazine*, which partially sponsored the visit, portrayed in a trivial fashion how the consensus was achieved (in a bar after the visit the participants made a show-of-hands vote and the acceptance of the site was unanimous) (Gore 1997). In the same vein, other scientific journals maintained a similar triumphalist tone (i.e. the editorial of *Current Research in the Pleistocene* 1997). Moreover, several articles claimed conclusively that after the visit 'the Clovis Curtain has

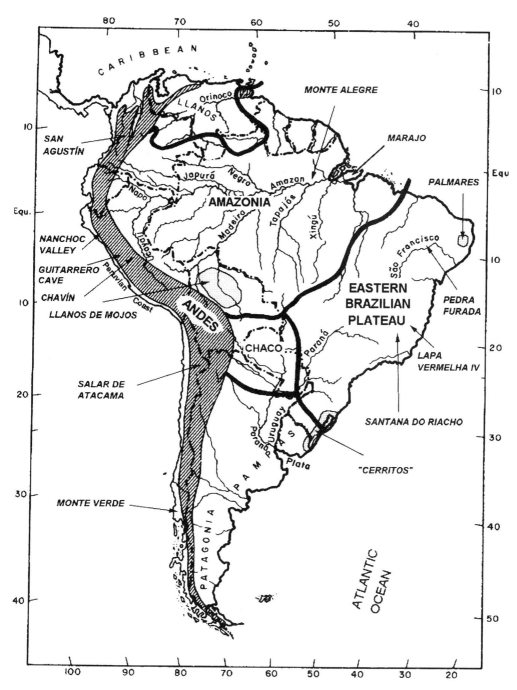

Figure 1. Map of South America showing the main areas and most of the sites and localities discussed in the text.

Figure 2. View of the Monte Verde site, in 1997, just before the start of systematic excavations (photo courtesy of Tom Dillehay).

fallen' (i.e. Adovasio and Pedler 1997). In agreement with other South American colleagues (Borrero 1995), I do not believe that these types of visit are that useful for resolving doubts or problems associated with a site. They are usually very short, occur after the excavations have taken place, and serve to 'officialize' the sites. However, it appears that this visit by well-known scholars was the turning point that has led to a 'resolution' of the debate. Tom Dillehay's years of investigating the site, including his most recent one thousand three hundred-page volume, were important but not enough. It would appear that the rite of passage had yet to be completed: the visit of the experts.

The new 'blue ribbon panel' published an article in *American Antiquity*. In their paper, Meltzer and his seven co-authors briefly comment on the findings from Monte Verde, accepting everything Dillehay had proposed and more besides. For example, in relation to the 33,000 year old date, to which Dillehay remains noncommittal, they state: 'at least some of them are clearly artifacts, there is no suggestion that they owe their position to disturbance and the associated radiocarbon determinations indicate an age of at least 33,000 BP. The chances seem good that these materials indicate a significantly early human occupation in the region' (Meltzer *et al.* 1997, 662).

In their two-day visit to Lexington, they listened to several lectures given by Dillehay, Adovasio, Collins and Rossen and examined and discussed the main part of the site collection. Contradictorily, in their abstract the authors inform us that the potential importance of the site prompted a 'detailed examination of the collections from the locality'. How can a detailed examination be performed in such a short time and covering such a wide variety of materials? However, the final statements made concerning every aspect of the site were conclusive: 'we have no doubt that they are genuine artifacts', and 'There is no doubt that the cordage, many of the wooden specimens and many seeds etc. were introduced into the site by humans', and so on (Meltzer *et al.* 1997, 661).

The group visited the site for one day — although the main occupation area of Monte Verde no longer existed, having been destroyed by the construction of a road. They actually examined only marginal stratigraphic sections attached to the site area, but this did not stop them continuing with their conclusive assertions: 'we saw no evidence of disturbance and no evidence of younger archaeological material that could have become incorporated into older sediments' (Meltzer *et al.* 1997, 661). Everything appeared to be clear from a one-day visit to a region unfamiliar to most of them.

Nevertheless, it seems some discussions and debates took place during the visit, but in the article these arguments are summarized in one short paragraph stating that they were secondary and focused on particular objects (Meltzer *et al.* 1997, 661). The substance of these disagreements is what is of interest, and perhaps a better contribution to the understanding of the cultural and natural processes that formed the site would have occurred had the authors shared their disagreements with the readers. My purpose here is not to question the high level of professionalism of either the excavators or the members of the party who visited the site, but rather to suggest that questions concerning the chronology, cultural status of some artefacts and their associations cannot be resolved by a short visit more than a decade after the excavation, and certainly not by an inspection of the stratigraphy visible in the remaining section. Few people today doubt the anthropogenic status of Monte Verde 2, but there are alternative positions to be taken concerning some of Dillehay's specific interpretations, as one would expect of such a complex site with a non-conventional archaeological deposit. For example, in a separate article Nuñez and Mena (the two Chilean participants in the visit), recognize the qualities of Monte Verde 2 but doubt the status of some so-called artefacts that they consider culturally over-valued. They also call attention to the reason for a settlement of such characteristics situated directly on gravel and damp sand, and to the lack of a record *in situ* of certain artefacts (Nuñez and Mena 1997, 41). Moreover, few people would accept Dillehay's conclusive statement that 'Monte Verde was a genuine and intact archaeological site . . .' and 'that both the geological and archaeological records at the site were intact' (Dillehay 1997, 1). What does intact mean? An abandoned site with all its cultural and natural material *in situ*, subsequently 'frozen' for more than 12,000 years with no natural factors affecting the disposition of the remains? Dillehay himself (1997, 20–1), some pages further on, recognizes some of the natural factors that would have affected the site, although he considers them as secondary and of minimal post-depositional effect. From my point of view, the very concept of 'intact' is unsustainable for any archaeological site. This does not detract from the merit of Dillehay's work, nor reduce confidence in the site; it simply places the site on a more objective and concrete footing. It is not necessary to demonstrate with an infinite variety of detailed analyses something theoretically impossible, such as an 'intact' site (the non-existence of pre-burial or post-burial agents affecting the deposit over thousands of years), in order to maintain that people have lived in southern Chile for over 12,000 years, and with a substantially different lifestyle to the Clovis foragers.

However, as Bray (1988) argues, what in practice saves archaeology from complete chaos is the fact that duplication does exist. Consequently, if Monte Verde 2 is a site as complex and well-preserved as is described and interpreted, the chances of finding similar sites in the same environment are undoubtedly high. This is one of the greatest potentials of Monte Verde 2: the generation of a model to be verified against new observations, and consequently to be able to identify patterns of behaviour of the early peoples of South America. These patterns will undoubtedly be far from the rigid schemes derived from the Clovis studies and will significantly widen the range of adaptability of the first populations of the continent.

Pedra Furada is the other site at the centre of the debate (Guidon 1986; Guidon and Parenti 1987). The site is located in a cave in the Serra da Capibara (Capibara Hills) in the Brazilian north-east (Fig. 3). The first excavations carried out at the site between 1978 and 1980 were aimed at establishing the chronology of the rock paintings. The discovery of hearths and lithic industries of quartz and quartzite in deeper strata prompted major excavations between 1982 and 1987. Today, 700 sq m have been excavated, which represents at least 80 per cent of the site. The chronology has been established with 55 radiocarbon dates, of which 46 (ranging from 6150 to more than 50,000 BP) were used to define six phases and sub-phases, Pedra Furada 1, 2 and 3 for the Pleistocene period, and Serra Talhada 1 and 2 and Agreste for the Holocene period. The Pleistocene phases show stable patterns through time, such as a unifacial technique without any flaking pattern and minimal retouch, which is considered an expedient technology which makes immediate use of natural fragments. According to Fabio Parenti (1996, 20), one of the principal investigators of the site, the whole chrono-stratigraphy presents no problems, is very secure and the 50,000 years BP should be considered as a minimum age.

The visit to Pedra Furada by a group of specialists in 1993 produced an effect contrary to that at Monte Verde. It resulted in an article by Meltzer *et al.* (1995) which severely questioned most aspects of the site and the research methodology. The replies from Guidon and Pessis (1996) and Parenti *et al.* (1996) failed to resolve some of the issues raised. The main criticisms from Meltzer and co-authors can be summarized as follows: 1) The sub-phases appear to have been based almost entirely

Figure 3. View of the Pedra Furada site during the 1993 site visit.

on the radiocarbon chronological hiatuses within the sequence. There is no clear stratigraphic separation and no difference in the artefacts or contexts. 2) There are no obvious mechanisms of contamination of the charcoal, but doubts are related to the source of the charcoal. Moreover, in the remaining stratigraphic profile of the site, the charcoal lenses were thick and diffuse, different from the discrete lenses and hearths from the Holocene levels. 3) All the artefacts reported in the Pedra Furada phase are made of quartz and quartzite, the source of which is a gravel bar which occurs 100 m directly above the site. This gravel bar is directly connected with the site deposits through chutes at either end of the shelter — material falls down from the drip line during the rains. These chutes are certainly a source of geofacts, since cobbles fall and crush one another.

Parenti (1996) developed certain criteria to identify the artefacts: 1) the number of flake scars; 2) the edge angle (less than 90 degrees); 3) the pattern of the flake scars on the working edge; and 4) the location of the object within the rock shelter. He argued that the rocks could not be geofacts because of the large number of flakes (more than three) removed from each one. Nonetheless, the fact remains that the artefacts were selected in the field from amidst countless rock. How many rocks? On one hand, Meltzer *et al.* (1995) calculated that even if the probability was very low, a rock could crush or be crushed by others, with the possibility of a few hundred putative artefacts accumulating over 50,000 years. On the other hand, the more-than-three flakes criterion assumes that there were only limited opportunities for the cobbles to be flaked (Meltzer *et al.* 1995).

Guidon and Pessis (1996) answered the criticisms made by Meltzer and colleagues by accusing the authors of not being specialists in archaeological excavation in the Pleistocene period of tropical regions. Such an argument is futile. Why then were they invited to visit, discuss and evaluate the findings at Pedra Furada? Guidon and Pessis respond to every point raised by Meltzer and co-authors with different degrees of success. For example, they state that in the entire site there are only waterfalls in the chutes at each end, and also defended the method of excavation used (*décapage*), and how Meltzer *et al.* had misinterpreted their explanation of the site. They further claimed that it was impossible that the material overlying the quartzite-laden bars had fallen directly into the interior of the shelter, behind the drip-line.

Some of the criticisms were successfully countered by Guidon and Pessis, but although Meltzer and his co-authors probably misinterpreted some aspects of the site and did not make detailed analyses of all the issues criticized, there are still obscure points in the interpretation of the site. One such point is the absence of detailed published site reports in spite of more than 20 years of continuous investigation. Another point is the lack of systematic studies of the site formation process, the type of research now obligatory for almost all archaeological sites. If there were 6000 artefacts in the Holocene levels and slightly less than 600 in the Pleistocene levels, is it possible that these artefacts could have migrated to a deeper level due to biological activity for example? The other weak point, in agreement with Meltzer *et al.*, is the selection process used in the field to pick out the 'artefacts' and discard the abundant naturally broken cobbles in the matrix.

If there were people living in the area more than 50,000 years ago who occasionally visited the cave (perhaps once every hundred years — averaging out the time span with the number of artefacts found), where are the remains of these people in the rest of the region? We should wait for the other sites generated by these early people to be uncovered — sites which could show, for example, artefacts made with non-local rocks or some kind of bone preservation. In summary, we need to await more data, especially detailed published data, and a better understanding of the site formation process before accepting Pedra Furada as a 'paradigm-breaking' site and the presence of people in the Brazilian *caatinga* more than 50,000 years ago.

The third important site in the discussion is Monte Alegre although the age of the deposit is para-Clovis rather than pre-Clovis. The site is located in the Caverna da Pedra Pintada, a cave located on a high plain 10 km west of the Lower Amazon River. In the deepest layer of the cave, Roosevelt and her team excavated 11 contiguous metre-sized squares to a maximum depth of 2.25 m and found, in the Paleoindian layers, approximately 30,000 flakes and 24 formal tools, including bifacial projectile points, some of which had tangs (Roosevelt *et al.* 1996). The quantity contrasts sharply with the mere 150 lithics found in the upper, Holocene, layers. The principal raw materials used were chalcedony, quartz crystal and quartz breccia, all of which occur locally, but none are from the cave itself. Researchers identified percussion and pressure flaking, bifacial and unifacial flaking, heat treatment and isolated platforms prepared with pecking and grinding. In the Paleoindian levels, carbonized wood in hearths, thousands of carbonized fruit and seeds from tropical rainforest trees were found. The species harvested during the Late Pleistocene occupation are still to be found in the tropical forest of the neighbouring area. Faunal remains were badly preserved and included small fragments of bone (some of them carbonized) of fish, rodents, bats, bivalves, molluscs, tortoises, turtles, snakes, amphibians and large land mammals (unidentified ungulates).

Fifty-six radiocarbon dates, ranging from 11,200–10,000 BP, were obtained from wood and carbonized plants. For Roosevelt and her collaborators the arrival of humans at the cave is marked by a cluster of four dates between 11,145 ± 135 and 10,875 ± 295 BP. In concluding, Roosevelt and her associates postulated that Paleoindians visited the cave periodically for more than 1200 years, and while there ate fruit and a wide variety of river and land game, painted the cave, manufactured stone tools and cut wood. They further proposed, through ethnographic analogy, that the rock paintings were used to define ancestral territory and celebrate initiation rituals.

The main criticism of the site is related to the age of the archaeological deposits and to the sensationalist way in which the site was presented to the press (see, for example,

The Observer, 23 June, 1996). C. Vance Haynes and K. Tankersley (quoted in Gibbons 1996) feel that 10,500 BP is a safer date, since they averaged the 14 earliest dates and arrived at this age. Dincauze (quoted in Gibbons 1996) agrees that the more recent dates are more reliable, noting that the earlier contain greater errors. Fiedel (1996) discusses the datings and their sigmas in relation to major C-14 anomalies in this period and concludes that 'there may have been an interval of anywhere from 700 to 2000 years between Clovis and the Initial Phase of Monte Alegre' (1996, 1823). The other set of criticisms point out that the evidence from Monte Alegre is not new, as other sites in Brazil had already demonstrated the existence of humans in the region before 10,000 BP (Dillehay 1996; Meggers 1996). However, whether or not the first human occupation is 11,200 years old or slightly younger, the early levels of Monte Alegre show quite clearly that people lived in the tropical rainforest at the end of the Pleistocene period. This new site, along with other Brazilian sites such as Santa Ana do Riacho, Lapa do Boquete (Prous 1997), or Lapa Vermehla IV (Neves *et al.* 1999), demonstrates the human occupation of South America and cannot be considered a post-Clovis expansion. Furthermore, the evidence from Monte Alegre has been supported from recent work by Behling (1996). He suggested that the appearance of particles of carbon in a core, from a level dated to 12,868–12,682 BP, from a lake close to the mouth of the River Amazon, could be due to the arrival of people in the region.

No conclusive statement can yet be made in regard to when and how people colonized South America. However, it is possible to propose the following: a) There were humans in South America while the Clovis people were hunting large mammals in the North American plains. Moreover, as has been demonstrated through detailed comparative studies (Nami 1997), there are important technological differences between the North American Clovis points and the so-called 'fishtail' points of the Southern Cone. Clearly, both models of projectile points demonstrate distinct manufacturing styles and cannot be considered as descended from each other as has been repeatedly postulated (e.g. Fiedel 1999; Lynch 1983; Morrow and Morrow 1997; Schobinger 1988); b) by the end of the Pleistocene period, during Clovis times, humans in South America were developing several different subsistence strategies. The tropical forest, the wet western foothills of the Andes and the southern plains of the Pampa and Patagonia were colonized by people who were exploiting different environments using a variety of economic strategies.

Instead of a model that sees the first colonizers schizophrenically advancing into a completely new environment along a north-to-south highway, I, like many other South American archaeologists, prefer to imagine a scenario of slow movements designed to people the new environment. Hunter-gatherers need to know the availability of resources, the location of water and raw material, and also need to conceptualize their space and sacralize the landscape. During the Late Pleistocene in the Americas the problem would not have been population pressure, but, rather, how to sustain a certain number of people in an area and maintain a mating system. Hence, from my perspective, there was no such driving force which pushed people to face all of these new challenges.

Amazonia: a green debate in the rainforest

The Amazonian rainforest is the largest rainforest in the world, comprising approximately seven million square kilometres. This area has usually been divided into the *várzea*, or flood plain of the Amazon river and its major Andean tributaries (the so-called 'white rivers'), and the *terra firme*, or inter-riverine uplands. While the *várzea* is restricted and occupies only 2 per cent of the basin, the *terra firme* are the dominant environment and make up the remainder of the territory. This division has been determinant in the study of human adaptation in Amazonia (see a recent review in Heckenberger *et al.* 1999). Whilst the fertility of the *várzeas* has been accepted and their potential to support large, fully sedentary villages has been recognized, the potential of the *terra firme* for sustaining a particular density of population has been questioned, and this has been transformed into a critical point of debate. Furthermore, recent studies have proposed that at least 11.8 per cent of the *terra firme* forest is anthropogenic (Baleé 1989; Fedick 1995).

The Amazonian rainforest has been one of the favoured places for testing models related to human adaptation and discussing the environmental constraints on human behaviour. It has also been one of the places where archaeological and ethnographic data were used and misused together in various ways in order to examine the multiple dimensions of human adaptation. Here, ethnic and especially linguistic pre-Hispanic boundaries were reconstructed from ceramic type distributions, historical documents and ethnographic analogy. Furthermore, the Amazon Basin is currently one of the areas in South America where problem-orientated research with a strong anthropological background is consistently carried out (Neves 1999). Finally, Amazonia has been a battlefield for strong theoretical, methodological, political and personal disagreements (for antagonistic interpretations and perspectives, see Lathrap 1968, 1970, 1977; Meggers 1971, 1992a, 1999; Roosevelt 1980, 1991, 1995). This debate, called the 'Amazon archaeology wars' by Denevan (Mann 2000), has been bitter, acrimonious and difficult to follow for those of us who do not know the details of the politico-academic disputes between the North American antagonists.

The idea that there are 'limiting' factors to the human occupation of the Amazonian rainforest has had a long-held tradition. Following *The Handbook of South American Indians* (Steward 1946–50), the Amazonian environment has been 'cited by cultural ecologists as a prime example of how the environment determines and limits sociocultural evolution' (Hames and Vickers 1983, 7). Moreover, Amazonia was considered limited in resources, not only for foragers (Bailey *et al.* 1989), but also for horticulturists. Poor soils, sparse faunal resources, the lack of efficient transportation and isolation from the main centres of cultural invention (the Andes) were presented as 'limiting factors' which explained the lack of social complexity in the region (Steward and Faron 1959). This was particularly marked in the *terra firme* (Meggers 1971), the inter-riverine areas with poor soils. Only in the *várzea*, where annual flooding produced silt-rich soils, were the limiting factors reversed.

Steward and Faron (1959) refer to the occupants of the poorer *terra firme* as 'marginal food nomads'. They argued that these people possessed a simpler level of egalitarian organization than those in the *várzea* because they 'barely met minimum subsistence needs and often fell far short of them' (Steward and Faron 1959, 60). Using Steward's model, Meggers concluded that the soils of the *várzea* provided a better environment for human exploitation (Meggers 1971). Carneiro (1970), who linked protein needs to circumscription and the emergence of social complexity, concluded that since the *terra firme* were poor in protein resources social development would not occur. Consequently, *terra firme* 'societies . . . remained small because they could adapt to resource depletion by simple geographical expansion' (Hames and Vickers 1983, 10). Lathrap (1968) continued to develop the idea of the poverty of the *terra firme* habitat but focused on the concept of devolution. According to his hypothesis, weaker groups were originally surrounded by far stronger ones. Once the stronger groups expanded into the interior they devolved as a result of the poverty of the interior forest, and became small, mobile bands of hunter-gatherers. Among many subsequent papers related to this issue (see reviews in Carneiro 1995; Hames and Vickers 1983; Neves 1999; Sponsel 1986), Gross (1975) deserves special mention since he expanded the model of animal protein as the limiting factor on Amazonian populations. Carbohydrate deficiency has also been put forward as another critical factor in population density (Milton 1984) and occupation of the *terra firme* generally.

The conclusions from these important studies have inspired a tradition in Amazonian research which explains human adaptation in the area by emphasizing that the lack of resources makes it particularly difficult for foragers to live in the *terra firme*. Scarcity, poverty and constraint are often used to describe the impact of the Amazonian landscape on human settlement. Since the negative aspects of Amazonia have been emphasized it is not surprising that environmental factors have emerged as the major limiting factor on human adaptation. This opened the way for Headland and Bailey's general hypothesis concerning the human use of *all* tropical rainforests, where adaptation, they argue, can only be sustained if some horticulture is practised or domesticated plants from neighbouring horticulturists are consumed. Their model was also inspired by work (Hart and Hart 1986; Hutterer 1983) which emphasized the scarcity of some resources in non-Amazonian rainforests. While the latter pointed out that 'it is the scarcity of carbohydrates rather than protein that represents a major limiting factor for low-density foraging population in rain forests' (Hutterer 1983, 179), the former stressed the precarious resource-base of the Ituri Forest in Zaire.

The Bailey–Headland model has been developed and proposed several times since 1986 (Bailey 1990; Bailey and Headland 1991; Bailey *et al.* 1989, 1991; Headland 1987; Headland and Bailey 1991), and has promoted a lively debate (Brosius 1991; Cavelier *et al.* 1995; Colinvaux and Bush 1991; Stearman 1991; Townsend 1990). In early papers Headland proposed that carbohydrates were the limiting factor, while Bailey and associates also took into account fat and other sources of nutrients (see similarities and differences in Headland and Bailey 1991). The Bailey–Headland model was also supported by Sponsel (1989, 45), who argued that in Amazonia foraging and farming are not only complementary but are also necessary to make human occupation viable.

Among these papers, Bailey *et al.* (1989) and Bailey and Headland (1991) were the most important for the discussion of the history of human occupation in tropical rainforests. Bailey *et al.* (1989) added time-depth to the nutritional argument by pointing out the lack of archaeological remains in tropical rainforests prior to the presence of horticulture. They discuss several archaeological examples, concluding that '. . . resources in pre-agricultural rain forest habitats were probably so poor, variable and dispersed that they could not support viable populations of human foragers' (Bailey *et al.* 1989, 62). They later expanded this hypothesis and proposed that humans could not inhabit these environments until they had developed 'ways to alter the distribution and abundance of edible resources through domestication of plants and clearing of forest' (Headland and Bailey 1991, 118).

The later paper (Bailey and Headland 1991) is significant because it followed a series of critical case studies which contradicted their model in various ways, especially case studies which demonstrated that populations of foragers are viable in tropical rainforests (Brosius 1991; Dwyer and Minnegal 1991; Endicot and Bellwood 1991; Stearman 1991). Most of the data presented in these studies, however, were regarded as 'largely anecdotal' and the arguments as 'mainly rhetorical' (Bailey and Headland 1991, 281). By refining the concept, they modified slightly their original proposition concluding that 'in the absence of purposeful forest clearing for the purposes of cultivation of domesticated or semi-domesticated plants, humans have never subsisted for sustained periods in tropical forest environments' (Bailey and Headland 1991, 266–7). Domestication and forest clearance were the two prerequisites for living successfully in the rainforest; without them foragers would not survive unless they obtained crops from neighbours. Finally, they reinforced the position that calories, not protein, are the limiting factor for tropical rainforest foragers.

However, the data presented by Stearman (1991) and Politis (1996b) for South American tropical rainforest foragers indicate that they can maintain viable populations based on the exploitation of non-domesticated resources, even though they practise some small-scale horticulture. The data recorded among the Nukak from the Colombian Amazon (Fig. 4) are significant as it appears that some heavily exploited fruit (i.e. *seje* (*Oenocarpus bataua*), *popere* (*Oenocarpus mapora*), *platanillo* (*Phenakospermum guianensis*),

Figure 4. Nukak foragers from the Colombian Amazonia. View of a winter residential camp with a nuclear family around the hearth. The woman is burning the hair of a monkey before cooking.

and *moriche* (*Mauritia flexuosa*)) provide enough carbohydrates, especially in the rainy season when other sources of calories, such as honey and fish, might not be so plentiful (Politis 1996b). These observations also provide support for the comments made by Townsend (1990) that palm fruits have been undervalued as a source of carbohydrates, with attention concentrated on tubers (Headland 1987; Milton 1984). They certainly contradict Sponsel's (1989, 40) argument concerning the 'relatively low accessibility of most wild plant resources in the interior forest'. In most analyses of the food potential of the *terra firme* such resources are regarded as secondary and only significant for a limited period of time.

> Many of the additional aquatic resources (fish, manate, caiman, turtle and eggs etc.) are either concentrated in, or limited to, the fluvial zone and so they are mostly, if not completely, irrelevant to the interfluves. Insects are rich in many nutrients including protein, but most are ephemeral and of limited quantity.
>
> (Sponsel 1989, 40)

However, in the case of the Nukak these so-called 'limited' resources form an important part of their diet, even though some are more abundant and predictable than others. For example, palm grubs are abundant in the rainy season, and there are strong reasons to believe that the Nukak augment their productivity by cutting *seje*, *moriche* and *chontaduro* (*Bactris gasipaes*) palms, as do other Amazonian groups (Dufour 1987). In addition, during the rainy season fish, tortoise and a little honey occasionally provide a modest quantity of supplementary food. Honey is extremely abundant and also predictable during the dry season. It must also be taken into account that a large quantity of honey, real jelly, rich-fat larvae, propolis, and even some types of pollen are immediately consumed at the foot of the fallen hives. These so-called secondary rainforest resources were exploited in a similar way by other Amazonian groups such as the Yuqui prior to contact (Stearman 1991). Fish is also abundant and predictable during the dry season when creeks and ponds reach their lowest levels. The Nukak are not the only inter-riverine group that consume fish; similar levels of fish use have been recorded amongst other groups, such as the Shipibo, where 45 per cent of their protein intake is from fish (Balée 1995).

The next part of the Bailey and Headland hypothesis which needs to be examined is the distribution of resources within the forest, since accessibility affects the cost/benefit return ratio of any resource. The issue of high productivity but poor yield lies at the heart of the Bailey and Headland model, as tropical rainforests are characterized by a high diversity of species, but individuals within a species tend to be widely scattered (Kricher 1989). In this sense, such habitats are considered to have uniform patchiness, which may limit the viability of human foragers (Bailey *et al.* 1989, 61) since they cannot gather their daily dietary requirement without travelling substantial distances. Such travel increases foraging costs and reduces the energy return until a point is reached where the exploitation of a given plant or animal becomes extremely expensive. These are a general characteristic of all rainforests, but this does not mean that a concentration of plants or animals can only be achieved by clearing the forest and planting domesticated species. The high diversity/low density of con-specific taxa is neither a universal condition at the scale of a single rainforest, nor for rainforests in general (Peter *et al.* 1989 in Stearman 1991). Furthermore, a great diversity of habitats have been recognized within what is understood as the rainforest, some of which contain resources in much higher concentrations than in other areas.

In the case of the Nukak, both situations are encountered. Some resources are concentrated in predictable locations while others are manipulated by the Nukak in order to increase their density. *Moriche*, fish and honey are examples of the former. These resources can be obtained in large quantities in restricted areas. The second situation covers *seje*, *platanillo*, *guana* (*Dacryodes peruviana*), palm grubs and probably many others that have not yet been recorded. These resources are almost inadvertently concentrated by the Nukak through various short-term activities with long-term effects on the management of their habitat. Residential mobility creates patches of edible resources — when the residential camp is moved, thousands of seeds from the plant species they have consumed are left behind. By leaving the forest canopy untouched, the camp area remains shaded which prevents colonization by vines and other high-light competitive species. The high concentration of seeds in a semi-cleared area provides an environment, which facilitates the growth of these plants, which are now relatively free from competition. This creates gardens of 'wild' species which the Nukak can revisit after some years and find a dense patch of edible plants (see discussion in Politis 1996a, 1996b, 1999). In this way, their frequent moves generate numerous patches of resources scattered within easy reach of their pathways. This further explains why camp sites are not reused, despite the fact that former dwelling structures are at times located in their immediate vicinity.

The Nukak are not alone in demonstrating such behaviour. Laden has noted a comparable pattern among the Efe of the Ituri Forest of Africa (Bailey and Headland 1991, 266). This raises another major question that I do not have space to do more than touch on here: How primary is the primary rainforest? We may now have in Amazonia an environment which has been modified by humans in many ways and at different levels of management since at least the Late Pleistocene (Denevan 1992; Kricher 1989; Stahl 1996). In particular areas and periods the manipulation of wild resources by foragers was a constant factor in the maintenance of the forest, while at other times slash-and-burn horticulture produced more visible results (Balée 1989; Meggers 1999). This view is also supported by archaeological studies from other areas in Amazonia, such as work by Herrera *et al.* (1992, 111), who state that in the pre-Hispanic Colombian Amazon, 'The [archaeological] data presented so far support recent ideas posited by researchers working in Amazonia, which present man conserving and managing resources instead of merely exploiting them.'

Of course, from historical ecology one could argue that equally the Nukak, the Yuqui or the Sirionó all live in an environment formed by thousands of years of intensive agriculture and settled village life (Balée 1989). However, until now there has been no evidence to support such an argument, at least in the Nukak area. Neither has it been shown that in every case (or in the majority of cases) do horticultural activities increase the density of animal populations, although they may serve to attract prey (e.g. Holmberg 1969).

While I would not claim the Nukak as a pristine group of foragers who provide us with a privileged glimpse of traditional rainforest adaptations, I would argue that those who adhere to the necessity of horticulture/agriculture for the sustained exploitation of this, one of the world's major habitat types, have been led to the wrong conclusion by the available ethnography. This ethnography, well exemplified in Amazonia by the much-cited works on the Makú (Hupdu and Bará, see Silverwood-Cope 1972 and Reid 1979), has always suffered from the problem that these peoples only became part of the ethnographic record *after* they adopted a significant agricultural component into their subsistence system, which included a degree of sedentism. They are only considered as foragers because we have historical knowledge that until recently their economy was based to a much larger extent on hunting and gathering. In the 1970s, when Reid (1979) carried out his fieldwork, he reported that the Hupdu-Makú only gathered significant quantities of fruit and nuts between April and June, and the main value of this food was to 'provide a pleasant diversion from the manioc-based vegetable diet, adding a variety of different flavours and textures to the monotony of cassava bread and starch drinks' (1979, 71).

Nor does the archaeology of Amazon foragers support a late colonization of the area by horticulturist groups or those dependent upon horticulturists. A strong example is the case of Monte Alegre (Roosevelt *et al.* 1996), where the represented trees (primarily rainforest palms) and their δ C13 ratios indicate that during the occupation of the cave the surrounding area was tropical rainforest. Other less well-known examples, like Gaviao Cave in the Carajá Hills (Magalhaes 1994) of the southern Amazon, and the open-air sites of the Itapipoca Phase (Miller 1992), both dated to the Early Holocene, do not support a late (horticulturist) colonization. The palaeo-ecological reconstruction for the Central/Lower Amazon also demonstrates that at the end of the Pleistocene period the area was already covered by dense rainforest (Adam and Faure 1997). If an environmental limit to foraging did exist, then I believe it will be found in a much earlier period of prehistory (see discussion in Politis and Gamble 1996). The first occupation of the Amazonian tropical rainforest may not have been contemporary with the first wave of human dispersal into South America, but neither is it possible to delay it until the appearance of swidden agriculture at a much later date.

As has been said, the debate over the sustainability of Amazonian soils and their agricultural potential has also led to the questioning of the possibility of cultural complexity in the Amazonian rainforest. The main 'battlefield' was, in this case, the archaeological sequence of Marajó Island, where Meggers and Evans (1957) reconstructed a sequence of five phases, four of which have characteristics compatible with the Tropical Forest Cultures and a fifth that incorporates elements that suggest some kind of hierarchical social organization (Meggers 1999). Meggers and Evans (1957) proposed that the rapid decline of the mound-builders of Marajó, the last phase, was the result of their inability to maintain an intensive agricultural production, basically due to environmental limitations. Brochado (1980) challenged this model, presenting an alternative in which Marajoara agriculture is seen as a large-scale undertaking of a chiefdom-like organization, based on the intensive cultivation of seed and root crops in naturally raised fields. Following this idea, the excavation in the site of Teso dos Bichos led Roosevelt (1991) to propose the existence of a long sequence of complex chiefdoms in the region, with intensive agriculture and urban-scale sites with earthen architecture and monumental mounds. The investigation at Teso dos Bichos has been questioned (e.g. Meggers 1992b, 1999) and it has been remarked that the site has not produced conclusive evidence of intensive cultivation of maize or even of maize being a staple in Marajó during the span of the Marajoara phase (Carneiro 1995; Neves 1999, 222). Moreover, it has recently been proposed as a counter-argument that some chiefdoms could have actually developed as a result of the European Conquest, instead of having being destroyed by it (Neves 1999).

One of the most significant problems in approaching this subject is the small sample analysed by Roosevelt and the data which have still only been presented in a preliminary fashion. On one side it is clear that Amazonian societies 'were neither ecologically prevented from settled village life nor narrowly constrained by an egalitarian ideology' (Heckenberger *et al.* 1999, 372), but on the other side the presence of large sedentary population aggregates does not presuppose that those societies were socio-politically integrated into centralized systems at local or regional levels (Clastres 1977; Fausto 1992). Were the mounds of Marajó the result of complex societies who were managing agriculture on a grand scale and had developed urban centres as Roosevelt argues? Or, on the contrary, are they the result of the relocation of the cultivated fields and the settlements of non-complex villages in cycles of periodic movement, as Meggers suggests? How many of the mounds and cultivated fields were occupied simultaneously? What quantity of cultivable land was controlled from each mound? At present, there is no conclusive evidence with which to reject or confirm any of the models proposed, although from my perspective, and in spite of the weakness of the evidence, some type of social hierarchization, whether chiefdom or chiefdom-like societies, would appear to have existed in several places and time periods in Amazonia.

The emergence of chiefdoms or some kind of social hierarchy has been discussed for several places on the periphery of Amazonia. Such places include the western Venezuelan *llanos* (Spenser and Redmond 1998) and the Llanos de Mojos, in the north-eastern savannahs of Bolivia. In the former case, the causeways that traverse the *llanos* and the public architecture led Spenser and Redmond (1998) to suggest that the society which built them was socio-politically organized into chiefdoms. In the latter area, there have been recorded thousands of mounds, causeways and channels created by humans in order to make this huge seasonally flooded plain habitable (Denevan 1966; Dougherty and Calandra 1984–5; Erickson 1995). Although this area is still poorly known, the extension of the earthworks and the connections between them (in terms of causeways and canals) led Erickson to suggest that they were erected by 'heterarchical societies: groups of communities, loosely bound by shifting horizontal links through kinship, alliances, and informal association' (Mann 2000, 789). Once again, when it becomes possible to determine more clearly the degree of contemporaneity between these earthworks it will be possible to have a better idea concerning their articulation and the type of social complexity necessary in order for the system to function.

Social complexity and food production in the Andes or *Sometimes, the paths in the labyrinth converge* (Borges 1941)

The issue of social complexity has been of continual interest to South American archaeology, but has been encumbered with methodological and conceptual problems related to the criteria used to define social complexity and the archaeological indicia used to trace it, as we noted in the previous section. In South America the existence of state-level societies was evident from the first moment of the Conquista, when Europeans made contact with the Inca. Since archaeology developed as a scientific discipline, the Inca have been considered as the most complete version of Andean civilization. It has been said that the Andes (especially the Central Andes) have been tinted with an 'Incarized' vision of the past, due to the pre-eminence of this empire within the indigenous context of the sub-continent (Roe 1994). Nonetheless, the concept of complexity has been questioned, and criticisms of neo-evolutionist typologies have been so forceful that types that supposedly attest to the growth of this complexity should now be considered only as operating tools and not socio-political formations on an evolutionary scale (Bawden 1989; Gnecco 1996; McGuire 1983; Paynter 1989). Currently, such types have little use beyond providing a framework for cross-cultural comparisons. Moreover, the definition of complexity is arbitrary, related only to the variables that are chosen to examine it. One criterion commonly used is the internal social differentiation of unequal access to goods and services which are controlled by a small sector of society (the élite). However, it remains unclear how this can be detected in the archaeological record. A large part of the problem is the different indicators used to discuss the existence of social complexity, such as major artefact variability, mortuary practices (Isbell 1988), public and monumental architecture (Burger 1992; Pozorski and Pozorski 1993), settlement pattern hierarchy and intensive agriculture (Stanish 1994).

An interest in understanding the origin, causes and processes involved in social complexity has been present in South America since the first systematic archaeological studies. For example, for the German archaeologist Max Uhle, the Andean cultures 'were products detached from a Central American trunk', or 'peripheral branches of the ancient Mayan expansion' (Amat Olazábal 1997, 10), while for the Peruvian archaeologist Julio Tello, their origins lay in the highlands of the Andes and corresponded to a process of autochthonous evolution. Larco Hoyle (1946) supported a coastal origin for the Andean civilization, while Lathrap (1975) proposed a tropical forest origin for the Valdivia culture (from coastal Ecuador) and stressed the importance of the Amazonian lowlands to ancient Andean civilization.

Recently, there has been renewed interest in social complexity in South America. A crucial point in current arguments is that variation in the demographic scale or the level of complexity can be characterized as vertical variations. Although important, this is not the only relevant distinction between complex societies (Drennan 1993). A comparative study of ethnographic data from societies with different degrees of complexity has led to the identification of horizontal variations in the function of leaders, differentiation in status, political activities and settlement models (Feinman and Neitzel 1984). In this sense, one of the most important conclusions from the last few decades of the study of complex societies in South America is that vertical variation is far more complicated than the classic neo-evolutionary models have allowed for; and, further, that an extremely rich horizontal variation exists which has recently begun to be examined (Drennan 1993). This exploration has fortunately come out of the so-called 'nuclear areas', and has focused on regions where social complexity had distinct trajectories and particular manifestations. Today we know that the archaeology of the chiefdoms of the Upper Magdalena River (Drennan *et al.* 1993) and the Sierras del Tairona (Gnecco 1996), or the builders of the 'cerritos' of south-eastern Brazil and eastern Uruguay (Andrade and López Mazz in press; Pintos 1998) can teach us as much as the societies of the Central Andes or the highlands of Mexico about processes such as social hierarchy or the development of authority.

Recent studies have stressed different motivating mechanisms for complexity and have characterized it according to different criteria (Earle 1997). What motivated isolated and relatively autonomous small villages to transform into intermediate-level polities such as chiefdoms? One of the more popular economic explanations is that the evolution of complexity in the Andes was due to the control of large irrigation systems in the valleys of the desert coast of Peru (Wittfogel 1957). This hypothesis argues that the increased control of water would have encouraged the generation of centralized political systems. Although this process has some explanatory power for social complexity on the coast, the hydraulic theory seems to be insufficient to explain the Andean highland chiefdoms, where irrigation systems were small-scale and few communities depended entirely upon them (Earle 1997). Although various causes could have triggered social complexity (i.e. environmental changes, demography, etc.) there are strong correlations suggesting that in South America complexity is a phenomenon derived from sedentism and food production.

It appears that in the region the domestication of plants is one of the first steps in the evolutionary process of Andean societies. Nonetheless, the process of domestication, which would have started at the beginning of the Holocene, occurred gradually over several millennia and did not initially produce important social changes. Almost simultaneously to the initial domestication of plants, a tendency towards sedentism, especially on the coast of Peru, is recorded. This is in some ways an atypical process, because it is regarded in other parts of the world as a prerequisite for the origin of agricultural societies (Price and Gebauer 1995). The exceptions are Mesoamerica and the Central Andes where early domestication and sedentism appeared together at approximately the same time. Drennan (1991) has compared six regional sequences of chiefdom trajectories in Formative Mesoamerica, Lower Central America and Northern South

America, which showed significant differences in the degree to which resources were mobilized for the construction of ritually-based public works and in the degree to which peer polity interaction can predict the pattern of appearance of chiefly centres. This variation in regional historical trajectories seems to be visible in the two or three centuries during the development of sedentary agricultural economies.

The seed of social complexity in the Andes has primarily been looked for in the archaic period, in the highlands as well as on the coast. Three large environmental zones are present in the Central Andes: the coastal desert, the highlands (or *sierra*) (Fig. 5), and the tropical forest of the eastern slope of the cordillera (the *selva*). This is referred

Figure 5. View of the Andean highlands. A llama in the *Puna*, the dry high plateau of the Andes.

to as the 'three worlds of the Andes' and it has provided a framework for the study of pre-Hispanic human adaptation. However, there is no consensus on the operational definition of coast and highlands. The placement of the boundary between these two zones has a significant effect on the spatial patterns studied (Shimada 1999). Llagostera (1992) summarized and discussed coastal adaptation from Chile to Ecuador and presented the variety of local strategies, which to him appeared to be related to increasing sedentism. Shady (1993 in D'Altroy 1997) analysed the transition between the Formative and the Archaic, concluding that in the Andean populations mixed foraging and farming occurred early and that the growth in the use of cultigens was associated with incipient social complexity in the highlands. This was based on the data obtained in the Nanchoc Valley sites on the north coast of Peru, where several small mounds, used some time between 6000 and 5000 BP, were interpreted as small-scale public architecture which probably served as a focus for communal activity (Dillehay *et al.* 1997, 51). The Ring site, on the south coast of Peru, also appears to have had early public architecture (Sandweiss *et al.* 1989), as did the Asana site (Aldenderfer 1991). Domestic elliptical huts, some of which would have been related to the use of the small mounds, and dated from 8500 to 5000 BP, were also excavated in the Nanchoc Valley. At these sites, which were used to define the Las Pircas and Tierra Blanca phases, several wild and semi-cultivated plants were recovered: squash (*Cucurbita* sp), peanuts (*Arachis hypogaea*), a quinua-like chenopod (*Chenopodium*), manioc (*Maniot esculenta*), cactus fruit, etc. (Dillehay *et al.* 1997). Ten radiocarbon dates obtained from this context matched the artefact stratigraphy and previous dates from the project (Rossen *et al.* 1996), which ranged from *c.*7600 to 8400 BP. However, a set of four radiocarbon dates taken directly from the archaeobotanical remains and processed using AMS produced extremely modern dates, from AD 1700 to 1950-5 (Rossen *et al.* 1996). The situation appears controversial and new studies will have to be completed to confirm the presence of early gardening activity in the Nanchoc Valley. Conversely, other candidates for the provision of evidence of early cultivated plants have been seriously questioned. In Guitarrero Cave, Callejón de Huaylas, Smith (1980) identified pepper, beans and various types of tubers and fruit in a context dated from 10,600 to 10,000 BP. In Tres Cuevas Cave, in the Chilca Canyon, three tubers (excluding manioc) were reported that dated from 10,000 to 6600 BP (Engel 1970; Martins 1976). Both contexts have been placed in doubt by the record of disturbances in the stratigraphy of the cave where the archaeobotanical remains were found (Bonavía 1984; Hastorf 1999; Vescelius 1981a, 1981b).

Organization into sedentary villages appears precariously on the coast of Peru at approximately 8000 BP, utilizing the 'fog meadows' (*lomas*) which occur amid the arid landscape (Fung Pineda 1988). From 5500–5000 BP the number of villages near the coast increases, by which time firm evidence of the cultivation of squash, gourds, kidney and lima beans and cotton has been recorded. However, the domestication of plants, which was the result of a several millennia-long process, seems not to have introduced notable social changes (Fung Pineda 1988). Based on the internal differentiation of the buildings and their forms, it has been proposed that in this period on the Peruvian coast a process of complexity began in the settlements (Fung Pineda 1988, 70).

The sites in the Nanchoc Valley (excluding for now the botanical context of semi-cultivated or cultivated plants) belong to a period defined as the Middle Pre-Ceramic period (*c.*8000–5000 BP), where the preconditions for monumental building were present (Moseley 1992). During this period, initial moves were made towards the domestication of plants and animal species, sedentism, technological innovation, occupational specialization and the construction of public architecture (Dillehay *et al.* 1997). In the case of domesticated animals, Bonavía (1999) concludes, after discussing the various sources of evidence and different hypotheses on camelid domestication, that llamas and alpacas were domesticated in the Central Andes at 4000–4900 m above sea-level between 5000 and 6000 BP. However, Bonavía also states that the ancestral form of camelid from which the llama and alpaca were domesticated, and the fundamental reason for such domestication, are still subject to debate. Another independent centre of domestication of camelids has been proposed for the south-central Andes, in the area of Salar de Atacama, at around 4300 BP (Nuñez 1981, 1992).

Recent work by Hastorf (1999) offers an alternative perspective on the process of plant domestication and social differentiation on the Peruvian coast. The first evidence of crop plants on the coast was found in what has been defined as the Preceramic III phase (10,000–8000 BP), but substantial agriculture, with more than 15 crops grown up and down the coast, and with irrigation systems associated with civic architecture, occurred some 4000–5000 years later (Hastorf 1999). What happened in this interval and in what way were the various crops incorporated into the coastal valley societies of Peru? Hastorf concludes that some crops (beans, chilli peppers, cotton and gourds) appeared around 8000 BP and were planted and consumed in many places on the coast, whilst other plants (guava, manioc and potatoes) arrived earlier but remained irregularly present for millennia. A third group entered later (6200–4500 BP). Some crops were adopted quickly, such as *achira*, while others were taken up more slowly and selectively over a period of years, such as maize and avocado. This sequence is explained by the symbolic value of some grains, since 'in the early phases of food production was influence by social identity and place, and the concept of domestication was active at many levels' (Hastorf 1999, 53). As such, the differential adoption of some crops on the Peruvian coast reflects nascent ethnic differences, each of which had their own food tradition, a situation which is highlighted by the avocado eaters and the maize eaters. In the Initial Period, 4000 years after the beginnings of agriculture, the generation of surplus food and labour began, with increasing civic–ceremonial construction and '. . . crop production and use with a political edge of hierarchy and internal difference' (Hastorf 1999, 53).

In the third millennium BP one observes a cultural phenomenon without precedent taking place in the Andes as a multitude of distinctive regional and local cultures coalesce into a pan-Andean horizon, usually known as the Chavín Horizon, which is considered by many archaeologists to be the source of Andean civilization (Burger 1988, 1992; Lumbreras 1989). Nonetheless, Chavín means many things. It has been used 'to denote a developmental stage in Andean culture–history (Lumbreras 1971), an archaeological period, a religious ideology and an empire (Willey 1951)' (Burger 1988, 106). For the majority of archaeologists, Chavín is considered as the expansion throughout much of the Peruvian Andes of a formalized religious ideology associated with an iconography whose most complete and sophisticated representation is found in the temple complex at the site of Chavín de Huantar, situated in the highlands at 3150 m above sea-level in the small Mosna Valley (Fig. 1). The processes and causes are still poorly understood; even the chronological framework remains controversial (Rick *et al.* 1998).

The site of Chavín de Huantar is formed by two juxtaposed masonry constructions, known as the Old and New Temples, which represent several main building phases spanning several hundred years (Shimada 1999). One of the problems in understanding the evolution of the construction of the temples and their relationship with regional ceramic phases, as well as explaining the development of the religious iconography, has been the lack of direct datings for the constructions, with the possible exception of two galleries (Lumbreras 1993; Rick *et al.* 1998). Burger (1984) has proposed three phases: Urabarriu (2800–2400 BP), Chakinani (2400–2350 BP) and Janabarriu (2350–2150 BP) and believes the construction of the Old Temple corresponds to the first phase, the first addition to the second phase and the second addition to the third phase. Lumbreras (1989), however, proposed that Chavín started earlier and has four developmental phases: Urabarriu (3150–2750 BP), Ofrendas (2750–2550 BP), Chikamani (2550–2350 BP) and Rocas or Janabarriu (2350–2150 BP). He associated the construction of the Old Temple with the first two phases and the construction of the New Temple with the other two younger phases.

One of the outstanding characteristics of Chavín is the approximately 200 stone carvings, most of them in the form of slabs with base-relief design and sculptured tenon heads (Shimada 1999). Based on iconographic studies of the carvings, Tello and Lathrap proposed that Chavín was an important centre pertaining to an eastern Andean cultural tradition that diffused out of Amazonia. However, most contemporary archaeologists prefer to see Chavín as the result of a period of intense interaction and unification, related to the spread of the Chavín cult, whose success was based on an ideological and organizational integration across horizontal (latitudinal) and vertical (altitudinal) dimensions in the Andes. The same type of integration, although in each case with particular characteristics, occurred twice more in the Andes, within what are known as the Tiawanaku-Huari and Inca horizons. In the first case, there is no doubt that there was some kind of interaction between the two large Tiawanaku centres (south of Lake Titicaca, in the Bolivian highlands) and Huari (in the highlands of Peru in the Ayacucho valley), and that both shared cultural attributes. Although it is not certain that Huari can be considered as the origin of Andean urbanization, it is clear that this site was the seat of '. . . a hierarchical organisation and highly centralised state government . . . it was the creator of a unique technique of revenue collection and vast administrative structure' (Isbell 1988, 188–9). The final period of integration, known as the Inca Horizon, was in effect when the Spanish arrived in South America in the beginning of the sixteenth century, and was evidenced by state control of a vast territory from Argentina to Ecuador. The Inca Empire was, without a doubt, the most complex expression of a long process of social differentiation which had begun several millennia earlier.

New trends and developments or *Centuries and centuries and only in the present do things happen* (Borges 1941)

In the last two decades South American archaeology has attempted to free itself from a culture–history strait-jacket through the adoption of alternative approaches based on actualistic studies. One such approach, derived from processualism, has the objective of developing up-to-date studies focused on site formation processes. This has led to a series of taphonomic and palaeo-ecological studies that have their most complete expression in South America in the work carried out by Borrero and his team of collaborators in southern Patagonia and Tierra del Fuego (Borella and Favier Dubois 1994–5; Borrero 1988, 1990; Borrero and Martin 1996; Borrero and Muñoz 1999; Borrero *et al.* 1997; Martin and Borrero 1997; Muñoz 1996). These studies have generated an as yet incipient information base, which is systematic and consistent, concerning the natural processes that affect archaeological deposits. They have especially advanced understanding of the pre-burial conditions of deposition and modification of the guanaco (*Lama guanicoe*), the most frequent prey of the Southern Cone hunter-gatherers. Furthermore, the contribution of carnivores and the possibility of identifying them as agents of the creation of bone assemblages and of the disturbance of archaeological sites have been carefully examined (Borrero *et al.* 1988). These studies are crucial, now that models of the early population of America, and especially the Southern Cone, are based on sites — many of them caves — which have a high chance of having been affected by severe pre- and post-burial processes.

Recently, detailed studies of the diagenesis of bone — a post-burial process — have been initiated, which use anthropogenic accumulations of guanaco bones from Pampean sites as case study material (Gutiérrez 1998). In a less systematic way, disturbance by rodents in archaeological sites has been studied, both in the actual deposits (Gómez 1996; Politis and Madrid 1988) and experimentally (Durán 1991). With a few exceptions (e.g Stahl 1995) such developments in taphonomy, which include long-term and systematic research projects, and their application to the study of archaeological sites in the regions of Pampa (Acosta 1997; Gutierrez *et al.* 1997; Silveira 1997), Patagonia (Cruz 1999; Lanata 1991) and the north-west (Elkin 1995; Nasti 1991, 2000; Mondini 1995; Olivera *et al.* 1991–2) appear to be an Argentinian development (Mondini and Muñoz 1996; Ratto and Haber 1988), and lack counterparts in other South American countries.

Ethnoarchaeology is a methodological development in South America which has only recently arrived in the region in spite of the richness and variety of indigenous societies in the sub-continent who could provide inspiration and a source for up-to-date studies. Amongst the first antecedents are studies of agro-pastoral societies in the Andes (Miller 1977), as well as the work of De Boer and Lathrap (1979) and Zeidler (1984) among the Shipibo and Ashuar of eastern Ecuador. In recent years far-reaching and systematic research programmes have followed the line established by the pioneer works and have been concentrated in two main themes: Andean herders (Kuznar 1995; Nielsen 1998; Tomka 1993; Yacobaccio 1995; Yacobaccio and Madero 1994; Yacobaccio *et al.* 1998) and tropical lowlands horticulturists (Assis 1995–6; Heckenberger *et al.* 1999; Wüst 1998). Other areas of research include hunter-gatherers of the tropical rainforest (Politis 1996a, 1996b, 1998, 1999), hunter-fisher-horticulturists of the tropical savannahs (Greaves 1996, 1997), and the Mapuches of the southern Andes (Dillehay 1998). The subjects focused on vary among others between ceramic production (Cremonte 1988–9; García 1988) and its function as a vehicle of social expression (Hosler 1996), technological organization and its relation with subsistence (Greaves 1997), bone and artefactual refuse in agro-pastoralist sites (Tomka 1993; Yacobaccio *et al.* 1998), the settlement patterns and the residential huts of lowland villagers (Assis 1995–6; Wüst 1998; Wüst and Barreto 1999), the relation between floor area and demography (Siegel 1990), the study of the material consequences of food taboos (Politis and Martínez 1996; Politis and Saunders in press), and the symbolic significance of the jaguar (Dillehay 1998).

At least three tendencies can be identified in the ethnoarchaeological studies in the region. The first tendency restricts case studies to the physical effects of behaviour defined within systems by variables that can, in principle, be well-controlled, as with, for example, ceramic production (García 1993) or the spatial distribution of discarded bones (Borrero and Yacobaccio 1989; Jones 1993). Scholars working from this perspective propose that effort should be directed towards particular cases within general theoretical models (Yacobaccio 1995). This group of investigations emphasizes the techno-economic function of material culture. The second tendency is orientated towards the study of more complex systems where the variables are harder to control, but which takes into account more diverse phenomena and attempts to discern the non-techno-economic meaning of objects through ethnographic case studies (for example Holser 1996). In the second approach, archaeological artefacts are not simply 'things in themselves', but rather are considered as the representation of ideas (Leach 1977, 16) and polysemic in character. Of course, both tendencies are tied to the material effects of behaviour and their respective properties (i.e. density, variability, etc.), but while the first attempts to establish non-ambiguous relationships and strong cross-cultural regularities, the second is directed towards understanding under what conditions (not only material, but also social and ideological) one can hope for certain kinds of archaeological records. In the second tendency the need to establish some generalizations is recognized, but it also valorizes the usefulness of context-specific cultural particularities, and explores the continuity of cosmovisions and meanings attached to specific symbols and icons (see discussion in Saunders 1998). The ethnoarchaeological study of symbolic and religious issues has been incorporated into this line of investigation through the medium of material derivations in egalitarian societies, such as Amazonian hunter-gatherers (Politis and Saunders in press), or societies with low levels of social hierarchy, such as the pastoralists of the Central Andes (Nielsen 1998) or the Mapuches of the southern Andes (Dillehay 1998).

The third tendency is represented by a group of research projects, above all in Brazil, which focus on gathering ethnoarchaeological data in order to reconstruct the historical processes of present-day Indians (i.e. Heckenberger 1996; Heckenberger *et al.* 1999; Wüst 1998; Wüst and Barreto 1999). In this trend the emphasis is on understanding the process of cultural continuity using both ethnographic and archaeological data obtained in the same area, where a genetic connection between contemporary people and the people who produced the archaeological deposit under investigation can be proven. Although the results obtained by this kind of research could be considered historically restricted, the potential for understanding some general cultural patterns, such as village and configuration size, village occupation and abandonment, formation of black soils, etc., in past Amazonian societies is enormous.

It is obvious that as we ascend through the levels of complexity and abstraction the capacity to control the variables in play and the strength of the relationship between behaviour and its material derivatives diminishes. However, is this an obstacle in the attempt to approach systematically the study of belief systems in order to identify in living societies generative principles and generalizations that can be tested against archaeological data? This has become commonplace for complex societies (see, among many others, González 1977, 1992; Reichel-Dolmatoff 1972), now that it is assumed, for example, that the production of objects with a symbolic character and the construction of monuments are inherent to social complexity, and consequently an archaeological record in which this is manifested is awaited. However, egalitarian societies not only produce objects, but also consume food or construct living spaces exclusively as a consequence of adaptation to the natural and social environment. There is no doubt, as ethnography and ethnohistory show us, that foragers as well as herders and villagers maintain highly developed belief systems and complex social rules which infuse all their activities and determine, for example, which animals and which parts of animals they will eat, where the encampment will be set up, or from which place they will bring the rocks used to manufacture artefacts. These social and ideological aspects have been gravely overlooked in the archaeology and ethnoarchaeology of South America. Information universally recorded in ethnographic studies of hunter-gatherer societies, such as food taboos or the existence of sacred places, have not even been considered as possible causes that contribute to the formation and distribution of the archaeological record in South America (for exceptions see Politis and Saunders in press). It has been proposed that the process of materialization is of primary importance to the under-standing of culture (De Marrais *et al.* 1996). Materialization, or the transformation of ideas, values, stories, myths and the like into a physical reality (Earle 1997), allows foragers as well as more socially complex groups to develop, maintain and manipulate ideology.

Applied archaeology

In the last decades, there have been a number of attempts to make archaeology a sci-ence of some practical and immediate use for indigenous, mestizo and rural com-munities. In some cases, such as the archaeological project developed by the Fundaçao Museum do Homem Americano in São Raimundo Nonato, archaeological research has been accompanied by plans for social development generated from within the same project. In other cases, above all in the Andean region, there has been a transference and rehabilitation of particular pre-Hispanic technologies with the goal of increasing the economic potential of some areas (e.g. Erickson 1986, 1992). Besides these, the archaeology of South America has recently developed a praxis that has broadened the borders of application of the discipline towards new fields and themes of immediate and direct applicability, amongst which forensic and Afro-American archaeology stand out. In both cases, the applications have moral and ethical connotations, because the results are of direct interest to the dispossessed classes or to relatives of the victims of state violence.

During the 1970s, the countries of South America were shaken by periods of intense violence and repression. The best-known cases were in Argentina, Bolivia, Brazil, Chile, Paraguay and Uruguay. In this period, severe and extensive human rights violations were committed, primarily by the state under the control of military governments. Dur-ing the early 1980s, these same countries successively entered into processes of democ-ratization, which promoted the investigation of the human rights violations of the recent past. Argentina returned to democracy in December 1983 and the new President, Dr. Raul Alfonsín, created the National Commission on the Disappearance of Persons (CONADEP), which requested the help of the American Association for the Advance-ment of Science (AAAS). The Association sent a delegation of American forensic and genetic scientists to Argentina, including Dr. Clyde Snow, one of the world's foremost experts in forensic anthropology. He called for a halt of non-scientific exhumations and brought together archaeologists, social anthropologists and physicians to undertake the scientific exhumation and analyses of skeletal remains. Dr. Snow returned to Argentina many times during the following five years, during which period he trained local scientists and helped establish the Argentine Forensic Anthropology Team (EAAF) (EAAF 1997).

The EAAF was formed in order to meet the historical need to exhume and attempt to identify the *desaparecidos*. Such identifications are a great source of solace to families suffering the trauma of having a loved one 'disappear'. The presence of archaeologists was crucial to the task, as they uniquely had the necessary expertise in recovering human skeletal remains and associated evidence in a scientific manner, and with the proper recording techniques for the use of such evidence in court cases. The EAAF currently consists of 12 people, both full- and part-time, who specialize in archaeological, social and physical anthropology, medicine, law and computing. In 1987 EAAF expanded its activities beyond Argentina and participated or conducted research in many countries of South America (i.e. Bolivia, Chile, Colombia, Brazil, Peru, Paraguay, etc.) and throughout the world (i.e. Bosnia, Croatia, the Democratic Republic of Congo, South Africa, Zimbabwe, etc.). Among the most resonant cases undertaken by the EAAF was the discovery in Bolivia of the remains of 'Che' Guevara, the guerrilla leader and icon of a whole generation (Fig. 6). In recent years, the EAAF has actively collaborated in the formation of new teams of forensic archaeologists in other countries where investigations into human rights violation were necessary.

Figure 6. Exhumation of the remains of the guerilla leader 'Che' Guevara, carried out by the Argentine Forensic Anthropology Team and a forensic team from Cuba (photo courtesy of Argentine Forensic Anthropology Team).

Without a doubt, the activity of the EAAF has consolidated a new field (sometimes mined!) for the application of archaeology in South America, and generated a new type of social demand on archaeologists. Currently, the investigations performed by forensic archaeologists not only serve to assist the relatives of the victims in their right to recover the remains of their loved ones, so they can perform the customary funeral and mourn their dead, but also contribute to the historical reconstruction of the recent past, which is often distorted or hidden by the parties or governmental institutions which are themselves implicated in the crimes under investigation.

Historical archaeology is a branch of archaeology which has developed recently in South America (Funari 1994) and has not escaped the tendency which has led it to be defined as 'the archaeology of the spread of European culture throughout the world since the fifteenth century and its impact on indigenous people' (Deetz 1977, 5). Although this is a one-sided definition, and the European emphasis comes from the parentage of the discipline of history (Little 1994), it is also the case that in South America historical archaeology has been the archaeology of the colonial process (see reviews in Funari 1994). In Argentina, interest has focused on urban studies, above all in cities such as Buenos Aires, Rosario, Cordoba and Mendoza, and in military settlements and Jesuit Missions. In Uruguay effort has concentrated above all on the urban and military archaeology of the colonial period, although more recently research has commenced on rural archaeology. In Brazil, work has focused on Jesuit Missions, Military Forts and, lately, on the archaeology of Afro-American peoples. This last subject added a new and original dimension to the archaeological study of the historical period in South America.

The 'invisibility' of African cultures in the structure of present-day South American populations has been noted with increasing vigour over the last decade. In Brazilian archaeology, the material production of the Afro-American population had been practically ignored until the initiation of systematic studies in the zone where the maroon state of Palmares was located. Palmares was created when slaves escaped from Portuguese settlements at the beginning of the seventeenth century and formed a free state in the hilly forest areas of north-eastern Brazil. It became the largest and most powerful maroon community in South America. Palmares was always considered a threat by the colonial powers, both Portuguese and Dutch, who sent various expeditions there during the seventeenth century and finally succeeded in destroying the Afro-American settlements (Funari 1999b).

In 1991 the Palmares Archaeological Project was created, under the direction of Ch. Orser Jr and Pedro Funari, in order to study maroon society using the methodology of historical archaeology (Funari 1999b). The research was conceived from its inception as a social archaeology and was an attempt to obtain new evidence on slave resistance and the struggle for freedom. Fieldwork was concentrated around the capital village, Macaco, now known as the Serra da Barriga, and 14 sites in the area were surveyed and test-pits were dug. Several interesting issues emerged from this study. For example,

Palmares had been characterized by historians as an African society, but the archaeological record shows something different and, in terms of ethnic composition, much more complex. The study of the ceramics from the sites at the Serra da Barriga indicated the presence of three principal ethnic types: Amerindian, European and local ('Palmarina'). Rejecting the maintenance of African, Amerindian and European traits in the material culture, Allen (1995) emphasizes the fact that the inhabitants of Palmares had shaped a syncretic culture. In this context, the ceramics acquired a significant value in the construction of identity, and made evident the integration of Palmares within a wider regional system, where the slaves that had fled were not isolated from the colonial context, but rather remodelled their social situation. The whole theme has emerged as an excellent case study for arguing the correlation between material culture, identity and ethnicity and to analyse the methodological possibilities of tracing the continuity of African cultures in South America through the archaeological record.

The days to come or *I leave to the various futures (not to all) my garden of forking paths* (Borges 1941)

Some years ago, Dillehay (1993, 255) stated that one of the promising areas of research in the Southern Cone (and by extension, the rest of South America) was the need to explain material culture not merely in terms of techno-economic adaptation and political organization, but also in terms of ideology. Although some advances have been made in this area, South American archaeology today is basically navigating between two waters: culture–historical reconstruction, and ecological functionalism in which adjustments to the natural environment are seen as the principal engine of cultural change and material culture is only a means to cope with the environment. Obviously, nobody can deny that human populations co-evolve with the environment in a relationship where both components co-vary, but likewise neither can one doubt that the inter-relationship is neither direct nor mechanical, but rather is mediated by complex social systems and beliefs that significantly influence the way in which human societies transform and generate their material culture. It is the social and symbolic aspects that have yet to be examined in sufficient depth to produce a conceptual body of work that can be tested against archaeological data in order to better understand the native societies of South America.

A subject which remains unsettled in South America is the reburial issue. Apart from rare exceptions, such as the case of the return of the bones of the *cacique* Inakayal who was kept in the Museum of La Plata for more than one hundred years, no bones of indigenous people have been sent back to their communities. Moreover, very few archaeologists or institutions in which they work have been confronted with indigenous claims for the return of human remains or archaeological objects (there is no parallel with what is happening in North America). This in part reflects the degree of subjection of the indigenous communities of South America, and the little power they have to make their claims heard. Nonetheless, it is unclear what the reaction of scientists will be when the claims begin to arrive. The recent excavation of several Inca mummies in the Andes (e.g. Reinhard 1996) has once again shown the discrepancy amongst archaeologists concerning 'ownership' of indigenous remains and the ethical questions related to the exhumation of human bones (*Ciencia Hoy* 1999). In the case of the skeleton of Inakayal, a number of archaeologists and physical anthropologists refused his return, claiming that the remains were the 'property' of the Museum of La Plata and an indivisible part of the scientific collection, whilst others of us defended the indigenous right to dispose of their dead. These examples exposed the existing tensions within the archaeological community and the disagreement over what to do with regard to future claims. In South America the ethical dimension of archaeological practice is occasionally erased by the unpleasant aftertaste of the European colonialism of the last centuries.

Several tens of South American archaeologists are currently carrying out postgraduate studies in North American universities, and others are scattered throughout the countries of Europe (essentially Great Britain, France and Spain). Such a high number of young archaeologists abroad is unprecedented. How will this impact South American archaeology in the years to come? Will these archaeologists — many of whom are destined to fill prominent positions in their respective countries — be the ones to produce a significant change in the archaeology of the region? Will they reproduce the North American academic model, or, on the contrary, will they generate a new model that recreates the characteristics peculiar to each one of their countries? Will these archaeologists, who have 'fed of the food of the beast and have even lived in its intestines' (as has been dramatically portrayed by McGuire and Navarrete 1999, 95), adopt a critical or complacent position? Which path will they choose or create when they return to the garden? To a great extent (although not exclusively of course), the future theoretical and political course of South American archaeology will depend upon the attitude of the new Ph.D.s and their insertion into local scenarios.

Concurrently, South American archaeology finds itself today at another forking path that will surely determine its development in the years to come. On one side, there is an attempt to reconstruct the past in order to contribute to science as a whole as an intellectual activity in order to satisfy the interests of contemporary Western society and place regional archaeology within the framework of a global discussion. For some, this is the only way of achieving a relevant archaeology while avoiding the limited and modest objectives of local archaeologies usually involving culture–historical reconstruction. For the others, who are fewer, archaeology should be an instrument of social action, destined to restore the dignity of the indigenous peoples, mestizos and dispossessed of the continent and to contribute to the legitimization of their moral as well as material rights. Furthermore, it should be a tool for the preservation of the archaeological heritage, not only for the purposes of tourism or for the scientific value, but more importantly for the symbolic value the archaeological heritage has for indigenous people in supporting their claims. This second group demands of archaeologists that they recognize their social responsibility. The justification of their labour can rest on idiosyncratic arguments, but praxis should be related to the social context of the country and the elaboration of a discourse that is of use to indigenous and mestizo groups and the dispossessed classes (Gnecco 1995).

The recent growth of historical archaeology also faces a crossroad. Will this nascent South American historical archaeology attempt to recuperate the active voice of the silent majority, as Beaudry *et al.* (1991) have stated? Or will it be the archaeology of colonialism and of European expansion in the continent? Both possibilities are at present latent in the multiple processes that are gestating across the length and breadth of the region.

In archaeological terms, South America can be considered metaphorically as a garden, in an idyllic way. The greater part of the continent is relatively unknown archaeologically and there are extensive areas where no systematic research has been carried out, which produces an important stimulant. There is an infinite variety of subject matters that can be approached in the region: from the initial colonization of *Homo sapiens*, to the formation of imperial societies such as the Inca. Furthermore, there are in existence present-day indigenous populations who still keep alive a large part of the rich pre-Hispanic cultural tradition, and who are eager to know the results of archaeological research and eventually appropriate them for themselves. The scientific potential and possible social uses of archaeology in South America are enormous. Nonetheless, this garden is crossed by many forking paths that will have to be confronted by the archaeologists who work in the region, especially the South Americans. The greatest challenge is either to try to build a supposedly objective and socially distant scientific discipline, or to attempt to create something else in order to achieve global scientific standards whilst simultaneously being a discipline which is of service to contemporary society. As in the garden imagined by Borges, there are innumerable futures that can be created, all of which are present at the same time. It only remains to be seen, therefore, which of these futures will prevail for South American archaeology. Needless to say, Borges would never accept a single, dominant future.

Acknowledgements

To Ben Alberti for the translation and comments. To Clark Erickson whose careful review helped me to amplify and clarify the discussion. Also to Pedro Funari, Cristobal Gnecco, Maria Gutiérrez, Eduardo Goés Neves, José Perez Gollán, and Verónica Willians for their comments and suggestions. Needless to say that any remaining mistakes are my own responsibility.

This research is part of the program of INCUAPA (Investigaciones Arqueológicas y Paleontológicas del Cuaternario Pampeano) which was founded by the Agencia Nacional de Promición Científica, el CONICET and the Universidad Nacional del Centro de la Pcia. de Buenos Aires.

References

ACOSTA, A. 1997: Estado de conservación y problemas de contaminación de las estructuras arqueofaunísticas en el extremo nororiental de la la Provincia de de Buenos Aires. In Berón, M. and Politis, G. (eds.), *Arqueología Pampeana en la década de los '90* (San Rafael, Museo de Historia Natural de San Rafael (Mendoza) — INCUAPA), 187–99.

ADAM, J. and FAURE, H. 1997: Preliminary vegetation maps of the world since the last Glacial Maximum: an aid to archaeological understanding. *J. Archaeol. Sci.* 24, 623–47.

ADOVASIO, J. and PEDLER, D.R. 1997: Monte Verde and the antiquity of humankind in the Americas. *Antiquity* 71, 573–80.

ALDENDERFER, M. 1991: Continuity and change in ceremonial structures in Late Preceramic Asana, southern Peru. *Latin American Antiquity* 2, 227–59.

ALLEN, S. 1995: Africanism, Mosaics and Creativity: the historical archaeology of Palmares (Unpublished M.A. dissertation, Brown University, Providence, USA).

AMAT OLAZÁBAL, H. 1997: Julio C. Tello. Paladín del Autoctonismo. In Amat Olazábal, H. (ed.), *Julio C. Tello. Forjador del Perú Auténtico* (Lima, Centro de Estudios Histórico-Militares del Perú), 9–18.

AMEGHINO, F. 1880: *La Antigüedad del Hombre en el Plata* (Paris and Buenos Aires).

ANDRADE, T. and LÓPEZ MAZZ, J. in press: La emergencia de complejidad entre los cazadores recolectores de la costa atlántica meridional sudamericana. *Boletín de Antropología Americana*.

ARDILA, G. 1992: El Norte de América del Sur: diversidad y adaptaciones en el final del Pleistoceno Tardío. In Politis, G. (ed.), *Arqueología en America Latina Hoy* (Bogotá), 88–115.

ASSIS, V.S. de 1995–6: Um Estudo da Casa Mbya pela Perspectiva Etnoarqueológica. *Coleçao Arqueologia* 1 (vol. 2), 519–26.

BAWDEN, G. 1989: The Andean State as a State of Mind. *J. Anthropol. Res.* 45, 327–32.

BAILEY, R. 1990: Exciting opportunities in Tropical Rain Forests: a reply to Townsend. *American Anthropologist* 92, 747–8.

BAILEY, R., HEAD, G., JENIKE, M., OWEN, B., RECHTMAN, R. and ZECHENTER, E. 1989: Hunting and Gathering in Tropical Rain Forest: Is it Possible? *American Anthropologist* 91, 261–85.

BAILEY, R. and HEADLAND, Th. 1991: The Tropical Rain Forest: Is it a productive Environment for Human Foragers? *Human Ecol.* 19(2), 261–85.

BAILEY, R., JENIKE, M. and RECHTMAN, R. 1991: Reply to Colinvaux and Bush. *American Anthropologist* 93, 60–162.

BALÉE, W. 1989: The culture of Amazonian forests. In Posey, D.A. and Balée, W. (eds.), *Resource Management in Amazonia: Indigenous and Folk Strategies. Advances in Economic Botany* (vol. 7) (New York Botanical Garden, Bronx), 1–21.

BALÉE, W. 1995: *Footprints of the forest: Ka'apor ethnobotany — the historical ecology of plant utilization by an Amazonian people* (New York).

BARRETO, C. 1998: Brazilian archaeology from a Brazilian perspective. *Antiquity* 72, 573–81.

BATE, L.F. 1977: *Arqueología y materialismo histórico* (México).

BATE, L.F. 1998: *El proceso de investigación en arqueología* (Barcelona).

BEAUDRY, M., COOK, L.J. and MROZOWSKI, S. 1991: Artifacts and active voices: material culture as social discourse. In Paynter, R. and McGuire, R. (eds.), *The Archaeology of Inequality* (Oxford), 150–91.

BEHLING, H. 1996: First report on new evidence for the occurrence of *Podocarpus* and possible human presence at the mouth of the Amazon during Late-glacial. *Vegetation History and Archaeobotany* 5, 241–6.

BENNETT, W. and BIRD, J. 1949: *Andean Culture History* (New York, American Museum of Natural History, Handbook Series no. 15).

BENNETT, W., BLEILER, E. and SOMMER, F. 1948: *Northwest Argentine Archaeology* (New Haven, Yale University Publications in Anthropology no. 38).

BERENGUER RODRÍGUEZ, J. (ed.) 1995: XXX Aniversario. Sociedad Chilena de Arqueología. Jornadas de Reflexión. 1963–1993. *Boletín de la Sociedad Chilena de Arqueología. Número Especial* (Punta de Tralca).

BONAVÍA, D. 1984: La importancia de los restos de papa y camote de época precerámica hallados en el valle de Casma. *J. de la Societé des Américanistes* 70, 7–20.

BONAVÍA, D. 1999: The domestication of Andean camelids. In Politis, G. and Alberti, B. (eds.) 1999, 130–47.

BORELLA, F. and FAVIER DUBOIS, C. 1994–5: Observaciones tafonómicas en la Bahía San Sebastián, Costa Norte de Tierra del Fuego. Argentina. *Palimpsesto* 4, 1–8.

BORGES, J.L. 1941: *Ficciones* (Buenos Aires).

BORRERO, L. 1986: La economía prehistórica de los habitantes del Norte de la Isla de Tierra del Fuego (Unpublished doctoral dissertation, Universidad de Buenos Aires, Argentina).

BORRERO, L. 1988: Estudios tafonómicos en Tierra del Fuego: Su relevancia para entender procesos de formación del registro arqueológico. In Yacobaccio, H. (ed.), *Arqueología Contemporánea Argentina. Actualidad y Perspectivas* (Buenos Aires), 13–32.

BORRERO, L. 1990: Taphonomy of Guanaco Bones in Tierra del Fuego. *Quat. Res.* 34, 361–71.

BORRERO, L. 1995: Human and natural agency: some comments on Pedra Furada. *Antiquity* 69, 601–2.

BORRERO, L., LANATA, J.L. and BORELLA, F. 1988: Reestudiando huesos: nuevas consideraciones sobre sitios de Última Esperanza. *Anales del Instituto de la Patagonia* 18, 133–56.

BORRERO, L. and MARTIN, F. 1996: Tafonomía de carnívoros: un enfoque regional. In Gómez Otero, J. (ed.), *Arqueología Sólo Patagonia* (Puerto Madryn, CENPAT-CONICET), 189–98.

BORRERO, L., MARTIN, F. and PRIETO, A. 1997: La Cueva Lago Sofía 4, Última Esperanza, Chile: una madriguera de felino del Pleistoceno Tardío. *Anales del Instituto de la Patagonia* 25, 103–22.

BORRERO, L. and MUÑOZ, A. 1999: Tafonomía en el bosque patagónico. Implicaciones para el estudio de su explotación y uso por poblaciones humanas de cazadores-recolectores. *Soplando en el viento. . . Actas de las Terceras Jornadas de Arqueología de la Patagonia* (San Carlos de Bariloche 1996), 43–56.

BORRERO, L. and YACOBACCIO, H. 1989: Etnoarqueología de Asentamientos Aché. *J. de la Societé des Américanistes* LXXV, 7–33.

BRAY, W. 1988: The Paleoindian debate. *Nature* 332, 107.

BROCHADO, J. 1980: The social ecology of the Marajoara chiefdom (Unpublished M.Sc. dissertation, University of Illinois, USA).

BROSIUS, P. 1991: Foraging in Tropical Rain Forest: the case of the Penan of Sarawak, East Malaysia. *Human Ecol.* 19(2), 123–50.

BRUHNS, K. 1996: *Ancient South America* (Cambridge).

BRYAN, A. 1973: Paleoenvironmental and Cultural Diversity in Late Pleistocene South America. *Quat. Res.* 3(2), 237–56.

BRYAN, A. 1975: Paleoenvironmental and Cultural Diversity in Late Pleistocene South America. A Rejoinder to Vance Haynes and a Reply to Thomas Lynch. *Quat. Res.* 5(1), 151–9.

BRYAN, A., CASAMIQUELA, R., CRUXENT, J.M., GRUHN, R. and OCHSENIUS, C. 1978: An El Jobo Mastodon Kill at Taima-taima, Venezuela. *Science* 200, 1275–7.

BURGER, R. 1984: *The prehistoric Occupation of Chavín de Huantar, Peru* (University of California Publications in Anthropology).

BURGER, R. 1988: Unity and heterogeneity within the Chavín Horizon. In Keatinge, R. (ed.), *Peruvian Prehistory* (Cambridge), 99–144.

BURGER, R. 1989: An overview of Peruvian Archaeology (1976–1986). *Ann. Rev. Anthropol.* 18, 37–69.

BURGER, R. 1992: *Chavín and the Origins of Andean Civilization* (London).

CABRERA PÉREZ, L. 1988: *Panorama retrospectivo y situación actual de la arqueología uruguaya* (Montevideo, Universidad de la República, Facultad de Humanidades y Ciencias).

CARNEIRO, R. 1970: A Theory on the Origin of the State. *Science* 169, 733–8.

CARNEIRO, R. 1995: The History of Ecological Interpretations of Amazonia: Does Roosevelt Have it Right? In Sponsel, L.E. (ed.), *Indigenous Peoples and the Future of Amazonia: An Ecological Anthropology of an Endangered World* (Tucson), 45–65.

CAVELIER, I., RODRIGUEZ, C., HERRERA, L.F., MORCOTE, G. and MORA, S. 1995: No sólo de caza vive el hombre. Ocupación del Bosque Amazónico, Holoceno Temprano. In Cavelier, I. and Mora, S. (eds.), *Ambiente y Ocupaciones Tempranas de la America Tropical* (Fundación Erigaie–Instituto Colombiano de Antropología, Santafé de Bogotá), 27–44.

CHATTERS, J.C. 1997: Encounter with an Ancestor. *Anthropol. Newslett.* 38(1), 9–10.

CHATTERS, J.C., NEVES, W.A. and BLUM, M. in press: The Kennewick Man: A first Multivariate Analysis. *Curr. Res. in the Pleistocene.*

CIENCIA HOY 1999: Editorial. *Ciencia Hoy* (March–April) 9(51), 10–11.

CLASTRES, P. 1977: *Society against the State: Essays in Political Anthropology* (New York).

COLINVAUX, P. and BUSH, M. 1991: The rain-forest ecosystem as a resource for hunting and gathering. *American Anthropologist* 91(1), 153–90.

COLLIER, D. 1982: One hundred years of Ecuadorian archaeology. In Marcos, J. and Norton, P. (eds.), *Primer Simposio de Correlaciones Antropológicas Andino-Mesoamericano* (Guayaquil, Escuela Superior Politécnica del Litoral (ESPOL)), 5–33.

CORREAL URREGO, G. 1981: *Evidencias Culturales y Megafauna Pleistocénica en Colombia* (Bogotá, Fundación de Investigaciones Arqueológicas Nacionales).

CREMONTE, B. 1988–9: Técnicas alfareras tradicionales en la Puna: Inti-Cancha. *Arqueología Contemporánea* 2(2), 5–29.

CRIVELLI MONTERO, E. 1990: Un campo de huesos secos: la arqueología argentina en el último decenio. In Berbeglia, C.E. (ed.), *Propuestas para una Antropología Argentina* (Buenos Aires), 111–31.

CRUXENT, J. and ROUSE, I. 1958: An archeological chronology of Venezuela. *Social Science Monographs* 1, 2–39.

CRUZ, I. 1999: Estepa y bosque: paisajes actuales y tafonomía en el noroeste de Santa Cruz. In *Soplando en el viento... Actas de las Terceras Jornadas de Arqueología de la Patagonia* (San Carlos de Bariloche 1996), 303–18.

D'ALTROY, T.N. 1997: Recent Research in the Central Andes. *J. Archaeol. Res.* 5(1), 3–73.

DEBOER, W. and LATHRAP, D. 1979: The Making and Breaking of Shipibo-Conibo Ceramics. In Kramer, C. (ed.), *Ethnoarchaeology. Implications of Ethnography from Archaeology* (New York), 102–38.

DEETZ, J. 1977: *Small Things forgotten. The Archaeology of Early American Life* (Garden City, NY).

DE MARRAIS, E., CASTILLO, L.J. and EARLE, T. 1996: Ideology, materialization and power strategies. *Curr. Anthropol.* 37, 15–31.

DENEVAN, W. 1966: *The aboriginal cultural geography of the Llanos de Mojos of Bolivia* (Berkeley, California, Ibero-Americana 48).

DENEVAN, W. 1992: The pristine myth: the landscape of the Americas in 1492. *Annals of the Association of American Geographers* 82(3), 369–85.

DILLEHAY, T. (ed.) 1989: *Monte Verde. A Late Pleistocene Settlement in Chile. Volume 1. Paleoenvironment and Site Context* (Washington and London).

DILLEHAY, T. 1993: Archaeological Trends in the Southern Cone of South America. *J. Archaeol. Res* 1(3), 235–66.

DILLEHAY, T. 1996: Letters. *Science* 274, 1824–5.

DILLEHAY, T. (ed.) 1997: *Monte Verde. A Late Pleistocene Settlement in Chile. Volume 2. The Archaeological Context and Interpretation* (Washington and London).

DILLEHAY, T. 1998: Felines, patronyms, and history of the Araucanians in the southern Andes. In Saunders, N. (ed.), *Icons of Power. Feline Symbolism in the Americas* (London), 203–28.

DILLEHAY, T., ROSSEN, J. and NETHERLY, P. 1997: The Nanchoc Tradition: The Beginning of Andean Civilization. *American Scientist* 85, 46–55.

DINCAUZE, D. 1984: An archeo-logical evaluation of the case for a pre-Clovis occupation. In Wendorf, F. and Close, A. (eds.), *Advances in World Archaeology* (Orlando), 275–323.

DINCAUZE, D. 1991: Review of *Monte Verde: a late Pleistocene settlement in Chile 1: Paleoenvironment and site context*, by T. D. Dillehay. *J. Field Archaeol.* 18, 116–19.

DOUGHERTY, B. and CALANDRA, H. 1984–5: Ambiente y Arqueología en el Oriente Boliviano: la Provincia Itenez del Departamento del Beni. *Relaciones de la Sociedad Argentina de Antropología* 14 (n.s), 37–61.

DRENNAN, R. 1991: Regional dynamics of chiefdoms in the valle de la Plata. *J. Field Archaeol.* 18, 297–317.

DRENNAN, R. 1993: Sociedades complejas precolombinas. Variación y trayectorias de cambio. In Uribe Tobón, C.A. (ed.), *La Construcción de las Américas* (Santafé de Bogotá, Universidad Nacional de Los Andes), 31–49.

DRENNAN, R., TAFT, M.M. and URIBE, C.A. (eds.) 1993: *Cacicazgos Prehispánicos del Valle de la Plata, Tomo 2: Cerámica-Cronología y Produccion Artesanal* (Pittsburgh, University of Pittsburgh memoirs in Latin American Archaeology no. 5).

DUFOUR, D. 1987: Insect as food: a case study from the Northwest Amazon. *American Anthropologist* 89(2), 383–97.

DURÁN, V. 1991: Estudios de perturbación por roedores del género *Ctenomys* en un sitio arqueológico experimental. *Revista de Estudios Regionales* 7, 7–31.

DWYER, P.D. and MINNEGAL, M. 1991: Hunting in lowland tropical rain forest: toward a model of non-agricultural subsistence. *Human Ecol.* 19(2), 187–212.

EARLE, Th. 1997: *How Chiefs come to power. The Political Economy in Prehistory* (Stanford).

EAAF. EQUIPO ARGENTINO DE ANTROPOLOGÍA FORENSE 1997: *Informe Bianual 1994–1995* (Buenos Aires).

ELKIN, D. 1995: Volume Density of South American Camelid Skeletal Parts. *Int. J. Osteoarchaeol.* 5, 29–37.

ENDICOT, K. and BELLWOOD, P. 1991: The possibility of independent foraging in the rain forest of Peninsular Malaysia. *Human Ecol.* 19(2), 151–85.

ENGEL, F.A. 1970: Exploration of the Chilca Canyon, Peru. *Curr. Anthropol.* 11, 55–8.

ERICKSON, C. 1986: Waru-Waru: una tecnología agrícola del altiplano pre-hispánico. In de la Torre, C. and Burga, M. (eds.), *Andenes y Camellones en el Perú Andino. Historia presente y futuro* (Lima, CONCYTEC-Perú), 59–84.

ERICKSON, C. 1992: Applied archaeology and rural development: archaeology's potential contribution to the future. *J. Steward Anthropol. Soc.* 20(1–2), 1–16.

ERICKSON, C. 1995: Archaeological methods for the study of ancient landscapes of the Llanos de Mojos in the Bolivian Amazon. In Stahl, P. (ed.), *Archaeology in the lowland American tropics. Current analytical methods and applications* (Cambridge), 66–91.

FAUSTO, C. 1992: Fragmentos de historia é cultura Tupinambá: da etnologia como instrumento crítico de conhecimiento etno-histórico. In Carneiro da Cunha, M. (ed.), *Historia dos indios no Brasil* (São Paulo, Companhia das Letras/FAPESP/SMC), 381–96.

FEDICK, S.L. 1995: Indigenous Agriculture in the Americas. *J. Archaeol. Res.* 3, 257–303.

FEINMAN, G. and NEITZEL, J. 1984: Too Many Types: an Overview of Sedentary Prestate Societies. In Schiffer, M. (ed.), *Advances in Archaeological Method and Theory* vol. 7 (New York).

FERNÁNDEZ, J. 1982: *Historia de la Arqueología Argentina* (Mendoza, Asociación Cuyana de Antropología).

FIEDEL, S. 1996: Letters. *Science* 274, 2824.

FIEDEL, S. 1999: Older Than We Thought: Implications of Corrected Dates for Paleoindians. *American Antiquity* 64(1), 95–116.

FUNARI, P.P.A. 1992: La arqueología en Brasil: Política y Academia en la encrucijada. In Politis, G. (ed.), *Arqueología en America Latina Hoy* (Bogotá), 57–69.

FUNARI, P.P.A. 1994: South American Historical Archaeology. *Latin American Hist. Archaeol.* 3, 1–14.

FUNARI, P.P.A. 1999a: Etnicidad, identidad y cultura material: un estudio del cimarrón Palmares, Brasil, Siglo XVII. In Zarankin, A. and Acuto, F. (eds.) 1999, 77–96.

FUNARI, P.P.A. 1999b: Brazilian Archaeology: A reappraisal. In Politis, G. and Alberti, B. (eds.) 1999, 37–27.

FUNG PINEDA, R. 1988: The Late Preceramic and Initial period. In Keatinge, R. (ed.), *Peruvian Prehistory* (Cambridge), 67–96.

GARCÍA, L.C. 1988: Etnoarqueología: Manufactura de Cerámica en Alto Sapagua. In Yacobaccio, H. (ed.), *Arqueología Contemporánea Argentina* (Buenos Aires), 33–58.

GARCÍA, L.C. 1993: Qué nos cuentan las cocinas. Etnoarqueología en Inca Cueva. *Palimpsesto* 3, 133–8.

GATHERCOLE, P. and LOWENTHAL, D. (eds.) 1990: *The Politics of the Past* (London, One World Archaeology Series).

GERO, J. 1991: Genderlithics: Women's Roles in Stone Tool Production. In Gero, J. and Conkey, M. (eds.), *Engendering Archaeology. Women in Prehistory* (Oxford), 163–93.

GERO, J. 1992: Feast and Females: Gender Ideology and Political Meals in the Andes. *Norwegian Archaeol. Rev.* 25(1), 15–30.

GIBBONS, A. 1996: First Americans: Not Mammoth Hunters, But Forest Dwellers? *Science* 272, 346–7.

GNECCO, C. 1995: Praxis científica en la periferia: Notas para una historia social de la arqueología colombiana. *Revista Española de Arqueología Americana* 25, 9–22.

GNECCO, C. 1996: Reconsideración de la complejidad social del suroccidente colombiano. *Dos Lecturas Críticas. Arqueología en Colombia. Cuaderno FPC 3* (Santafé de Bogotá, Fondo de Promoción de la Cultura), 43–74.

GNECCO, C. 1999: *Multivocalidad histórica. Hacia una cartografía postcolonial de la arqueología* (Santafé de Bogotá, Universidad de Los Andes).

GÓMEZ, G. 1996: Los pequeños mamíferos del sitio Arroyo Seco 2 (Partido de Tres Arroyos, Provincia de Buenos Aires). Aspectos relacionados con la subsistencia, tafonomía y paleoclima (Unpublished Tesis de Licenciatura, Facultad de Ciencias Sociales (Olavarría) UNCPBA, Argentina).

GONZÁLEZ, A.R. 1977: *Arte Precolombino de la Argentina. Introducción a su historia cultural* (Buenos Aires).

GONZÁLEZ, A.R. 1992: *Las placas metálicas de los Andes del Sur. Contribución al estudio de las religiones precolombinas* (Mainz am Rhein).

GORE, R. 1997: Los Americanos más antiguos. *Nat. Geogr.* (edición española) octubre, 92–8.

GREAVES, R. 1996: Ethnoarchaeology of wild root collection among savanna foragers of Venezuela. Paper presented at the 54th Annual Plains Anthropological Conference, October 31, Iowa City, Iowa.

GREAVES, R. 1997: Hunting and Multifunctional Use of Bows and Arrows. Ethnoarchaeology of Technological Organization among the Pumé Hunters of Venezuela. In Knecht, H. (ed.), *Projectile Technology* (New York), 287–320.

GREENBERG, J.H., TURNER II, C.G. and ZEGURA, S.L. 1986: The settlement of the Americas: a comparison of linguistic, dental and genetic evidence. *Curr. Anthropol.* 27, 477–97.

GROSS, D.R. 1975: Protein capture and cultural developments in the Amazon Basin. *American Anthropologist* 77, 526–49.

GUIDON, N. 1986: A sequencia cultural da área Sao Raimundo Nonato. *Clio* 3(8), 137–44.

GUIDON, N. and PARENTI, F. 1987: Toca do Boquerao do Sitio da Pedra Furada: excavaçoes. *Dédalo* Publicaçoes avulsas 1, 57–67.

GUIDON, N. and PESSIS, A.-M. 1996: Leviandade ou falsidade? Uma resposta a Meltzer, Adovasio & Dillehay. *FUNDHAMentos. Revista da Fundaçao do Homem Americano* 1(1), 379–94.

GUTIÉRREZ, M. 1998: Taphonomic effects and state of preservation of the guanaco (*Lama guanicoe*) bone bed from Paso Otero 1 (Buenos Aires Province, Argentina) (Unpublished Master thesis in Interdisciplinary Studies, Texas Tech University, USA).

GUTIÉRREZ, M., MARTÍNEZ, G., JOHNSON, E., POLITIS, G. and HARTWELL, W. 1997: Nuevos análisis óseos en el sitio Paso Otero 1 (Partido de Necochea, Provincia de Buenos Aires). In Berón, M. and Politis, G. (eds.), *Arqueología Pampeana en la década de los '90* (San Rafael, Museo de Historia Natural de San Rafael (Mendoza) — INCUAPA), 213–28.

HABER, A. 1997: La casa, el sendero y el mundo. Significados culturales de la arqueología, la cultura material y el paisaje en la Puna de Atacama. *Estudios Atacameños* 14, 373–98.

HAMES, R.B. and VICKERS, W.T. (eds.) 1983: *Adaptive Responses of Native Amazonians* (New York).

HART, T.B. and HART, J.T. 1986: The Ecological Basis of Hunter-Gatherer Subsistence in African Rain Forests: The Mbuti of Eastern Zaire. *Human Ecol.* 14(1), 29–55.

HASTORF, C. 1991: Gender space and food in prehistory. In Gero, J. and Conkey, M. (eds.), *Engendering Archaeology. Women in Prehistory* (Oxford), 132–59.

HASTORF, C. 1998: The cultural life of early domestic plant use. *Antiquity* 72(278), 773–82.

HASTORF, C. 1999: Cultural implications of crop introduction in Andean Prehistory. In Gosden, C. and Hather, J. (eds.), *The Prehistory of Food. Appetites for change* (London), 35–58.

HAYNES, C.V. 1974: Paleoenvironment and Cultural Diversity in the Late Pleistocene South America: A Reply to A.L. Bryan. *Quat. Res.* (4)3, 378–82.

HEADLAND, Th.N. 1987: The Wild Yam Question: How Well Could Independent Hunter-Gatherers Live in a Tropical Rainforest Environment? *Human Ecol.* 15(4), 463–91.

HEADLAND, Th.N. and BAILEY, R.C. 1991: Introduction: have hunter-gatherers ever lived in Tropical Rain Forest independently of agriculture? *Human Ecol.* 19(2), 115–22.

HECKENBERGER, M. 1996: War and Peace in the Shadow of Empire: Sociopolitical Change in the Upper Xingu of Southeastern Amazonia, ca. A.D. 1400–2000 (Ph.D. dissertation, University of Pittsburgh, Pittsburgh, USA).

HECKENBERGER, M., PETERSON, J. and NEVES, E.G. 1999: Village size and permanence in Amazonia: two archaeological examples from Brazil. *American Antiquity* 10(4), 353–76.

HERRERA, L., CAVELIER, I., RODRÍGUEZ, C. and MORA, S. 1992: The technical transformation of an agricultural system in the Colombian Amazon. *World Archaeol.* 24(1), 98–113.

HOLMBERG, A. 1969: *Nomads of the long bow: the Sirionó of Eastern Bolivia* (New York).

HOSLER, D. 1996: Technical choices, social categories and meaning among the Andean potters of Las Animas. *J. Material Culture* 1(1), 63–92.

HRDLIČKA, A. 1912: Early Man in South America. *Bulletin 52, Smithsonian Institution, Bureau of American Ethnology* (Washington, D.C.).

HUTTERER, K. 1983: The natural and cultural history of Southeast Asian agriculture. Ecological and evolutionary considerations. *Anthropos* 78, 169–212.

ISBELL, W. 1988: City and state in Middle Horizon Huari. In Keatinge, R. (ed.), *Peruvian Prehistory* (Cambridge), 164–89.

JONES, K. 1993: The Archaeological Structure of a Short-Term Camp. In Hudson, J. (ed.), *From Bones to Behaviour. Ethnoarchaeological and Experimental Contributions to the Interpretation of Faunal Remains* (Center for Archaeological Investigations, Occasional Paper No. 21, Southern Illinois University at Carbondale), 101–14.

KIPNIS, R. 1998: Early hunter-gatherers in the Americas: perspectives from Central Brazil. *Antiquity* 72(227), 581–92.

KOHL, Ph. and FAWCETT, C. (eds.) 1997: *Nationalism, Politics and the Practice of Archaeology* (Cambridge).

KRICHER, J. 1989: *The Neotropical Companion* (Princeton).

KUZNAR, L.A. 1995: *Awatimarka: The Ethnoarchaeology of an Andean Herding Community* (Fort Worth).

LAHR, M.M. 1997: A origem dos ameríndios no contexto da evoluçao dos povos mongolóides. *Revista USP* 34, 58–69.

LANATA, J.L. 1991: Según pasan los años. Hacia un modelo regional de los procesos naturales que afectan el registro arqueológico en Península Mitre, Tierra del Fuego. Paper presented at the 47th International Congress of Americanist, New Orleans.

LANATA, J.L. and BORRERO, L.A. 1999: The Archaeology of hunter-gatherers in South America. In Politis, G. and Alberti, B. (eds.) 1999, 76–89.

LARCO HOYLE, R. 1946: A cultural sequence for the North Coast of Peru. In Steward, J. (ed.), *The Handbook of South American Indians* vol. 2 (Washington, Bureau of American Ethnology), 149–82.

LATHRAP, D. 1968: The "Hunting" Economies of the Tropical Forest Zone of South America: an Attempt at Historical Perspective. In Lee, R. and DeVore, R. (eds.), *Man the Hunter* (Chicago), 23–9.

LATHRAP, D. 1970: *The Upper Amazon* (London).

LATHRAP, D. 1975: *Ancient Ecuador: culture, clay and creativity, 3,000–300 BC* (Chicago, Field Museum of Natural History).

LATHRAP, D. 1977: Our Father the Cayman, Our Mother the Gourd: Spinden Revisited or a unitary Model for the Emergence of Agriculture in the New World. In Reed, C.D. (ed.), *Origins of Agriculture* (The Hague), 713–51.

LAVALLÉE, D. 1995: *Promesse D'Amérique. La préhistoire de l'Amérique du Sud* (Paris).

LEACH, E. 1977: A View from the Bridge. In Spriggs, M. (ed.), *Archaeology and Anthropology* (Oxford, BAR Supp. Ser. 19), 161–76.

LITTLE, B. 1994: People with History: An Update of Historical Archaeology in the United States. *J. Archaeol. Method and Theory* 1(1), 8–40.

LLAGOSTERA, A. 1992: Fisherman on the Pacific coast of South America. *Andean Past* 3, 87–109.

LÓPEZ MAZZ, J.M. 1999: Some aspects of the French influence upon Uruguayan and Brazilian archaeology. In Politis, G. and Alberti, B. (eds.) 1999, 38–58.

LORENZO, J.L., PÉREZ ELÍAS, A. and GARCÍA BÁRCENA, J. 1976: *Hacia una Arqueología Social: Reunión de Teotihuacán* (México, Instituto Nacional de Antropología e Historia).

LUMBRERAS, L. 1971: Towards a re-evaluation of Chavín. In Benson, E.P. (ed.), *Dumbarton Oaks on Chavín* (1968) (Washington, D.C., Dumbarton Oaks Research Library), 1–28.

LUMBRERAS, L. 1974: *La Arqueología como ciencia social* (Lima).

LUMBRERAS, L. 1989: *Chavín de Huantar en el nacimiento de la Civilización Andina* (Lima).

LUMBRERAS, L. 1993: Chavín de Huantar Excavaciones en la Galería de las Ofrendas. *Materialien zur Allgemeinen und Vergleichenden Archaeologie 51* (Mainz am Rhein).

LUMBRERAS, L. and CISNEROS, L. 1986: Estado de la enseñanza en arqueología en el área Andina. In Alvarez, S. (ed.), *Guía histórico informativa. Centro de Estudios Arqueológicos y Antropológicos de la ESPOL* (Guayaquil, ESPOL), 29–40.

LYNCH, Th. 1974: Early Man in South America. *Quat. Res.* 4(3), 356–77.

LYNCH, Th. 1983: The South American Paleo-Indians. In Jennings, J. (ed.), *Ancient Native Americans* (San Francisco, 2nd edition), 87–137.

LYNCH, Th. 1990: Glacial-Age Man in South America: A Critical Review. *American Antiquity* 55, 12–36.

MAGALHAES, M. 1994: *Arqueologia de Carajás: A presença Pré-Histórica do Homen na Amazonia* (Rio de Janeiro).

MANN, Ch. 2000: Earthmovers of the Amazon. *Science* 287, 786–9.

MARTIN, F. and BORRERO, L.A. 1997: A Puma Lair in Southern Patagonia: Implications for the Archaeological Record. *Curr. Anthropol.* 38(3), 453–61.

MARTIN, P. 1973: The discovery of America. *Science* 179(4077), 969–74.

MARTINS, R. 1976: New Archaeological Techniques for the study of Ancient Root Crops in Peru (Ph.D. thesis, University of Birmingham, England).

MCGUIRE, R. 1983: Breaking down cultural complexity: inequality and heterogeneity. In Schiffer, M. (ed.), *Advances in Archaeological Method and Theory* vol. 6 (New York), 91–142.

MCGUIRE, R. and NAVARRETE, R. 1999: Entre motocicletas y fusiles: las arqueologías radicales anglosajona y latinoamericana. *Boletín de Antropología Americana* 34, 89–110.

MEGGERS, B. 1971: *Amazonia: Man and Culture in a Counterfeit Paradise* (Chicago).

MEGGERS, B. 1992a: Cuarenta años de colaboración. In Meggers, B. (ed.), *Prehistoria sudamericana: nuevas perspectivas* (Santiago de Chile).

MEGGERS, B. 1992b: Amazonia: real or counterfeit paradise? *Rev. Archaeol.* 13, 25–40.

MEGGERS, B. 1996: Letters. *Science* 274, 2825.

MEGGERS, B. 1999: *Ecología y biogeografía de la Amazonía* (Quito, Biblioteca Abya-Yala No. 62).

MEGGERS, B. and EVANS, C. 1957: Archaeological investigation at the mouth of the Amazon. *Bulletin 167, Smithsonian Institution, Bureau of American Ethnology* (Washington, D.C.).

MELTZER, D., ADOVASIO, J. and DILLEHAY, T.D. 1995: On the Pleistocene human occupation at Pedra Furada, Brazil. *Antiquity* 68, 695–714.

MELTZER, D., GRAYSON, D.K., ARDILA, G., BARKER, A., DINKAUZE, D., VANCE HAYNES, C., MENA, F., NUÑEZ, L. and STANFORD, D. 1997: On the Pleistocene Antiquity of Monte Verde, Southern Chile. *American Antiquity* 62(4), 659–63.

MENA, F. 1991: Prehistoric resource space and settlement at the Rio Ibañez Valley (Unpublished Ph.D. dissertation, UCLA).

MENDONÇA DE SOUZA, A. 1991: *História da Arqueologia Brasileira* (São Leopoldo, Instituto Anchietano de Pesquisas (Antropologia 46)).

MENGONI GOÑALONS, G. 1988: El estudio de huellas en arqueofaunas: una vía pararereconstruir situaciones interactivas en contextos arqueológicos: aspectos teórico-metodológicos y técnicas de análisis. In Ratto, N. and Haber, A. (eds.) 1988, 17–28.

MILLER, E. 1992: *Arqueologia nos emprendimientos hidroelétricos da Eletronorte; resultados preliminares* (Brasília).

MILLER, G. 1977: An introduction to the ethnoarchaeology of Andean camelids (Unpublished Ph.D. dissertation, University of California, Berkeley).

MILTON, K. 1984: Protein Carbohydrate Resources of the Makú Indians of Northwestern Amazonia. *American Anthropologist* 86, 7–25.

MIOTTI, L. and CATTÁNEO, R. 1997: Bifacial Technology at 13,000 Years Ago in Southern Patagonia. *Curr. Res. in the Pleistocene* 14, 62–5.

MIOTTI, L., VÁZQUEZ, M. and HERMO, D. 1999: Piedra Museo, un *Yamnagoo* pleistocénico de los colonizadores de la meseta de Santa Cruz. El estudio de la arqueofauna. *Soplando en el viento. . . Actas de las Terceras Jornadas de Arqueología de la Patagonia*, 113–36.

MONDINI, N. 1995: Artiodactyl prey transport by foxes in Puna rock shelters. *Curr. Anthropol.* 36, 520–4.

MONDINI, N. and MUÑOZ, A.S. 1996: El desarrollo de la tafonomía en la Arqueología Argentina. Estado Actual y Perspectivas. *Comunicación de la II Reunion de Tafonomía y Fosilización*, 255–8.

MORELL, V. 1998: Kennewick Man's Trials Continue. *Science* 280, 190–2.

MORLAN, R. and CINQ-MARS, J. 1982: Ancient Beringians: Human Occupation in the Late Pleistocene of Alaska and the Yukon Territory. In Hopkins, D., Matthews Jr., J., Scheweger, Ch. and Young, S. (eds.), *Paleoecology of Beringia* (New York), 353–81.

MORROW, J. and MORROW, T. 1997: Geographic Patterning in Fluted Point Morphology in the New World. Paper presented at the 62nd Annual Meeting of the Society for American Archaeology, Nashville.

MOSELEY, M. 1992: *The Incas and their ancestors* (London).

MUÑOZ, A.S. 1996: Análisis de marcas naturales en arqueofaunas de los sitios Bloque Errático 1 y Maria Luisa A3. In Gómez Otero, J. (ed.), *Arqueología, Sólo Patagonia* (Puerto Madryn, CENPAT-CONICET), 271–8.

NAMI, H. 1997: Investigaciones actualísticas para discutir aspectos técnicos de los cazadores-recolectores del Tardiglacial: el problema Clovis-Cueva Fell. *Anales del Instituto de la Patagonia (Punta Arenas)* 25, 151–86.

NASTI, A. 1991: Tafonomía de vertebrados en contextos sedimentarios modernos de la Puna Sur: chances de enterramiento y formación del registro arqueológico. *Shincal* 3, Tomo 1, 234–51.

NASTI, A. 2000: Modification of Vicuña Carcasses in High-Altitude Deserts. *Curr. Anthropol.* 41(2), 279–83.

NEVES, E.G. 1999: Changing perspectives in Amazonian archaeology. In Politis, G. and Alberti, B. (eds.) 1999, 216–43.

NEVES, W., POWELL, J., PROUS, A., OZOLINS, E. and BLUM, M. 1999: Lapa Vermelha IV Hominid 1: morphological affinities of the earliest known American. *Genetics and Molecular Biology* 22(4), 461–9.

NEVES, W. and PUCCIARELLI, H. 1989: Extra-continental biological relationships of early South American human remains: a multivariate analysis. *Ciencia e Cultura* 41, 566–75.

NEVES, W. and PUCCIARELLI, H. 1991: Morphological affinities of the first Americans: an exploratory analysis based on early South American human remains. *J. Human Evol.* 21, 261–73.

NIELSEN, A. 1998: Tráfico de caravanas en el sur de Bolivia: observaciones etnográficas e implicancias arqueológicas. *Relaciones de la Sociedad Argentina de Antropología* XXII–XXIII, 139–78.

NUÑEZ, L. 1981: Asentamientos de cazadores tardíos de la Puna de Atacama: hacia el sedentarismo. *Chungara* 8, 137–68.

NUÑEZ, L. 1992: *Cultura y conflicto en el Oasis de San Pedro de Atacama* (Santiago).

NUÑEZ, L. and MENA, F. 1997: El caso Monte Verde: ¿hacia un veredicto final? *Boletín de la Sociedad Chilena de Arqueología* 24, 38–44.

OCHSENIUS, C. and GRUHN, R. (eds.) 1979: *Taima-taima. A Late Pleistocene Paleo-Indian kill site in Northwestern South America — Final Reports of 1976 excavations* (South American Quaternary Documentation Program).

OLIVERA, D. 1988: La opción productiva. Apuntes para un análisis de sistemas adaptativos de tipo Formativo en el Noroeste argentino. *Precirculados IX Congreso Nacional de Arqueología Argentina*, 83–101.

OLIVERA, D., NASTI, A., DE AGUIRRE, M.J. and HORSEY, A. 1991–2: Tafonomía en desierto de altura. *Anales de Arqueología y Etnología* 46–7, 75–106.

ORELLANA RODRÍGUEZ, M. 1996: *Historia de la Arqueología en Chile* (Santiago de Chile).

OYUELA-CAYCEDO, A. (ed.) 1994: *History of Latin American Archaeology* (Aldershot).

OYUELA-CAYCEDO, A., AMAYA, A., ELERA, C.G. and VALDEZ, L. 1997: Social Archaeology in Latin America?: Comments to T.C. Patterson. *American Antiquity* 62, 365–74.

PARENTI, F. 1996: Problemática da Pré-História do Pleistoceno superior no Nordeste do Brasil: o abrigo da Pedra Furada em seu contexto regional. *FUNDAMentos. Revista da Fundaçao Museu do Homem Americano* 1(1), 15–54.

PARENTI, F., FONTUGNE, M. and GUÉRIN, C. 1996: Pedra Furada, Brasil e a sua "presumida" evidencia: limitaçoes e potencial dos dados disponiveis. *FUNDAMentos. Revista da Fundaçao Museu do Homem Americano* 1(1), 395–408.

PAYNTER, R. 1989: The archaeology of equality and inequality. *Ann. Rev. Anthropol.* 18, 366–99.

PÉREZ GOLLÁN, J. 1981: *Presencia de Vere Gordon Childe* (México, Instituto Nacional de Antropología e Historia).

PINTOS, S. 1998: Actividad monumental: la construcción del paisaje entre los cazadores-recolectores de la región Este de Uruguay. *Arqueología Espacial* 19–20, 529–42.

POLITIS, G. 1992: Política nacional, arqueología y universidad en Argentina. In Politis, G. (ed.), *Arqueología Latinoamericana Hoy* (Bogotá, Editorial del Fondo de Promoción de la Cultura), 70–86.

POLITIS, G. 1995: The socio-politics of archaeology in Hispanic South America. In Ucko, P. (ed.) 1995, 197–235.

POLITIS, G. 1996a: Moving to produce: Nukak mobility and settlement patterns in Amazonia. *World Archaeol.* 27, 492–510.

POLITIS, G. 1996b: *Nukak* (Santafé de Bogotá, Instituto SINCHI).

POLITIS, G. 1998: Arqueología de la Infancia: una perspectiva etnoarqueológica. *Trabajos de Prehistoria* 55(2), 5–19.

POLITIS, G. 1999: Plant exploitation among the Nukak hunter-gatherers of Amazonia: between ecology and ideology. In Gosden, C. and Hather, J. (eds.), *The Prehistory of Food. Appetites for Change* (London), 99–126.

POLITIS, G. and ALBERTI, B. (eds.) 1999: *Archaeology in Latin America* (London).

POLITIS, G. and GAMBLE, C. 1996: Los Nukak y los límites ambientales de los *foragers*. In Politis, G. 1996b, 335–54.

POLITIS, G. and MADRID, M. 1988: Un hueso duro de roer: análisis preliminar de la Tafonomía del sitio Laguna Tres Reyes 1 (Pdo. de Adolfo Gonzáles Chaves). In Ratto, N. and Haber, A. (eds.) 1988, 45–52.

POLITIS, G. and MARTÍNEZ, G. 1996: La cacería, el procesamiento de las presas y los tabúes alimenticios. In Politis, G. 1996b, 231–80.

POLITIS, G. and SAUNDERS, N. in press: Archaeological correlates of ideological activity: food taboos and spirit-animals in an Amazonian hunter-gatherer society. In Miracle, P. (ed.), *Consuming Passions. Archaeological studies of material culture* (Cambridge, McDonald Institute).

POZORSKI, T. and POZORSKI, S. 1993: Early complex society and ceremonialism on the Peruvian north coast. In Millones, L. and Onuki, Y. (eds.), *El mundo ceremonial andino* (National Museum of Ethnology, Osaka, Japan, Senri Ethnological Studies no. 37), 45–68.

PRICE, D.T. and GEBAUER, A. 1995: New perspectives on the transition to agriculture. In Price, T.D. and Gebauer, A. (eds.), *Last Hunters-First Farmers* (Santa Fé, New Mexico), 3–19.

PROUS, A. 1991: Santa Ana do Riacho — Tomo 1. *Arquivos do Museu de História Natural* 12, 3–384.

PROUS, A. 1992–3: Santa Ana do Riacho — Tomo II. *Arquivos do Museu de História Natural* 13, 143–420.

PROUS, A. 1997: O povoamento da América visto do Brasil: uma perspectiva crítica. *Revista USP* 34, 8–21.

RATTO, N. and HABER, A. (eds.) 1988: *De Procesos, Contextos y otros Huesos* (Buenos Aires, ICA (Sección Prehistoria) FFyL, UBA).

REICHEL-DOLMATOFF, G. 1972: *San Agustín: a culture of Colombia* (New York and Washington, D.C.).

REID, H. 1979: Some Aspects of Movement, Growth, and Change among the Hupdu Maku Indians of Brazil (Unpublished Ph.D. dissertation, University of Cambridge, England).

REINHARD, J. 1996: Peru's Ice Maidens. *Nat. Geogr. Soc.* 189(6), 62–81.

RICK, J. 1980: *Prehistoric Hunters of the High Andes* (New York).

RICK, J., RODRÍGUEZ KEMBEL, S., MENDOZA RICK, R. and KEMBEL, J. 1998: La Arquitectura del complejo ceremonial de Chavín de Huantar: Documentación tridimencional y sus implicancias. *Boletín PUCP* 2, 181–214.

ROE, P. 1994: Ethnology and Archaeology: Symbolic and Systemic Disjunction or Continuity? In Oyuela-Caycedo, A. (ed.) 1994, 183–208.

ROOSEVELT, A. 1980: *Parmana: Prehistoric maize and manioc subsistence along the Amazon and Orinoco* (New York).

ROOSEVELT, A. 1991: *Mountbuilders of the Amazon: geophysical archaeology on Marajo Island, Brazil* (San Diego).

ROOSEVELT, A. 1995: Early pottery in the Amazon. Twenty years of scholarly obscurity. In Barnett, W. and Hoopes, J. (eds.), *The emergence of Pottery. Technology and innovation in Ancient Societies* (Washington, D.C.), 115–31.

ROOSEVELT, A.C., LIMA DA COSTA, M., LOPES MACHADO, C., MICHAB, M., MERCIER, N., VALLADAS, H., FEATHERS, J., BARNETT, W., IMAZIO DA SILVEIRA, M., HENDERSON, A., SILVA, J., CHERNOFF, B., REESE, D.S., HOLMAN, J.A., TOTH, N. and SCHICK, S. 1996: Paleoindian Cave Dwellers in the Amazon: The Peopling of the Americas. *Science* 272, 373–84.

ROSSEN, J., DILLEHAY, T. and UGENT, D. 1996: Ancient Cultigens or Modern Intrusions?: Evaluating Plant Remains in an Andean Case Study. *J. Archaeol. Sci.* 23, 391–407.

SALAZAR, E. 1995: Between Crisis and Hope: Archaeology in Ecuador. *Soc. American Archaeol. Bull.* 13(4), 34–7.

SALOMON, F. and SCHWARTZ, S. (eds.) 1999: *The Cambridge History of the Native Peoples of the Americas, Vol. III. South America* (Cambridge).

SANDWEISS, D., RICHARDSON III, J., RITZ, E., HSU, J. and FELDMAN, R. 1989: Early maritime adaptations in the Andes: Preliminary studies at the Ring site, Peru. In Rice, D., Stanish, C. and Scar, P. (eds.), *Ecology, Settlement and History in the Osmore Drainage, Peru* (Oxford, BAR Int. Ser. 546), 35–84.

SAUNDERS, N. 1998: Architecture of Symbolism: The feline image. In Saunders, N. (ed.), *Icons of Power: Feline Symbolism in the Americas* (London), 12–52.

SCHOBINGER, J. 1988: *Prehistoria de Sudamérica* (Madrid).

SHIMADA, I. 1999: Evolution of Andean Diversity: regional formations. In Salomon, F. and Schwartz, S. (eds.) 1999, 350–517.

SIEGEL, P. 1990: Demographic and Architectural Retrodiction: An Ethnoarchaeological Case Study in the South American Tropical Lowlands. *Latin American Antiquity* 1(4), 319–46.

SILVEIRA, M. 1997: Ausente sin aviso. Tafonomía regional ósea en la llanura interserrana bonaerense. In Berón, M. and Politis, G. (eds.), *Arqueología Pampeana en la década de los '90* (San Rafael, Museo de Historia Natural de San Rafael (Mendoza) — INCUAPA), 229–42.

SILVERWOOD-COPE, P. 1972: A Contribution to the Ethnography of the Colombian Maku (Unpublished Ph.D. dissertation, University of Cambridge, England).

SMITH, C.E. 1980: Plant remains from Guitarrero Cave. In Lynch, T. (ed.), *Guitarrero Cave. Early Man in the Andes* (New York), 87–119.

SPENSER, Ch. and REDMOND, E. 1998: Prehispanic Causeways and Regional Politics in the Llanos de Barinas, Venezuela. *Latin American Antiquity* 9(2), 95–110.

SPONSEL, L. 1986: Amazon Ecology and Adaptation. *Ann. Rev. Anthropol.* 15, 67–97.

SPONSEL, L. 1989: Farming and Foraging: A necessary complementary in Amazonia? In Kent, S. (ed.), *Farmers as Hunters: the implications of Sedentism* (Cambridge), 37–47.

STAHL, P. 1995: Differential preservation histories affecting the mammalian zooarchaeological record from the forested neotropical lowlands. In Stahl, P. (ed.), *Archaeology in the Lowland American Tropics* (Cambridge), 154–80.

STAHL, P. 1996: Holocene Biodiversity. An Archaeological Perspective from the Americas. *Ann. Rev. Anthropol.* 25, 105–26.

STANISH, C. 1994: The hydraulic hypothesis revisited: Lake Titicaca raised fields in theoretical perspective. *Latin American Antiquity* 5(4), 312–32.

STEARMAN, A.M. 1991: Making a living in the Tropical Forest: Yuqui Foragers in the Bolivian Amazon. *Human Ecol.* 19(2), 245–60.

STEELE, D.G. and POWELL, J.F. 1992: Peopling of the Americas: Paleobiological evidence. *Human Biol.* 64, 303–36.

STEWARD, J. 1946–50: *The Handbook of South American Indians* 6 vols. (Washington, Bureau of American Ethnology).

STEWARD, J. and FARON, L. 1959: *Native People of South America* (New York).

STUART, D.E. 1977: Seasonal phases in Ona subsistence, territorial distribution and organization: Implications for the archaeological record. In Binford, L. (ed.), *For Theory Building in Archaeology* (New York), 251–83.

TAYLOR, R., HAYNES JR, C.V., KIRNER, D. and SOUTHON, J. 1999: Radiocarbon analysis of modern organics at Monte Verde, Chile: no evidence for a local reservoir effect. *American Antiquity* 64(3), 455–60.

TAYLOR, R., HAYNES JR, C.V. and STUIVER, M. 1996: Clovis and Folsom age estimates: stratigraphic context and radiocarbon calibration. *Antiquity* 70, 515–25.

TOMKA, S. 1993: Site abandonment behavior among transhumant agro-pastoralists: the effects of delayed curation on assemblages composition. In Cameron, C.M. and Tomka, S., *Abandonment of Settlement and Regions* (Cambridge), 11–24.

TOWNSEND, P.K. 1990: On the possibility/impossibility of Tropical Forest hunting and gathering. *American Anthropologist* 92, 745–7.

TRIGGER, B. 1992: *Historia del Pensamiento Arqueológico* (Barcelona).

TURNER II, C.G. 1983: Dental evidence of the peopling of the Americas. In Shutler Jr., R. (ed.), *Early Man in the New World* (Beverly Hills), 147–57.

UCKO, P. (ed.) 1995: *Theory in Archaeology. A World Perspective* (London).

VARGAS ARENAS, I. and SANOJA OBEDIENTE, M. 1992: Revisión crítica de la arqueología sudamericana. In Meggers, B. (ed.), *Prehistoria Sudamericana. Nuevas Perspectivas* (México), 35–44.

VARGAS ARENA, I. and SANOJA OBEDIENTE, M. 1999: Archaeology as a social science. In Politis, G. and Alberti, B. (eds.) 1999, 59–75.

VESCELIUS, G.S. 1981a: Early and/or not-so-early man in Peru: the case of Guitarrero Cave. *Quart. Rev. Archaeol.* 2, 11–15.

VESCELIUS, G.S. 1981b: Early and/or not-so-early man in Peru: the case of Guitarrero Cave. *Quart. Rev. Archaeol.* 2, 19–20.

WEST, F. 1993: Review of Paleoenvironment and Site Content at Monte Verde. *American Antiquity* 58(1), 166–7.

WILLEY, G. 1951: The Chavín problem: a review and critique. *Southwestern J. Anthropol.* 64, 1–14.

WILLEY, G. 1958: Estimated Correlations and Dating of South and Central American Culture Sequences. *American Antiquity* 23, 353–78.

WILLEY, G. and SABLOFF, J. 1980: *A History of American Archaeology* (San Francisco, 2nd edition).

WILSON, D. 1999: *Indigenous South Americans of the Past and Present: An Ecological Perspective* (Boulder).

WITTFOGEL, K. 1957: *Oriental despotism* (New Haven).

WÜST, I. 1998: Continuities and discontinuities: archaeology and ethnoarchaeology in the heart of the Eastern Bororo territory, Mato Grosso, Brazil. *Antiquity* 72, 663–75.

WÜST, I. and BARRETO, C. 1999: The Ring Village of Central Brazil: A Challenge for Amazonian Archaeology. *Latin American Antiquity* 10, 3–23.

YACOBACCIO, H. 1995: El aporte de la Etnoarqueología al conocimiento del registro arqueológico pastoril andino. *Actas del XIII Congreso Nacional de Arqueología Chilena, Hombre y Desierto* 9(1) (Antofagasta, Chile), 309–16.

YACOBACCIO, H. and MADERO, C. 1994: Etnoarquelogía de pastores surandinos: una herramienta para conocer el registro arqueológico. *Jornadas de Arqueología e Interdisciplinas* (Buenos Aires, CONICET-Programa de Estudios Prehistóricos), 203–36.

YACOBACCIO, H., MADERO, C. and MALMIERCA, M. 1998: *Etnoarqueología de Pastores Surandinos* (Buenos Aires, Grupo Zooarqueología de Camélidos).

ZARANKIN, A. and ACUTO, F. (eds.) 1999: Sed Non Satiata, *Teoría Social en Arqueología Latinoamericana Contemporánea* (Buenos Aires).

ZEIDLER, J. 1984: Social space in Valdivia Society: Community patterning and domestic structure at Real Alto, 3,000–2,000 B.C. (Unpublished Ph.D. dissertation, Urbana, Illinois).

Theatrum Oceani: Themes and arguments concerning the prehistory of Australia and the Pacific

RHYS JONES AND MATTHEW SPRIGGS

Wherever the geologist can explore the earth's surface, he can read much of its past history . . . but wherever oceans and seas now extend, he can do nothing but speculate on the very limited data afforded by the depth of the waters. Here the naturalist steps in, and enables him to fill up this great gap in the past history of the earth. (A.R. Wallace 1869, 15)

Introduction

If one were to tip a terrestrial globe so that one's perspective was centred on a location situated over Turkmenistan (lat. 40° north and long. 60° east), the subtended view would represent a hemisphere almost entirely covered by land (Fig. 1). From east to west is the mass of Eurasia, with northern Africa curving away out of view to the south. This is how the ancient Greek geographers conceived of the inhabitable world; the *ekumene* surrounded by the great circumscribing ocean. By an irony, when Aristotle's most famous student at the Lyceum, Alexander, reached the shores of the Caspian Sea, he thought that he had actually found the edge of this *okeanos*, whereas in reality he was close to the very geographical centre-point of an expanded *ekumene* (Glacken 1956). Had he in his militarized expeditions been able to travel further east beyond even *India trans Gangem*, he would indeed have reached the western edge of a great ocean that might have seemed to have circumscribed the entire world of humankind.

In its historical development, the discipline of prehistory over the past one hundred and fifty years has been largely developed from the analyses of the archaeological record of the historical events that have occurred over this vast and largely continuous terrain. In general, the oceans surrounding these central land masses have been seen to have played only a marginal influence, restricted perhaps to regional scales such as the

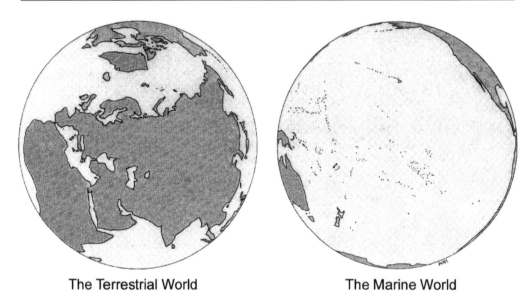

The Terrestrial World   The Marine World

Figure 1. The terrestrial world and the marine world.

littoral shores and islands of the European Atlantic or the gulfs and northern waters of the Indian Ocean. It was only the enclosed seas, in particular the aptly named Mediterranean, which, penetrating into the western heart of the land mass, have provided major interpretive themes for its prehistory.

There is another viewpoint of the globe, that centred on Christmas (or Kiritimati) Island (lat. 2° north and long. 157° west) in the Line Islands chain of Kiribati in the central Pacific. From here, one sees a global hemisphere almost entirely covered by sea. The western coasts of the Americas fringe the right hand margin like the concave edge of a new crescent moon; to the left there is the faintest edge of the coast of China; and to the south-east, just the eastern coastline of Australia and New Guinea. The very south has the ice edge of the Antarctic shore. The centre view consists of a vast oceanic world, with a scatter shot of islands. Some of these are of course large, such as the two main islands of New Zealand; and the combined land masses of Australia and New Guinea are themselves continental in scale. Yet it is our contention that despite great differences in geographic size and isolation of the various islands, and the differences of scale in the timing and intensities of their human occupations, there still remain some unifying principles in one's interpretation of all of their prehistories. We take the term 'theatre' as used by the Renaissance geographer Abraham Ortelius of Antwerp, in his pioneering atlas *Theatrum Orbis Terrarum* of 1571, to exemplify the grand geographical terrains upon which the histories of human lives have been carried out. These reflect the prehistoric signature of an oceanic world, and it is this that we would like to attempt to explore in this present essay.

Only a very limited number of themes can be addressed within the word-length available and the vast area to be covered geographically. Archaeology is a young discipline in the Pacific region. Its history has been explored in recent essays by Golson (1986), McBryde (1986), Mulvaney (1993) and by one of us (Jones 1993, 1998, 1999). We are still much concerned with the 'when' of prehistory and still working out the implications of this for the 'why' which justifies its study. It is thus the 'when' which we stress here in an overview of the settlement of the region, and the difficulties involved in establishing acceptable chronologies. These are difficulties of techniques of dating beyond the 'radiocarbon barrier' of about 40,000 years, where small changes of parameter in experimental method can make major changes to the numbers produced. Difficulties of interpretation of stratigraphy at major sites, both in Southeast Asian and Australian fossil hominid and early occupation sites, also present major differences in the possible stories to be told. At the other end of the chronological and geographic spectrum in East Polynesia, with a less than 2000-year archaeological record and in some areas a less than 600-year prehistory prior to European contact, the problems are those of the interpretation of radiocarbon dates themselves. Problems of old wood, natural or cultural burning and proper calibration of marine shell samples loom large in sometimes spirited discussion. Figures 2, 3 and 4 display the islands and in some cases the individual sites mentioned in this paper in the Southeast Asian, Australian and New Guinea, and Pacific Islands regions.

It is our contention that to get the dates 'right' is a primary task in Oceania, and one that is not yet accomplished. The implications are enormous, as we shall show. Knowing when something happened, even if only relative to something else, itself tells you something about it — fast or slow, old or recent, same time or different. If we take an issue such as the spread of modern humans into our region, timing is critical in order to examine questions such as whether the spread was contemporary with the spread of modern humans elsewhere out of Africa, whether it related to particular world-scale glacial events or cycles, whether it was a slow adaptation or a rapid spread by an environmentally super-flexible species, whether there were absolute environmental limits to the spread or major pauses, and whether the spread coincided with the extinction of Australia and New Guinea's marsupial megafauna and thus might be implicated in that extinction. As we shall see below, when particular grades of hominid, *Homo sapiens* and before them *Homo erectus* entered the area are the subjects of major debate. Until such debates are settled, we shall have no idea of the tempo of cultural change or of its relation to environmental changes we can witness in other biological and fossil records.

Bathymetry and biological history

If we wish to consider the biological histories of this vast array of islands, it is not so much their present geographic delineation as on the pages of an atlas which is so

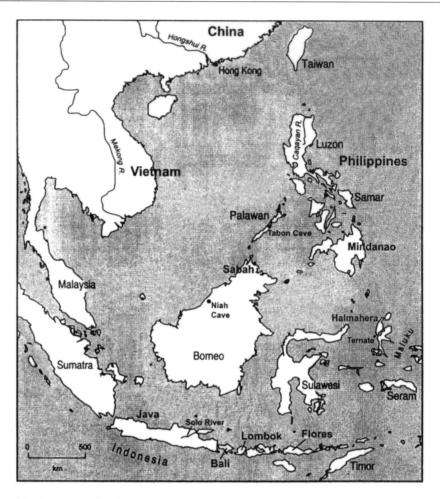

Figure 2. Islands mentioned in the text in Southeast Asia.

important, but rather the bathymetry of the shelves from which they emerge. To extend our metaphor of an observer from far out in Space, what is critically important is to be able to look down through the blue surface of the sea to its bed. Glacio-eustatic theory shows that periodically throughout the Pleistocene, glacial low sea-levels have descended to depths of about 130 m below present levels. During such phases, shallow continental shelves were exposed and islands on them were joined to their adjacent continents. This allowed periodic faunal recruitment. Conversely during periods of interglacial isolation, processes of extinction occurred due to the limiting factors of reduced habitat size, according to the laws of island biogeography succinctly enunciated by MacArthur and Wilson (1967). Beyond such continental shelves are the true oceanic islands to which faunal access has always been across water. In these cases the

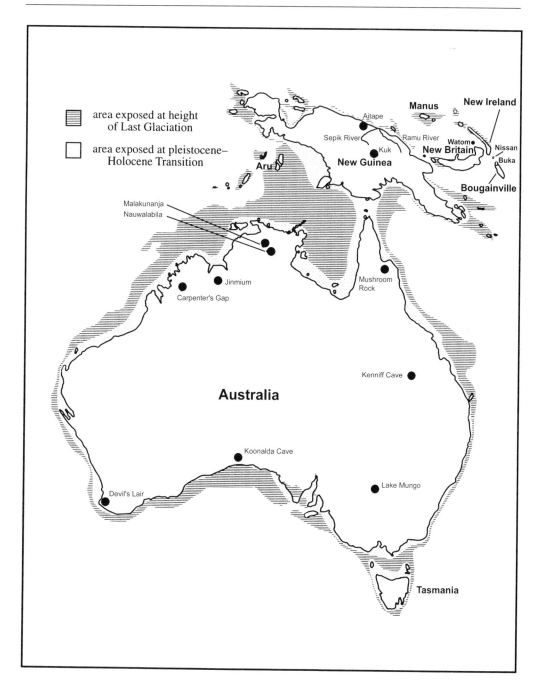

Figure 3. Sites and areas mentioned in the text in Australia and New Guinea (map after Beaton 1995).

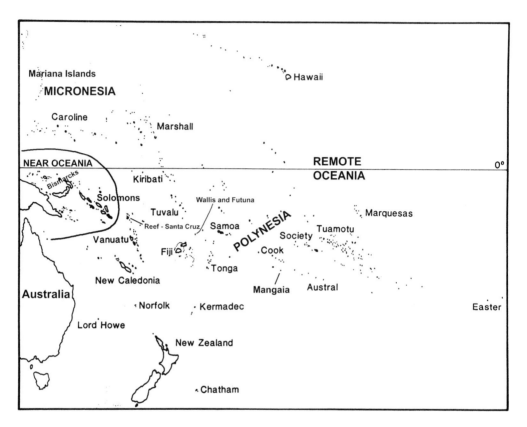

Figure 4. Islands and archipelagoes mentioned in the text in the Pacific region.

probability of any particular species being able to colonize was based on their trans-marine survival capacity and also inversely according to the distances to be travelled.

The great Victorian naturalist Alfred Russell Wallace instinctively saw some of these patterns during his travels through the Indo-Malay Archipelago in the mid-1850s. Sailing a short distance eastwards from the small spice-rich island of Ternate to Halmahera, to the west of the 'Bird's Head' or Vogelkop peninsula of the island of New Guinea, he met for the first time Papuan people, and commented on how different they seemed to be to the Malays of the eastern part of the archipelago. That, 'on drawing the line which separates these races, it is found to come near to that which divides the zoological regions, but somewhat eastwards of it; a circumstance which appears to me very significant of the same causes having influenced the distribution of mankind that have determined the range of other animal forms' (1869, 15). Wallace made explicit that his original 'conviction that the eastern and western halves of the Archipelago belonged to distinct primary regions of the earth' derived initially from these ethnological observations (ibid.). As adjusted by Thomas Huxley (1868), this boundary has been called 'Wallace's Line' ever since and it marked the south-eastern extent of the Eurasian fauna.

The ancient fauna of Java is Eurasian. The island itself was only formed tectonically in Plio-Pleistocene times and its fossil fauna consisting of such mammalian taxa as bovids, elephants and primates resembles that of the Siwaliks on the Himalayan foothills of India. Yet between the islands of Bali and Lombok there is a profound change in faunal composition. Wallace himself put it that, 'The strait here is fifteen miles wide, so that we may pass in two hours from one great division of the earth to another, differing as essentially in their animal life as Europe does from America' (op. cit., 11). Beyond this narrow strait was a series of island chains, highly depauperate in their land fauna, and beyond these again to the east and south, the Australian continent, with its own distinctive land fauna. These great biogeographical distributions were only finally explained in the mid-1960s with the development of the theory of plate tectonics (Campbell 1975). Australia, part of the original super-continent of Gondwanaland, has never been joined to Asia. Its archaic biological affinities are with southern Africa, South America and India. Since its final separation from Antarctica, Australia has been slowly drifting northwards, and its collision with the Asian and Pacific plates has formed the spine of the New Guinea Highlands and a series of tectonically uplifted island chains (including the greater Sunda Chain containing Sumatra and Java) separated by abyssal oceanic straits. Between the continents of Asia and Australia lies a region of islands and straits, referred to as Wallacea. Here was the gateway to the human colonization of the Pacific world when moving from Sunda — the Southeast Asian continental extension of Greater Asia — to Sahul, the Pleistocene continent made up of Australia, New Guinea, the Aru Islands and Tasmania (Jones 1989, 743–6).

Ancient hominids

Ever since the discovery by Eugene Dubois of the calvaria of his original *Pithecanthropus* at Trinil on the banks of the Solo River in 1891 (Dubois 1894), the island of Java has been the source of more fossil specimens of what is now referred to as *Homo erectus* than any other part of the world. This has been partly due to taphonomic processes, whereby fluvial deposits were accumulated in shallow deltaic contexts, conducive to the accumulation of fossil bones, and then tectonically uplifted as in the deposits of the classic Sangiran Dome sequence of south central Java. Indeed during the early part of the century it was considered by some scholars including Dubois himself that Southeast Asia was the original homeland for humankind, which is why he had originally gone to the Dutch East Indies as a colonial government official in order to initiate his field enquires. Concerning the dating of these Javanese hominids, their earliest appearance is within the stratigraphic context of the uppermost part of the Pucangan beds of the Sangiran sequence.

The classic Sangiran 17 hominid fossil (*Pithecanthropus* VIII), which has its upper facial features preserved, came from the middle part of the overlying Kabuh beds. Dates obtained by the fission track method on zircon crystals within stratified tuffs in the Pucangan gave values of about one million years ago, consistent with the reverse magnetic polarity of the deposit, and the Kabuh was dated by the same methods to about 750 ka years ago (Itihara *et al.* 1985, 376; Suzuki *et al.* 1985, 329–30), a value which seemed to have support from an assessment of a normal magnetic polarity for these higher deposits. At the site of Mojokerto in north central Java, the calvaria of a *Homo erectus* child was found in 1936 within river sands intercalated in marine deposits ascribed to the Djetis beds of the Pucangan formation (Jacob 1975, 105–6) and later dated on the basis of detailed palaeomagnetic studies to *c.*970 ka (Hyodo *et al.* 1993), a figure considered by de Vos (1994) to be consistent with the faunal component of these deposits.

    However, research by Swisher *et al.* (1994; Swisher 1994), based on ^{40}Argon/^{39}Argon isotope measurements of hornblende minerals within pumice recovered from both Sangiran and at Mojokerto, proposed dates some 900 ka older than either of the values quoted above, with an age for Mojokerto of 1.8 ma. In the case of Mojokerto, the argon dates were carried out on samples of pumice taken from a conglomerate which may have been substantially reworked and redeposited since the original volcanic ejection (de Vos 1994). At Sangiran, however, a new ^{40}Ar/^{39}Ar study was carried out, based on developments in laser incremental heating of hornblendes (Swisher and Curtis 1998), and this was integrated with palaeomagnetic studies based on detailed stratigraphic sampling across the critical hominid-bearing layers. This yielded a series of dates of between 1.7 ma to 1.0 ma, which were chronologically consistent with their stratigraphic positions (Swisher *et al.* 1998); and all of the *H. erectus* fossils occurred within reverse polarity rocks. The critical differences compared with the previous results from the same site were attributed, firstly, to anomalously young fission-track dates and, secondly, to a misinterpretation whereby a 'normal polarity' signal was attained by a contemporary field overprint, derived from surface weathering (Swisher *et al.* 1998). If these dates gain critical acceptance, then they establish the presence of *H. erectus* in Southeast Asia almost instantaneously, in terms of the discrimination of our dating methods, with their first appearance in Africa, and confirm the first great geographical spread of advanced hominids from their ancestral home.

    There has also been recent controversy concerning the youngest age for the Javanese *erectus* hominids. At Ngandong, on the Solo River of central Java, a celebrated series of hominid fossils was recovered originally in 1931 from a high terrace of the Solo River (Oppenoorth 1932; von Koenigswald 1933). Morphologically these were considered to represent the final form of the Asian *erectus* lineage (Weidenreich 1951) and there is a general consensus that the geomorphological context of the fossils would indicate an Upper Pleistocene age. ESR and uranium series dates were assayed by Swisher *et al.* (1996) on fossil bovid tooth enamel, excavated from a small pit adjacent to the original excavations of the 1930s where some of the hominids had been found (Oppenoorth 1932; von Koenigswald 1933; Jacob 1975, 107). They gave values as recent as between 27 ka and 53 ka, the large error range reflecting uncertainties in the uranium uptake histories. If this age were true, then it would imply that the final *erectus* population had been living contemporaneously with modern *sapiens* populations within this region. This would have huge implications not only for general issues of human evolution but also specifically to the question of the colonization of Australia and the affinities of its oldest human forms (Swisher *et al.* 1996, 1870). The critical question concerning this study is the assumption that the dated bovid remains within this deposit have had a similar taphonomic history to the hominid remains (op. cit., 1871). This is unlikely to have been the case, however, since unlike the other fauna, the hominid fossils were heavily mineralized and dark, almost black in colour, and had most probably been reworked into the upper Ngandong terrace by fluvial action from older deposits (Grün and Thorne 1997). The most recent estimate, based on direct non-destructive gamma-ray spectrometric uranium series measurements on two of the skulls (Solo 1 and Sambungmacan), indicates a value older than 200 ka (Yokoyama *et al.* 1998).

The only *Homo sapiens* fossil of substantial age from Indonesia is the Wadjak hominid, recovered from a breccia deposit within a limestone cliff crevice in southern Java and, on present evidence, dated to terminal Pleistocene times, perhaps 10 ka years ago (Jacob 1975, 115–16; von Koenigswald 1956). From its first discovery its rugged morphology has been compared to that of Australian Aborigines (Dubois 1920), and it represents a population clearly pre-dating the modern Javanese one. Elsewhere in Southeast Asia fossil skulls with sapient morphology, recovered from the caves of Niah on the island of Borneo and Tabon on Palawan island in the Philippines, have come from deposits carbon dated to *c.*40 ka and 26 ka respectively (Harrisson 1959; Fox 1970). However, given the less-precise excavation methods of a generation ago, there is a possibility that these fossils might have been inserted into older deposits due to burial customs or other taphonomic processes. There is now the urgent need to get direct dates on them using the most recent dating methods before further historical speculations are embarked upon (Jones 1989, 750–2).

Concerning the cultural capacities of the Southeast Asian *H. erectus* hominids, and their archaeological signature, there has long been controversy. Throughout most of the century it was assumed that with a primitive hominid, so also a primitive stone technology. The absence of Acheulean-type handaxes led Movius (1944) to propose an east Asian equivalent called the 'Chopper-chopping tool tradition', based largely on unifacial and bifacial flaked cobbles. Part of the formulation for this came from his study of the surface collection made by von Koenigswald and Tweedie of large core and thick flake tools from the Baksoka Valley near Pacitan in southern Java. It was originally assumed from their typological appearance of large size and simplicity of form that they were of Middle Pleistocene age (von Koenigswald 1939). However, detailed field research by Bartstra (1984) within the type area of this industry has shown them to be derived from terminal Pleistocene times or even later. In his opinion, the oldest reliable finds of stone artefacts from Java or indeed elsewhere from Sundaland are restricted to industries consisting of small flakes and casually struck cores from locations such as the 'Old River Gravel' at Ngebung within the youngest deposits of the Sangiran sequence, and at the Solo River High Terrace, both dated to no older than the middle part of the Upper Pleistocene (Bartstra 1985, 103–8; Jones 1989, 748–50).

The issue is also potentially confused by problems concerning the identity, in some cases, of genuine humanly made stone artefacts as opposed to pieces, which, while showing some percussion fractures, were formed entirely by natural causes, in particular by being knocked against each other in high energy cobble-bedded streams. The problem partly lies in the common occurrence of easily fractured silicified tuffs, which can often show quasi-artefactual phenomena, and unfortunately there has also been a lack of analytical rigour by some observers concerning the unequivocal criteria to be applied in identifying humanly fashioned artefacts. These issues are similar to those concerning the 'eolith' problem in the early 1900s when Tertiary age artefacts were claimed from gravel deposits in England and France. Objective criteria for an unquestionable human agency for percussion have been discussed in an Australian context by Wright (1971, 50, 56–7) in his analysis of the flaked flint pieces from Koonalda Cave in the Nullarbor Plain of South Australia.

The capacities of the Southeast Asian *Homo erectus* hominids both to make stone tools and also to cross narrow oceanic barriers have been brought into focus by new examinations of the site of Mata Menge in south central Flores, situated under the shadow of a large volcano. Here claims were made as long ago as 1970 of the stratigraphic association of flaked stone tools with fossils of the now extinct elephant-like *Stegodon trigonocephalus* (Verhoeven 1958; Maringer and Verhoeven 1970; Glover 1973, 122–5). The stegodons were one of the few large Asian mammals to have been able to colonize some of the islands of Wallacea, such as Flores, Timor, Sulawesi (the Celebes) and both Luzon and Mindanao in the Philippines (Hooijer 1975), perhaps through their ability to swim substantial cross-sea distances. Reanalysis of the Mata Menge site by palaeontologists found further flaked stones within the same deposits as the *Stegodon* fossils (Sondaar *et al.* 1994), which they dated as lying immediately above the Brunhes-Matuyama magnetic reversal, indicating an age of *c.*700 ka. At least one flake illustrated by van den Bergh *et al.* (1996, fig. 5) is unquestionably an artefact. These deposits were later dated by fission track method, indicating the arrival of *H. erectus* in Flores by about 850 ka ago, with an absence in deposits slightly older (Morwood *et al.* 1997; Morwood *et al.* 1998). A further regional survey has revealed more sites within the same region, where bones of *Stegodon* have been reported associated with *in situ* flaked stone tools (Morwood *et al.* 1999, 285).

It is our responsibility to address the evidence with the utmost scrutiny because of its importance regarding the capacity of early hominids to cross sea straits (Bednarik

1997). Our final question is one of geomorphology, whether or not there have been episodes of massive regional slumping of fluvio-volcanic deposits, with resultant mixing, perhaps due to monsoonal-rain or tectonic events? (Cf. Fennema 1996.) New data indicate stratified stone tools and fauna in basal levels of the limestone cave of Liang Bua in central Flores, which will probably settle the issue (Schulz 2001).

For the record, one of us (RJ, in association with Indonesian and Australian colleagues in 1993) failed to find any stone artefacts within extensive exposed deposits, probably of Early or Middle Pleistocene age and which yielded fossils of *Stegodon*, near Atambua, in West Timor close to the border with East Timor. Other reporters have been more sanguine in this regard (Verhoeven 1964, 1968, 402; Glover and Glover 1970, 188–90): some stone tools found from surface locations in Timor, as described in these latter reports, have some typological resemblances with the Pacitanian, and are different to those excavated by Glover (1986) from limestone cave sites in East Timor and dated by him to a maximum antiquity of about 14 ka. At the cave of Lene Hara, East Timor, shell midden debris has been dated to between 30 and 35 ka ago (Dayton 2001).

The oldest Australian dates

The systematic application of radiocarbon dating, beginning in the early 1960s, caused a revolution in prehistoric research in Australia. As recently as 1961, it was considered that the oldest reliable direct dates for human occupation of the continent lay only within the mid-Holocene (Mulvaney 1961; Clark 1961, 243). A year later in 1962, a date of 12,000 years before present was obtained from Kenniff Cave in the highlands of south-east Queensland and this was quickly followed by the measurement of a slightly lower sample dated to 16,000 years ago (Mulvaney and Joyce 1965). Within the next decade, this antiquity had been extended to more than 30,000 years ago (Jones 1973).

An important discovery which dramatically tied the archaeological evidence to parallel basic discoveries which were also being made concerning the geomorphic and palaeoclimatic history of the continent was at Lake Mungo in the arid south-western corner of New South Wales (Bowler *et al.* 1970). Here, in 1969, the cremated remains of a young woman, now referred to as the Mungo 1 hominid, were found in a carbonate-encrusted pit within the core of an eroded crescent-shaped sand dune or lunette, bordering the eastern shore of a now-extinct lake. From this same eroded surface were recovered numerous *in situ* stone artefacts made from quartzite, which included dome-shaped horsehoof cores and steep-edge scrapers. A series of small hearths contained evidence of a broad spectrum foraging economy, including fishing, possibly using woven nets to drive fish such as golden perch (*Plectroplites ambiguus*) to the shore (Allen 1998), freshwater mussel gathering and the hunting of small marsupials. Radiocarbon dates on burnt human bone, and charcoal from adjacent and stratigraphically equivalent hearths, indicated an age of c.26 ka (Bowler et al. 1972), which at that time was the oldest date for human occupation of the Australian continent. Further research showed freshwater mussel shell middens in adjacent lunettes of the same fossil lake system which dated to 32 ka (Barbetti and Allen 1972), and the oldest date for a stratified shell midden at nearby Lake Arumpo was between 34 and 37 ka bp (Bowler 1976, 59). Within the Mungo Sand Unit itself, excavations were carried out in the early 1970s, with stone artefacts found throughout its upper half. A carbon date (ANU-1263), on black organic material located above the lowest artefact, gave a value barely indistinguishable from background, with an ascribed value of '40,000 years or more' (Shawcross 1975, 30; Shawcross 1998, 190). One of us speculated a decade ago that, 'these lower artifacts (might) have a general antiquity of c. 40–45 ka at least' (Jones 1989, 762).

During the 1970s and 1980s, radiocarbon dates of the order of 35–37 ka were obtained from a variety of sites, mostly sandstone rockshelters or limestone caves but also including open sand dunes and swamps. These were located over the full extent of the Australian continent, and also in Papua New Guinea (Jones and Bowler 1980). Latitudinally they spanned slightly over 40° of latitude from the Equator to southern Tasmania, equivalents in the northern hemisphere being from Belfast to the Congo. Within the Sahul land mass, the ecological regions occupied during this time included all of the major ecological zones, from the montane valleys of New Guinea and the savannas of northern Australia to the desert core of the continent and to its temperate extremities, both in the extreme south-west of Western Australia, and to southern Tasmania (Jones 1989, 1995; Smith and Sharp 1993; Allen and O'Connell 1995; O'Connell and Allen 1998). Human occupation also extended to the truly oceanic islands of the Bismarck Archipelago close to New Guinea, indicating significant ocean-crossing capacities in these tropical waters at that time.

The oldest conventional radiocarbon dates from a securely stratified archaeological context in Australia have been obtained at Carpenter's Gap which is a large open rockshelter in the cliff face of a Devonian-age fossilized coral reef fringing the southern edge of the Archaean-age Kimberley massif of north-western Australia. The oldest pair of AMS dates were 39,220±870 and 39,700±1000 BP (O'Connor 1995), and work which is still in progress using the most advanced methods of charcoal sample pre-treatment (Bird et al. 1999; Fifield et al. 2001) confirms the order of magnitude of these dates.

The question remained whether this continental pattern dated the first arrival of humans or whether these values simply reflected the technical limits of the radiocarbon method? The problem lies with the physics of radiocarbon dating, so that by about 35–40 ka, we are close to the asymptote of the decay curve, whereby only one per cent potential contamination of a sample of infinite age would give a radiocarbon value of about 37 ka. This is the 'radiocarbon barrier' (Jones 1982, 30; Roberts *et al.* 1994a; Allen and Holdaway 1995; Chappell *et al.* 1996; Jones 1999, 46) which may still not be fully appreciated by some archaeological practitioners and commentators. The technical issues are complex and have been discussed with clarity by Gillespie (1998, 170–3) and Bird *et al.* (1999). There are questions concerning both the limiting capacity of the measuring system itself and also of sample purity. The absolute limit is the signal that is measured within a laboratory system when no ^{14}C has been added to it. An apparent radiocarbon age which is calculated by these measurements is described by Gillespie (op. cit., 170) as the 'system background', and it also includes a contribution from the chemical processes used in sample preparation: the more steps involved, the greater the chances of contamination. Charcoal samples may contain mobile organic compounds that at the limiting edge are extraordinarily hard to eliminate totally. As Gillespie (op. cit., 171) put it, 'A point of diminishing returns is reached with radiocarbon analysis at about 45–50 ka, beyond which both physics and chemistry are against sensible measurements being made — the absolute amount of 14 C remaining is too small and the analytical chemistry is too hard.'

Luminescence dating

A solution to this problem was offered by the application of new developments in the luminescence dating of sand sheets and other deposits (Roberts and Jones 1994; Roberts 1997). These depend on the measurement of trapped electrons within faults in the crystal lattices of grains of silica. The electrons are driven into these traps due to the effects of radiation, derived largely from the decay of primordial radionuclides within the soil, with some contribution from cosmic rays. They are bleached by a brief exposure to sunlight, and thus 'zeroed' of signal until reburied. Measurements of both the trapped electron signal and the background radiation flux will give an age estimation since the time when the sand grains were last exposed to sunlight. The trapped electrons are measured with a photomultiplier system when they are released either through heating as in thermoluminescence (TL) or by light in optically stimulated luminescence (OSL).

A series of luminescence dates were obtained from deep sand sheet deposits within two occupied sandstone rockshelters in the Kakadu region in the Top End of the Northern Territory. At Malakunanja, a column of 4.6 m of sand had 10 TL dates with a basal value of 107 ka (Roberts *et al.* 1990; Roberts and Jones 1994, 14). Within every excavation unit of the upper 2.60 m of the deposit there were numerous flaked stone artefacts, with the lowest ones bracketed by TL dates of between 53 and 60 ka ago. Where charcoal was available in higher levels, a series of cross-checks was carried out, with good concordance between TL and ^{14}C values. Underneath the lowest artefacts was a further 2.0 m of sand utterly devoid of any cultural evidence. The absence of human evidence within the time period of slightly older than 60 ka to 110 ka, as opposed to the upper half of this sequence, is critically important. At Nauwalabila, paired OSL and ^{14}C dates back to *c*.25 ka were in excellent concordance, but below that visible charcoal ceased to exist. OSL dates from the basal part of the deposit, including a tightly packed rubble which contained flaked artefacts down to the bottom, were again between 53 and 60 ka (Roberts *et al.* 1993; Roberts *et al.* 1994b).

These results, adding as they did some 50 per cent on to the previously accepted age of human occupation of the Australian continent, have not met universal acceptance (Bowdler 1990; Mulvaney and Kamminga 1999, 142; O'Connell and Allen 1998, 139). A constructive criticism by Hiscock (1990) was based on whether or not artefacts might have been displaced by human or other taphonomic agencies into lower and older sand levels. This is of course potentially the case in all archaeological deposits, and paradoxically the luminescence dating methods are superior in this regard to radiocarbon, in that what is dated is the last time that the silica grains in the deposits have been exposed to sunlight. Any reworking of the surface due to human or animal disturbance would thus result in an almost instantaneous zeroing of its luminescence signal, whereas charcoal pieces can be endlessly recycled without changing their age.

Potential problems with the application of some luminescence methods in Australian field conditions were experienced in the dating of the site of Jinmium, situated near the Keep River on the border of the Northern Territory and Western Australia. This was a slanting sandstone slab, sticking out of a sand sheet, and its sheltered face was covered with pecked, shallow, semi-circular 'cupules' which were weathered and believed on comparative rock art studies to be ancient. The sand deposit in this shelter was only 1.50 m deep and it showed no particular pedological evidence of great age, such as oxidized orange weathering of the sands.

However, TL dates suggested that a fallen fragment of rock within the deposit featuring some of these cupules was bracketed between 58 and 75 ka; that red ochre existed in levels dated to between 75 and 116 ka; and that there were flaked stone artefacts below 116 ka, with the very base of deposits dated to 176 ka (Fullagar *et al.* 1996, 764–5, 771). If this was true, the implications would have been not only a huge antiquity for art, but also that the colonization of the Australian continent might have been carried out prior to the appearance of *Homo sapiens*. Naturally this caused immediate international controversy both in the popular science press (Dayton and Woodford 1996; Wilford 1996) and in academic reviews (Bahn 1996; O'Connell and Allen 1998).

The problem with these TL dates was that they had been distorted by the inclusion of sand which had been derived from friable *in situ* weathered bedrock, which had never been exposed to sunlight and which therefore carried a large residual signal (Spooner 1998). This presented a serious methodological challenge for the reliable application of the luminescence method within tropical Australian archaeological sites. The solution lay in the development of sophisticated methods of dating of an array of individual grains of sand so that those which had been fully bleached before burial could be distinguished from those which carried an older signal (Galbraith *et al.* 1999; Roberts *et al.* 1999). Single-grain OSL dating, backed by AMS radiocarbon with a rigorous pre-treatment of the samples to remove contaminants, showed that none of this deposit was older than 20 ka, and that most of it probably dated to less than 10 ka (Roberts *et al.* 1998).

The question then obviously extended to the original Malakunanja claims, which had also been based on TL dating, although here the sand column consisted of homogeneous sand with no rubble. Nevertheless, another programme of dating was carried out on the two critical samples at Malakunanja that bracketed the first stratigraphic appearance of flaked stone artefacts. These confirmed the general order of the original results, with values from the multiple aliquot (*c*.800 quartz grains) assays of between 46±4 and 61±8 ka and values of 44±5 ka and 56±8 ka respectively from the same samples according to single-grain measurements (Roberts *et al.* 1998, 22; Jones 1999, 52–3; Roberts and Jones 2001). Both the consistency of palaeodose estimates for single grains from these samples and the fact that the flakes were found flat within tightly bound, lightly cemented sands indicate the lack of any significant post-depositional disturbance of these sediments and that the artefacts were highly unlikely to have been intruded from above into these lower levels (Roberts and Jones 2001).

The dating of the Mungo 3 hominid

The application of this arsenal of new dating techniques has also recently transformed our views of the chronology of the critical Mungo–Willandra Lakes sequence discussed above. Detailed geomorphological studies by Bowler (1998) have refined this sequence and here we will concentrate on the uppermost part of the Lower Mungo Sedimentary Unit (Unit C), where some of the oldest archaeological finds are located. This unit consists of pure quartz beach sands, reflecting a lake full stage.

The transition to the Upper Mungo Unit D was a gradual one, with a low percentage of poorly sorted sands and clay pellets mixed with beach sands. There is also the first appearance of long-distance desert-derived *wüstenquarz* dust, the term coming from the German word *wüst*, namely wilderness or wasteland. These mineralogical indicators reflect the first subtle onset of arid conditions. A soil was formed and, as Bowler (op. cit., 138) put it, this was 'the land surface which sustained many human generations'. Eventually, arid conditions increased with the abrupt formation of the overlying Upper Mungo Unit when the prevailing westerly winds blew from the floor of the often-dry lake bed the greyish brown sandy clays (PCD: namely pelletal clay dunes) which mantled the Mungo stratigraphic complex (Bowler op. cit., 130, fig. 9). On the grounds of regional correlation with other critical sections in the Willandra Lakes system, the onset of the full Upper Mungo arid phase occurred about 40 ka years ago (Bowler op. cit., 150).

On stratigraphic grounds, Bowler believed that it was during this transitional phase of the beginning of aridification at the very end of the Lower Mungo phase that the grave of the extended burial called the Mungo 3 hominid was dug. In part, the evidence for this was calcareous deposition around the bones showing that the burial event pre-dated major carbonate mobilization associated with the process of soil formation (Bowler 1998, 150). In the original publication of this find, based on conventional radio-carbon chronology, it was estimated to have occurred between 28 ka and 30 ka ago, a value then considered to be 'as precise as both present and future circumstances will allow' (Bowler and Thorne 1976, 138). In his paper published in 1998, Bowler stated that thin sections of the grave fill (sample MP 55) and also of the surrounding quartz sands (sample MP 54) were 'almost entirely free of both Wüstenquarz and PCD facies indicating burial before any such onset of PCD deposition' (1998, 150). The small percentage represented in the mineral counts 'is attributed simply to later bioturbation in the upper metre of Unit C sediments near the contact with the higher Unit D deposits' (Bowler 1998, 150, 130 and fig. 9). Yet in a response to new independent dating results, discussed below, Bowler and Magee (2000) have since revised this analysis, stating that the above explanation was incorrect. Their new stratigraphic drawing (Bowler and Magee 2000, fig. 2: based on Bowler 1998, fig. 9) now shows the pelletal clays to extend not only within the grave fill itself, but also within the surrounding deposit into which it had been dug, whereas in the original drawing they did not.

A new dynamic has been injected by the application of luminescence and other dating techniques to this and other critical sites within the Mungo sequence. Concerning the Mungo 3 burial itself, Oyston (1996) obtained three samples that he dated with the TL method. Two superimposed samples from the Upper Mungo Unit gave values of 19.5±2.3 and 24.6±2.4 ka in the correct stratigraphic order. The critically important sample J 3 from the Lower Mungo Unit, only two metres away from the feet of the burial, gave a value of 43±3.8 ka (Oyston 1996, 748). An independent study was done by Price from these same locations and this gave values respectively of 22.4±2.1 ka, 29.3±3.1 ka and 41.4±6.7 ka, which were all within acceptable error limits of the previous series (Bowler and Price 1998, 160). Bowler's conclusion as recently as 1998 (1998, 150) was that the Mungo 3 burial had occurred within the time range of 42 to 45 ka ago.

This evaluation has, however, been put into serious doubt by yet another independent multi-method dating programme (Simpson and Grün 1998; Thorne et al. 1999). This consisted of OSL measurements of the Lower Mungo sands and, for the first time, direct dating of the bones themselves using electron spin resonance (ESR) on tooth enamel and uranium series dating. The latter involved using both thermal ionization mass spectrometry (TIMS) methods on shavings from long bones and gamma-ray spectrometry (Th/U and Pa/U) on the cranium itself (Simpson and Grün 1998, 1009). The U-series work was at the technical limits of the method and this constitutes the first multiple, direct-dating study of a hominid fossil undertaken anywhere in the world. Because of the ethics of the situation concerning permission from the relevant Aboriginal communities, these involved the use either of minimal samples or, in the case of the gamma-ray work, of non-destructive methods.

Mass spectrometric results on four samples of bone shavings gave values of $c.50$, 55, 58 and 70 ka respectively (Thorne *et al.* 1999, table 1 and fig. 4a). This range shows that some uranium mobilization had taken place, the sequence of ages being explained both by delayed U-uptake and recent U-loss (op. cit., 598). There are two fundamental problems with uranium dating: namely whether or not there had been early or linear uptake, and also the question of more recent leaching. To attempt to assess these issues, Grün and his team measured the ratios of the daughter chains of two separate isotopes ^{234}U and ^{238}U which showed that the uranium had migrated into the bones at about the same time that the carbonate around them was precipitated. The carbonate matrix itself was dated to 82 ± 21 ka, the large error being due to the low uranium concentration and also the small spread in the ratios of two isotopes of thorium ($^{230}Th/^{232}Th$) (ibid., 601).

Combining the ESR and U-series dating, the mean age of the Mungo 3 skeleton was estimated as 62 ± 6 ka, the ESR estimate being significantly less affected by uranium mobilization than the U-series results. While it was acknowledged that, given the possibility of uranium loss, the correct age of the sample might be younger, the authors nevertheless considered that it was difficult 'to invent explanations that could accommodate combined U-series/ESR ages of less than 50 ka' (Thorne *et al.* 1999, 605).

Two OSL samples (ANU$_{OD}$174a and ANU$_{OD}$174d) were collected by Spooner from the Lower Mungo Unit, 350 m and 450 m east and west respectively from the LM3 burial, in stratigraphic locations 30 cm below the carbonate horizon. Mineralogically, they consisted entirely of beach sands, with the absence of clay pellets. These gave age estimates of 59 ± 3 and 63 ± 4 ka respectively, with a weighted mean of 61 ± 2 ka. This is the maximum constraining age for the LM3 human, since the deposition of this sediment unit obviously pre-dated the burial event (Thorne *et al.* 1999, 605). These values are significantly older than those of Oyston and Price quoted above. A possible explanation for the discrepancy may be due to different assessments of the extremely low background radiation levels from the almost pure sand, where cosmic ray contribution may be as much as 40 per cent of total dose. The issues are beyond the scope of this present paper and have been addressed in a series of recent arguments (Bowler and Magee 2000; Gillespie and Roberts 2000; Grün *et al.* 2000).

The direct dating of the LM3 hominid has removed any possible doubt that it had been interred into old deposits from a much more recent ground level and, at the very least, has securely placed it in the time of the Lower Mungo transition some 43 ka ago. The calibre of the multi-method dating methods involved, combining both ESR and U-series, is a powerful approach and allows for an accurate assessment of U-mobilization. Considering the limiting constraint of the OSL dates on the deposits, the broad concordance of direct-dating results gives support to a conclusion that the LM3 hominid may lie between 56 ka and 61 ka.

Burial and ochre

The grave was that of an extended male skeleton, his hands arranged to cover his pelvic region. Anatomically it conforms with a modern Aboriginal morphology, and as such represents one of the oldest examples of *Homo sapiens* in the world (Bowler and Thorne 1976; Thorne *et al.* 1999, 610; Thorne and Curnoe 2000). Palaeogenetics of this skeleton indicates the presence of an mtDNA lineage not present in any modern human population (Adcock *et al.* 2001). Critically important from a cultural point of view was that the body had been covered from head to groin with ochre, calculated to have required at least a kilogram of haematitic minerals (Bowler 1998, 151). The closest source of such material was within mineralized veins in Proterozoic rocks near Broken Hill, some 200 km to the west. A large lump of such haematite, show-ing clear grinding facets, was found by Bowler (ibid.) on the surface of the eroding Lower Mungo soil surface and is believed to date from the same cultural phase as that involved in the mortuary decoration of the LM3 person. This corresponds in age with similar ground haematite pieces from the Kakadu sites in northern Australia (Jones 1999, 57; Jones and Johnson 1985). Concerning the archaeological evidence contained within the Upper Mungo soil, here was a palimpsest of both the economic and ritual lives of ancient Australian people, pushed back by a time period of almost 20 ka, through a new revolution in dating technology, from previous assessments made only 25 years ago.

Human occupation at Isotope Stage 3

The oldest stone artefacts at the site were recovered by excavation below this soil, down to a depth of 1.50 m within the Lower Mungo Unit (Bowler and Price 1998, 162; Shawcross and Kaye 1980; Shawcross 1998, 191–3). Six TL dates (W1801–6) were obtained from an auger column adjacent to the excavation, and a date (W1804), equiv-alent to a stratigraphic position just above the lowest artefact, was assayed at 61±8 ka

(Bowler and Price 1998, 159). Because of the large error estimates from each of these individual TL dates, a depth–age regression line was drawn derived from the entire dataset (op. cit., 162). According to this, and taking into account Spooner's additional OSL data, we estimate that the first occurrence of stone artefacts at this site probably occurred within the time envelope of 55±5 ka near the beginning of Isotope Stage 3. Also, significantly, the basal half of the Lower Mungo Unit was entirely devoid of arte-facts. So here as at other sites, such as Malakunanja, Devil's Lair in the extreme south-west of Western Australia (Turney *et al.* 2001), and Mushroom Rock in Cape York (Wright 1964; Morwood *et al.* 1995; Roberts 1997, 860), we have stratigraphic sequences which precisely mark the first indications of human presence. We are now confident in positing the human colonization of Australia within the probable time envelope of between 55 ka and 60 ka at the beginning of Isotope Stage 3. It is also likely that core areas of the continent such as the braided river systems of the eastern interior were occupied relatively swiftly; perhaps even to be seen as an archaeologically 'instanta-neous' event, given the large error bars of the dating methods.

It is also important at this point to consider the question of a proven absence of human occupation at a certain time period, an issue raised originally by Bowler (1976). We may say that there has been no hint of any evidence of hominid presence in Australia within deposits dated to the Last Interglacial. Some of these relate to what might have been highly desirable locations, had there been people here at that time. Key locations would include the Gol Gol formation, underlying the Mungo sequence and dated by TL to *c.*140 ka–180 ka (Oyston 1996, table 4), and an extensive system of fossil beach ridges inland of old coastal lagoons associated with the higher Last Interglacial sea-level, and which extend as extensive landforms over hundreds of kilometres along the coasts of southern Queensland and New South Wales. The contrast with the situa-tion at the Cape of Good Hope in South Africa is striking. Here, west of the Cape, sparse shell middens have been consistently found within Last Interglacial dunes, indicating sea shore exploitation dated back to 120 ka (Parkington 1999, 27). One could find close environmental and geomorphic equivalents in such locations as the perched coastal dunes in north-west Tasmania, western Victoria or the south-west of Western Australia. Yet here, nothing has ever been found. We are confident in asserting that there has not been any hominid incursion into the Australian–New Guinea continent as far back as Last Interglacial times.

Homo sapiens expansion

A secure dating for this first occupation is important, not only for its own sake but also for more general issues concerning the origins and the first global geographical spread of *Homo sapiens*. The central premise of what has been tagged the 'out of Africa' model, which was derived from studies both in DNA genetics and palaeo-anatomy, is that modern *sapiens* people first emerged in sub-Saharan Africa within the savanna region perhaps 150 ka ago (Cann *et al.* 1987; Stringer 1992; Clark and Willermet 1997; Foley this volume). This has gained archaeological support with the ESR re-dating programme at Border Cave in the Kwa-Zulu land of South Africa, confirming the presence of anatomically modern human fossils by about 130 ka ago, and the typologically advanced Howiesons Poort stone industry with its standardized tools of flake-blades, backed or blunted into geometrical shapes that implies hafting (Deacon 1989, 559–60) and dated to c.66±5 ka (Grün and Beaumont in press; Miller *et al.* in press). The conclusion of a review by Deacon, written over a decade ago (1989, 561), was that 'not only were people in the Southern Cape some 100,000 years ago anatomically modern, but they were also behaviourally modern'. Their descendants may have extended their geographic range northwards, with several severe genetic bottlenecks, out of north-east Africa into the Arabian–Levantine region some 80–50 ka ago (Tishkoff *et al.* 1996).

Some would wish to date the spread beyond this point according to the west Eurasian chronology of the appearance of the Upper Palaeolithic (Klein 1995). Here, apparently, there is a 'consensus model' whereby there was 'a rapid expansion of anatomically and behaviorally modern humans out of Africa into southwest Asia 45,000 to 50,000 years ago, then into Europe and the southern margins of Siberia and across to east and southeast Asia by about 40,000 years ago' (O'Connell and Allen 1998, 143). Let us briefly examine the basis of these statements. On the coast of the Levant, the key land link between Africa and Eurasia, the earliest Upper Palaeolithic is characterized by the production of flake-blades which still carry some elements of the preceding Levallois technology such as faceted platforms. But the formal retouched tools are dominated by Upper Palaeolithic forms such as end scrapers and burins (Kuhn *et al.* 1999, 506).

Concerning absolute dating, there are some revealing admissions that 'most investigators assume that the earliest Upper Palaeolithic dates to sometime between 40,000 and 45,000 years ago' (Kuhn *et al.* 1999, 507; cf. Bar-Yosef *et al.* 1996); and that 'not coincidentally, this interval corresponds with the conventional dates for the Middle–Upper Palaeolithic transition throughout Eurasia' (Kuhn *et al.* op. cit., 507). Indeed! But this concordance may also be a reflection of the technical limits of the radiocarbon dating methods that had been applied at these sites.

As regards actual radiometric dates, a study published in 1983 at the open air site of Boker Tachtit in the Israeli Negev yielded radiocarbon dates extending back to 45 ka at the base and one of 33.1±4.1 ka at the top (Marks 1983; Kuhn *et al.* 1999, 507). At the rockshelter site of Ksar Akil, near the Lebanon coast, there is one of the longest archaeological sequences of the Upper Pleistocene of Eurasia, with no less than 22 m of deposit, spanning the transition from the Mousterian throughout the Upper Palaeolithic. A dating programme of ^{14}C dates from two separate laboratories, using both conventional and AMS methods on charcoal, established a coherent age–depth sequence within its upper part which extended back to 31–32 ka ago (Mellars and Tixier 1989, 763–5). Concerning the deposit which underlay this, spanning no less than 10 m and which included both the earliest Aurignacian and the transitional industries from the underlying Middle Palaeolithic, an assessment of its antiquity was made by extrapolating the average age–depth relationship derived from higher up in the sequence and taking into account relevant depositional regimes. This implied an age for the boundary between the 'transitional' and the underlying Middle Palaeolithic industries of c.50–52 ka (op. cit., 766). A single radiocarbon date of 44 ka which was obtained from a late Mousterian layer stratigraphically beneath this served to stress only that such a number merely reflected the methodological limits of the ^{14}C-method. At the recently reported cave of Üçagizli in Turkey, located where the ancient Orontes River reaches the Mediterranean coast close to Antioch, two AMS radiocarbon determinations were made of the initial Upper Palaeolithic levels at 39.4±1.2 and 38.9±1.1 ka ago (Kuhn *et al.* 1999, 514–15).

Finally, concerning Europe itself, the oldest typologically distinctive industry made by fully modern sapient people is the Aurignacian. It may be that there was an autochtonous European expression with its earliest manifestation either in the southeastern Balkans or on the plains of western Eurasia. If this were the case, then the cave sites of Bacho Kiro and Temnata in Bulgaria are of critical importance. Here AMS dates for the Aurignacian layers were obtained of c.38 ka to 46 ka, and 44 ka from Istállóskö in Hungary with large error bars (Straus 1997, 241). Elsewhere in western Europe, Straus (op. cit., 241–2) has listed 24 sites from which the carbon dates for the earliest Aurignacian or equivalent industries have been bracketed as between 37 ka and 43 ka ago. At first glance this may seem to be an extremely impressive conclusion, or is it only another example of the 'event horizon' phenomenon discussed above? Some internal causes for doubt might come from the first TL dates obtained from Temnata which were 45 to 46 ka in age.

Our view is that the security of the earliest dating of the Upper Palaeolithic in west Eurasia might be more illusory than would first appear from the vast published literature on the subject. From our perspective, very old carbon dates seem to be published and discussed with an insouciance that does not belie much anxiety as to the limits of the dating method itself, issues which are central in the hard-contested field of Australia. Our experience convinces us that a reappraisal of the dating of the transition from the Middle to the Upper Palaeolithic of Europe and the Middle East is now required, using the same range of methods and intensity of dating techniques that have been discussed above.

Even if the European chronological scenario survives the new inspection, it has no dominant relevance to the issue of the first human colonization of Australia which as all scholars are agreed was carried out by modern *sapiens* people. There is no coherent reason why Australia should have been settled at some respectful time after Europe, nor that the oldest Australian dates should be discarded merely to fit with some pre-conceived theoretical time framework (O'Connell and Allen 1998, 143; Allen 2000, 68). A case can be made for the first spread of modern *sapiens* out of Africa, extending from west to east along the Parallel of the tropical savanna. This was the obvious new terrain, involving little ecological adaptation for peoples emerging from similar conditions in East Africa (Jones 1999, 55). There is much genetic support for this view that both New Guineans and Australian Aborigines have ancient lineages that might reflect such an early migration event (Wood 1997, 120). To cross to the Sahul continent, the critical new invention was that of watercraft, competent enough to transport people across sub-stantial cross-sea distances within tropical waters. It is highly possible that the first occupation of the higher latitudes of the Eurasian continent by modern *sapiens* people may well have occurred a substantial time period after this initial latitudinal spread across the route of the tropical savannas.

Extinction of the giant marsupials

During the Late Quaternary, there occurred a massive phase of extinction of the Australian land fauna. During that time, all Australian land mammals, reptiles and birds weighing over 100 kg became extinct, as did about 60 per cent of those within the weight range of 10–100 kg (Flannery 1990). Of this megafauna, over 90 per cent of species were marsupials. About a third of all marsupial genera became extinct during this time. These included the cow-like *Diprotodonts*, the stocky, kangaroo-like *Sthenurids* and short faced *Protemnodons*, as well as much larger species within some existing genera such as the *Macropod* kangaroos. This megafauna had been palaeonto-logically recognized and described from fossil and other deposits from as far back as the middle of the nineteenth century. Richard Owen, who made the original descrip-tions, even then had considered that they had survived into the Upper Pleistocene and that the probable cause for their extinction had been due to human hunting influence (1877). His views fell into obscurity over the following century, largely because it became widely believed that Aboriginal people had only a short antiquity on the continent.

Despite numerous field discoveries, including those of full skeletons of *Diprotodonts*, the dating of the extinction event or events has proved extremely elusive. Two independent reviews of the data published over 30 years ago by Merrilees (1968) and one of us (Jones 1968) came to similar conclusions that a wide suite of the extinct megafauna had existed across the entire range of Australian and New Guinean eco-logical zones until tantalizingly recent times; seemingly always just beyond the first appearance of human artefacts such as stone tools, which were present and sometimes numerous in deposits immediately overlying the megafaunal ones. This was the case in stratigraphic sequences within fossil dunes bordering lake systems in western New South Wales; in the dry lake bed deposits of the arid core of the continent near Lake Eyre; in limestone cave deposits; and in peat lake beds of the wet temperate south-east of the continent. In our separate reviews, we both considered that the giant marsupials had survived just up to the time of the arrival of people on the continent, and since this event seemed not to be associated with any great climatic or environmental crisis, such as the height of the Last Ice Age, then the primary cause for the extinction event must be pointed towards a human impact. A problem for this theory was that at the time of writing these papers, as is still the case, there is no convincing direct field association of megafaunal remains within the structure of a human kill or other prey-processing archaeological site. Jones' (1968) assessment of the timing of these events was predicated on the available chronometric data at that early research phase in the application of ^{14}C dating techniques to Australian archaeological and geomorphological sites. In the same way that the earliest dates for human arrival seemed to lie within the time range of about 25 to 30 ka, so also the available dates for the last megafaunal remains were also seen within this time frame (op. cit., 202–5); both sets of data are now seen to have been false.

The past 30 years of research have stubbornly refused to yield convincing direct associations of the megafaunal remains within Australian archaeological sites. The situation has been made more frustrating in that a series of such claims, initially convincing (Flood 1995, 183), have consistently failed the tests of further stratigraphic or chronometric analyses. A single *Sthenurus* bone from levels dated to 23 ka containing flaked stone artefacts at the limestone cave of Cloggs Cave in south-east Victoria was almost certainly derived from an older deposit within the cave system. Fossilized *Diprotodont* teeth fragments associated with numerous stone artefacts in the mound spring site at Tambar Springs in north-east New South Wales were excavated from deposits dated to as recently as about 6 ka ago, yet direct Ur dating on the teeth showed them to be older than 60 ka, indicating that they had been reworked into the younger deposits through fluvial processes of the mound springs themselves. Swamp sites have also proved elusive. Perhaps the best researched have been those in southern Victoria, such as Spring Creek (White and Flannery 1995), and at Lancefield (Van Huet *et al.* 1998). At the latter site, excellent excavations by archaeological and palaeontological specialists in their fields (Gillespie *et al.* 1978) seemed to show unequivocal stratigraphical association between *Diprotodont* remains and stone artefacts, within swamp deposits dated by radiocarbon on various materials to between 20 and 27 ka. Subsequent work showed that there may have been slumping of older swamp deposits, and that the bones came from a quite older facies. Direct ESR dating on a *Diprotodont* incisor at this site gave decisive values of 50 to 56 ka, which is probably the true age of the bone (Van Huet *et al.* 1998). Association has been proposed at Cuddie Springs, a swamp at the very end of the Macquarie river system in north-western New South Wales (Field and Dodson 1999). Here numerous stone artefacts have been found in close strati-graphic association with long bones of *Diprotodont* and the giant *Genyornis* bird. The association was within a sticky clay, overlain by deposits dated to the last Glacial Maximum. The clay had charcoal, AMS dated to between 29 and 33.5 ka BP, and an OSL date of 35.5 ka BP. It might seem thus to be a secure case. But in the opinion of one of us (RJ), the issue is far from concluded. The bones themselves are heavily mineralized and are devoid of all but traces of amino acids; there is no hint of the smashing of bones, typi-cal of a human midden; and in the critical level, many are aligned at random oblique angles into the sticky clay. It is possible that these bones have been derived from an adjacent older deposit within the swamp system. At the very least, direct dates on these bones using Ur and ESR methods now need to be obtained.

The fundamental problem with the dating of the extinction of the megafauna has been exactly the same as that of the arrival of the first humans — that it occurred beyond the 'event horizon' of conventional radiocarbon dating. As with the archaeo-logical issues, new dating technologies have had to be deployed. The first systematic demonstration of the chronology of extinction of any of this megafauna has been done in the case of the giant bird, *Genyornis newtoni*. Biologically related to the goose family and weighing about twice the weight of an emu, its egg shells, as is the case with emus, are common within Upper Pleistocene sand deposits in central Australia. A dating study on over 1000 egg shells from both species, using amino acid racemization, showed that whereas the emu survived all of the changes of climate and environment, including the extremely arid phase of the Last Glacial Maximum, the *Genyornis* sud-denly collapsed across all regions studied during the time period of 50 ± 5 ka years ago (Miller *et al.* 1999).

A systematic study has also been carried out using both OSL and Ur dating on artic-ulated remains of giant marsupials from a variety of sites across the south of the con-tinent (Roberts *et al.* 2001). By restricting the study to fossils which had bones in articulated anatomical positions, this ensured that the animals had died close to the site and time of their ultimate burial. There was a continental-wide extinction event within a period of about 46.5 ± 5 ka BP. The conjunction of this timing with the *Genyornis* extinc-tion is striking. The dates rule out the Last Glacial Maximum as the cause of extinction. However they do coincide closely with the time of initial spread of people throughout the continent, which after an initial landfall was probably occurring within the same time envelope of 55 ± 5 ka. The hand of humans as the ultimate cause of this extinction event seems inescapable.

Fire

The issue of how this might have occurred has been discussed extensively (e.g. Flood 1995, 182–7). There was the direct impact of hunting, with the arrival on the isolated continent of a supremely intelligent placental predator, heavier than any existing marsupial predator, and one armed with a sophisticated hunting technology and a culture of the chase. There was also perhaps the more profound impact of the systematic use of fire. Fire has been a natural feature of the Australian landscape since Tertiary times, with key elements of its biota, such as the radiation of Eucalypt tree species, responding to a progressively drier and more fire-prone climate, as the continent itself has experienced a long-term trend of desertification. However the arrival of people would have increased the fire frequency within any one area by orders of magnitude. Ethnographic studies have shown the systematic use of fire by Aborigines across the entire continent. Few parts of contemporary Arnhem Land in the tropical north were not burnt every year. The reasons for burning were manifold, the key factor being the desire to burn off tall dry grass at the beginning of the dry season, to give access for movement, and to reduce mosquitoes and the danger of snakes. The green regrowth which often occurred after early season fires provided a new feed for wallabies, which in their own turn were hunted (Jones 1969).

Such an impact would have had ecological consequences, capable of being analysed within the pollen record, and numerous detailed studies on past fire regimes have been carried out. Some of these sequences come from deep terrestrial lake cores (Singh and Geissler 1985), and also from offshore marine cores, both off the north-east Australian coast and also within the shallow neighbouring Indonesian seas (Wang *et al.* 1999). The modern consensus is that fire frequency on the Australian continent increased markedly in Upper Pleistocene times, and that this increase cannot solely be ascribed to climatic changes (Kershaw *et al.* in press). One can argue for a significant human component, one that changed the distribution of major vegetation communities: in the tropical north extending the range of fire-adapted savanna at the expense of the fire-sensitive vine thickets and rain forest communities; in the centre, aiding the spread of the fire-adapted spinifex landscape. These issues are hotly debated and a full exposition is beyond the range of this paper. From our broadest archaeological perspective, however, our region can be looked at as a 'natural laboratory' for the discussion of the impact of the geographical spread of modern humans into new areas, with their native faunas.

The Australian case has been at a continental scale, and some of the main events may have taken place early within the process of the global expansion of our species. We turn now to the vast oceanic spaces of the Pacific, and to time scales one and two orders of magnitude less than the ones which dominate the prehistoric research agenda of Australia. The processes of colonization and of impact however show remarkable similarities.

Pauses and pulses in human colonization of the Pacific

The human colonization of the Pacific Islands beyond what is now the island of New Guinea shows an interesting pattern of pauses and then rapid pulses of migration. Whether the initial move beyond what was then the continent of Sahul represents the first such pause is as yet unclear. There are radiocarbon dates of 35,000 BP from both New Britain and New Ireland, with the only-known Pleistocene site in the Solomon Islands dating to 29,000 BP (Spriggs 1997a, chapter 2; Leavesley and Allen 1998). As the other dating techniques mentioned above which can go beyond the radiocarbon barrier have not yet been deployed in this relatively little-studied part of the Pacific, it is impossible to know if there was any significant pause before this part of Near Oceania was settled after New Guinea was reached. Near Oceania is defined as that part of the western Pacific settled prior to the spread of the agricultural and pottery-using Lapita culture: the Bismarck Archipelago and the main Solomon Islands (the definition is by Green 1991a). Recent intensive work across that boundary in 'Remote Oceania' (the rest of the Pacific beyond the Solomons) in Vanuatu and New Caledonia now makes it seem most unlikely that humans penetrated beyond the main Solomons until around 3000 years ago. As sea gaps are very small along the main Solomons chain (indeed for most of the Pleistocene a lot of the chain was joined as the island of 'Greater Bougainville'), it would seem likely that the Near Oceania boundary at its southern end on the island of Makira (San Cristobal) would have been reached soon after 29,000 BP at the latest. It remained an impermeable barrier for a further 26,000 years of hunting and gathering occupation of the Solomons and Bismarcks.

A recent feature of the study of colonization of the Pacific region is that as well as the dates getting earlier at the lower end, now extending beyond the 'radiocarbon barrier' in the case of the Australian dates as we have discussed above, they are now getting ever younger as we move east and into Polynesia. Dates for the founding Lapita culture in Near and Remote Oceania are also becoming constricted, both in terms of start date and in terms of the end of the distinctive Lapita design system and its most common expression on dentate-stamped decorated vessels. A few years ago dates back to about 4000 BP were being posited for the start of Lapita culture in Island Melanesia. Now, even 3500 BP seems too early and 3300 BP seems more likely in the Bismarck Archipelago 'homeland' (Specht and Gosden 1997). The spread of this culture beyond Near Oceania is now thought to start about 3100 BP in the Reef-Santa Cruz Group of the south-east Solomons, 3000 BP in Vanuatu and New Caledonia and 2900 to 2800 BP in Fiji and Western Polynesia (primarily Tonga and Samoa). Relevant recent references include Bedford *et al.* (1998) for Vanuatu, Sand (1997) for New Caledonia, Anderson and Clark (1999) for Fiji, and Burley *et al.* (1999) for Western Polynesia.

In Island Southeast Asia too, as discussed by Peter Bellwood in his contribution to this volume (see also Bellwood 1997; Spriggs 1999a), the timing of the spread of pottery-using Neolithic cultures is being tightened (Spriggs 1989) and pauses are becoming evident there as well, the first between the settlement of Taiwan perhaps 6500 to 6000 BP (the earliest phases of occupation are extensive but virtually undated) and points south, the second between the settlement of Northern Luzon at about 5000 BP and soon after it the Mariana Islands in Western Micronesia, and the settlement of Sulawesi and Eastern Indonesia beginning about 4000 BP. The extension of this Island Southeast Asian Neolithic culture into the Pacific (excluding earlier-settled Western Micronesia) is the Lapita culture. From Sulawesi to Samoa the spread takes just over a thousand years. A thousand-year pause then takes place in Western Polynesia before the first well-attested evidence of Eastern Polynesian settlement, which again represents a rapid expansion across a vast area.

Lapita-style dentate-stamping has been claimed previously to continue in some areas of the western Pacific to 2000 BP or later. An end everywhere to the Lapita distribution now seems likely about 2800 to 2700 BP, with cultural continuity to 'post-Lapita' cultures becoming more obvious as key sites in Island Melanesia and Fiji are explored in more detail and redated. Although the evidence is by no means all in, it seems a plausible hypothesis to suggest that a wide area of the western Pacific remained in interaction, albeit perhaps increasingly sporadic, until at least 1500 BP. Much of the extreme regionalization in pottery, artistic styles, and social and religious systems in the Island Melanesian region seems to be a product of 'cultural drift' since that time period (Spriggs 1997a, chapter 6). First to drop out of the interaction system was Western Polynesia, recalling that East Polynesia was still uninhabited at the time. Indeed one can only really define Polynesia in opposition to Melanesia in cultural terms from about 2300 BP onwards. Fiji remained part of the western Pacific mainstream for some centuries and occasional interaction with areas to the west, including probably significant in-migration, continued even later. As late as 1500 BP in areas from Central Vanuatu through to Buka and Manus in the north there are remarkable parallels in pottery decoration which must betoken continued even if irregular contact between potting communities over thousands of kilometres.

Pottery-making eventually died out throughout all areas of Polynesia where it had previously been practised and indeed in many parts of Island Melanesia too. Cultural 'drift' in pottery styles developed as potters across the region no longer saw each other's products when intermediary centres ceased production. Isolation then set in, particularly after 1000 BP (see below).

A growing consensus seemed to be developing by the beginning of the 1990s that earlier dates than those conventionally accepted for the settlement of Western and Eastern Polynesia would be substantiated by further work. The high water mark of this optimism was reached in 1991 with palaeoenvironmental evidence from Mangaia in the Cook Islands suggesting to Kirch and his colleagues (1991) that people had reached the Southern Cooks by 2500 BP, some 1500 years earlier than the first direct evidence for occupation of the island in the form of cultural deposits in a rockshelter. They used this evidence to support the arguments of Irwin (1980, 1992) that there was no pause between the settlement of West and East Polynesia. The growing consensus was shattered in 1993 with the publication of a critical review of all early dates for Eastern Polynesia (Spriggs and Anderson 1993; see also Anderson 1995) which suggested that a much shorter chronology was likely. Since that date all 'early' dates for Fiji, West and East Polynesia have confirmed this conservative position. The current picture is that areas of Central-East Polynesia were first settled between AD 300 to 600, with the fringes settled much later: Hawaii after about AD 800, Easter Island perhaps as late as AD 800 (Skjølsvold 1994, 105–7, 113–14; Steadman *et al.* 1994), and New Zealand at about AD 1250 (Higham *et al.* 1999).

The implications of a short chronology for Eastern Polynesia are profound. The large populations attested in places such as Hawaii built up in only 1000 years. The New Zealand evidence suggests the construction of forts as a witness of increasing internecine warfare began only 200–300 years after first landfall. The hierarchical political systems of much of the region must owe more to ancestral forms than, as some have seen them, to inevitable and largely independent evolutionary trajectories in the different island groups. In addition, human impacts on the biotic and non-biotic environments of the various island groups were often rapid and catastrophic in their effects. Even in the case of the large forested island of New Ireland, close to New Guinea and with a modern bird fauna rich in comparison with those of the more remote Pacific islands, at least 12 species out of a total of 50 recorded from all of the excavated sites became extinct in the time period since 15 ka ago (Steadman *et al.* 1999). On the evidence presented, they may well have become extinct only within the last 3000 years. Further out into Oceania, it has been claimed that the extinction of bird species on Pacific Islands attendant upon human expansion represents the greatest vertebrate extinction 'event' since the demise of the dinosaurs (Steadman 1995).

The very pattern of early human impacts suggests in part a 'push' factor to continued settlement. Many species of birds disappear within two to three hundred years of initial human colonization. Pollen and geomorphological evidence suggests that deforestation was rapid on many islands and led to increased landscape instability. A sequence of initial settlement, destruction of much of the local fauna, increased erosion rates and subsequent local abandonment sometimes for hundreds of years is commonly found in the histories of many island groups (Spriggs 1997b). But after a while, moving on to the next valley or next island was no longer an option, and more conservation-oriented land management practices came into operation. It is probably no coincidence that we start to see the first evidence of human occupation in Eastern Polynesia precisely at the point in time that Western Polynesian islands appear to become fully occupied, with substantial inland as well as coastal populations. At the time of European contact it was often the Eastern Polynesian islands that had the most impressive intensive agricultural systems of irrigated taro gardens or managed tree-cropping. Once the fringes were settled, there was nowhere else to go.

Having got people out to all the Pacific Islands over a period from at least 35,000 to 700 years ago, let us examine some findings on their various lifestyles over that period.

Innovative hunter-gatherers and the 'game park' strategy

Any constraints posed to a hunter-gatherer existence in northern Sahul (now New Guinea) are multiplied considerably in Island Melanesia (Chappell *et al.* 1994). If early hunter-gatherers could live in Island Melanesian rainforests then they could certainly live in New Guinea. This is because of the relative poverty of the natural flora and fauna of Island Melanesia compared to New Guinea. The boundary between the latter island and New Britain marks the end of the distribution of primary division freshwater fish, some 265 extant bird species found on the east coast of New Guinea are reduced to 80 in New Britain, and very few terrestrial mammals crossed the same gap unassisted by humans (Green 1991a). The flora is also considerably depauperate compared to New Guinea.

Within Island Melanesia there are two further major biogeographic boundaries: the Remote Oceania boundary between the main Solomons and the Santa Cruz group to the south, and that between Vanuatu and New Caledonia. Beyond the main Solomons chain in the nearest regions of Remote Oceania all terrestrial mammals except bats have been humanly transported, 30 genera of extant land birds and 162 genera of seed plants find their eastern limits, and major disjunctions occur in the natural distribution of other fauna and flora. It is very unlikely that a hunter-gatherer way of life was viable beyond Near Oceania and this, rather than questions of voyaging capability, delayed settlement until a fully-agricultural way of life became available with the spread of the Lapita culture about 3000 years ago.

The area inhabited by humans in the Pleistocene — the Bismarck Archipelago and the main Solomons — was almost certainly rainforest throughout the period of human settlement, although this may not have been the case for Vanuatu and New Caledonia further south. In the Bismarcks and Solomons we are within a few degrees of the equator and it is postulated that there was no major difference in the Pleistocene from the weather systems existing today (Enright and Gosden 1992). There would still have been an equatorial band of shelter between cyclone belts. Warm air would still have risen in the region of the equator, drawing in the wind from north and south. The rotation of the earth created the same prevailing trade winds. The faunal and limited pollen evidence from the region also suggest continuity in rain forest habitat from the Pleistocene to the last few thousand years.

There are at present less than ten Pleistocene archaeological sites known in the Island Melanesian region and so our reconstructions of lifestyle are tentative. All of the sites bar one are rockshelters and only four are any significant distance from the coast. What are the frameworks for interpretation of what we might find as more sites are investigated? In previous publications, one of us (Spriggs 1993, 1996a) has gone into the terminological distinctions needed to consider the range of behaviours which occur between the poles of simple foraging and intensive agriculture, that grey area where live Zvelebil's (1986) 'complex hunter gatherers' and Guddemi's (1992) 'hunter-horticulturists'.

Spriggs has largely followed the lead of David Harris' discussions (1989, 1996) on the subject. Rather than seeing the presence of domesticated plants and animals as the important threshold between hunter-gatherers and agriculturists, it is important to identify for any given cultural sequence when dependence upon agriculture began, defined in terms of the creation of agro-ecosystems which limit subsistence choice because of environmental transformation or labour demands (Yen 1995). This threshold has greater implications for changes in human behaviour and organization than whether cultivated plants are 'domesticated' in the morphological sense or whether indeed some form of cultivation of crops is being carried out. None of the sites known in the Bismarcks and Solomons had crossed the agricultural threshold during the period under consideration. A fully agricultural lifestyle did not come into being in Island Melanesia until about 3300 BP with the advent of the Lapita culture (Bellwood 1996).

For the Bismarck Archipelago, the pre-20,000 BP fauna of New Ireland is the best known (Flannery 1995; Flannery and White 1991). The island's vertebrate fauna consisted of a narrow range of edible species of lizards and snakes, a single large rat species (*Rattus sanila*), a small rat *Melomys rufescens,* and an unknown number of species of birds. Exploitation of various local species of bats completes the list of hunted mammals. Some of these were quite large, such as the fruit bats *Pteropus neohibernicus* and *Dobsonia anderseni.* At 2–4 kilograms *Varanus indicus,* the biggest of the lizards, was one of the largest sized land animals around, and its importance as a protein source should not be underestimated. The rest of the Bismarck Archipelago was probably comparably endowed in edible terrestrial fauna.

The Solomon Islands were considerably better provided with edible species, with a rich fauna of bush rats, including an endemic genus *Solomys* (Flannery and Wickler 1990). These rats and various fruit bats, lizards (including *Varanus indicus*), snakes and birds would have provided valuable protein sources for the archipelago's early human inhabitants. The reasons for this difference in natural endowment are unclear, although the Solomons appear to have received some of their species from an Australian source. Both the Bismarcks and the Solomons have a comparatively rich marine fauna, similar in many ways to New Guinea and tropical Asia and therefore familiar to the first colonists.

Our knowledge of this critical formative period of settlement of Island Melanesia is very scant at present. Gosden (Enright and Gosden 1992, 173; cf. Gosden 1995) has put forward an interesting overall model of this period, in part based on certain contrasts with the period that succeeds it. He notes that despite the lack of land resources, the early colonists would have had two factors in their favour: by moving into an uninhabited area they could live where they liked, and they could balance the poverty of the land resources with the richness of those of the sea.

Gosden argues that for the first few thousand years the sea was important for the mobility it allowed in moving between scarce resources as well as being an important food source. Low population densities would have given people room to move through the landscape between its dispersed resources, but on the other hand would have made human contacts extremely important for securing necessary marriage partners and for keeping in touch with the wider world. The lack of land resources may be more apparent than real, given the evidence for plant exploitation at the Pleistocene site of Kilu on Buka in the northern Solomons (Loy *et al.* 1992; Wickler and Spriggs 1988), or there may be a real difference between the Solomons and the Bismarcks in this respect (Wickler 1990). The richer fauna of the Solomons may have provided a less precarious existence for its human inhabitants at this period.

It was mentioned earlier that pre-agricultural settlement does not appear to have extended south of the main Solomons. Although it is harder to get to Vanuatu and New Caledonia, they may not have been outside the technological ability of Pleistocene voyaging. The real problem is lack of food. Wild relatives of major food plants such as *Colocasia* and *Cyrtosperma* taros do not occur in Vanuatu forests. In the absence of introduced plants and animals, sustained human occupation of Remote Oceania may have been impossible. Bailey *et al.*'s (1989) judgment on the lack of edible plant food in tropical rainforests in general applies most forcefully to Vanuatu. As far as the early inhabitants of Island Melanesia were concerned, the archipelago may indeed have been a 'green desert'.

Gosden's model of contrast between the archaeological record before and after 20,000 BP forms a useful starting point for consideration of economic change during this period. In the pre-20,000 BP period he detects a strategy whereby people moved themselves between scarce resources. In the subsequent period there is evidence that resources are being moved, possibly between more settled groups.

The major changes were the apparently deliberate introduction of wild animal species such as the marsupial possum *Phalanger orientalis* into the New Ireland forests from 20,000 BP onwards and a different species of phalangerid and a bandicoot into Manus before 13,000 BP, the transplantation of nut trees such as *Canarium* to New Ireland and Buka by the end of the Pleistocene and perhaps much earlier in Manus, and the movement of obsidian from New Britain to New Ireland from 20,000 BP onwards and from offshore islands to the Manus mainland from 13,000 BP (summarized in Spriggs 1997a, chapter 3). Making a conscious move to recreate the richer environment of the New Guinea forests or at least to compensate for the poverty of the ones they fetched up in, the early Island Melanesians overcame the natural productivity limits of the forest environment and took an active part in shaping it. Although foraging to wild food production as a sequence demonstrates a continuum rather than a sharp break, it is clear that the system from 20,000 BP represents the latter kind of economy. The economy of the first settlers may also have gone beyond simple foraging by necessity, but the evidence is much clearer for this later period.

If we look at the period from 10,000 BP to the first evidence of an agricultural lifestyle in the region after 3300 BP we find that agriculture did not represent an inevitable development from what had gone before. There was no period of 'incipient agriculture' leading up to the adoption of full-on agriculture in the region. It arrived with new migrants bringing domesticated animals and a suite of plants with them from Southeast Asia, the makers and users of Lapita pottery and its associated material culture (Spriggs 1996b). They also brought with them a totally different attitude to the landscape and the place of humans within it. Their environmental impact was sudden and dramatic, and it quickly so transformed Island Melanesian landscapes that a hunter-gatherer lifestyle was no longer sustainable for the region's inhabitants. Subsistence choice rapidly narrowed towards a fully agricultural economy throughout Island Melanesia.

In the depauperate forests of Island Melanesia, transplanting of useful plant species from more productive habitats may have been necessary from initial occupation of areas beyond the coastal fringe. Thus, there may never have been true foragers in the region's rainforests, a condition of regular exploitation being a form of wild plant-food production from the beginning. The overall effect of this and the introduction of wild animal species beyond their natural range were to mimic the diversity of the New Guinea forests from whence the early settlers presumably came.

Bailey and his colleagues (1989) therefore may be right in one sense. Perhaps foragers could not have lived in these forests, but people did not have to wait for the advent of agricultural colonists to open up the canopy through clearance for gardens. Wild plant-food production and cultivation may have been developed early on as a set of strategies to allow occupation of the forests, starting with initial settlement in Island Melanesia (cf. Groube 1989 for mainland New Guinea).

There is a vast gulf in lifestyle implied by the terms hunter-gatherer and agriculturalist, and a vast gulf in attitude to the environment. The Pacific Islands are a good place to demonstrate this. When full-on agriculture did reach the area with the Lapita culture, patterns of settlement, population density, land use, degree of human impact on the environment and material culture were radically changed. The obvious continuities in Island Melanesian cultural sequences from at least 20,000 BP onwards until the moment of agriculture at about 3300 BP, and the radical re-assortment that followed, are eloquent witness to the gulf between two very different ways of life.

The presence of swamp cultivation systems evident in the New Guinea Highlands from at least the mid-Holocene and possibly back as far as 9000 BP (Golson 1977; Hope and Golson 1995) has been taken by some to suggest that an agricultural lifestyle was general throughout the region pre-Lapita. But there are questions as to the scale of the systems and the specificity of Highland adaptations. Were such swampland garden systems within the capabilities of low-population hunter-horticultural groups, just another local response to the challenges of the region's environments? The Highland environments of New Guinea may have necessitated specialized subsistence systems to allow sustained human use of the area. The remains at Kuk and other Highland swamps may, in their early phases, represent one such system just as the transport of plants and animals into the Bismarcks allowed greater certainty of human tenure there in the face of particular environmental challenges. The question is whether the dense populations of the Highlands 'discovered' by white explorers in the 1930s resulted from these early subsistence innovations. Or whether some further input of crops and domestic animals, ultimately of Southeast Asian origin and associated with the spread of the Lapita culture, changed population and cultural directions to the fully-agricultural lifestyle of recent observation there (Bayliss-Smith 1996). A challenge for the future of New Guinea archaeology is to give context to what remain isolated incidents of swamp drainage with no associated settlements and thus no idea of settlement pattern or population densities in the pre-2000 BP period. The articulation of early Highlands societies with the lowlands and possible pathways of agricultural spread from coastal entry points will also occupy researchers well into the next century.

The origins and spread of the Lapita culture

This is a difficult time to write a neatly encapsulated description of the Lapita phenomenon, as we have reached the end of a cycle of study and publication, represented by major syntheses of the 'orthodox' view of Lapita culture and its origins (Bellwood 1997, chapter 7; Kirch 1997; Spriggs 1997a, chapters 3 and 4). The arguments of the proponents of this view are well known, as are those of its detractors (most recently Ambrose 1997; Terrell and Welsch 1997; Terrell et al. 1997). It is time to move on, but the new cycle of research and model-building is only nascent.

In this review of the evidence we will (briefly) go over the old ground and then attempt to chart where the discussion of Lapita might be headed. The main ammunition for a new direction is provided by a series of intensive field projects currently under way in Vanuatu, New Caledonia, Fiji and Tonga, along with the presentation of detailed results from earlier research in the Bismarck Archipelago in a recently-presented Ph.D. thesis by Summerhayes (1996, 2000). Summerhayes' thesis represents an important reinterpretation of stylistic change in Lapita pottery. Taken together, the new research requires a major rethink of the nature of Lapita. But first to what we think we know.

Early recognition of Lapita was based on the elaborately decorated pottery, much of it executed by what was later recognized as a series of small toothed or 'dentate' stamps, perhaps resembling in form tattooing chisels. Much of the pottery found in association was undecorated. Lapita pottery was generally coated with a red slip and some designs were highlighted using a white infill of clay or lime.

Lapita was first reported in the literature before the First World War by Father Meyer, a Catholic missionary on the island of Watom off the north-east coast of New Britain (Meyer 1909). Subsequently similarities were recognized between this and pottery recovered from New Caledonia (from the site of Lapita itself) and Tonga between the wars. Gifford and Shutler's 1952 excavations at the site of Lapita and the recognition of these wide-ranging similarities led to the definition of a Lapita style which had been distributed from the Bismarcks to Polynesia prior to the Christian era (Gifford and Shutler 1956).

This distribution immediately became the main puzzle of Pacific archaeology, and a focus on Lapita and its distribution has remained central to Pacific archaeology to this day. Since that time a suite of associated artefacts and a distinct settlement pattern have led to the definition of a full cultural complex and it is now known to have been distributed even further afield, as far as Wallis and Futuna and Western Samoa. The only finds of Lapita pottery on the island of New Guinea or adjacent to it are of sherds from a single vessel from Aitape on the central north coast, and a dentate-stamped sherd from Ali Island, just off Aitape (Terrell and Welsch 1997, 558–9).

Three sub-styles of Lapita pottery have been recognized, conventionally called Far Western, Western and Eastern (Anson 1983, 1986), which have geographical and chronological significance. The tendency in Lapita pottery is for simplification through time, as the style spread from west to east.

A link between the west to east spread of the Lapita cultural complex from Island Melanesia to Western Polynesia and the spread of Austronesian languages in this area was first suggested in the 1970s (Shutler and Marck 1975; Bellwood 1978). The idea that this spread was linked to a major dispersal of peoples out of Asia, through Southeast Asia and on into Polynesia was also explicit in these early formulations.

The orthodox view is that the most widespread archaeological phenomenon in the Southeast Asian–Pacific region and the most widespread language group in the same area are intimately linked. It is uncontroversial that the foundations of Polynesian languages and cultures go back to the eastern extension of Lapita in a region previously uninhabited. That the immediate Lapita 'homeland' is further west in the Bismarck Archipelago is now also well accepted. It is also generally agreed that Austronesian languages, whether in Polynesia or the Bismarcks, are derived from even further to the west in Southeast Asia and ultimately in Taiwan. It is hard to imagine a process to get these languages from Taiwan to Island Melanesia and Polynesia that would not leave an archaeological trace, and the obvious trace at the appropriate time period (which has to be no later than initial settlement of Polynesia about 2900 years ago) is Lapita in Island Melanesia and Polynesia.

The orthodox view of Lapita origins is not without its archaeological critics in Southeast Asia and more so in Melanesia (see for instance Allen and White 1989; Terrell *et al.* 1997). If we list what is new about the Lapita culture, then the evidence for major cultural discontinuity in the Bismarcks — and therefore the likelihood of a population intrusion — is made plain:

1 The most visible attribute is the pottery, its very occurrence and its distinctive decorative system using dentate-stamping, incising and some other minor techniques. There are clear antecedents in terms of vessel form and red-slipping, and possibly decoration, in Island Southeast Asia (Bellwood 1997) and claims for early pottery in New Guinea have not achieved general acceptance (Spriggs 1996b, 329, 334).

2 Lapita represents the first convincing evidence for full-on agriculture in the region, indicated by evidence for accelerated erosion consistent with gardening on hillslopes, the extension of settlement to areas where a non-agricultural subsistence base would be unlikely or impossible, i.e. Remote Oceania (Polynesia in particular), and the very size and nature of Lapita settlements as large settled villages. It has been argued that many of the associated plants are of New Guinea origin, however (Yen 1998).

3 It marks the first appearance of the three Pacific domesticates: pig, dog and chicken, and therefore the beginnings of Pacific animal husbandry. All are of Southeast Asian origin. There is now scepticism concerning claims for early pigs in New Guinea (Spriggs 1996b, 335).

4 The already mentioned settlement pattern is itself new: large villages often consisting of stilt houses over lagoons or on small offshore islands in the Bismarcks and main Solomons, but on the ground and on large islands further out in the Pacific. Lapita sites do not generally re-occupy previously used locations apart from where Lapita deposits occur in rockshelters. The settlement pattern in the Bismarcks and main Solomons suggests a defensive posture or avoidance of mainland situations where malaria could have been rife.

5 There is a distinctive Lapita stone adze kit not paralleled in previous assemblages in the area (Green 1991b). In addition, although edge-ground adzes occur pre-Lapita, there are no examples of fully-ground stone adzes from earlier periods in Island Melanesia.

6 There is a distinctive range of shell ornaments, interpreted by Kirch (1988) as shell valuables, again not paralleled by earlier forms. These include *Conus* shell rectangular units, beads, rings and disks, *Tridacna* rings and *Spondylus* beads and long units.

7 Lapita represents a major extension in the range of New Britain and Manus obsidian. In the pre-Lapita era, Manus obsidian is not found outside that island group. In contrast it is found in Lapita sites throughout the Bismarcks, Solomons and into

Vanuatu. New Britain obsidian was distributed pre-Lapita to the west on the New Guinea mainland as far as the Sepik-Ramu basin (Swadling *et al.* 1988), and to the south and east in New Ireland and on Nissan. In Lapita times its spread encompassed Sabah in Borneo to the west (Bellwood and Koon 1989) and Fiji in the east (Best 1987), a spread of some 7000 km.

8   In Remote Oceania south and east of the main Solomons, Lapita appears to be the founding culture, representing initial human colonization. It is thus evidence that a threshold in voyaging technology and navigation skill was reached at that time (Irwin 1992, 1998). There is at present no evidence of a pre-Lapita extension of voyaging range (and therefore developments in boat technology) in Island Melanesia post-dating 20,000 BP. All of the island groups reached pre-Lapita show evidence of Pleistocene settlement: the Bismarcks, Solomons and the Admiralty Islands (Manus).

9   A process is needed to explain the pattern of genetic markers among populations of the region, particularly the presence of the 9 base-pair deletion found in mitochondrial DNA samples in Polynesia and in coastal and near-coastal populations in Island Melanesia and New Guinea. Its origin is clearly Asian and the spread of the Lapita culture as deriving ultimately from a Southeast Asian source provides the only plausible mechanism for its spread which is visible in the archaeological record. See Merriweather *et al.* (1999, 261–6) for a recent comprehensive discussion of this point.

The recent re-analysis by Summerhayes (1996, 2000) of Lapita pottery decoration and form shows that temporal differences far outweigh regional ones in the division of Lapita decoration into sub-styles by Anson (1983, 1986) and before him Green (1979). Summerhayes (1996, 262, 2000) calls for a re-naming of the sub-styles as Early, Middle and Late Lapita. There are of course no hard and fast breaks between them. The changes are continuous over a span of about 500–600 years, and any divisions we construct are somewhat arbitrary within this continuum, serving mainly to illustrate breaks in the settlement sequence.

1   Early Lapita is what Anson called Far Western or, as I preferred to call it, 'Early Western' (Spriggs 1997a, 70). This sub-style is limited to the Bismarck Archipelago and dates from about 3300 to 3100 BP or slightly later. This sub-style has produced the most complex vessel forms and the most elaborate decorative motifs, often executed using extremely fine dentate stamps.

2   Middle Lapita (Anson's Western Lapita) is found after 3100 BP until about 2900 BP in the Bismarcks and represents the earliest Lapita pottery in the Solomons, Vanuatu and New Caledonia. It consists of less elaborate decoration, fewer vessel forms and generally the use of coarser stamps.

3   Late Lapita (Anson's Eastern Lapita) is found in Fiji and Western Polynesia from first settlement around 2900 BP. Very similar material is identified by Summerhayes (1996, 198–201) from the Arawe Islands assemblages in the Bismarcks and comparable

material can be found elsewhere in Island Melanesia. The motifs are simpler still than Middle Lapita and there are fewer vessel forms. A coarse dentate-stamping is often used. The style lasts until the end of dentate-stamped Lapita which may be around 2700 BP throughout the range of its distribution, with some possibility that it continues later in parts of the Bismarcks.

As noted above, Lapita *sensu stricto* may well end in all areas about 2700 BP, the pottery then becoming a plain ware with lip notching until about 2500 BP. There is a usually rare incised component associated with this material. Subsequently, this incised component becomes a common form of decoration, along with fingernail impression. Lasting until about 2300 BP, this goes along with a further decrease in the range of vessel forms produced. After that date pottery goes out of use in several areas, but where it persists there is a change in decoration to incised and applied relief decoration on simple vessel forms, often called the Mangaasi style after a site on Efate in Central Vanuatu. See Sand (1995), Green (1997), Spriggs (1997a), Bedford *et al.* (1998) and Wahome (1998) for discussion of post-Lapita sequences in the region. The material culture that accompanied Lapita pottery continues in these post-Lapita sequences (Spriggs 1984), although over time the range of shell ornament types is reduced.

Given the probable role of shell valuables in Lapita exchange, the changes in the range of ornaments produced are surely as significant as the cessation of dentate-stamped pottery itself in signalling societal changes following the end of the Lapita settlement period.

Once the Lapita expansion had reached its geographical limits and communities had settled into their new homes, the need for displaying whatever Lapita designs symbolized was gone, at least on the non-perishable media where they had been prominently displayed. The spiritual assistance of the ancestors may no longer have been needed (an implication of Kirch 1997, 143–4), or the cult or ritual may have lost its function or meaning (Terrell and Welsch 1997, 568). But this wasn't directly because of isolation. The fact that pottery style change across the entire Lapita range continued in step for at least a further 400–500 years after 2700 BP, and over much of it perhaps for a further 1200 years, testifies to continued social interaction between these far-flung communities.

The causes of the migration associated with the spread of Lapita remain obscure, although as Anthony has argued in a general study of prehistoric migration processes, causes are often extremely complex and in many prehistoric cases can no longer be identified (1990, 898). The migrants' initial success in establishing settlements in the Bismarcks and Solomons may have been due to the demographic advantages imparted by an integrated animal husbandry and agricultural economy in an area previously inhabited by small populations of hunter-gatherer or hunter-horticultural groups. Bellwood (1996, 487) has suggested that the existence of an already in-place agricultural (or at least tree-crop managing) economy on the mainland of New Guinea may explain why significant Austronesian settlement there appears to have been delayed for over a thousand years after the Bismarcks were settled. He also notes that malaria may have been an added or alternative factor discouraging settlement (cf. Groube 1993). A Lapita trail along the north coast of New Guinea might still await the archaeologist, however.

Conclusions

We have inevitably had to miss out many significant research findings and directions in a contribution of this kind, choosing to concentrate particularly on questions of 'when' rather than 'why'. 'When' remains surely the more basic question and one which inevitably takes priority at an early stage of research. We have identified areas of recent controversy and pointed out the directions we think research should take in considering the chronology of human colonization of the Pacific. For such a vast and comparatively little-studied region, where basic cultural sequences are often lacking, the perhaps somewhat unromantic tasks of cultural sequence building are still the building bricks needed before convincing theory-building and synthesis can occur.

We have avoided discussion of areas such as New Zealand and some other parts of Polynesia where this pioneering stage of research is already over, to highlight areas such as most of the vast island of New Guinea and much of Australia beyond the heavily-populated eastern coastal fringe. Here for the most part, we still do not have detailed cultural sequences, nor many systematic data concerning changing settlement patterns and densities through time, which might allow deeper analysis into cultural process. The basic challenge, even after an energetic half century of research, remains that of gaining fundamental, indeed even first order archaeological knowledge, and of secure sequence building. This is not proposed as some sort of naïve positivist agenda, but is drawn from our direct experiences working in the region.

Within Oceania, we are also actors in a complex political world, where the results of archaeology increasingly 'matter' in nationalist discourse and that of indigenous minorities within larger nations of ultimately settler origins (cf. Spriggs 1999b). It might be considered to be a serious fraud to put our undigested ideas innocently out into such an interested arena, but conversely, the craft of archaeology has some fundamental historical truths which it must tell.

Acknowledgements

We would like to thank Bob Cooper and Darren Boyd for the preparation of the figures at extremely short notice.

References

ADCOCK, G.J., DENNIS, E.S., EASTEAL, S., HUTTLEY, G.A., JERMIIN, L.S., PEACOCK, W.J. and THORNE, A. 2001: Mitochondrial DNA sequences in ancient Australians: Implications for modern human origins. *Proc. Nat. Acad. Sci.* 98, 537–42.

ALLEN, H. 1998: Reinterpreting the 1969–72 Willandra Lakes archaeological surveys. *Archaeol. in Oceania* 33(3), 207–20.

ALLEN, J. 2000: A matter of time. *Nature Australia* Spring, 60–9.

ALLEN, J. and HOLDAWAY, S. 1995: The contamination of Pleistocene radiocarbon determinations in Australia. *Antiquity* 69, 101–12.

ALLEN, J. and O'CONNELL, J.F. (eds.) 1995: *Transitions. Pleistocene to Holocene in Australia and Papua New Guinea. Antiquity* 69, Special Number 265.

ALLEN, J. and WHITE, J.P. 1989: The Lapita Homeland: Some New Data and an Interpretation. *J. Polynesian Soc.* 98, 129–46.

AMBROSE, W.R. 1988: An Early Bronze Artefact from Papua New Guinea. *Antiquity* 62, 483–91.

AMBROSE, W.R. 1997: Contradictions in Lapita Ware, a Composite Clone. *Antiquity* 71, 525–38.

ANDERSON, A. 1995: Current Approaches in East Polynesian Colonisation Research. *J. Polynesian Soc.* 104(1), 110–32.

ANDERSON, A. and CLARK, G. 1999: The Age of Lapita Settlement in Fiji. *Archaeol. in Oceania* 34(1), 31–9.

ANSON, D. 1983: *Lapita Pottery of the Bismarck Archipelago and its Affinities* (Unpublished Ph.D. thesis, Department of Anthropology, University of Sydney).

ANSON, D. 1986: Lapita Pottery of the Bismarck Archipelago and its Affinities. *Archaeol. in Oceania* 21, 157–65.

ANTHONY, D.W. 1990: Migration in Archaeology: the Baby and the Bathwater. *American Anthropologist* 92, 895–914.

BAHN, P.G. 1996: Further back down under. *Nature* 383, 577–8.

BAILEY, R.C., HEAD, G., JENIKE, M., OWEN, B. and RECHTMAN, R. 1989: Hunting and Gathering in Tropical Rainforests: Is It Possible? *American Anthropologist* 91, 59–82.

BARBETTI, M. and ALLEN, H.R. 1972: Prehistoric man at Lake Mungo, Australia, by 32,000 years BP. *Nature* 240, 46–8.

BARTSTRA, G.-J. 1984: Dating the Pacitanian: some thoughts. *Courier Forschungsinstitut Senkenberg* 69, 253–8.

BARTSTRA, G.-J. 1985: Sangiran, the stone implements of Ngebung, and the Palaeolithic of Java. *Modern Quat. Res. in Southeast Asia* 9, 99–113.

BAR-YOSEF, O., ARNOLD, M., BELFER-COHEN, P., GOLDBERG, P., HOUSELEY, R., LAVILLE, H., MEIGNEN, L., MERCER, N., VOGEL, J.C. and VANDERMEERSCH, B. 1996: The dating of the Upper Palaeolithic layers in Kebara Cave, Mt Carmel. *J. Archaeol. Sci.* 23, 297–307.

BAYLISS-SMITH, T. 1996: People-Plant Interactions in the New Guinea Highlands: Agricultural Hearthland or Horticultural Backwater? In Harris, D.R. (ed.), *The Origins and Spread of Agriculture and Pastoralism in Eurasia* (London), 499–523.

BEATON, J.M. 1995: The Transition on the Coastal Fringe of Greater Australia. In Allen, J. and O'Connell, J.F. (eds.) 1995, 798–806.

BEDFORD, S., SPRIGGS, M., WILSON, M. and REGENVANU, R. 1998: The Australian National University–National Museum of Vanuatu Archaeology Project: a Preliminary Report on the Establishment of Cultural Sequences and Rock Art Research. *Asian Perspectives* 37(2), 165–93.

BEDNARIK, R.G. 1997: The earliest evidence of ocean navigation. *Int. J. Nautical Archaeol.* 26, 1–10.

BELLWOOD, P.S. 1978: *Man's Conquest of the Pacific* (London).

BELLWOOD, P.S. 1996: The Origins and Spread of Agriculture in the Indo-Pacific Region: Gradualism and Diffusion or Revolution and Colonization. In Harris, D.R. (ed.), *The Origins and Spread of Agriculture and Pastoralism in Eurasia* (London), 465–98.

BELLWOOD, P.S. 1997: *Prehistory of the Indo-Malaysian Archipelago* (Honolulu, 2nd edition).

BELLWOOD, P.S. and KOON, P. 1989: 'Lapita Colonists leave Boats Unburned!' The Question of Lapita Links with Island Southeast Asia. *Antiquity* 63, 613–22.

BEST, S. 1987: Long Distance Obsidian Travel and Possible Implications for the Settlement of Fiji. *Archaeol. in Oceania* 22, 31–2.

BIRD, M.I., AYLIFFE, L.K., FIFIELD, L.K., TURNEY, C.S.M., CRESSWELL, R.G., BARROWS, T.T. and DAVID, B. 1999: Radiocarbon dating of 'old' charcoal using a wet oxidation, stepped-combustion procedure. *Radiocarbon* 41, 127–40.

BOWDLER, S. 1990: 50,000 year old site in Australia — is it really that old? *Australian Archaeol.* 31, 93.

BOWLER, J.M. 1976: Recent developments in reconstructing late Quaternary environments in Australia. In Kirk, R.L. and Thorne, A.G. (eds.), *The Origin of the Australians* (Canberra, Australian Institute of Aboriginal Studies), 55–77.

BOWLER, J.M. 1998: Willandra Lakes revisited: environmental framework for human occupation. *Archaeol. in Oceania* 33, 120–55.

BOWLER, J.M., JONES, R., ALLEN, H. and THORNE, A.G. 1970: Pleistocene human remains from Australia: a living site and human cremation from Lake Mungo, western New South Wales. *World Archaeol.* 2, 39–60.

BOWLER, J.M. and MAGEE, J.W. 2000: Redating Australia's oldest human remains: a sceptic's view. *J. Human Evolution* 38, 719–26.

BOWLER, J.M. and PRICE, D.M. 1998: Luminescence dates and stratigraphic analyses at Lake Mungo: review and new perspectives. *Archaeol. in Oceania* 33, 156–68.

BOWLER, J.M. and THORNE, A.G. 1976: Human remains from Lake Mungo. In Kirk, R.L. and Thorne, A.G. (eds.), *The Origin of the Australians* (Canberra, Australian Institute of Aboriginal Studies), 127–38.

BOWLER, J.M., THORNE, A.G. and POLACH, H.A. 1972: Pleistocene man in Australia: age and significance of the Mungo skeleton. *Nature* 240, 48–50.

BURLEY, D.V., NELSON, E. and SHUTLER, R., Jr. 1999: A Radiocarbon Chronology for the Eastern Lapita Frontier in Tonga. *Archaeol. in Oceania* 34(2), 59–70.

CAMPBELL, K.S.W. (ed.) 1975: *Gondwana Geology. Papers presented at the Third Gondwana Symposium, Canberra, Australia, 1973* (Canberra).

CANN, R.L., STONEKING, M. and WILSON, A.C. 1987: Mitochondrial DNA and human evolution. *Nature* 325, 31–6.

CHAPPELL, J., HEAD, J. and MAGEE, J. 1996: Beyond the Radiocarbon Limit in Australian Archaeology and Quaternary Research. *Antiquity* 70, 543–52.

CHAPPELL, J., OMURA, A., MCCULLOCH, M., ESAT, T., OTA, Y. and PANDOLFI, J. 1994: Revised Late Quaternary Sea Levels between 70 and 30 Ka from Coral Terraces at Huon Peninsula. In Ota, Y. (ed.), *Study on Coral Reef Terraces of the Huon Peninsula, Papua New Guinea: Establishment of Quaternary Sea Level and Tectonic History* (Yokohama, Department of Geography, Yokohama National University), 155–65.

CLARK, G.A. and WILLERMET, C.M. (eds.) 1997: *Conceptual Issues in Modern Human Origins Research* (New York).

CLARK, J.G.D. 1961: *World Prehistory: An Outline* (Cambridge).

DAYTON, L. 2001: East Timor's prehistoric picnic a feast for archaeologists. *The Australian* Wednesday, March 28, 4.

DAYTON, L. and WOODFORD, J. 1996: Australia's date with destiny. *New Scientist* 152, 28–31.

DEACON, H.J. 1989: Late Pleistocene palaeoecology and archaeology in the Southern cape, South Africa. In Mellars, P. and Stringer, C.B. (eds.), *The Human Revolution: Behavioral and Biological Perspectives on the Origins of Modern Humans* (Edinburgh), 547–64.

DUBOIS, E. 1894: *Pithecanthropus erectus: eine Menschenaehnliche Uebergangsform aus Java* (Batavia).

DUBOIS, E. 1920: De proto-Australische fossiele mensch van Wadjak (Java). *Versl. Gewone Vergad. Akad. Amsterdam* 29, 88–105.

ENRIGHT, N.J. and GOSDEN, C. 1992: Unstable Archipelagoes: South-West Pacific Environment and Prehistory since 30,000 B.P. In Dodson, J. (ed.), *The Naive Lands: Prehistory and Environmental Change in Australia and the South-West Pacific* (Melbourne), 160–98.

FENNEMA, K. 1996: *Een Eiland Te Ver* (Doctoraalscriptie, Facultiet der Pre-en Protohistorie, Rijks Universieit, Leiden).

FIELD, J. and DODSON, J. 1999: Late Pleistocene megafauna and archaeology from Cuddie Springs, south-eastern Australia. *Proc. Prehist. Soc.* 65, 275–301.

FIFIELD, L.K., BIRD, M.I., TURNEY, C.S.M., HAUSLADEN, P.A., SANTOS, G.M. and di TAPA, M.L. 2001 in press: Radiocarbon dating of the human occupation of Australia prior to 40 ka B.P. – successes and pitfalls. *Radiocarbon*.

FLANNERY, T.F. 1990: Pleistocene faunal loss: implications of the aftershock for Australia's past and future. *Archaeol. in Oceania* 25, 45–67.

FLANNERY, T.F. 1995: *Mammals of the South West Pacific and Moluccan Islands* (Sydney).

FLANNERY, T.F. and WHITE, J.P. 1991: Animal Translocation. *National Geographic Research and Exploration* 7(1), 96–113.

FLANNERY, T.F. and WICKLER, S. 1990: Quaternary Murids (Rodentia: Muridae) from Buka Island, Papua New Guinea, with Descriptions of Two New Species. *Australian Mammalogy* 13, 127–39.

FLOOD, J. 1995: *Archaeology of the Dreamtime: The Story of Prehistoric Australia and its People* (Sydney and London, 2nd edition).

FOX, R.B. 1970: *The Tabon Caves* (Manila, National Museum of the Philippines, Monograph 1).

FULLAGAR, R.L.K., PRICE, D.M. and HEAD, L.M. 1996: Early human occupation of northern Australia: archaeology and thermoluminescence dating of Jinmium rock-shelter, Northern Territory. *Antiquity* 70, 751–73.

GALBRAITH, R.F., ROBERTS, R.G., LASLETT, G.M., YOSHIDA, H. and OLLEY, J.M. 1999: Optical dating of single and multiple grains from Jinmium rock shelter, Northern Australia: Part I, experimental design and statistical models. *Archaeometry* 421, 339–64.

GIFFORD, E.W. and SHUTLER, R.J. 1956: *Archaeological Excavations in New Caledonia* (Berkeley and Los Angeles, Anthropological Records 18(1)).

GILLESPIE, R. 1998: Alternative timescales: a critical review of Willandra Lakes dating. *Archaeol. in Oceania* 33, 169–82.

GILLESPIE, R., HORTON, D.R., LADD, P., MACUMBER, P.G., RICH, T.H., THORNE, R. and WRIGHT, R.V.S. 1978: Lancefield Swamp and the extinction of the Australian megafauna. *Science* 200, 1044–8.

GILLESPIE, R. and ROBERTS, R.G. 2000: On the reliability of age estimates for human remains at Lake Mungo. *J. Human Evolution* 38, 727–32.

GLACKEN, C.J. 1956: Changing ideas of the habitable world. In Thomas, W.L. (ed.), *Man's Role in Changing the Face of the Earth* (Chicago), 70–92.

GLOVER, I.C. 1973: Island southeast Asia and the settlement of Australia. In Strong, D.E. (ed.), *Archaeological Theory and Practice* (London), 105–29.

GLOVER, I.C. 1986: *Archaeology in Eastern Timor, 1966–67. Terra Australis* 11 (Canberra, Department of Prehistory, Research School of Pacific Studies, The Australian National University).

GLOVER, I.C. and GLOVER, E.A. 1970: Pleistocene flaked stone tools from Timor and Flores. *Mankind* 7, 188–90.

GOLSON, J. 1977: No Room at the Top: Agricultural Intensification in the New Guinea Highlands. In Allen, J., Golson, J. and Jones, R. (eds.), *Sunda and Sahul: Prehistoric Studies in Southeast Asia, Melanesia and Australia* (London), 601–38.

GOLSON, J. 1986: Old guards and new waves: reflections on antipodean archaeology 1954–1975. *Archaeol. in Oceania* 21, 2–12.

GOSDEN, C. 1995: Arboriculture and Agriculture in Coastal Papua New Guinea. In Allen, J. and O'Connell, J.F. (eds.) 1995, 807–17.

GREEN, R.C. 1979: Lapita. In Jennings, J.D. (ed.), *The Prehistory of Polynesia* (Canberra), 27–60.

GREEN, R.C. 1991a: Near and Remote Oceania: Disestablishing 'Melanesia' in Culture History. In Pawley, A. (ed.), *Man and a Half: Essays in Pacific Anthropology and Ethnobiology in Honour of Ralph Bulmer* (Auckland, The Polynesian Society, Polynesian Society Memoir), 491–502.

GREEN, R.C. 1991b: The Lapita Cultural Complex: Current Evidence and Proposed Models. In Bellwood, P.S. (ed.), *Indo-Pacific Prehistory 1990* vol. 2 (Canberra and Jakarta, IPPA and Asosiasi Prehistorisi Indonesia; Bulletin of the Indo-Pacific Prehistory Association 11), 295–305.

GREEN, R.C. 1997: Linguistic, Biological and Cultural Origins of the Initial Inhabitants of Remote Oceania. *New Zealand J. Archaeol.* 17 (1995), 5–27.

GROUBE, L. 1989: The Taming of the Rainforests: a Model for Late Pleistocene Forest Exploitation in New Guinea. In Harris, D.R. and Hillman, G.C. (eds.), *Foraging and Farming: the Evolution of Plant Exploitation* (London), 292–317.

GROUBE, L. 1993: Contradictions and Malaria in Melanesian and Australian Prehistory. In Spriggs, M., Yen, D.E., Ambrose, W., Jones, R., Thorne, A. and Andrews, A. (eds.), *A Community of Culture; the People and Prehistory of the Pacific* (Canberra, Department of Prehistory, Research School of Pacific Studies, The Australian National University, Occasional Papers in Prehistory 21), 164–86.

GRÜN, R. and BEAUMONT, P. in press: Border cave revisited. Revised ESR chronology and an update on hominids BC1 to BC8. *J. Human Evolution.*

GRÜN, R., SPOONER, N.A., THORNE, A., MORTIMER, G., SIMSON, J.J., MCCULLOCK, M.T., TAYLOR, L. and CURNOE, D. 2000: Reply to J.M. Bowler and J.W. Magee, 'Redating Australia's oldest human remains: A sceptic's view', and R. Gillespie and R.G. Roberts, 'On the reliability of age estimates from human remains at lake Mungo'. *J. Human Evolution* 38, 733–41.

GRÜN, R. and THORNE, A. 1997: Dating the Ngandong humans. *Science* 276, 1575.

GUDDEMI, P. 1992: When Horticulturalists are like Hunter-Gatherers: the Sawiyano of Papua New Guinea. *Ethnology* 31(4), 303–14.

HARRIS, D.R. 1989: An Evolutionary Continuum of People-Plant Interaction. In Harris, D.R. and Hillman, G.C. (eds.), *Foraging and Farming: the Evolution of Plant Exploitation* (London), 11–26.

HARRIS, D.R. 1996: The Origins and Spread of Agriculture and Pastoralism in Eurasia: an Overview. In Harris, D.R. (ed.), *The Origins and Spread of Agriculture and Pastoralism in Eurasia* (London), 552–73.

HARRISSON, T. 1959: Radio-carbon C-14 dating from Niah: a note. *Sarawak Mus. J.* 13, 136–8.

HIGHAM, T.G.F., ANDERSON, A.J. and JACOMB, C. 1999: Dating the First New Zealanders: the Chronology of Wairau Bar. *Antiquity* 73, 420–7.

HISCOCK, P. 1990: How old are the artefacts in Malakunanja II? *Archaeol. in Oceania* 25, 122–4.

HOOIJER, D.A. 1975: Quaternary mammals east and west of Wallace's Line. *Modern Quat. Res. in Southeast Asia* 1, 37–46.

HOPE, G. and GOLSON, J. 1995: Late Quaternary Changes in the Mountains of New Guinea. In Allen, J. and O'Connell, J.F. (eds.) 1995, 818–30.

HUXLEY, T.H. 1868: On the classification and distribution of the Alectoromorphae and Hetero-morphae. *Proc. Zoological Soc. London* 1868, 367–78.

HYODO, M., WATANABE, N., SUNATA, W., SUSANTO, E.E. and WAHYONO, H. 1993: Magnetostratigraphy of hominid fossil bearing formations in Sangiran and Mojokerto, Java. *Anthropol. Sci.* 101, 157–96.

IRWIN, G. 1980: The Prehistory of Oceania: Colonization and Culture Change. In Sherratt, A. (ed.), *The Cambridge Encyclopaedia of Archaeology* (Cambridge), 324–32.

IRWIN, G. 1992: *The Prehistoric Exploration and Colonisation of the Pacific* (Cambridge).

IRWIN, G. 1998: The Colonisation of the Pacific Plate: Chronological, Navigational and Social Issues. *J. Polynesian Soc.* 107(2), 111–43.

ITIHARA, M., KADAR, D. and WATANABE, N. 1985: Concluding remarks. In Watanabe, N. and Kadar, D. (eds.), *Quaternary Geology of the Hominid Fossil Bearing Formations in Java* (Bandung, Indonesia, Geological Research and Development Centre, Ministry of Mines and Energy, Special Publication no. 4), 367–78.

JACOB, T. 1975: Indonesia. In Oakley, K.P., Campbell, B.G. and Molleson, T.I. (eds.), *Catalogue of Fossil Hominids. Part III Americas, Asia, Australasia* (London, British Museum of Natural History), 103–16.

JONES, R. 1968: The geographical background to the arrival of man in Australia and Tasmania. *Archaeol. and Physical Anthropol. in Oceania* 3, 186–215.

JONES, R. 1969: Firestick farming. *Australian Nat. Hist.* 16, 224–8.

JONES, R. 1973: Emerging picture of Pleistocene Australians. *Nature* 246, 278–81.

JONES, R. 1982: Ions and eons: some thoughts on archaeological science and scientific archaeology. In Ambrose, W. and Duerden, P. (eds.), *Archaeometry: an Australasian Perspective* (Canberra, Department of Prehistory, Research School of Pacific Studies, The Australian National University), 22–35.

JONES, R. 1989: East of Wallace's Line: issues and problems in the colonization of the Australian continent. In Mellars, P. and Stringer, C. (eds.), *The Human Revolution: Behavioural and Biological Perspectives on the Origins of Modern Humans* (Edinburgh), 743–82.

JONES, R. 1993: A continental reconnaissance: Some observations concerning the discovery of the Pleistocene archaeology of Australia. In Spriggs, M., Yen, D.E., Ambrose, W., Jones, R., Thorne, A. and Andrews, A. (eds.), *A Community of Culture; The People and Prehistory of the Pacific* (Canberra, Department of Prehistory, Research School of Pacific Studies, The Australian National University, Occasional Papers in Prehistory 21), 97–122.

JONES, R. 1995: Tasmanian archaeology: establishing the sequences. *Ann. Rev. Anthropol.* 24, 423–6.

JONES, R. 1998: Folsom and Talgai: Cowboy Archaeology in Two Continents. In Bolitho, H. and Wallace-Crabbe, C. (eds.), *Approaching Australia. Papers from the Harvard Australian*

Studies Symposium (Cambridge, MA, Harvard University Committee on Australian Studies), 3–50.

JONES, R. 1999: Dating the human colonization of Australia: Radiocarbon and luminescence revolutions. *Proc. Brit. Acad.* 99, 37–65. And in Coles, J., Bewley, R. and Mellars, P. (eds.), *World Prehistory: Studies in Memory of Grahame Clark* (Oxford), 37–65.

JONES, R. and BOWLER, J. 1980: Struggle for the savanna: northern Australia in ecological and prehistoric perspective. In Jones, R. (ed.), *Northern Australia: Options and Implications* (Canberra, Research School of Pacific Studies, The Australian National University), 3–31.

JONES, R. and JOHNSON, I. 1985: Deaf Adder Gorge: Lindner Site, Nauwalabila 1. In Jones, R. (ed.), *Archaeological Research in Kakadu National Park* (Canberra, Australian National Parks and Wildlife Service, Special Publication 13), 165–227.

KERSHAW, A.P., MOSS, P.T. and WILD, R. in press: Patterns and causes of vegetation change in the Australian wet tropics over the last 10 million years. In Moritz, C. and Bermingham, E. (eds.), *Tropical Rainforests: Past and Future* (Chicago).

KLEIN, R.G. 1995: Anatomy, behavior and modern human origins. *J. World Prehist.* 9, 167–98.

KIRCH, P.V. 1988: Long-Distance Exchange and Island Colonisation: the Lapita Case. *Norwegian Archaeol. Rev.* 21(2), 103–17.

KIRCH, P.V. 1997: *The Lapita Peoples: Ancestors of the Oceanic World* (Oxford).

KIRCH, P.V., FLENLEY, J.R. and STEADMAN, D.W. 1991: A Radiocarbon Chronology for Human-Induced Environmental Change on Mangaia, Southern Cook Islands, Polynesia. *Radiocarbon* 33(3), 317–28.

KOENIGSWALD, G.H.R. von 1933: Ein neuer Urmensch aus dem Dilivium Javas. *Zentbl. Miner. Geol. Palaeontologie* (Stuttgart), 29–42.

KOENIGSWALD, G.H.R. von 1939: Das Pleistocän Javas. *Quartär* 2, 28–53.

KOENIGSWALD, G.H.R. von 1956: The geological age of Wadjak man from Java. *Proc. Koninkl. Nederl. Akadamie van Wetenschappen-Amsterdam* (B) 59, 455–7.

KUHN, S.L., STINER, M.C. and GÜLEÇ, E. 1999: Initial Upper Palaeolithic in South-Central Turkey and its Regional Context: a Preliminary Report. *Antiquity* 73, 505–17.

LEAVESLEY, M. and ALLEN, J. 1998: Dates, Disturbance and Artefact Distributions: Another Analysis of Buang Merabak, a Pleistocene Site on New Ireland, Papua New Guinea. *Archaeol. in Oceania* 33(2), 63–82.

LOY, T.H., SPRIGGS, M. and WICKLER, S. 1992: Direct Evidence for Human Use of Plants 28,000 Years Ago: Starch Residues on Stone Artefacts from the Northern Solomon Islands. *Antiquity* 66, 898–912.

MACARTHUR, R.H. and WILSON, E.O. 1967: *The Theory of Island Biogeography* (Princeton).

MCBRYDE, I. 1986: Australia's once and future archaeology. *Archaeol. in Oceania* 21, 13–28.

MARINGER, J. and VERHOEVEN, T. 1970: Die steinartefakte aus der Stegodon-Fossilschicht von Mengeruda auf Flore, Indonesien. *Anthropos* 65, 229–47.

MARKS, A. 1983: The Middle to Upper Palaeolithic transition in the Levant. In Wendorf, F. and Close, A. (eds.), *Advances in World Archaeology*, 2 (New York), 51–98.

MELLARS, P. and TIXIER, J. 1989: Radiocarbon-accelerator dating of Ksar 'Aqil (Lebanon) and the chronology of the Upper Palaeolithic sequence in the Middle East. *Antiquity* 63, 761–8.

MERRILEES, D. 1968: Man the destroyer: late Quaternary changes in the Australian marsupial fauna. *J. Roy. Soc. Western Australia* 51, 1–24.

MERRIWEATHER, D.A., FRIEDLAENDER, J.S., MEDIAVILLA, J., MGONE, C., GENTZ, F. and FERRELL, R.E. 1999: Mitochondrial DNA variation is an Indicator of Austronesian Influence in Island Melanesia. *American J. Physical Anthropol.* 110, 243–70.

MEYER, O. 1909: Funde Prähistorischer Töpferei und Steinmesser auf Vuatom, Bismarck-Archipel. *Anthropos* 4, 251–2, 1093–5.

MILLER, G.H., BEAUMONT, P.B., DEACON, H.J., BROOKS, A.S., HARE, P.E. and JULL, A.J.T. in press: Earliest modern humans in southern Africa dated by isoleucine epimerization in ostrich eggshell. *Quat. Geochronology.*

MILLER, G.H., MAGEE, J.W., JOHNSON, B.J., FOGEL, M.L., SPOONER, N.A., MCCULLOCH, M.T. and AYLIFFE, L.K. 1999: Pleistocene extinction of genyornis newtoni: Human impact on Australian megafauna. *Science* 283, 205–8.

MORWOOD, M.J., AZIZ, F., BERGH, G.G., VAN DEN SONDAAR, P.Y. and DE VOS, J. 1997: Stone artefacts from the 1994 excavation at Mata Menge, west central Flores, Indonesia. *Australian Archaeol.* 44, 26–34.

MORWOOD, M.J., AZIZ, F., O'SULLIVAN, P., NASRUDDIN, HOBBS, D.R. and RAZA, A. 1999: Archaeological and palaeontological research in central Flores, east Indonesia: results of fieldwork 1997–98. *Antiquity* 73, 273–86.

MORWOOD, M.J., L'OSTE-BROWN, S. and PRICE, D.M. 1995: Excavations at Mushroom Rock. In Morwood, M.J. and Hobbs, D.R. (eds.), *Quinkan Prehistory: the Archaeology of Aboriginal Art in S.E. Cape York Peninsula, Australia* (St Lucia, Brisbane, Anthropology Museum, University of Queensland, Tempus 3), 133–46.

MORWOOD, M.J., O'SULLIVAN, P., AZIZ, F. and RAZA, A. 1998: Fission track age of stone tools and fossils on the east Indonesian island of Flores. *Nature* 392, 173–6.

MOVIUS, H.L. 1944: *Early Man and Pleistocene Stratigraphy in South and East Asia* (Cambridge, MA, Papers of the Peabody Museum, 19, no. 3).

MULVANEY, D.J. 1961: The stone age of Australia. *Proc. Prehist. Soc.* 27, 56–107.

MULVANEY, D.J. 1993: From Cambridge to the bush. In Spriggs, M., Yen, D.E., Ambrose, W., Jones, R., Thorne, A. and Andrews, A. (eds.), *A Community of Culture; The People and Prehistory of the Pacific* (Canberra, Department of Prehistory, Research School of Pacific Studies, The Australian National University, Occasional Papers in Prehistory 21), 18–26.

MULVANEY, D.J. and JOYCE, E.B. 1965: Archaeological and geomorphological investigations on Mt Moffatt Station, Queensland, Australia. *Proc. Prehist. Soc.* 31, 147–212.

MULVANEY, J and KAMMINGA, J. 1999: *Prehistory of Australia* (Sydney).

O'CONNELL, J.F. and ALLEN, J. 1998: When did humans reach Australia and why is it important to know? *Evolutionary Anthropol.* 6, 132–6.

O'CONNOR, S. 1995: Carpenter's Gap Rockshelter I: 40,000 years of Aboriginal occupation in the Napier Ranges, Kimberley, WA. *Australian Archaeol.* 40, 58–9.

OPPENOORTH, W.F.F. 1932: Ein neuer diluvialer Urmensch von Java. *Natur Museum* 62, 271–9.

OWEN, R. 1877: *Researches on the Fossil Remains of the Extinct Mammals of Australia* (London).

OYSTON, B. 1996: Thermoluminescence age determinations for the Mungo III human burial, Lake Mungo, southeastern Australia. *Quat. Sci. Rev.* 15, 739–49.

PARKINGTON, J. 1999: Western Cape landscapes. In Coles, J., Bewley, R. and Mellars, P. (eds.), *World Prehistory: Studies in Memory of Grahame Clark* (Oxford), 25–35.

ROBERTS, R.G. 1997: Luminescence dating in archaeology: from origins to optical. *Radiation Measurements* 27, 819–92.

ROBERTS, R.G., BIRD, M., OLLEY, J., GALBRAITH, R., LAWSON, E., LASLETT, G., YOSHIDA, H., JONES, R., FULLAGAR, R., JACOBSEN, G. and HUA, Q. 1998: Optical and radiocarbon dating at Jinmium rock shelter in northern Australia. *Nature* 393, 358–62.

ROBERTS, R.G., FLANNERY, T.F., AYLIFFE, L.K., YOSHIDA, H., OLLEY, J.M., PRIDEAUX, G.J., LASLETT, G.M., BAYNES, A., SMITH, M.A., JONES, R. and SMITH, B.L 2001: New ages for the last Australian megafauna: continent-wide extinction about 46,000 years ago. *Science* 292, 1888–92.

ROBERTS, R.G., GALBRAITH, R.F., OLLEY, J.M., YOSHIDA, H. and LASLETT, G.M. 1999: Optical dating of single and multiple grains of quartz from Jinmium rock shelter, Northern Australia: Part II, results and implications. *Archaeometry* 41, 365–95.

ROBERTS, R.G. and JONES, R. 1994: Luminescence dating of sediments: new light on the human colonisation of Australia. *Australian Aboriginal Stud.* 2, 2–17 (Canberra, Australian Institute of Aboriginal and Torres Strait Islander Studies).

ROBERTS, R.G. and JONES, R. 2001: Chronologies of carbon and of silica: evidence concerning the dating of the earliest human presence in northern Australia. In Tobias, P.V., Raath, M.A, Moggi-Cecchi, J. and Doyle, G.A., assisted by Kuykendall, K.L. and Soodyal, H. (eds.), *Humanity from African Naissance to Coming Millennia: Colloquia in Human Biology and Palaeoanthropology* (Florence), 239–48.

ROBERTS, R.G., JONES, R. and SMITH, M.A. 1990: Thermoluminescence Dating of a 50,000 Year Old Human Occupation Site in Northern Australia. *Nature* 345, 153–6.

ROBERTS, R.G., JONES, R. and SMITH, M.A. 1993: Optical dating at Deaf Adder Gorge, Northern Territory, indicates human occupation between 53,000 and 60,000 years ago. *Australian Archaeol.* 37, 58–9.

ROBERTS, R.G., JONES, R. and SMITH, M.A. 1994a: Beyond the Radiocarbon barrier in Australian prehistory. *Antiquity* 68, 611–16.

ROBERTS, R.G., JONES, R., SPOONER, N.A., HEAD, M.J., MURRAY, A.S. and SMITH, M.A. 1994b: The human colonisation of Australia: optical dates of 53,000 and 60,000 bracket human arrival at Deaf Adder Gorge, Northern Territory. *Quat. Sci. Rev.* 13, 575–83.

ROBERTS, R., YOSHIDA, H., GALBRAITH, R., LASLETT, G., JONES, R. and SMITH, M. 1998: Single-aliquot and single-grain optical dating confirm thermoluminescence age estimates at Malakunanja II rock shelter in northern Australia. *Ancient T.L.* 16, 19–24.

SAND, C. 1995: *'Le Temps d'Avant': la Préhistoire de la Nouvelle-Calédonie. Contribution à l'Etude des Modalités d'Adaptation et d'Evolution des Sociétés Océaniennes dans un Archipel du Sud de la Mélanésie* (Paris).

SAND, C. 1997: The Chronology of Lapita Ware in New Caledonia. *Antiquity* 71, 539–47.

SCHULZ, D. 2001: The bones of the family. *The Sydney Morning Herald* Monday, July 9, 9.

SHAWCROSS, F.W. 1975: Thirty thousand years and more. *Hemisphere* 19, 26–31.

SHAWCROSS, F.W. 1998: Archaeological excavations at Mungo. *Archaeol. in Oceania* 33, 183–200.

SHAWCROSS, F.W. and KAYE, M. 1980: Australian archaeology: implications of current interdisciplinary research. *Interdisciplinary Sci. Rev.* 5, 112–28.

SHUTLER, R.J. and MARCK, J.C. 1975: On the dispersal of the Austronesian Horticulturalists. *Archaeol. and Physical Anthropol. in Oceania* 13(2 and 3), 215–28.

SIMPSON, J.J. and GRÜN, R. 1998: Non-destructive gamma spectrometric U-series dating. *Quat. Geochronology* 17, 1009–22.

SINGH, G. and GEISSLER, E.A. 1985: Late Cainozoic history of vegetation, fire, lake levels and climate, at Lake George, New South Wales, Australia. *Phil. Trans. Roy. Soc. London*, Series B 311, 379–447.

SKJØLSVOLD, A. 1994: Archaeological Investigations at Anakena, Easter Island. In Skjølsvold, A. (ed.), *Archaeological Investigations at Anakena, Easter Island* (Oslo, Kon Tiki Museum Occasional Papers 3), 1–121.

SMITH, M.A. and SHARP, N.D. 1993: Pleistocene sites in Australia, New Guinea and Island Melanesia: Geographic and temporal structure of the archaeological record. In Smith, M.A.,

Spriggs, M. and Fankhauser, B. (eds.), *Sahul in Review. Pleistocene Archaeology in Australia, New Guinea and Island Melanesia. Occasional Papers in Prehistory* 24 (Canberra, Department of Prehistory, Research School of Pacific Studies, The Australian National University), 37–59.

SONDAAR, P.Y., VAN DEN BERGH, G.D., MUBROTO, B., AZIZ, F., DE VOS, J. and BATU, U.L. 1994: Middle Pleistocene faunal turn-over and colonisation of Flores (Indonesia) by *Homo erectus. Comptes Rendues de l'Academie des Sciences Paris* 319, 1255–62.

SPECHT, J. and GOSDEN, C. 1997: Dating Lapita Pottery in the Bismarck Archipelago, Papua New Guinea. *Asian Perspectives* 36(2), 175–99.

SPOONER, N.A. 1998: Human occupation at Jinmium, northern Australia: 116,000 years ago or much less? *Antiquity* 72, 173–8.

SPRIGGS, M. 1984: The Lapita Cultural Complex: Origins, Distribution, Contemporaries and Successors. *J. Pacific Hist.* 19(4), 202–23.

SPRIGGS, M. 1989: The Dating of the Island Southeast Asian Neolithic: an Attempt at Chronometric Hygiene and Linguistic Correlation. *Antiquity* 63, 587–613.

SPRIGGS, M. 1993: Pleistocene Agriculture in the Pacific: Why Not? In Smith, M.A., Spriggs, M. and Fankhauser, B. (eds.), *Sahul in Review: Pleistocene Archaeology in Australia, New Guinea and Island Melanesia. Occasional Papers in Prehistory* 24 (Canberra, Department of Prehistory, Research School of Pacific Studies, The Australian National University).

SPRIGGS, M. 1996a: Early Agriculture and What Went Before in Island Melanesia: Continuity or Intrusion? In Harris, D.R. (ed.), *The Origins and Spread of Agriculture and Pastoralism in Eurasia* (London), 524–37.

SPRIGGS, M. 1996b: What is Southeast Asian about Lapita? In Akazawa, T. and Szathmary, E. (eds.), *Prehistoric Mongoloid Dispersals* (Oxford), 324–48.

SPRIGGS, M. 1997a: *The Island Melanesians* (Oxford).

SPRIGGS, M. 1997b: Landscape Catastrophe and Landscape Enhancement: Are Either or Both True in the Pacific? In Kirch, P.V. and Hunt, T. (eds.), *Historical Ecology in the Pacific Islands: Prehistoric Environmental and Landscape Change* (New Haven).

SPRIGGS, M. 1999a: Archaeological Dates and Linguistic Sub-Groups in the Settlement of the Island Southeast Asian–Pacific Region. In *Indo-Pacific Prehistory: The Melaka Papers*, Vol. 2 (Bulletin of the Indo-Pacific Prehistory Association 18), 17–24.

SPRIGGS, M. 1999b: Pacific Archaeologies: Contested Ground in the Construction of Pacific History. *J. Pacific Hist.* 34(1), 109–21.

SPRIGGS, M. and ANDERSON, A. 1993: Late Colonization of East Polynesia. *Antiquity* 67, 200–17.

STEADMAN, D.W. 1995: Prehistoric Extinctions of Pacific Island Birds: Biodiversity Meets Zooarchaeology. *Science* 267, 1123–31.

STEADMAN, D.W., CASANOVA, P.V. and FERRANDO, C.C. 1994: Stratigraphy, Chronology and Cultural Context of an Early Faunal Assemblage from Easter Island. *Asian Perspectives* 33(1), 79–96.

STEADMAN, D.W., WHITE, J.P. and ALLEN, J. 1999: Prehistoric birds from New Ireland, Papua New Guinea: Extinctions on a large Melanesian island. *Proc. Nat. Acad. Sci. USA* 96, 2563–8.

STRAUS, L.G. 1997: The Iberian situation between 40,000 and 30,000 B.P. in light of European models of migration and convergence. In Clark, G.A. and Willermet, G.M. (eds.) 1997, 235–52.

STRINGER, C.B. 1992: Replacement, continuity and the origin of Homo sapiens. In Bräuer, G. and Smith, F.H. (eds.), *Continuity or Replacement: Controversies in Homo sapiens Evolution* (Rotterdam), 9–24.

SUMMERHAYES, G.R. 1996: *Interaction in Pacific Prehistory: an Approach Based on the Production, Distribution and Use of Pottery* (Unpublished Ph.D. thesis, La Trobe University, Melbourne).

SUMMERHAYES, G.R. 2000: *Lapita Interaction. Terra Australis* 15 (Canberra, ANH Publications and the Centre for Archaeological Research, ANU).

SUZUKI, M., BUDISANTOSO, W., SAEFUDIN, I. and ITIHARA, M. 1985: Fission track ages of pumice tuff, tuff layers and javites of hominid fossil bearing formations in Sangiran area, central Java. In Watanabe, N. and Kadar, D. (eds.), *Quaternary Geology of the Hominid Fossil Bearing Formations in Java* (Bandung, Indonesia, Geological Research and Development Centre, Ministry of Mines and Energy, Special Publication no. 4), 309–57.

SWADLING, P., SCHAUBLIN, B.W., GORECKI, P. and TIESLER, F. 1988: *The Sepik-Ramu: an Introduction* (Boroko, PNG, National Museum).

SWISHER, C.C. 1994: Response to de Vos. *Science* 266, 1727.

SWISHER, C.C. and CURTIS, G.H. 1998: $^{40}Ar/^{39}Ar$ dating of Plio-Pleistocene hornblendes from Java, Indonesia, using CO2 laser incremental heating techniques. In Raath, A., Soodyall, H., Barkhan, D., Kuykendall, K.L. and Tobias, P.V. (eds.), *Abstracts of Contributions to the Dual Congress 1998* (Johannesburg, International Association for the Study of Human Palaeontology and the International Association of Human Biologists), 16.

SWISHER, C.C., CURTIS, G.H., JACOB, T., GETTY, A.G., SUPRIJO, A. and WIDIASMORO 1994: Age of the earliest known hominids in Java, Indonesia. *Science* 263, 1118–21.

SWISHER, C.C., RINK, W.J., ANTON, S.C., SCHWARCZ, H.P., CURTIS, G.H., SUPRIJO, A. and WIDIASMORO 1996: Latest *Homo erectus* of Java: Potential contemporaneity with *Homo sapiens* in Southeast Asia. *Science* 274, 1870–3.

SWISHER, C.C., SCOTT, G.R., CURTIS, G.H., BUTTERWORTH, J., ANTÓN, S.C., JACOB, T., SUPRIJO, A., WIDIASMORO, SUKANDAR and KOESHARDJONO 1998: The antiquity of *Homo erectus* in Java: $^{40}Ar/^{39}Ar$ dating and palaeomagnetic study of the Sangiran area. In Raath, A., Soodyall, H., Barkhan, D., Kuykendall, K.L. and Tobias, P.V. (eds.), *Abstracts of Contributions to the Dual Congress 1998* (Johannesburg, International Association for the Study of Human Palaeontology and the International Association of Human Biologists), 31.

TERRELL, J., HUNT, T. and GOSDEN, C. 1997: The Dimensions of Social Life in the Pacific: Human Diversity and the Myth of the Primitive Isolate. *Current Anthropol.* 38(2), 155–95.

TERRELL, J. and WELSCH, R. 1997: Lapita and the Temporal Geography of Prehistory. *Antiquity* 71, 548–72.

THORNE, A. and CURNOE, D. 2000: Sex and significance of Lake Mungo 3: reply to Brown 'Australian Pleistocene variation and the sex of Lake Mungo 3'. *J. Human Evolution* 39, 587–600.

THORNE, A., GRÜN, R., MORTIMER, G., SIMPSON, J.J., MCCULLOCH, M., TAYLOR, L. and CURNOE, D. 1999: Australia's oldest human remains: age of the Lake Mungo 3 skeleton. *J. Human Evolution* 36, 591–612.

TISHKOFF, S.A., DIETZSCH, E., SPEED, W., PAKSTIS, A.J., KIDD, J.R., CHEUNG, K., BONNE-TAMIR, B., SANTACHIARA-BENERECETTI, A.S., MORAL, P., KRINGS, M., PAABO, S., WATSON, E., RISCH, N., JENKINS, T. and KIDD, K.K. 1996: Global patterns of linkage disequilibrium at the CD4 locus and modern human origins. *Science* 271, 1380–7.

TURNEY, C.S.M., BIRD, M.I., FIFIELD, L.K., ROBERTS, R.G., SMITH, M.A., DORTCH, C.E., GRUN, R., LAWSON, E., MILLER, G.H., DORTCH, J., CRESSWELL, R.G. and AYLIFFE, L.K. 2001: Breaking the radiocarbon barrier and early human occupation at Devil's Lair, southwestern Australia. *Quat. Res.* 55, 3–13.

VAN DEN BERGH, G.D., MUBROTO, B., AZIZ, F., SONDAAR, P.Y. and DE VOS, J. 1996: Did Homo erectus reach the island of Flores? In Bellwood, P. (ed.), *Indo-Pacific Prehistory: the Chiang Mai Papers 1 (Proceedings of the 15ᵗʰ IPPA Congress, Chiang Mai, Thailand 1994)* (Canberra, Indo-Pacific Prehistory Association), 27–36.

VAN HUET, S., GRÜN, R., MURRAY-WALLACE, C.V., REDVERS-NEWTON, N. and WHITE, J.P. 1998: Age of the Lancefield megafauna: a reappraisal. *Australian Archaeol.* 46, 5–11.

VERHOEVEN, Th. 1958: Pleistozäne funde in Flores. *Anthropos* 53, 264–5.

VERHOEVEN, Th. 1964: Stegodon-Fossilien auf der Insel Timor. *Anthropos* 59, 634.

VERHOEVEN, Th. 1968: Vorgeschtliche Forschungen auf Flores, Timor und Sumba. In *Anthropica Gedenkschrift zum 100sten, Geburtstag von P. Wilhelm Schmidt* (St. Augustin, Studia Instituti Anthropos, 21), 393–403.

DE VOS, J. 1994: Dating hominid sites in Indonesia. *Science* 266, 1726–7.

WAHOME, E. 1998: *Pottery in Manus Prehistory* (Unpublished Ph.D. thesis, Australian National University, Canberra).

WALLACE, A.R. 1869: *The Malay Archipelago. The Land of the Orang-Utan and the Bird of Paradise. A Narrative of Travel with Studies of Man and Nature* (London).

WANG, X., KAARS, S. VAN DER, KERSHAW, P., BIRD, M. and JANSEN, F. 1999: A record of fire, vegetation and climate through the last three glacial cycles from Lombok Ridge core G6-4, eastern Indian ocean, Indonesia. *Palaeogeography, Palaeoclimatology, Palaeoecology* 147, 241–56.

WEIDENREICH, F. 1951: Morphology of Solo man. *Anthropol. Pap. American Mus. Nat. Hist.* 43, 203–90.

WHITE, J.P. and FLANNERY, T. 1995: Late Pleistocene fauna at Spring Creek, Victoria: a re-evaluation. *Australian Archaeol.* 40, 13–17.

WHITE, J.P. and O'CONNELL, J.F. 1982: *A Prehistory of Australia, New Guinea and Sahul* (Sydney).

WICKLER, S. 1990: Prehistoric Melanesian Exchange and Interaction: Recent Evidence from the Northern Solomon Islands. *Asian Perspectives* 29(2), 135–54.

WICKLER, S. and Spriggs, M. 1988: Pleistocene Human Occupation of the Solomon Islands, Melanesia. *Antiquity* 62, 703–6.

WILFORD, J.N. 1996: In Australia, signs of artists who predate *Homo sapiens. New York Times* 29 September.

WOOD, B. 1997: Ecce Homo — behold mankind. *Nature* 390, 120–1.

WRIGHT, R.V.S. 1964: Probing Cape York's past. *Hemisphere* 8, 12–16.

WRIGHT, R.V.S. 1971: The flints. In Wright, R.V.S. (ed.), *Archaeology of the Gallus Site, Koonalda Cave* (Canberra, Australian Institute of Aboriginal Studies, Australian Aboriginal Studies, 26), 48–58.

YEN, D.E. 1995: The Development of Sahul Agriculture with Australia as Bystander. In Allen, J. and O'Connell, J.F. (eds.) 1995, 831–47.

YEN, D.E. 1998: Subsistence to Commerce in Pacific Agriculture: some Four Thousand Years of Plant Exchange. In Etkin, N.L., Harris, D.R., Houghton, P.J. and Prendergast, H.D.V. (eds.), *Plants for Food and Medicine* (Kew, Royal Botanic Gardens), 161–83.

YOKOYAMA, Y., JACOB, T., FALGUÈRES, C. and SÉMAH, F. 1998: Direct dating of Homo erectus skulls of Solo Man in Java by non-destructive gamma-ray spectrometry. In Raath, A., Soodyall, H., Barkhan, D., Kuykendall, K.L. and Tobias, P.V. (eds.), *Abstracts of Contributions to the Dual Congress 1998* (Johannesburg, International Association for the Study of Human Palaeontology and the International Association of Human Biologists), 57.

ZVELEBIL, M. 1986: Mesolithic Societies and the Transition to Farming: Problems of Time, Scale and Organisation. In Zvelebil, M. (ed.), *Hunters in Transition: Mesolithic Societies of Temperate Eurasia and their Transition to Farming* (Cambridge), 167–88.

Note added in proof by M.S.

Rhys Jones passed away on 19 September 2001 after a three-year battle with leukaemia, bravely fought. This paper was originally drafted and sent in at the end of 1999 after his cancer had been diagnosed and initially treated, and Rhys oversaw the correction of the final proofs just a month before his death. The jointly-conceived introduction and conclusions and my section on the Pacific Islands are, bar some updates of referencing, largely as submitted. This is not true of the Australian and early Southeast Asian archaeology sections, which Rhys wrote and which I edited, sometimes savagely, in order to keep them at least close to the word limits we were given. As new discoveries were made and absorbed by the Australian archaeological community, Rhys was continually adding and deleting paragraphs, mainly adding. Every time I went off on field-work or to a conference, I would return to find the Australian section again growing like topsy, and in need of judicious pruning. Rhys knew his time might be short and attempted to distill the conclusions of a lifetime of study of the region into what has in fact turned out to be his last word on the subject.

He, of course, had the last word of either of the authors too. I was to be in the field when the final proofs had to be corrected, and Rhys agreed to undertake the task on his own. I realised there was a great risk that another major rewrite would ensue and hoped the editors would be indulgent. By the time I returned to Australia, Rhys was gravely ill but the proofs were in. About 25 lines had been deleted, and he had been careful to add the same amount so as not to disturb the compositors too much. Apart from further gentle editing of my own section, he added lines on the latest discoveries on Flores, which had obviously allayed some of his scepticism of the earlier claims for an early hominid presence there, and also an update on the latest archaeological results from East Timor. He shortened the section on the dating of Mungo 3 as further studies were published and the exegesis required of 'pers. comm.' information was no longer required, but added the latest reference on the DNA analysis of the Mungo skeleton. Finally, he added in the implications of the recent paper by Roberts *et al.* (of which he was a co-author) on the dating of megafaunal extinction in Australia. The proofs were sent off on 13 August. And now silence. Like many other colleagues and friends, I miss him terribly.

South and Southeast Asia

K. PADDAYYA AND PETER BELLWOOD

Reminiscing about his experiences in (undivided) India from 1944 to 1948 as the Director General of its Archaeological Survey, Sir Mortimer Wheeler wrote that 'In India it is possible to dig almost anywhere below a living level and to discover the vestiges of civilisation layer by layer. This is not of course true of a great many regions of the world' (Wheeler 1976, 66). One would presume that Wheeler, if an occasion ever arose, would have gladly expanded the geographical scope of the compliment he paid to the richness of India's archaeological record to cover other parts of South Asia and even Southeast Asia. This is one region in the Old World where not only the cultural heritage has a vast time-depth but also the images and concepts drawn from the past still pervade day-to-day life.

The aim of this paper is two-fold: a) to evaluate the results of archaeological research carried out so far in the two regions, and b) to identify the issues or themes that are likely to dominate the scene in the coming decades. This paper is a joint contribution by Paddayya and Bellwood but, in keeping with their respective areas of specialization, the work was shared between them as follows: Paddayya prepared the part dealing with South Asia, and the section on Southeast Asia was written by Bellwood. Arising from certain major differences between the archaeological records of the two regions and the research traditions developed for their study, the two sections have orientations of their own.

SOUTH ASIAN ARCHAEOLOGY: LOOKING AHEAD

Introduction

South Asia, comprising the sovereign states of India, Pakistan, Nepal, Bangladesh, Bhutan and the island nation of Sri Lanka, constitutes a subcontinent; it is neatly marked off from the main Asiatic land mass by the arc-shaped Himalayan massif in the north and by sea on the other sides (Fig. 1).

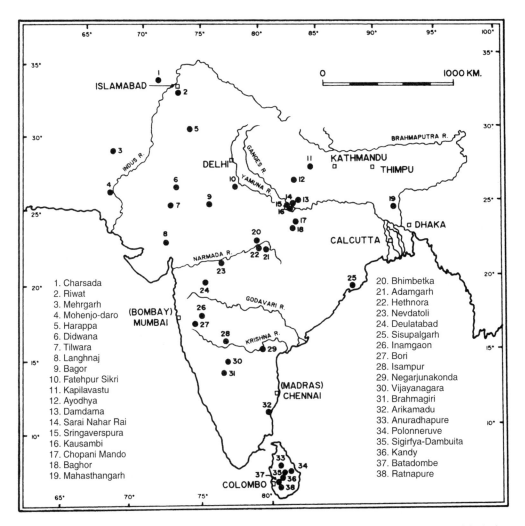

Figure 1. Map of South Asia showing important archaeological sites mentioned in the text. Modified after B. Allchin and F.R. Allchin (1997).

Within this larger geographical entity there is tremendous diversity: the high snow-clad Himalayan chain in the north; the Hindukush range in the north-west; the arid Thar desert in the west; the vast Indus and Gangetic alluvial plains in the north; the hill-tract of north-east India supporting a rich tropical rainforest ecosystem; and the triangular-shaped plateau of peninsular India drained by east- or west-flowing rivers and flanked on either side by narrow hill-chains running close to the seaboard. The central highlands, northern lowlands and southern rolling plains are the chief geographical units of Sri Lanka.

South Asia is an area of monsoonal climate. The peninsular block receives its precipitation from the south-west monsoon. The mountain tract in the north lies in the winter rainfall belt of the northern hemisphere; precipitation derives from winter storms and melt snows. The extreme southern part of the peninsula and Sri Lanka depend on the rainfall received from the north-east monsoon. Add to this geographical and climatic variability the all-too-obvious ethnic, religious and linguistic diversity, and the area then presents a challenging setting to students of past and present human adaptations.

In retrospect

Colonial contributions

The study of the antiquarian remains of South Asia forms part of the larger story of the development of oriental studies during the colonial period. The establishment of the Asiatic Society in Calcutta in 1784 by Sir William Jones (Fig. 2), a true product of the Age of Enlightenment, placed on an organized footing the individual antiquarian pursuits of European travellers and traders who had visited the South Asian lands during the previous three centuries (Kejariwal 1988). The next half-century witnessed significant developments in the study of ancient history, scripts, coins, classical languages and monuments of various parts of South Asia (for details, see Chakrabarti 1988; Wijesekera 1990).

Antiquarian studies took a more definite shape during the second half of the last century. The four really outstanding contributions included James Fergusson's prolonged study (1829 to 1847) of ancient Indian architecture; Meadows Taylor's discovery in the 1840s of megalithic monuments of the Iron Age in lower Deccan; Alexander Cunningham's unparalleled foot-survey (1862 to 1885) of the historical sites in the northern part of the subcontinent; and Robert Bruce Foote's discovery of prehistoric sites (1863 to 1890s) in the southern part of the peninsula. These laid firm foundations, respectively, for branches of study now called art-history, protohistory, historical archaeology and prehistory. Viewed in a larger context, these developments were a

Figure 2. Sir William Jones (1746–94), the founder of the Asiatic Society in Calcutta. After S. Roy (1961).

reflection of the important changes that were coming up in Victorian anthropology of the mid-nineteenth century — the initial lack of interest in the colonial peoples followed by the development of evangelical and administrative interests, which were finally replaced by an intellectual or scientific bent of mind (Stocking 1987).

John Marshall dominated South Asian archaeology in the first quarter of the twentieth century. The outstanding achievement of this period was the discovery of a Bronze
Age civilization in the Indus valley. Mortimer Wheeler's four-year tenure as the Director General of the Archaeological Survey of India was the last major episode of colonial
archaeology in South Asia. His most enduring contribution lay in the organization of
field schools in archaeology and the introduction of the concept of strategic planning
which he put into practice with remarkable results by his excavations at Arikamedu,
Brahmagiri and Harappa.

Post-colonial achievements

An eye-striking development of the last half-century concerns the formidable increase
in the number of institutions engaged in archaeological research (Chakrabarti 1989,
1–17). This is represented by the expansion of government departments in India,
Pakistan and Sri Lanka; the introduction of archaeology as a regular discipline in the universities, particularly in India and Sri Lanka; the emergence of archaeology as a multi-
disciplinary study thanks to the establishment of laboratories for archaeological
chemistry, archaeozoology, archaeobotany, palaeontology, sedimentology and geomorphology, and palaeoanthropology at the Deccan College, Pune and, to a lesser extent, in
Baroda University as well as the creation of dating facilities at the Physical Research
Laboratory in Ahmedabad and the Birbal Sahni Institute of Palaeobotany in Lucknow;
and collaboration with many foreign teams. The infrastructural expansion led to important developments at the substantive level. A large number of regional surveys and
excavations were initiated and these brought to light an immense body of fresh data.
Consequently South Asia emerged as an important centre for the study of ancient
human societies (for major syntheses, see Sankalia 1977a; Agrawal 1982; Thapar 1985;
Dani 1988; Mughal 1990; Deraniyagala 1992; Chakrabarti 1992, 1998; Allchin and
Allchin 1997).

In Stone Age prehistory the major developments included the reporting of stone
artefacts dated to two million years by palaeomagnetism from Riwat near Peshawar
(Dennell *et al.* 1988), which has served to refocus attention on South Asia as a possible
centre of the origins of Early Man; the recognition of an elaborate and well-dated
culture sequence (Lower Palaeolithic to Mesolithic) in the sand dune deposits near
Didwana in Rajasthan and its interpretation in terms of changes in climate and landscape (Misra 1995); the discovery of an Acheulean site at Bori in the Deccan dated to
670,000 years by the argon-argon method[1] (Mishra *et al.* 1995); the excavation of a major

---

[1] I would however like to draw the attention of readers to the controversy regarding the dating of the tephra
formation at Bori which has been correlated with the youngest Toba ash eruptions dated to about 74,000 years
(Shane *et al.* 1995).

Figure 3. View of the excavated area at the quarry-cum-workshop near Isampur, India, showing Acheulean cultural material resting on limestone surface. Ravi Dhamapurkar, Deccan College, Pune.

Acheulean quarry-cum-workshop at Isampur (Fig. 3) in the Deccan (Paddayya and Petraglia 1997; Petraglia *et al.* 1999); the recovery of a hominid cranium (an archaic form of *Homo sapiens*) from Hathnora on the Narmada river (Kennedy *et al.* 1991); the discovery of sites belonging to the Lower, Middle and Upper Palaeolithic and Mesolithic phases — a Stone Age culture sequence homotaxial with that of Europe — in diverse ecological settings and their dating by radiometric methods (Misra 1989; Mishra 1992);[2] the excavation of a probable late Upper Palaeolithic shrine at Baghor in central India connected with the worship of a mother goddess (Kenoyer *et al.* 1983); the discovery of a pebble tool tradition called the Ratnapura industry in Sri Lanka and the dating of cultural levels yielding geometric microliths at the Batadomba cave to 28,500 years BP (Deraniyagala 1990, 1992); the availability of excavated data from Langhnaj, Bagor,

[2] The time-ranges of the various cultural phases computed by the uranium-thorium series, thermoluminescence and radiocarbon methods are as follows: Lower Palaeolithic (400,000 yrs BP to 150,000 yrs BP); Middle Palaeolithic (150,000 yrs BP to 50,000 yrs BP); Upper Palaeolithic (40,000 yrs BP to 10,000 yrs BP); and Mesolithic (10,000 yrs BP to 5000 yrs BP).

Tilwara, Adamgarh and Bhimbetka in western and central India and from Sarai Nahar Rai, Damdama and Chopani Mando in the Ganga valley for reconstructing dwelling structures, burial practices, and subsistence and mobility strategies of the Mesolithic populations (Misra 1976; Pandey 1990); and the discovery of over 500 cave and rock-shelter sites, particularly in central India, yielding evidence of rock art dating from the terminal part of the Stone Age to the historical period (Neumayer 1993; Sharma and Tripathi 1996).

Coming to the protohistoric phase (from c.3000 BC to the middle of the first millennium BC) — an apt designation in the South Asian context not only because of the availability of some written materials like the (undeciphered) Indus script and the Vedic texts but also because of the continuity of many of the cultural traditions into the historical period, one must first refer to the prolonged excavations at Mehrgarh in Baluchistan, which take the beginnings of settled life based on agropastoral economy to

Figure 4. View of the Neolithic settlement at Mehrgarh, Pakistan, showing brick-built structures used for human occupation, storage and animal penning. After M. Lechevallier and G. Quivron (1981).

the seventh millennium BC (Fig. 4). Prior to 1947 the Indus Civilization was known only in its full-fledged urban form and was confined to the Indus basin proper. Subsequent research in India and Pakistan brought to light a staggering number of sites on both the western and eastern sides of the Indus, such that this culture is now said to occupy an area larger than those of its Egyptian and Mesopotamian counterparts (Lal 1997). These discoveries included many major excavations and provided a good understanding of the stages preceding and post-dating the urban phase. Over 1000 sites were discovered in the Indian territory east of the Indus river, stretching up to Jammu in the north, Delhi in the east and the river Godavari in the south. Prompted by a dense concentration of sites along the 'lost' Saraswati river (the present-day Ghaggar-Hakra channel in the Thar desert) referred to in the Vedic literature, some Indian archaeologists even rechristened this Bronze Age culture as the Saraswati Civilization.

A second major contribution made by post-colonial research to protohistoric studies was that other parts of the Indian subcontinent, far from entering what Wheeler called a Dark Age, witnessed the rise of a dozen or so village farming (Neolithic–Chalcolithic) cultures based on settled life, agropastoral economy, rich lithic and ceramic traditions, and chiefdom-based socio-political organization (Dhavalikar 1997). A considerable amount of literature came up suggesting archaeological correlates of the original Indo-Aryan-speaking people; interpretations refer to cultures ranging from the Mature/Late Harappan phase to the Painted Grey Ware and megalithic cultures (Allchin and Allchin 1989, 298–308; Dhavalikar 1997, 288–303).

As concerns the megalithic culture of the Iron Age which marks the terminal phase of the protohistoric period, a few dozen burial sites were excavated in peninsular India. This new work brought into focus significant regional variability in tomb types and also provided a fresh understanding of iron metallurgy, socio-economic organization and belief systems of the megalith-builders (Deo 1985; Moorti 1994). In Sri Lanka, too, several burial sites have been excavated in recent years (Seneviratne 1990, 1998).

The study of human skeletal data from the Mesolithic and protohistoric sites emerged as a distinct subfield. From what were initially attempts to designate 'racial' types, palaeoanthropology began to address various issues of human skeletal biology including palaeodemography (Kennedy 1980; Walimbe and Tavares 1995).

Historical archaeology (including the medieval period) also progressed to a considerable extent (Mehta 1979; Allchin 1995; Dhavalikar 1999). Sites like Sisupalgarh, Kausambi, Nagarjunakonda, Sringaverapura, Fatehpur Sikri, Daulatabad and Vijayanagara in India, Mahasthangarh in Bangladesh, Kapilavastu in Nepal, and Charsada, Butkara, Udegram, Nimogram and Chatpat in Pakistan were excavated on a large scale. In Sri Lanka under the Cultural Triangle Project (1980–90) intensive field studies were carried out at Anuradhapura, Sigiriya (Fig. 5), Polonnaruva and Kandy. Noteworthy is the settlement pattern study carried out in the Sigiriya-Dambulla region (Bandaranayake *et al.* 1990a). Marine (Rao 1988) and maritime archaeology also came into being during this period (Bhandaranayake *et al.* 1990b; Ray 1999). These are only a limited number of studies and there is tremendous potential for further work in this branch of archaeology. Some of the historians now freely admit that written sources are

Figure 5. View of part of a water-garden with fountains exposed at Sigiriya, Sri Lanka. After K. Dahanayake (1990).

practically exhausted for studying this period and that new insights will have to come from the spadework of the archaeologist.

Issues ahead

The foregoing review should not generate a feeling that all is well in South Asian archaeology and that nothing more needs to be done. In fact the discipline in this part of the world is yet to shed its innocence. The intense debates that were generated in Anglo-American archaeology during the last three decades have found but very negligible response on South Asian soil. Soul-searching and agenda-setting contributions such as the ones by Binford (1962, 1964), Clarke (1973) and Hodder (1982) are far from widely read. While it is true that a worker like Sankalia (1977b; see also Paddayya 1990, 1995) examined the relevance of the New Archaeology in the Indian context almost immediately after its genesis and even used some of the new ideas in his work, the general attitude towards theoretical and methodological debates is still one of indifference and sometimes even cynicism.

The central issue in South Asian archaeology, I believe, is not one of wholesale importation of any one paradigm or perspective from outside but one of recognizing the character of the specific problem or issue that one has before oneself and accordingly formulating one's research strategies to tackle it. In this connection it is good to know that culture history, New Archaeology and postprocessual archaeology are now seen as complementary and not mutually exclusive approaches (Hodder 1991).

Improvements in the conceptual framework

South Asian archaeology needs to overcome inadequate exposure to the theoretical underpinnings of the discipline. If concepts are accepted as building blocks of any scheme of knowledge, one cannot overemphasize the need to be clear about their meanings. In the South Asian case their usage ranges from the vague to the highly whimsical, reminding one of David Clarke's famous phrase 'undisciplined empirical discipline'. It is essential that workers have a clear understanding of the meanings of regular concepts like culture, adaptation and settlement system as well as those of higher order concepts like hypothesis, causality, generalization, explanation and theory. Postprocessual archaeology, apart from calling for changes in the meanings of some of the above concepts, has introduced into the discipline a whole group of new concepts ranging from text and context to mediation, agency and hermeneutic cycle. Archaeologists in South Asia should no longer feel shy of crossing disciplinary boundaries and equipping themselves with a basic understanding of the theory and method of science.

Culture history paradigm still?

In spite of the 200-year-old tradition of field studies and the large-scale expansion in more recent times in the agencies undertaking archaeological research, there are vast tracts of land in South Asia where archaeologists are yet to set their feet. If not every village, every district and every taluk in it has some archaeological sites or other, be they Stone Age lithic scatters, Buddhist stupas or medieval forts, which still lie unreported. What does one do in a situation like this? I think that the answer lies in redoubling the application of the culture history approach which in the early days of New Archaeology invited much derision. It is good to know that even the workers in the West have now begun to realize the strengths of this research orientation and the strong basis that it formed for the rise of New Archaeology and later trends. South Asian archaeologists are yet to exhaust the potential of this approach. As ready examples to illustrate this point of view, I will cite the discovery in recent years of Stone Age sites in many hitherto unexplored areas of the Indian mainland such as the west coast of India producing evidence of Palaeolithic and Mesolithic cultures (Guzder 1980; Rajendran 1989), the Late Palaeolithic assemblages of fossilwood from Lalmai in Bangladesh and from the adjoining Tripura state in north-east India (Ramesh 1986; Chakrabarti 1998) and the sub-Himalayan zone of Nepal containing sites ranging in age from the Palaeolithic to the Neolithic (Corvinus 1996). One could easily multiply examples from other areas and other cultural phases. Despite these new discoveries the South Asian landscape is dotted with a large number of areas which are still archaeologically *terra incognita*. Wheeler's concept of building up first of all regional time-tables of cultural development serves as a valid proposition for initiating work in such areas. Pending a sound understanding of the spatio-temporal and cultural dimensions of the archaeological record of these unexplored areas, our reconstruction of the ancient societies of South Asia will remain incomplete and tentative.

Need for culture process-oriented studies

I have mentioned before that Sankalia initiated in the mid-seventies the debate on the relevance of New Archaeology in the Indian context. No longer satisfied with the study of various Neolithic–Chalcolithic sites in terms of the grouping of ceramic and stone tool assemblages, he and his colleagues realized the need for horizontal excavations to identify the various other components of these cultures and their interrelationships. Sites like Inamgaon in the Deccan were excavated on a large scale and aspects like structures of various kinds, social organization and religious practices could be reconstructed (Dhavalikar *et al.* 1988). Archaeobotanical and archaeozoological studies revealed the agropastoral character of the economy (Kajale 1991; Thomas and Joglekar 1995). Temporal changes in the culture were sought to be explained in terms of decline in rainfall (Dhavalikar 1988). The lithic blade industry of Navdatoli in central India was studied from the point of view of its socio-economic significance (Sankalia 1967). In short, a culture process perspective was adopted in the study of this cultural phase. The use of this perspective in the case of Neolithic ashmounds of lower Deccan showed that, far from being just heaps of burnt cow-dung, these sites represent regular pastoral settlements adapted to a hilly landscape and consist of functionally differentiated areas (cattle penning and garbage dumping areas, settlement area, lithic workshop, animal butchering platform, etc.) (Allchin 1963; Paddayya 1998). A few other studies employing the settlement pattern perspective were carried out by younger workers, e.g. the work of Lal (1984) and Erdosy (1988) on the protohistoric and early historic phases of the upper Ganga basin and that of Shinde (1998) on the Chalcolithic phase in northern Deccan.

This process-oriented approach, based on intensive field surveys and ethnographic studies, was employed in Stone Age research too in central and southern India and the Deccan (Jacobson 1975; Murty 1981, 1985; Raju 1988; Pappu and Deo 1994). I made an attempt to study the Acheulean culture of the Hunsgi and Baichbal valleys in lower Deccan from a settlement system perspective (Paddayya 1982). The main observation emanating from this study is that the Acheulean groups of the two valleys adopted an annual resource management strategy consisting of wet season dispersal all over the valley and dry season aggregation near perennial water sources formed by spring flows. A seasonal mobility strategy was also suggested for the Mesolithic groups of the central Ganga valley (Sharma 1973). Deraniyagala (1992) made a comprehensive attempt to study the Sri Lankan Stone Age from an ecological perspective.

However studies of the type mentioned above are exceptions. Much of the work in South Asian prehistory and protohistory is still rooted in a space–time framework and Childean conception of culture. Archaeologists are yet to realize the implications of the wide geographical and climatic diversity that exists in South Asia, both at the macro and micro levels, for understanding variability in past human adaptations. They are still in a mindset where the Palaeolithic and Mesolithic cultural stages and the proto-historic culture complexes are seen as homogeneous, pan-regional entities. Very few attempts have been made to look at these cultural phases in terms of a series of sub-regional variants adapted to their respective ecological settings (Mohanty 1988; Selvakumar 1996; Cooper 1997). The differences in tool types and their proportions need to be evaluated as possible reflections of specific patterns of human adaptations, each geared to a set of terrain features and food, water and raw material resources. A critical factor like seasonality of climate and its implications for human adaptations deserves serious consideration. North-east India which has in recent years yielded pre-Neolithic cultural assemblages offers excellent scope for investigating diversity in human adaptations. Forming as it does a halfway house between the Indian mainland and Southeast Asia, this area probably enabled early societies to develop individual identities of their own. This emphasis on the study of sub-regional adaptations applies no less to the historical period. For example, in the case of Sri Lanka it has been rightly pointed out that the island, far from being a mere geographical and cultural appendage to the Indian mainland, was the scene of many innovative religious as well as art and architectural traditions.

I firmly believe that a set of conceptual and methodological strategies drawn from the basic tenets of New Archaeology alone can remedy this situation and help realize the goal of identifying intra-regional diversity in past human adaptations. These strate-gies include treating human cultures as functioning wholes and not merely as aggrega-tions of similar-looking artefactual assemblages; a shift of emphasis from locating secondary sites to identification of sites preserved in their original contexts; a lateral approach shifting the focus of field research from major rivers to interior areas; the selection of areas in terms of well-defined ecological zones in lieu of the earlier practice of using present-day administrative units; intensive regional surveys as against earlier 'hit and run' surveys; a shift of focus from big sites to an approach geared to the discovery of all possible types and sizes of sites; and the replacement of the simplistic ways of giving meaning to the archaeological record by formation processes research

(Paddayya 1987; Petraglia 1995; Jhaldiyal 1997). Also the role of natural sciences should be reoriented from the preparation of enumerative accounts to the recognition of man –environment relationships which form an integral part of process-oriented studies in archaeology (Paddayya 1995). These research strategies will surely elevate the study of South Asian archaeology to the intellectually more challenging level of explaining diversity in the behavioural patterns of ancient societies.

Wheeler's (1949) concept of strategic planning nearly fell on deaf ears in the post-independence period. There is a whole host of topics which could be meaningfully understood with reference to problem-oriented investigations, e.g. the origins of the Neolithic–Chalcolithic cultures; the transition between the Neolithic–Chalcolithic phase and the Iron Age; the relationships between village farming and hunting-gathering communities; settlement organization of the megalithic groups and possible survival of the megalithic traditions into the historical period; the re-emergence of urban life in the second half of the first millennium BC; and urban decline (Second Deurbanization?) in the late historical period (AD 400 to 1000).

Role of interpretive approaches

Some of the ideational approaches to the archaeological record being advocated by the postprocessualists were already being adopted in South Asia half a century earlier. I must make a specific reference here to the contributions made from the 1920s through to the 1940s by Ananda Coomaraswamy. Based upon his unparalleled knowledge of ancient Indian culture, religion, philosophy and literature, Coomaraswamy developed an interpretive framework which, while not denying the importance of 'more mechanical tasks of description', sought to lay bare the symbolic meanings of ancient Indian art and architectural forms. For example, he viewed the Indian temple not merely as a building giving shelter to the image and the worshipper but as the image of the cosmos itself representing the drama of disintegration and reintegration. Equally remarkable are Coomaraswamy's views about the Buddha image. Totally dismayed by the inability of European workers[3] to recognize the symbolism contained in it, he called for the role of empathy and contextual analysis. He wrote that 'In order to understand the nature of the Buddha image and its meaning for a Buddhist, we must, to begin with, reconstruct its environment, trace its ancestry and remodel our own personality. . . We are to see, not the likeness made by hands but its transcendental archetype; we are to take part in a communion . . . The image is one of Awakened' (Coomaraswamy 1986, 147–8).

---

[3] Ridiculing the Dhyani-Buddha figure from Indonesia, Sir George Birdwood, for example, in a lecture delivered in London in 1910 remarked that 'by its immemorial fixed pose, (it) is nothing more than an uninspired brazen image, vacuously squinting down its nose to its thumbs, knees and toes. A boiled suet pudding would serve equally well as a symbol of passionless purity and serenity of soul' (as quoted in Chandra 1983, 51–2).

Coomaraswamy's pioneering studies in South Asian art history were developed further by later workers. A recent study pointed out that the famous rock-cut Kailas temple in the Deccan is a symbolic expression of Advaita philosophy (Deshpande 1995). It is unfortunate that workers in South Asia failed to explore the relevance of these indigenous interpretive approaches to archaeology. One had to wait until the eighties for their reintroduction under the guise of postprocessual archaeology. Fritz's (1986) interpretation of the layout of the medieval city of Vijayanagara as evoking association with Ayodhya, the capital of epic king Rama, and Darsana's (1998) view treating the distribution of the Iron Age stone circles and dolmens in south India as markers of social division of the landscape are some examples.

South Asian archaeology, particularly protohistory and historical archaeology, has enormous benefits to derive from the application of the ideational orientations to the archaeological record. Perspectives like Tilley's (1994) phenomenological approach giving meaning to various components of the landscape and Julian Thomas's (1996) Heideggerian archaeology investigating how meanings, far from being fixed in things and places, are generated continuously in networks of human relationships sound very promising. There are many aspects of the Neolithic–Chalcolithic and Iron Age megalithic phases, be they lithic or ceramic records, human or animal burials and structural features including garbage disposals, which are fit topics for employing these approaches. Correspondingly, ethnoarchaeological research in India will have to rise above the level of descriptive studies of hunting-gathering technologies, ceramic traditions and wild plant and animal foods to encompass even the worldviews of human groups and how they give meaning to the human and physical landscapes in which they are placed (Miller 1985; Sinopoli 1991). The oral traditions preserved in the existing simple societies could serve as good starting points, e.g. Allchin's (1963) work on the place-names and folk religious traditions of southern Deccan and their relevance for reconstructing the Neolithic pastoral practices of the area; and the work of Murty and Sontheimer (1980) on the genesis of sheep–goat pastoralism in the same region.

South Asia has an ancient thought of its own; the Hindu, Buddhist and Jain epistemological traditions do provide clues for an indigenous conception of the scientific method (Datta 1967). The Hindu tradition recognizes several sources of knowledge: perception, inference, authority, knowledge based on similarity, postulation, noncognition, intuitive knowledge and unbroken tradition. According to the *Nyayasutra* of Gautama (suggested age ranging from fourth century BC to fourth century AD), doubt (*samasya*) is the chief incentive to inquiry. He then prescribes an elaborate process for arriving at a theory (*vada*) which will remove doubt. The relevance of these notions to empirical research is worth exploring.

Ancient Indian hermeneutics is another potential source of ideas. It has been used for interpreting the meanings of texts ranging from the Vedic literature to the writings of medieval saints (Sundara Rajan 1991; Arapura 1986). Interpretation, known as *tika* (elucidation) and *bhasya* (commentary), was used for this purpose (Kapoor 1991). Indigenous notions of concepts like time, space and causality are also worth exploring. Of particular interest is the Buddhist theory of causation known as *paticca samuppada* or dependent coarising. It clearly anticipates the basic principles of general systems theory (Macey 1992). One needs to explore the usefulness of this concept for dealing with complex archaeological issues like the origins, functioning and end of cultures.

Critical historiography of archaeology

Developments like Kuhn's (1962) radical reformulation of the history of science and Said's (1978) serious indictment of western scholarship have given rise to a critical historiography of oriental studies. I would propose the following topics in South Asian archaeology as components of this critical trend.

Contrary to the long-held views about the ahistorical attitude of Indians, it is now clear that ancient India had its own historical trend called the *itihasa-purana* tradition stretching back to Vedic times (Thapar 1991, 1992). It underwent elaboration from time to time, emerging as a full-fledged secular tradition by the tenth to twelfth centuries AD, as exemplified by the text *Rajatarangini* of Kalhana which is not merely a history of Kashmir but also comments on the method and purpose of history.

Was there also an indigenous antiquarian tradition? In South Asia too there are several instances of what Bradley and Williams (1998) have recently designated as 'The Past in the Past'. Artists of the Gupta period (fourth to sixth centuries AD) deriving inspiration from the art work of the Mauryan rulers, excavation done by the Sri Lankan king Parakramabahu IV (fifteenth century AD) at Sigiriya for checking measurements; Firuz Shah Tughlak's (fourteenth century AD) keen interest in the stone pillars from Meerut and Ambala bearing Asoka's royal edicts and their eventual transportation to Delhi are some instances that should serve to underscore the need for more comprehensive studies on this interesting topic. Based on a large number of instances drawn from ancient texts and epigraphical records of India, Nagaraja Rao (in press) has argued that structural conservation of monuments and repairs to mutilated sculptures (this practice was known as *jirnoddhara* or *navikarana*) were being undertaken since early times and continued until the nineteenth century.

Said's views treating orientalism as colonial discourse have already led to a considerable amount of discussion aimed at a critical evaluation of the motives and interests underlying oriental scholarship (for a recent critique of Said's views, see Trautmann 1997, 19–25). Chakravarti's book *Colonial Indology* (1997) is one of the most recent shots fired in this direction. There is no doubt that this hypercritical trend should continue but one would of course not go to the extent of throwing away the baby with the bathwater. This hypercritical trend notwithstanding, foreign collaborations should be encouraged, while ensuring that theoretical and method-ological overkills common in the West are not repeated on South Asian soil. More-over, as warned by Bandaranayake (Mydral-Runebjar 1990, 39) 'such interchange should not become a back door to enter a field that cannot be entered by the front door'.

There is tremendous scope for continuing historiographical research at the descrip-tive level. The contributions of the erstwhile princely states in India as well as those made by a number of lesser known European workers like Colin Mackenzie and Meadows Taylor and the impact of rediscovery of the South Asian past on the nationalist move-ment at the national and regional levels are fit topics for research (Kopf 1969).

Apart from experiencing major stirrings in its epistemological realm, the discipline of archaeology has in recent times also witnessed a seesaw change in its sociological dimension. Tilley (1989) captured this change very well when he called archaeology as socio-political action in the present. The time has arrived for South Asian archaeology to give up its ivory-tower stance. In my view there are two aspects which need imme-diate attention.

Heritage management

Heritage management is one topic which hardly excites interest among the work-ers. The number of publications on this topic could literally be counted on one's fingers (Allchin *et al.* 1989; Thapar 1992; Deshpande 1997). It is true that over the last 100 years the governments in India and Sri Lanka have framed legislative measures for protecting monuments. Major rescue excavations like the one at Nagarjunakonda were undertaken. In recent times other developments have taken place like the creation of the Indian National Trust for Cultural Heritage and the Heritage Society and the placement of major sites on the World Heritage List. But the realization is yet to come that the scope of archaeological heritage in South Asia is tremendously vast. The landscape is strewn with literally hundreds of sites of lesser visibility but of no mean cultural significance — be they Acheulean lithic scatters, Neolithic mounds, megalithic burials or small isolated historical temples and forts. This small site record has come under serious threat due to various developmental activities such as reclamation of virgin lands for agriculture, creation of major and minor irrigation projects, proliferation of industrial projects, and hous-ing and roadway projects (Paddayya 1996). There is an urgent need to enact Cul-tural Resource Management legislation so that the agencies responsible for land development are obliged to have all archaeological sites investigated and recorded before they are erased out of existence. Also heritage protection could be made an aspect of the larger movement of environment conservation.

Misuse of the past in the present

The second and equally disturbing trend pertains to the use of the past for present partisan (religious or political) ends. The pulling down of the mosque at Ayodhya by the Hindu groups and the LTTE bombing of the temple at Kandy enshrining the tooth-relic of the Buddha are well-known examples. The Ayodhya incident clouded a major event in the discipline like the World Archaeological Congress III held in New Delhi in 1994. Rivalry among the various political and ethnic groups has now become so intense that they have also begun using ideas and images from the past to influence public opinion (Rao 1994). Naming a political party after an ancient ruler or after a particular language or culture and, still worse, displaying cut-outs showing politicians in their former cinema roles playing heroes from ancient Indian mythology are some of these vulgar uses of the past. Another disturbing trend that has surfaced is the use of academic positions to mediate situations of power.

Archaeology and public education

The situation is not beyond redemption. Educating the public about the past is of the utmost importance both for highlighting the need for heritage preservation and for enabling society to form a balanced perception of the past which, to use Lowenthal's (1985) phrase, by and large still remains as 'a Foreign Country'. In the past a worker like Sankalia, apart from carrying out horizontal excavations and examining the relevance of newly developed research perspectives to South Asian archaeology, made a multi-sided attempt to bring archaeology to the masses. He wrote popular books and published extensively in English and vernacular languages about various discoveries. He held exhibitions, gave lectures even in schools and threw open to the public the museum he had created at the Deccan College in Pune. It is sad that most of the workers now are unwilling to go beyond their individual research projects.

The role of archaeology in public education should first and foremost be aimed at inculcating in the ordinary citizen a perception that would both allow him to appreciate the unity of human culture underlying its spatio-temporal diversity and also create in him a feeling that the past is a common legacy and that it is sacred and stands above use for subserving narrow ethnic, religious and political purposes. The Nobel Laureate Amartya Sen (1996) put the case very well when he wrote that the Indians need to adopt a critical openness of mind towards the pluralistic past and present of the land and their place in the global context. Quoting Rabindranath Tagore, he warned that we should avoid the situation of being haunted by the ghost of the past.

There are positive indications that efforts to educate the public about the past will have a high degree of success. Both government and privately owned mass media (print as well as electronic) are playing a laudable role in taking knowledge of the past

to society at large. By regularly announcing archaeological discoveries, publishing feature articles and by running TV serials on various themes drawn from the past including the epics *Ramayana* and *Mahabharata*, these media have succeeded in creating in the
public a positive attitude towards their heritage. How else could one understand hap-
penings like a senior advocate moving the Supreme Court about the neglect of Moghul
monuments in Delhi or a resident of the hill-station of Mahabaleshwar in the Deccan
sending an agitated letter to a newspaper decrying the decision of the municipality to
raise a public building on a plot housing a British period cemetery?

It is a happy development that this interest in and concern for the cultural heritage is spreading very fast even into the remote countryside. Poverty and mass illit-
eracy notwithstanding, people have started developing strong emotional bonds with
the past including the remote Stone Age. As realized by C.J. Thomsen in the last century, the visual character of the archaeological record, as against the written documents forming the source material of history, can be a great asset in public
education. Also helpful is the fact that respect for the past is part of the South Asian
ethos; so is the Indian conception of time providing for a long period of human history. I have the memorable experience of being requested by the village council of
Hunsgi in the Deccan region, where I have been working for the last 30 years, to
organize from the funds drawn from their meagre annual budget a permanent display of local heritage material stretching from the Lower Palaeolithic to the British
period. This display has become very popular and there are proposals from other
places to put up similar displays. Instances like these also serve to highlight the
importance of spreading the museum movement.

I would like to conclude by observing that the study of the past in South Asia cannot just be a matter of intellectual or romantic adventure. The matter is certainly not like
saying with Edmund Hillary that 'I climbed Mount Everest, because it is there.' The
study of the past has the greatest social relevance. Pandit Nehru (1960, 22) put the matter in his inimitable style and wrote that : 'The past oppresses me or fills me sometimes
with its warmth when it touches on the present, and becomes, as it were, an aspect of
that living present. If it does not do so, then it is cold, barren, lifeless, uninteresting.' In
a similar vein Amartya Sen argues that, over and above economic growth, development
has a more foundational aspect which is connected with the enhancement of the quality of life and 'the expansion of capability of people to do the things that they have reason to value and choose' (Sen 1997). A sensible approach to the study of the past and its
pragmatic use in the present would be important components of Sen's broad-spectrum
approach to the human science of development and serve as the anchor-ground for the
attainment of *Ramarajya* (a state of righteousness and well-being of all), as envisioned
by M.K. Gandhi. The renowned historian R.G. Collingwood talked of history as providing self-knowledge to man. Kalhana, the great chronicler of Kashmir, gave expression to this notion of self-knowledge very well when he said that 'This saga which is

properly made should be useful for (a) king as a stimulant or as a sedative, like a psychic, according to time and place' (Majumdar 1961, 21). Even after 800 years Kalhana's message has not lost its value and will guide the South Asian peoples into the next millennium.

Acknowledgements

I am grateful to Professor M.K. Dhavalikar for going through the manuscript and offering helpful comments. I deeply appreciate the editorial assistance rendered by Dr. Richa Jhaldiyal. I also thank Mr. D.D. Phule for preparing the map of South Asia and Mr. S.I. Amin for typing the manuscript.

References

AGRAWAL, D.P. 1982: *Archaeology of India* (London).

ALLCHIN, B. and ALLCHIN, F.R. 1989: *The Rise of Civilisation in India and Pakistan* (New Delhi).

ALLCHIN, B. and ALLCHIN, F.R. 1997: *Origins of a Civilization: the Prehistory and Early Archaeology of South Asia* (New Delhi).

ALLCHIN, B., ALLCHIN, F.R. and THAPAR, B.K. (eds.) 1989: *Conservation of the Indian Heritage* (New Delhi).

ALLCHIN, F.R. 1963: *Neolithic Cattle-Keepers of South India: a Study of the Deccan Ashmounds* (Cambridge).

ALLCHIN, F.R. 1995: *The Archaeology of Early Historic South Asia: the Emergence of Cities and States* (Cambridge).

ARAPURA, J.G. 1986: *Hermeneutical Essays on Vedantic Topics* (Delhi).

BHANDARANAYAKE, S., MOGREN, M. and SENEVIRATNE, E. (eds.) 1990a: *The Settlement Archaeology of the Sigiriya-Dambulla Region* (Colombo, Postgraduate Institute of Archaeology).

BHANDARANAYAKE, S., DEWARAJA, L., SILVA, R. and WIMALARATNE, K.D.G. 1990b: *Sri Lanka and the Silk Road of the Sea* (Colombo, The Sri Lanka National Commission for UNESCO and The Central Cultural Fund).

BINFORD, L.R. 1962: Archaeology as anthropology. *American Antiquity* 28, 217–25.

BINFORD, L.R. 1964: A consideration of archaeological research design. *American Antiquity* 29, 425–41.

BRADLEY, R. and WILLIAMS, H. (eds.) 1998: *The Past in the Past: the Reuse of Ancient Monuments* (=*World Archaeology* Vol. 30, No. 1) (London).

CHAKRABARTI, D.K. 1988: *A History of Indian Archaeology from the Beginning to 1947* (New Delhi).

CHAKRABARTI, D.K. 1989: *Theoretical Issues in Indian Archaeology* (New Delhi).

CHAKRABARTI, D.K. 1992: *Ancient Bangladesh* (New Delhi).

CHAKRABARTI, D.K. 1997: *Colonial Indology: Sociopolitics of the Ancient Indian Past* (Delhi).

CHAKRABARTI, D.K. 1998: *The Issues in East Indian Archaeology* (New Delhi).

CHANDRA, P. 1983: *On the Study of Indian Art* (Cambridge, MA).

CLARKE, D.L. 1973: Archaeology: the loss of innocence. *Antiquity* 47, 6–18.

COOMARASWAMY, A.K. 1986: The nature of Buddhist art. In Lipsey, R. (ed.), *Coomaraswamy 1: Selected Papers (Traditional Art and Symbolism)* (Delhi) (Originally published in 1938), 147–78.

COOPER, Z. 1997: *Prehistory of the Chitrakot Falls, Central India* (Pune).

CORVINUS, G. 1996: The prehistory of Nepal after 10 years of research. *Bull. Indo-Pacific Prehistory Assoc.* 14, 43–55.

DAHANAYAKE, K. 1990: Some geological aspects of the Sigiriya fortress (5th century A.D.), Sri Lanka. In Seneviratne, S. *et al.* (eds.), *Perspectives in Archaeology* (Peradeniya, University of Peradeniya), 107–10.

DANI, A.H. 1988: *Recent Archaeological Discoveries in Pakistan* (Tokyo, UNESCO and Centre for East Asian Studies).

DARSANA, S.B. 1998: Megaliths in the Upper Palar Basin, Tamil Nadu — a new perspective. *Man and Environment* 23(2), 51–64.

DATTA, D.M. 1967: Epistemological methods in Indian philosophy. In Moore, C.A. (ed.), *Indian Mind: Essentials of Indian Philosophy and Culture* (Honolulu), 118–35.

DENNELL, R.W., RENDELL, H. and HAILWOOD, E. 1988: Early tool-making in Asia: two-million year-old artefacts in Pakistan. *Antiquity* 62, 98–106.

DEO, S.B. 1985: The megaliths: their culture, ecology, economy and technology. In Deo, S.B. and Paddayya, K. (eds.), *Recent Advances in Indian Archaeology* (Pune, Deccan College), 89–99.

DERANIYAGALA, S.U. 1990: The prehistoric chronology of Sri Lanka. In Seneviratne, S. *et al.* (eds.), *Perspectives in Archaeology* (Peradeniya, University of Peradeniya).

DERANIYAGALA, S.U. 1992: *The Prehistory of Sri Lanka: an Ecological Perspective* (Parts 1 and 2) (Colombo, Archaeological Survey of Sri Lanka).

DESHPANDE, M.N. 1995: Influence of the philosophy of Sankaracharya on Hindu temple architecture and symbolism. *Man and Environment* 20(2), 21–8.

DESHPANDE, M.N. 1997: *First Convocation Address* (Pune, Deccan College).

DHAVALIKAR, M.K. 1988: *First Farmers of the Deccan* (Pune).

DHAVALIKAR, M.K. 1997: *Indian Protohistory* (New Delhi).

DHAVALIKAR, M.K. 1999: *Historical Archaeology of India* (New Delhi).

DHAVALIKAR, M.K., SANKALIA, H.D. and ANSARI, Z.D. (eds.) 1988: *Excavations at Inamgaon* (Vol. I, Parts 1 and 2) (Pune, Deccan College).

ERDOSY, G. 1988: *Urbanisation in Early Historic India* (Oxford, BAR Int. Ser.).

FRITZ, J.M. 1986: Vijayanagara: authority and meaning of a South Indian imperial capital. *American Anthropologist* 88, 44–55.

GUZDER, S. 1980: *Quaternary Environment and Stone Age Cultures of the Konkan, Coastal Maharashtra* (Pune, Deccan College).

HODDER, I. 1982: Theoretical archaeology: a reactionary view. In Hodder, I. (ed.), *Symbolic and Structural Archaeology* (Cambridge), 1–16.

HODDER, I. 1991: Archaeological theory in contemporary European societies: the emergence of competing traditions. In Hodder, I. (ed.), *Archaeological Theory in Europe: the Last Three Decades* (London), 1–24.

JACOBSON, J. 1975: Early Stone Age habitation sites in eastern Malwa. *Proc. American Phil. Soc.* 119, 280–97.

JHALDIYAL, R. 1997: *Formation Processes of the Prehistoric Sites in the Hunsgi-Baichbal Basins, Gulbarga District, Karnataka* (Unpublished Ph.D. thesis, University of Pune).

KAJALE, M.D. 1991: Current status of Indian palaeoethnobotany: introduced and indigenous food-plants with a discussion of the historical and evolutionary development of Indian agriculture and agricultural systems in general. In Renfrew, J. (ed.), *New Light on Early Farming: Recent Developments in Palaeoethnobotany* (Edinburgh), 155–89.

KAPOOR, K. 1991: Some reflections on the interpretation of texts in the Indian tradition. In Gill, H.S. (ed.), *Structures of Signification*, Vol. 1 (New Delhi), 208–71.

KEJARIWAL, O.P. 1988: *The Asiatic Society of Bengal and the Discovery of India's Past 1784–1838* (Delhi).

KENNEDY, K.A.R. 1980: Prehistoric skeletal record of man in South Asia. *Annual Rev. Anthropol.* 9, 391–432.

KENNEDY, K.A.R., SONAKIA, A., CLEMENT, J. and VERMA, K.K. 1991: Is the Narmada hominid an Indian *Homo erectus*? *American J. Physical Anthropol.* 86, 475–96.

KENOYER, J.M., CLARK, J.D., PAL, J.N. and SHARMA, G.R. 1983: An Upper Palaeolithic shrine in India? *Antiquity* 58, 88–94.

KOPF, D. 1969: *British Orientalism: Bengal Renaissance* (Berkeley, CA).

KUHN, T.S. 1962: *The Structure of Scientific Revolutions* (Chicago).

LAL, B.B. 1997: *The Earliest Civilisation of South Asia — Rise, Maturity and Decline* (New Delhi).

LAL, M. 1984: *Settlement History and the Rise of Civilization in the Ganga-Yamuna Doab* (Delhi).

LECHEVALLIER, M. and QUIVRON, G. 1981: The Neolithic in Baluchistan: new evidence from Mehrgarh. In Härtel, H. (ed.), *South Asian Archaeology 1979* (Berlin), 71–92.

LOWENTHAL, D. 1985: *The Past is a Foreign Country* (Cambridge).

MACEY, J. 1992: *Mutual Causality in Buddhism and General Systems Theory: the Dharma of Natural Systems* (Albany, NY).

MAJUMDAR, R.C. 1961: Ideas of history in Sanskrit literature. In Philips, C.H. (ed.), *Historians of India, Pakistan and Ceylon* (London), 13–28.

MEHTA, R.N. 1979: *Medieval Archaeology* (Delhi).

MILLER, D. 1985: *Artefacts as Categories* (Cambridge).

MISHRA, S. 1992: The age of the Acheulian in India. *Current Anthropol.* 33, 325–8.

MISHRA, S. 1995: Chronology of the Indian Stone Age: the impact of recent absolute and relative dating attempts. *Man and Environment* 20(2), 11–16.

MISHRA, S., VENKATESAN, T.R., RAJAGURU, S.N. and SOMAYAJULU, B.L.K. 1995: Earliest Acheulian industry from peninsular India. *Current Anthropol.* 36, 847–51.

MISRA, V.N. 1976: Ecological adaptations during the terminal Stone Age in western and central India. In Kennedy, K.A.R. and Possehl, G.L. (eds.), *Ecological Background of South Asian Prehistory* (Ithaca, Cornell University), 28–51.

MISRA, V.N. 1989: Stone Age India: an ecological perspective. *Man and Environment* 14, 18–64.

MISRA, V.N. 1995: Geoarchaeology of the Thar desert, northwest India. In Wadia, S., Korisettar, R. and Kale, V.S. (eds.), *Quaternary Environments and Geoarchaeology of India* (Bangalore, Geological Society of India), 210–30.

MOHANTY, P. 1988: Five seasons of explorations in Keonjhar district, Orissa. *Bull. Indo-Pacific Prehistory Assoc.* 7, 47–53.

MOORTI, U.S. 1994: *Megalithic Culture of South India: Socio-Economic Perspectives* (Varanasi).

MUGHAL, M.R. 1990: Archaeological field research in Pakistan since independence: an overview. *Bull. Deccan College Res. Inst.* 49, 261–78.

MURTY, M.L.K. 1981: Hunter-gatherer ecosystems and archaeological patterns of subsistence behaviour on the southeast coast of India: an ethnographic model. *World Archaeol.* 12, 47–58.

MURTY, M.L.K. 1985: Ethnoarchaeology of the Kurnool cave areas. *World Archaeol.* 17, 192–205.

MURTY, M.L.K. and SONTHEIMER, G.D. 1980: Prehistoric background to pastoralism in the southern Deccan in the light of oral traditions and cults of some pastoral communities. *Anthropos* 75, 163–84.

MYRDAL-RUNEBJAR, E. 1990: *Archaeo Lanka* (Sweden, Riksantikvarieamtet).

NAGARAJA RAO, M.S. in press: The concept of Jirnoddhara. *Bull. Deccan College Res. Inst.* 60.

NEHRU, J. 1960: *The Discovery of India* (London).

NEUMAYER, E. 1993: *Lines on Stones: The Prehistoric Rock Art in India* (New Delhi).

PADDAYYA, K. 1982: *The Acheulian Culture of the Hunsgi Valley (Peninsular India): a Settlement System Perspective* (Pune, Deccan College).

PADDAYYA, K. 1987: The place of the study of site formation processes in prehistoric research in India. In Nash, D.T. and Petraglia, M.D. (eds.), *Natural Formation Processes and the Archaeological Record* (Oxford, BAR Int. Ser. 352), 74–85.

PADDAYYA, K. 1990: *The New Archaeology and Aftermath: a View from Outside the Anglo-American World* (Pune).

PADDAYYA, K. 1994: Investigation of man-environment relationships in Indian archaeology: some theoretical considerations. *Man and Environment* 19, 1–28.

PADDAYYA, K. 1995: Theoretical perspectives in Indian archaeology: an historical review. In Ucko, P. (ed.), *Theory in Archaeology: a World Perspective* (London), 110–49.

PADDAYYA, K. 1996: Modern impacts on archaeological sites in India: a case study from the Shorapur Doab, Karnataka. *Man and Environment* 21(2), 75–88.

PADDAYYA, K. 1998: Evidence of Neolithic cattle-penning at Budihal, Gulbarga district, Karnataka. *South Asian Studies* 14, 141–53.

PADDAYYA, K. and PETRAGLIA, M.D. 1997: Isampur: an Acheulian workshop site in the Hunsgi Valley, Gulbarga district, Karnataka. *Man and Environment* 22(2), 95–100.

PANDEY, J.N. 1990: Mesolithic in the middle Ganga valley. *Bull. Deccan College Res. Inst.* 49, 311–16.

PAPPU, R.S. and DEO, S. 1994: *Man-Land Relationships During Palaeolithic Times in the Kaladgi Basin* (Pune, Deccan College).

PETRAGLIA, M.D. 1995: Site formation research in India. In Wadia, S., Korisettar, R. and Kale, V.S. (eds.), *Quaternary Environments and Geoarchaeology of India* (Bangalore, Geological Society of India), 446–65.

PETRAGLIA, M.D., LAPORTA, P. and PADDAYYA, K. 1999: The First Acheulian quarry in India: stone tool manufacture, biface morphology and behaviours. *J. Anthropol. Res.* 55, 39–70.

RAJENDRAN, P. 1989: *The Prehistoric Cultures and Environment of Kerala* (New Delhi).

RAJU, D.R. 1988: *Stone Age Hunter-Gatherers: an Ethnoarchaeology of Cuddapah Region, South-East India* (Pune).

RAMESH, N.R. 1986: Discovery of Stone Age tools from Tripura and its relevance to the prehistory of southeast Asia. *Bull. Geol. Soc. Malaysia* 20, 289–310.

RAO, N. 1994: Interpreting silences: symbol and history in the case of Ram Janamabhoomi Babari Masjid. In Bond, G.C. and Gilliam, A. (eds.), *Social Construction of the Past: Representation as Power* (London), 154–64.

RAO, S.R. (ed.) 1988: *Progress and Prospect of Marine Archaeology in India, Goa: First Indian Conference on Marine Archaeology of Indian Ocean Countries* (Goa, National Institute of Oceanography).

RAY, H.P. (ed.) 1999: *Archaeology of Seafaring: the Indian Ocean in the Ancient Period* (Delhi).

ROY, S. 1961: *The Story of Indian Archaeology 1784–1947* (New Delhi, Archaeological Survey of India).

SAID, E.W. 1978: *Orientalism* (New York).

SANKALIA, H.D. 1967: The socio-economic significance of the lithic blade industry of Navdatoli, Madhya Pradesh, India. *Current Anthropol.* 8, 262–8.

SANKALIA, H.D. 1977a: *Prehistory of India* (New Delhi).

SANKALIA, H.D. 1977b: *New Archaeology: its Scope and Application to India* (Lucknow, Ethnographic and Folk Culture Society).

SELVAKUMAR, V. 1996: Archaeological investigations in the upper Gundar basin, Madurai district, Tamil Nadu. *Man and Environment* 21(2), 27–42.

SEN, A. 1996: *On Interpreting India's Past* (Calcutta, Asiatic Society).

SEN, A. 1997: *Development Thinking at the Beginning of the 21st Century* (London, London School of Economics).

SENEVIRATNE, S. 1990: A life after death: continuity and change in the religious symbolism of the Iron Age. In Seneviratne, S. *et al.* (eds.), *Perspectives in Archaeology* (Peradeniya, University of Peradeniya), 145–52.

SENEVIRATNE, S. 1998: Looking for lineage ancestors: the archaeology of early Iron Age megaliths in Sri Lanka. *Annual Meeting of the Archaeological Institute of America* (Washington, D.C.), 1–6.

SHANE, P., WESTGATE, J., WILLIAMS, M. and KORISETTAR, R. 1995: New geochemical evidence for the youngest Toba tuff in India. *Quat. Res.* 44, 200–4.

SHARMA, G.R. 1973: Mesolithic culture in the Ganga Valley. *Proc. Prehist. Soc.* 39, 129–46.

SHARMA, R.K. and TRIPATHI, K.K. (eds.) 1996: *Recent Perspectives on Prehistoric Art in India and Allied Subjects: Essays in the Honor of S.K. Pandey* (New Delhi).

SHINDE, V.S. 1998: *Early Settlements in the Central Tapi Basin* (New Delhi).

SINOPOLI, C.M. 1991: Seeking the past through the present: recent ethnoarchaeological research in South Asia. *Asian Perspectives* 20, 177–92.

STOCKING, G.W., Jr. 1987: *Victorian Anthropology* (New York).

SUNDARA RAJAN, R. 1991: *Studies in Phenomenology, Hermeneutics and Deconstruction* (New Delhi, Indian Council of Philosophical Research).

THAPAR, B.K. 1985: *Recent Archaeological Discoveries in India* (Tokyo, UNESCO and Centre for East Asian Studies).

THAPAR, B.K. 1992: *Our Cultural Heritage: Reappraisal of the Existing Legislation and Role of INTACH and its Preservation* (New Delhi, The Indian National Trust for Arts and Cultural Heritage).

THAPAR, R. 1991: Genealogical patterns as perceptions of the past. *Studies in History* 7, 1–36.

THAPAR, R. 1992: *Interpreting Early India* (Delhi).

THOMAS, J. 1996: *Time, Culture and Identity: an Interpretive Archaeology* (London).

THOMAS, P.K. and JOGLEKAR, P.P. 1995: Faunal studies in archaeology. In Wadia, S., Korisettar, R. and Kale, V.S. (eds.), *Quaternary Environments and Geoarchaeology of India* (Bangalore, Geological Society of India), 496–514.

TILLEY, C. 1989: Archaeology as socio-political action in the present. In Pinsky, V. and Wylie, A. (eds.), *Critical Traditions in Contemporary Archaeology: Essays in the Philosophy, History and Socio-Politics of Archaeology* (Cambridge), 104–16.

TILLEY, C. 1994: *A Phenomenology of Landscape: Places, Paths and Monuments* (Oxford).

TRAUTMANN, T.R. 1997: *Aryans and British India* (New Delhi).

WALIMBE, S.R. and TAVARES, A. 1995: Evolving trends in skeletal biology in the Indian sub-continent: a case study on the incipient agricultural populations of the Deccan plateau. In Wadia, S., Korisettar, R. and Kale, V.S. (eds.), *Quaternary Environments and Geoarchaeology of India* (Bangalore, Geological Society of India), 515–29.

WHEELER, R.E.M. 1949: Archaeological fieldwork in India: planning ahead. *Ancient India* 5, 4–11.

WHEELER, R.E.M. 1976: *My Archaeological Mission to India and Pakistan* (London).

WIJESEKERA, N. (ed.) 1990: *History of the Department of Archaeology* (Colombo, Archaeological Survey of Sri Lanka).

Additional bibliographic notes

There are three national level societies in India, promoting the interests of South Asian archaeology. These are: the Indian Archaeological Society (New Delhi), the Indian Society for Prehistoric and Quaternary Studies (Pune) and the Association for the Study of History and Archaeology (New Delhi). As part of their activities these Societies hold annual conferences. The former two societies also regularly bring out journals called *Puratattva* and *Man and Environment*, respectively. Other periodicals exclusively devoted to archaeology include *Ancient Pakistan* (Peshawar), *Pakistan Archaeology* (Karachi), *Ancient India* (New Delhi), *Indian Archaeology — A Review* (New Delhi), *Ancient Nepal* (Kathmandu) and *Ancient Ceylon* (Colombo). *Journal of the Asiatic Society of Bengal* (Calcutta), *Journal of Indian History* (Trivandrum), *Studies in History* (New Delhi), *Indian Historical Review* (New Delhi), *Man in India* (Ranchi), *Eastern Anthropologist* (Lucknow), *Indica* (Bombay), *Bulletin of the Deccan College Research Institute* (Pune), and *Bharati* (Varanasi) are some other periodicals which also regularly publish papers devoted to archaeology. The European Association of South Asian Archaeologists (Cambridge) and the Indo-Pacific Prehistory Association (Canberra) are two outside organizations looking after the interests of South Asian archaeology. These two societies hold biennial conferences and publish their proceedings; they also publish annual periodicals entitled *South Asian Studies* and *Bulletin of the Indo-Pacific Prehistory Association*, respectively. Over and above the works of synthesis already cited in the references, other major publications include Misra, V.N. and Mate, M.S. (eds.), *Indian Prehistory 1964* (Pune, Deccan College, 1965); Sankalia, H.D., *Prehistory and Protohistory of India and Pakistan* (Pune, Deccan College, 1974); Agrawal, D.P. and Chakrabarti, D.K., *Essays in Indian Protohistory* (Delhi, 1979); Misra, V.N. and Bellwood, P. (eds.), *Recent Advances in Indo-Pacific Prehistory* (New Delhi, Oxford and IBH, 1985); Possehl, G.L. (ed.), *Harappan Civilization* (New Delhi, Oxford and IBH, 1982); Possehl, G.L. (ed.), *South Asian Archaeology Studies* (New Delhi, Oxford and IBH, 1992); and Ghosh, A. (ed.), *An Encyclopaedia of Indian Archaeology, Vol. 1 (Subjects) and Vol. 2 (Gazetteers)* (New Delhi, 1989).

SOUTHEAST ASIAN PREHISTORY AND ARCHAEOLOGY AT THE TURN OF THE MILLENNIUM

Introduction

A region during this century of both tourist delights and political torments, Southeast Asia (Fig. 6) comprises a remarkable array of peoples and cultures located across two geographical divisions. These are *Mainland Southeast Asia* (Burma, Laos, Thailand,

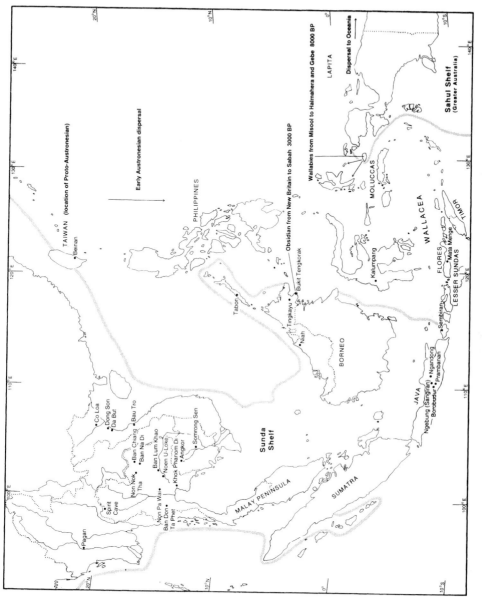

Figure 6. Map of Southeast Asia showing sites and regions referred to in the text.

Cambodia, Vietnam, Peninsular Malaysia) and *Island Southeast Asia* (Taiwan, Philippines, East Malaysia, Indonesia, Brunei). During the Pleistocene, except for short interglacial periods like the one we are in now, Mainland Southeast Asia was for long periods extended by land bridges to the Sunda Shelf islands of Sumatra, Java, Borneo and Bali, forming a huge south-easterly extension to the Asian continent. Taiwan was also joined to the Chinese mainland. However, the islands of the Philippines and eastern Indonesia (Sulawesi, Moluccas, Lesser Sundas) were never land bridged either to Asia or to Greater Australia (Australia plus New Guinea and Tasmania). These eastern Indonesian islands belong to the biogeographical province of *Wallacea*, through which human migration beyond the Sunda Shelf has always involved sea crossings.

So far, our knowledge of the prehistory and archaeology of Southeast Asia is a little uneven, not only in geographical coverage — many countries such as Burma, Laos and Cambodia are only just commencing archaeological research on pre-Classical periods — but also in content. For instance, we have a good fossil record for *Homo erectus* in Java, but rather poor information about chronology and tool-use. Excellent evidence is now to hand for the first recorded human water crossings perhaps 60,000 years ago or more in Wallacea, but chronological precision beyond the range of C14 is a problem here, and there is still only a very limited Wallacean human skeletal record. We have an excellent burial, economic and inter-settlement pattern record for the Neolithic and Bronze–Iron Ages on the mainland of Southeast Asia, but almost no data on the internal housing plans of settlements. Much of the Holocene information on hunter-gatherers and farmers from Malaysia and Indonesia is derived from caves and rock-shelters, so we know little here of open site distributions but we have good data on lithics and pottery sequences. Some of the lacunae reflect the nature of the tropical environment — preservation is never good in the equatorial zone and leaching is also a major problem in the monsoonal tropics. However, the monsoon regions of Thailand, Cambodia and Vietnam do have the benefit of excellent site visibility in the form of settlement mounds belonging to the agricultural period, an advantage denied in the equatorial regions of Malaysia and Indonesia.

Environmental underpinnings

To understand the creation of a human cultural kaleidoscope on the scale of Southeast Asia, we need first an awareness of some of the major environmental factors, presented here as three axes of variation (Bellwood 1992, 1997):

   1   There is increasing dry season length as one moves beyond 5 degrees north and south of the equator, along which rain falls during much of the year. Equatorial populations tend to be small, and in eastern Indonesia often dependent for subsistence on tubers and tree crops such as yams, taro, sago and bananas. The major cereals, especially rice and foxtail millet, evolved in tropical to temperate monsoon (long dry season) regions, with rice being domesticated in the Yangzi Basin by 6000 BC. Today, and in the agricultural past, the greatest population densities occur in these monsoon regions, especially in alluvial lowland landscapes in southern China and Mainland Southeast Asia north of the Malay Peninsula, and in alluvial/volcanic landscapes in Luzon, Java and Bali. Archaeology suggests that earlier hunter-gatherer densities were similarly differentiated, with a notable lack of evidence for major Pleistocene (pre-Hoabinhian) activity in the rainforests of the Malay Peninsula and the large equatorial islands of Indonesia.

   2   Continentality (Asian mainland, the large Sunda Shelf islands, Greater Australia) versus insularity (Wallacea) is another very significant axis of differentiation. Pleistocene low sea-levels increased the sizes of the Asian and Australian continents, but never caused land bridges to stretch across eastern Indonesia. Interestingly, the colonization of Australia occurred perhaps 60,000 years ago, and even Middle Pleistocene *Homo erectus* colonizations might have reached Flores. Both these events involved the crossing of sea gaps, not huge ones, but nevertheless hardly swimmable ones. Human colonization beyond the Sunda Shelf was not dependent on the existence of land bridges.

   3   Continentality tends to equate with faunal and floral richness, insularity with endemicity and depauperization. The Asian mainland, together with the Sunda Shelf islands, has varied placental mammal faunas. Australia and New Guinea have marsupial faunas. But colonists in Wallacea, particularly the Lesser Sundas and Moluccas, had precious few mammalian faunal resources until they learnt the values of animal translocation. The first evidence for this practice falls in the Late Pleistocene and Early Holocene, when marsupials were taken from New Guinea to the northern Moluccas Islands and Bismarck Archipelago.

Southeast Asian archaeology in the mid-twentieth century

To understand where Southeast Asian archaeology is headed in 2000, and upon what achievements it is based, we need to examine the foundations. Fifty years ago, an archaeologist asked to summarize the essence of Southeast Asian cultural evolution prior to AD 1000 would probably have noted four high points of knowledge:

   1   The discovery of *Pithecanthropus* in Java, at that time a hominid not associated positively with artefacts, despite some uncertain claims and some sterling field research effort by von Koenigswald, Movius, de Chardin and others. Nevertheless, Javan *Pithecanthropus* at that time was a hominid firmly believed by most scholars to be on the evolutionary pathway to modern humans.

   2   The results of cave excavations by the French in Tonkin, the Dutch in the East Indies and the British in Malaya, showing the presence of a series of flaked stone tool industries ('Hoabinhian' on the Southeast Asian mainland, various flake and point

industries in Indonesia), followed by a hazy 'Neolithic' with polished stone tools and pottery, often cord-marked. Putatively Neolithic assemblages were also known from a number of open sites, the best known perhaps being Somrong Sen in Cambodia, Da But and Bau Tro in Vietnam, and Kalumpang in Sulawesi, Indonesia.

3   Awareness of an array of bronze and iron objects, some found under obscure circumstances as at Somrong Sen, others found under more controlled circumstances as in the North Vietnamese site of Dong Son, still others (including many bronze drums) simply kept as heirlooms by villagers.

4   An understanding of the roles played by Han dynasty China and the emerging Hindu and Buddhist kingdoms of South Asia, the former having influenced northern Vietnam via political and military interference since the second century BC, the latter entering the scene via trade contacts at about the same time. The oldest inscriptions in Indic scripts appeared some centuries later (AD 300–500), initially for the most part in the Sanskrit language, but soon afterwards in Southeast Asian languages such as Mon, Khmer, Cham, Malay, Javanese and Balinese. Indian contact culminated about 800–1200 years ago in some of the most stupendous Hindu and Buddhist monuments ever erected — Borobudur and the Prambanan temples in Java, the Angkor complex in Cambodia, Pagan in Burma, to name just the brightest stars. Since art historians and epigraphists have never been in short supply in Southeast Asia we are not lacking in interpretations of such monuments, but of stratigraphic archaeology (as opposed to monument stabilization and reconstruction), there had been very little prior to 1950.

The 1950s archaeologist, if asked to provide a coherent cultural scenario for the two middle phases listed above (late hunter-gatherer and Neolithic to Iron Age), would perhaps have offered multiple observations based on Heine Geldern's rather masterly, and extremely influential, paper of 1932 (Heine Geldern 1932). Heine Geldern used data from three main sources — linguistics, museum material culture (especially stone adzes), and ethnology. He favoured three phases of migration into Southeast Asia, all from mainland Asian sources, the first being that of the Papuan-speaking peoples of New Guinea with their Walzenbeilkultur (oval cross-sectioned stone adze culture), then the Austroasiatic speakers (including Vietnamese and Khmers) with their Schulterbeilkultur (shouldered stone adze culture), finally the Austronesians with their Vierkantbeilkultur (untanged rectangular cross-sectioned stone adze culture). Since the 1960s it has become rather fashionable to discard Heine Geldern 1932 as something not belonging to our modern world of elegant anthropological theory. But his reconstruction of how Southeast Asian cultural history had been structured within the past 10,000 years was a major achievement for its day, even down to his guess-work pre-C14 chronology, based on Chinese and European dates transferred to the prehistoric cultures of Southeast Asia. His date for the beginning of Austronesian dispersal at 1750 BC was not far off the mark, although his immediate homeland (Malaya) was not in accord with modern archaeolinguistic homeland views (Taiwan).

During the 1950s and early 1960s, post-war prosperity increased the flow of knowledge but overall interpretations changed little. In 1964, the French historian Coedès (1968, 4–13) was still obliged to summarize pre-Classical Southeast Asia in much the same terms as had Heine Geldern, 32 years before. Until the mid-1960s it was still widely believed that Southeast Asia had been something of a cultural backwater, languishing in tribal darkness until contact with India, China and the West introduced the wonders of bronze-casting early in the first millennium BC.

When it came, the revolution was dramatic. In 1966, W.G. Solheim II began excavation at the Bronze Age site of Non Nok Tha in north-eastern Thailand. Continued by his student Donn Bayard, and later by another student Chet Gorman at the sites of Spirit Cave and Ban Chiang, this research catapulted Southeast Asia into world prominence as a likely origin locus for the oldest agricultural economies and bronze-casting industries (Solheim 1972; Bayard 1972; Gorman 1970; Gorman and Charoenwongsa 1976). Thirty years later, we know that such enthusiasm was no more than the result of a misinterpretation of radiocarbon dates — Thai bronze-casting is no older than Chinese, and Thai agriculture is several millennia younger than that of the Yangzi. But the impetus which this frothy delight of 1960s and 1970s discovery gave to the overall discipline of archaeology in Southeast Asia was almost unimaginable. For the first time, Southeast Asia actually *mattered* in world prehistory. Heads were held high.

At the same time as these developments in Thailand, hints were also arising of intriguing prehistoric developments at and beyond the eastern end of Southeast Asia, in Australia and the Pacific. The realization that people had to cross the ocean to reach Australia about 40,000 years ago came as a surprise in the 1960s, as did the emerging evidence for Early Holocene agriculture in the New Guinea Highlands (Golson 1977) and the remarkable Lapita expansion of initial human settlement through Island Melanesia into Polynesia at about 3500–3000 years ago. When the first radiocarbon dates began to flow from China, it was also realized that millet and rice agriculture had Early Holocene beginnings there, back to at least 5000 BC.

During the 1960s and 1970s, stratigraphic excavation of both caves and open sites in Southeast Asia continued apace. At the same time, advances in two other crucial disciplines brought archaeology into a new multidisciplinary alignment. Comparative linguists in the Pacific were using both lexicostatistical and cladistics methodologies to determine the histories of the major language families and their subgroups. This research rapidly attracted the interest of archaeologists, as did new developments in the field of genetics, initially in blood-based genetic systems but developing rapidly in the 1970s into the study of mitochondrial DNA variation. Today, the study of archaeology in Southeast Asia is truly a part of a vast multidisciplinary array of investigation into the human past.

Southeast Asian archaeology at the turn of the twenty-first century

Southeast Asia is no longer presented as a primary centre of agricultural or urban development. But it still scores impressively in the one-upmanship stakes. Eastern Indonesia (helped by Australia) has the oldest evidence in the world for ocean crossing, presumably by raft. Together with western Melanesia it also has the world's oldest evidence for animal translocation. Island Southeast Asia later served as the genesis region for the greatest ethnolinguistic dispersal in world history prior to AD 1500, that of the Austronesians (Bellwood 1991; Blust 1995). Bronze-working in Thailand is now known to date from at least 1500 BC, perhaps not quite as old as in China or Sumer, but still pre-dating the chronological estimates of the 1950s by a millennium or so. Furthermore, many regions of Mainland Southeast Asia witnessed a development of mid to late first millennium BC iron-based social complexity long before the first Indic temples and inscriptions appeared. Indian influences in Southeast Asia were of fundamental importance, but they seem to have been invited, not imposed. The people of Southeast Asia are today biologically and linguistically Southeast Asian, whatever cultural influences (linguistic, religious, and philosophical) they might have absorbed from India and China. Of course, some populations have moved south from China into Southeast Asia in historical times, Thais and Hmong-Mien for instance, but the overall fact remains that the great Hindu and Buddhist kingdoms of Southeast Asia were created by indigenous peoples and their leaders, not by Indian colonists or conquering armies. In this regard, these civilizations differ greatly from the recent expansion of European civilization, with its massive investment in colonization, and also of course from conquest-based ancient civilizations such as Han Dynasty China and the Roman Empire.

The big issues

Let us now turn to the new data. What broad-scale problems are likely to galvanize the archaeologists of the new millennium? How are they being approached? How can Southeast Asian data assist interpretation and understanding in other arenas of world archaeology?

Homo erectus in Indonesia: a dead end or an ancestor?

Pithecanthropus in its modern guise, as *Homo erectus*, has now acquired some degree of cultural status as a toolmaker at Ngebung in the Sangiran region in Java and across the Wallace Line at Mata Menge and other sites in Flores (Simanjuntak and Sémah

1996; van den Bergh *et al.* 1996; Morwood *et al.* 1998, 1999). The making of stone tools and an ability to cross sea gaps about 20–25 km wide by 800,000 years ago now appear very likely, if not 'proven' with absolute certainty. The Flores evidence is particularly interesting since stone flakes, but not yet any human fossils, occur in association with bones of *Stegodon* in sediments dated by the fission track method on zircon to between 840,000 and 700,000 BP. These claims are raising debate on the role of *Homo erectus* in modern human evolution, even if the majority of palaeoanthropologists today regard this unfortunate species as 'extinct', with the possibility that its youngest members might have survived at Ngandong in Java until as recently as 25,000 to 55,000 years ago (Swisher *et al.* 1996). The issue is open and hotly debated. The date of initial appearance of hominids in Java is also under dispute, with a rather unsatisfactory estimate between 1.8 and 1 million years being most likely (Bellwood 1997). Dating *Homo erectus* does matter, for Java has yielded a very long sequence of fossils belonging to this hominid species and the tempo at which they evolved in terms of brain size will doubtless be very significant for eventual determination of their true place in human ancestry.

Anatomically-modern humans in Southeast Asia

Hard data in fossil form for the arrival of modern humans in Southeast Asia have not grown much during the past 50 years, beyond the discovery of the Niah and Tabon remains, believed to date to between 25,000 and 40,000 years ago on C14. The main current revelation, from Australia, is that one of the Lake Mungo skeletons from western New South Wales, originally dated to about 30,000 BP by correlated C14 data, may actually date to about 60,000 years ago according to ESR, uranium series and optical luminescence dating (Thorne *et al.* 1999). Since the Mungo burials are of undisputed modern and not *erectus* status, these dates obviously raise questions about the true antiquity of modern humans outside Africa and especially in Indonesia, from where the Mungo population must have been drawn in an immediate sense. They also raise questions about the validity of radiocarbon dating towards the older limit, because organic materials are subject to levels of younger C14 contamination such that they are unlikely ever to become totally inert. This means that C14 dates older than perhaps 35,000 years could be very much older than the laboratory calculations indicate. Thus, as far as Southeast Asia is concerned, there are legitimate questions concerning the true ages of the Niah Deep Skull and the lower layers in many excavated caves which have C14 dates in the 30,000s and 40,000s, but these issues will not be resolved until non-C14 absolute dating methods such as those used at Lake Mungo are applied. So far, these methods have not been available to Southeast Asian researchers, but hopefully they will be in the near future.

Stone tools and modern humans

There are two major observations about the 'Late Palaeolithic' in Southeast Asia, which are of striking importance. Firstly, stone tool industries in some regions (e.g. eastern Indonesia) are mostly very simple in terms of technology, often reflecting little more than core smashing, with more careful directional flaking only occurring when good quality fine-grained materials such as chert were available. True, there are important exceptions, for instance the Tingkayu biface industry of Sabah, the bifacial Hoabinhian industries of the Malay Peninsula, and the blade-like and point industries in Holocene Sulawesi and the Philippines (summarized in Bellwood 1997). Yet for many regions we must face the fact that totally modern humans, capable of ocean voyaging and animal translocation, made and used stone tools down to the Neolithic of types that elsewhere in the world would rank with the Oldowan. So the equations which one often reads for Africa and Europe, between evolving humanity and evolving stone tool technology, *probably do not work* for Southeast Asia at all. In the Moluccas, for instance, stone tools of 3000 BP are generally not differentiable from those of 30,000 BP (Bellwood *et al.* 1998), or even of 800,000 BP in nearby Flores. In Southeast Asia, there clearly is much more to modern humans than the ability to strike blades from a prismatic core.

The second observation concerning the Late Palaeolithic is that there is still a remarkable lack of evidence for any major occupation of the deep-inland equatorial rainforest belt during the last glacial maximum. This is surprising, since drier conditions then might, in theory, have made the forest easier to enter and exploit. But current distributions of C14-dated Hoabinhian sites in Peninsular Malaysia suggest that the colonization of the interior rainforest was very much a Holocene event, occurring mostly within the past 10,000 years. Why the relative lateness? It is possible that increased Holocene rainfall enhanced river erosion and the destruction of older deposits in Malaysian rock shelters, thus masking the true story. Interior Borneo and Sumatra are also still relatively unresearched, so perhaps we are being fooled by missing data.

On the other hand, however, there are very good reasons for regarding the observed distributions as 'real'. The vast extension of the late glacial Sunda Shelf as dry land would have made areas that are a long way inland today far more distant from coastlines then, and much less accessible. Hoabinhian colonization of the Malay Peninsula in Holocene times might also have been assisted by developments in trapping and plant exploitation. We do not know the answers here, but the question of when humans first penetrated deep rainforest interiors is an important one. If some hunter-gatherers really did have problems living in equatorial deep interiors hundreds/thousands of kilometres from the sea, as maintained in a quantity of relatively recent literature (Bailey *et al.* 1989; and see also discussion of this issue in *Human Ecology* Vol. 19, 1991), then we have legitimate questions of how *Homo erectus* was able to reach Java, an island on the other side of the rainforest from a mainland Asian perspective, located quite far south of the equator. 'Dry season corridors',[4] ocean crossings, coastal migrations — all merit some thought. We know that human existence on *small* equatorial islands was never difficult within the past 35,000 years, as witnessed by the archaeological record in the Moluccas and Island Melanesia. But interior Borneo still remains a Palaeolithic mystery in terms of the archaeological record.

The great Neolithic divide?

Ethnographically, the vast majority of the recorded cultures of Southeast Asia have agricultural economies, with professional hunters and gatherers surviving only in interstices, particularly in equatorial rainforest. Thus, there are Negrito hunter-gatherers in Peninsular Malaysia and the Philippines, and rather more 'Mongoloid' hunter-gatherers in parts of Borneo, Sumatra, Halmahera and northern Thailand. These peoples are unable to withstand agriculturist expansion and have survived in the past because of relative isolation, also because they have often been able to forge useful trade and exchange relationships with surrounding farmers. The big questions are obvious: how do the modern hunter-gatherers relate to those in the archaeological record, where do the farming peoples come from and how did farming emerge in Southeast Asia, and how does the spread of farming relate to the spread of the major language families? We start with the languages.

Language families and their implications (see Blust 1995, 1996; Bellwood *et al.* 1995)

Southeast Asia has several major language families. Austronesian covers the largest area, being distributed through all of Island Southeast Asia and Oceania (excepting Australia and most of New Guinea) and is striking because of its unbroken distribution in most regions. The mainland families — Austroasiatic, Tai, Hmong-Mien, Tibeto-Burman — are more mosaic-like in their distributions, for reasons which are uncertain but which certainly reflect more complex migration and replacement histories than in Indonesia and the Philippines. The essential observation to be made about these language families, all well-defined and relatively well-studied, is that their histories reflect expansions from homeland regions, either by outright migration or by slow population expansion with more gradual linguistic separations. Furthermore, proto-language reconstructions indicate that we are dealing, in the case of all of these major families, with foundation societies with agricultural economies rather than hunter-gatherers. In the case of Austronesian, comparisons of regional proto-languages in the Philippines, Indonesia and western Oceania suggest that dispersal

---

[4] Such must have existed during Pleistocene periods of relative deglaciation, but it is not possible in this chapter to deal with Pleistocene environmental changes. For a summary see Bellwood 1997.

was *geographically and temporally rapid*, leading to a rake-like rather than a tree-like structure of subgroup relationships.

We must remember two provisos, however. These expansions are of *languages, not necessarily peoples*, since it is possible under certain circumstances for people to change their linguistic affiliations. Secondly, absolute dates cannot be calculated easily from comparative linguistic data alone and we lack inscriptions more than about 1700 years old in this part of the world. Just how rapid, for instance, was the spread of Austronesian languages from Taiwan to Samoa? Relating linguistic observations to the archaeological and genetic records may not be easy, and opinions on just how such entities can relate can often become quite heated.[5]

The two main language families of Neolithic Southeast Asia were probably Austronesian and Austroasiatic. Historical linguistic data, not summarized here, indicate that Tai and Hmong-Mien represent later spreads from southern Chinese homeland regions. Some of the Tibeto-Burman languages might represent Neolithic dispersal (van Driem 1999), but unfortunately there are very few archaeological records relevant for Tibeto-Burman prehistory and these languages are not discussed further here. Today, the Austroasiatic languages include Mon and Khmer, Vietnamese, the Aslian languages of central Peninsular Malaysia, Nicobarese, and many other linguistic pockets scattered over northern mainland Southeast Asia and north-eastern India. The initial spread of the Austroasiatic languages can be related to the settlement of mainland Southeast Asia by rice-growing populations from southern China, probably during the third millennium BC (Higham and Thosarat 1998; Higham 1996a). The initial spread of the Austronesian languages also began initially amongst southern Chinese agricultural populations (Blust 1995, 1996), but the clearest episode of dispersal can be related to the colonization by agriculturalists of the islands of Southeast Asia, from Taiwan through the Philippines and Indonesia into western Oceania, during the second millennium BC (Bellwood 1991, 1997, 1998).

The archaeological record of early agriculture in Southeast Asia

Given the strength of the linguistic evidence for the dispersal of these language families we might ask if there are corresponding episodes of major change in the archaeological record. Indeed there are, as the previous paragraph has already foreshadowed. Between 3000 and 1000 BC (with a tendency to be earlier in the north, later in the south and east) the pre-ceramic lithic industries of Southeast Asia were replaced by quite different assemblages with pottery, polished stone adzes, bones of domesticated animals (dog, pig and poultry widespread, with cattle restricted to the Asian mainland) and,

---

[5] The genetic evidence is, of course, very relevant for issues of population origin, but space precludes discussion here.

most importantly, evidence for rice husk tempers or impressions in pottery (except in eastern Indonesia). There has been a long tradition in Southeast Asia, going back to the 1970s claims for extremely ancient agriculture in Thailand, to regard these massive changes in material culture and economy as a result of internal developments alone. But, unfortunately, no sites anywhere reveal a convincing transition from the Hoabinhian or other pre-ceramic lithic tradition into the regional Neolithic. In this sense, Southeast Asia is not another China or Levant. Agriculture represents a techno-logical introduction from southern China and many Epipalaeolithic hunting and gathering communities were doubtless absorbed into the ensuing economic mosaic.

High points of Neolithic research in Southeast Asia include the excavations by Charles Higham, Rachanie Thosarat and colleagues of long and complex burial and economic sequences at Khok Phanom Di in central Thailand (c.2500–1500 BC; Higham and Thosarat 1994), the identification of ceramic complexes from the Malay Peninsula (c.2000 to 500 BC) and Vietnam (c.3000–1500 BC), and the discovery of a very wide-spread tradition of red-slipped pottery within the Philippine and eastern Indonesian Neolithic (c.1500–1200 BC), this latter undoubtedly being associated with Austronesian settlement of these regions and onwards into Oceania (Bellwood 1997). The island of Taiwan also has a very significant Neolithic sequence from which the Island Southeast Asian red-slipped pottery tradition must in part be drawn. The site of Beinan in south-eastern Taiwan is especially significant, being a village of aligned stone-walled dwelling and storage houses dating to about 1000 BC (Lien 1993).

Bronze, iron and pre-Indic social complexity

The burial records from Thailand sites such as Non Nok Tha, Non Pa Wai, Khok Phanom Di, Ban Nadi, Ban Lum Khao and Ban Chiang (Higham 1996b; Higham and Thosarat 1998; White 1995) indicate a presence of lineage-based social ranking and set-tlement autonomy in Neolithic times, continuing without special elaboration into the Bronze Age, beginning c.1500 BC. But during the Iron Age, after 500 BC, major devel-opments into stratified and hierarchically structured societies occurred. Iron-working clearly fuelled a revolution in food production and population growth, being probably associated with the initial use of the plough in Southeast Asia and cattle and perhaps water buffalo for traction (pigs, cattle and dogs were domesticated during Neolithic times). Large areas of the fairly dry southern Khorat Plateau region of north-eastern Thailand were apparently first settled by agriculturalists during the Iron Age, an inter-esting circumstance which suggests that earlier agricultural communities were quite widely dispersed and that large areas might have remained the preserve of hunters and gatherers until almost historical times.

The earlier phase of bronze-working in Southeast Asia was restricted to the main-land, with the copper/bronze items themselves being mainly simple forms cast in bivalve moulds or by the lost wax method (socketed axes, spear and arrowheads, bracelets). Settlements in Thailand during this period were not over 5 ha in size. The Iron Age, between about 500 BC and AD 500, was therefore a time of major cultural change, involving not just internal developments of social and settlement hierarchy, with the largest ('moated') settlements in Thailand being recorded up to 55 ha in size, but also the beginnings of contact with India and China (Glover 1990, 1996). Also associated with this phase was a widespread distribution from southern China to eastern Indonesia of massive Dongson bronze drums and other bronze vessels, seemingly manufactured in northern Vietnam. This latter region, during its Dongson Phase (c.500 BC to AD 1), witnessed the apogee of pre-Han socio-political development in Southeast Asia, with numerous very rich burial assemblages (Higham 1996b) and claims that the earthwork defences of the settlement of Co Loa near Hanoi might have enclosed 600 ha. Indonesia and the Philippines, hitherto universally Neolithic, now entered a combined Bronze–Iron Age, with a contemporary appearance of both metals to as far east as the Moluccas. The bronze, at least, was worked locally according to the finding of casting moulds in several Indonesian, East Malaysian and Philippine sites by at least the mid-first millennium AD.

It is actually very difficult to tease apart the different threads of Iron Age complexity to such a degree that they can be regarded as independent strands of development. Indeed, it seems very possible that all the above developments were historically related as one 'complex' and reflected a growing role for Southeast Asia, with its spices and forest products, in the growing world of international commerce stretching from the Mediterranean to China. Indian Rouletted Ware in quite large quantities was reaching Bali by about 2000 years ago (Ardika and Bellwood 1991). Iron, Dong Son drums, glass beads, Indian pottery, Chinese imports (in northern Vietnam), and the beginnings of metal usage in Island Southeast Asia all appear in the last few centuries BC. Do they appear as reflections of a closely related set of historical circumstances?

Historical ('Classical') archaeology in Southeast Asia

Important research efforts are currently under way to provide archaeological backgrounds for the major Indic civilizations of Mainland Southeast Asia during the late first and early second millennia AD (for several summaries see Stark and Allen 1998), particularly using the remarkably rich burial records from sites such as Ban Don Ta Phet and Noen U-Loke in Thailand (Glover 1991; Higham and Thosarat 1998). Historical archaeology extends into the Islamic era in Indonesia, and there are also projects examining the rise of pre-Spanish social complexity in the Philippines. The complexity of regional cultures during this period means that summary is no longer an easy matter, a situation not really helped by the great linguistic diversity of this region and the decreasing availability of materials in translation, an understandable but problematic result of the ending of the colonial era with its domination by European languages. This paper does not offer sufficient space for a significant review of the archaeology of the past 1500 years in Southeast Asia, but the signs are clear that this will be a major growth area in the twenty-first century.

Historical archaeology does bring up one final observation of significance. It is clear that the oldest Neolithic pottery styles in Southeast Asia — the curvilinear incised and cord-marked patterns on much mainland pottery, the Neolithic tripod vessels of the Malay Peninsula, the red-slipped pottery in eastern Indonesia — cover much greater extents than any earthenware complexes of historical times (glazed ceramic trade wares from China, Thailand and Vietnam must, of course, be excluded from this generalization). In terms of cultural dispersal, the Neolithic was a very significant period indeed in terms of large-scale population and cultural dispersal. There are no signs of such processes in the historical period, when the emphasis seems to have been on contact-based trade and diffusion between independent regional cultures and early states, with localized patterns of stylistic variation as the result. Such, perhaps, suggests that human history has not always been witness to uniform rates of cultural change through time and across space.

Where to after 2000?

Southeast Asian archaeology is now such a vast enterprise that it is difficult to predict what will be the major questions of the immediate future. But four major issues, which will probably be debated well into the new millennium, are as follows:

1   The chronology and cultural capability of *Homo erectus,* and the relations between this hominid and the first modern humans to traverse Wallacea and to reach Australia more than 40,000 years ago.

2   The chronology and mechanics for agricultural spread through Southeast Asia. Here we have major issues of migration versus hunter-gatherer adoption, combined with considerations of language family histories.

3   Reasons for the apparent concatenation of growth markers during the mid–late first millennium BC. Internal or external stimuli, and what roles for India, China, iron-working and world trade?

4   Explanations for the rise of the Hindu–Buddhist and Islamic kingdoms of Classical and Early Modern Southeast Asia. Compared to our knowledge of many other early civilizations, our archaeological knowledge of the kingdoms of Classical Java or Thailand, not to mention Burma, is still very much limited to aspects of art and architectural history.

So archaeology in Southeast Asia still has a long way to go to yield the density of information available for other regions such as Europe or North America. However, the

1998 Congress of the Indo-Pacific Prehistory Association in Melaka brought together 225 presenters from 36 countries, suggesting that the will to expand understanding of the Southeast Asian past across national borders will remain in active mode into the foreseeable future.

References

NB: Only a small number of references have been listed in the text. These are followed by a general note on bibliographic sources for current research in Southeast Asian archaeology.

ARDIKA, I.W. and BELLWOOD, P. 1991: Sembiran: the beginnings of Indian contact with Bali. *Antiquity* 65, 221–32.

BAILEY, R., HEAD, G., JENIKE, M., OWEN, B., RECHTMAN, R. and ZECHENTER, E. 1989: Hunting and gathering in tropical rain forest: is it possible? *American Anthropologist* 91, 59–82.

BAYARD, D. 1972: Early Thai bronze: analysis and new dates. *Science* 176, 1411–12.

BELLWOOD, P. 1991: The Austronesian dispersal and the origin of languages. *Scientific American* 265 (1), 88–93.

BELLWOOD, P. 1992: Southeast Asia before history. In Tarling, N. (ed.), *The Cambridge History of Southeast Asia* (Cambridge), 55–136.

BELLWOOD, P. 1997: *Prehistory of the Indo-Malaysian Archipelago* (Honolulu).

BELLWOOD, P. 1998: La dispersion des Austronisians. In Newton D. (ed.), *Arts des Mers du Sud* (Paris, Sociiti Nouvelle Adam Biro), 8–17.

BELLWOOD, P., FOX, J. and TRYON, D. (eds.) 1995: *The Austronesians* (Canberra, Department of Anthropology, RSPAS, Australian National University).

BELLWOOD, P., NITIHAMINOTO, G., IRWIN, G., GUNADI, WALUYO, A. and TANUDIRJO, D. 1998: 35,000 years of prehistory in the northern Moluccas. *Modern Quat. Res. Southeast Asia* 15, 233–75.

BLUST, R.A. 1995: The prehistory of the Austronesian-speaking peoples: a view from language. *J. World Prehist.* 9, 453–510.

BLUST, R. 1996: Beyond the Austronesian homeland: the Austric hypothesis and its implication for archaeology. In Goodenough, W. (ed.), *Prehistoric Settlement of the Pacific* (Philadelphia, American Philosophical Society).

COEDÈS, G. 1968: *The Indianized States of Southeast Asia* (translation of 1964 French original) (Canberra).

GLOVER, I.C. 1990: *Early Trade between India and South-East Asia* (Hull, Centre for SE Asian Studies, University of Hull, 2nd edition).

GLOVER, I. 1991: Ban Don Ta Phet. In Glover, I. and Glover, E. (eds.), *Southeast Asian Archaeology 1986* (Oxford, BAR Int. Ser. 561), 139–84.

GLOVER, I.C. 1996: Recent archaeological evidence for early maritime contacts between India and Southeast Asia. In Ray, H.P. and Salles, J.F. (eds.), *Tradition and Archaeology* (New Delhi), 129–58.

GOLSON, J. 1977: No room at the top. In Allen, J., Golson, J. and Jones, R. (eds.), *Sunda and Sahul* (London), 601–38.

GORMAN, C. 1970: Excavations at Spirit Cave. *Asian Perspectives* 13, 79–108.

GORMAN, C. and CHAROENWONGSA, P. 1976: Ban Chiang: a mosaic of impressions from the first two years. *Expedition* 18, 14–26.

HEINE GELDERN, R. 1932: Urheimart und früheste Wanderungen der Austronesier. *Anthropos* 27, 543–619.

HIGHAM, C. 1996a: Archaeology and linguistics in Southeast Asia: implications of the Austric hypothesis. *Bull. Indo-Pacific Prehistory Assoc.* 14, 110–18.

HIGHAM, C. 1996b: *The Bronze Age of Southeast Asia* (Cambridge).

HIGHAM, C. and THOSARAT, R. 1994: *Khok Phanom Di* (Orlando).

HIGHAM, C. and THOSARAT, R. 1998: *Prehistoric Thailand* (Bangkok).

LIEN, C.M. 1993: Pei-nan: a Neolithic village. In Burenhult, G. (ed.), *People of the Stone Age* (San Francisco), 132–3.

MORWOOD, M.J., AZIZ, F., O'SULLIVAN, P., NASRUDDIN, HOBBS, D. and RAZA, A. 1999: Archaeological and palaeontological research in central Flores, east Indonesia. *Antiquity* 73, 273–86.

MORWOOD, M.J., O'SULLIVAN, P.B., AZIZ, F. and RAZA, A. 1998: Fission-track ages of stone tools and fossils on the east Indonesian island of Flores. *Nature* 392, 173–6.

SIMANJUNTAK, H.T. and SÉMAH, F. 1996: A new insight into the Sangiran flake industry. *Bull. Indo-Pacific Prehistory Assoc.* 14, 22–6.

SOLHEIM, W.G.I. 1972: An earlier agricultural revolution. *Scientific American* 226, 34–41.

STARK, M. and ALLEN, J. (eds.) 1998: The Transition to History in Southeast Asia. *Int. J. Historical Archaeol.*, Special Issues Vol. 2, Nos. 3 and 4.

SWISHER, C., RINK, W., ANTON, S., SCHWARTZ, H., CURTIS, G., SUPRIJO, A. and WIDIASMORO 1996: Latest *Homo erectus* of Java. *Science* 274, 1870–4.

THORNE, A., GRÜN, R., MORTIMER, G., SPOONER, N., SIMPSON, J., MCCULLOCH, M., TAYLOR, L. and CURNOE, D. 1999: Australia's oldest human remains: age of the Lake Mungo 3 skeleton. *J. Human Evolution* 36, 591–612.

VAN DEN BERGH, G., DE VOS, J., SONDAAR, P.Y. and AZIZ, F. 1996: Did *Homo erectus* reach the island of Flores? *Bull. Indo-Pacific Prehistory Assoc.* 14, 27–36.

VAN DRIEM, G. 1999: A new theory on the origin of Chinese. *Bull. Indo-Pacific Prehistory Assoc.* 18, 43–58.

WHITE, J. 1995: Incorporating heterarchy into theory on socio-political development. In Crumley, C.L. and Levy, J.E. (eds.), *Heterarchy and the Analysis of Complex Societies* (Arlington, VA, American Anthropological Association, Archaeological Papers, Vol. 6), 101–23.

Additional bibliographic notes

The European-language major journals which deal with Southeast Asian archaeology are *Asian Perspectives* (Honolulu), *Bulletin of the Indo-Pacific Prehistory Association* (Canberra), *Jurnal Arkeologi Malaysia* (Kuala Lumpur), *Journal of Southeast Asian Archaeology* (Kagoshima, Japan), *Journal of the Siam Society* (Bangkok), *Bulletin de l'Ecole Française d'Extrême-Orient* (Paris) and *Modern Quaternary Research in Southeast Asia* (Rotterdam). General accounts of the prehistoric and early historical archaeology of Southeast Asia can be found in *The Cambridge History of Southeast Asia* (Tarling, N. (ed.), 1992) and in the books referenced above as Bellwood *et al.* (ed.) 1995; Bellwood 1997; Glover 1990; Higham 1996b; Higham and Thosarat 1994 and 1998. For recent research in Taiwan, see Li, Paul J-K *et al.* (ed.), *Austronesian Studies Relating to Taiwan* (Symposium Series No. 3 of the Institute of History and Philology, Academia Sinica, Taipei, Taiwan). For recent compilations on early historical archaeology, mainly covering Mainland SE Asia, see Glover, I. (ed.), *Southeast Asian Archaeology 1990* (Centre for Southeast Asian Studies, University of Hull, UK, 1992); Glover, I., Suchitta, P. and Villiers, J. (eds.), *Early Metallurgy, Trade and Urban Centres in Thailand and SE Asia* (Bangkok, 1992); and Bulbeck, D. and Barnard, N. (eds.), *Ancient Chinese and Southeast Asian Bronze Age Cultures* (2 volumes, Taipei, 1996–7).

Eurasia east of the Urals

C.F.W. HIGHAM

Introduction

Eastern Eurasia is a region of such diversity that encapsulating the essential details of its prehistoric past would have to cover the origins and expansion of *Homo erectus* and anatomically modern humans, a myriad of distinct hunter-gatherer traditions from the arctic north to the tropical south, the expansion of hunter-gatherers from Siberia into the Americas (Dumond and Bland 1995), the indigenous origins of agriculture in the far east, and the expansion of agriculture from the far west. It would also include the adoption of bronze technology, with particular reference to single or multiple origins, linked with the antiquity and the nature of the transmission of people and ideas across what came to be known as the Silk Route. Documents in Tocharian, an Indo-European language, and presence by 2000 BC of the desiccated remains of people who look like Europeans in the Tarim Basin, demand scrutiny and explanation. There is likewise the expansion into the Americas, and of agricultural societies in a region where we deal not with one, but at least five language families, not to mention the subsequent development of the world's longest-lived civilization. These various themes have in common a recent and major surge in concentrated research, with new results tumbling over their predecessors and requiring at the same time concentrated thought and a surgeon's willingness to wield a scalpel on entrenched interpretations. To this situation must be added a research environment in which hermetically sealed areas have recently been opened to Western scholarship, with an inevitable clash of traditional and innovative theoretical approaches (Fig. 1).

This paper will not attempt to penetrate the dense mist which still shrouds the timing and expansion of *Homo erectus* into this area, nor the evolution of anatomically modern humans. Rather, it will begin with the end of the Pleistocene when already, hunter-gatherer communities in Japan were making pottery vessels, and the first adaptive steps towards the cultivation of rice and millet were being taken in the valleys of the Yangzi and Huang He rivers. Hunter-gatherers adaptive to the steppes, the forest

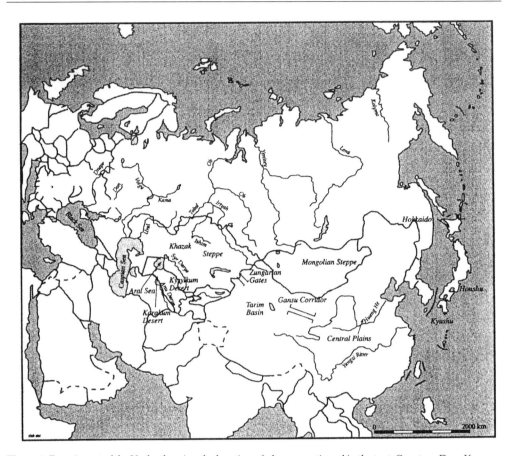

Figure 1. Eurasia east of the Urals, showing the location of places mentioned in the text. Courtesy Dora Kemp.

belt, tundra and internal drainage systems feeding the Aral and Caspian seas add to the immense variety of different adaptations (Sinor 1990).

   Four major themes will be considered. The first explores the transition to rice and millet cultivation and its implications both for the expansion of agricultural communities, and the growth of populations and cultural complexity in the heartlands. This necessarily incorporates the rich coastal hunter-gatherers of Japan and Korea. The next topic addresses the evidence for the transmission of ideas, and the movement of peoples, across the steppes. It will trace the eastward movement of bronze technology and discuss a possible western origin not only for Chinese metallurgy but also the domestic horse and the chariot (Puett 1998). Bronze-working in China soon took on a distinctly local flavour, the products being employed in aristocratic rituals. In discussing the development of civilization, particular attention will be given to the new evidence for regional states beyond the traditional area of Shang dominance in the Central Plains of the Huang He Valley.

Aspects of the environment

The vast area between the Urals and Gansu may be divided from north to south into first the bitterly cold tundra, then the deep taiga belt of coniferous forests. These zones are drained by south–north flowing rivers, the lower reaches of which freeze for much of the year with attendant flooding. The steppe to the south comprises grasslands suited to grazing stock, but given the continental high temperatures in summer and freezing months in winter, it is a region which does not favour agriculture. On the other hand, the Kazakh and Mongolian steppes provide the opportunity for uninterrupted east to west passage, particularly once the horse was domesticated, and wheeled vehicles were available. Low rainfall on the southern fringes of the steppe leads to desertic conditions. The Karakum and Kyzylkum deserts east and south of Aral Sea, for example, receive less than 10 cm of rain on average per annum. The Taklamakan desert in the centre of the Tarim Basin is one of the world's driest places, but its fringes, where rivers originating in the Pamir, Tien Shan and Kunlun mountains reach the piedmont, are characterized by fertile oases. This is particularly so in the Turfan Depression which, being well below sea-level, enjoys a relatively long and warm growing season (Taaffe 1990). The Zungarian gates and Gansu corridor link the Kazakhstan steppe with the Huang He River system, routes by which a series of innovations, such as metallurgy, the domestic horse and the chariot, probably reached China. The Huang He Valley, particularly in its western sector, is continental in climate with cold dry winters and hot summers during which most rainfall is experienced (Keightley 1999a). Under natural conditions, this region would sustain a broad-leaved deciduous forest, able to tolerate the considerable variations in rainfall which may be double or half the mean from year to year. This variation might help explain the Shang kings' regular enquiries of their diviners for weather forecasting. The Yangzi Valley to the south is on the northern margins of the area affected by the monsoon, and supports a subtropical mixed evergreen and deciduous forest. A vital feature of this great river system is the quantity of water carried by the Yangzi and its tributaries. This far exceeds that seen in the Huang He system, and sustains many large lakes and extensive swamps. Recent palaeoenvironmental research has also revealed marked climatic changes over the past 12,000 years, which are an essential component of any consideration of agricultural origins (Zhao et al. 1991).

The origins of rice cultivation

The amount of research dedicated to understanding the origins of agriculture in the Levant dwarfs that applied to the major river valleys of China, and only now are the main elements of the sequence being assembled. As a pattern slowly emerges, so it is possible to recognize intriguing parallels between events in the Near East and China that persuasively indicate that similar variables were operating. In the first instance, it is necessary to summarize the major environmental changes, which took place towards the end of the Pleistocene and into the early Holocene periods, and then relate them to the archaeological sequence.

It is becoming increasingly apparent that the transition to economies which incorporated rice cultivation took place in the middle reaches of the Yangzi Valley, with a possible extension in the Huai River, one of its major tributaries. This low-lying lacustrine region lies at the northern limits of wild rice, and it is highly likely that the availability of wild rice changed with climatic fluctuations. There is little likelihood that rice was available to the hunter-gatherers of the Yangzi Valley during the particularly cold spell which lasted until 15,000 years BP. Cold dry continental conditions would have favoured small groups of hunter-gatherers. Between 15,000 and 13,700 BP, there was a distinct warming, bringing the mean temperature close to its present level. The pollen spectra reveal that oak, pine, elm and willow began to invade the region, and that moister conditions prevailed. Cyclic weather patterning then saw a return to cold conditions, and a prevalence of drought-resistant herbs in what would have been a decidedly steppic habitat (Winkler and Wang 1993; Higham and Lu 1998). A further mild and moist episode followed until about 11,300 BP, when it again descended to the cold and dry conditions of the Younger Dryas. There followed a long period of warming which lasted until a further cold period commenced just after 9000 BP (Fig. 2).

Recent research has highlighted the importance of excavations in a series of rock shelters, which command swampy or lacustrine habitats in the middle Yangzi Valley (Yasuda 1999). These reveal deep stratigraphic sequences, which span the Pleistocene–Holocene boundary. The application of standard methods for the recovery of plant remains, as well as fastidious attention to the provenance of ceramic, stone and bone artefacts now permits the integration of the cultural and climatic sequences. There remains, however, a difficult problem in that at the key site of Diaotonghuan, the radiocarbon dates are unrealistically early. However, by cross dating with other sites on the basis of material culture, a general idea of the chronology there can be presented (Zhao 1998). The excavators have divided the long sequence into cultural zones B to O within a 5-m build up of deposits. The rice phytoliths can be diagnosed as probably of a wild variety, a domestic form, or one intermediate between the two. Moreover, it is possible to distinguish between phytoliths from the leaf or the glume. Until zone G, phytoliths were rare, no layer yielding more than 15. This number surged by a factor of 10 with zone G, which was, if anything, thinner than its predecessors. Twenty-nine phytoliths from this layer were examined and measured, all but two being either of the wild form or indeterminate. The remaining two might have been from a cultivated plant, but their rarity makes this unlikely. This zone is thought to date from about 12,000 BP, during one of the warm periods when wild rice could have been adaptive to the prevailing moist conditions. Zhao considers it likely that the hunters and gatherers of Diaotonghuan were collecting wild rice at this juncture (Fig. 3).

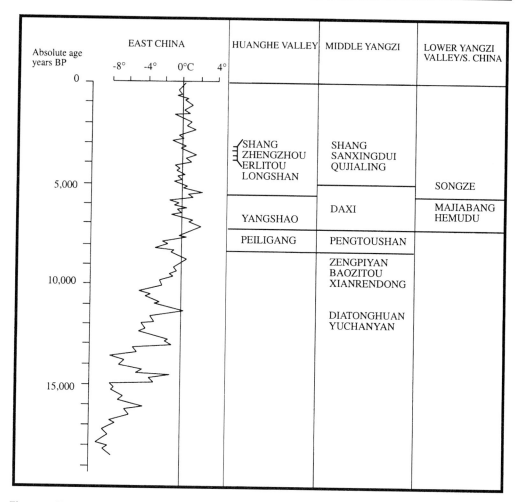

Figure 2. Changes in the mean temperature in east China in relation to the main archaeological sites.

There was a sharp fall in the frequency of rice phytoliths with zone F, which is thought to correspond to the cold of the Younger Dryas when wild rice would probably have retreated to its southern refugia. However, rice remains were back in force during the accumulation of zones D and E, which correspond, it is thought, to the long period of warming between 10,000 and 8000 BP. Perhaps significantly, it was during zone E that the first pottery sherds were recovered. The form of the phytoliths suggests that half are probably from a wild stand, the others are closer to the cultivated form. During zone C, phytoliths remained abundant, and the majority fall into the domestic range of form and size. Moreover, as more domestic phytoliths were found, so glumes were more frequently represented than leaves. This suggests grain harvesting, rather than the fortuitous arrival of rice remains in the cultural deposits. The site reveals a

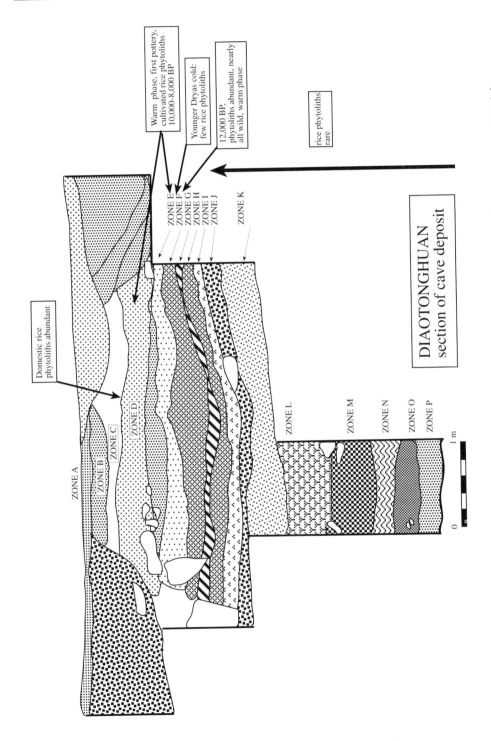

Warm phase, first pottery, cultivated rice phytoliths 10,000-8,000 BP

Younger Dryas cold: few rice phytoliths

12,000 BP, phytoliths abundant, nearly all wild, warm phase

rice phytoliths rare

Domestic rice phytoliths abundant

ZONE A
ZONE B
ZONE C
ZONE D
ZONE E
ZONE F
ZONE G
ZONE H
ZONE I
ZONE J
ZONE K
ZONE L
ZONE M
ZONE N
ZONE O
ZONE P

DIAOTONGHUAN
section of cave deposit

0   1 m

Figure 3. Section through the cave deposits of Diaotonguan, showing the relationship between the layers and presence of rice phytoliths.

sequence in which the domestic form of rice grew steadily in numbers relative to the wild, and reveals a harmony between the presence of rice and the changing climate. The first pottery from the site is potentially most significant, since ceramic vessels often reflect a more sedentary lifestyle, while rice has been found within a pot at the later site of Hemudu. It is likely that an increasing emphasis on cereals in the diet and using pottery vessels for cooking were linked. Similarly early evidence for an early ceramic industry has been found at Yuchanyan, another cave site overlooking low-lying, swampy terrain. This cave yielded the remains of fish, birds, 40 species of seeds and husks of rice transitional between wild and domestic. It is said to date in the region of 12,500 BP (Yuan and Zhang 1999). Xianrendong, a third major cave site, is located only a few hundred metres from Diaotonghuan and incorporates a similar cultural sequence.

These recent excavations disclose that the long warming period between approximately 10,000–8000 BP saw the northward expansion of rice into the Yangzi Valley, linked with an increase in the frequency of rice remains, much if not all of it wild. Pottery made an appearance in cultural contexts where the prevailing stone industry still included forms common during the earlier phases of the late Pleistocene. It is suggested that hunter-gatherers were becoming sedentary as they incorporated more rice into their diet.

The sequel to this trend is to be found in a new form of settlement, in which houses, cemeteries, pits and the remains of domestic activity accumulated as low mounds away from the limestone bluffs and onto the plains surrounding the major lakes of the middle Yangzi. The first and best known such site is Pengtoushan (Yan Wenming 1991). Excavations have revealed the remains of houses, a flourishing ceramic industry in which rice was used to temper the clay, and an inhumation cemetery in which the dead were accompanied by siltstone ornaments and pottery vessels. The radiocarbon dates cover rather a wide range, and it is best to concentrate on those AMS dates derived from rice remains used as a ceramic temper. These lie within the period 8000–9000 BP. More recent research in this area has uncovered similar remains from Bashidang, a mounded site only 20 km from Pengtoushan, and on the same plain surrounding Lake Dongting. The upper of the two cultural layers is dated to about 8000 BP. Excavations between 1993–7 revealed a defensive ditch and an old river bed, which preserved many plant remains, including over 15,000 grains of rice claimed to have been of a cultivated variety (Pei 1998). Twenty other plants were represented, including the water caltrop and lotus, both of which are easily propagated in the site's watery habitat. The survival of organic remains includes wooden spades, which could have been used in agriculture, vestiges of houses raised on piles, pottery tempered with rice husks and the bones of cattle, pigs, deer and chicken. A cemetery containing at least 100 inhumation graves is compatible with a long-term, permanently-occupied village (Higham and Lu 1998). Zhang and Wang (1998) have extended the search for early village communities into the Huai River valley and at Jiahu, they have uncovered the substantial area of 2400 sq m, finding wooden spades as well as stone sickle blades, knives and grinding stones.

These, in addition to the carbonized remains of rice grains, husks and phytoliths suggest that rice was being cultivated there within the period 9000–6800 BP. The significant point about these village communities is that they were established when the climate became colder after a long period of increasing warmth.

By integrating the cultural and climatic data, it is possible to propose a model for the transition to rice cultivation which recalls aspects of that proposed for the Levant at the same period (Bar-Yosef and Meadow 1995). The Yangzi Valley lies at the northern limit of wild rice under warm conditions, but a fall in mean temperature makes it marginal, if not impossible, for this plant's survival. Predominantly wild phytoliths from Diaotonghuan were abundant during a late Pleistocene warm phase, but fell away with the Younger Dryas cold. The long warming period which immediately followed saw phytoliths, now probably of a cultivated variety, increase markedly in conjunction with the earliest pottery making, but only so far in cave sites. When the climate again cooled at about 9000 BP, there was no retraction in the economic role of rice, but rather an expansion into permanent open villages. Here, the material culture took on a new aspect as spades and sickles appeared, more pottery was made from clay tempered with rice chaff, and the dead were interred in permanent cemeteries. It is suggested that, having become increasingly familiar with rice manipulation during the long warm phase, incipient or early rice agriculturalists withstood the next cold phase through a commitment to increasing the area under a now domestic strain.

The Huang He River cuts through the loess uplands before it reaches the Central Plains, home of the Shang Civilization. Here, the temperature has always been too cold for wild rice, but it is adaptive to *Setaria viridis*, the wild millet. In tandem with the transition to rice cultivation further south, the late Pleistocene hunter-gatherers of this region brought millet under cultivation, and we encounter the same variety of village communities. Peiligang is the best known, over 2000 sq m having been excavated. There are many parallels, in terms of community structure and material remains, with the contemporary rice-growing sites of the middle Yangzi. Pottery was widely employed, and even fired in the controlled atmosphere provided by closed kilns. Stone sickles with serrated edges were made, querns raised on four feet appeared and the dead were interred in communal cemeteries accompanied by pottery vessels, polished stone adze-heads and querns (HATIA 1984). Cishan is a second site with clear evidence for the cultivation of millet, and the domestication of pigs, dogs and possibly cattle. Continued manufacture of bone projectile points and the collection of nuts and seeds indicate how the new productive economy continued alongside traditional hunting and gathering. Yet the importance of millet in the maintenance of these communities was considerable, as may be seen in the size and number of deep storage pits, presumed to have been used to store grain for the winter.

The long-term implications of these transitions are considerable, for they project this part of East Asia into the forefront of the debate on the potential links between archaeology, linguistics and human biology. If sedentary agriculture promoted population growth and settlement fission, so the analysis of language distributions and human DNA should allow us to track the progress of human expansion. Thus, the distribution of Austroasiatic and Austronesian languages, and the southern Mongoloid human type, might reflect the intrusive thrust of agricultural societies outward from an original homeland in the Yangzi Valley. The mechanics of the introduction of rice cultivation to the northeast, into Korea and Japan, also bear scrutiny. In the Yangzi Valley itself, the establishment of an increasingly dense network of agricultural villages ascribed to the Daxi culture reflects a growing human population, linked with sharper social divisions within the community. In the Huang He Valley, the Yangshao and Dawenkou cultures, dated from about 7000 BP, reveal the development of mature and increasingly complex agricultural societies.

Coastal hunter-gatherers

During the extreme cold of the late Pleistocene, the world's oceans were considerably lower than at present, thus exposing extensive coastal lowlands. Land bridges linked Asia with Alaska, and Hokkaido with the mainland. The other islands of Japan became one land mass, and only the narrowest of straits separated Honshu from Korea to the west, and Hokkaido to the north. The sharp climatic amelioration of the Holocene saw the sea-level rise even beyond its present position, thereby drowning the former plains and creating raised beaches inland. The latter are marked by prehistoric settlements which become archaeologically visible from about 6000 BC (Fig. 4).

From the Pacific coast of Siberia to the tropical shore of Australia, this marine habitat was host to a myriad of coastal hunter-gatherer communities. In some areas, there was a pattern of long-term stability at least in terms of the subsistence base, in others there were marked changes. First and foremost, it must be stressed that the coast, particularly where punctured by major estuaries, is a rich habitat in terms of bio-productivity. A combination of fish, shellfish, marine mammal and terrestrial food resources makes possible a degree of sedentism in foraging communities which provides, at least in Japan and Korea, a degree of stability which encouraged marked social complexity.

The earliest ceramic industry known is but one of the indices of such settlement stability, for pottery vessels are not adaptive to a mobile lifestyle. Pottery has long been associated with the Holocene Jomon culture sites. Now, it is possible to trace the origins of ceramic industries back into the late Pleistocene. At Shimomouchi, far from the coast in central Honshu, pottery sherds have been found sealed by pumice deposited by Mt Asama. Radiocarbon dates indicate an age in the vicinity of 16,000 years ago. Other examples of this undecorated style of so-called Mumondoki pottery have come from Oodaiyamamoto near Shimomouchi, Ushirono north-east of Tokyo and Kamino just

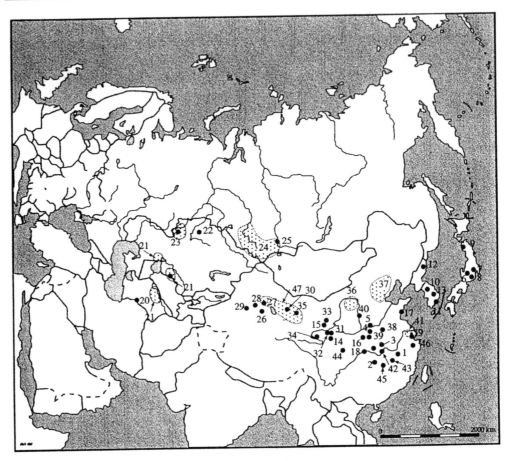

Figure 4. The distribution of the sites and cultures mentioned in the text.
1. Diaotonghuan, Xianrendong 2. Pengtoushan, Bashidang, Chengtoushan 3. Jiahu, Qujialing 4. Peiligang, Meishan, Erlitou, Zhengzhou 5. Cishan, Anyang 6. Shimomouchi 7. Ushirono 8. Kamino 9. Kazahari 10. Osanni 11. Tongsamdong 12. Sopohang 13. Hupori 14. Linjia 15. Liuwan 16. Puyang 17. Chengzi 18. Daxi 19. Songze 20. Djeitun 21. Area of the Kelteminar culture 22. Botai 23. Area of Surtanda culture 24. Afanasievo culture core area 25. Minusinsk 26. Gumugou 27. Aidinghu, Turfan 28. Xintala 29. Haladun 30. Dunhuang 31. Qinweijia 32. Dahezhuang 33. Huangniangniangtai 34. Gamatai 35. Huoshaogou 36. Area of the Zhukaigou culture 37. Area of the lower Xiajiadian culture 38. Pingliangtai 39. Wangchenggang 40. Taosi 41. Area of the Liangzhu culture 42. Panlongcheng 43. Wucheng, Xin'gan 44. Sanxingdui 45. Yuchanyan 46. Hemudu 47. Area of the Siba culture.
Courtesy Dora Kemp.

west of Tokyo. Tsutsumi (1999) has suggested that vessels may have been used for cooking acorns: some sherds still bear traces of soot. A second early style of pottery known as Ryutaimonndoki ware has been identified in southern Kyushu.

With the rising sea-level, we find that many coastal sites ascribed to the long period of the Jomon culture based their sedentary way of life on the wealth of the coast. The archaeological record for this period, arguably the most completely documented for any prehistoric society in the world, includes many shell mounds which incorporate pit houses, fishing implements, and an economy which incorporated sea mammals, shell-fish collecting, fishing, and the collection of nuts. The ritual life, which flourished on this rich subsistence base, included extraordinarily complex pottery vessels and richly-endowed individuals in the cemeteries. The people must have had considerable skill in deep-sea navigation, given the similar pot forms found in Japan and in contemporary Korean sites. There was also an element of specialization to be seen in the clear evidence for community craft industries, and exchange patterns.

Rice grains have been found in late and final Jomon, between the late second and mid first millennia BC, and rice remains have been uncovered in association with final Jomon pottery (Yoshizaki 1997). But the adoption of rice agriculture was not universally grasped, particularly in northern Honshu and Hokkaido, where there is a growing body of evidence in favour of some local domestication of food plants, such as the beefsteak herb and barn-yard grass (Crawford and Takamiya 1990; Barnes 1993). Indeed, the critical importance of flotation for the accurate portrayal of late Jomon subsistence is nowhere more clearly seen than at Kazahari in north-eastern Honshu. Fifteen genera were represented in a sample of 367 seeds recovered from a pit house, of which 15 came from exotic domestic plants: seven specimens of rice and eight of millet (D'Andrea *et al.* 1995).

Riverine and coastal settlements incorporating pit houses in Korea stretch from the Yalu and Tumen rivers in the north to the southern coast. Far less is known about these Chulmun (comb ware) sites than their contemporaries in Japan. Certainly dating between 6000–2000 BC, some sites could be as early, on the grounds of ceramic typology, as the initial Jomon. Speculation reigns on the origins of this ceramic tradition, whether it be from the south, or represents an intrusive movement from the north. Too little is known on the degree to which agriculture co-existed with the abundant evidence for maritime hunting and gathering, and only few burials have been found. However, sites like Osanni, dating between 6000–4500 BC, reveal the existence of round to oval dwellings centred upon hearths. Numerous stone fishhooks and weights, which proba-bly represent net fishing, reveal a maritime orientation. Tongsamdong in Pusan Bay to the south comprises a shell midden incorporating the remains of sharks, tuna, cod, sea lions and whales. Wild cattle and pig were also hunted. Sopohang, on the Tumen River near Russian Siberia, is a large mound in which oyster shells predominate, the superim-posed house floors indicating a degree of permanence in settlement. One house yielded 40 bone awls, perhaps due to some form of specialization (Nelson 1993). There is no equivalent to the rich mortuary data from the Jomon sites, but an element of ritual is seen in the 130 large polished stone axes from a grave at Hupori, set out in parallel rows and surrounded by a circle of stones. Animal and human figurines are also found in many Chulmun sites. The recovery of the remains of millet, as well as slate hoes, suggests that some form of agriculture was introduced into the region from the west, much as the knowledge of rice was to reach Japan.

The expansion of agriculture

The expansion of rice and millet agriculturalists has attracted much attention over the past two decades, but the nature of their interaction with coastal hunter-gatherers is of equal interest. One can, indeed, follow several themes in considering the implications of the domestication of millet, rice and domestic animals. There is the inexorable expansion of settled village communities from centres of innovation, which in due course saw farmers intrude into eastern India, Southeast Asia, Taiwan south to Island Southeast Asia and beyond, and the knowledge of farming reach Korea and Japan. Each region presents opportunities for a combination of archaeological, linguistic and human biological research to establish how and when these developments occurred. There is also the issue of consequential changes in society in the heartlands, so to speak, of the Neolithic Revolution in East Asia.

Hitherto, most research on the latter has concentrated in the so-called nuclear area of the Huang He Valley. Now that the Yangzi Valley has been identified as the focus of early rice cultivation, this region too holds centre stage in any review of increasing social complexity prior to the transition to the state. The archaeological sequence in the Yellow River valley saw a proliferation of villages with an economy based on millet cultivation, sites assigned to two large groupings, the Yangshao in the west, and the Dawenkou to the east. Both can be subdivided regionally and chronologically over two millennia from about 5000 BC. Settlements of the Majiayao phase of the Gansu Yangshao culture, for example, incorporate semi-subterranean houses equipped with hearths, a wide repertoire of painted pottery vessels and extensive cemeteries containing inhumation graves. A storage pit at Linjia contained nearly 2 cubic metres of millet (GPMNNC 1984). Some of the excavations in subsequent Yangshao sites in this area have furnished among the largest samples of mortuary remains for this type of site anywhere. Liuwan, for example, has yielded about 1500 burials belonging to the Banshan and Machang phases (2700–2000 BC). Social differentiation was probably well developed, to judge from variations in the quantity of grave goods from virtually none to over 90 pottery vessels. At Yuanyangchi, graves were found in rows and included pottery vessels and stone blades held in a wooden handle as offerings (GPM 1982). The spiritual world of the Yangshao farmers is to be seen in the remarkable burial of a shaman, flanked by a dragon and a tiger formed by shells, from Puyang (Chang 1999).

The Dawenkou culture of Shandong, which dates between approximately 4500–2400 BC, is best documented by mortuary remains. Successive phases reveal an increasing hierarchy based upon the quantity and nature of associated offerings, and the degree of energy expended in, for example, the provision of ledges to contain the grave goods. In the earliest of Chang's proposed three phases, there is no major difference in grave wealth, but at Liulin, the graves are set out in groups suggestive of people related to each other within one community (NM 1965). Pearson (1981) has shown that the distinctions are based on sex rather than status, men being buried with adzes and chisels, women with spindle whorls. During the middle phase at Dawenkou and Chengzi, individuals in wooden coffins were increasingly superimposed over their predecessors, and certain graves became particularly rich, incorporating large assemblages of fine black pottery vessels and jade ornaments. This trend continued into the final phases, the presence of exotic jades and outstanding pottery vessels suggesting the possibility of craft specialization in the service of the élite in society.

In the middle Yangzi Valley, the transition to an economy based on rice agriculture saw the development of the Daxi culture. As with Yangshao and Dawenkou, it can be subdivided into several phases (Li Wenjie 1986). Sites incorporating houses of clay and bamboo are found on elevated ground commanding wetlands suitable for rice cultivation. Much rice has been found, in association with the remains of domestic cattle and pigs. At Daxi itself, the 208 excavated graves indicate increasing emphasis on the provision of jade ornaments over time, and the incorporation of pottery vessels as grave goods at the expense of stone and bone tools (MSP 1981). A similar trend is seen lower down the Yangzi Valley, where the Songze site has yielded clustered inhumation graves accompanied by a much greater variety of exotic goods than the preceding Majiabang sites. Again, jades in the form of pendants and split rings reveal increasing social differences.

In those areas which witnessed an indigenous transition to agriculture, be it based on millet or rice, there was an ensuing period of population growth, an increasing density in the distribution of settlements, and a sharpening in social ranking as jade and ceramics were converted into objects of mortuary display. During the three millennia involved, items of metal were either absent or sufficiently rare as to suggest a lack of firm provenance. From the beginning of the new millennium, about 2000 years BC, however, there were major changes.

The steppe and the Bronze Age

One of the most important avenues of research in this vast region is the timing and nature of cultural contact across the expanse of steppe, which provides east–west passage from Hungary to Gansu in western China. Only a few of the many topics worthy of examination can be reviewed. These include the establishment of agriculture, and the degree to which a knowledge of bronze and later, iron technology spread from west to east, or had independent centres of innovation. There are also the origins and implications of the domestication of the horse and invention of wheeled vehicles and the war chariot, and the reasons underlying the presence of Indo-European Tocharian languages in the Tarim Basin, an area which has also yielded the desiccated remains of people who look like Europeans, and who wore clothes paralleled far to the west of their settlements (Mair 1995, 1998a).

With the ameliorating climate at the end of the last glacial, it is evident that hunter-gatherer groups with a microlithic stone industry were engaged in hunting and fishing in the south-eastern flanks of the Urals. The environment at that period, to judge from the presence of bones from the elk, beaver and bear, would have been a relatively temperate forest. The steppe, however, was not far off, as many sites also contain the remains of wild horses. Matiushin (1986) has suggested, on the basis of the microlithic industries, that there were connections with northern Iraq and Iran. East of the Caspian, however, hunting and gathering communities continued to exploit the steppe environment until well into the third millennium BC. Anthony (1998), for example, has drawn attention to a series of cultures which flourished in this environment, while the early agricultural settlements such as Djeitun were confined to the well-watered tracts further to the south (Matiushin 1986). Several groups of hunter-gatherers have been identified. The Kelteminar culture, for example, exploited the Aral Basin, particularly along the courses of the Amu Darya and the Syr Darya, during the fourth into the third millennium BC. The same situation obtained with the Botai and Surtanda cultures of the steppes north of the Aral Sea (Dolukhanov 1986).

The Botai culture of the third millennium BC is particularly interesting, because although still based on hunting and gathering, domestic horses were in use (Kislenko and Tatarintseva 1999). Many large settlements have been investigated, some attaining an area of 15 ha, home, according to the density of semi-subterranean dwellings, to a substantial population. At Botai itself, the remains of 158 such houses have been found, disposed in a linear fashion along what look like streets up to 50 m long (Fig. 5). Circular houses incorporated a central hearth, an area for sleeping and another where ritual or cult objects predominated. There was a major interest in horses, which are represented in extraordinary numbers. Over 70,000 individual animals have been counted on the basis of the bone sample, from a mere 2.5 per cent of the site. Moreover, the burials, placed in old houses, were associated with what looks like a horse cult with the animals' crania being set round the walls. The material culture also provides evidence for horse-riding in the form of bone pieces for bridles, but other elements of the material culture, the knives, for example, spearheads and stone maces indicate either a commitment to hunting, or perhaps inter-group conflict. The quarry for the former included wild cattle, bison, elk and roe deer.

Kislenko and Tatarintseva (1999) have described evidence which links the Botai sites with the Afanasievo culture of the Irtysh, Ob and Yenesei valleys. This complex of many sites appears as an intrusive element east of the Urals, and it may well represent an eastward movement of people belonging to the Yamnaya culture. The latter, which concentrates west of the Urals and dates in its earliest phase to about 3500 BC, is significant not only for the presence of copper-based metallurgy, but also for the presence of domestic horses and wheeled carts (Anthony 1998). The potential of rapid transport by horse, and the movement of heavy goods through the use of baggage

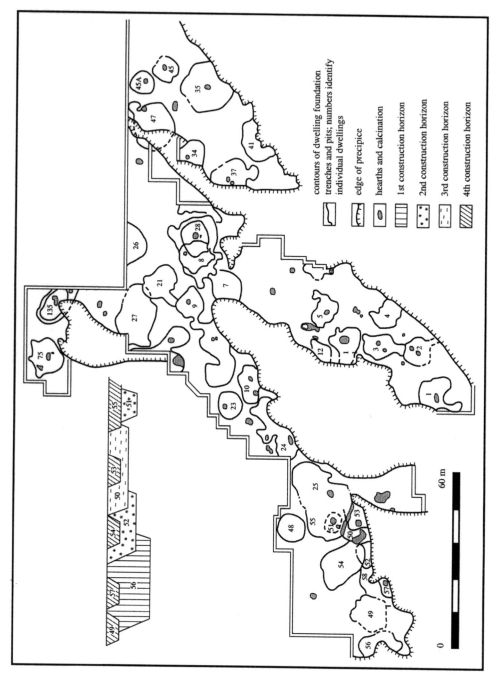

Figure 5. The south-western portion of the Botai excavations, showing the distribution of dwellings. Courtesy Dora Kemp.

trains, would clearly have opened wide vistas for the settlement of the steppes. This move east is a likely explanation for the thick distribution of Afanasievo sites.

Most Afanasievo sites are cemeteries, in which the dead were interred in the main with pottery vessels but occasionally one encounters copper beads, and gold and silver ornaments, as well as the remains of horses, sheep and cattle. Graves, singly or in groups, were ringed by a stone wall or stones set in a circle. The greatest density of sites lies in the copper-rich Minusinsk Basin in the middle reaches of the Yenesei Valley (Okladnikov 1990). It is claimed that the form of the crania of these people matches that found to the west, and was of Europoid affiliations. The metal industry became much more sophisticated in the succeeding Okunevo sites, for by now copper was being alloyed, and cast into knives, awls, fish hooks and bangles. The presence of tin suggests that the rich deposits of the Rudny Altai were by now exploited.

An Zhimin has considered the expansion of copper-based industries further east still, into the eastern margin of the Tarim Basin, as being evidence for contact of one form or another with the Afanasievo culture. Demonstrating this would stress the impact of horse transport during the Steppe Bronze Age. The Gumugou cemetery of the Könchi River valley is a key site in appreciating the chronology and cultural affiliations of the Tarim Basin Bronze Age. During the early period, dated between 2000–1500 BC, grave goods include copper, bone and jade ornaments, together with wheat grains but no pottery. During the middle period, dating to 1500–1000 BC, painted pottery, woollen clothing, bronze knives, arrowheads, awls, needles, mirrors and plaques were recovered from graves. The late period (1000–400 BC) incorporated collective burials with bronze, gold, silver, bronze knives, awls, arrow and spearheads, mirrors and belt buckles. A number of small iron items were also found.

Gumugou is rightly renowned for the survival of a wide range of organic remains which, if one takes the most likely set of radiocarbon results, date in the vicinity of 1700–1500 BC. Kuzmina (1998) has described the recovery of 42 graves lined with wood, in which the dead lay on a bed of twigs and birch bark. Barber's (1998) investigation of the clothing has revealed a tradition based on sheep's wool, in which the fabric was tailored on a loom rather than cut and stitched. One woman wore a cap and a woven woollen wrap. Boots and trousers have also survived. Extraordinarily, the plaid twills from this cemetery are similar to fragments from far to the west at Hallstatt in Austria. She has suggested that these two distant groups inherited the same textile tradition from a common source. Further details of the Gumugou burial rituals hint at an origin in the Afanasievo culture, including the provision of animal remains and the enclosing of the graves by a fence. Similar copper-based knives, awls, bracelets and earrings are also found. There is also convincing evidence, in the form of the remains of domestic goats, sheep, cattle and wheat, that the Gumugou economy incorporated agriculture and stock raising, in association with hunting and gathering. The preferred location of this and related sites was emphatically along the oases where rivers flowed from the surrounding mountains into the arid Tarim Basin.

Gumugou is but one of many cemeteries located along the northern and southern margins of the basin. He Dexiu (1998) has described the burials from Zughanluq, a site that extends over 80 ha. Four desiccated corpses were found in one of the tombs. The primary interment was of an old woman, laid out on a blanket of wool and felt. She wore a woollen robe of a purple colour, and leather boots. A piece of red wool had been inserted into each of her nostrils. Her hands, eyelids and forehead had been tattooed with delicate patterns and she was accompanied by millet cakes. This tomb was covered by a roof of logs from the poplar tree, reeds and various branches, and a child had, according to the excavator, been forced head first into the tomb chamber while still alive. Perhaps the most unexpected feature of the dead in this and all the related graves in the Tarim Basin is that they look like Europeans.

Chen and Hiebert (1995) have considered all the known Xinjiang sites of this period, and have emphasized the singular adaptation to the oases set on the margins of one of the driest and most desolate of regions. Much attention has been given to the early occupants of these sites as possible arrivals from far to the west, and hence their potential role in the transmission of ideas and goods into China. But these sites should also be considered with a local, regional focus, particularly the growing body of evidence for long-term stability once established in the oasis enclaves. Although there are regional variations, the contemporary cultures of Gumugou, Aidinghu, Haladun and Xintala all reflect a similar adaptation to the Tarim Basin oases, each anticipating a degree of continuity which endured well into the first millennium BC. Again, the physical remains have been seen as similar to those of the Afanasievo culture to the west.

This finding has alerted many specialists to the need to place these people relative not only to other archaeological sites to east and west, but also to explore their DNA, and the possible affiliations of their language. The application of ancient DNA sequencing to the resolution of relationships between populations in prehistory is still in its infancy. The first results of this vital new technique, however, are revealing in that the European-looking corpses have a mitochondrial DNA pattern which falls into haplogroup H. This concentrates in Europe (Francalacci 1998). At the least, such a finding hints at a western origin for these communities of the Tarim Basin.

An understanding of the possible linguistic affiliations of these remote prehistoric people entails proceeding forwards in time to the seventh century AD (Mair 1998b). As Boltz (1999) has explained, manuscripts from ancient cities in the Tarim Basin near Kucha, Turfan and Karashahr were written in an Indic script derived from Brahmi. The languages employed in these texts are Indo-European and fall into two groups. Tocharian A or Agnean was a liturgical language, which survived in monastic texts. Tocharian B or Kuchean survived into the first millennium AD in commercial and religious texts. Their relationship with other Indo-European words can be seen in a number of cognates. A hundred, in Tocharian B, is *kante*, but *centum* in Latin. The word for honey in Tocharian B is *mit*, in Sanskrit *madhu*, and in English, the cognate survives in the word mead. The name Tocharian comes from Ptolemy who, in the second century AD, referred to Thagouroi in Gansu, and Thochoroi in Sogdiana. Linguists have pointed out that Tocharian separated early from other Indo-European languages. Indeed, a consensus is almost forming round the hypothesis that Proto-Tocharian was probably already spoken by about 3000 BC on the steppes (Renfrew 1998). Mallory (1995, 1998), in reviewing possible archaeological contexts within which Proto-Tocharian was spoken, has identified the Afanasievo culture of about 2500 BC as the most likely candidate.

Bronze, chariots and Chinese civilization

Given the uniquely gifted skills of Chinese bronze workers, and the ritual and festive importance of their output, it is at first strange that the earliest evidence for bronze-casting should be found in the remote reaches of Gansu, far to the west of the earliest states. A consideration of the geography of this area, however, poses an important possibility. This region of early metallurgy is linked by the Gansu corridor and the Zungarian gates to the open grasslands of Kazakhstan. The corridor is almost 1000 km long and 80 km wide, and while arid, incorporates a series of oases fed by the waters of the Nan Shan Range. This natural conduit, centred on oases at sites such as Dunhuang, is a likely route for the transmission of the knowledge of copper-based metallurgy into China.

Linduff (2000) has described sites of the Majiayao and Machang cultures in Gansu, Qinghai and Xinjiang which include cast and forged copper knives and other tools dated between 2740–1900. This third-millennium bronze industry in far western China was maintained in the Qijia culture. This comprises a series of agricultural villages dated between 2300–1800 BC, several of which have been excavated. At Qinweijia, for example, two burial areas were uncovered, the dead being accompanied by pottery vessels, needles, polished stone adze heads and pigs' mandibles (GATIA 1975). Some graves overlie storage pits, which contained a few objects in bronze and copper. An axe and a ring are of leaded bronze, a disc is of copper (Sun Shuyun and Han Rubin 1981). The industry appears fully fledged, for the axe was cast in a stone mould and hardened by annealing. Excavations at Dahezhuang have opened a substantial area of burials and house remains (GATIA 1974). The burials were on the same orientation as at Qinweijia, and contained similar bone implements, pottery vessels and pigs' jaws. One pot also contained millet, and millet was also found adhering to a copper knife found beside one of the houses. Copper-based knives, chisels, awls and rings have also been recovered (Chang 1986). Huangniangniangtai has provided 32 copper-based items, including knives, awls, chisels, and a possible hairpin. While the knife and three awls analysed by Sun Shuyun and Han Rubin (1981) were of unalloyed copper, a mirror from the related site of Gamatai included 9.6 per cent of tin.

The Siba culture of the same region dates between 1900–1600 BC. Huoshaogou is the best documented of these sites, incorporating 312 excavated burials set out in five groups. Grave goods include gold and bronze earrings, bronze knives, daggers, spearheads and socketed axes more akin to those of the Andronovo culture of southern Siberia than the later examples on the Central Plain of China (Chernyk 1992). The methods of heating and hammering these implements recall western methods of metalworking, rather than the techniques practised on the Central Plain of the Huang He (Linduff 1998, 2000).

Several other cultures on the northern and western margins of the Central Plain saw an early development of bronze-working (Linduff 1998). The Zhukaigou culture of northern Shaanxi Province also incorporated bronze needles, awls and knives in phase 2, which recall Qijia forms (Linduff 1995), and the lower Xiajiadian culture of southeastern Inner Mongolia involves village communities, often concentrating round a larger one, sustained by domestic stock and millet cultivation. Again, copper and bronze ornaments, knives and axes accompany the dead.

These sites, in particular those from Gansu, question the indigenous origins of the Chinese bronze tradition. An Zhimin (1998) has noted the western parallels in copper- and bronze-working, and the strategic location of the Qijia sites adds weight to the possibility that horse transport across the steppes in the third millennium BC brought not only speakers of an Indo-European language, but also the technological expertise developed in the west.

The first rare bronze artefacts east of Gansu occur in a series of settlements ascribed to the Longshan culture. These feature a major innovation in settlement archaeology, for they are surrounded by stamped-earth walls. Pingliangtai, for example, incorporates a walled area of 5 ha entered through gateways on the northern and southern walls, within which lies an inner enclosure of 185 sq m. One pit contained what might be the remains of a copper-based artefact. At Wangchenggang, the defences enclose an area of 0.75 of a hectare, and the walls contain further foundations of stamped earth which incorporate what are probably sacrificial skeletons. A fragment of a bronze vessel from a late pit could well date to the early second millennium BC. Mortuary remains from this period are best represented in the sample of over 1000 graves excavated at Taosi (Shanxi-ATIA 1980). The trends to increasing social complexity seen in the preceding phases were further intensified: nine of the graves, all those identified being male, were exceptionally rich, grave goods including jade rings and axes, and a wooden drum covered in crocodile skin (Pearson and Underhill 1987). Eighty graves fall into a middle category in terms of wealth, while the large number of remaining interments contained few, if any, offerings. Only one bronze object, part of a bell with 1.5 per cent of tin, was recovered. Meishan has furnished domestic house foundations as well as two fragments of crucible, enough to confirm that a knowledge of bronze-casting, which was to dominate the material culture of this area in due course, was entering the Huang He Valley at this juncture.

A similar pattern of increasing complexity based on Daxi culture foundations can be recognized in the Yangzi Valley. Research here is in its infancy, but the period and area must represent one of the most promising, for at Chengtoushan on the plains surrounding Lake Dongting, part of an 8-ha walled settlement has been uncovered (He Jiejun 1995). There are many remarkable findings: a wooden bridge spanned a stream, human remains within the stamped-earth walls, a street 2 m wide, and a wooden oar. Five hundred burials have been examined, and sufficient organic remains survive to document a diet based on rice, but including gourds and walnuts. This is one of many sites now known, a corpus belonging to the Qujialing culture. Once again, similar trends may be detected in the lower Yangzi on the basis of the well-known Liangzhu culture. The burial of a young man at Sidun included 24 jade rings and 33 tubes (cong) embellished with animal mask and bird designs, which probably reflect his shamanic powers (NM 1984). Bronzes in the Yangzi Valley appear slightly later than the Qujialing or Liangzhu contexts, and as seen at the walled city of Panlongcheng, probably derive from contact with the Huang He Valley during the Erligang phase.

Civilization

Erlitou, located on the bank of the Luo River, resembles in its first two occupation phases the other sites of the early second millennium in the Huang He Valley. There are the same stamped-earth walls and the dead, in their individual graves, were accompanied by pottery vessels, jades and a small number of bronzes, including bells. The less fortunate were dumped in pits with no ceremony (EATIA 1980; Zhao Ziquan 1985). The third and fourth phases, beginning in the sixteenth century BC, saw major changes. The foundations of two palaces have been uncovered, the first incorporating a central hall over 30 m in length which dominated a private courtyard measuring 100 by 100 m. Pits dug into the raised terrace below this complex contain human skeletons of individuals who were probably sacrificed. The second structure incorporated an outstandingly large tomb, which, though plundered and virtually empty when excavated, indicates by its very size a new departure in energy expended on high-status burials. Flannery (1998, 1999) has suggested that palaces are a consistent and compelling indicator of the presence of a state. At Erlitou, this is reinforced by the presence of less august housing remains, as well as the substantial area given over to bronze-casting. Previous castings were of a relatively simple kind: knives, trinkets and bells. But the new Erlitou specialists essayed much more demanding items of which the two dozen or so *jue* wine goblets raised on tripod feet are best known. These involved the novel technique of piece

moulds, whereby a clay core and outer clay pieces were formed over a model. Having decorated these clay moulds with the intended pattern to appear on the bronze, the pieces were fitted tightly together and the bronze poured into the space vacated by the original model in one action. Other bronzes include *ge* dagger axes and knives, and ornamental discs inlaid with turquoise (Barnard 1987). Jades also proliferated in élite graves, including the *yazhang* blades, a *ge* blade and one *cong* tube. All these élite grave goods were incorporated in burials provided with painted wooden coffins. The Erlitou site was not unique, and its extensive excavations indicate how an élite commanded a large labour force, and had access by an exchange network to exotic goods including copper, tin, turquoise, jade and shell.

The rise of regional states

The distorted image of state formation in China, resulting from a concentration of fieldwork in the Central Plains, has been redressed in the past decade through fieldwork and chance finds. Hitherto, syntheses of Chinese civilization have concentrated on the state of Shang, with particular reference to the late capital of Anyang. This situation is easily understood, for it was at Anyang that the Shang royal tombs have been explored, and whence virtually the entire documentary record derives (Keightley 1999b).

The preceding phase of the Shang state is best documented on the basis of the Erligang phase at Zhengzhou (1500–1300). This city was surrounded by massive walls made of stamped earth which, even today, survive to a basal width of 22 m and a height of nearly 10 m. These enclose an area of about 300 ha, but settlement and industrial sites outside the walls cover 2500 ha. The extramural area includes a series of specialist workshops the products of which reveal technological advances over the Erlitou piece-mould technique, incorporating multiple pours of bronze to fashion much larger and more complex feasting vessels. A *ting* tripod found in a burial outside the walled area weighs 86.4 kg, an indication of the increasing scale of bronze production. There is also a bone workshop producing weaponry, often with human remains as the raw material. An Chin-huai (1986) has described the earth foundations for large structures within the city walls, incorporating a columned building and a concentration of jades. Unfortunately, Zhengzhou lies under a modern city, thus limiting the degree to which excavation can illuminate this vital phase of the Shang polity. No élite royal graves, for example, have yet been identified.

Some indication of the potential wealth of such élite graves can be perceived at Lijiazui, a burial area associated with the walled settlement of Panlongcheng. We have seen how the Qujialing culture sites such as Chengtoushan match the early walled settlements of the Central Plains. Panlongcheng shows that the Yangzi Valley was also

deeply involved in progress towards regional states in the Middle Shang period, for here we encounter another example of a city wall of stamped earth, albeit not as large as Zhengzhou. There is a foundation for what might well have been an élite palace within the walled precinct and at Lijiazui, the richest known burial of this period in China has been uncovered. The rectangular pit incorporated at least two wooden, painted coffins and ledges to retain three sacrificed individuals and a host of grave goods in jade, bronze, ceramics and wood. The recognition of bronze workshops indicates that many of the vessels were locally manufactured, although clearly of Erligang inspiration. Indeed, Bagley (1999) has suggested that this site might represent an Erligang period outpost to secure the supply of copper from southern mines.

Wucheng lies even further south of the alleged seminal area of Chinese civilization, in the valley of the Gan River south of Lake Poyang. Even the Shang dominance of early writing systems is challenged here, for some ceramic vessels incorporate passages in an undeciphered script. The ceramic industry itself is highly sophisticated, and was probably the centre for exporting wares into the Central Plains. The most significant find from this region, however, was made 20 km away at Xin'gan: the richest burial of this period in China, excepting only that of Fu Hao, a royal consort, at Anyang (Bagley 1993). The mortuary offerings include over 50 bronze vessels, many tools and weapons, and hundreds of items in jade. Although some bronzes show Erligang influence, the majority of the assemblage from Xin'gan reveals local innovations, such as the casting of tigers to adorn the handles of a huge *fangding* cauldron.

Sanxingdui is located north of Chengdu in Sichuan Province. The city walls, 40 m wide at the base, enclose an area of 260 ha but again, there are many signs of occupation outside the walled and moated precinct. It is considered likely that the city dates within the period 1700–1100 BC, and must represent the local development of a state raised on the rich agricultural potential of the Sichuan Basin. The site is best documented on the basis of the contents of two extraordinary ritual pits (SPCRAC 1987; Bagley 1988). The first contained cowrie shells, elephant tusks and items of gold, jade and bronze. The bronzes included a number of life-sized heads not known elsewhere in China. The second pit incorporated first a layer of jade items, then bronzes and finally a layer of 60 elephant tusks. The bronzes have attracted most attention for they, too, are unmatched elsewhere. There are three trees bearing fruit and feeding birds, one of which is almost 4 m in height. Huge human face masks, still retaining fragments of gold leaf, reach an extraordinary size: one is 1.38 m wide and its eyes protrude on stalks 16 cm long. Then there is a human figure, cast in one pouring which took over 180 kg of bronze, and stands 2.62 m high on its podium. Ritual vessels were cast in the form of a dragon, a tiger, and a bird. There are but two ritual pits, in which objects were burnt and inhumed, it is thought, as offerings to the ancestors. Further excavations at sites such as Sanxingdui can only further redress the imbalance caused by the concentration of research at Anyang.

Anyang and the late Shang state

The importance of Anyang lies in the clarity with which it is possible to penetrate the internal organization of an early Chinese state. This reflects the discovery in the royal archives of inscriptions stored on turtle plastrons and bovid scapulae, the examination of thousands of graves from the kings' down to the humblest sacrificial victims', the excavation of élite secular structures and the uncovering of specialist workshops. The written records cover the last nine of the 29 recorded kings of Shang, from the reign of Wu Ding to the last sovereign, Di Xin. Tribute offerings to the royal court included the bones required for divination. Holes were punctured into these bones, and the cracks, which resulted from the application of heat, were interpreted by an élite group of diviners. Their predictions were then recorded in writing on bones ultimately destined for the archives. Over 200,000 such texts are known. The texts reveal what most interested the Shang court, and thereby provides clues on the organization of the state in terms of subsistence, political alliances, warfare and ideology. Prospects for the millet harvest, for example, are often mentioned along with weather forecasts and floods. There are references to military strategy, the taking of prisoners and formation of alliances. The prospects for a male infant, then as now, preoccupied Chinese families, as did the causes of illness and ritual cures.

The inscriptions reveal concern with the ancestors and the rituals necessary to communicate with them and obtain their benediction. The king was seen as a mediator between the present and the powers imbued in the ancestors. Rituals to appease the ancestral spirits gave the king immense cult power, and this was put into practice by feasting and sacrifice. Indeed, to understand the importance of the royal ancestors is the key to appreciating the intense energy expended in mortuary rituals and the provision of bronzes. The bronze industry was dedicated to ritual objects rather than tools or weaponry. Colossal vessels, for example, were employed in the feasts involved in communicating with the deities. Offerings of wine and animals were undertaken on a large scale. Human sacrifices involved the shedding of blood and dismemberment, the largest recorded number of victims being in the vicinity of 400. Human sacrifice and the immolation of great wealth were also part of the rituals whereby a dead ruler became an ancestral divinity. The size of the royal graves at Anyang represents a considerable investment of labour. The deep pits, reached by four ramps and surrounded by ledges, would have contained a wooden chamber vestiges of which survive despite the attentions of generations of looters. High-status retainers, perhaps even some relatives, were interred without mutilation in the lower part of the grave, often in their own wooden coffin in association with mortuary gifts. Sacrificial victims, often young men and children, were usually found decapitated in groups, either in the grave fill of tamped earth, on the ramps or with up to 10 individuals in pits set out in rows alongside the royal tomb. None of the kings' burial pits has survived intact, but the grave of a royal

consort, Fu Hao, was found undisturbed. It contained over 440 bronzes weighing 1.5 tonnes and 590 jades, some of which were probably heirlooms over a millennium old when buried.

The archaeological and epigraphic evidence points to a substantial urban centre at Anyang. Over 5000 burials have been examined. The sample of 939 in the western cemetery falls into eight spatial groups, each subdivided into what seem to have been lineage plots of up to 40 graves. In contrast to royal wealth, only 67 included bronzes, and most were accompanied only by a handful of pottery vessels. But these people, whose average age fell in the mid 30s, would have contributed to the specialized workforce commanded by the sovereign for the casting of ceremonial bronzes, weapons and agricultural implements, or the vigorous industry in fashioning bone weaponry and ornaments. Some may have been skilled in the manufacture of the chariots, which represent a major innovation at Anyang compared with preceding Shang royal centres.

These chariots, along with a corpus of exotic bronzes, provide compelling evidence for contact with the eastern steppes. The chariot arrived fully developed in China, and words used to describe the chariot, parts of the wheel and the axle were borrowed from Indo-European sources (Lubotsky 1998). Even the word for horse, a cognate in Mongolic, Korean, Japanese and Chinese, suggests to Janhunen (1998) a single origin, possibly during one wave of contact across the steppes. Yet, as in the case of bronze technology, the Chinese took the innovation and embellished it, including, for example, far more spokes than are seen in the west.

Both the Shang and their rivals may well have applied chariots to warfare. As in most, if not all, archaic states, there was always the problem of securing control over peripheral polities who might see themselves as vassals under certain circumstances, and as independent under others. Hence the concern expressed in the texts for alliance structures and warfare. Again, the durability of the state depended ultimately upon the energy provided by surplus agricultural production. In the case of the Shang, this involved millet, a plant no less susceptible than others to disease. Hence the Shang countryside would have included dependent villages surrounded by their fields, as well as royal domains in which the king's workforce produced the surpluses necessary to maintain the centre. The recovery of thousands of stone sickles at Anyang, many unfinished, is just a reflection of the role played by central specialists in agricultural production.

The mature Shang polity exhibits many of the essentials of all later Chinese states: the deployment of large reserves of human labour in ritual, war and production, the intercession by the king and royal family in rituals for the ancestors, the maintenance of an army and a shifting pattern of alliances with potential rivals. It was one such rival, the Zhou, which brought the line of 29 kings to a close towards the end of the second millennium BC.

Conclusions

The last decade has seen a tiny crack open in terms of access to vast areas of archaeological potential. Each of the themes explored above stands at the threshold of a deeper understanding which only intensive research can achieve. Opening an extensive area of a second millennium BC Tarim Basin cemetery, linked with the analysis of the human biology and material culture of those buried, would in all likelihood permit a deeper appreciation of the expansion eastward of early speakers of Indo-European languages. Further excavations in late Pleistocene hunter-gatherer sites in the major river valleys of China, linked with palaeoclimatic and environmental studies, will sharpen our appreciation of the context in which only the second major transition to agriculture in the Old World matured. The interior of a site such as Sanxingdui has the potential to be a second Anyang, and greatly increase our understanding of Oriental civilization. Whatever the area, each topic has potential, drawing upon multidisciplinary teamwork, to add a significant chapter to a world prehistory.

References

AN CHIN-HUAI, A. 1986: The Shang city of Cheng-Chou and related problems. In Chang, K.-C. (ed.), *Studies of Shang Archaeology* (New Haven), 15–48.

AN ZHIMIN 1998: Cultural complexes of the Bronze Age in the Tarim Basin and surrounding areas. In Mair, V.H. (ed.), *The Bronze Age and Early Iron Age Peoples of Eastern Central Asia* (Philadelphia, The Institute for the Study of Man and the University of Pennsylvania Museum Publications), 45–62.

ANTHONY, D.W. 1998: The opening of the Eurasian steppe at 2000 BCE. In Mair, V.H. (ed.), *The Bronze Age and Early Iron Age Peoples of Eastern Central Asia* (Philadelphia, The Institute for the Study of Man and the University of Pennsylvania Museum Publications), 94–113.

BAGLEY, R. 1988: Sacrificial pits of the Shang period at Sanxingdui in Guanghan county, Sichuan. *Arts Asiatiques* XLIII, 78–96.

BAGLEY, R. 1993: An early Bronze Age tomb in Jiangxi Province. *Orientations* 24, 20–36.

BAGLEY, R. 1999: Shang archaeology. In Loewe, M. and Shaughnessy, E.L. (eds.), *The Cambridge History of Ancient China* (Cambridge), 124–231.

BARBER, E.J.W. 1998: Bronze Age cloth and clothing of the Tarim Basin: the Kroran (Loulan) and Qumul (Hami) evidence. In Mair, V.H. (ed.), *The Bronze Age and Early Iron Age Peoples of Eastern Central Asia* (Philadelphia, The Institute for the Study of Man and the University of Pennsylvania Museum Publications), 647–55.

BARNARD, N. 1987: Bronze casting technology in the peripheral 'barbarian' regions — preliminary assessments of the significance of technical variations between these regions and the metallurgy of the *Chung-yuan. Bull. Metal Mus.* 12, 3–37.

BARNES, G.L. 1993: *China, Korea and Japan. The Rise of Civilization in East Asia* (London).

BAR-YOSEF, O. and MEADOW, R.H. 1995: The origins of agriculture in the Near East. In Price, T.D. and Gebauer, A.B. (eds.), *Last Hunters — First Farmers: New Perspectives on the Prehistoric Transition to Agriculture* (Santa Fe, American School of Prehistoric Research), 39–94.

BOLTZ, W.G. 1999: Language and writing. In Loewe, M. and Shaughnessy, E.L. (eds.), *The Cambridge History of Ancient China* (Cambridge), 74–123.

CHANG, K.-C. 1986: *The Archaeology of Ancient China* (New Haven).

CHANG, K.-C. 1999: China on the eve of the historical period. In Loewe, M. and Shaughnessy, E.L. (eds.), *The Cambridge History of Ancient China* (Cambridge), 37–73.

CHEN, K.T. and HIEBERT, F.T. 1995: The late prehistory of Xinjiang in relation to its neighbors. *J. World Prehist.* 9(2), 243–300.

CHERNYK, E.N. 1992: *Ancient Metallurgy in the USSR: the Early Metal Age* (Cambridge).

CRAWFORD, G.W. and TAKAMIYA, H. 1990: The origins and implications of late prehistoric plant husbandry in northern Japan. *Antiquity* 64, 889–911.

D'ANDREA, A.C., CRAWFORD, G.W., YOSHIZAKI, M. and KUDO, T. 1995: Late Jomon cultigens in northeastern Japan. *Antiquity* 69, 146–52.

DOLUKHANOV, P.M. 1986: Foragers and farmers in West-Central Asia. In Zvelebil, M. (ed.), *Hunters in Transition. Mesolithic societies of Eurasia and their Transition to Farming* (Cambridge), 121–32.

DUMOND, D.E. and BLAND, R.L. 1995: Holocene prehistory of the northernmost North Pacific. *J. World Prehist.* 9, 401–51.

EATIA (Erlitou Archaeological Team, Institute of Archaeology, CASS) 1980: Excavation of a Shang site at Erlitou in Yanshi, Henan in autumn 1980 (in Chinese). *Kaogu* 1980, 199–216.

FLANNERY, K.V. 1998: The ground plans of archaic states. In Feinman, G.M. and Marcus, J. (eds.), *Archaic States* (Santa Fe), 15–57.

FLANNERY, K.V. 1999: Process and agency in early state formation. *Cambridge Archaeol. J.* 9, 3–21.

FRANCALACCI, P. 1998: DNA analysis on ancient desiccated corpses from Xinjiang (China): further results. In Mair, V.H. (ed.), *The Bronze Age and Early Iron Age Peoples of Eastern Central Asia* (Philadelphia, The Institute for the Study of Man and the University of Pennsylvania Museum Publications), 537–47.

GATIA (Gansu Archaeological Team, Institute of Archaeology, CASS) 1974: Excavations of the remains of Ch'i Chia culture at To-Ho-chuang in Yungching County, Kansu Province (in Chinese). *Kaogu Xuebao* 1974, 29–62.

GATIA (Gansu Archaeological Team, Institute of Archaeology, CASS) 1975: The excavation of a Ch'i Chia culture cemetery at Chin-wei-chia in Ying-Ching County, Kansu Province (in Chinese). *Kaogu Xuebao* 1975, 57–96.

GPM (Gansu Provincial Museum) 1982: Banshang-Machang tombs at Yuanuangchi, Wuwei, Gansu (in Chinese). *Kaogu Xuebao* 1982, 199–227.

GPMNNC (Gansu Provincial Museum and Northeast Normal College) 1984: Studies on remains of millet and hemp unearthed from a Majiayao culture site in Linjia, Gansu (in Chinese). *Kaogu Xuebao* 1984, 54–5.

HATIA (Henan Archaeological Team, Institute of Archaeology, CASS) 1984: Excavation of the Neolithic site of Peiligang (in Chinese). *Kaogu Xuebao* 1984, 23–52.

HE DEXIU 1998: A brief report on the mummies from the Zaghunluq site in Charchan County. In Mair, V.H. (ed.), *The Bronze Age and Early Iron Age Peoples of Eastern Central Asia* (Philadelphia, The Institute for the Study of Man and the University of Pennsylvania Museum Publications), 169–74.

HE JIEJUN 1995: Early Neolithic relics in Hunan. In Yueng Chung-tong and Li Wai-ling (eds.), *Archaeology in Southeast Asia* (Hong Kong, the University Museum and Art Gallery), 371–8.

HIGHAM, C.F.W. and LU, T.L.-D. 1998: The origins and dispersal of rice cultivation. *Antiquity* 72, 867–77.

JANHUNEN, J. 1998: The horse in East Asia: reviewing the linguistic evidence. In Mair, V.H. (ed.), *The Bronze Age and Early Iron Age Peoples of Eastern Central Asia* (Philadelphia, The Institute for the Study of Man and the University of Pennsylvania Museum Publications), 415–30.

KEIGHTLEY, D.N. 1999a: The environment of ancient China. In Loewe, M. and Shaughnessy, E.L. (eds.), *The Cambridge History of Ancient China* (Cambridge), 30–6.

KEIGHTLEY, D.N. 1999b: The Shang, China's first historical dynasty. In Loewe, M. and Shaughnessy, E.L. (eds.), *The Cambridge History of Ancient China* (Cambridge), 232–91.

KISLENKO, A. and TATARINTSEVA, N. 1999: The eastern Ural steppe at the end of the Stone Age. In Scarre, C. (ed.), *Late Prehistoric Exploitation of the Eurasian Steppe* (Cambridge, McDonald Institute Monographs), 183–216.

KUZMINA, E.E. 1998: Cultural connections of the Tarim Basin people and the pastoralists of the Asian steppes in the Bronze Age. In Mair, V.H. (ed.), *The Bronze Age and Early Iron Age Peoples of Eastern Central Asia* (Philadelphia, The Institute for the Study of Man and the University of Pennsylvania Museum Publications), 63–93.

LI WENJIE 1986: On the classification and periodization of the Daxi culture (in Chinese). *Kaogu Xuebao* 1986(2), 131–52.

LINDUFF, K. 1995: Zhukaigou, steppe culture and the rise of Chinese civilisation. *Antiquity* 69, 133–45.

LINDUFF, K.M. 1998: The emergence and demise of bronze-producing cultures outside the Central Plain of China. In Mair, V.H. (ed.), *The Bronze Age and Early Iron Age Peoples of Eastern Central Asia* (Philadelphia, The Institute for the Study of Man and the University of Pennsylvania Museum Publications), 619–43.

LINDUFF, K.M. 2000: Metallurgists in ancient East Asia: the Chinese and who else? In Linduff, K.M. (ed.), *Beginnings of Metallurgy in China* (Lampeter), 1–28.

LUBOTSKY, A. 1998: Tocharian loanwords in Old Chinese: chariots, chariot gear, and town building. In Mair, V.H. (ed.), *The Bronze Age and Early Iron Age Peoples of Eastern Central Asia* (Philadelphia, The Institute for the Study of Man and the University of Pennsylvania Museum Publications), 379–90.

MAIR, V.H. 1995: Prehistoric Caucasoid corpses of the Tarim Basin. *J. Indo-European Stud.* 23, 281–307.

MAIR, V.H. 1998a: Priorities. In Mair, V.H. (ed.), *The Bronze Age and Early Iron Age Peoples of Eastern Central Asia* (Philadelphia, The Institute for the Study of Man and the University of Pennsylvania Museum Publications), 4–41.

MAIR, V.H. 1998b: Die sprachamobe: an archaeolinguistic parable. In Mair, V.H. (ed.), *The Bronze Age and Early Iron Age Peoples of Eastern Central Asia* (Philadelphia, The Institute for the Study of Man and the University of Pennsylvania Museum Publications), 835–55.

MALLORY, J.P. 1995: Speculations on the Xinjiang mummies. *J. Indo-European Stud.* 23(3) and (4), 371–84.

MALLORY, J.P. 1998: A European perspective on Indo-Europeans in Asia. In Mair, V.H. (ed.), *The Bronze Age and Early Iron Age Peoples of Eastern Central Asia* (Philadelphia, The Institute for the Study of Man and the University of Pennsylvania Museum Publications), 169–201.

MATIUSHIN, G.N. 1986: The Mesolithic and Neolithic in the southern Urals and Central Asia. In Zvelebil, M. (ed.), *Hunters in Transition. Mesolithic societies of Eurasia and their Transition to Farming* (Cambridge), 133–50.

MSP (Museum of Sichuan Province) 1981: The third season of excavation at the Daxi site in Wushan County (in Chinese). *Kaogu Xuebao* 1981, 461–90.

NELSON, S. 1993: *The Archaeology of Korea* (Cambridge).

NM (Nanjing Museum) 1965: Excavations (second season) of the Neolithic site of Liulin, P'i Hsien, Kiangsu Province (in Chinese). *Kaogu Xuebao* 1965, 9–47.

NM (Nanjing Museum) 1984: Excavations of the Sidun site at Changzhou in Jiangsu in 1982 (in Chinese). *Kaogu Xuebao* 1984, 109–29.

OKLADNIKOV, A.P. 1990: Inner Asia at the dawn of history. In Sinor, D. (ed.), *The Cambridge History of Early Inner Asia* (Cambridge), 41–96.

PEARSON, R. 1981: Social complexity in Chinese coastal Neolithic sites. *Science* 213, 1078–86.

PEARSON, R. and UNDERHILL, A. 1987: The Chinese Neolithic: recent trends in research. *American Anthropologist* 89, 807–22.

PEI, A. 1998: Notes on new advancements and revelations in the agricultural archaeology of early rice domestication in the Dongting Lake region. *Antiquity* 72, 878–85.

PUETT, M. 1998: China in early Eurasian history: a brief review of recent scholarship on the issue. In Mair, V.H. (ed.), *The Bronze Age and Early Iron Age Peoples of Eastern Central Asia* (Philadelphia, The Institute for the Study of Man and the University of Pennsylvania Museum Publications), 699–715.

RENFREW, A.C. 1998: The Tarim Basin, Tocharian, and Indo-European origins: a view from the west. In Mair, V.H. (ed.), *The Bronze Age and Early Iron Age Peoples of Eastern Central Asia* (Philadelphia, The Institute for the Study of Man and the University of Pennsylvania Museum Publications), 202–12.

SHANXI-ATIA (Shanxi Archaeological Team, Institute of Archaeology, CASS) 1980: Excavations of a Neolithic site at Taosi in Xiangfen, Shanxi (in Chinese). *Kaogu* 1980, 18–31.

SINOR, D. 1990: Introduction: the concept of Inner Asia. In Sinor, D. (ed.), *The Cambridge History of Early Inner Asia* (Cambridge), 1–18.

SPCRAC (Sichuan Province Cultural Records Administrative Committee) 1987: The site of Sanxingdui in Guanghan (in Chinese). *Kaogu Xuebao* 1987, 227–54.

SUN SHUYUN and HAN RUBIN 1981: A preliminary study of early Chinese copper and bronze artefacts (in Chinese). *Kaogu Xuebao* 1981, 287–302.

TAAFFE, R.N. 1990: The geographic setting. In Sinor, D. (ed.), *The Cambridge History of Early Inner Asia* (Cambridge), 19–40.

TSUTSUMI, T. 1999: The oldest pottery in Japan archipelago. *Newsletter of the Grant-in-Aid Program for COE Research Foundation of the Ministry of Education, Science, Sports and Culture in Japan* 2(1), 4–5.

WINKLER, M.G. and WANG, P.K. 1993: The late Quaternary vegetation and climate of China. In Wright, H.E., Kutzbach, J.E., Webb, T., Ruddiman, W.F., Street-Perrott, F.A. and Bartlein, P.J. (eds.), *Global Climates Since the Last Glacial Maximum* (Minneapolis), 221–64.

YAN WENMING 1991: China's earliest rice agriculture remains. *Bull. Indo-Pacific Prehist. Assoc.* 10, 118–26.

YASUDA, Y. 1999: Recent archaeological discoveries in the middle Yangtze Basin, China. *Newsletter of the Grant-in-Aid Program for COE Research Foundation of the Ministry of Education, Science, Sports and Culture in Japan* 2, 1–2.

YOSHIZAKI, M. 1997: Domesticated plants of the Jomon Period. *Quat. Res.* 36, 343–6.

YUAN JAIRONG and ZHANG CHI, 1999: The origins of pottery and rice cultivation in China. *Newsletter of the Grant-in-Aid Program for COE Research Foundation of the Ministry of Education, Science, Sports and Culture in Japan* 2(1), 3–4.

ZHANG, Z. and WANG, X. 1998: Notes on the recent discovery of ancient cultivated rice at Jiahu, Henan Province: a new theory concerning the origin of *Oryza japonica* in China. *Antiquity* 72, 897–901.

ZHAO, S.Z., CHEN, F., PAN, B.T., CAO, J.X., LI, J.J. and DERBYSHIRE, E. 1991: Environmental change during the Holocene in Western China on a millennial timescale. *Holocene* 1, 151–6.

ZHAO ZIQUAN 1985: On the ancient site of Erlitou. *Annali Istituto Universitario Orientale Napoli* 45, 287–302.

ZHAO, Z. 1998: The Middle Yangtze region in China is one place where rice was domesticated: phytolith evidence from the Diaotonghuan Cave, Northern Jiangxi. *Antiquity* 72, 885–97.

Western Eurasia

A.F. HARDING

Western Eurasia, or Eurasia west of the Urals, can for all practical purposes be taken to mean 'Europe', since the Urals define the eastern limit of the continent. This land mass, though large, is not as large and varied as that east of the Urals, but it has over the millennia played host to such a bewildering number and variety of human cultures that the story to be told about it is no less complex; indeed, arguably more so. This, of course, is the standpoint of a western European archaeologist; but since the modern discipline of archaeology developed largely in this area (and in North America) the 'widening debate' is one that has a special importance for the development and future direction of the subject.

In terms of archaeological practice, Europe is an 'old' continent. Most of the standard histories of archaeology deal mainly with the development of the subject as it occurred in European countries. It has generally been the practices of European scholars that — until the emergence of North America as a major force in world archaeology — defined the ways that archaeologists proceed in their attempts to understand the cultures of past ages. It has been their preoccupations that defined the 'debate', the things that people thought important about the past and the ways in which we should study it. Perhaps, inevitably, this has meant that archaeological practice in Europe has been slow to change, since the methods and theories of the founding fathers of the subject can, within their own frames of reference, and with the limited goals that were set, be thought adequate even for a rapidly changing age like our own.

But this simple statement of fact indicates that the 'debate' in Europe has been held, and continues to be held, on a variety of different levels. On the one hand, a substantial number of practitioners believe that archaeology is a positivist discipline, with large and obvious sets of data, clearly defined methodologies, and well-established links to historical, geographical and literary modes of study. In this sphere of activity, archaeology is clearly a historical science, which aims to describe and understand human actions in the past. On the other hand, though, recent approaches see the subject in a host of different ways, that eschew the positivist, empirical and 'scientific' and concentrate instead on the contextual, the phenomenological, or the ideological. These

developments are covered elsewhere (see Ian Hodder, this volume) but they are relevant here insofar as they are influencing the way in which European archaeologists
are thinking, and changing their practices. It is within this context that we shall, in this
chapter, look at the ways in which the archaeological debate in Europe is widening, or
changing.

The fact is that many archaeologists are today doing different things from what they
or their predecessors were doing 50 or even 20 years ago. True, academics working in
universities are still — for the most part — engaging in research by means of writing
books and papers, though the drive to 'accountability' of recent years and the consequent increase in bureaucracy mean that research output can be in danger of decreasing in quantity or quality or both. But university academics are a minority of practising
archaeologists in Europe. The largest number today are those who work in the field,
typically on small projects and on short contracts. The privatization of archaeological
fieldwork has proceeded very far and very fast, so that in most European countries the
majority of work conducted in advance of development is carried out by commercial
enterprises, large or small. Furthermore, it has become a requirement in many countries
that archaeological assessments and, where appropriate, investigations precede the
development, and that the developer should pay for the work. This practice was virtually unknown in Europe 30 years ago, and its advent has been greeted with mixed feelings by those involved. It is arguable that this represents the largest single aspect of the
widening of the archaeological debate in Europe. The rationale is the retrieval of as
much information as possible prior to destruction; a worthy aim, one might think. In
practice, many of the small-scale projects rarely come up with anything of much archaeological significance, and even if they do, they may not find their way into the public
domain through publication.[1] Yet many archaeologists today do this work, and they do
it in the name of science and knowledge. But the question remains, *cui bono*? Has the
general public any interest in such relatively undramatic and (in terms of spectacular
finds) unproductive work? Is it in fact not the preserve of a self-appointed managerial
élite, who have succeeded in imposing conditions of this sort on a not very willing construction and industrial sector? I do not attempt to answer these questions here; but
they are important questions, and illustrative of one way in which the debate has
widened, and will continue to widen, within Europe as economic development takes
place. Pressure on agricultural land from such development is acute in booming
economies such as those of Ireland, but it is scarcely less so in countries of the former
socialist bloc where free enterprise as a consequence of privatization and the inflow of
foreign capital is blossoming. The situation of rescue archaeology in the former DDR,
Poland, Hungary and the Czech Republic is striking in this regard.

---

[1] In Britain, as a result of this regrettable lack of dissemination of information from commercial operations,
R. Bradley (University of Reading) is currently engaged on assembling information from this source, apparently with interesting results.

In this context, it is very striking that a quite new set of priorities has been mooted by some of the leading theorists of today. Driven by the knowledge that much of what archaeologists 'discover' is abstruse or trivial, J. Barrett (1995 and elsewhere) has argued that there is a duty to work more effectively with those who pay for archaeological work to be undertaken, and that practical and theoretical archaeology need to work more closely together. The professionalization of field archaeology has brought with it, in his view, a dehumanizing of the subject, with the cold, dispassionate recording of contexts removing the need for interpretation and with it the chance to make the subject exciting. Hodder, too, has argued that field archaeology needs to become reflexive, to interpret as it excavates, and to contextualize both the circumstances of original production and the circumstances of excavation (1999). Examples of this type of approach, for instance those illustrated by Hodder himself on Çatalhöyük or the Ice Man, the discussion of fieldwork on Bodmin Moor by Bender et al. (1997), or the approach to landscape adopted by Edmonds (1999), may be found exhilarating, depressing, or hilarious, depending on your point of view. What one may question is whether practice, as engaged in by the vast majority of practitioners, has actually changed very much. Most archaeologists on the ground have little to do with issues of this kind as they earn their daily crust. A quick survey of recent site reports does not reveal any great move in this direction, though it may be argued that time is needed for the methodology to become embedded.

In spite of a lively debate about the philosophical foundations of science between sociologists and scientists, there is little sign in the published output of the latter that the basic principles of scientific investigation have changed significantly in recent years. This inevitably means that an archaeology which attempts to follow the course recommended for it by Hodder will find itself further and further apart from 'science', something which Hodder's incorporation of a few selected aspects of the natural sciences in archaeology will do little to alter.

In the rest of this chapter, I shall explore some of the debates that are currently engaging both intellectuals and the general public in the wider European scene.

Ethnogenesis: the origins of Europe's peoples

Europe today is in a state of flux. While the western half is generally stable in political terms, the eastern half is either unstable or moving fast towards the western model. This leads to a paradoxical situation where on the one hand there are moves towards integration of the separate nation-states into an overarching federation or 'union', and on the other towards the fissioning of existing entities into numbers of smaller parts. The states emerging from the former Soviet Union and from Yugoslavia are the most obvious, but the separatist movements of Scotland, Corsica or the Basque country are not so far behind, and the 'Euroscepticism' that is present in a number of countries (not just in Britain) is symptomatic of a deeper feeling of unease. In this, the concept of 'Europeanness' is a crucial element, and it necessarily raises with it the question of what Europeans are ethnically, where they came from and when — the question of European ethnogenesis, to use the technical term. This is a big question, and I can only touch on some elements of it here. I will take as my example the Celtic question, though one could equally validly discuss the identity and origins of the Scythians, the Illyrians, the Germans, or many other ancient peoples who are traditionally believed to have developed over time into the modern peoples whom we see in Europe today. In most of these cases, there is considerable room for debate; in only a minority is there general agreement — with the Hungarians, for instance, whose arrival in Europe in the ninth century AD is relatively well-documented, and for whom an immediate origin point in the area between the Siret and the Dnieper is attested by Byzantine historians (though their ultimate origin may have lain further east).

The question of the Celts indicates nicely the way in which the debate over ethnic origins has changed in recent years. Since the early historians of Greece, and later those of Rome, identified various peoples to their north to whom they gave the name of Celts (Κέλτοι, *Celtae*), it has been the normal assumption that the archaeological cultures of central Europe from at least 600 BC, and particularly the creators of the La Tène art style from around 400 BC onwards, were 'Celtic', in other words, the bearers of those cultures (the makers of particular styles of pottery, metalwork, and so on) spoke a language identifiable as belonging to the Celtic group of languages, and were through language and material culture separate from adjacent peoples. On this analysis, it is possible to classify as Celtic the Iron Age cultures of much of Central Europe, as well as France and Spain in the west and — because of the historical records attesting a migration of the 'Galatians' to Asia Minor — Anatolia in the east. What is more, since language studies show that Britain and Ireland were occupied by speakers of Celtic languages, those islands too were Celtic — even though the term 'Celts' is not specifically used by the Roman historians of their inhabitants. Traditionally, therefore, 'Celtic' culture means Iron Age culture, as numerous basic and well-respected textbooks indicate (Powell 1958; Filip 1976; Spindler 1983; etc).

Now if this is so, there is a clear implication that — unless we wish to believe, as some have, that the Celts arrived with the developed Hallstatt culture of the earliest Iron Age — there must have been a Bronze Age background to the Iron Age manifestations of the Celts in Europe, which implies that at the very least the 'Urnfield' cultures of Europe, clearly ancestral in terms of material culture to the succeeding Hallstatt phases, were 'Celtic'. And if that is the case, then maybe the ancestry can be traced back even further, into the Neolithic. Were the Celts even the indigenous population of Europe (unlikely), or perhaps to be identified with the first farmers arriving on the European scene from the hearth of domestication in the Near East, as Renfrew (1987) has argued?

One of the many problems surrounding this debate is that of language. All the primary literary evidence, in the form of texts in a Celtic language, is much later than the references in Greek historians, and in the case of 'Insular' Celtic, very much later; and in any case the early texts are relatively few and far between. Consequently there is little agreement on where, how and when Celtic originated and spread, or on what relationship its various constituent languages bear to the archaeological manifestations. A clear summary of the current position is provided by Ellis Evans (1995).

This picture of a continent largely populated by several large ethnic groups, among whom the Celts occupied most of the centre and west, is familiar, but today controversial. A number of scholars have argued that it is not possible to accept the word of the Greek and Roman historians and geographers at face value (Chapman, M. 1992; Collis 1997; James 1999). Certainly it is unlikely that Hecateios of Miletus, let alone Herodotus, actually visited 'Celtic' lands and had first-hand knowledge of them. When Herodotus spoke of the Scythians, occupants of the area north of the Black Sea, he was drawing on descriptions provided by travellers and traders, not his personal experience; when he ventured further afield to the north and east, his accounts become frankly fantastical. So it is certainly arguable that his identification of large ethnic blocks, among whom the Celts, Illyrians and Scythians are the most important, was a rationalization of a complex situation of which he had little or no direct knowledge, in an attempt to order the world for tidy Greek minds.

Against the apparently reasonable correlation of Iron Age, and especially La Tène, archaeology with the Celts, Collis has argued that the definition of the ancient Celts is ambiguous in the ancient authors and that the distribution of La Tène art only partly correlates with the distribution of the ancient Celts; the identification of archaeological cultures with ancient ethnic groups is methodologically wrong, according to Collis. He is among several recent authors to point out that the supposed 'Celticity' of Britain and Ireland is a construct of scholarship in the last 300 years, and that although 'Celtic' languages were spoken in these islands, the inhabitants were not 'Celtic' in the sense that the Greeks and Romans recognized.

The case of the Germans is not dissimilar. As Todd points out, the Germani 'had no collective consciousness of themselves as a separate people, nation or group of tribes. There is no evidence that they called themselves "Germani" or their land "Germania". These were terms applied by writers in the Mediterranean world and they can be traced with certainty no further back than the time of Poseidonius' (Todd 1992, 8). It is possible, as with several other ancient peoples, that the Germani were originally just one of a number of tribal groupings in north-west Europe, who happened to come to the notice of Greek and Roman writers and whose name was adopted by them to represent all the inhabitants of the area. As with the Celts, opinions have therefore differed about where they originated; some archaeologists have favoured an identification with Neolithic or Copper Age cultural groups (Kilian 1988), while others are much more cautious. Nor does language assist us much: the earliest known piece of text in a Germanic language comes from the famous Negau helmets in Austria, probably dating to the first century BC, though it is generally assumed that Germanic speakers were present in central and northern Europe much earlier than this. The situation with the Illyrians is very similar.

The lines of this debate are thus clearly set out. It illustrates something of the dilemma that students of the ancient world now find themselves in: on the one hand, the testimony of ancient writers such as Herodotus is interesting and certainly gives the impression of being authoritative; on the other, there are notable problems in tying it in with the material culture as uncovered by archaeologists. But this is part of a wider debate about ethnicity, a subject that has attracted much attention in recent years (Jones 1997; Graves-Brown *et al.* 1996), and to which I return shortly.

First, however, a still more fundamental problem: when did the speakers of Indo-European language first arrive in Europe? This is very far from being a new problem, but that does not make it any the less intriguing. Generally speaking, archaeologists (as opposed to linguists) have sought to introduce these 'new people' at a time when there is a marked break in the archaeological record, with new elements of material culture suggesting the immigration of a new stock. Opinions over the years have varied considerably: for some, basing their judgment on the belief that the European Iron Age represented a Celtic world, it was with the start of the Iron Age; for others it was with the 'Beaker folk' (i.e. those who made and used Beaker pottery); yet others thought that the widespread adoption of the practice of cremation in Europe after about 1300 BC was the tell-tale pointer; notably, or notoriously, depending on your point of view, the late Marija Gimbutas argued over many years that Proto-Indo-Europeans were to be identified with the 'Kurgan culture' (Neolithic–Copper Age barrow-building groups) of the south Russian steppe (e.g. Gimbutas 1970). When in 1917 the decipherment of Hittite showed that an Indo-European language was spoken in the Late Bronze Age in Anatolia, and in 1952 that of the Linear B tablets of Knossos and Pylos showed that Greek was present in Late Bronze Age Greece, the search for Indo-European origins went back to the supposed beginnings of Hittite and Mycenaean culture in the Middle Bronze Age, in the first half of the second millennium BC. All these positions can be, and have been, argued at length. Renfrew's position, that the spread of Indo-European language occurred at the time of the spread of farming through the Old World, was certainly different, though no less controversial for philologists — however tempting the idea may have seemed at first sight to archaeologists.[2]

In fact this theory is now seen to raise just as many questions as it answers. In particular, ideas about the spread of culture in the Neolithic have changed markedly

---

[2] And subsequently modified somewhat, following the objections raised by Zvelebil (1995).

in recent years. On the one hand, Hodder (1990) has set out a model of the Neolithic transformation in which as well as a physical shift from domesticated to wild plants and animals, there was also a metaphorical shift from wild to domestic, *agrios* to *domus* as he puts it, which saw people regarding the world around them in quite different and new ways. Similarly, Thomas (1988, 1992) has argued that the shift to farming was less an economic change, more a change of attitude or ideology, allowing monuments to be built and pottery created, perhaps in connection with new ideas concerning the preparation of food. The willingness of native populations to adopt innovations might then 'be connected with their aspirations towards a more intensive ceremonial life and more involved social relations' (Thomas 1988, 64). In retrospect, the idea of a wholesale replacement of Mesolithic populations by Neolithic ones, as envisaged by most commentators over the years and modelled most recently by Ammerman and Cavalli-Sforza (1984), seems astonishingly oversimplistic, allowing little or no room for human agency in the transition, for instance for the role of long-standing interaction between Mesolithic groups across the European continent, and particularly across stretches of water like the Baltic or the North Sea and going back to times when they were no more than marshlands and creeks in the 'Doggerland' of B. Coles (1998).

Seen in this light, Renfrew's hypothesis seems less attractive. And yet the linguistic facts cannot simply be explained away. Europe's peoples do for the most part share a common linguistic ancestor or ancestors, and unless one imagines that Proto-Indo-Europeans were always there, i.e. came in with modern humans at the start of the Upper Palaeolithic (impossible, given what is known about the speed of linguistic divergence, and other factors), they had to have arrived at some specified point.

At this point, the newest research on genetic markers must be brought in to the argument, and the reader is referred to Chapter 3, by C. Renfrew (also Renfrew 2000). The remarkable results obtained from analysis of mitochondrial DNA and Y-chromosome DNA do, on the face of it, lend support to the notion that farming was diffused, perhaps along with Indo-European language, after the Last Glacial Maximum. On the other hand, the age estimates are broad, and it is not even possible to be sure whether the spread of the relevant genetic markers might not have occurred in the Palaeolithic rather than the Neolithic. At present the fit to observed archaeological data is not so close that reasonable certainty is possible; but it may be predicted that within a few years, greater clarity will have been achieved. Even if a close link-up of genetic types and languages is not ultimately possible, certainly much more will soon be known about the genetic origin of the peoples of Europe. Those who want to demonstrate that the English are different genetically as a 'race' from the French are likely to be disappointed; those who want to use race for political ends will not find any support from science.

Identities in archaeology

Where then does this leave the question of the identity of Europeans, in physical, linguistic, or other terms? Recent discussions of ethnicity in archaeological contexts have
focused upon the ways in which material culture can express the group adherence of
those who possess it. While for anthropologists looking at living populations a variety of conceptual and philosophical issues are at stake (cf. the 'primordialist' and
'instrumentalist' approaches, as discussed by Jones 1997), for archaeologists the problems are at once simpler and more complex. Simpler, in that objects of material culture, i.e. archaeological artefacts, are the given data and in themselves cannot lie to us;
more complex, in that the relationship of material culture to ethnic groups is at best
uncertain and at worst unknowable or negatively correlated. Nonetheless, archaeologists (and others) continue to brave the shark-infested waters of material culture and
its meaning.

   Much of what European archaeologists study is variation in material culture, and
specifically variation in style, i.e. how people in different places, or the same people at
different times, or even the same people at the same time, did things (made objects) in
different ways. The study of style in archaeology and anthropology has now generated
a significant literature (e.g. Wobst 1977; Plog 1980; Wiessner 1983; Conkey and Hastorf
1990; review in Jones 1997, 110 ff.), though tangible outcomes are harder to specify. The
study of romanization is a notable case (ibid., 29 ff., 129 ff.), since it involved an apparent transformation of 'indigenes' to 'Romans', over a relatively short time and — a few
high profile instances apart — with relatively little demur from those being romanized.
Metropolitan Roman authors such as Livy, Caesar or Tacitus tell us something, but of
course it is a metropolitan point of view, and the absence of indigenous viewpoints at
the time of the initial transformation is a serious drawback, for which material culture
can only partly compensate.

   Discussions of ethnicity in the archaeological record can take on a very pessimistic
tone, in contrast to the optimistic assertions of earlier generations. Jones (1996, 72)
questions the very existence of homogeneous ethnic entities except 'at an abstract conceptual level', believing that 'configurations of ethnicity, and consequently the styles
of material culture involved in the signification and structuring of ethnic relations,
may vary in different social contexts and with relation to different forms and scales of
social interaction'. Artefact assemblages, which is what archaeologists have to work
with, must be studied and understood in their cultural context. Since the reconstruction of past cultural contexts is a difficult, maybe an impossible, procedure, one might
be forgiven for a feeling of pessimism. On the other hand, Renfrew has argued that
'ethnicity in this [the construction of a European identity] ... is a current reality,
dependent above all upon our present awareness of who we are and of who we want
to be ... There is no *a priori* European identity available to us which might persuade

us that we should want to be "Europeans". But there are indeed abundant ingredients for the construction of such a European identity: linguistic, genetic, cultural, religious and in terms of shared history from which such a common myth may be created' (Renfrew 1996, 134).

While the identification of national or trans-national identities may still be problematic, there is much more that can be said today about individual identities in the past on the basis of archaeological evidence. Here the representation of gender in archaeological material culture is of particular importance, and has been the subject of a number of recent studies (notably Stig Sørensen 2000). In an archaeological context, the fact that material objects are so frequently 'gendered' is of major significance, even if it is not always evident to which gender a particular object was assigned by the people who made and used it. Dress is the most obvious way that personal identities are expressed. Archaeologically, the common practice of burying dress objects with the dead is an inestimable advantage. Among the many examples of gendered dress ornaments, the case of Bronze Age women in central Germany is particularly impressive (Wels Weyrauch 1989; Stig Sørensen 1997). Not only can women from different areas of Germany be clearly differentiated, but it is also possible to argue in specific instances that women with different ranks and/or different roles are discernible; the same is no doubt true for the burials of Bronze Age Denmark, both male and female.

Other areas where identity is particularly expressed are those of the house, where the variety of activities carried out must have been specific to person and sometimes to gender, and of food preparation and consumption (Stig Sørensen 2000, 99 ff.). The creation of personalized vessels for eating and drinking is a notable case in point. Copper Age Bell Beakers, for instance, can be studied on one level as an exercise in providing individuals with a specific identity through the means of a personalized pot. In part, the variability seen from one pot to the next cross-cuts with the need to adopt particular styles of decoration (cf. above), and the end-product is as much an expression of its creator as of its user; but ultimately, it was the visible process of a person using her or his pot, marked with its specific decoration, that ensured the attribution of a particular identity to that person in the eyes of the beholder.

This indicates something of the power of objects to express more than their mere decorative arrangement would imply. That power is only now beginning to be studied. The notion that artefacts have a 'social life', and that it is possible to write a biography of them is now well appreciated (Appadurai 1986), though detailed studies of this kind are still thin on the ground. Most recently a study of 'fragmentation' has been undertaken to illustrate just such possibilities (Chapman, J.C. 2000); if the conclusion that objects in many archaeological contexts are broken intentionally and are incomplete through design rather than accident seems remarkable, it is merely another reminder that human behaviour is infinitely variable and never loses its capacity to surprise.

Band, tribe, chiefdom and state: relevant models?

Traditionally, our understanding of how ancient societies were organized was based on the evolutionary sequence suggested by Lewis Henry Morgan in *Ancient Society* (1871). Adopted by Engels and to a lesser extent by Marx, the progression from 'savagery' through 'barbarism' to 'civilization' appeared to many thinkers to encapsulate what they needed by way of a descriptive framework within which to set the social manifestations of the ancient past. For European archaeologists, the adaptation of the Morgan scheme by Gordon Childe has been of greatest significance, for instance in his *Social Evolution* of 1951. True, Childe pointed out (1951, 23) that 'fresh data accumulated by more recent field studies . . . have played havoc with the contents of Morgan's scheme', but he believed that in spite of its failings 'it remains the best attempt of its kind', though he proposed new criteria for each stage. Thus the Palaeolithic and Mesolithic were assigned to savagery, and the Neolithic, Bronze and Iron Ages to barbarism (including, perhaps surprisingly, the early societies of the east Mediterranean, Egypt and Mesopotamia). Civilization, then, is restricted to Classical Greece and Rome. Curiously, in a work originally written in 1942 but revised in 1954, *What happened in history*, Childe adopted the more usual position that saw 'barbarism' as restricted to the Neolithic and the Bronze Age of continental Europe, while the Bronze Age cultures of Greece, Crete, Egypt, Anatolia and Mesopotamia were called 'civilizations', characterized by cities and/or palaces, writing, higher forms of organization, and advanced arts and crafts. A not dissimilar position, though expressed much less explicitly, was adopted by other Anglo-Saxon writers (e.g. Clark and Piggott 1965).

Childe speculated in these writings on how exactly social divisions might have been organized, in particular whether barbarian societies were subject to the authority of a chief. In the 1960s, such preoccupations became explicit with the appearance of a number of works from the pens of American anthropologists, notably E.R. Service, whose *Primitive Social Organization* (1962/1975) and *Origins of the State and Civilization* (1975) set the agenda for the next generation of archaeological writers. In these seminal works, based mainly on ethnographic case-studies, Service distinguished between band, tribe, chiefdom and state organization, bands being organized on the basis of family groups, mainly involved in hunting and foraging, and small in extent (a few tens or scores of individuals); tribes consist of a larger number of 'economically self-sufficient residential groups', with leadership being personal in nature and stemming from the charismatic qualities of individuals; but the organization is essentially small-scale and fragmented, 'segmental' to use the favoured term. Lastly, chiefdoms embrace a range of organizational forms, but all unified by a hierarchical system characterized by the presence of a few rich and powerful individuals at the top of the pyramid of power. Population typically numbers in the thousands on a regional level, often centred on a specific location from where the organization is carried out; craft specialization and the redistribution of goods and materials are frequent concomitants.

Clearly none of these things qualify chiefdoms to be called states, for which a still more complex level of organization is necessary. States could vary considerably in size, and it is arguable that one is not talking about the same thing in organizational terms when one compares the city-states of Iron Age and Classical Greece with either Dynastic Egypt or with Republican Rome — let alone Imperial Rome. Greek city-states may well be compared with the statelets of the Bronze Age Near East, often centred on a single city and its hinterland, and frequently acting independently — to the chagrin of its more powerful neighbours. Obviously such city-states were quite different from states that embraced the equivalent of a whole modern country (Egypt or Italy), though many aspects of their organization could be paralleled.

Service's evolutionary sequence has held sway for a good many years, though many writers have expressed dissatisfaction with it, varying from a general uneasiness that it was hard to see a close fit between Service's ethnographic observations and the archaeological record, to an outright denial that such things as chiefdoms exist at all. Although the rules appeared to be clear as to what constituted each type of organization, in practice the situation is much more varied, and for archaeologists the indications much less clear-cut, than the model would predict. Nowadays many observers accept the general premise of increasing complexity without going along with the idea that any particular stage of human development should fit exactly into one of Service's stages.

For some, these distinctions are not issues of great significance. Hodder (1999, 180) argues that this debate, like those of the 'origins of agriculture' or the Stone–Bronze–Iron Age system, are merely products of 'a particular perspective on the past, appropriate to a particular time and place . . . they may have general validity, but only from a specific local perspective'; as universal claims, they can be locally situated and challenged. The extreme relativism of these statements makes one wonder in what way archaeological data can ever be used to assure two different people that a given interpretation is valid (though of course this is intentional, since Hodder would maintain that many different interpretations of the past can be equally valid).

This said, for most archaeologists studying the sequence of periods of the past, a framework within which particular manifestations of human endeavour may be understood is a useful, indeed a necessary, thing. Thus in spite of fashionable critiques that emphasize the difficulty or irrelevance of such attempts, they continue unabated. Chiefdoms in particular have exercised the minds of many. Sahlins (1968), Renfrew (1974), Carneiro (1981, 1991) and most recently Earle (1987, 1991, 1997) have written extensively about what chiefs are and how they come to occupy and maintain positions of power. All have been concerned to correlate recovered material culture with inherent structures that were responsible for ordering the ways in which societies regulated themselves. In essence, chiefdoms have been seen as the ordering principle behind those societies in which riches, power and authority are vested in a small number of people, with the bulk of the population in varying positions of subservience. In general, it has been supposed that European societies from the Neolithic through to the Early Iron Age were tribal and that most of them were chiefdoms, certainly in the Bronze and Iron Ages. One of the problems has been to account for the apparent lack of social division in the Neolithic, when (in western Europe, at least) large-scale monuments requiring the communal labour of scores of people were erected. Renfrew (1974) coined the term 'group-oriented' to describe this sort of chiefdom, as opposed to the 'individualizing' chiefdoms of the Bronze Age, where status artefacts became common in graves. In fact, there are a number of prestige artefacts — such as the magnificent flint macehead from Knowth (Eogan 1986, 141–2, fig. 57 pl. X) — which do suggest differential provision of goods, and plausibly the expression of power, so the assumption of social divisions is not entirely based on inference from monuments. In any case, humankind has numerous ways of creating divisions between people that do not involve visible differences in material culture.

Three principal mechanisms have been seen as responsible for promoting the rise of chiefdoms: economic, military and ideological (Mann 1986; Earle 1997; Mann includes political mechanisms as a fourth). In fact, all of them cross-cut the others. Control of economic resources, including particularly that of trade and traded objects, has long been considered a major factor in developmental terms (cf. Frankenstein and Rowlands 1978 on the rise of 'paramount chiefs' in south-west Germany in the Early Iron Age). Military control has been most vocally advanced by Carneiro as a mechanism for the rise of both states and of chiefdoms (1970, 1981). Carneiro's view depends on the notion of competition for resources, including land, and the consequent rise of inter-group hostilities where the resources were scarce. In a broader sense, warfare, commonly occurring in the Europe of later prehistory, can be seen as a mechanism by which individuals could promote and maintain their rank position, especially where individual combat between heroes was the principal means of conflict (in the manner suggested by Homer). Ideological control is perhaps subtler and less easy to detect archaeologically. Ideological factors are those that reflect the world view of the society in which they appear, and this means principally the world view of the dominant sector of society, as expressed through a variety of mainly symbolic activities and objects. Some of these may relate to forms of dress, or to the carrying of weaponry; some may be concerned with particular forms of treating the dead, for instance through a concern to impose the presence of ancestors on living communities through the erection of large monuments that may (or occasionally may not) have contained their bodily remains. Others may relate to the creation of institutions (places and practices) in which activities we may describe as ritual or religious were founded, for instance in the great henge monuments of which Stonehenge and Avebury are pre-eminent (though atypical) examples.

All these mechanisms, however, are concerned primarily with *control* rather than representing ends in themselves. What we remain uncertain about is whether specifying the means of control is also specifying the means of achieving the dominant position where control could be exercised. In other words, did chiefs become chiefs because they were great war leaders (or wise counsellors, or a priestly élite)? Or did their role as war leaders follow from some other predisposition to be chiefs? Did, for instance, factors such as the investment of labour in economically important projects (ploughing, shipbuilding, vine and olive production, irrigation) bring about a situation where labour-providers had an inbuilt incentive to maintain a *status quo* in which their labour was brought under the control of others, as Gilman (1981) and others have suggested?

In this, an alternative system to the hierarchical one which dominates most thinking on the topic is that which favours the existence of 'heterarchies'. Although Earle and others have argued strongly for the existence of chiefdom societies in later prehistory in Europe, others have pointed out that in a number of ways the situation on the ground does not seem to reflect what might be expected from a chiefly system; in particular, that settlements rarely exhibit what may be interpreted as chiefly residences. Heterarchies (Crumley 1987, 1995) would allow for a less rigid means of organization, so that different aspects of control might be exercised simultaneously by different people, or different sites, in different ways, allowing for a much more fluid representation of power relations. Potentially heterarchical structures have thus been examined, and the concept found useful, in a number of Eurasian (and other) situations, for instance Bronze and Iron Age Wessex (Ehrenreich 1995), Bronze Age Denmark (Levy 1995), early medieval Ireland (Wailes 1995) and elsewhere (Crumley 1987).

These reflections do, of course, compel some consideration of the relationship between early and late complex societies, and in particular the recognition of early state organizations. Separating developed chiefdoms from early states is neither easy nor, perhaps, necessary (Arnold and Blair Gibson 1995, 2, 7–8; Brun 1995). It is, however, noteworthy that a variety of political forms that lie somewhere on the borders of the two things have been mooted. I have already referred to the sites of the 'paramount chiefs' of Frankenstein and Rowlands; this is in itself an adaptation of what the Germans call *Fürstensitze* and the French *'résidences princières'*; aspects of what in recent French literature has become known as the *'phénomène princier'* (Brun and Chaume 1997). It is of course undeniable that parts of Europe in the Early Iron Age were characterized by a set of sites and artefacts that suggests very marked ranking, to the extent that in the sixth century BC it is common to talk of 'princes/ses' or 'chiefs'. Equally, by the first century the rise of *oppida*, along with what we know of political organization from literary sources, suggest that formations suggestive of a more complex form of organization were in place — some might talk of 'states' or at least 'proto-states', though others would stick with the designation of 'tribes'. This very divergence of opinion illustrates, however, that while the notion of the tribe may have some explanatory value in terms of internal organization, it says little or nothing about political matters. What needs to be defined in any given instance is the degree to which administrative and political structures were in place, and what were their implications for the society in question.

In Egypt and Mesopotamia, most authorities have identified the emergence of states in the third millennium BC, as seen most fully in the Egyptian situation (Wilkinson 1996, 1999). A proper consideration of even one of these cases is outside my present scope. It does, however, bring home forcefully how far the scholarly world is from accepted definitions of these overarching terms, and reinforces the need to contextualize each situation as it occurs.

World systems, cores and peripheries

Attempting to understand the nature of social and political organization within societies in early Europe raises a series of questions about how their internal arrangements impinged on the outside world. Even in the smallest-scale societies, human groups cannot have existed in isolation, if for the simple reason that maintenance of group size and fitness would have necessitated interaction with adjacent groups in order to ensure reproductive success. As groups grew larger, such matters will still have been of concern, though they may have been easier to satisfy. Contact with the outside world, however, is a demonstrable fact in most areas of later prehistoric Europe, since materials and artefacts can frequently be shown to emanate from areas other than those in which they were found.

This contact appears to increase in extent and importance as the later millennia BC pass. While in the Neolithic the main materials moved were stone (for axes and blades) and shells (for ornaments), in the Bronze and Iron Ages a whole series of materials were moved around: most notably metals but also such other materials as coral, amber, or glass. It is also in these periods (third–first millennia BC) that the great palace civilizations of the east Mediterranean area developed, and later the states or proto-states of the central Mediterranean. This led to a notable phenomenon: the requirement for large quantities of raw materials for the complex societies of the south and east, principally but by no means exclusively metals. The need for these minerals is obvious; less so was the requirement for exotic materials such as amber or lapis lazuli, or even special woods (a large piece of ebony was discovered on the Kaş shipwreck: Bass *et al.* 1989, 9 f., fig. 17).

Now while there are undoubtedly a number of sources of metal ores in the general area of the east Mediterranean (Cyprus being the prime example), it is generally supposed that at least some of the metal wealth must have emanated from sources outside that area: maybe far to the east in distant Afghanistan, maybe to the north in the

Carpathian Mountains, maybe to the west in Sardinia or even further afield, in Spain, France or Britain. The facts are not yet fully resolved, as disagreements over the interpretation of data from the physical sciences have brought about a temporary halt to progress in this field. By contrast, theoretical positions which seek to model how such contact might occur have occupied a large part of the literature in recent years, and look set to do so: the debate continues. What is involved is the application of 'World Systems Theory', otherwise known as the Core-Periphery debate, to various situations in the second and first millennia BC in the area between Mesopotamia and northern Europe.

World Systems Theory (WST) developed as a means of visualizing the situation of early modern Europe, and was largely the brainchild of the economic historian Immanuel Wallerstein (originally 1974), who believed that it was only applicable to the capitalist world which developed in the fifteenth and sixteenth centuries AD. Nonetheless, a series of commentators have suggested that it can be applied to much earlier periods. Archaeologists such as K. Kristiansen (e.g. 1987, 1994) and A. Sherratt (1993) have explored the possibilities of WST in the context of Bronze Age Europe, but it has mostly been left to economists and political theorists to apply the results to the Ancient Near East (e.g. Frank 1990, 1993; Gills and Frank 1993; Frank and Gills 1993).

WST is essentially a means of understanding, or at least describing, how one area becomes dependent on another, so that developments in one will affect the other. Specifically, it has been seen as a way to model the means by which goods and materials moved between the two can structure not only economic but also social practice. For instance, prestige goods manufactured in the 'core' area can be introduced into the 'periphery', where they may play an important role in articulating social divisions. WST would go further; since economies typically experience cycles (in their simplest form upward and downward trends, but in more extreme form cycles of boom and bust), one might expect to see cyclical patterns in both core and periphery — though not necessarily going in the same direction. Kristiansen has suggested just such a set of cycles for the course of the European Bronze Age; Frank believes that similar cycles were in play during the Bronze Age of the Near East. A much more sophisticated analysis by Bintliff (1997) has examined the situation in Iron Age Greece, and suggested that such cycles are connected with long-term structural changes.

It is the writings of Andre Gunder Frank that have promoted in its most developed form the notion that WST is an appropriate way to view the remote past. According to this view, there was a '5000-year old World System', one that was 'the *one* central world system', that extended in 'unbroken historical continuity between the central civilization/world system of the Bronze Age and our contemporary modern capitalist world system', and which has allegedly stayed the same system in spite of various modifications undergone over the years (Frank 1993, 387). Frank appears to believe that any situation in which one can demonstrate trade connections, and a tendency to growth and decline, would qualify for admission into the category of a World System. An even more extreme position is adopted by Chase-Dunn and Hall (1991 and elsewhere; Hall 1999), who argue that World Systems can be traced back as far as the start of the Neolithic. Other observers, such as Sherratt, have been much more pragmatic in their approach to the problem; it is in fact arguable whether WST in Sherratt's sense qualifies as WST in Frank's or Hall's, and the same is true of a number of archaeological contributors to Kardulias 1999.

Since a number of recent works (e.g. Kristiansen 1998; various contributions to Kardulias 1999) depend so heavily on the incorporation of WST, it is certain that the debate will continue, whether or not one takes seriously the extreme position adopted by Frank and others. So what are the grounds for thinking that an approach of this kind is helpful or appropriate?

On the positive side, WST does provide a good mechanism for understanding the role of traded commodities in given situations, both at the macro level of exchange between regions (or 'peoples') and at the micro level of enabling discrimination within communities through differential possession of imported (and thus élite) goods. It is particularly applicable in cases involving long-distance trade and exchange. 'These concepts do provide a general framework within which it is possible to analyse in very precise terms the specific conditions in which the relationships between polities at different levels of economic, political or technological development did, in specific cases, produce changes in those polities' (Champion 1989, 10; cf. Kardulias 1999). It is, of course, arguable how one is to recognize and define cores and their peripheries, but a working hypothesis would appear to be that they exist where there is a flow of goods between unequal partners — unequal in technology, in craft production, and by implication in social and political development. Thus the movement of wine amphorae from the Mediterranean into Gaul and Britain in the Iron Age, or of Etruscan bronze vessels into Burgundy, would qualify as examples of such movement that indicated unequal partners in trade and thus a 'world system' (or part of one). On the other hand, 'core-periphery exploitation needs to be demonstrated, not simply assumed' (Kardulias 1999, xviii).

More negatively, it is possible to question whether the overarching theory that is represented by WST is a necessary concomitant to the study of ancient trade and exchange; or whether the scale at which it is supposed to have operated is an appropriate one. The approach adopted by Kristiansen, for instance, is to assume that a World System existed, and then to point to aspects of the archaeological record that allegedly stem from the fact. A striking case is that exemplified by his distribution map of solid-hilted Bronze Age swords (his fig. 83, after Müller-Karpe 1961, pl. 98). This map allegedly depicts chiefly centres from northern Italy to northern Europe, in the form of the distribution of two particular varieties of sword. There are 33 symbols on the map, mostly scattered thinly across this vast area. Kristiansen, however, has drawn circles round five 'groups' of swords that purport to represent the chiefly centres. But of these, three contain only two swords, not found especially close together. The other two are those centred on the Bologna region of Italy, and on Lac Léman in west Switzerland (the lake sites of Grandson and Bex, canton Vaud). It is certainly true that Bologna has a special claim to be considered an important area that may relate to high-status individuals, but the deposition of bronzes in Swiss lake sites is a much more difficult issue. Production of high-status bronzes certainly occurred there, but why they were deposited is a matter of debate: they are not in graves, but in or near settlement sites, and it has been argued that they are part of the wider phenomenon of bronze deposition that forms so visible a feature of the Bronze Age world. Kristiansen's case might have been strengthened immeasurably if he had included in the map those swords that are closest in form to the ones depicted.[3] As it is, the map can only be considered a case of wishful thinking, demonstrating the advisability of becoming familiar with one's sources before leaping to conclusions.

Why should one consider the world of 2000 BC, or 1000 BC, as a 'world system'? What reasons are there for supposing that modern ideas of a 'world view' might be applicable to situations hundreds or thousands of years ago? In what ways can one show that it was a system at all, given that most of the communities involved were small-scale, technologically unadvanced, and pre-literate? The answers to these questions are not immediately apparent. I have argued (2000, 450) that alternative ways of visualizing the societies of later prehistory in Europe are very much more helpful, and other recent authors appear to be suggesting the same (e.g. Bintliff 1997; Morris 1999). To begin with, it is necessary to get a handle on the scale of communities at different stages of the past, and, if possible, obtain some idea of the extent to which they were open systems rather than closed ones. For this, extensive and detailed information on settlement patterns is needed, along with the best available data on artefact form and provenance. Modern techniques are able to provide such information; the best modern studies of settlement and landscape give unrivalled quality and quantity of data, while provenance studies coupled with sensitive artefact analysis have already solved many aspects of ancient production and distribution. While world views (if not systems) have their place in the study of ancient societies, regional studies are simpler and founded on much more secure evidence, at least in prehistory. Thus a view of Europe as a series of individual core areas, each with its own 'periphery', is much more consonant with the size and frequency of sites that are to be found. Bintliff (1997) has argued along similar lines for Greece, taking into account a series of other factors and other explanatory models, which lie beyond my present scope.

---

[3] In any case, the data are long out of date and have been superseded by volumes of the *Prähistorische Bronzefunde* series.

One may take this line further. A now famous article by A. Jockenhövel (1991) isolated what he termed *'fremde Frauen'*, that is, women moving in marriage between adjacent groups as defined by their characteristic dress ornaments placed in graves. This takes us back to the arguments about identity (above), but what is noteworthy here is the information this provides on the size of the groupings who used similar ornaments — a core area some 100 km across is suggested, with a 'halo' or periphery outwards up to another 50 km from the centre (i.e. total radius 100 km). This suggestion has been enthusiastically followed up by a number of scholars, most recently in a study of tumuli on the Grosse Heide at Ripdorf (Uelzen) in Lower Saxony (Geschwinde 2000). This information is subtle, accurate, and — in my opinion — the way forward. Certainly the approach adopted by Frank, to judge from his most recent pronouncements (1999) — simply to rubbish his opponents while offering no new data or arguments — will not widen this or any other debate.

Conclusion: widening the debate on ancient Europe

Widening the debate in and about archaeology is only part of what is now needed. Deepening it is no less important and in some ways more so.

How can archaeology in Europe become more inclusive without becoming less rigorous? As the present British Prime Minister remarked of his political priorities at the time of his election in 1997, 'Education, education and education'. TV programmes on archaeology are popular, but most professionals find it hard to see much in common between these programmes and what they themselves do for a living. In such circumstances, it is hardly surprising that developers who are forced to pay for archaeological evaluations and investigations of sites see no advantage to them to pay for further study and publication. It is indeed ironic that those calling most loudly for a new approach to fieldwork and publication are precisely those whose writings are found most impenetrable by the layperson. So there needs to be a half-way point at which professionals and laypeople can meet. Jargon-ridden texts that require a university degree in sociology or philosophy to understand must be frowned on; but the media must play their part in promoting a more realistic view of what archaeology is and does, in presenting accurately the live issues in the subject today, and in demonstrating the theoretical and factual underpinnings of the subject.

I have presented here a brief overview of four current debates, which each touch on many more. Yet none of them (with the possible exception of the first) has found any favour with those who control our media; none would be familiar to the 'person on the Web' (today's version of the 'man on the Clapham omnibus'). Education is indeed the way forward, and it is to be hoped that the present volume will play an important role in this task.

References

AMMERMAN, A.J. and CAVALLI-SFORZA, L.L. 1984: *The Neolithic Transition and the Genetics of Populations in Europe* (Princeton).

APPADURAI, A. (ed.) 1986: *The Social Life of Things. Commodities in Cultural Perspective* (Cambridge).

ARNOLD, B. and BLAIR GIBSON, D. 1995: Introduction. Beyond the mists: forging an ethnological approach to Celtic studies. In Arnold, B. and Blair Gibson, D. (eds.), *Celtic Chiefdom, Celtic State* (Cambridge), 1–10.

BARRETT, J.C. 1995: *Contemporary Archaeology* (Oxford, Oxbow Lecture 2).

BASS, G.F., PULAK, C., COLLON, D. and WEINSTEIN, J. 1989: The Bronze Age shipwreck at Ulu Burun: 1986 campaign. *American J. Archaeol.* 93, 1–29.

BENDER, B., HAMILTON, S. and TILLEY, C. 1997: Leskernick: stone worlds; alternative narratives; nested landscapes. *Proc. Prehist. Soc.* 63, 147–78.

BINTLIFF, J.L. 1997: Regional survey, demography, and the rise of complex societies in the ancient Aegean: Core-Periphery, Neo-Malthusian, and other interpretive models. *J. Field Archaeol.* 24(1), 1–38.

BRUN, P. 1995: From chiefdom to state organization in Celtic Europe. In Arnold, B. and Blair Gibson, D. (eds.), *Celtic Chiefdom, Celtic State* (Cambridge), 13–25.

BRUN, P. and CHAUME, B. 1997: Introduction: une approche multiscalaire. In Brun, P. and Chaume, B. (eds.), *Vix et les éphémères principautés celtiques. Les VIe-Ve siècles avant J.-C. en Europe centre-occidentale. Actes du colloque de Châtillon-sur-Seine* (Paris), 9–11.

CARNEIRO, R.L. 1970: A theory of the origin of the state. *Science* 169, 733–8.

CARNEIRO, R.L. 1981: The chiefdom as precursor of the state. In Jones, G. and Kautz, R. (eds.), *The Transition to Statehood in the New World* (Cambridge), 37–79.

CARNEIRO, R.L. 1991: The nature of the chiefdom as revealed by evidence from the Cauca Valley of Columbia. In Rambo, A.T. and Gillogly, K. (eds.), *Profiles in Cultural Evolution. Papers from a Conference in Honor of Elman R. Service* (Ann Arbor, University of Michigan Museum of Anthropology), 167–90.

CHAMPION, T.C. 1989: Introduction. In Champion, T.C. (ed.), *Centre and Periphery. Comparative Studies in Archaeology* (London, One World Archaeology, 11), 1–21.

CHAPMAN, J.C. 2000: *Fragmentation in Archaeology* (London).

CHAPMAN, M. 1992: *The Celts: the construction of a myth* (London).

CHASE-DUNN, C. and HALL, T.D. (eds.) 1991: *Core/Periphery Relations in Precapitalist Worlds* (Boulder).

CHILDE, G. 1951: *Social Evolution* (London).

CHILDE, G. 1954: *What happened in history* (Harmondsworth, 2nd edition).

CLARK, G. and PIGGOTT, S. 1965: *Prehistoric Societies* (London).

COLES, B.J. 1998: Doggerland: a speculative survey. *Proc. Prehist. Soc.* 64, 45–81.

COLLIS, J. 1997: Celtic myths. *Antiquity* 71, 195–201.

CONKEY, M.W. and HASTORF, C.A. (eds.) 1990: *The uses of style in archaeology* (Cambridge).

CRUMLEY, C. 1987: A dialectical critique of heterarchy. In Patterson, T.C. and Gailey, C.W. (eds.), *Power Relations and State Formation* (Washington, D.C., American Anthropological Association), 155–9.

CRUMLEY, C. 1995: Heterarchy and the analysis of complex societies. In Ehrenreich, R.M., Crumley, C.L. and Levy, J.E. (eds.), *Heterarchy and the Analysis of Complex Societies* (Arlington, Archeological Papers of the American Anthropological Association, 6), 1–5.

EARLE, T.K. 1987: Chiefdoms in archaeological and ethnohistorical perspective. *Annu. Rev. Anthropol.* 16, 279–308.

EARLE, T.K. 1991: The evolution of chiefdoms. In Earle, T.K. (ed.), *Chiefdoms: Power, Economy and Ideology* (Cambridge), 1–15.

EARLE, T.K. 1997: *How chiefs come to power. The political economy in prehistory* (Stanford).

EDMONDS, M. 1999: *Ancestral Geographies of the Neolithic. Landscape, monuments and memory* (London).

EHRENREICH, R.M. 1995: Early metalworking: a heterarchical analysis of industrial organization. In Ehrenreich, R.M., Crumley, C.L. and Levy, J.E. (eds.), *Heterarchy and the Analysis of Complex Societies* (Arlington, Archeological Papers of the American Anthropological Association, 6), 33–9.

ELLIS EVANS, D. 1995: The early Celts: the evidence of language. In Green, M.J. (ed.), *The Celtic World* (London), 8–20.

EOGAN, G. 1986: *Knowth and the Passage Tombs of Ireland* (London).

FILIP, J. 1976: *Celtic Civilisation and its Heritage* (Prague).

FRANK, A.G. 1990: A theoretical introduction to 5000 years of world-system history. *Review* 14, 155–248.

FRANK, A.G. 1993: Bronze Age world system cycles. *Curr. Anthropol.* 34(4), 383–429.

FRANK, A.G. 1999: Abuses and uses of World Systems Theory in archaeology. In Kardulias, P.N. 1999, 275–95.

FRANK, A.G. and GILLS, B.K. (eds.) 1993: *The World System: Five Hundred Years or Five Thousand?* (London).

FRANKENSTEIN, S. and ROWLANDS, M.J. 1978: The internal structure and regional context of early Iron Age society in southwest Germany. *Bull. Inst. Archaeol.* 15, 73–112.

GESCHWINDE, M. 2000: *Die Hügelgräber auf der Großen Heide bei Ripdorf im Landkreis Uelzen* (Neumünster, Göttinger Schriften zur Vor- und Frühgeschichte 27).

GILLS, B.K. and FRANK, A.G. 1993: World system cycles, crises, and hegemonic shifts, 1700 BC to 1700 AD. In Frank, A.G. and Gills, B.K. 1993, 143–99.

GILMAN, A. 1981: The development of social stratification in Bronze Age Europe. *Curr. Anthropol.* 22(1), 1–23.

GIMBUTAS, M. 1970: Proto-Indo-European culture: the Kurgan culture during the 5th to the 3rd millennia B.C. In Cardona, G., Koenigswald, H.M. and Senn, A. (eds.), *Indo-European and Indo-Europeans* (Philadelphia), 155–98.

GRAVES-BROWN, P., JONES, S. and GAMBLE, C. (eds.) 1996: *Cultural Identity and Archaeology: the construction of European identities* (London).

HALL, T.D. 1999: World-Systems and evolution: an appraisal. In Kardulias, P.N. 1999, 1–23.

HARDING, A.F. 2000: *European Societies in the Bronze Age* (Cambridge).

HODDER, I. 1990: *The Domestication of Europe* (Oxford).

HODDER, I. 1999: *The Archaeological Process. An Introduction* (Oxford).

JAMES, S. 1999: *The Atlantic Celts: ancient people or modern invention?* (London).

JOCKENHÖVEL, A. 1991: Räumliche Mobilität von Personen in der mittleren Bronzezeit des westlichen Mitteleuropa. *Germania* 69, 49–62.

JONES, S. 1996: Discourses of identity in the interpretation of the past. In Graves-Brown, P., Jones, S. and Gamble, C. (eds.), *Cultural Identity and Archaeology: the construction of European communities* (London), 62–80.

JONES, S. 1997: *The Archaeology of Ethnicity. Constructing identities in the past and present* (London).

KARDULIAS, P.N. (ed.) 1999: *World-Systems Theory in Practice. Leadership, production and exchange* (Lanham).

KILIAN, L. 1988: *Zum Ursprung der Germanen* (Bonn).

KRISTIANSEN, K. 1987: Center and periphery in Bronze Age Scandinavia. In Rowlands, M., Trolle Larsen, M. and Kristiansen, K. (eds.), *Centre and Periphery in the Ancient World* (Cambridge), 74–85.

KRISTIANSEN, K. 1994: The emergence of the European World System in the Bronze Age: divergence, convergence and social evolution during the first and second millennia BC in Europe. In Kristiansen, K. and Jensen, J. (eds.), *Europe in the First Millennium BC* (Sheffield, Sheffield Archaeological Monographs, 6), 7–30.

KRISTIANSEN, K. 1998: *Europe before History* (Cambridge).

LEVY, J.E. 1995: Heterarchy in Bronze Age Denmark: settlement pattern, gender and ritual. In Ehrenreich, R.M., Crumley, C.L. and Levy, J.E. (eds.), *Heterarchy and the Analysis of Complex Societies* (Arlington, Archeological Papers of the American Anthropological Association, 6), 41–54.

MANN, M. 1986: *The Sources of Social Power. Vol. I. A History of Power from the Beginning to AD 1760* (Cambridge).

MORGAN, L.H. 1871: *Ancient Society* (New York).

MORRIS, I. 1999: Negotiated peripherality in Iron Age Greece: accepting and resisting the East. In Kardulias, P.N. 1999, 63–84.

MÜLLER-KARPE, H. 1961: *Die Vollgriffschwerter der Urnenfelderzeit aus Bayern* (Munich).

PLOG, S. 1980: *Stylistic Variation in Prehistoric Ceramics: Design Analysis in the American Southwest* (Cambridge).

POWELL, T.G.E. 1958: *The Celts* (London).

RENFREW, C. 1974: Beyond a subsistence economy: the evolution of social organisation in prehistoric Europe. In Moore, C.B. (ed.), *Reconstructing Complex Societies: an archaeological colloquium* (Bulletin American Schools of Oriental Research, Supplement 20), 69–95.

RENFREW, C. 1987: *Archaeology and Language. The puzzle of Indo-European origins* (London).

RENFREW, C. 1996: Prehistory and the identity of Europe, or, Don't let's be beastly to the Hungarians. In Graves-Brown, P., Jones, S. and Gamble, C. (eds.), *Cultural Identity and Archaeology: the construction of European communities* (London), 125–37.

RENFREW, C. 2000: At the edge of knowability: towards a prehistory of languages. *Cambridge Archaeol. J.* 10(1), 7–34.

SAHLINS, M. 1968: *Tribesmen* (Englewood Cliffs).

SERVICE, E.R. 1962/1975: *Primitive Social Organization, an evolutionary perspective* (New York).

SERVICE, E.R. 1975: *Origins of the State and Civilization: The process of cultural evolution* (New York).

SHERRATT, A.G. 1993: What would a Bronze Age world system look like? Relations between temperate Europe and the Mediterranean in later prehistory. *J. European Archaeol.* 1(2), 1–57.

SPINDLER, K. 1983: *Die frühe Kelten* (Stuttgart).

STIG SØRENSEN, M.L. 1997: Reading dress: the construction of social categories and identities in Bronze Age Europe. *J. European Archaeol.* 5(1), 93–114.

STIG SØRENSEN, M.L. 2000: *Gender Archaeology* (Cambridge).

THOMAS, J. 1988: Neolithic explanations revisited: the Mesolithic–Neolithic transition in Britain and south Scandinavia. *Proc. Prehist. Soc.* 54, 59–66.

THOMAS, J. 1992: *Rethinking the Neolithic* (Cambridge).

TODD, M. 1992: *The Early Germans* (Oxford).

WAILES, B. 1995: A case study of heterarchy in complex societies: early Medieval Ireland and its archaeological implications. In Ehrenreich, R.M., Crumley, C.L. and Levy, J.E. (eds.), *Heterarchy and the Analysis of Complex Societies* (Arlington, Archeological Papers of the American Anthropological Association, 6), 55–69.

WALLERSTEIN, I. 1974/1980: *The Modern World-System*, Vols. 1–2 (New York).

WELS-WEYRAUCH, U. 1989: Mittelbronzezeitliche Frauentrachten in Süddeutschland (Beziehungen zur Hagenauer Gruppierung). In *Dynamique du bronze moyen en Europe occidentale* (Actes du 113e Congrès National des Sociétés Savantes, Strasbourg 1988) (Paris), 117–34.

WIESSNER, P. 1983: Style and social information in Kalahari San projectile points. *American Antiquity* 48, 253–76.

WILKINSON, T.A.H. 1996: *State Formation in Egypt: Chronology and Society* (Oxford, BAR Int. Ser. 651; Cambridge Monographs in African Archaeology 40).

WILKINSON, T.A.H. 1999: *Early Dynastic Egypt* (London).

WOBST, M. 1977: Stylistic behavior and information exchange. In Cleland, C.E. (ed.), *For the Director: Research Essays in Honor of James B Griffin* (Ann Arbor, Museum of Anthropology, University of Michigan), 317–42.

ZVELEBIL, M. 1995: Indo-European origins and the agricultural transition in Europe. *J. European Archaeol.* 3(1), 33–70.

The first civilizations in the Middle East

NICHOLAS POSTGATE

The arena

Between 3500 and 3000 BC the lower reaches of the Nile and of the Tigris and Euphrates witnessed a transformation in human society from which the world has never looked back. Different though they are in detail, Egypt and Mesopotamia at this crucial juncture have much in common, and give or take a century, they are contemporary: twins, but not identical. They are similar in their scale, their geographical environment, their advances in technology, and their cultural sophistication as expressed in writing, art and architecture. These are some of the criteria which have been used since Gordon Childe to define a state, or a complex society. If in our title we revert to the less clinical term 'civilization' it is to stress that their significance lies not only in the history of humanity's social and political institutions, but also in its material and intellectual creativity.[1] What is more, as in Classical Greece, the phenomenon of civilization in Mesopotamia was a koine which extended beyond the limits of any single state: it may perhaps go hand in hand with the formation of states in the region, but not of a single state, and this, to a lesser extent, seems to apply to Egypt too.[2]

Of course the ancient Near East is not just these two centres: Anatolia and Iran, not to mention the small matter of Palestine, all belong within the wider orbit of these two main civilizations, but culturally and politically, for most of the time between the invention of writing and Cyrus the Great, the initiative comes from one or the other. Apart from their primacy, a crucial aspect of their cultural sophistication is the use of written records, which distinguishes them among contemporary cultures, and the survival of those records which informs us of their administrative and cultural activities. The fascination of Egypt is immediate and enduring; Mesopotamia, with its changing

---

[1] Usage is of course elastic, but even within the sphere of social order some broader term than 'state' is needed. Baines and Yoffee use 'civilization' for 'the overarching social order in which state governance exists and is legitimized' (Feinman and Marcus 1998, 254), but even this does not sufficiently acknowledge those cultural aspects of a society which are later described as art and literature.
[2] Kemp 1989, 31 ff.; Wilkinson 1999.

dynasties and capitals is less easy to grasp, but commands equal attention for reasons summed up in the sub-title of one of S.N. Kramer's books: 'From the tablets of Sumer: twenty-five firsts in man's recorded history' (New York 1959). No wonder they both continue to attract the interest of academics and the general public alike.

When we ponder what might be happening 20, 50 or 100 years from now it becomes plain that there are two active ingredients at work which will between them dictate the nature of 'Middle Eastern archaeology': one is the spirit of intellectual enquiry, and the other is the physical presence of archaeological remains on and under the ground. While in academic minds the pursuit of knowledge may be setting the agenda, in practical terms it is likely to be the facts on the ground which dominate the archaeological scene, and that is where we will look first.

With the establishment of separate nation states from the dissolution of the Ottoman empire, local identities have certainly awakened political interest in the visible archaeology of the region. Governments have taken command of their own past, and antiquities departments and museums are an invariable ingredient of the state apparatus. On the political stage the 'heritage' of these lands has indeed been adopted by their rulers as a draw for tourism and an emblem of national identity. During the next few decades it is likely that proprietorial and hereditary motivation will grow within the consciousness of the population so that they too see themselves as inheritors and the early civilizations as 'their' forebears.

A recent stimulating collection of articles on nationalism and archaeology strikingly fails to include our part of the world, as the editors themselves note: 'We particularly regret lack of coverage on the nationalist practices of archaeology in Israel, Turkey, and other Middle Eastern countries.'[3] We are politely not told the reason for this lack, but at least one reason may well be that those competent to write on it felt that an honest assessment would prejudice their chances of continuing to work in the countries of their choice, so starkly does the past play a role in the ideology of the governments currently in place. The tensions are most evident in areas of open tension such as Cyprus and Israel. To cite just one comment from the same volume: 'The goals of Israeli archaeology have meant that very little state support is accorded to the study of the archaeology of the Christian and particularly the Islamic periods, since this would be counterproductive from a nationalistic point of view.'[4] But political distortions are always present. At best conscious or unconscious bias can set the agenda, making one type or period of research more congenial, and there are many stages beyond this, ranging from the deliberate or instinctive suppression of evidence to the wilful destruction of sites, threatened though mercifully not realized during the extremes of the Iranian revolution.

---

[3] Kohl and Fawcett 1995, 3. I gather that a second tranche of papers will soon fill this gap.
[4] Kohl and Fawcett 1995, 271.

Despite the strong pan-Arab sentiment of most of the countries in our arena, and the historical awareness that Arabic-speakers first entered a country long after the most spectacular periods of its history, there is a natural inclination to see in the earlier inhabitants of a country one's own forebears. Of course the surviving Aramaean-speaking communities, and the Copts in Egypt represent a link reaching back long before Islam, but this is not essential. Like the Chinese, even in the eighteenth century BC Mesopotamian kings included previous and unrelated dynasties in the funerary rites for their ancestors. The desire to claim affinity with these 'cradles of civilization' is reflected, for instance, in the pressure placed on Iraqi academics in the 1970s to demonstrate that Sumerian was a dialect of Arabic. That Sumerian is to the best of our knowledge totally unrelated (whereas Akkadian, which is attested almost as far back in time, emphatically is related) merely reflects the fact that political agendas do not always need to pay regard to academic opinion. In Turkey kindred sentiments in the years after the establishment of the modern state led to banks being named after the Hittites or the Sumerians, and the adoption of Sumerian surnames expressed an affinity to the founders of Near Eastern civilization who also shared an agglutinative non-Semitic and non-Indo-European language (though not in fact demonstrably related to Turkish).

This is not to suggest that there is anything bogus about the interest in the past. The combination of western scholarship and the spread of Islam tends to obscure real continuities. The search for the genesis of the western world regularly takes us back to these twin cultures which lie behind Classical Greece like primeval gods in one of their theogonies. For they are viewed through the mediation of Greece in particular. Alexander saw to it that a thin membrane of Hellenism was stretched across all these lands and beyond, and until the decipherment of the scripts all our knowledge of Egypt and Mesopotamia was derived from the Bible and classical authors. While we may see ancient Egypt and Mesopotamia as the grandparents of modern western culture, so we forget that they had other grandchildren, our cousins who now occupy their lands. There must indeed be a substantial persistence of genetic stock, and in vocabulary, religious practice, and other cultural aspects it is not only the Copts, the Mandaeans and the Christians who inherit through Aramaic from the pre-Hellenistic world of the ancient Near East.

Development problems and conservation

Being the inheritors of the world's first civilizations has proved a mixed blessing. Governments of such countries are like the owners of stately homes: deeply committed to maintain the splendour with which they are surrounded, but deeply over-committed to the banking fraternity by the cost of so doing. Expected to bear the costs themselves, but at the same time expected to do nothing detrimental to their slice of the common heritage in the eyes of those who do not bear the cost. The traditional solution is of course to let the public in, set up funfairs in the grounds, and in the last resort to sell the family silver. It means paying extra staff, and installing public conveniences, but some of this will work.

The value of tourism to governments in the Middle East, especially those which do not produce their own oil, is considerable, and if it is the archaeological monuments which draw them in it seems fair that income from tourism should contribute to their upkeep. Nevertheless, archaeological services have not traditionally been the best-funded of government departments, and tensions are often present between Ministers of Tourism and Directors of Antiquities. Yet even outside Egypt the example of Petra, and the recent rise of tourism in Syria, demonstrate that archaeological heritage is a significant economic resource. It is however a goose that must be carefully tended if it is to continue to lay its golden eggs.

The foundation of archaeological research in the Middle East was laid by Western Europeans operating in the context of rivalries between the three major powers of Britain, France and later Germany. Napoleon's invasion of Egypt was accompanied by a remarkable episode of what today might be called data collection, recently characterized by Edward Said as the beginning of 'orientalism' (1978, 76 ff.), though this cannot undermine the seriousness of its purpose and the scale of its achievement, not least in areas of natural science which have no overtones of cultural imperialism. Mesopotamian archaeology was virtually initiated by a French Vice-Consul in Mosul (P.-E. Botta) and an agent of the British ambassador to the Sublime Porte (A.H. Layard).[5] The massive investigation of the ancient capitals of Assur, Babylon and Uruk took place at the time the Berlin to Baghdad railway was under construction, under the auspices of the Deutsche Orient-Gesellschaft which had close relations with the Kaiser. While their devotion to the acquisition of knowledge in the face of considerable personal discomfort and danger is beyond dispute, they were also acquiring objects for the adornment of museums and even patrons' mantelpieces. Along with their genuine academic endeavour aspiring Middle Eastern archaeologists took advantage of political conditions which secured them financial support and some measure of diplomatic cover. Apart from Egypt, most of the Middle Eastern arena still fell under the Ottoman cloak. Finds from American excavations at Nippur were apparently presented personally to Hilprecht by the Sultan himself, and the granting of firmans to Layard for his work in Assyria in the teeth of local resistance was directly the result of the influence of his patron back in Istanbul.

Conditions may have changed in many ways, but the underlying structure is still the same. The academic motivation on the part of the western academic world persists, though with different emphases, and joined by Japan and more recently Korea. Almost without exception researchers from outside the region are allowed in to play their part in the recovery of antiquity. Why, from the host's point of view, one may reasonably

---

[5] Larsen 1996.

ask? The colonial era is long gone, and there are home-grown archaeologists, often with doctorates from western universities, who might be expected to experience proprietorial feelings about their country's sites and monuments. The answer is largely one of numbers: antiquities staffs (and their university colleagues) are stretched beyond their human and financial resources by the scale of their task. There is also the force of tradition, where foreign participation has been hallowed by decades, and the awareness that workers from abroad can introduce new technologies and methods. Not least, there is a generous instinct for hospitality.

Though a comfortable relationship has often thus been established, with benefit to both sides, there remain tensions. Host countries, for various reasons, prefer foreign expeditions to base themselves in long-term projects. Security services like to know where foreign nationals are supposed to be. Academics may wish to flit from flower to flower, but an antiquities service granting the concession to a major site has a right to expect a major commitment in time and finance. I was once asked by the Iraqi Director-General whether the British had 'finished' the excavation of Nimrud, and if not, why we wished to cease work there. I could have been asked the same of Ur, or any other urban site in Mesopotamia. There are of course some obvious responses — the sheer size of the Middle Eastern sites making 'complete' excavation a matter of centuries, the undesirability of leaving nothing for posterity, the need for pauses for reflection and publication — but there are also enough sites which have been broached and abandoned to give some validity to such concerns. And there are academic reasons for long-termism: despite the predilection in Britain for short (five-year) projects, especially among funding bodies, in Egypt and Mesopotamia it is the long-term projects which in the end 'yield the true glory', as the examples of Elephantine, Tell el-Dab'a, Tell Mardikh and Sheikh Hamad demonstrate.

If the rich of the world expect to be allowed to pursue their academic goals in less rich countries, they may also expect to pay for the privilege. Regional projects are now more of a comprehensive geographical description than the placing of dots on a blank sheet of paper to represent places where sherds were located, but there is every reason to incorporate such results into a 'Sites and Monuments Record' maintained by the local directorates. Hard-pressed governments may sometimes allow foreign expeditions with cash to spend to work in their territories purely because it boosts the local economy, perhaps running counter to sentiment which sees no reason for foreigners to benefit from the local cultural heritage. This soon becomes a version of economic imperialism. Wider issues surface: where a foreign expedition has exposed significant remains of the past, they should be expected to conserve them for the future, but how far does that commitment extend? Can a foreign country take over financial liability for an entire ancient city, visited by thousands of tourists each year to the benefit of the local economy? Hardly. Archaeological budgets, even in the most generous countries, are not limitless or open-ended. The host country must in any case retain overall control of the site and will end up holding the baby if and when the foreign team becomes unable or unwilling to meet its demands.

If a sovereign state decided to destroy a major archaeological site the rest of the world would not stand aside unmoved, but would it dig in its pockets? There is a stand-off here, with undertones of cultural blackmail. Where a developing country identifies an economic imperative to alter the landscape — whether by building barrages, or grading a plain, or simply via urban growth — the material welfare of the present population usually comes before the cultural heritage of future generations. Governments are not unaware of the clash of interests, but they do not have the resources to resolve it. If an international agency is invited to contribute to the development, it can impose conditions, and the World Bank, for instance, may require assessments of both environmental and cultural loss. Despite a commendable beginning with the Aswan Dam rescue campaign in Nubia, the premier international cultural agency, UNESCO, suffers from lack of cash and of political support from major players (e.g. the USA and the UK). It does what it can. Its World Heritage Committee has listed 582 sites of cultural or natural value, and one of the Committee's main responsibilities is to provide technical co-operation where local resources are insufficient, and emergency assistance in the case of properties threatened with imminent destruction. But of course this is but a drop in the ocean, the tip of the iceberg. Take Turkey, a country which has, in the memorable formulation of a previous Director-General, more Greek cities than Greece and more Roman cities than Italy. As of December 1998 there were nine World Heritage sites listed in Turkey. These include Troy and Hattusha, but what of Pergamon, Ephesus, Miletus, Halicarnassus, Çatalhöyük, Side, Perge, Aphrodisias, Sagalassos, Termessos, Van, Gordion, Kül Tepe, Dara, Ani, Aghthamar, and all the fortresses of Urartu? Iraq, the centre of one of the two founding civilizations of the Eurasian world, has one site listed: the Parthian desert city of Hatra. Not Uruk, Ur, Babylon or Nineveh. With the best will in the world, as things stand at present the World Heritage list may protect the occasional site, but it is not going to resolve any country's problems.

Two patterns may come to play an increasing role. Money may be directed at specific targets by external agencies, for a variety of motives. At the time of writing, the *Economist* reports on payments of $30,000 and $60,000 secured by the Egyptian government from American sources for press rights to archaeological discoveries, and also in Egypt huge sums have been put into a major conservation programme by the US government, though its effectiveness is hurt by its bureaucratic constraints. A Berlin project has contributed the cost of a major museum display in the Syrian town of Deir az-Zor (Fig. 1), museums have been built at Tell el-Dab'a and Elephantine. This is not something that seems likely to attract public funding in the UK, but the Çatalhöyük project has been granted 6-figure funding towards a site museum by the European Union.[6]

---

[6] Examples of collaborative site conservation from Turkey and Honduras are cited in Winter 1997, 140 note 4.

Figure 1. Collaboration between guests and hosts. Deir az-Zor Museum, eastern Syria: Neolithic house from Tell Bouqras. A life-size reconstruction carried out as a Syrian-German collaboration. Photo Ulrich Runge, 1996; courtesy Prof. Dr. Hartmut Kühne, Freie Universität Berlin.

The other pattern has the foreigner as a hired employee rather than a donor, carrying out contract archaeology, where the demand is coming from a host country which is prepared to pay for the work to be done by experts: this is after all nothing new to governments, who do it all the time in the field of civil engineering. In recent UNESCO-sponsored work in Lebanon an archaeological team was brought from Britain, and in the Gulf some governments have invited archaeological teams in and paid for them to carry out research rather than rescue projects. Plainly there is plenty of room for tension between the desires of the paymasters and the academic motivation of the excavators, but this is a pattern which will inevitably expand, and has of course come to play a major role in British archaeology. Here indeed over 75 per cent of money going into archaeological fieldwork comes from developers who are obliged by new regulations to carry it out as a condition of planning permission. This is a lesson which host countries could learn: the funding of major barrage construction or urban development needs to have an element built in from the start to cover archaeological salvage operations.

For destruction of sites will continue (Fig. 2). As the populations grow and standards of living rise, important sites are threatened by the housing and civil engineering

Figure 2. The march of progress. The tumuli of the world's largest prehistoric cemetery (left) give way to the bulldozer in favour of the demands of modern housing, near Saar, Bahrain. Photo courtesy Dr. J. Moon, copyright London–Bahrain Archaeological Expedition.

needs of modernization. This has been most obvious in the case of barrages on the major rivers: the Aswan dam has had many successors on the Tigris, the Euphrates and their tributaries. The extreme is represented by the GAP project in south-eastern Turkey, which will soon lock up the headwaters of the Tigris and Euphrates within the Turkish borders, and in the process drown much of their valleys, prime environments for human settlement in the past. The wealth of archaeological remains in some of these areas far exceeds the possibilities for controlled excavation. In general the antiquities services have done their very best to stretch their resources and personnel to rescue something. (They do have better laws than e.g. the UK, and often their government has more teeth.) Foreign teams have also been invited, tempted by favourable conditions such as allocation of antiquities (Syria), provision of free labour (Iraq), less formal and restrictive conditions (Turkey), or 'blackmailed' by making participation in the rescue project an explicit or implicit condition of permission to work at a site of their own choosing.

The fact that the agenda has been set by a civil engineering requirement in another country has sometimes made it difficult for foreign teams to raise finance from their own government sources. In Canada rescue excavation at one time, perhaps still, explicitly disqualified a project from consideration, and it can certainly be a negative factor in the UK as well. Yet here we run into one of the principal issues which will affect archaeology abroad in the coming century. The scale of the problem is so large, that excavation will only recover a fraction of what will be lost, and by that token, there will be plenty of scope for projects to exercise their own judgement and suit their own academic objectives in selecting a site.

Movable heritage

Of the strategies for the survival of the stately home the most controversial part is selling the family silver, and it often happens clandestinely. Governments universally have laws prohibiting or at least strictly controlling the export of antiquities, but they continue to haemorrhage across the frontiers. Here the international community must share a good deal of the blame. Even if we accept (and not all parties do) that in practice the status quo (defined perhaps by where things were in 1970) is likely to remain, opinion and practice in the developed countries are far from acknowledging the unacceptable face of the international trade in antiquities. Museums have by and large put their act in order, but the trade is a different matter. Expressed charitably, their position is that an item is innocent until proven guilty. Respectable dealers would not handle a piece they knew to be stolen, but in their book (and in accordance with the legal systems of many countries) theft from an individual or institution should be distinguished from export from a country in contravention of that country's laws. And even where an item can be shown to have been stolen, under the law of some Western European countries this may not render its purchase illegal.

One particularly vicious effect of the art market is the demand it fosters for fresh sources. Individual objects can, physically, be repatriated, but sites turned over by treasure-hunters can never be restored. One looks enviously at the wild-life movement: when a customs officer seizes a piece of ivory the onus of proof is on the importer, but not for a unique piece of another country's past. Yet archaeological sites and artefacts, unlike elephants, don't breed. The issue is actively debated, though without much sign of progress. There may be some solutions. Tighter controls on the source are very difficult to implement, not least because of political chaos. In Iraq and Afghanistan entire contents of museums have been looted, and where the state's control does run it has higher priorities than guarding ancient mounds. One way to reduce demand might be to flood the market. Trade in antiquities might be decriminalized if governments were sufficiently sure of themselves to identify and market items from their cultural heritage which they consider 'surplus to requirements'. Thus after the first million mummified ibises, the Egyptian cultural heritage would not be seriously depleted if some were exported. But in the long run we need a change of culture in the collecting countries, hand in hand with a determined effort to convince farmers and shepherds — not to mention government ministers — that the antiquities under their feet belong to them and their children and should remain where they can see them.[7]

The academic enterprise

Like it or not, then, the opportunities for archaeological activity will be largely dictated by the inhabitants of these lands past and present. How will the academic world adapt its enterprise to these constraints? To understand (and perhaps to improve) the study of the ancient Near East — and in the context of this volume we are concerned with the time between the 'end of prehistory' and Alexander the Great — one has to be aware of the existence of the different micro-environments in which the practitioners operate. Like our early states, our academic polities are complex and fractured both horizontally and vertically. The vertical lines of division are of various kinds: geographical, topical and methodological.

As far as the geographical barriers are concerned, to some extent the lines were drawn up for us in antiquity, or are prescribed for us by modern political frontiers, but we have certainly allowed them to set the agenda. We are looking at four academic microcosms: Egypt and the Egyptologists, the Bible and biblical scholars, Greece and Rome and the classical community, and the ancient Near Eastern types. The negative effects of this are most apparent precisely where the four communities intersect, in the eastern Mediterranean in the second and first millennia BC. If we take a Swan's cruise round the littoral, we need a Classicist to tell us about Pylos and Knossos, an ancient Near Eastern wallah to deal with Ugarit, a biblical archaeologist at Ashdod and of course an Egyptologist at Tell el-Dab'a. It is a rare bird that is at home in more than a couple of these environments.

Egypt, today as in antiquity, is a world of its own. Although in museums and universities ancient Egypt is often grouped with the rest of the ancient Near East, it almost always retains its individual identity, assisted not a little by its unequivocal name, and scholars expert in the language, textual record, history and archaeology of Egypt rarely step outside its disciplinary frontiers.[8] There are good reasons for this in the nature of the subject of investigation. Although there are links with both Semitic and Hamitic languages, the ancient Egyptian language is peculiar to its territory, and its script was not adopted outside the frontiers. The physical geography of the land of Egypt holds it together through the uniformity of its subsistence base, and at the same time circumscribes it so that by sea and desert the rest of the world has been held at arm's length. Despite regular economic links with the outside, and the occasional foreign incursion, it retained its individual character with consummate ease.

[7] On many of these issues in the Near Eastern context see Winter 1997.
[8] Cf. Trigger 1993, 2, citing Eyre, citing Herodotus.

The rest of the area is altogether more diverse and permeable. The diversity is reflected in our modern nomenclature. Ancient Near East, or Middle East, Western Asia, the Levant, the Fertile Crescent, Mesopotamia, Anatolia, they are all imprecise, but we use them because in antiquity the names changed from age to age as populations and boundaries shifted. Yet there was some kind of interaction zone. One traditional cohesive force is the Semitic language group, the members of which rub shoulders in time and place and interact readily with loanwords and idiom. This is reflected in recent scholarship: in the good old days of the nineteenth century serious philologists reckoned to know Hebrew, Syriac and Aramaic, Arabic and perhaps Ethiopic. They were probably also familiar with Latin and Greek, and thereby could control the bulk of the written sources relating to the Middle East through time. Few except hard-core comparative philologists can match this today, not least because we have to add Ugaritic, Akkadian, Amorite, Eblaite to the list, but in the second millennium the diffusion of the cuneiform script and the accompanying Akkadian language, and in the first millennium the use of the alphabet and Aramaic language, corresponded to an interaction sphere which holds modern scholarship in a similar loose embrace. Boundaries for such a sphere are inevitably imprecise, but the editors of the *Reallexikon der Assyriologie* apply as a rule of thumb the use of cuneiform script and cylinder seals, which seems to work as well as any more sophisticated or complicated scheme.

The fields of research

These are not the only divides. Our subject area is subdivided into topical fields: art history, field archaeology, ceramics, philology, anthropology, and so on. Each offers rich grazing so that specialists do not always feel the need to look over the fence for greener pastures. A recent collection of articles addressed the study of the ancient Near East in the twenty-first century, to salute the memory of W.F. Albright who worked in an unrivalled range of fields (Cooper and Schwartz 1996). One word which keeps recurring in it is 'contextualization', and this seems to mean taking account of how each scholar's narrow field of research intersects with and is thereby affected by neighbouring fields. In the case of the ancient Near East it is not difficult to find a host of ways in which ancient Near Eastern research requires 'contextualization', so as to counteract another seven-syllable concept, 'compartmentalization'. Time and again the specialists have neither presented their data in a form accessible to specialists in neighbouring disciplines, nor themselves interpreted the material they have quarried.

This goes for art history (to use the traditional term),[9] but perhaps the prime example in Mesopotamia is the reconstruction of Sumerian literature. Within the ivory tower of

[9] Work on linking the traditional concerns of art history to other aspects of ancient Near Eastern civilization, such as (dare I use the term?) ideology, has been in the doldrums but is now gathering pace, thanks in no small part to I.J. Winter.

Sumerology the enterprise has been exciting and rewarding. Fundamental work was done by S.N. Kramer in making the raw texts available to scholarship, and text editions followed on both sides of the Atlantic in the 1950s to 1970s. A body of texts has been reconstituted which is attractive and varied, but also difficult to understand on various levels. Tablets with new compositions, or more often with additions to known ones, will continue to surface in museum collections and one day again from the soil of ancient Sumer. Those competent to work on them have tended to treat the texts as philological assault courses rather than literary compositions. Their difficulty makes errors inevitable, and a stern philologist's ethic generates pathological anxiety among Sumerologists not to have missed a single reference. Nor has it helped that for many years the text and content of some of the texts has been privy to a few scholars, creating the insecurity of knowing that somewhere in the world a colleague has a fuller or better version. For all these reasons it is fair to say that for such a fascinating body of texts from so early in human history, Sumerian literature has been shamefully underexploited. With the idiosyncratic exception of Thorkild Jacobsen, extremely little serious analysis has been written by hard-core Sumerologists about the content of these jewels they have rescued from the surface of the clay tablets.[10]

Happily this may soon change. The electronic corpus of Sumerian literature, now accessible in an on-line web-site at Oxford, breaks new ground not only in making the most up-to-date texts widely available in a consistent format, but also in achieving a change of ethic whereby members of the field have pooled their academic capital in a single communal investment. Nevertheless, there is a long way to go in exploiting this new asset, and even today one of the most stimulating works on Sumerian literature was written 30 years ago by a Professor of Greek without knowledge of the language.[11]

And lest a reader is inclined to ask what all this has to do with archaeology, let me cite chapter and verse! One epic about bilateral missions between Uruk in south Mesopotamia and Aratta, reached by traversing seven mountain ranges, has often — however questionably — featured in discussions of third-millennium trading networks. A short composition of the early second millennium BC gives in poetic form detailed instructions for the annual farming calendar, and should be a starred item on the Mesopotamian archaeologist's reading list, whether or not the farmers themselves paid much heed to it. These are just examples: more important is the entire corpus as one facet of the world we are looking at: the facet turned to the archaeologist belongs to the same world and one cannot wisely be studied without awareness of the other.

---

[10] The principal exceptions are Alster, Black, and Van Stiphout and Wilcke, but all these scholars have tended to concentrate more on formal aspects than on the content.
[11] Kirk 1970.

Archaeology and the texts

There should be no call to apologize for allowing texts to intrude on the austere world of archaeology proper, but one sometimes encounters a conviction, perhaps fostered by fear of the unknown, that mixing the two sources is a methodological sin. The idea that one could write the history of the Old Kingdom of Egypt without including a reference to the pyramids, or that one should study the pyramids without using historical information about the time when they were constructed is of course preposterous. No one can control all the different classes of evidence, but that is no excuse for ignoring their existence, and calls instead for collaboration. Co-operation with the philologist, or more generally with historians, is one area where the archaeologist is not constrained by the cost of fieldwork or the restrictions of political geography, yet we have been lamentably lax in profiting from this extra source of information and in using it to refine and target our fieldwork.

In his exhaustive and percipient book on historical archaeology Andrén writes 'Historiographic surveys [of archaeology] should therefore also comprise the historical archaeologies as well, and bear in mind that archaeology borders not just on anthropology and history but also on aesthetics, philology, European ethnology, American folk studies, and religious studies.'[12] Indeed so. Few prehistorians explicitly despise the archaeologist working on historical societies, but there is a divide, perhaps most acute among purists who eschew the corrupting influence of the written record. Specialists are often pinned down in time and place by the investment needed to acquire competence in the language or artistic tradition of a historical complex society. Global theories which may seem applicable in the uncrowded tracts of prehistory become less easy to reconcile with the increasing density of information and cultural variation. Am I the only one to wonder if prehistorians have more time to think deep thoughts because they are less bogged down in detail?

The extent to which archaeology can contribute will vary according to the extent which history can cover (see Andrén 1998, 121). The Finley view, that the less of a society is described by historical sources the greater the potential role of archaeology, is not untrue by its own lights, but it is only a very partial truth. For one thing, the role of archaeology within a single society will vary, depending on the extent to which different sectors were engaged in the literate scene.[13] However rich and detailed the documentation — and in our civilizations it outdoes anything before the Middle Ages — archaeology can contribute an extra dimension to social and economic history in much the same way as contemporary fieldwork is used by anthropologists and sociologists to provide context and extra detail for studies otherwise based on recorded information.

[12] Andrén 1998, 3.
[13] Andrén 1998, 124, bottom; cf. also p. 126.

In the ancient Near East it is obvious that the society's written records by their very existence differentiated it qualitatively from illiterate contemporaries of the time, and by their survival to the present day provide the modern researcher with an information source parallel to and of equal standing with archaeology 'proper'. All the more reason to strive to overcome the operational gulf between the philologist and the archaeologist. There are of course specific areas of overlap in the representation of 'archaeological' types of information within the written sources, and the occurrence of written artefacts as archaeological items in their own right and in archaeological contexts; but the imperative is much deeper than that, since each dataset constitutes one facet of a single phenomenon. The integration of the two types of evidence is fundamental, yet there is all too little collaborative work. It is true that the steady growth of data in both areas prevents individuals from controlling both sides in detail, but this does not absolve us from making the effort to match them.

The primacy of both Mesopotamia and Egypt in both mathematical and astronomical expertise was acknowledged by the Greeks themselves, and recent trends in the history of science have seen a revival of interest in the early civilizations. Through architecture in particular archaeological fieldwork can contribute to precisely these subjects, but more generally the cultures which provided the environment for these discoveries also fostered a methodical approach to other aspects of the natural world. The technical expertise of Egyptian and Mesopotamian craftsmen led in one direction to the formation of a body of traditional knowledge or even trade secrets, but also went hand in hand with a more general spirit of enquiry and classification. By more attentive study of the surviving artefacts we can certainly contribute to the history of technical expertise. Once again, work along these lines has usually been initiated by historians of science. Much can be done by the laboratory analysis of securely datable artefacts, and ceramic and metal analyses have been with us for decades, but there is a long way to go before the objectives of this kind of research are fully integrated into the agenda of most field archaeologists. Industrial sites need to be sought out deliberately, and careful attention needs to be paid to the evidence for manufacturing techniques to establish the chronology of changes or innovations in production, and locate them within their social context.

The wider audience

Fieldwork is of course an all-engrossing activity in which it is all too easy to get bogged down. As with the textual side, so with the archaeology the actual excavators have tended to allow others to think grand thoughts. Robert McC. Adams is one fieldworker who has used his raw data to address the wider issues: but as survey data they were deliberately collected with this in mind, and although he dug at the small Sassanian site of Abu Serifa it was an experience which brought home to him the indigestibility of most excavated data. Another writer on wider issues, Henry T. Wright, has also excavated from time to time, and his work has tended to be modest in scale, and on 'lesser' settlements, not in the capitals or urban supernovas. It has also been published.

It is not a coincidence that these are Americans. Egypt and Mesopotamia were firmly positioned in global prehistory by Gordon Childe, but in Europe the shadow of the nineteenth century still looms, and work in the Middle East has not been uninfluenced by modern politics and links with the biblical and classical scenes. European specialists have been too busy with their own tasks to worry about the rest of the world, and the unfashionableness of diffusionism has provided an excuse; while the density of our self-contained compartments has not encouraged interaction. It seems to have been easier for Americans with their more distant perspective, and their placing of archaeology within anthropology, to see the ancient Near East in a truly global context. Unlike Europeans they have treated it less as a phase in the evolution of Western European civilization, and more as a phenomenon in its own right, a product of circumstances which are understood through an anthropological approach rather than that of cultural history, and have a relevance for comparative studies in other parts of the world, notably the independent civilizations of Central and South America. Egypt has been even more resistant to globalization, and the attempt by Trigger to drag Egyptology into the wider anthropological scene by a methodical comparison with other early states across the world is remarkable more because it stands alone than for any blinding revelations.

The concerns of the social anthropologist, as opposed to the historian, have tended to foster generalization by the specialist less than specialization by the anthropologist. This is typical of a systematic malaise of the discipline. The publication of excavation and survey, the preparation of corpora of texts and artefacts, all proceed virtuously, but those best able to do it are swamped by the volume of material they need to process. Excellent work is being done at the rock-face, but the resulting material often stands around in unworked blocks. We have plenty of plain, untargeted, data (settlement patterns, city sizes, subsistence evidence, buildings public and private) and rescue work will ensure that more turns up. To take a different metaphor, at present the study of the ancient Near East and Egypt is like a large but failing restaurant. Behind the swing-doors there are chefs and their minions, some chopping onions, others preparing dishes with consummate care, but there is a shortage of waiters, and most of the diligence and experience of the kitchen labourers has not been reaching the appreciative audience it surely deserves. It is hardly surprising, therefore, that from time to time the kitchen is raided by hungry customers.

That an important study of Sumerian literature was written by a Professor of Greek has already been mentioned. One of the rare books on Mesopotamian religion, and one of the best, was written by an Old Testament scholar (albeit one thoroughly competent in Akkadian).[14] In recent years the ancient Near East in the third and second millennia BC has been hailed by an alliance of prehistorians and economic historians as an early manifestation of a (or the) 'World System'.[15] No doubt it is flattering that there is a demand for our fare, but we should be bringing it to the customers ourselves. They are not only academics in neighbouring disciplines, but the more general public. For them there is a shortage of authoritative and recent secondary literature, although there is no shortage of demand for Egypt in particular, and it is not surprising that there are plenty of take-away fast-food joints serving up ice-cream pyramids or deep-fried mummies.

This is an aspect of the discipline which can't be ignored. Even without its biblical connections, Pharaonic Egypt has an eternal allure which endears it to authors of romantic novels and television producers. It has much to do with the durable spectacularity of some of their funeral arrangements: the preservation of the mummy through the collusion of deliberate science and the climate, the masonry of the pyramids and the painted interiors of so many lesser tombs. It is also sustained by the instant visual appeal of the hieroglyphic script. Self-avowed fiction uses the fascination and photogenic qualities of ancient Egypt to good effect: witness *Stargate*, *Prince of Egypt*, *The Mummy*, three box-office successes of recent years. For a best-selling airport novel, there is *River God*, complete with Hyksos chariotry battles, with its sequel presenting a melodramatic resuscitation of amateur tomb-robbing, exciting to the reader however reprehensible to the kill-joy academic.

Even other parts of the ancient world can provide copy for authors of science fiction, as the novel (originally conceived as a cartoon strip) *Snow Crash*[16] can show: like other products of the role-playing sci-fi and Tolkien-derivative culture, it creates an atmosphere of authenticity by drawing on works of genuine scholarship, in this case citing the works of the reputable Sumerologists S.N. Kramer and B. Alster. This shares some of the ethos of the war-games fraternity, whose search for authenticity has generated an illustrated manual on ancient Near Eastern armies which has drawn responsibly on the academic literature and attempts to give accurate facts over a wide range of time and place.[17]

Neither of these creations should cause any unease for us back-room boffins. One is transparently fictional, the other subscribes to our own creed in a different forum. More worrying are works which adopt the style of academic respectability but generate something which can only mislead. Egyptologists and others are less than enthused with prime-time television series which present a hypothesis, appealing to dubious geological and astronomical evidence, that the Sphinx was carved around 10,500 BC, and linking it to other phenomena across the world (e.g. at Angkor Wat) which can only be connected by the wildest imaginative leaps. We also still suffer from the gravitational

[14] Van der Toorn 1985.
[15] E.g. Frank and Gills 1993; Moore and Lewis 1999; Kaufman 1997.
[16] Stephenson 1992.
[17] Stillman and Tallis 1984.

distortion of the Bible. Some impatience is inevitable when we are treated yet again to the 'discovery' of Noah's Ark on Mount Ararat, once again in prime television time, one recent version being not miscellaneous lumps of wood but a boat-shaped geological formation in solid rock.

Is such impatience justified? One might hope that such things have their day and then sink without trace, arks and all, while solid academic progress gets built into the structure of scholarship, so that in the long term what deserves to survive does so. Woolley had no qualms about using the Biblical Flood to generate interest and finance for his work at Ur. And in any case, in this commercial world is not all publicity good? Perhaps so, but some anxiety is warranted. In Egypt, for instance, there is no doubt that astronomy *was* used for various symbolic purposes to do with religion and architecture. The constant appeals to astronomy by idiosyncratic theories run the risk that better founded research in such an area will be tarred with the same brush. Similarly, a recent TV programme reconstructed a geological event around 5500 BC, in which the waters of the Mediterranean flowed into the previously independent Black Sea basin. The original scientific evidence, which seemed impeccable at the time, was yoked uneasily to Noah's Flood, something inherently improbable given the geographical context of the two hypothetical events.[18] Of course attempts to link archaeological, and indeed geomorphological, evidence to historical or mythical events will continue, and we note that even Sodom and Gomorrah have recently been subjected to a scientific resurrection. The coverage afforded to such hypotheses is symptomatic. 'Experts' from outside the field tend to be taken at their own estimation, and because their facts seem to be 'hard' there is a danger that not only the general public but also the archaeologists will subject them to less scrutiny than they should. The same phenomenon accounts for the prevalence of earth-shaking theories in the fields of chronology and astronomy, where the usual historical criteria of probability and judgement often struggle unequally with the apparent incontrovertibility of the precise sciences.

But we must not bury our heads in the sand, with our sights set ruthlessly on the next research assessment exercise. While we cannot allow our agenda to be set by the media, academics have a clear duty to inform of their work and to justify it, and glossy magazines are not all to be viewed with suspicion. Rather contrary to current perceptions, it may well be that the world-wide web will come to the aid of the specialists in keeping them in touch with the general public. While it may mean keeping strange company, one web page is as accessible as the next, whatever its contents, and via the web academic matter can become accessible to audiences as large as those for the prime-time television programmes and inflated print-runs given to sensationalizing works on antiquity.

---

[18] Ryan *et al.* 1997; Ryan and Pitman 1998. The fact that the scientific case seems to have been successfully challenged in Aksu *et al.* 1999 merely underlines the potential for embarrassment posed by academics straying outside the confines of their familiar world. My thanks to Kate Spence for these references.

Aims and techniques

The demand from outside should encourage us to take the time and trouble to ask new questions of our data, but at the same time it reminds us that the case for further primary research in both areas is as strong as ever. In the abstract search for knowledge it would be perfectly proper for archaeology to proceed like the march of nineteenth-century geography, filling in blanks on the map but with the added fourth dimension of time. There are plenty such blanks still to be filled in, and the undertaking is promoted by the existence of state boundaries and identities, which encourage coverage to be extended into areas and periods merely because they are there. 'New' cultural phases, regional sub-cultures, dynasties, and such like will continue to be resurrected, but as with the nineteenth-century explorers, undertakings on the ground must interact with innovations in theory and technique, more often than not borrowing both from the collective consciousness of the discipline of archaeology as a whole.

What can be done depends of course on the reconciliation of research objectives with external and internal constraints. Strategies have rarely been adopted and carried through with anything like the ideal agenda one could devise. This is the consequence of human inadequacies on various fronts, but the two principal hindrances are politics and finance. In the twentieth century the archaeology of south Mesopotamia has been brutally interrupted, along with the lives of the modern inhabitants of that land, by four major conflicts (and some minor ones). As for finance, few fieldworkers would claim to have received what they really require to carry out and bring to publication their ideal programme of research. How should we move forward? It should not be too difficult to improve on our past record.

There might at first sight seem to be a problem of scale. There is no denying the value of small excavation projects tailored carefully to specific research queries and the testing of methodology (such as Abu Serifa or Sakheri Saghir mentioned above), but in the end they cannot replace larger operations on a scale commensurate with massive urban sites. Put in a nutshell, the size of an investigation needs to be commensurate with the size of the phenomenon to be investigated. Individual buildings on some Near Eastern sites can be as big as entire settlements in other places or times. One house in a city does not tell the full story of urban life: we need data on the size of the settlement as a whole and the quantitative and qualitative variability within it. Funds will never sustain adequately controlled and recorded excavation of an entire settlement, whether for pure research or rescue purposes, nor could the accumulated data be processed in a reasonable time span. Even in the carefree 1930s noble attempts to excavate a complete tell were overwhelmed by the sheer volume of soil to be moved, and these days such an ambition is unrealistic even if it were laudable. Unlike civil engineering, archaeology cannot usually save either time or money by bringing in heavy earth-moving machinery. As wages in the host country creep towards the norms of the guest countries, tightening standards of observation and recording are banishing the gangs of labourers on Middle Eastern sites to nostalgic sepia photographs of the past. Rigorous and judicious selectivity is therefore imperative whether choosing a site in a landscape littered with the ruins of earlier occupation or a few cubic metres within the site itself.

One way to achieve the necessary horizontal coverage is the exploitation of non-invasive techniques. Insofar as political constraints permit, landscape archaeology in the Near East can be enormously fruitful, with swathes of territory where past human activity supplies the most conspicuous features, and it is significantly enhanced where aerial photography and other remote sensing techniques can be brought in.[19] These can help to reconstruct settlement patterns, but also deliver evidence of their own for the extent and layout of major settlements. Combined with resistivity, other geomagnetic procedures, or even judicious surface clearance where mud-brick rules these out, and especially where applied to extended single-period sites, these techniques can provide important results (Fig. 3).[20] They will not only permit the broad reconstruction of settlement layout, but also identify individual components in the plan which will yield up either a typical or an atypical body of evidence: in other words, enable us to focus on both the norm and the abnormal for further description.

One sometimes gains the impression that 'invasive' archaeology is faintly indecent, but new data need to be generated to keep the subject alive, and even the most arm-chair-bound theorist must welcome 'the role of fieldwork in maintaining an element of the unexpected in any study of the ancient past'.[21] The royal tomb and the unexpected archive are nothing to be ashamed of, even if they have a tendency to distort painfully assembled statistics from a hundred less glitzy projects. But even on a more humble plane the archaeology of the advanced urban society has a leading role to play, a role which has not yet been fulfilled because of the plethora of more spectacular data.

Changes in archaeological technique are so much a matter of course that we take it for granted that work carried out by earlier generations will lack rigour and precision, and we tend also to assume that our own work will be overtaken by the march of time. More often than not it has been the new techniques that have made the running, with science generating solutions before the questions have been formulated, and in the past, it has not been the early civilizations which have supplied the testing ground for new methodology and techniques. There is every reason for this to change. The questions we wish to put to complex early settlements are equally delicate as those of interest in Palaeolithic times, and the nature of our evidence is equally sensitive. The more complex and varied a society the better the correlation between human activity and archaeological evidence is crystallized. It takes no great insight to guess that lifestyles in

[19] See Kennedy 1998.
[20] Compare the combination of such techniques in the work of Geoff and Françoise Summers at Kerkenes Dag east of Ankara: http://www.metu.edu.tr/home/wwwkerk/index.html.
[21] Adams in Cooper and Schwartz 1996, 409.

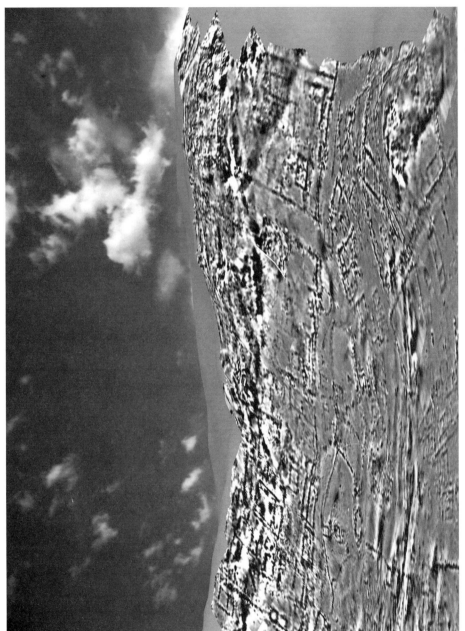

Figure 3. New methods for ancient sites 1. The NE sector of Kerkenes Dag, central Turkey, fortified sixth-century BC capital: a terrain model produced by kinematic survey with a Global Positioning System, with a geomagnetically generated plan draped over it. Buildings and other features clearly discernible. Courtesy Dr. G.D. Summers, Middle East Technical University, Ankara.

different parts of an urban settlement may have varied more than within a village. Not merely as to the size of individual dwellings, but also in the specialization of activities within the settlement and within each dwelling unit, and in the value and quantity of the artefacts which might be recovered there. Clarity of correlation is afforded by the larger sites, and can suggest the criteria to which the excavator of the smaller (or earlier) site should be sensitized. We don't need new sites to achieve this sort of advance, merely fresh techniques.

A variety of techniques could contribute, but let me cite one example familiar to me. When trying to work out how space was actually used some traces of use are obvious, others less so. A good proportion of most Middle Eastern sites will consist of periodically reconstructed dwellings from which anything of value is likely to have been carefully cleared out on each occasion, leaving a tedious sequence of uninformative surfaces separated by secondary matter which says very little about the use of the space, let alone about its date.[22] Even less stimulating can be the echoing halls of public buildings, kept clean by under-employed sweepers and under-inhabited for most of their existence, which could linger on for centuries. At first sight there is little in either type of context to restore the busy hum of men, but by magnifying the record something can be done. The technique of micro-morphological thin-sections offers a direct view of what the assiduous housewife has not removed: still in its early days in its archaeological applications, it can distinguish carefully laid flooring from natural layers, identify water use, locate minute traces of specific activities, e.g. fragments from grindstones, and so on (Fig. 4).[23]

Last but not least, in the struggle to describe a large and varied phenomenon on the basis of a proportionately small investigation we can better our chances by acknowledging that all archaeology is a sampling procedure, and making use of appropriate quantitative controls. In any record of human activity there will be some norms and spectrums of variation, and with the help of even the crudest statistical controls these can be defined. Only when what we are observing falls within an already established range are we really relieved of the responsibility for extracting every last millimetre of information from each spoonful of earth.

Page or screen?

One way in which archaeology is being transformed by information technology is in the meaning and purpose of publication. It is the tedious quantity of frequently unrewarding data that lies behind the perennial problem of projects unfinished because unpublished. All too often glamorous results rapidly see the light of day, but the underpinning

---

[22] Cf. for a Nubian parallel Rowley-Conwy 1994.
[23] Matthews *et al.* 1994.

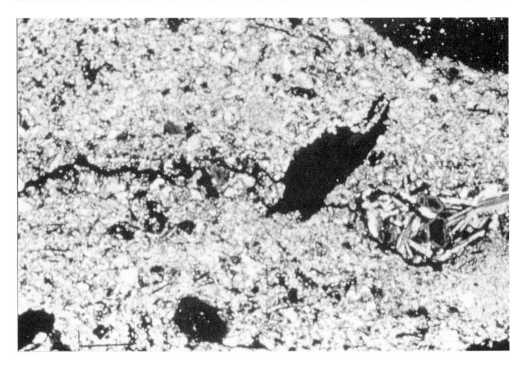

Figure 4. New methods for ancient sites 2. Micro-morphological thin-section through floors in an urban residence at Abu Salabikh (Early Dynastic III, *c*.2400 BC): dark basalt grindstone fragments associated with voids from decayed plant remains, suggesting one of the activities in a kitchen annexe. Photo courtesy Dr. W. Matthews (see Matthews *et al.* 1994, 211).

detail resides in archives gathering metaphorical and indeed literal dust. To consult an excavation's primary archives it used to be necessary to visit the place where notebooks and plans were stored, or at least to secure a photographic record of them. This unsatisfactory situation is relieved by computing in two areas: in the creation of datasets and in their dissemination. Most projects must by now be using computer databases to store part of their excavation data. Because a database must be pre-planned, logical, and internally consistent, the same constraints are imposed on the collection of data; so that used properly it creates automatically a coherent body of raw data which can easily be disseminated without a conventional publication.

That it can be done does not mean that it should, but with a computerized object catalogue, from which the details of any object to be published are taken, there seems very little point in excerpting parts of some entries for inclusion in a publication, rather than making the entire dataset accessible, with its opportunities for searching and statistical manipulation. Moreover, improvements in the quality and reductions in the cost of digital imaging will soon mean that drawings and photographs can be routinely included. In that case it might well seem an indefensible waste of both publishers' and readers' money to include in a book an entire illustrated catalogue rather than the occasional image of particular importance to the text. On the other hand the detailed record of the excavation process is another matter, since without considerable explanation much of it would surely remain meaningless. In any case, although progress is being made with GIS systems, we are still some way from dispensing with notebook and pencil altogether. The computer will standardize and stream-line access to the stratigraphic and architectural record of a site but it does not replace the excavator's report.[24]

Scepticism is often voiced about the possibility that on-line electronic data could ever replace the printed word. It is certainly not the same thing. Those who protest that it is not acceptable to restrict access to those with the right wiring and software have a point, but there is a much weightier point in favour of electronic dissemination. In the developed countries anyone who wishes to engage with on-line archaeology can do so. In less developed countries this will take time, but real costs continue to fall and before long a terminal will open an enormous range of information to people who may never have seen a book on archaeology and could certainly never afford to buy one. Which is more accessible to the world in general, a web-site or a beautifully printed excavation report with a print-run of 500 largely absorbed by institutional libraries in the G8 countries? These questions are not unique to the ancient Near East, although some of our publications have been particularly large and expensive. It is too early to say whether the printed report is going to go the way of the illuminated manuscript.

The future

Whatever the political and financial constraints, the incentive to carry forward the archaeology of Egypt and Mesopotamia will not diminish. There is no shortage of challenging and rewarding tasks ahead. For some the civilizations provide in themselves adequate justification to explore them further as a phenomenon. We can see them as founder members of the club of pristine states, in which one of the major transformations of human history can be observed. They share this distinction with China and the Maya, though with the added attraction of written sources from an early stage. Closer examination may unravel attributes which are either shared by some or all pristine states, or peculiar to one or the other. In Trigger's words 'a comparative study of the traits common to all, or even some, of the early civilizations may assist us to understand ancient Egypt better. At the same time, the features unique to ancient Egypt are equally important for understanding all other early civilizations' (Trigger 1993, 5).

---

[24] Of course, while the original paper archives remain accessible for as long as they physically survive, electronic data need to be assiduously curated to keep them accessible. This problem has already been foreseen in archaeology in general, and in the UK the York ADS is committed to updating electronic archives entrusted to its care, although of course the long-term security of funding is unforeseeable. For a really idiosyncratic opinion on the use of the computer in Near Eastern archaeology, see Buccellati 1998.

For those interested in procedures of the discipline itself, there is much scope for methodological advance. These pristine states lie at the interface between the prehistorian and the historian, but relations between the two have not been as intimate as they should be. Especially with Mesopotamia the crucial period of state formation tends either to form the last chapter of a book by a prehistorian, or the introduction to one by a historian, and to be given very different treatment as a result. It should of course be the focus of investigation in its own right, and hence of intense collaboration between the two approaches. The historians of early Mesopotamia, most of whom are still at heart philologists, have not risen to the challenge, and have still done little to target their exploration of the sources to address the economic and social processes which are frequently invoked by prehistorians in their attempts to account for the material record.[25] Prehistorians likewise have tended to disregard the insights potentially offered by historical sources into issues which concern them, no doubt largely because of their intractability or sheer inaccessibility. As observed some time ago by Snodgrass,[26] the archaeology of a historical period has a paradigmatic value in establishing parallels for times and places without written documentation. Yet to take just one instance, recent work which has revived interest in reconstructing the distribution of linguistic groups has not drawn on the 5000-year history of languages in the Middle East, which might have been expected to provide the best opportunities to observe the processes of linguistic change in their historical context. Even where prehistorians have laudably quarried historical times for comparative material, it sometimes feels as though the examples are kidnapped from the embrace of the historian and carried back across the frontier, suggesting that there is much more scope for collaboration between the two sides.[27]

The anthropological concern for explaining process and causation has sometimes diverted attention from the phenomenon itself, and from the fact that what we later call art, literature, philosophy and science are as much a part of early civilizations as social stratification, cores and peripheries, and redistribution. Egypt and Mesopotamia supply the first full chapter in the history of science and technology. The early history of chemistry, agriculture, stockbreeding, medicine, hawking, horses, astronomy, not to mention law, begins here. Through the Greek world they have a direct ancestral relationship to modern Western European culture, but their influence spread elsewhere, into India for instance, and for this reason among others we can expect that in the next millennium academics from South and East Asia will play an increasing role in this forum as well as in the discipline as a whole.

---

[25] The papers in Hudson and Levine (eds.) 1999 are an interesting mix of papers, including some which bravely step outside their field and others which stick cautiously to their own.

[26] Snodgrass 1985, 34, referring back to David Clarke.

[27] Flannery 1999. This article brings the global sweep of anthropological prehistory into historical times in a most stimulating fashion: but in its use of only relatively recent historical sources (which are not exempt from distortion by virtue of being more recent) it rather perpetuates the reluctance of the prehistorian to engage with ancient history.

For social and economic historians and anthropologists the time span of two millennia and more of recorded history should be irresistible. Durées are even longer in the Near East. It provides us with case studies in the ebb and flow of history. The relationship between material culture and political or ethnic boundaries is a major topic which poses but may also answer questions, while historical archaeology too has much to say on how social stability and instability can be reflected in standardization and differentiation in the material record. Whatever terminology may be fashionable, periods of prosperity and strong government alternate with 'Intermediate Periods' or 'Dark Ages' and social disintegration.[28] With the disappearance of written record in times of trouble the historian needs the archaeologist to help see what was happening. If those who wish to resurrect and understand these two first civilizations can make common cause with those entrusted with their material remains, the archaeology of Egypt and Mesopotamia will not have lost any of its compelling allure a hundred years from now.

Acknowledgements

Many thanks to Barry Kemp and Kate Spence, who each read a first draft, corrected my ignorance of Egyptological matters, and suggested a range of improvements. For providing, and allowing the reproduction of, their photographs, I am very grateful to Prof. Dr. Hartmut Kühne, Dr. Jane Moon, Dr. Wendy Matthews, and Dr. Geoffrey Summers. Thanks are also due to Deniz Kutay for producing Figure 3.

References

AKSU, A.E., HISCOTT, R.N. and YAŞAR, D. 1999: Oscillating Quaternary water levels of the Marmara Sea and vigorous outflow into the Aegean Sea from the Marmara Sea — Black Sea drainage corridor. *Marine Geol.* 153, 275–302.

ANDRÉN, A. 1998: *Between artefacts and texts: Historical archaeology in global perspective* (New York and London).

BUCCELLATI, G. 1998: Review of J. Aviram and H. Shanks (eds.), *Archaeology's Publication Problems*. *Near Eastern Archaeol.* [formerly *Biblical Archaeologist*] 61/ii (June), 118–20.

COOPER, J.S. and SCHWARTZ, G.M. (eds.) 1996: *The Study of the ancient Near East in the Twenty-First Century; The Willian Foxwell Albright Centennial Conference* (Winona Lake, IN).

FEINMAN, G.M. and MARCUS, J. (eds.) 1998: *Archaic States* (Santa Fe, New Mexico).

FLANNERY, K. 1999: Process and agency in early state formation. *Cambridge Archaeol. J.* 9, 3–21.

FRANK, A.G. and GILLS, B.K. (eds.) 1993: *The world system: Five hundred years or five thousand?* (London).

HUDSON, M. and LEVINE, B. (eds.) 1999: *Urbanization and land ownership in the ancient Near East* (Cambridge, MA, Peabody Mus. Bull. 7).

---

[28] Cf. Kemp 1991.

KAUFMAN, S.J. 1997: The fragmentation and consolidation of international systems. *Int. Organization* 51, 173–208.

KEMP, B.J. 1989: *Ancient Egypt: Anatomy of a civilization* (London).

KEMP, B.J. 1991: Explaining ancient crises. *Cambridge Archaeol. J.* 1, 239–44.

KENNEDY, D. 1998: Declassified satellite photographs and archaeology from the Middle East: case studies from Turkey. *Antiquity* 72, 553–61.

KIRK, G.S. 1970: *Myth. Its meaning and functions in ancient and other cultures* (Cambridge/Berkeley and Los Angeles).

KOHL, P.L. and FAWCETT, C. (eds.) 1995: *Nationalism, politics, and the practice of archaeology* (Cambridge).

LARSEN, M.T. 1996: *The conquest of Assyria* (London).

MATTHEWS, W., POSTGATE, J.N., PAYNE, S., CHARLES, M.P. and DOBNEY, K. 1994: The imprint of living in an early Mesopotamian city: questions and answers. In Luff, R. and Rowley-Conwy, P. (eds.), *Whither environmental archaeology?* (Oxford, Oxbow Monogr. 38), 171–212.

MOORE, K. and LEWIS, D. 1999: *Birth of the Multinational. 2000 years of ancient business history — From Ashur to Augustus* (Copenhagen).

ROWLEY-CONWY, P. 1994: Dung, dirt and deposits: Site formation under conditions of near-perfect preservation at Qasr Ibrim, Egyptian Nubia. In Luff, R. and Rowley-Conwy, P. (eds.), *Whither environmental archaeology?* (Oxford, Oxbow Monogr. 38), 25–32.

RYAN, W.B.F., PITMAN III, W.C., MAJOR, C.O., SHIMKUS, K., MOSKALENKO, V., JONES, G.A., DIMITROV, P., GÖRÜR, N., SAKINÇ, M. and YÜCE, H. 1997: An abrupt drowning of the Black Sea shelf. *Marine Geol.* 138, 119–26.

RYAN, W. and PITMAN, W. 1998: *Noah's Flood* (New York).

SAID, E.W. 1978: *Orientalism: western conceptions of the Orient* (London).

SCHWARTZ, G. 1994: Rural economic specialization and early urbanization in the Khabur Valley, Syria. In Schwartz, G. and Falconer, S. (eds.), *Archaeological views from the countryside: Village communities in early complex societies* (Washington, D.C.), 19–36.

SNODGRASS, A. 1985: The New Archaeology and the Classical Archaeologist. *American J. Archaeol.* 89, 31–7.

STEPHENSON, N. 1992: *Snow crash* (New York).

STILLMAN, N. and TALLIS, N. 1984: *Armies of the Ancient Near East, 3000 BC to 539 BC* (Warminster).

TRIGGER, B.G. 1993: *Early civilizations: Ancient Egypt in context* (Cairo).

VAN DER TOORN, K. 1985: *Sin and sanction in Israel and Mesopotamia* (Assen/Maastricht).

WILKINSON, T.A.H. 1999: *Early Dynastic Egypt* (London).

WINTER, I.J. 1997: Packaging the past: the benefits and costs of archaeological tourism. In Sitter-Liver, B. and Uehlinger, C. (eds.), *Partnership in Archaeology. Perspectives of a cross-cultural dialogue* (Fribourg University Press).

The Mediterranean

ANNA MARIA BIETTI SESTIERI, ALBERTO CAZZELLA AND
ALAIN SCHNAPP

Focusing on the central role of interaction in the development of human cultures and societies is an appropriate starting point for a discussion of the present and future state of the archaeology of the Mediterranean: indeed, in our discipline this part of the world has always been considered as the privileged area of contact, and, more importantly, of deeply effective interaction between structurally different polities.

In addition, the Mediterranean is also the crossroad of the different, and often contrasting, cultural paradigms and disciplinary traditions which coexist in the current practice of archaeology.

The 'interior sea' is the cradle of archaeology, born in the Renaissance as the study of Roman and subsequently Greek art, with essential support from the ancient historical sources. The ideological basis for its progressive change from antiquarianism to a proper academic discipline, which was achieved by the nineteenth century, was the world primacy of European civilization, which in turn was founded upon Greek and Roman culture. The role of the heritage of the classical world, and therefore of classical archaeology, as one of the main ideological components of European cultural imperialism, was firmly established in the nineteenth century, and was explicitly propounded especially by German scholars such as Theodor Mommsen.

Oriental archaeology and philology, including the special branch of Egyptology, also had a substantial ideological impact on the discipline as a whole, which can be summarized as the *ex Oriente lux* paradigm. This is partly justified, since Mesopotamia, Anatolia and the Levant together with Egypt are among the core areas which saw the emergence of two of the most important evolutionary developments in the history of mankind: food production and urbanization. From the Neolithic, and throughout the Bronze Age, powerful states and city-states were the dominant socio-political form in this part of the world, while tribal and chiefdom communities occupied the central and western Mediterranean and Europe.

In the overall field of Mediterranean archaeology, the acknowledgment of this primacy had the disconcerting result of creating the almost complete separation between oriental archaeology — Egyptology and the other branches of the discipline.

In nineteenth-century Europe the classicist claim to supremacy was soon challenged by the nationalist revival, focusing on local prehistoric and later cultures. In this case, the basic research method relied on environmental and material culture studies rather than on written sources. The use of archaeological research as a means for enhancing and reinforcing national identity is still quite popular throughout the world, although in the Mediterranean area it may coincide or overlap with the idea of the classical–oriental primacy.

Combined with the classicist paradigm, that of *ex Oriente lux* has often diverted archaeologists' interest away from the contextual analysis of local cultures and polities beyond the Aegean, as well as their diachronic development. The main agent of structural change has been generally identified as an eastern or Aegean influence of some kind, without too much attention being paid to the actual ability (let alone the interest) of the east Mediterranean and Aegean polities to introduce changes to the west. A somewhat similar perspective is common in the current practice of the archaeology of the Roman period. Thus, in the analysis of local contexts, the archaeological data, which may be seen as indicating an eastern or Aegean influence, as well as the most visible evidence for the process of romanization, are invariably used as the privileged evidence for both synchronous and historical reconstruction.

If considered from the point of view of their effects on the current practice of archaeology, rather than on the grounds of their theoretical principles, the trends which appeared in the last few decades, namely new ('processual') and postprocessual archaeology, produced some significant changes. The most important is the general adoption of an anthropological perspective, and a focus on contextual studies. The latter was exemplified by the emphasis placed by L. Binford (1982) on the value to archaeological theory of decoding the individual material record, and by I. Hodder's (1982) reference to the inherently contextual significance of material culture, as well as being enhanced by the steady improvement of survey and excavation methods and analytical techniques.

Overall, these new directions, which have been received by archaeologists in the Mediterranean countries with varying degrees of caution and enthusiasm, have helped to modify archaeological thinking and approaches. The focus of research began to shift from a belief in the significance of oriental–Aegean influence on the central and west Mediterranean regions to the analysis of local cultures and processes of interaction (see for example Renfrew 1973; Chapman 1990). More comprehensive analyses and reconstructions of contemporary developments on an interregional scale, and of long-term historical processes, can only be based on the results of a number of local contextual studies. This may appear to be a somewhat cumbersome procedure, and certainly one which does not allow the ready publication of essays of worldwide interest; however, it is the only truly archaeological means at our disposal for exploiting the archaeological record to its full potential.

On the other hand, in the field of archaeology (both prehistoric and classical) as it is practised in the Mediterranean countries, a very effective means for leaving things just as they have always been consists of borrowing from contextual research some models and theoretical aspects, while ignoring the methodological changes which should go with them: for example, the adoption of anthropological models is not usually thought of as implying that the archaeological record should be analysed by any other means than the usual systems of chrono-typological classification.

Some recent trends in archaeological research are already contributing to a smooth restoration of traditional thinking, which in Mediterranean archaeology has always been notably strong and not amenable to theoretical and, in particular, to practical innovation. This is the case in the various attempts to build an archaeologically-based global history by such means as the generalized application of the world systems theory, or the total rejection of substantivist as opposed to formalist approaches to the study of ancient and even prehistoric economies. The difference between core-periphery relationships and overall oriental/Aegean influence as the key factor in the study of the Mediterranean, as well as of Europe at large, is very slight indeed.

There is a very serious theoretical drawback which prevents the adoption of modern-contemporary categories in the study of interaction in the ancient world: namely that a specific agent of the acceleration of the worldwide processes of change in the modern era is precisely the exponential increase in the effectiveness of interaction in all its forms, from communication and transport to trade and warfare. Thus by no means could the analysis of modern or contemporary processes generate a model suitable for understanding contact and interaction in Neolithic, Bronze Age, and even Roman Europe.

However, the main reason for the recurrent obstacles to the emergence of an archaeological normal science (*sensu* Kuhn 1970) such as contextual archaeology, particularly evident in the Mediterranean regions, might be described in old-fashioned Marxist terms as a structural contradiction: as it pertains to the group of disciplines labelled as humanities, which implies a substantially lesser status as compared with the 'hard' sciences, contextual archaeology is disproportionately expensive in terms of financial resources, time, and energy to be sustainable, even in comparison with other disciplines in the same general area as, for example, ancient history or philology. In fact, the only current major projects involving systematic, extensive and long-lasting archaeological excavations are those spectacular enough to enhance the scientific prestige of important universities, as well as the cultural role of the states (or the interest of the private sponsors) which support them. In the Mediterranean regions, this is essentially the case with the great excavation projects in Anatolia, the Levant and Egypt, as well as the excavations of some key historical sites, as for example the urban centre of Rome. The implication is that contemporary archaeology is still rather heavily biased by ideological and economic factors, but so are other scientific disciplines, including hard sciences such as physics or chemistry.

From a purely academic point of view, the main drawback of archaeology is that a systematic research project comprising both fieldwork and analysis of the material record is likely to take as much as ten years of a researcher's active life to be completed, whereas in any other scientific area the duration of a standard research project does not usually exceed one or two years.

Thus the attempt to identify some kind of absolute archaeological indicator is common to the great majority of past and present theoretical and methodological approaches to archaeology, a discipline which responds to the need to bridge the gap between overwhelming material evidence and 'historical' interpretation on an interregional or wider scale. Also, the recent claim that the archaeological record is nothing but a few fragmentary material traces of the past (Hamilakis 1999), and that archaeologists should accept the responsibility resulting from the acknowledgment of this self-evident truth, is another way to elude the (awkward) methodological and practical idiosyncrasies of the discipline.

From the beginning of food production to early forms of social stratification by Alberto Cazzella

Ever since the Early Neolithic when navigation skills were developed, or better still when Neolithic man decided to exploit this potential to the full, the Mediterranean with its particular configuration and the presence of peninsulas and islands, provided the ideal background for cultural contacts, even though the nature of such contacts differed widely in the various phases of prehistory and between the different regions. Some recent studies on the Mediterranean in its entirety, or more often on specific contexts, have allowed us better to understand the specific characteristics of the historical processes that took place, providing us with new perspectives for research and debate. In this paper particular attention will be focused on the non-African regions of the Mediterranean whose history throughout the period under examination differed widely from that of the African regions.

The first aspect to be considered is the development of a farming economy beyond the area of origin in the Near East. In a paper written some years ago, T.H. van Andel and C.N. Runnels (1995) once again considered this topic, stressing the high degree of selectivity in the choice of environment by the first Neolithic groups which moved from Anatolia towards the nearby European regions. Within the generally accepted idea (movement of small groups, rather than the autonomous or induced transformation of local Mesolithic groups), this partly modifies the Wave of Advance model proposed by A. Ammerman and L. Cavalli Sforza (1984), and also accepted by C. Renfrew (1987), wherein the variable factor is the rate of demographic growth combined with time and distance. As regards the Mediterranean this advance could and in several cases seems to have occurred by sea, thus adding a further element of variability together with that of the selection of specific environments. Even though the picture produced by radiocarbon dates is not as yet totally coherent, some aspects of the process are problematic at any rate as regards the central Mediterranean, where even the model proposed by van Andel and Runnels could be inadequate. Given its proximity to north-western Greece and the Ionian Islands (Papathanassopoulos 1996), and the presence of areas compatible with the model proposed by van Andel and Runnels, it seems plausible that south-east Italy was involved in the process of neolithization as early as the beginning of the sixth millennium cal BC (Tiné 1996). The situation is less clear in the Tyrrhenian area as far as south-east France, and including the three major islands (Camps 1988; Contu 1997; Demoule and Guilaine 1986; Guilaine *et al.* 1987; Moscoloni 1992; Tusa 1997), as regards the rhythm of advance, the incidence of geomorphological and pedo-logical factors, and the shift from the Aegean/Near East Neolithic model. The need to adapt cultivated crops (cereals and legumes) and domesticated animals (sheep and goats) to new and different ecological zones, the different weight given to farming in relation to hunting and gathering, the various models of settlement and diffusion in the territory, all point to a more varied situation than that usually observed in south-east Italy. In addition, radiocarbon dates are not consistent with a presumed geographic pro-gression, from south-east towards north-west. Some calibrated dates in the Tyrrhenian area are as early as the seventh millennium BC (perhaps due to contamination) and the beginning of the sixth (Skeates and Whitehouse 1994, 1995–6; Trump 1995–6; for south-ern France see Voruz 1995).

In south-east Italy the early phases of the Neolithic show a strong incidence of agriculture and animal husbandry (sheep and goats) derived from the Aegean/Near Eastern model along with some cultural homogeneity as regards subsistence activities, even though other elements, such as settlement organization, tend to diverge from that model. On the other hand, in the Tyrrhenian area, apart from some similarities in pot-tery production, there is no evidence of a similar homogeneity; economic strategies and settlement types show a wide range of variation from the Early Neolithic up to the beginning of the fourth millennium cal BC. In fact, from Sicily to southern France, all of the following occur: cave sites, villages (including those on lake shores: Fugazzola Delpino 1998), coastal and inland settlements, sites where hunting and animal husbandry prevailed, and others settled by farming communities.

Apparently, in this period a wide range of solutions for the integration with the local environments was tried. At the same time, even though there are no radiocarbon dates, which might give a more precise chronological sequence, the phenomenon of maritime exploration in the central Mediterranean appears. This goes beyond the interest in the major islands (which is found also in the east Mediterranean), and includes several minor islands, some of which were permanently or temporarily settled (Cazzella 1988; Cherry 1981, 1990; Patton 1996). These islands were generally dry, had poor land and were sometimes far from the coast. Only a few could have been a source of raw mate-rials, especially obsidian, although the exploitation of this resource did not necessarily imply a stable occupation of the islands: this is the case of Pantelleria and Palamarola, where obsidian was extracted from the beginning of the Neolithic but no clear traces of permanent settlement have been found. The stable occupation of several minor islands in the central Mediterranean remains difficult to explain, although a general explanation would be that it dates to the period of experimentation with the various economic strategies described above (for example, fishing along with primary food production). In the central Mediterranean, the models of development of a farming economy based on the Wave of Advance model or on the selection of ecologically suitable areas apparently do not account for the complexity of local situations and the variety of contexts which characterize this area. Further research should provide more information about specific regional environments as well as a sounder chronological framework. A substantially different process seems to have taken place in south-west France and along the Spanish coast (Geddes 1980; Lopez 1988; Martì Oliver 1978; Munoz 1986; Schumacher and Weniger 1995; Vaquer 1990). Early dates are documented for animal husbandry and the adoption of ceramics, while developed agriculture and permanent villages seem to have occurred much later.

Another theme of particular interest is the intensification of primary farming activities or, to use a term which has been widely adopted in prehistoric research on continental Europe, the 'secondary products revolution' (Sherratt 1981, 1983). As regards the Mediterranean, it is necessary to reconsider some hypotheses, which were proposed several years ago, regarding the changing role of animal husbandry after the initial phases of the Neolithic, in connection with the specific climatic characteristics of these areas. These studies (Bailloud and Mieg de Boofzheim 1955; Pericot Garcia 1950; Puglisi 1959) focused on the increase in the range of animal resources, as well as on the number of animals reared, presumably in connection with the former factor. In a region in which pasturing and water resources were scarce in the summer months at the low altitudes, the problem represented by breeding a greater number of animals could have been solved by the adoption of some forms of seasonal, not necessarily long-distance, movement of sheep, goats and cattle. The pioneering studies of the fifties can be supported by the results of recent research, which provide both a deeper critical insight and a more precise chronological framework for these developments (Bartosiewicz and Greenfield 1999; Maggi et al. 1991–2). Rather than the opposition of these two factors, what now seems to emerge is the possible integration between an increase in breeding and an improvement in agricultural technique, due to the potential for the use of animals as fertilizers and for tillage.

There are still chronological problems as regards this period: direct data can only be related to some evidence of ard-marks, for example at Aosta, Trescore Balneario, Gricignano, in Italy (Marzocchella 1998; Mezzena 1997; Poggiani Keller 1998). Moreover, some relevant elements, such as those relating to changes in the mortality patterns of domestic animals, in tools and vases connected with the use of secondary animal products, and in trace elements found in human skeleton remains that indicate changes in diet, apparently point to an early emergence of this process. In better documented regions of Europe, the appearance of these elements can be dated to the beginning of the fourth millennium cal BC, which generally corresponds to the advanced phases of the Neolithic.

Another open question is the chronology of the first tree cultivation in the Mediterranean, especially of vine and olive. C. Renfrew (1972) has emphasized the relevance of the cultivation of these plants in the development of Aegean society at the transition between the fourth and the third millennia BC; the criticism of this hypothesis (Hansen 1988; van Andel and Runnels 1988) is well known. Early evidence of vine and olive domestication, as well as of control of the water supply, has been recorded for the same period in the Iberian peninsula (Chapman 1990). It is probable that this type of agriculture, which was characteristic of these areas until the last decades, became fully established in the Mediterranean in the following centuries. Based on this substantial continuity in the use of pastoral and agricultural techniques, a number of ethnoarchaeological studies have been carried out (Bartosiewicz and Greenfield 1999; Lugli and Vidale in press; Maggi *et al.* 1991–2). More of this kind of research is urgently needed, as the traditional Mediterranean subsistence economy is rapidly disappearing.

A topic in Mediterranean archaeology which has received renewed attention in the last few years is the origin and early development of metallurgy. At present, the social as well as technical nature of metallurgy is generally acknowledged: the problem is no longer whether a cultural context in which a metal artefact has appeared should be considered as Neolithic or Eneolithic. Rather, the emphasis is on the role played by metal production, as well as by the presence itself of metal objects in a given context. The question goes even further beyond the traditional alternative between diffusion and autonomous regional development. There is general agreement on the possibility that an information chain regarding technical processes linked central eastern Anatolia to the Aegean, the Aegean to the Italian peninsula, and Italy to the western Mediterranean regions (which, in turn, were exposed to Balkan and central European stimuli). Nevertheless, it is also quite likely that different regions developed particular local technical trends. The first phases of metallurgy in the Aegean are not yet well documented (Demoule and Perlés 1993; McGeehan Liritris 1996; Muhly 1996; Zachos 1996), while Sitagroi apparently is more directly linked to the Balkan tradition. The earliest metal objects in 'Neolithic' contexts in eastern Italy are thought to be imports from the Balkan or central European world, and the emergence of metallurgy in this area probably resulted from these interregional relations (Barfield 1996; Cazzella 1994; Skeates 1993). On the other hand, it is still doubtful whether the earliest mining and metallurgy in the Tyrrhenian area (Lipari, Sardinia, Corsica, western Tuscany, Liguria, in the first half of the fourth millennium or slightly later) were inspired by Aegean models. An autonomous development of metallurgy in the Iberian peninsula has been recently proposed on the grounds of new evidence (Delibes de Castro *et al.* 1996). However, if the close chronological correspondence

between these developments in the Iberian peninsula and in other areas of the Mediterranean and of central Europe (first half of the fourth millennium BC) is taken into
account, the hypothesis of complete autonomy seems unlikely.

On the other hand, later developments in metallurgical technique were clearly stimulated by technical innovations in the Aegean. Highly complex artefacts, probably of
Aegean origin, such as daggers (or halberds) with a biface midrib and cast in a bivalve
mould, dated between the end of the fourth and the beginning of the third millennia,
have been found along the coast of Montenegro, in Italy, sporadically in southern
France and as far as the Iberian peninsula (Barfield 1996; Eluère and Mohen 1996;
Montero Ruiz 1994; Primas 1996). The marked symbolic significance of metal daggers,
as indicated by 'menhir statues' and by widespread rock-cut representations, has also
been identified (Bagolini 1981).

Another aspect concerning the Mediterranean world before the end of the third millennium and the subject of recent debate among scholars is the development of forms
of social distinctions, both horizontal and vertical. Cemeteries with structures designed
to hold multiple burials or with spatially differentiated areas which are at least partly
contemporary are widely documented from the second half of the fourth millennium,
and probably represent the funerary correlate of sub-groups existing within the communities. In turn, the competition between these horizontal sub-groups could be the
basis for the beginning of forms of accepted vertical differentiation. This kind of situation occurred in many Mediterranean contexts, though with a wide range of local variation and date. For example, it is seen at several Aegean sites already around the
mid-third millennium BC, although, rather than in the cemeteries, it is more evident
from the organization of the settlements or from the occurrence of luxury goods. The
evidence includes the citadel of Troy with its monumental buildings, the corridor
houses (probably the prototypes of palaces: see a synthesis of the debate in Shaw 1990)
in continental Greece and at Egina, and the jewellery found at some Aegean sites. This
process seems to have been much slower in the other areas of the Mediterranean. Based
on the evidence of the megalithic temples, C. Renfrew (1973) assumes the existence of
chiefdoms in the Maltese archipelago from the second half of the fourth millennium,
although the majority of archaeological indicators usually associated with a hierarchical social organization of this kind are lacking (Fig. 1). A more plausible social model
would be closer to a tribal organization, characterized by a strong internal cohesion that
controls and limits the expansionary tendencies of sub-groups that together form the
social whole, without the development of an élite. A development of the same kind
might be suggested by the building of the sanctuary of Monte d'Accoddi in Sardinia,
around the middle of the fourth millennium (Tiné and Traverso 1992). In the Italian
peninsula some burial sites with special grave offerings and/or structures (male burials in the Tomba della Vedova in Lazio, Tomba del Capo Tribù in Campania, tomb of
the contrada Pane e Vino in Basilicata) have been the subject of debate among scholars

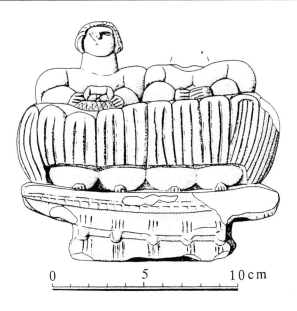

0   5   10 cm

Figure 1. Brochtorff circle, Gozo. Twin seated figures, 3000–2500 BC (from Malone *et al.* 1995).

as regards the presence or absence of permanent vertical social differences at the beginning of the third millennium or slightly earlier (Bailo Modesti and Salerno 1998; Barker 1981; Cazzella 1992; Cremonesi 1976; Miari 1994). These are individual burials rather than collective tomb structures used by a whole social sub-group, which might have been an indication of the sub-group's élite status; moreover, the differences in comparison with other burials are slight. These two combined elements would suggest that, rather than being an indication of permanent social stratification, these burials were meant to signal prominent individuals whose status was achieved rather than inherited.

There has also been much discussion on the social organization typical of south-east Spain between the fourth and third millennia. From a recent study by R. Chapman (1990) of the data available and models proposed the picture that emerges is that of social ranking rather than social stratification (though it should be considered that there is no clear definition of the term 'social ranking'). Chapman assumes a situation of privileged access to prestige goods for some family groups that were part of a community (with particular reference to Los Millares), which did not imply an acquired right from birth. This would mean that the differences among family groups were not institutionally recognized but were acquired through forms of internal competition due to success in economic activities, group cohesion, etc. Chapman also correctly points out that, due to the high degree of variability among local groups in a given area and period, it is not possible to group the various patterns observed, in one schematic whole. However, one cannot exclude the possibility that, rather than being the expression of a political hierarchy based on two levels of control (as Chapman proposes), the dimensional difference (and in the case of Los Millares the complex fortification walls) between settlements in south-east Spain during the Copper Age is a reflection of different settlement patterns (aggregate as opposed to small cores) co-existing in the same area, the variability of behaviour within a social context being perhaps stronger than normally imagined.

Mediterranean interaction in the second and early first millennia BC
by Anna Maria Bietti Sestieri

The subsequent period — c.2200–750 BC — is marked by the evidence of increasingly systematic contacts throughout the Mediterranean; thus the focus of archaeological research shifts more decidedly to a specific, and partly new, range of problems. First, the technical and organizational constraints on economic and political expansion throughout the Mediterranean Bronze Age should be considered. In the modern and contemporary world, expansion of territory, etc. has been increasingly, though not always effectively, supported by two crucial elements: overwhelming technological and military power, and the ability to disseminate relevant information, that is, to induce a widespread process of symbolic and ideological entrainment by such means as political or religious propaganda; in recent times this has been further enhanced by control of the mass-media. As it is apparent that none of these factors was in operation in the Bronze Age, it is necessary to try and identify the ways and means by which interaction could be effectively established and maintained. In the Mediterranean, a strategic factor is access to and control of the major islands. The characteristics of these islands, which can be described as mini-mainlands, have been outlined by J.F. Cherry (1981, 1990). Owing to their substantial size, along with their physical and cultural separation from the adjacent mainland, they represented an ideal place for the establishment of a systematic cultural relationship with the indigenous communities, based on regular voyages. A process of this kind, which can be observed in the archaeological record especially in Sicily, was likely to generate a deep structural integration between local and foreign groups, which, in turn, would constitute a crucial factor in the emergence of socio-political complexity. Thus the major islands offered the best possible conditions for the establishment of permanent bases, which could play an essential intermediary role in long-distance interaction. Striking archaeological evidence of this, observed by B. Knapp (1990), is that ox-hide ingots, apparently the most important means for the maritime circulation of metal in the second millennium BC, concentrate in Cyprus, Crete, and Sardinia.

Other important problems are the structural differences between the Aegean/east Mediterranean as opposed to the central and western Mediterranean communities; the roles played by the polities and communities involved in long-distance relationships in this area, as well as the possible (and indeed very likely) discrepancies between the aims of the contact as planned at the source and its outcome once its target region had been reached; and the balance and relative effectiveness of economic and political components and symbolic–ideological entrainment as active factors in the contact.

As far as the central and western Mediterranean is concerned, the most exciting aspect of research is the possibility of identifying political and ethnic entities, and even some historical events, via the analysis of the archaeological record. In a few cases, this can even be used to verify the scanty information on this period which has been preserved by the literary sources.

The eastern kingdoms and city-states were not directly involved in seaborne trade beyond the Aegean during the second and early first millennia BC, except for the Canaanite Syro-Palestinian regions (including Cyprus) and subsequently Phoenicia, Crete, and mainland Greece with the Aegean islands. However, a ship whose voyage had been organized by a single east Mediterranean or Aegean region was likely to carry some goods, as well as a few individuals, from one or more different parts of the whole area. This is clearly illustrated by the Ulu Burun cargo. The ship probably set off from a Canaanite or Cypriot harbour and carried goods from several different sources (Knapp 1990, 120; INA web site) along with a pair of Mycenaean armed men. This particular feature of long-distance seaborne trade should be taken into account when considering the ways and means by which Aegean and east Mediterranean sailors acquired their knowledge of the Mediterranean sea-routes, and the varied provenances of the exotica which reached some regions of the central and western Mediterranean in the Bronze and Early Iron Ages.

Absolute dates and the related relative chronological phases: c.2200–1200 BC (MH to LHIIIB in the Aegean, Early Bronze Age, Middle Bronze Age and beginning of the Late Bronze Age in the central and western Mediterranean); c.1200–750 BC (LHIIIC to Middle Geometric, and Late Bronze Age to Early Iron Age).

c.2200–1200 BC

Central and southern Greece's interaction with its northern neighbours (Epirus and Albania, northern Thessaly, Macedonia, Chalcidice and Bulgaria) was substantially different from its relationships with the central and west Mediterranean. The former is mainly indicated by some similarities in pottery, bronzes and house-plans, and by a few actual imports. More substantial evidence of Mycenaean impact can be recognized in northern Thessaly from LHIIIA and in Macedonia and the central Balkan area during LHIIIB and C (Coles and Harding 1979, 388 ff.; Harding 1984; Dickinson

1994, 249–50). The interaction belongs in the same category with those linking adjacent regions of Bronze Age Europe, although, given the structural difference between
the partners, it may have triggered a more significant process of symbolic–ideological
entrainment resulting in an acceleration in the emergence of socio-political complexity. It is also possible that, at the end of the Mycenaean era, these groups were partly
responsible for the final collapse of the palaces (Kristiansen 1998, 386 ff.).

On the other hand, maritime activity is particular to the Aegean polities, as is indicated by their intensive interaction with Anatolia and the east Mediterranean, as well
as by the early takeover of Crete by mainland Greece. Organized voyages to the west
appeared at a very early date, possibly from the Middle Helladic period, as is indicated by some distinctive features of the Early Bronze Age Castelluccio culture in
Sicily (Tusa 1992, 325 ff.), and they probably played a strategic role in the process of
increasing economic and political complexity which led to the development of the
complex chiefdoms documented by the fossa-graves at Mycenae (MHIII–LHI transition), and culminated in early state formation and the Mycenaean palaces (LHIIIA1 to
IIIB) (Shelmerdine 1997). The systematic westward drive might indicate that the emerging Aegean polities were looking to this part of the Mediterranean for alternative
sources of raw materials (mainly metals, though other ones, like sulphur, have been
suggested recently: Castellana 1998) where no competition from their powerful eastern
neighbours was to be expected.

Direct as well as considerably complex Aegean interactions with the local communities can only be identified in a few areas of the central Mediterranean. Apparently, the
fossa-grave period marked a definite shift towards more systematic and directional
relationships. The Adriatic and Ionian coasts of southern Italy, Sicily, and possibly
Malta were selected for these early voyages, but the main evidence concentrates on a
few locations on small Tyrrhenian islands (Vivara and Filicudi, in the Phlegraean and
Aeolian archipelagoes) and coastal promontories (Capo Piccolo and Monte Grande, on
the southern coasts of Calabria and Sicily) (Vivara 1991, 1994; Cavalier and Vagnetti
1983; Bianco 1991–2; Marazzi 1998; Cazzella and Moscoloni 1991). The combination of
features of local and Aegean type qualifies these as small ports-of-trade, settled by
mixed indigenous and Aegean communities, which were able to participate in the local
networks of coast-to-coast and terrestrial trade.

The subsequent developments, LHIIIA to early C, show an increasing divergence
between the Ionian and the Tyrrhenian area. In the former, many of the indigenous
coastal settlements apparently sheltered groups of Aegean residents, but the level of
integration was generally low: painted and grey wheel-turned pottery of Aegean type
was produced locally, although the difference in clay sources as well as in technique
indicates that this process was entirely separate from the making of the local impasto
ware (Jones 1993; Bietti Sestieri 1996, 248–9). Moreover, Aegean pottery is never found
in the local élite collective burials, which probably indicates a rather effective resistance

by the local communities to ideological and symbolic entrainment. A likely interpretation of this evidence is that the Aegean residents were only able to gain access to, though not control of, the local resources and raw materials by participating in the indigenous trade networks (Bietti Sestieri 1988).

A very different process developed in the Tyrrhenian area, in which Sicily with the Aeolian archipelago played a central role. Bronze Age Sicily was an autonomous cultural and political entity. Owing to its central position on Mediterranean sea-routes, it was an important landing place where groups from different regions had been integrated into the local communities from Neolithic times. During the second millennium BC Aegean interaction with this favourable milieu produced a deep cultural and structural integration: a number of archaeological indicators of structural complexity, most of which have a distinctly Aegean flavour, characterize both the Middle Bronze Age Thapsos-Milazzese and the Late Bronze Age Pantalica cultures (Bietti Sestieri 1988; Cultraro 1998).

The consolidation in Sicily and the Aeolian islands of a group of territorially based polities, which were connected to the Aegean both culturally and through regular voyages, apparently resulted in an attempt to manage the interaction with the indigenous communities of the southern Tyrrhenian coast of Italy by violence rather than by integration: a few Thapsos-Milazzese settlements were established on the coast of Calabria, while evidence of depopulation characterizes the Campanian coast (Bernabò Brea *et al.* 1989, 210 ff.).

This trend, which can be dated to the fifteenth and fourteenth centuries BC, eventually led to a strong reaction from the indigenous 'Ausonian' communities of the southern Tyrrhenian coast, resulting in the total destruction of the Milazzese settlements on the Aeolian islands, a long-lasting advance into eastern and central Sicily, and the final (Early Iron Age) takeover of the ancient stronghold of Pantalica (Bietti Sestieri 1997b, 1998). These events can be approximately dated between the thirteenth and the ninth to eighth centuries BC.

These two trajectories of direct Aegean interaction with the central Mediterranean, which can be clearly identified from the analysis of south Italian and Sicilian contexts, clearly show the inherent limitations of its impact on the indigenous communities, especially as regards its ability to produce structural changes, either by symbolic entrainment or by the use of force.

Throughout the local Early and Middle Bronze Ages, Sardinia did not play a role comparable to that of Sicily in Mediterranean interactions.

Regular voyages from the east to the central and western Mediterranean are barely visible archaeologically prior to the final centuries of the second millennium BC. From the fourteenth to thirteenth century, the occurrence of some imports (especially from Cyprus) in Italy and Sicily (Lo Schiavo *et al.* 1985, 4 ff., fig. 2; Wilson 1988, 112) probably is an indication that Cypriot and Levantine merchants were present in the Aegean ships regularly sailing towards the central Mediterranean, as well as in the Mycenaeanized ports-of-trade on Sicily such as Thapsos.

Cyprus, Crete and Sardinia seem to have played an essential role in movements from the east Mediterranean. During the Minoan Final Palatial period (*c.*1490–1300 BC: Rehak and Younger 1998), Canaanite (and Egyptian) imports appeared in Crete, while Minoan pottery reached Cyprus, the Aegean, Italy and Sardinia.

Significant north Syrian and Cypriot influence, which produced a structural change in local metallurgical production, can be identified from the fourteenth century BC in Sardinia (Bartoloni in press). The limited amount of Late Helladic material from this island (e.g. the LHIIIA2 angular alabastron from Nuraghe Arrubiu and the ivory head from Mitza Purdia: Moscati *et al.* 1997; Lo Schiavo 1997, fig. 187), as well as the two LHIIIA or IIIB sherds from Montoro in the middle Guadalquivir valley (Martin de la Cruz 1992), may well be prestige goods brought to the west by east Mediterranean ships.

Apparently, a process of increasing structural complexity, based on direct cultural and economic interaction with Aegean sailors, can be identified in Sicily. A similar process, triggered by frequent voyages from the east Mediterranean, possibly emerged during the Nuragic period in Sardinia.

As far as contemporary developments in other regions of the central and western Mediterranean are concerned, the Aegean presence was just one among various external factors which played a role in local autonomous processes. A number of socio-political and territorial entities of considerable complexity emerged, based on specific environmental and locational factors and on active systematic interaction with adjacent or more distant regions. The Aegean was probably included among the final destinations of raw materials circulating within and between local trade networks, especially for metals from the ore deposits of Etruria, as is possibly indicated by the few Aegean sherds found in these regions (Vagnetti 1982, 189 ff.). However, the bulk of the archaeological evidence shows that the main factors causing structural change stemmed from the particular characteristics of the indigenous regional systems, including local trade networks and interregional interaction.

An interesting example is a group recently identified in the highly distinctive regional environment of south-eastern Italy, characterized by fortified coastal settlements (e.g. Coppa Nevigata, Roca Vecchia) often located on ancient lagoons, relying on an agricultural hinterland and on intensive seaborne trade with the Balkan coast opposite (Cinquepalmi and Radina 1998). Collective chamber tombs with funerary assemblages comprising sets of weapons and lavish personal ornaments (e.g. Toppo Daguzzo, Trinitapoli: Cipolloni 1986; Borgognini Tarli *et al.* 1991–2; Tunzi Sisto 1991–2) indicate the presence of warrior élites. The development in this area, in which Aegean material is rather rare, is markedly distinct from that of the adjacent region (southern Salento and the Gulf of Taranto), which has the highest concentration of Mycenaean material on the Italian mainland. A similar situation possibly emerged in Etruria, as is indicated by scanty traces of collective élite burials with rich funerary assemblages (d'Ercole *et al.* 1995).

Another regional system developed in northern Italy: from the Early Bronze Age lake dwellings of the Polada culture (Cardarelli 1992), in the Alpine regions, closely connected to southern France, Switzerland, southern Germany and Slovenia, to the Middle and Recent Bronze Age Terramare (ditch and embankment settlements) of the central Po Plain (Bernabò Brea *et al.* 1997), which were related to the eastern Alps, Slovenia, and the Hungarian Plain, by similarities in environmental conditions, settlement type and material culture. The rich bronze industry of these regions depended on the copper ores of the eastern Alps, the Carpathian Basin, and Etruria. The emergence of warrior aristocracies in the Middle Bronze Age is indicated by the long decorated swords of east European type (especially the Sauerbrunn–Boiu group) from male inhumation burials in northern Italy (Salzani *et al.* 1992), and from tumulus graves further east (Bronasta Doba 1987, 65 ff.).

Although it was probably reached by voyages from the east from a relatively early date, the Iberian peninsula was not the object of systematic contacts, comparable to those seen in the central Mediterranean. A relative isolation also from Europe beyond the Pyrenees characterizes the local Bronze Age. The development of the Argaric culture, the best known regional group in this period, centred in eastern Almeria and southern Murcia (Coles and Harding 1979, 214 ff.; Chapman 1990), was based on agricultural intensification and the development of metallurgy (including silver), and reached a considerable degree of complexity and social stratification, indicated by the local fortified settlements and élite burials. However, Argaric society was never able to achieve early state organization, and apparently declined in the Late Bronze Age. A recent study of the Bronze Age of the Sierra de Huelva region, in the interior southwestern part of the peninsula (Garcia Sanjuan 1999), shows a similar trend of demographic growth, settlement nucleation, and the development of mining and metallurgy, resulting in the emergence of a hierarchical settlement system and the transition to social stratification, which was to be fully achieved in the Iron Age.

c.1200–750 BC

During the thirteenth-century BC crisis in the Aegean and east Mediterranean, the LHIIIB–IIIC transition (*c*.1200 BC) marked the final collapse of the Mycenaean palaces along with their economic and territorial organization (Morris 1996).

Some LHIIIC pottery is found in Italy, both in the south of the peninsula and at different locations as far apart as the Po Plain, Sicily and Sardinia (Fig. 2) (Vagnetti 1982, 30–1, figs. 2, 5, 1997), but Submycenaean and Protogeometric material is lacking. The most interesting evidence in this period is the occurrence of bronzes and other artefacts of Italian 'Protovillanovan' and Early Iron Age type in mainland Greece, the islands, and Cyprus: from type II swords and violin bow fibulae to the stilted arch fibulae from Submycenaean graves in the Kerameikos cemetery, to some of the earliest bronzes from the Greek sanctuaries, especially Olympia, which can be dated to the Late Bronze Age –Early Iron Age transition (Kilian 1985; Bietti Sestieri 1973, 1988; Matthäus 1980; Lo Schiavo and Peroni 1979, 553, fig. 3; von Hase 1997, 297, fig. 4.1). The possible implication is that during the Dark Age the initiative of the Aegean–central Mediterranean interaction shifted from Greece to Italy.

From the twelfth to eleventh century, Cypriot and Phoenician voyages to the central and western Mediterranean seem to immediately follow earlier ones from the Levant and Cyprus. Crete was intensively visited (Morris 1996), and Sardinia became the intermediate landing place for voyages heading towards the far west. The symmetrical role of these two islands is indicated by the occurrence of Cretan pottery in Sardinia (Jones and Day 1987), as well as of Sardinian pottery in Crete (Watrous 1989; Vagnetti 1989). Sardinian material, especially bronzes, occurs along the whole Phoenician sea route, including Cyprus (Karageorghis and Lo Schiavo 1989). The concentration of LHIIIB2 and IIIC pottery in Sardinia, especially at Nuraghe Antigori (Vagnetti 1982, 165–87; Knapp 1990, 126–7; Moscati *et al.* 1997, 8) might indicate a limited Aegean presence in this period; however, Sardinia's long-lived connection to the east Mediterranean is far more important.

Figure 2. Termitito, Basilicata. A fragment of locally made LHIIIC pottery from the Bronze Age site.

The integration of east Mediterranean and subsequently Phoenician groups in Sardinia bears a striking resemblance to the Aegean interaction with Sicily which developed throughout the previous period, and apparently was made possible by the complex socio-political structure of the Nuragic communities (Lo Schiavo 1981, 1997).

The Italian Final Bronze Age (c.twelfth to eleventh century) marks the emergence of some well-structured territorial polities as the outcome of complex local processes (Bietti Sestieri 1997a, 378 ff.). Some general factors of change, which appear at this time over many regions of Europe (Kristiansen 1998, 384 ff.), include a definite shift in the perception and function of metal, from prestige and warfare to a wide range of utilitarian uses, the intensification in subsistence techniques, especially agriculture, but also animal breeding, fishing and hunting, and an overall demographic growth. In Italy, complex developments appear in Etruria and in the 'Ausonian' south-west (Calabria and eastern Sicily). The emergence of complexity in Etruria was linked to the collapse of the Terramare system. Combined with a steady progress in social hierarchy and settlement organization, this collapse enabled the flourishing metal industry of central and northern Etruria to extend its trade network to the Po Plain, trans-Alpine Europe and the Balkan regions, possibly including Greece. A parallel development took place in southern Etruria, whose distinctive metal industry circulated through a southward trade network including Lazio, Abruzzi, Campania, Calabria and Sicily. A seaborne connection with Greece is indicated by some specific types of bronzes found in Submycenaean contexts (Bietti Sestieri 1988, fig. 7).

The Bronze Age–Iron Age transition is marked by a dramatic reorganization in the political and territorial setting of Etruria and by the formation of the proto-urban Villanovan centres both in Etruria and along the trade routes established in the previous period: Fermo, Verucchio and Bologna on the northward route; Capua, Pontecagnano and Sala Consilina on the southward one.

The development was later in the 'Ausonian' regions (Calabria and eastern Sicily: Albanese Procelli 1994; Leighton 1996; Bietti Sestieri 1997b), and the local territorial setting did not go beyond a two-tiered settlement hierarchy. Approximately from the eleventh century BC, and probably based on the exploitation of the copper ores of both Sicily and Calabria (Giardino 1995), a distinctive metal industry emerged in this area, with strong connections throughout southern Italy and as far north as Lazio. In the Calabrian and Sicilian contexts iron was used along with bronze from the end of the Bronze Age. Some bronze objects from this area reached Greece and the Aegean between the end of the second and the beginning of the first millennia BC (Lo Schiavo and Peroni 1979, 553, fig. 3; von Hase 1997, 297, fig. 4.1). An interesting feature of these regions is the evidence of Sardinian, Cypriot and Phoenician contacts in the Final Bronze and Early Iron Ages: in Sicily Sardinian pottery comes from Lipari and Pantalica (Vagnetti 1989, 357), and bronze vessels possibly of Cypriot type have been found at Caldare and Milena (Lo Schiavo et al. 1985, 30 ff., fig. 12.1, 2, 4). East Mediterranean and

Phoenician imports appear in the Early Iron Age cemetery of Torre Galli in Calabria (Pacciarelli 1999, 58 ff.); a possible parallel for the bronze-sheet cups from Torre Galli believed to be of Phoenician origin or inspiration is in the Sicilian hoard of San Cataldo (Albanese Procelli 1993, 67 ff., 100, fig. 25.1). An active link between Sardinia and the Tyrrhenian regions of Italy, which apparently involved the transmission of Cypriot and Atlantic bronzes, developed along with the Bronze Age–Iron Age transition and in the Early Iron Age (Lo Schiavo and Ridgway 1986).

The archaeological information on the Iberian Late Bronze Age is still rather sketchy. From the thirteenth century BC east Mediterranean groups sailed to the eastern and south-eastern zones of the peninsula, where permanent settlements and social stratification had developed throughout the Bronze Age. Interior sites in a favourable position, like Villena, in the middle Guadalquivir valley, probably were indigenous points of reference for the east Mediterranean sailors and merchants, as is indicated by the Cypriot and Sardinian connections of the finds from an important local hoard.

In the Final Bronze Age (c.tenth to eighth century BC) western Spain and Portugal, where rich copper and tin ores are concentrated, participated in the revival of the Atlantic trade route. The Iberian centres apparently provided the link between the latter and the western end of the Mediterranean route followed by the Phoenicians (Ruiz Galvez Priego 1995, 1997). Sardinia was both the recipient of Atlantic bronzes and the intermediary for their movement further east, from Tyrrhenian Italy and Sicily to the east Mediterranean (Lo Schiavo and Ridgway 1986, 397 ff.; Karageorghis and Lo Schiavo 1989).

Throughout the central and western Mediterranean, the pre-colonial period, including the earliest phase of Greek and Phoenician colonization (especially ninth to eighth century BC), is characterized by the phenomenon recently described by David Ridgway (in press) as general expansion, which in many respects appears as the direct sequence to the movements in the previous phase: Euboean sailing in the central Mediterranean began as early as the ninth century; however, Euboean pottery was also carried by Phoenician ships and distributed along the coasts of Sardinia (S. Imbenia) and northern Africa (Carthage). Both the Phoenicians and the Greeks extended their exploration of the Mediterranean coasts and their interaction with the indigenous communities to regions which were not to be involved in the proper colonization process: southern Etruria and Lazio apparently were reached by the Euboeans; Phoenician sailings, steadily supported by the participation of Sardinian natives, headed towards the eastern and north-western coasts of Sardinia, the Tyrrhenian coasts of Italy (Etruria and the 'Ausonian' regions), possibly the northern Adriatic area, and the whole Mediterranean and Atlantic coasts of Iberia.

However, the Phoenician and Greek colonization shows quite clearly that the main areas of influence were well defined and followed the traditional lines which had been established throughout the Bronze Age: the Greek colonies were concentrated in the central Mediterranean, including southern Italy along with eastern and central Sicily;

the Phoenician ones consistently selected the west: Sicily's western end, south-western Sardinia and southern Iberia. As far as the northern African coast is concerned, it might have been one of the targets of east Mediterranean voyages during the Bronze Age.

To sum up, the most promising lines for future research on the second and early first millennia BC in the Mediterranean are the thorough analysis of local contexts, although seen from a wider geographical and chronological standpoint. An essential factor in long-distance interaction in this area is represented by the specific role played by the great Mediterranean islands: at different times, Cyprus, Crete, Sicily, and Sardinia apparently became the main bases which enabled east Mediterranean and Aegean groups to organize further sailings and contacts. Indeed, it seems rather likely that the end of the Aegean sailings in the Dark Age depended at least as much on the collapse of the Mycenaean palaces as on the 'Ausonian' takeover of their traditional Bronze Age bases in Sicily and in the Aeolian islands. On the contrary, one of the basic conditions for the Phoenicians' expansion to the far west was their ability to integrate Sardinia as an active partner in their trade network.

A further important point emerges from a diachronic overview of the Mediterranean in the Bronze and Early Iron Ages. Along with the structural contingencies which determined the systematic sailings, and finally the colonial enterprises from Greece and Phoenicia (Aubet 1993; Tsetskhladze and De Angelis 1994; Snodgrass 1994; Moscati *et al.* 1997; Bartoloni in press), at least as far as the European side of the Mediterranean is concerned, another crucial factor should be considered. The necessary condition for the establishment of contacts of a permanent kind between groups from the east and the indigenous communities of the central and western Mediterranean was that the two partners should possess an overall comparable level of development. It is interesting to note that interaction in the Bronze Age was basically different from that documented in the colonial period. The Bronze Age establishment of permanent interaction apparently was via cultural integration in the favourable environment provided by the major Mediterranean islands, and exemplified by the Mycenaean integration in Sicily and the east Mediterranean and Phoenician connection with Sardinia. The colonial foundations should rather be described under the heading of political relationships (not necessarily friendly) between approximately peer polities: the Etruscans apparently were the Euboeans' active partners in Campania, while rich and relatively structured local communities occupied the regions selected by the Phoenician and Greek colonists in southern Italy, Sicily, Sardinia and Iberia.

A future for classical archaeology by Alain Schnapp

In a recent essay on the future of archaeology, Ian Morris (1994) warned classical archaeologists against the temptations of the *status quo*. Between 1870 and 1930, classical archaeology reached its height. As regards intellectual achievement, a full body of methodology as well as a substantial body of conclusive results had been attained. The basic exploration of the different component regions of the classical world had been completed, with the establishment of permanent missions by the archaeological institutions from the main western countries at the most important Mediterranean sites.

In the fifties, while pre- and protohistoric research was developing new methods for fieldwork and interpretation, the archaeology of the classical world did not progress. The most spectacular changes appeared at both ends of historical archaeology: Aegean archaeology was revolutionized by the methods of proto-history, while the research on Late Antiquity was deeply affected by the progress of historical research on the Middle Ages.

The idea of the pre-eminence of Greek culture over all the contemporary cultures of the 'classical' period is no longer feasible, and neither is that of the primacy of classical archaeology over archaeology as a whole: 'this situation is even more difficult as regards classical archaeology. Since the latter was invented at the end of the 19th century as a technique bound to isolate and idealize ancient Greece against dangerously conspicuous facts . . . once the context of ideas it ought to support has been given up, it finds itself deprived of its own object' (Morris 1994, 42; see also Holscher 1995).

Greek studies have long since lost their role as the adornment as well as the justification of political powers. Classical archaeology is no longer the leader over other archaeologies. Rather, its task consists of holding both ends of the obligations of the discipline: being in full command of the Greek historical sources as well as responding to the new methodological and practical rules of archaeology. All in all, this is simply what is required from any archaeologist, be he/she a student of Mesopotamian, Chinese or other archaeologies.

The uneasiness highlighted by Morris goes far beyond classical archaeology, as it expresses the Altertumswissenschaft's deeply perceived self-criticism. One might regret that within this trend of internal critique certain fields are scarcely represented, thus agreeing with Morris (1994, 45) when he states that the data should be taken as a means rather than as an end in itself. On the other hand, Anthony Snodgrass (1987) reminds us that the health of a discipline depends on its ability to keep a balanced and bilateral relationship with other fields which at first sight might appear as entirely different. Not without difficulties, classical archaeology has been able to establish such a relationship with philology. The schedule for the near future, which was foreshadowed several years ago by scholars like Jane Harrison, is to build up a similar connection with history, prehistory, and anthropology.

In the last half century, the most successful trends in archaeological research undoubtedly were those which relied on these three fields. First of all, on history. Although we know it will never be possible to write a history of the Greek economy like the one envisaged by Heichelheim, the work of M.I. Finley, E. Lepore and E. Will granted a substantial progress in the history of trade, especially for the archaic period (Descat 1995). In the next few decades, classical archaeology will obviously feel the effects of the approach of these scholars to economic history. On the other hand, the economic history of the ancient cities and of their relations with the indigenous societies should be based on anthropological analyses of such mechanisms as trade, imitation and acceptance. The colloquium in honour of F. Villard recently held in Paris (Rencontres 1999) exemplifies this approach.

As stated above, archaeology can be fostered by economic history as well as by anthropology. Several archaeological studies on mortuary practices and rituals depend on models elaborated in the field of funerary anthropology. The social dimension of funerary practices represents one of the few meeting points of classical and 'new' archaeology. Focusing on funerary behaviour stimulates a more careful approach to cemetery excavation, in order to identify biological and social variables which have seldom been considered in the past.

The study of environmental data was a decisive factor in the development of pre- and protohistoric archaeology. The set of recent studies of agricultural and pastoral activities shows that the history of rural Greece has been radically changed through the contact with other branches of archaeology.

Systematic surveys and the reconstruction of landscapes and territories, which were an essential component of epigraphic research in the term's broad meaning proposed by L. Robert, have been totally overturned by the adoption of the methods of Anglo-Saxon archaeology. Greece is presently the subject of surveys and multidisciplinary research: the historical relevance of this new approach is exemplified, among others, by the work of A. Snodgrass.

The same approach has been recently applied to Roman archaeological and historical research. In those regions where the Roman infrastructure was better preserved, Tchalenko's pioneering work on northern Syria has been integrated with palaeo-environmental and spatial data. From the Middle East to Maghreb, soil archaeology produced a huge progress in the understanding of land management and exploitation. Both in northern and southern Europe, this kind of research was stimulated by the new methods in historical and geographical research (Leveau *et al.* 1993). The surveys of the Italian countryside organized by the British School at Rome have been followed by integrated projects of excavation and regional survey, such as those of Settefinestre and of the Istituto Gramsci (Carandini *et al.* 1981). In turn, fieldwork combining extensive surveys and excavation has been carried out along the *Limes* in Great Britain and in Germany, and at Alésia in France. G. Duby's launching of a renewed rural history is also connected to this research trend (Bertrand *et al.* 1982).

Huge enterprises in topographic exploration, such as those at Olympia, Delphi and the Athenian Agora, did not take place in the last decades. However, the results of recent research at key sites such as Pithekoussai, Megara Hyblaea, Kalapodi, Eretria and Ephesus indicate that the topography and religious history of the Greek cities are a promising research field, provided that archaeological methods be integrated with historical and anthropological models. This approach to urban history has been adopted in Italy by Greco and Mertens (Greco 1992), in Greece by Hoepfner and Schwandner (1994), and was also applied in recent research on Roman urban centres. More information on urban history has been gathered from excavations in Rome in the last twenty years than in the whole previous century (Coarelli 1983, 1985, 1988; Carandini 1997). Throughout Europe, the history of ancient and medieval centres has been effectively analysed by emergency excavations as well as by a better integration of archive and textual data with excavation strategies.

The resumption of the explorations of Alexandria and Dura Europos, and the publication of important sites such as Ai-Khanoum in Afghanistan, make crucial contributions to the urban history of antiquity. Moreover, besides expanding in space, Greek and Roman archaeology has been able to import new techniques from the natural sciences. Pioneering tools such as geophysical prospection methods and remote sensing are steadily changing our understanding of the relationship between cities and their territories. Nautical archaeology, focusing on both shipwrecks and harbours, is enhancing our knowledge of ancient economic systems. The discovery of Kition's harbours on Cyprus, as well as the excavation of the docks of Marseille, and the exceptionally well-preserved Roman ships at Pisa constitute invaluable indicators of the new trends in the history of trade.

The renewal of classical archaeology depends on a greater openness to the present trends of archaeology itself. Anthropology (Hoffmann 1997) and philology are both helping to transform our idea of Greece. The influence of the school of structural mythology is the main reason for the success of a work such as 'La cité des images'. Within the same area, some recent studies, for example those by M. Shanks (1999) on archaic Greece, M. Torelli (1997) on the Roman world, and B. d'Agostino and L. Cerchiai (1999) on the Etruscans, all indicate that Warburg's, Panofsky's and Gombrich's efforts to provide iconography with a scientific basis have proved extremely productive for archaeology.

By losing its pre-eminence, classical archaeology simply became a part of archaeology; born in Great Britain in the late nineteenth century, the Altertumswissenschaft's self-criticism ends up in a confrontation between classical archaeology and archaeology as a whole. In archaeological practice, be it the use of historical or anthropological models, the acquisition of data by excavation and survey, or analytical procedures, there should be no difference between classical archaeology and archaeology *tout court*. True, the tension between art history and archaeology is still there, but this can be considered as a primary source of knowledge in a disciplinary field relying on written texts as well as on material evidence, as is shown by the work of F. Coarelli (1996).

The future of classical archaeology is not confined to the study of landscape, funerary practices or production techniques; rather, it comprises a new approach to its traditional topographic, architectural and iconographic sources. Indeed, the laicization of the Altertumswissenschaft is an achievement which by no means should imply its abandonment.

References

ALBANESE PROCELLI, R.M. 1993: *Ripostigli di bronzi della Sicilia nel Museo Archeologico di Siracusa* (Palermo, Accademia Nazionale di Scienze, Lettere e Arti).

ALBANESE PROCELLI, R.M. 1994: Considerazioni sulla necropoli di Madonna del Piano di Grammichele (Catania). In *La presenza etrusca nella Campania meridionale* (Firenze), 153–69.

AMMERMAN, A.J. and CAVALLI SFORZA, L.L. 1984: *The Neolithic Transition and the Genetics of Population in Europe* (Princeton).

AUBET, M.E. 1993: *The Phoenicians and the West* (Cambridge).

BAGOLINI, B. (ed.) 1981: *Il Neolitico e l'età del Rame. Ricerca a Spilamberto - S. Cesario 1977–1980* (Vignola).

BAILLOUD, G. and MIEG DE BOOFZHEIM, P. 1955: *Les civilisations Néolithiques de la France dans leur contexte Européen* (Paris).

BAILO MODESTI, G. and SALERNO, A. 1998: *Pontecagnano II.5. La necropoli eneolitica* (Napoli, Istituto Universitario Orientale).

BARFIELD, L.H. 1996: The Chalcolithic in Italy: Consideration of metal typology and cultural interaction. In Bagolini, B. and Lo Schiavo, F. (eds.), *The Copper Age in the Near East and Europe* (Forlì), 65–74.

BARKER, G. 1981: *Landscape and Society in Prehistoric Central Italy* (London).

BARTOLONI, P. in press: La Sardegna fenicia e il mondo etrusco. *XXI Convegno di Studi Etruschi e Italici, Sassari*.

BARTOSIEWICZ, L. and GREENFIELD, H.J. (eds.) 1999: *Transhumant Pastoralism in Southern Europe* (Budapest, Amulett '98 KFT).

BERNABÒ BREA, M., CARDARELLI, A. and CREMASCHI, M. (eds.) 1997: *Le Terramare, la più antica civiltà padana* (Milano).

BERNABÒ BREA, L., BIDDITTU, I., CASSOLI, P., CAVALIER, M., SCALI, S., TAGLIACOZZO, A. and VAGNETTI, L. 1989: *La grotta Cardini (Praia a Mare, Cosenza). Giacimento del bronzo* (Memorie dell'Istituto Italiano di Paleontologia Umana, n.s. 4).

BERTRAND, G., DUBY, G. and WALLON, A. 1982: *Histoire de la France rurale I, La formation des campagnes françaises des origines au XIV° siècle* (Paris).

BIANCO, S. 1991–2: La media età del bronzo della Calabria. In *L'età del bronzo in Italia nei secoli dal XVI al XIV a.C.* (*Rassegna di Archaeologia* 10), 509–22.

BIETTI SESTIERI, A.M. 1973: The metal industry of continental Italy, 13th–11th century, and its Aegean connection. *Proc. Prehist. Soc.* 39, 383–424.

BIETTI SESTIERI, A.M. 1988: The 'Mycenaean connection' and its impact on the central Mediterranean societies. *Dialoghi di Archaeologia* I(6), 23–51.

BIETTI SESTIERI, A.M. 1996: *Protostoria, teoria e pratica* (Roma).

BIETTI SESTIERI, A.M. 1997a: Italy in Europe in the Early Iron Age. *Proc. Prehist. Soc.* 63, 371–402.

BIETTI SESTIERI, A.M. 1997b: Sviluppi culturali e socio-politici differenziati nella tarda età del bronzo della Sicilia. In Tusa, S. 1997, 472–91.

BIETTI SESTIERI, A.M. 1998: Oral traditions, historical sources and archaeological data: reconstructing a process of ethnogenesis in the Italian Late Bronze Age. In *Papers from the EAA 3rd Annual Meeting, Ravenna 1997.* Volume I: *Pre- and Protohistory* (Oxford, BAR Int. Ser. 717), 280–3.

BINFORD, L. 1982: Meaning, inference and the material record. In Renfrew, C. and Shennan, S. (eds.), *Ranking, resources and exchange* (Cambridge).

BORGOGNINI TARLI, S., CANCI, A., FRANCALACCI, P. and REPETTO, S. 1991–2: Un approccio antropologico integrato alla ricostruzione delle condizioni di vita e del popolamento in Italia durante la media età del bronzo. In *L'età del bronzo in Italia nei secoli dal XVI al XIV a.C.* (*Rassegna di Archaeologia* 10), 593–601.

BRONASTA DOBA 1987: *Bronasta doba na Slovenskem* (*The Bronze Age in Slovenia*) (Ljubljana Narodni Muzej).

CAMPS, G. 1988: *Préhistoire d'un ile. Les origines de la Corse* (Paris).

CARANDINI, A. 1997: *La nascita di Roma. Dei, lari eroi e uomini all'alba di una civiltà* (Torino).

CARANDINI, A., GIARDINA, A. and SCHIAVONE, A. 1981: *Società romana e produzione schiavistica. L'Italia: insediamenti e forme economiche* (Bari).

CARDARELLI, A. 1992: Le età dei metalli nell'Italia settentrionale. In Guidi, A. and Piperno, M. (eds.), *Italia Preistorica* (Bari), 366–419.

CASTELLANA, G. 1998: *Il santuario castelluciano di Monte Grande e l'approvvigionamento di zolfo nel Mediterraneo nell'età del bronzo* (Agrigento, Regione Siciliana, Soprintendenza ai Beni Culturali e Ambientali, Museo Archeologico Regionale).

CAVALIER, M. and VAGNETTI, L. 1983: Frammenti di ceramica 'matt-painted' da Filicudi. *Mélanges de l'Ecole française de Rome* 95(1), 335–44.

CAZZELLA, A. 1988: Frontiers of neolithization in Italy and adjacent islands. *Berytus* 36, 87–99.

CAZZELLA, A. 1992: Sviluppi culturali eneolitici nella penisola italiana. In *Neolitico ed Eneolitico* (Bologna), 355–643.

CAZZELLA, A. 1994: Dating the Copper Age in peninsular Italy and adjacent islands. *J. European Archaeol.* 2(1), 1–19.

CAZZELLA, A. and MOSCOLONI, M. 1991: Gli scavi alla punta di Mezzogiorno. In Vivara 1991, 48–74.

CHAPMAN, R. 1990: *Emerging Complexity* (Cambridge).

CHERRY, J.F. 1981: Pattern and process in the earliest colonization of the Mediterranean islands. *Proc. Prehist. Soc.* 47, 41–68.

CHERRY, J.F. 1990: The first colonization of the Mediterranean islands: a review of recent research. *J. Mediterranean Archaeol.* 3(2), 145–221.

CINQUEPALMI, A. and RADINA, F. (eds.) 1998: *Documenti dell'età del bronzo. Ricerche lungo il versante adriatico pugliese* (Fasano).

CIPOLLONI, M. 1986: La tomba 3 dell'acropoli di Toppo Daguzzo (Potenza): elementi per uno studio preliminare. In *Annali dell'Istituto Universitario Orientale di Napoli. Archeologia e Storia Antica* 8, 1–40.

COARELLI, F. 1983, 1985: *Il foro romano* (1 and 2) (Roma).

COARELLI, F. 1988: *Il foro boario* (Roma).

COARELLI, F. 1996: *Revixit ars, arte e ideologia a Roma dai modelli ellenistici alla tradizione repubblicana* (Roma).

COLES, J.M. and HARDING, A.F. 1979: *The Bronze Age in Europe* (London).

CONTU, E. 1997: *La Sardegna preistorica e nuragica* (Sassari).

CREMONESI, G. 1976: Tomba della prima età dei metalli presso Tursi (Matera). *Rivista di Scienze Preistoriche* 31, 109–34.

CULTRARO, M. 1998: La cultura di Pantalica Nord in Sicilia nei suoi rapporti con il mondo egeo. In *Preistoria e protostoria in Etruria* 3 (Firenze), 301–12.

D'AGOSTINO, B. and CERCHIAI, L. 1999: *Il mare, la morte, l'amore* (Roma).

DELIBES DE CASTRO, G., MONTERO RUIZ, I. and ROVIRA LLORENS, S. 1996: The first use of metals in the Iberian peninsula. In Bagolini, B. and Lo Schiavo, F. (eds.), *The Copper Age in the Near East and Europe* (Forlì), 19–34.

DEMOULE, J.-P. and GUILAINE, J. (eds.) 1986: *Le Néolithique de la France. Hommage à Gérard Bailloud* (Paris).

DEMOULE, J.-P. and PERLES, C. 1993: The Greek Neolithic: a new review. *J. World Prehist.* 7(4), 355–415.

D'ERCOLE, V. *et al.* 1995: Prato di Frabulino (Farnese, Viterbo). Tomba a camera dell'età del bronzo. In *Preistoria e protostoria in Etruria, Atti del secondo incontro di studi* (Milano), 81–110.

DESCAT, R. 1995: L'économie antique et la cité grecque, un modèle en question. In *Annales ESC* 50(5), 961–89.

DICKINSON, O. 1994: *The Aegean Bronze Age* (Cambridge).

ELUERE, CH. and MOHEN, J.-P. 1996: La première metallurgie en France au Chalcolithique. In Bagolini, B. and Lo Schiavo, F. (eds.), *The Copper Age in the Near East and Europe* (Forlì), 35–40.

FUGAZZOLA DELPINO, M.A. 1998: La vita quotidiana del Neolitico. Il sito della Marmotta sul lago di Bracciano. In Pessina, A. and Muscio, G. (eds.), *Settemila anni fa il primo pane* (Udine, Museo Friulano di Storia Naturale), 184–91.

GARCIA SANJUAN, L. 1999: Settlement patterns, economy and social organization in the Iberian Bronze Age. *Antiquity* 73(280), 337–51.

GEDDES, D. 1980: *De la Chasse au Troupeau en Méditerranèe Occidentale: les Débuts de l'Elevage dans la Vallèe de l'Aude* (Toulouse, Centre d'Anthropologie des Societés Rurales).

GIARDINO, C. 1995: *Il Mediterraneo occidentale fra XIV e VIII sec. a.C.* (Oxford, BAR S612).

GRECO, E. 1992: *Archeologia della Magna Grecia* (Bari).

GUILAINE, J., COURTIN, J., ROUDIL, J.L. and VERNET, J.L. (eds.) 1987: *Premières communautés paysannes en Méditerranée occidentale* (Paris, CNRS).

HAMILAKIS, Y. 1999: La trahison des archéologues? Archaeological practice as intellectual activity in postmodernity. *J. Mediterranean Archaeol.* 12(1), 26–57.

HANSEN, J.M. 1988: Agriculture in the prehistoric Aegean: Data versus speculation. *American J. Archaeol.* 92, 39–52.

HARDING, A. 1984: *The Mycenaeans and Europe* (London).

HODDER, I. 1982: *Symbols in action* (Cambridge).

HOEPFNER, W. and SCHWANDNER, E.L. 1994: *Haus und Stadt im klassischen Griechenland, 2 Auflage* (München).

HOFFMANN, H. 1997: *Sotades, symbols of immortality in Greek vases* (Oxford).

HOLSCHER, T. 1995: Klassische Archäologie am Ende des 20. Jahrhunderts: Tendenzen, Defizitz, Illusionen. In Schwinge, E.R. (ed.), *Die Wissenschaften, vom Altertum am Ende des 2. Jahrtausends n. Chr.* (Leipzig), 197–227.

JONES, R.E. 1993: Laboratory analyses of Aegean-type Late Bronze Age pottery in Italy: review and future prospects. *Studi Micenei ed Eegeo-Anatolici* 32, 131–4.

JONES, R.E. and DAY, P. 1987: Aegean-type pottery in Sardinia: identification of imports and local imitations by chemical analysis. In Balmuth, M.S. (ed.), *Studies in Sardinian Archaeology* 3 (Oxford, BAR Int. Ser. 387), 257–70.

KARAGEORGHIS, V. and LO SCHIAVO, F. 1989: A west Mediterranean *obelos* from Amathus. *Rivista di Studi Fenici* 17(1), 15–29.

KILIAN, K. 1985: Violinbogenfibeln und Blattbügelfibeln des griechischen Festlandes aus mykenischer Zeit. *Praehistorische Zeitung* 60(2), 145–203.

KNAPP, A.B. 1990: Ethnicity, entrepreneurship and exchange: Mediterranean inter-island relationships in the Late Bronze Age. *Annu. Brit. Sch. Athens* 85, 115–53.

KRISTIANSEN, K. 1998: *Europe before history* (Cambridge).

KUHN, T. 1970: *The structure of scientific revolutions* (Chicago).

LEIGHTON, R. 1996: From chiefdom to tribe? Social organisation and change in later prehistory. In Leighton, R. (ed.), *Early societies in Sicily* (London, Accordia Specialist Studies on Italy, vol. 5), 101–16.

LEVEAU, PH., SILLIERES, P. and VALLAT, J.P. 1993: *Campagnes de la Méditerranée romaine* (Paris).

LOPEZ, P. (ed.) 1988: *El Neolìtico en Espana* (Madrid).

LO SCHIAVO, F. 1981: Economia e società nell'età del nuraghi. In Pugliese Carratelli, G. (ed.), *Ichnussa* (Milano), 254–347.

LO SCHIAVO, F. 1997: Sardegna. *Enciclopedia dell'Arte antica, classica e orientale. Secondo supplemento, 1971–1994* (Roma, Istituto dell'Enciclopedia Italiana), 141–57.

LO SCHIAVO, F., MACNAMARA, E. and VAGNETTI, L. 1985: Late Cypriot imports to Italy and their influence on local bronzework. *Pap. Brit. Sch. Rome* 53, 1–71.

LO SCHIAVO, F. and PERONI, R. 1979: Il Bronzo Finale in Calabria. *Atti della XXI Riunione Scientifica dell'Istituto Italiano di Preistoria e Protostoria* (Firenze), 551–70.

LO SCHIAVO, F. and RIDGWAY, D. 1986: La Sardegna e il Mediterraneo allo scorcio del II millennio. *Atti del 2° Convegno 'Un millennio di relazioni fra la Sardegna e il Mediterraneo'* (Cagliari, Assessorato alla cultura), 391–417.

LUGLI, F. and VIDALE, M. (eds.) in press: *Atti del I Convegno Italiano di Etnoarcheologia.*

MAGGI, R., NISBET, R. and BARKER, G. 1991–2: *Archeologia della pastorizia nell'Europa meridionale* (Bordighera, Istituto Internazionale di Studi Liguri).

MALONE, C., STODDART, S., BONANNO, A., GOUDER, T. and TRUMP, D. 1995: Mortuary ritual of 4th millennium BC Malta: the Zebbug period chambered tomb from the Brochtorff circle at Xaghra (Gozo). *Proc. Prehist. Soc.* 61, 303–45.

MARAZZI, M. 1998: I siti di Monte Grande e Vivara: due capisaldi delle più antiche frequentazioni egee in occidente. In Castellana, G. 1998, 319–31.

MARTIN DE LA CRUZ, J.C. 1992: La peninsula iberica y el Mediterraneo en el II milenio a.C. *Catalogo de la exposicion 'El mundo Micénico: cinco siglos de la primera civilisacion europea, 1600–1100 a.C.'* (Madrid, Ministerio de Cultura), 110–14.

MARTÌ OLIVER, B. 1978: El Neolitico de la Peninsula Ibèrica. *Saguntum* 13, 59–98.

MARZOCCHELLA, A. 1998: Tutela archeologica e preistoria nella pianura campana. In Guzzo, P.G. and Peroni, R. (eds.), *Archeologia e Vulcanologia in Campania* (Napoli), 97–133.

MATTHÄUS, H. 1980: Italien und Griechenland in der ausgehenden Bronzezeit. *JdI* 95, 109–39.

McGEEHAN LIRITZIS, V. 1996: *The Role and Development of Metallurgy in the Late Neolithic and Early Bronze Age of Greece* (Göteborg).

MEZZENA, F. 1997: La valle d'Aosta nel Neolitico e nell'Eneolitico. *Atti della XXXI Riunione Scientifica dell'Istituto Italiano di Preistoria e Protostoria* (Firenze), 17–133.

MIARI, M. 1994: Il rituale funerario della necropoli eneolitica di Ponte S. Pietro (Ischia di Castro — Viterbo). *Origini* 18, 351–90.

MONTERO RUIZ, I. 1994: *El origen de la metalurgia en el Sudeste de la peninsula ibèrica* (Almeria, Instituto de Estudios Almerienses).

MORRIS, I. 1994: Archaeologies of Greece. In Morris, I., *Classical Greece, ancient histories and modern Archaeologies* (Cambridge), 8–48.

MORRIS, I. 1996: Greece in the Iron Age. In Bietti Sestieri, A.M. (ed.), *The Iron Age in the Mediterranean area, Colloquium 23. Proceedings of the XIII UISPP Conference, Forlì*, 127–43.

MOSCATI, S., BARTOLONI, P. and BUONDÌ, S.F. 1997: *La penetrazione fenicia e punica in Sardegna - 30 anni dopo. Memorie dei Lincei* s. IX, vol. XI.1 (Roma).

MOSCOLONI, M. 1992: Sviluppi culturali neolitici nella penisola italiana. In *Neolitico ed Eneolitico* (Bologna), 11–354.

MUHLY, J.D. 1996: The first use of metals in the Aegean. In Bagolini, B. and Lo Schiavo, F. (eds.), *The Copper Age in the Near East and Europe* (Forlì), 75–84.

MUNOZ, A.M. 1986: El Neolitico y los comienzos del Cobre en el sureste. In *Homenaje a Luis Siret 1934–1984* (Sevilla, Consejeria de Cultura de la Junta de Andalucia), 152–6.

PACCIARELLI, M. 1999: *Torre Galli. La necropoli della prima età del ferro* (Catanzaro).

PAPATHANASSOPOULOS, G.A. (ed.) 1996: *Neolithic Culture in Greece* (Athens, N.P. Goulandris Foundation).

PATTON, M. 1996: *Islands in Time* (London and New York).

PERICOT GARCIA, L. 1950: *Los Sepulcros Megaliticos Catalanes y la Cultura Pirenaica* (Barcelona, Instituto de Estudios Pirenaicos del Consejo Superior de Investigaciones Cientificas).

POGGIANI KELLER, R. 1998: Trescore Balneario (Bergamo). Il sito del Canton tra Neolitico V.B.Q. e Campaniforme. In Nicolis, F. and Mottes, E. (eds.), *Simbolo ed enigma. Il bicchiere campaniforme e l'Italia nella preistoria europea del III millennio a.C.* (Trento, Servizio Beni Culturali della Provincia Autonoma), 87–91.

PRIMAS, M. 1996: *Velika Gruda* I (Bonn).

PUGLISI, S.M. 1959: *La civiltà appenninica* (Firenze).

REHAK, P. and YOUNGER, J.C. 1998: Review of Aegean prehistory VII: Neopalatial, Final Palatial and Postpalatial Crete. *American J. Archaeol.* 102(1), 91–173.

RENCONTRES 1999: *Céramiques et peintures grecques, modes d'emploi. Rencontres de l'Ecole du Louvre. La documentation française* (Paris).

RENFREW, C. 1972: *The Emergence of Civilisation* (London).

RENFREW, C. 1973: *Before Civilization* (Cambridge).

RENFREW, C. 1987: *Archaeology and Language* (London).

RIDGWAY, D. in press: Rapporti dell'Etruria con l'Egeo e il Levante: prolegomena sarda. *XXI Convegno di Studi Etruschi e Italici, Sassari*.

RUIZ GALVEZ PRIEGO, M. (ed.) 1995: *Ritos de paso y puntos de paso. La ria de Huelva en el mundo del Bronce Final Europeo* (Madrid, Universidad Complutense).

RUIZ-GALVEZ PRIEGO, M. 1997: The west of Iberia: meeting point between the Mediterranean and the Atlantic at the end of the Bronze Age. In Balmuth, M., Gilman, A. and Prados Torreira, L. (eds.), *Encounters and transformations: the archaeology of Iberia in transition* (Sheffield).

SALZANI, L. *et al.* 1992: Olmo di Nogara (Verona). Relazione preliminare sulle campagne di scavo 1991–92. *Padusa* 28, 7–52.

SCHUMACHER, T.X. and WENIGER, G.-C. 1995: Continuidad y cambio. Problemas de la neolitizacion en el Este de la Peninsula Ibérica. *Trabajos de Prehistoria* 52(2), 83–97.

SHANKS, M. 1999: *Art and the early Greek state, an interpretive archaeology* (Cambridge).

SHAW, J.W. 1990: The Early Helladic II corridor house: Problems and possibilities. In Darcque, P. and Treuil, R. (eds.), *L'habitat égéen préhistorique* (*Bulletin de Correspondance Hellénique* suppl. 19), 183–94.

SHELMERDINE, C.W. 1997: Review of Aegean prehistory VI: The Palatial Bronze Age of the southern and central Greek mainland. *American J. Archaeol.* 101(3), 537–85.

SHERRATT, A. 1981: Plough and pastoralism: aspects of the secondary products revolution. In Hodder, I., Isaac, G. and Hammond, N. (eds.), *Patterns of the Past* (Cambridge), 261–305.

SHERRATT, A. 1983: The secondary exploitation of animals in the Old World. *World Archaeol.* 15(1), 90–104.

SKEATES, R. 1993: Early metal-use in the central Mediterranean region. *The Accordia Res. Pap.* 4, 5–48.

SKEATES, R. and WHITEHOUSE, R. (eds.) 1994: *Radiocarbon Dating and Italian Prehistory* (London, Archaeological Monographs of the British School at Rome, 8).

SKEATES, R. and WHITEHOUSE, R. 1995–6: New radiocarbon dates for prehistoric Italy 2. *The Accordia Res. Pap.* 6, 179–91.

SNODGRASS, A. 1987: *An archaeology of Greece: the present state and future scope of a discipline* (Berkeley).

SNODGRASS, A. 1994: The nature and standing of the early western colonies. In Tsetskhladze, G.R. and De Angelis, F. 1994, 1–10.

TINÉ, S. and TRAVERSO, A. (eds.) 1992: *Monte d'Accoddi. Dieci anni di nuovi scavi* (Genova, Istituto Italiano di Archeologia Sperimentale).

TINÉ, V. (ed.) 1996: *Forme e tempi della neolitizzazione in Italia Meridionale e in Sicilia* (Catanzaro).

TORELLI, M. 1997: *Il rango, il rito e l'immagine* (Milano).

TRUMP, D. 1995–6: Radiocarbon dates from Malta. *The Accordia Res. Pap.* 6, 173–7.

TSETSKHLADZE, G.R. and DE ANGELIS, F. (eds.) 1994: *The archaeology of Greek colonisation* (Oxford).

TUNZI SISTO, A.M. 1991–2: L'ipogeo di Madonna di Loreto (Trinitapoli, Foggia). In *L'età del bronzo in Italia nei secoli dal XVI al XIV a.C.* (*Rassegna di Archeologia* 10), 545–52.

TUSA, S. 1992: *La Sicilia nella preistoria* (Palermo).

TUSA, S. (ed.) 1997: *Prima Sicilia* (Palermo).

VAGNETTI, L. (ed.) 1982: *Magna Grecia e mondo Miceneo, nuovi documenti* (Taranto, Istituto per l'archeologia e la storia della Magna Grecia).

VAGNETTI, L. 1989: A Sardinian askos from Crete. *Annu. Brit. Sch. Athens* 84, 355–60.

VAGNETTI, L. 1997: L'area Padana. In Bernabò Brea, M., Cardarelli, A. and Cremaschi, M. 1997, 616–20.

VAN ANDEL, T.H. and RUNNELS, C.N. 1988: An essay on the 'emergence of civilisation' in the Aegean world. *Antiquity* 62, 234–47.

VAN ANDEL, T.H. and RUNNELS, C.N. 1995: The earliest farmers in Europe. *Antiquity* 69, 481–500.

VAQUER, J. 1990: *Le Néolithique en Languedoc occidental* (Paris, CNRS).

VIVARA 1991: *Vivara — centro commerciale mediterraneo dell'età del bronzo.* Vol. I, *Gli scavi dal 1976 al 1982* (Roma, Bagatto Libri).

VIVARA 1994: *Vivara — centro commerciale mediterraneo dell'età del bronzo.* Vol. II, *Le tracce dei contatti con il mondo egeo (scavi 1976–1982)* (Roma, Bagatto Libri).

VON HASE, F.W. 1997: Presences étrusques et italiques dans les sanctuaires grecs (VIIIe–VIIe siècle av. J.-C.). In *Les étrusques, les plus religieux des hommes* (*Rencontres de l'école du Louvre* XII), 293–323.

VORUZ, J.L. (ed.) 1995: *Chronologies Néolithiques de 6000 à 2000 avant notre ère dans le Bassin Rhodanien* (Ambérieu-en-Bugey, Editions de la Société Préhistorique Rhodanienne).

WATROUS, L.V. 1989: A preliminary report on imported 'Italian' wares from the Late Bronze Age site of Kommos on Crete. *Studi Micenei ed Egeo-anatolici* 27, 69–79.

WILSON, R.J.A. 1988: Archaeology in Sicily 1982–87. *Archaeological Reports* 34, 105–50.

ZACHOS, K.L. 1996: Metallurgy. In Papathanassopoulos, G.A. 1996, 140–3.

Timeless time: Africa and the world

MARTIN HALL

The art in the artefact

In 1995, the Royal Academy's exhibition *Africa — The Art of a Continent* opened in London. There were more than eight hundred objects, ranging from southern Africa to the Mediterranean and from five thousand years ago to the present. In the words of the curator, Tom Phillips, 'it is a privilege to celebrate for the first time, in these rooms, the fertile contribution to the visual culture of the world from the whole of this vast and infinitely various continent; and to make here a praise song for Africa' (Phillips 1995, 20). For activist and academic Cornel West, 'this monumental exhibition is unprecedented in the history of the art world. Never before has there been gathered such a rich and vast array of African art-objects and artefacts from such a broad timespan. And rarely has any exhibition embraced the artistic treasures of the whole of Africa, from Egypt to Ife to Great Zimbabwe' (West 1995, 9).

Yet, despite such accolades, *Africa — The Art of a Continent* provoked hostile responses. Simon Jenkins of *The Times* wrote:

> On Monday night I put on my best suit and attacked the African art show, talk of the town at the Royal Academy. I was immediately stumped. Outside were a dozen prancing Zulu war drummers, skimpily clad in raffia briefs, beaming and whooping at the passing guests. The guests had no idea how to react. Were these renegade militants, satirising the white man's image of Africa? Or were they one of the exhibits, 'performance art' courtesy of the Bank of Ulundi. Should we throw coloured beads, or raise a fist in salute? Ambassadorial limousines cruised the forecourt menacingly, as if about to spew AK47s and mow us all down. . . (Jenkins 1995)

Jenkins was no happier inside the Royal Academy where, in the matter of Art, Africa was just not up to standard:

> I can appreciate a well-crafted meat platter from KwaZulu or an intricate Nigerian Igbo-Ukwu bowl. The decoration is pretty. I can see that the ubiquitous masks may have served their purpose in amusing or horrifying the communities for whose

religious beliefs they had meaning. But put them on a pedestal, light them and declare them to be something quite different — art — and my eye judges them as such, and judges the selector. The daubs and rock paintings and carvings are awesome echoes of the past. But most of the exhibits are 'found objects' of the past century. They are crude and — a word detested by the politically correct — primitive. . . . (Jenkins 1995)

Jenkins' compatriot, Richard Dowden of *The Spectator,* came to the same conclusion: 'Is there any art in the continent? You may pronounce a Zulu platter beautiful but it is only a meat dish. Can it therefore be art? You may say Kente cloth from Ghana is magnificent but it is only Asante proverbs woven into cloth through signs and symbols. . .' (Dowden 1995). Dowden then went on to offer his readers a paragraph of potted history which let them off the legacy of four centuries of invasion, pillage and plunder. For him, 'the greatest problem of all' is, again, 'political correctness':

The PC line on Africa is that it was the Garden of Eden before the Europeans pitched up and ruined it. Since then everything wrong with Africa, from genocide in Rwanda to drought in Sudan, is blamed on outsiders . . . If it were true that African culture had been wiped out by imperialism, Africans would simply be copying European art, building neo-classical houses, painting like Rembrandt and writing like Jane Austen. But Africans are not doing this. The fact is that Africa survived imperialism rather well. Its spirit was not crushed. Its culture and society, especially the family, remain as strong as ever. Faced with imperialism, war or drought, Africa falls back on its greatest strength: survival. Conservative but adaptable, Africa absorbed the impact of European intervention and did well out of it. The Europeans, so full of plans and dreams for Africa, were finally defeated, their plans and dreams swallowed up in Africa's mysterious maw and transformed into something quite different. (Dowden 1995)

Commentaries such as these cast Africa's history and culture as, at best, an amusing side-show, a vast colourful craft market, a mass of people whose purpose is merely to survive. Such positions are hardly new. They are the millennial version of the sentiments that made an industry from Africa's exoticism, whether early modern fables of Prester John and the Queen of Sheba, Rider Haggard's wildly successful novels such as *King Solomon's Mines* and *She,* Wilbur Smith's airport blockbusters (*Sunbird*) or Disney's *Lion King* (Hall 1995a, 1995b, 1996).

Such reactions are profoundly ironic. It is as if Africa's material world — its treasure house of work in all conceivable media — has been used up. Having inspired Napoleon and droves of adventurers after him to plunder the Nile valley, the British to raid Benin for its bronzes, and the Belgians to strip the Congo for King Leopold II's collections, Africa has no 'art' that can satisfy British taste. The turning point for Western art may have been Pablo Picasso's visit, in 1907, to the Musée d'Ethnographie in the Palais de Trocadéro and the force and form that he saw in African masks (Duncan 1968), but this cuts no ice with Simon Jenkins — such sources of inspiration have no place in the Academy. Europe's derivations from Africa are 'art' but their raw materials — the primary sources from which they are drawn — are archive. In a way, responses such as these are the purest form of colonialism, Franz Fanon's robbery of the soul (Fanon 1963).

But such reactions are also strange. It would hardly be credible to argue that European perceptions of Africa are frozen in some sort of false consciousness that would yield comments from a high-brow journalist at the end of the twentieth century that are indistinguishable from the popular fiction of a hundred years earlier. This small example of the Royal Academy's exhibition introduces a contradiction that will frame my argument in the rest of this chapter. This contradiction can be given form by turning to the programme notes that accompanied the show. In the catalogue, the curator tells us that his aim was to present Africa 'as it really is', stripped of the influence of the outside world. Nothing that was syncretic or cosmopolitan, nothing that diluted the strong streams of Africa's 'authentic' artistic traditions, would be allowed into the show (Phillips 1995). Such 'contemporary work' was for satellite exhibitions, scheduled for other venues in London. The consequence was the depiction of a continent frozen in an 'ethnographic present', a relative chronology in which the absolute dates of objects in the show varied widely from place to place (from early dynastic Egypt in the north to the ninth-century AD Lydenburg sculptures in the south), but in which the time horizon was always before Europe's 'influence'. African cultures could be seen to affect one another, but not to be influenced, or to exert influence, beyond the continent's periphery. Africa was a continent in a glass jar, an unearthed spectacle, at which the Academy's visitors could gaze and wonder (Hall 1996).

This, then, is the contradiction. Africa is the 'timeless continent': Joseph Conrad's *Heart of Darkness*, the apocalyptic encounter of civilization and its nemesis (Achebe 1988). It is Karl Jung's 'collective unconscious', the unchanging baseline of the human psyche (Jung 1973) and Karen Blixen's *Out of Africa* (1954), the herds of antelope sweeping across the Serengeti. But at the same time, Africa is the continent of origins: the precolonial cities of Great Zimbabwe and Jenne-jeno, mathematics, architecture and astronomy in early Egypt, animal husbandry and crop cultivation, artistic representation. Above all else, it is the continent in which humanity itself originated. How can Africa be both at the hub of history, and out of time?

Colonial days

But what is Africa? For the commentators such as Richard Dowden, Africa was always there, 'conservative but adaptable', albeit with a 'mysterious maw' (Dowden 1995). A reading of the exhibition catalogue would have pointed to a more complex situation. Here is Kwame Anthony Appiah:

> Take, first, 'Africa': through the long ages of human cultural life in the continent, and, more particularly, in the half dozen or so millennia since the construction of the first great architectural monuments of the Nile Valley, most people in the continent have lived in societies that defined both self and other by ties of blood or power. It would never have occurred to most of the Africans in this long history to think that they belonged to a larger human group defined by a shared relationship to the African continent . . . Only recently has the idea of Africa come to figure importantly in the thinking of many Africans, and those that took up this idea got it, by and large, from European culture. (Appiah 1995, 21–240)

Appiah's dissection of the idea of Africa is part of a stream of critical writing that questions the assumption that the unitary geography, history and culture of the continent is a given — that it provides a frame of comparison with 'Europe', 'Asia' or 'America'. V.Y. Mudimbe has explored Africa as 'invention' and 'idea', while Simon Gikandi identifies an 'Africanist' style of writing, akin to Edward Said's orientalism, in which the continent is inevitably a place of forests and primitive peoples (Gikandi 1996; Mudimbe 1988, 1994; Said 1985).

What was to become 'Africa' started as a vague shape of rumours, assumptions and prejudices in religious and popular early modern tales, manuscripts and early books. Sailors and settlers carried conceptual baggage along with trinkets for trade and armaments for subjection — prior concepts moulded the relationships that developed between the colonizers and the indigenous communities they were to encounter (Greenblatt 1991). Dante's *Divine Comedy*, written for a popular audience, cast the earth as a sphere, solid except for the cavity of Hell. In the south, in Africa, 'Garamantes' coped with the heat by going naked (Binyon 1952). The widely popular *Mandeville's Travels* saw the world in much the same way (Moseley 1983). Available in every major European language by the end of the fourteenth century, the fictitious 'Sir John Mandeville' described his travels away from Jerusalem, the centre of the world. Here are the parahuman inhabitants of 'Lamary', living under the 'Antarctic Star':

> In [Lamary] it is extremely hot; the custom there is for men and women to go completely naked and they are not ashamed to show themselves as God made them . . . In that land there is no marriage between man and woman; all the women of that land are common to every man . . . When women are delivered of a child, they give it to whom they want of the men who have slept with them. And in the same way the land is common property. So one year a man has one house, another year another; each man takes what pleases him, now here, now there. For all things are common, as I said, corn and other goods too; nothing is locked up, and every man is as rich as another. But they have an evil custom among them, for they will eat human flesh more gladly than any other. Nevertheless, the land is abundant enough in meat and fish and corn, and also gold and silver and other goods. Merchants bring children there to sell, and the people of the country buy them. Those that are plump they eat;

those that are not plump they feed up and fatten, and then kill and eat them. And
they say it is the best and sweetest flesh in the world. (Moseley 1983, 127–8)

Such antipodean images were closely associated with heat and suffering. Dante characterized India — the extreme east of the known world — as a land where the sand was
too hot to walk upon. The Third Ring of the Seventh Circle of Hell had the same burning sand. Here, the sexually deviant — the 'violent against nature' — were condemned
to walk forever. Burning sand signified the doom of Sodom and Gomorrah, while
'Libya's sand' was associated with the serpents and 'breeds so strange beside' in the
Seventh Chasm of the Eighth Circle (Sayers 1949, 160). Such tumbled confusions of
images must have been prominent in the minds of the lowliest seventeenth-century
sailor as Africa was sighted on the port bow. These vague shapes took ever more specific form in a series of cartographies. Descriptive fragments were brought together in
early travel accounts and influenced early medieval maps and charts, while the cartography of the continent was given clearer form from the closing years of the fifteenth
century with the first Portuguese voyages of discovery (Boxer 1957; Crone 1968). With
time the Catalan atlases, with their strange, elliptical representations of unrecognizable
land masses surrounding Europe and the Mediterranean, were replaced by Ortelian
globes and Mercator's Projection (Crone 1968). By 1588 Livio Sanuto could describe
Table Mountain from his knowledge of travellers' tales, bringing together contemporary cartography and a long-standing mythological tradition: 'Upon the top of this
promontory Nature . . . hath formed here a great plain, pleasant in situation, which with
the fragrant herbs, variety of flowers, and flourishing verdure of all things, seems a terrestrial paradise' (van Wyk Smith 1988, 9). Although Ortelius's and Mercator's new
globes did not map the location of Paradise, their contemporaries knew that it existed
and, throughout the following centuries of colonial expansion, sailors setting out from
Europe could expect that an unplanned deviation from the established sea lanes could
bring them to the Island of Purgatory or to other celebrated lands.

This creation of Africa from the periphery snaked into the interior, following the
lines of rivers and other routes. On the way, new observations were made and trophies
collected, yielding in time to the systematic procedures of collecting and classifying that
are the distinctive mark of the discipline of Archaeology. Alongside the creation of such
'travelling epistemologies' (Carter 1988) Africa was segmented into colonial divisions
— the spoils of Empire — with boundaries that followed lines of latitude and longitude,
or of major topographic features, reflecting the histories of disputes between European
powers. The end result was the modern map of Africa — a graphic representation of a
century of high colonialism and five hundred years of European settlement, and the
'invented continent'.

This colonial geography framed and directed the intellectual development of archaeology in Africa, and has left an ineluctable impression on the archive of knowledge about

the past. Language had a major influence. West Africa was the colonial territory of Britain, Belgium and France, and colonial officials who became interested in collecting artefacts corresponded with museums in London, Brussels and Paris, relating in turn again to different intellectual traditions of archaeological interpretation. Distribution maps of archaeological sites in southern Africa show sharp declines along the eastern boundaries of South Africa, as amateur collectors working in South Africa came to the borders of Portugal's colony, Moçambique. Studies of rock paintings in South-West Africa (now Namibia) were published in German, while studies of rock art belonging to the same pan-San pre-colonial tradition, but located in neighbouring Botswana, were published in English. In some cases, politics played an equally influential role. The most striking example here, of course, is the relationship between South Africa and the rest of the continent. Thus *The Archaeology of Africa: Food, Metals and Towns* (Shaw *et al.* 1993), presented as a comprehensive overview of the continent's past, contained virtually nothing on the archaeology of the south. The history of South Africa's pre-colonial people was eradicated in punishment for the sins of their own oppressors.

The consequence of these engagements is a rich discourse of texts and collections that links the earliest expeditions with today's museums, and recent publications with their antecedents. The first part of the continent to attract the West's attention was Egypt. Early interest was given great impetus by Napoleon's invasion in 1798, and the description of Egyptian antiquities, published in the *Description de l'Egypte* between 1809 and 1813 (Fagan 1977). In Martin Bernal's words:

> The whole Expedition is a fascinating turning point in European attitudes to the East. In many ways the elaborate surveys, maps and drawings, and the stealing of objects and cultural monuments to embellish France, was an early example of the standard pattern of studying and objectifying through scientific enquiry that became a hallmark of European imperialism and a basis of the 19th-century 'Orientalism' described so well by Edward Said. On the other hand, there were still many traces of the older attitude towards Egypt, and among the scientific members of the Expedition there was the belief that, in Egypt, they could learn essential facts about the world and their own culture and not just exotica to complete Western knowledge — and domination — of Africa and Asia. (Bernal 1991, 184)

Similarly, collections of artefacts were made from the early years of colonial possession and settlement in other areas, and were based on the same premises that inspired archaeologists in nineteenth-century Europe: Charles Lyell's *Principles of Geology* (1833) and the principle of uniformitarianism, C.J. Thomsen's technological phases, and the interpretations of stone tools made by pioneers such as Boucher de Perthes. The evolutionary synthesis that was brought together in Darwin's *Origins of Species* in 1859 provided a basis for recognizing human fossils and stimulated the classification of living societies, which were seen as representative of the various stages that European civilization had passed through before attaining its cultural superiority. Some of the earliest descriptions of

such as these, many African archaeologists have been forced into intellectual exile in Europe and North America in order to survive within their chosen profession.

Archaeology in South Africa faces its own problems, largely the consequence of its divergent history following the introduction of apartheid. Although South Africa has an internationally recognized tradition of archaeological research, its framing within an education structure organized by race and racial exclusion has resulted in an almost complete divide between the practice of archaeology and popular engagement with the past (Hall 1984, 1988, 1990). South Africa shares none of the national enthusiasm of Egypt, Nigeria or Zimbabwe for the archaeology of its past, comparatively few black students study archaeology in South African universities and there are very few professional archaeologists who are black. The contrast is evident in the responses to archaeology's heritage to the north and south of the Limpopo River. To the north, Great Zimbabwe is renowned both as national symbol and now as World Heritage Site. To the south Mapungubwe, the twelfth-century town that was precursor to Great Zimbabwe, stands isolated at the South African border, unknown even to local inhabitants.

The contradiction of timeless time

The years between the sunset of high colonial archaeology and the end of the millennium have, then, seen the emergence of an African archaeology practised by Africans for Africans. This distinctly African archaeology has been limited by endemic crises of resources for developing education and public institutions such as revitalized museums — problems that have been clearly identified and articulated, in particular, in the pages of the *African Archaeological Review* and other journals (see Musonda 1990; Karega-Munene 1996; Kusimba 1996; Andah *et al.* 1994). In the south, the persistence of institutionalized racism has inhibited the development of the broad consciousness of archaeology as history and identity that is a prerequisite for an enduring commitment to research (Shepherd 2000). But despite these limitations, some two hundred papers were delivered by archaeologists living and working in countries from all parts of Africa at the 1995 Pan African Association for Prehistory meeting in Harare (the first time there had been such representation since 1947 — Pwiti and Soper 1996). In 1999 the World Archaeological Congress met in Cape Town, again drawing participants from all parts of Africa (as well as the rest of the world) and hosting a variety of distinctly African symposia. Although, as Shepherd (2000) has pointed out in a comprehensive review of the Cape Town Congress, there is a chronic underdevelopment of indigenous archaeologies in Africa, extensive 're-colonization' of the continent by archaeologists from Europe and North America and 'a new and mercenary spirit in the handling of issues of heritage', there can be no doubt that, with the notable exception of South Africa, the second half of the twentieth century has seen the emergence of a distinctly continental tradition of research.

But still the contradiction persists. Despite the weight of evidence to the contrary, the popular image of Africa as the land that time forgot persists. Highbrow movies, such as Bertolucci's *The Sheltering Sky* (1990), cast Africa as an empty place, suitable for the redemption of the innermost self — a sort of psychological safari that seeks Jung's collective unconscious in the emptiness of the desert. For family entertainment Disney's *Lion King* offers an Africa in which the animals rule and people are altogether absent.

Contemporary popular Africa can be illustrated in two examples. Wilbur Smith can justifiably claim to be one of the kings of the airport novel — the world's best-selling fiction writer in 1981 with a string of subsequent successes to his name. His *Sunbird* (1972) continues the tradition of Rider Haggard's *King Solomon's Mines* a century after its publication (Hall 1995a). *Sunbird* is a political allegory that mourns the fading days of Rhodesia through images of the past. Ben Kazin, the hero archaeologist, believes that Carthaginians had a formative influence on Africa's past, although the academic world has yet to take him seriously. Kazin's friend and patron, the fabulously wealthy mining magnate and entrepreneur Louren Sturvesant, shows Kazin an aerial photograph, which reveals the outline of a lost city in the deserts of northern Botswana. Against the scepticism of the international academic community, the infidelity of Kazin's beautiful assistant Dr. Sally Benator, and the terrorist activities of Kazin's one time linguistic specialist, Timothy Mageba, Kazin finds his site, to the acclaim of all. But this lost city carried a curse; a fungal infection that kills Sturvesant and takes Kazin into a prolonged dream of the past, in which the destruction of this earlier civilization is acted out. Through this experience, Kazin becomes the custodian of 'the legend of the ancients', 'a race of fair-skinned golden-haired warriors' who had come from across the sea and had 'mined the gold, enslaved the indigenous tribes, built walled cities and flourished for hundreds of years before vanishing almost without trace'. Their capital had been Opet, a far more substantial place than Great Zimbabwe (which was merely the garrison for the 'Middle Kingdom'). Like the Ophir of the Bible, this was a land of fabulous plenty, a hunter's paradise teeming with game, a repository of immense wealth. The economy was fuelled by Opet's extensive gold mines, and subject tribes from the rest of the sub-continent brought tribute.

All this was swept away by the dark disaster of the 'Bantu migration', an episode of 'diabolical fury', 'an almost superhuman destructive strength', 'a solid mass of black humanity'. Here, Wilbur Smith plies back and forth between his imagined history and his political present. The attack on Opet is led by Manatassi, King of the Vendi, while the attack on white Rhodesia is under the command of Major-General Timothy Mageba, of the People's Liberation Army. Kazin, the historian and archaeologist of Africa, sums up the connection for the reader: '. . . it came to me then that this man was not unique, Africa had bred many like him. The dark destroyers who had strewn her plains with the white bones of men, Chaka, Mzilikazi, Mamatee, Mutesa, and hundreds of others that history had forgotten. Timothy Mageba was only the latest in a long line of warriors which stretched back beyond the shadowy, impenetrable veils of time' (Smith 1972, 231).

In Wilbur Smith's imagination, then, all 'civilization' in Africa is extra-territorial; all Africans can do is wipe away the gains brought from outside the continent through waves of barbaric rejection. This image appealed enormously to Rider Haggard and Joseph Conrad's readers in the nineteenth century, and equally to Wilbur Smith's innumerable readers a century later — the attraction of the plot lies in the way that it plays to well-entrenched stereotypes. It appeals equally to visitors to Sun International's 'Lost City', a high priced hotel and casino complex north of Johannesburg (Hall 1995a).

The Lost City is a sort of theme park. It is presented as a ruin, destroyed by an earthquake three thousand years ago, resulting in a maze of crumbled towers, heaps of stone and broken carvings (although, despite these ravages of time, there are restaurants, lounge bars, swimming pools and 300 guest rooms, equipped with bedspreads woven with animal spoor and zebra-stripped pencils by the telephones). The architecture of the Lost City is an eclectic *mélange* — a post-modern architectural dream complete with its own mythology, framed at the Californian corporate headquarters of Wimberly Allison Tong and Goo, international resort designers, and distributed as part of the resort's publicity pack. According to this 'Legend of the Lost City', a nomadic tribe long ago set out from northern Africa to seek a new place to settle. They found a secluded valley, gradually building a rich civilization. But one day their city was largely destroyed by an earthquake, which left only the Palace standing. Three thousand years later this lost valley was discovered by an explorer, who vowed to restore it to its original splendour. With the aid of futuristic technology, the past was brought back to life.

In the words of architect Gerald Allison,

> the 'Legend of the Lost City' is based purely on fantasy, but colored by the heritage of Africa. As is consistent with the legend, we have tried to create a totally new architecture developed by a people completely isolated from any outside human influences. The architecture is the result of several centuries of such isolated development. The greatest influences were the weather, materials available, the skills of the craftsmen, and most importantly the flora and fauna of the region that existed during the time that the Palace was supposedly built. Some of the architectural forms were influenced by the legends and stories that the ancient ones passed on from generation to generation. These stories, both true and mythological, told of their forefather's life in northern Africa where great cities dominated by soaring, domed spires and high arched facades were common. As we developed this 'new architecture', we tried very hard to recall in a mystical manner a conglomeration of historical influences instead of a specific north African heritage. (in Hall 1995a)

But although Allison may believe his story to be original, his inspiration has an unnerving similarity with the age-old mythology of Africa as the empty continent, out of time. An early civilization, derived from the north, is destroyed by Africa's untamed forces:

'One day, the winds screamed, the sky blackened and the jungle took on a dark and menacing look. The earth beneath the beautiful city began to shake with thunderous power. A mighty force destroyed walls and hurled buildings as if they were pebbles tossed from the hands of an angry giant' (from the 'Legend of the Lost City' — in Hall 1995a). With time, the enchanted ruins are discovered — Cecil Rhodes' Great Zimbabwe as the home of the Queen of Sheba, Wilbur Smith's Opet, and Sun International's casino and hotel complex, which continues to attract well-heeled tourists from both East and West, lured by their dream of Africa.

Some contradictions, however, can be resolved. How can it be that, whatever advances are made in the field of African archaeology in its contemporary, post-colonial modes of practice, the colonial assumptions of primitivism and timelessness continue to grasp the imagination of the West, whether this imagination is gratified in high-brow culture, popular entertainment or holiday destinations?

The key, I want to suggest, lies in archaeology's epistemology. Much has been written about postprocessual archaeology, and there have been many responses to critiques of broadly post-modern readings of the past. These arguments are well known, and this is not the place to rehearse them. But what is striking is the way in which archaeology — both in Africa and other parts of the world — returns repeatedly to a comfort zone of sequences, artefacts, plant remains, faunal assemblages and other collections of objects. The 1995 Pan African meeting in Harare heard four papers on Hominid Evolution (including a presentation on one part of the human pelvis), five papers on Palaeoenvironmental Studies, twenty-nine papers on the Early, Middle and Late Stone Ages (mostly concerned with the typology of stone tools), three papers on rock art studies, twenty-one papers on aspects of early farming society, twenty-four papers on complex societies and twelve papers on Cultural Resource Management (Pwiti and Soper 1996). None of the presentations at the conference was concerned with the history of archaeological practice in Africa, or with the relationship between theory and practice. The 'scientific programme' for the meeting of the Southern African Association of Archaeologists in April 2000 identified three themes: 'Archaeology 2000', 'Archaeology in the Community' and 'Regionality in Archaeology'. But apart from one more contemplative session, the bulk of the paper titles were concerned with material from individual sites: 'The rock art of Bongani Game Reserve', a full session on forensic archaeology, 'Excavations at Blombos Cave', 'Burnt Bones from Swartkrans' (www.wits.ac.za/archaeology/conference/program.htm).

There is no reason why the West's postprocessual theories should become the paradigm for archaeology in Africa, or why African archaeology should not foster a strongly empirical tradition of research that serves to define its own intellectual identity. However, the tendency never to return from the materiality of evidence and its minutiae does have the particular consequence of stifling any tradition of reflective practice. It is as if the evidence continually 'speaks for itself', irrespective of the historical and social contexts that influenced the formulation of research problems and structured the ways in which fieldwork was conducted and artefact collections assembled. The frustration that follows from the combination of alien theory and empiricism was well expressed by Francis Musonda a decade ago, in a review of archaeology in Africa which is still pertinent today:

> Who expects me, for instance, to spend hours on end trying to digest the thoughts and ideas advanced in such publications as *Analytical Archaeology* . . . which offer no immediate solution to my country's problems? Do I need to engage in unraveling archaeological problems through application of theories that are of no immediate relevance to solving our pressing cultural, social and scientific difficulties? (Musonda 1990, 18)

This detachment of the 'archaeological present' from what Bourdieu would call habitus and field — 'generative principles of distinct and distinctive practices' (Bourdieu 1998, 8–9) — is particularly difficult for intellectual work in Africa because of the burden of colonial practices — the inevitable frames of racial distinction and colonialism that I have reviewed earlier in this paper. The wish to disregard archaeology's colonial origins in the name of a new start leaves popular discourse about Africa — the tradition of Conrad, Rider Haggard and a legion of contemporaries — unchallenged and likely to sneak back into the archaeological narrative.

Two examples illustrate the point. One of Africa's most important areas of archaeological work is the investigation of human origins, particularly in the East African rift valley. But such work depends on sponsorship and a play to popular perceptions of Africa. As Donna Haraway (1991) has shown, this in turn perpetuates classic stereotypes about Africa, timelessness, the jungle and apes: the Tarzan genre that inspired Johannesburg's *Lost City*. One of Africa's most important sites is Great Zimbabwe. But the application of structuralist theory — which sacrifices time for the sake of explanation — perpetuates the notion that Africa is in a permanent ethnographic present (Hall 1998).

Recognizing the inevitability of a connection between past and present interpretations of Africa illuminates in turn the reactions to Tom Phillips' Royal Academy exhibition. In *Africa — the Art of a Continent*, the curator was intent on demonstrating an 'African aesthetic' by allowing the objects to 'speak for themselves' (Phillips 1995). The catalogue — a massive 600 pages — presented its artefacts against bland and featureless backgrounds: white, dove-grey and black. Similarly, in the exhibition itself, the objects were displayed in darkened rooms, spot-lit: 'when you leave these galleries, gloomy beyond the call of conservation, the lingering feeling is that in 1995, as in 1895, Africa is the dark continent. . . .' (Hall, J. 1995). The essays in the catalogue, surveying the collections region-by-region, are by professional museum curators and art historians. In the gallery labelling was minimal and context understated; 'mystifyingly minimalist' (Hall, J. 1995). Overwhelmingly absent are the voices and lives of the people who made and used these things. However, this device merely served to ensure that the exhibition was a mirror for the prior assumptions of its viewers. Rather than putting Africa back into history, the Royal Academy exhibition reinforced for many the belief that Africa was timeless. By leaving out anything that showed outside influence, this idea of a continent out of time was strengthened by the perception that such timelessness was situated in a space apart.

Not surprisingly, given the extreme form of its recent history, this contradiction is being played out in a particularly marked manner in the archaeology of South Africa at the close of the millennium. Because apartheid almost exclusively restricted the profession of archaeology to those South Africans who were classified as white, knowledge of the pre-colonial past through archaeological evidence was denied to almost all black South Africans. Denied a domestic field of support, or connections with the rest of the continent, archaeologists working in South Africa built, intentionally or by default, their strongest connections with the international community. Given the increasing pressure against engagement with South Africa from the early 1980s onwards, these foreign partnerships were dominated by those who were interested in archaeological science and generalizing theories and approaches such as structuralism and logical positivism that denied or downplayed the role of the politics of the present in the interpretation of the past. The niche for white South African archaeologists in the complex ecology of apartheid was of apolitical practitioners working for a higher goal (science) in a living laboratory with abundant possibilities. This was most strongly expressed in Botswana in 1984, when the Southern African Association of Archaeologists failed to pass a resolution condemning apartheid, causing Zimbabwean and Mozambican archaeologists to withdraw from the organization, and preparing the ground for the formal academic boycott of South African archaeology the following year, with the withdrawal of invitations to what would be the first meeting of the World Archaeological Congress in Southampton in 1986 (Shepherd 2000).

Now, at the end of the millennium, South African archaeology is paying a high price for this history, for the unavoidable consequences of apartheid, and for decisions such as that taken in Botswana in 1984. In the second democratic government, funding is tight. There are many competing priorities, of which education is one. But archaeology has little popular base. There is a call to study the past and to establish the history of the continent as the baseline for an 'African renaissance'. But, because the reality of archaeology has made so little impact in the experience of those in the new government (whether elected or appointed, or at the national or local level), this sense of the importance of the past does not translate into a priority for the discipline of archaeology. Many archaeologists in South Africa, for years opposed to the racial politics of apartheid, had expected 1994 to usher in their time. Instead, they have watched as funding for museums has diminished and as other priorities have dominated public debate about heritage.

The third millennium

My argument has been that trends in the practice of archaeology in Africa over more than a century have shown that present practices carry with them the burdens of their pasts. Following from this, the key to resolving the contradiction of an Africa both in and out of time lies in reflective practice — a recognition of the relationship between past and present, and the use of a critical understanding of the past to inform practice in the future. This seems to me the only way to achieve both a genuinely post-colonial archaeology and also a broad-based support for the work that archaeologists do in public discourse, both within Africa and in the rest of the world.

Logically, then, this becomes a key issue for the future: how can insight into the burden of the present help with anticipating, and to some extent directing, an archaeology of the future?

One key determinant of the course of archaeology in the twentieth century was the transition from colonial territory to nation state — the roll-out of independence from colonial and minority rule that began in the late 1950s and which reached its logical conclusion in 1994, with South Africa's first democratically-elected government. The creation of African nation states in mid-century formed an African archaeology responsive to issues of national history and identity, while the continuation of minority domination in the South has left South African archaeology cut off from a broad, popular base.

The political direction, and economic capacity, of the nation state will continue to be central to the framing of the public culture of which archaeology is a part. As in other continents, museums and universities are key nodal points in the ongoing development of research. Throughout Africa, such institutions remain critically dependent on government — local, regional or national, for financial support and viability. Consequently, the health of such institutions is critically linked to the ability of government to accumulate and direct resources for civic expenditure. More specifically, museums and universities are the repositories of key collections of material, reflecting archaeology's strange characteristic of transforming its evidence base as it explores it. Increasingly — as in the rest of the world — research on excavated collections will become as important as new fieldwork. As for fieldwork, this will be critically affected by the availability of infrastructure and conditions in which fieldwork is possible. At the time of writing, large parts of west-central and north-east Africa are sites of open conflict and warfare, rendering fieldwork difficult or impossible.

The crisis of the nation state in Africa is an aspect of global changes that, to a large extent, serve to define the new millennium. These changes have been drawn together by Manuel Castells:

> A new world is taking shape at this end of millennium. It originated in the historical coincidence, around the late 1960s and mid-1970s, of three independent processes:

the information technology revolution; the economic crisis of both capitalism and statism, and their subsequent restructuring; and the blooming of cultural social movements, such as libertarianism, human rights, feminism, and environmentalism. The interaction between these processes, and the reactions they triggered, brought into being a new dominant social structure, the network society; a new economy, the informational/global economy; and a new culture, the culture of real virtuality. The logic embedded in this economy, this society, and this culture underlies social action and institutions throughout an interdependent world. (Castells 1998, 336)

Castells' argument is nuanced. On the one hand, the effectivity of the nation state is declining as it loses its traditional controls and revenues — a widely recognized consequence of globalization. But, on the other hand, Castells concludes that the nation-state is far from dead. This is because a response to declining financial control is to assert more strongly the political claims of nationalism. What does this mean for public culture — and archaeology — in Africa? Fifty years after the formation of the first postcolonial nation states in Africa, the consequences of arbitrary borders, with their disrespect of earlier political structures, are far from worked through, and will become more contentious as the economic authority of Africa's mid-nineteenth-century nations declines. However much this results in Castells' inverse effect — the assertion of nationalism because of its declining saliency — it seems inherently improbable that nation states in Africa will be in a position to increase support for archaeology through museums and universities, or to spend more on the management and development of archaeological collections.

But while the ability of 'developing economies' to support public culture from public revenues seems set to decline, a second aspect of Castells' 'network society' is likely to increase in importance: local identity. The stress on locale is the answer to many to the dis-identification that follows from globalization. Whether manifested in nationalism or in new forms of ethnicity, the politics of local identity are a rising tide that is matching the trend to cosmopolitan, intercontinental communities (Appadurai 1996). Many local identity issues are populist and anti-intellectual. But many of them involve a mobilized awareness of history and an enthusiasm for its material manifestations — the artefacts that are the very stuff of archaeology (Hall 2000). Whether Hindu fundamentalism, ethnic mobilization in West Africa, Serbian identification with the monastic art of the medieval orthodox church or Celtic nationalism in Britain, the 'theatre of memory' (to use Raphael Samuel's phrase) is playing to packed houses (Samuel 1994).

The growing saliency of identity interests will cast an increasingly difficult role for archaeology. Very often, the attraction of historical — and archaeologically enhanced — identity lies in the projection of the past onto the future to mask the conditions of the present. Archaeologists will need to steer between, on the one hand, meeting a demand for information about the past — information which will probably be invented if it is not given — and, on the other hand, developing a critique of populist interpretations.

This is already placing archaeologists in difficult positions. For example, archaeology was used to legitimate the concept of a Greater Serbia that laid part of the intellectual foundations for atrocities in Bosnia and Kosovo and a visit to a museum in Croatia is vivid testimony to the way in which archaeological research is used to validate a Croat ethnic identity that is rooted deep in the past. Neo-nazi, millennial hate sites cite archaeological work (such as Colin Renfrew's overview of European prehistory) to claim Aryan superiority (Hall 2000). Some claims to a pre-colonial and 'pre-Bantu' identity in the southernmost parts of Africa claim a Khoikhoi culture that is 'in the blood'. Which archaeologist can contribute to an emerging popular culture that espouses the genetic transfer of culture, and is the archaeologist faced with this request not obliged to point out that this was the basis for the theory of racial domination that was apartheid?

For the archaeologist, then, as for practitioners of other historical and cultural disciplines, the development of populist local identity issues means that the practitioner must occupy the difficult space of the 'public intellectual', working to maintain Habermas' 'public sphere' as a place of critique and the application of logic and evidence (Habermas 1989). This will not be the comfortable, authoritative space of the academic expert — the museum scientist or university lecturer of a passing age whose opinion demands respect and silences opposition through intellectual authority. In the new knowledge economies of today and the future, everyone is potentially an 'organic intellectual', as Edward Said (1994) has observed. Rather than the laboratory or the podium, the archaeologist of the future will need to be familiar with the school, community hall and library. Rather than persuasion by authority, the archaeologist of the future will depend on persuasion by critique. Fieldwork and primary research will depend on engagement with local communities. There are good precedents for such practices in African archaeology: village archaeology in post-independence Mozambique, local community museums in West Africa. The latecomer is South African archaeology, fatally detached from a local community base, and with a lot of catching up to do.

This is not to say that such shifts will be easy. It is easier to idealize past paragons than it is to replicate them, and this will particularly be the case in the world that Castells maps out, in which it will be difficult or impossible to escape the forces of the market, and in which the distinction will become ever greater between those within the golden web of the information society and those who are in its new peripheral zones. The challenges to social justice that will follow in this 'postsocialist' age have been mapped out by Nancy Fraser, who argues for what she terms 'subaltern counterpublics' — 'arrangements that accommodate contestation among a plurality of competing publics', and which thereby avoid the bracketing of cultural and economic differences which is the condition for a single, liberal, public sphere (Fraser 1997, 81). Whether in the community hall, classroom or cyberspace, tomorrow's public intellectuals will face huge challenges.

Intersecting with archaeology at this local level, but playing to a very different audience, is the global marketplace of cosmopolitan heritage. This trend is fuelled by key aspects of globalization: the widening gap between the rich and the poor, and the vora-cious market for new experiences — world tourism and the intelligent traveller. Here, there is a direct connection with the long heritage of Africa as the exotic continent. Underpinned by UNESCO and other international agencies, there is a rapidly expand-ing market for heritage destinations, whether the medieval city of Fez, Great Zimbabwe or the rock art of southern Africa. This opens a second set of opportunities for archae-ology in Africa — Cultural Resource Management. Whether funded by international agencies or by governments responding to the possibilities in their cultural heritage, archaeologists are increasingly finding opportunities in commercial or development-related projects. This trend brings with it a set of well known problems that include potential conflicts of interest and the difficulty of research beyond mitigation.

What are the common features of these future directions? Whether public intellec-tuals working with local communities, or cultural resource managers working for inter-national agencies or commercial interests, archaeologists of the new millennium will need to be effective communicators and sensitive to the politics of their points of engagement. And here lies the hope of avoiding the contradictions of the past. There is little future prospect for the sort of practice that isolated archaeologists from their publics in the name of science, allowing the colonial myths of earlier centuries to become the media images of popular literature and media. Whether this brings the fur-ther marginalization and decline of Africa that is Manuel Castells' gloomy prediction or Thabo Mbeki's 'African Renaissance' is in the hands of those who will make the history of the future.

References

ACHEBE, C. 1988: *Hopes and Impediments: Selected Essays 1965–1987* (London).

ANDAH, B., ADANDE, A., FOLORUNSO, C.A. and BAGODO, O. 1994: African archaeology in the 21st century; Or, Africa, cultural puppet on a string? *West African J. Archaeol.* 24, 152–9.

APPADURAI, A. 1996: *Modernity at Large: Cultural Dimensions of Globalization* (Minneapolis).

APPIAH, K.A. 1995: Why Africa? Why Art? In Phillips, T. (ed.), *Africa. The Art of a Continent* (London, Royal Academy of Arts), 21–6.

ASOMBANG, R.N. 1990: Museums and African identity: the museum in Cameroon — a critique. *West African J. Archaeol.* 20, 188–98.

BENT, J.T. 1895, 1969: *The Ruined Cities of Mashonaland* (Bulawayo, Books of Rhodesia).

BERNAL, M. 1991: *Black Athena. The Afroasiatic Roots of Classical Civilization. Volume One. The Fabrication of Ancient Greece, 1785–1985* (London).

BINYON, L. 1952: *Dante's Inferno* (London).

BLIXEN, K. 1954: *Out of Africa* (London).

BOURDIEU, P. 1998: *Practical Reason* (Cambridge).

BOXER, C.R. 1957: *The Dutch in Brazil, 1624–1654* (Oxford).

BURKE, E.E. (ed.) 1969: *The Journals of Carl Mauch, 1869–1872* (Salisbury, National Archives of Rhodesia).

CARTER, P. 1988: *The Road to Botany Bay. An Exploration of Landscape and History* (Chicago).

CASTELLS, M. 1998: *The Information Age: Economy, Society and Culture. Volume 3. End of Millennium* (Oxford).

CATON-THOMPSON, G. 1931: *The Zimbabwe Culture. Ruins and Reactions* (Oxford).

CLARK, J.D. 1967: *Atlas of African Prehistory* (Chicago).

CRONE, G.R. 1968: *Maps and their Makers* (London).

DE BARROS, P. 1990: Changing paradigms, goals and methods in the archaeology of francophone West Africa. In Robertshaw, P. (ed.), *A History of African Archaeology* (London), 155–72.

DEACON, J. 1990: Weaving the fabric of Stone Age research in Southern Africa. In Robertshaw, P. (ed.), *A History of African Archaeology* (London), 39–58.

DIOP, C.A. 1979: *Nations Negres et Culture* (Paris).

DOWDEN, R. 1995: Africa and its art may be a PC fiction created by the West's guilty conscience. *The Spectator* (London).

DUNCAN, D.D. 1968: *Picasso's Picassos* (New York).

FAGAN, B.M. 1977: *The Rape of the Nile. Tomb Robbers, Tourists and Archaeologists in Egypt* (London).

FANON, F. 1963: *The Wretched of the Earth* (New York).

FRASER, N. 1997: *Justice Interruptus: Critical Reflections on the 'Postsocialist' Condition* (New York).

GARLAKE, P. 1973: *Great Zimbabwe* (London).

GIKANDI, S. 1996: *Maps of Englishness. Writing Identity in the Culture of Colonialism* (New York).

GREENBLATT, S. 1991: *Marvelous Possessions. The Wonder of the New World* (Oxford).

HABERMAS, J. 1989: The public sphere: an encyclopedia article. In Brunner, S. and Kellner, D. (eds.), *Critical Theory and Society* (New York).

HALL, J. 1995: It's hard not to see African art through modernist European eyes. *Weekly Mail and Guardian* (Johannesburg).

HALL, M. 1984: The burden of tribalism: the social context of southern African Iron Age studies. *American Antiquity* 49(3), 455–67.

HALL, M. 1988: Archaeology under apartheid. *Archaeology* 41(6), 62–4.

HALL, M. 1990: 'Hidden history'. Iron Age archaeology in Southern Africa. In Robertshaw, P. (ed.), *A History of African Archaeology* (London), 59–77.

HALL, M. 1995a: The Legend of the Lost City; or, The Man with Golden Balls. *J. Southern African Stud.* 21(2), 179–99.

HALL, M. 1995b: Great Zimbabwe and the Lost City: the cultural colonization of the South African Past. In Ucko, P.J. (ed.), *Theory in Archaeology: a World Perspective* (London), 28–45.

HALL, M. 1996: *Archaeology Africa* (Cape Town).

HALL, M. 1998: Snakes and crocodiles: power and symbolism in ancient Zimbabwe (review feature). *South African Archaeol. Bull.* 52, 129–32.

HALL, M. 2000: *Archaeology and the Modern World: Colonial Transcripts in South Africa and the Chesapeake* (London).

HARAWAY, D. 1991: *Simians, Cyborgs, and Women: the Reinvention of Nature* (London).

HOLL, A. 1990: West African archaeology: colonialism and nationalism. In Robertshaw, P. (ed.), *A History of African Archaeology* (London), 296–308.

JENKINS, S. 1995: Out of Africa and out of context. Why is the Royal Academy using artefacts of African life to adorn walls that have hung Rembrandt and Titian? *The Times* (London).

JUNG, C.C. 1973: *Memories, Dreams, Reflections* (London).

KAREGA-MUNENE 1996: The future of archaeology in Kenya. *African Archaeol. Rev.* 13(2), 87–90.

KUSIMBA, C.M. 1996: Archaeology in African museums. *African Archaeol. Rev.* 13(3), 165–70.

MOSELEY, C.W.R.D. (ed.) 1983: *The Travels of Sir John Mandeville* (Harmondsworth).

MUDIMBE, V.Y. 1988: *The Invention of Africa* (Bloomington).

MUDIMBE, V.Y. 1994: *The Idea of Africa* (Bloomington).

MUSONDA, F. 1990: African archaeology: looking forward. *African Archaeol. Rev.* 8(1), 3–22.

NZEWUNWA, N. 1980: *The Niger Delta. Aspects of its Prehistoric Economy and Culture* (Oxford, BAR).

PHILLIPS, T. 1995: Introduction. In Phillips, T. (ed.), *Africa. The Art of a Continent* (London, Royal Academy of Arts), 11–20.

PWITI, G. and SOPER, R. (eds.) 1996: *Aspects of African Archaeology: Papers from the 10th Congress of the Pan African Association for Prehistory and Related Studies* (Harare).

RANDALL-MACIVER, D. 1906: *Medieval Rhodesia* (London).

ROBERTSHAW, P. 1990: The development of archaeology in East Africa. In Robertshaw, P. (ed.), *A History of African Archaeology* (London), 78–94.

SAID, E. 1985: *Orientalism* (Harmondsworth).

SAID, E. 1994: *Representations of the Intellectual* (New York).

SAMUEL, R. 1994: *Theatres of Memory* (London).

SAYERS, D.L. (ed.) 1949: *The Comedy of Dante Alighieri the Florentine. Cantica 1. Hell* (Harmondsworth).

SHAW, T., SINCLAIR, P., ANDAH, B. and OKPOKO, A. (eds.) 1993: *The Archaeology of Africa. Food, Metals and Towns* (London).

SHEPHERD, N. 2000: World archaeology in the white south. *Public Archaeol.* 2.

SINCLAIR, P., MORAIS, J.M.F., ADAMOWICZ, L. and DUARTE, R.T. 1993: A perspective on archaeological research in Mozambique. In Shaw, T., Sinclair, P., Andah, B. and Okpoko, A. (eds.) 1993, 409–31.

SMITH, W. 1972: *Sunbird* (London).

STOW, G.W. 1905: *The Native Races of South Africa* (London).

TOBIAS, P.V. 1978: The VIIth Pan-African Congress on Prehistory, Nairobi, 1977 and the opening of the Louis Leakey Institute. *South African Archaeol. Bull.* 33(127), 5–11.

VAN WYK SMITH, M. 1988: *Shades of Adamastor. Africa and the Portuguese Connection* (Grahamstown, Institute for the Study of English in Africa).

WANDIBBA, S. 1990: Archaeology and education in Kenya. In Stone, P. and Mackenzie, R. (eds.), *The Excluded Past. Archaeology in Education* (London), 43–9.

WEST, C. 1995: Preface. In Phillips, T. (ed.), *Africa. The Art of a Continent* (London, Royal Academy of Arts), 9–10.

Marriages of true minds: Archaeology with texts

MARTIN CARVER

Introduction — a visit to the Picts

The sites of early historic Scotland are dark brown and sandy buff, the colours of camouflage. Its buildings are notoriously elusive — wandering stones and walls of irregular shape, difficult to plan and date. By contrast the art, as exemplified in stone carvings such as Hilton of Cadboll, or an illuminated manuscript such as the Book of Kells (both of the late eighth century AD) is brilliant, geometric, decisive, intricate, full of straight lines, perfect circles, elegant scrolls and portraits of aristocrats out hunting on sprightly horses, or clerics, hypnotic with conviction. More hypnotic still are the stories which have survived in early texts, however suspect their authors. The briefest encounter with Adomnan's *Life of St Columba* or Bede's *History of the English Church* is sufficient to convince the modern reader that these writers have a preferred past, skewed in favour of their missions, but their authority nevertheless remains undiminished. The conversion of the Picts is one of the major topics recounted, but in such a way as to leave the modern interpreter plenty to debate. Was it the shadowy Briton Ninian operating from his White House at Whithorn in the fifth century? Or the adventurous Irishman Columba, leaving Iona in 565, enduring the first recorded encounter with the Loch Ness Monster and bearding Brude son of Mailchu at his elusive headquarters near Inverness? Or was it the cunning of Bede's own English Northumbria, which convinced the Pictish King Nechtan in 710 to buy into the English model of Roman Christianity? Each of these missions could have succeeded partially and intermittently, and modern Scots have their own preferences too, seeing in one or the other model the more beneficial modern alliance. Or it may be that the Picts (who are no longer players on the UK stage) treated each of these ideological initiatives with equal circumspection, aware that their good land had something to do with the rough wooing of the neighbours (Carver 1998a).

This is a study area that contains much of the agenda for this paper. *Our* preferred past (and present), expressed in learned disquisitions, is largely drawn from *their* preferred past (and present), expressed in surviving texts, pictures, artefacts and other forms of material culture. The differences between these media are often stressed and some believe they merit independently managed disciplines of their own; but for me differences between media are less significant than the differences in the purposes of expression within them. Just as mice hide in the ornament of Kells, and real bridles furnish the heads of Hilton's horse, so the pages of Bede and Adomnan are not unrelieved rhetoric: detached comment keeps breaking in. Text and artefact are equally artful at conveying their meaning. Pictures on stone slabs were texts in the sense that the observer could read their messages, even if we cannot, and the references and metaphors used in building churches and forts were often explicit: 'Send us architects to build stone churches in the manner of the Romans,' wrote Nechtan king of Picts to Ceolfrid, Abbot of Jarrow, 'so our people can follow the customs of the Roman church — notwithstanding our remoteness from the Roman people and from Roman speech' (paraphrased from Bede V.21).[1] Ceolfrid in turn was concerned to ensure recognition by the Pope and made three enormous Bibles, each weighing about 90 lb (and requiring the skins of 515 calves), and in 715/6 set off with one of them (the *Codex Amiatinus*) to Rome (Bruce-Mitford 1969). These strategies of alignment involved the use of material culture as text and text as material culture.

Once established in the psyche, texts and sculptures became 'monumental' in that they continued to have the potential to influence the politics of every successive generation: they went on talking. Books offer history but they also make it. So Bede's *History*, and for that matter the Gospels are as important for what they did as what they said. Monuments also have an afterlife, in which they challenge and influence the politics of subsequent generations that see them. Cathedrals, standing crosses, burial mounds, stone circles, the pyramids have all set agendas (cf. Bradley 1987). Some may be impatient with the primacy of great art, and wish it were not so. With such glamorous partners strutting their stuff, archaeologists can feel overshadowed and react by demanding their own audience; irritated by the loud confident voices and chinking glasses, they slink into the next room with a few like-minded folk to swap potsherds and talk about social structure. But the history that relies mainly on arguments from books or monuments is the history taught to the people who never become historians. The discoveries made by archaeologists, no matter how remote from the subjects of the written record, are inevitably drawn into the forum of texts, not least by the public for whom texts underpin their education. All of us, maybe, are accustomed to vocalize every thought, but only a few of us communicate our dilemmas and delights by carving logs or making pots. Dependence on words, said or written, is deeply rooted (Kemp 1984; Hills 1997). Empty ditches, straggling stones, plant macrofossils and enigmatic scraps cannot but feel the strong magnetism of the well-dated Book, pulling the crude radiocarbon

---

[1] Bede, *A History of the English Church and People* (trans. L Sherley-Price) (Harmondsworth, 1968).

determinations into their web. In the study of the past there is a varying imbalance of academic power, from continent to continent and millennium to millennium, caused by an imbalance in the distribution of the written word. Scientists command the earliest times; in non-Classical central Europe, prehistorians rule the roost, and in twentieth-century Europe, historians set the agenda. The hybrids, the medieval, post-medieval and historical archaeologists are lords of smaller kingdoms, wracked by anxieties of alignment.

Since material culture and text are equally powerful forms of expression, such anxieties are not, in my view, endemic in the study of peoples who have left us both. They have been induced by the professionalization of academic life, the formation of economically supported cartels, which are likely to be dismantled in the course of the present century, thanks to revolutions in both attitudes and electronics. The most inhibiting of these cartels is that dedicated to professional theory-making in archaeology, which with its global aspiration has obscured much good thinking at a local, relativist level, especially in historical periods. If historical archaeologists suffer crises of identity, this is largely because their loyalty to material culture is being continually put to the test by theorists. There is of course no general theory of material culture, any more than there is of textual analysis. Archaeologists worry about whether their study is to be text-guided, text-aided or text-hindered. But I would like to suggest that the difference between a text and an artefact is a less important difference than that between the expressive and inert, the conscious and the unconscious, the emic and the etic, which can be found in each medium. The active and the passive voice are detectable in text, art and material culture of all kinds; these and the grades of expressive or rhetorical purpose between them provide the real contrast, whether in a book, a sculpture or a rampart. The study of texts, art and archaeology already has much common theory, a common purpose, common approaches and a shared agenda. The problem for some Atlantic countries is that due to incidents of temporary power in university administrations, those that study the same past of the same people do not necessarily work together. This is a situation that can be remedied, even though it will mean challenging the present edifice of academic competition and assessment.

Discussions about texts and archaeology could range over a number of different fields: *theory* which asks us whether we understand text and material culture to be subject to the same or different theoretical frameworks — or to be seen as living freely together as cohabiting relativists. *Programming*, which asks us to decide whether the type of archaeology which studies historic periods should develop its own special methodology or just its own special agenda. And *organization*: whether, consequent on these decisions, the past in historic periods should be studied in single or multi-discipline departments or within the kind of flexible relationship hinted at in my title.

Theory: Text is archaeology is text

Kate Atkinson in *Behind the Scenes at the Museum* (1995) uses artefacts to provide the prompt for her flashbacks; so the rabbit's foot pendant worn by Ruby's mother while giving birth had also got her father through the First World War, as revealed in a 'foot-note'. Objects and monuments that carry memories or imply power and plot are famil-iar to writers of novels, and the idea that artefacts carry texts, have dialogues with texts and indeed are texts has been implicit in much writing since Jonathon Swift called his teapot Percy, or Hrothgar named his hall Heorot. Before 1967 James Deetz had pointed to a relationship between words and things: 'The structural units and rules which govern the form of a language have an interesting parallel in the structural rules which govern material objects. In fact words and artifacts have a lot more in common than it would seem at first glance' (1967, 86), and went on to mention that language has a vocabulary, which is easily transferred from one culture to another, and a grammar which is not. Material culture studies should attempt to distinguish and classify an equivalence of vocabulary and grammar, the distinction between signs and the mean-ing of signs. This has become a hot issue in archaeology, led along somewhat meander-ing and thorny tracks by critical philosophy. The 'reading' of material culture as though it were a text has been widely and profitably explored (Hodder 1986), as has its con-verse, the idea that texts should be investigated using a kind of 'archaeology'. In his *Montaillou* (1978) Emmanuel Le Roy Ladurie used the term 'archaeology' to mean a kind of dispassionate analysis applied to the written record in order to reveal social habits and customs embedded in replies to questions put by the Inquisition. Part 1 of this description of a Cathar village was an 'ecology' of the district, which includes both the environment and the normative economy of the village. In part 2, the 'archaeology' of Montaillou, the evidence deposed by individuals is used to infer behaviour, gestures, sexual habits and concepts of space and time; all things now on the archaeological agenda, if they were not then.

It is taken for granted that texts are not to be taken (only) literally, but must them-selves be interrogated for the interesting secrets they conceal. 'Ever since a discipline such as history has existed, documents have been used, questioned and have given rise to questions; scholars have asked not only what these documents meant, but also whether they were telling the truth, and by what right they could claim to be doing so, whether they were sincere or deliberately misleading, well-informed or ignorant, authentic or tampered with' (Foucault 1972, 6); and to this description of the historian's mission one could add 'and why?', since within the motive for fraud lies a clue to the agenda of the writer's community. Michel Foucault proposed that all ideas were embedded in deep layers of fossilized intelligence, layers more numerous and more complex than Braudel's streams of geographical, social and individual time (1972, pref-ace), but similarly varying from the deep and slow to the lively and shallow. In this way he attempted to eliminate the primacy of the creative individual and with it the authority of a text's author. Individuals' own sad attempts to access these layers and claim the results as discovery (their 'discourse') were contrasted with Foucault's own project of investigation which he termed, confusingly, 'archaeological'. His use of the metaphorical term calls up quite a merry vision of archaeology, one which dissects, rummages, burrows and bulldozes, sometimes taking much of the structure of human thinking with it and tipping it on the spoil heap. On this model, text and material culture are interchangeable metaphors for each other: 'The domain of things said is called the archive; the role of archaeology is to analyze that archive' . . . 'In our time history is that which transforms documents into monuments . . . history aspires to the condition of archaeology, to the intrinsic description of the monument' (Foucault 1972, 7). Archaeology is seemingly being praised for its ability to depersonalize and generalize, which indeed became its mission for the next 20 years. 'To speak is to do something — something other than express what one thinks . . .' (1972, 209). So, people draw on deep roots when they talk and are incapable of saying 'immediately and directly what they think, believe or imagine'. If true of people in the past as well as the present this sets a stern agenda for writers of history; but note that it applies equally to both text and material culture. The implication is not only that the past cannot be accessed because it is too deeply camouflaged by ulterior motives, but that we cannot evoke it either, because our ability to be creative, innovative, imaginative, is actually an illusion. However it appears that we can always detect the presumption of creativity in someone else. This encourages us to abandon creativity for the sterile arenas of critique and irony (Shanks and Tilley 1987, 213). If, on the other hand, material culture and its investigation turn out to be subject to exactly the same uncertainties as text, there is no independent basis for a critique there. But it is possible that, like text and material culture, creativity and critique have been artificially opposed. Critique, like everything else, will turn out to depend on the imagination, which must therefore not be disqualified.

In 'The writing lesson' described in *Tristes Tropiques*, Lévi-Strauss observed how the Nambikwara mimicked writing in the form of wavy horizontal lines, which a chief then pretended to read out with authority, listing gifts that he expected to receive (Lévi-Strauss 1955, 339–40). The text was thus transformed into an artefact, in this case a weapon of dominance supplied by an anthropologist who perceived himself guilty of placing it in hitherto innocent hands. Jacques Derrida used this incident as a primary exercise in deconstruction (Johnson, C. 1997), showing that the Nambikwara had plenty of guile and dominance routines of their own, and that Lévi-Strauss, in spite of himself, wrote as a sentimental westerner rather than as a detached scientist. Administering the *coup de grâce* to the dream of the noble savage, Derrida asserted that the structures of violence have always been with us, but could be very variously expressed. This variety was confusingly defined by extending the meanings for the word 'writing', to include practically every form of self-expression, including tattooing and marks on pots, in general what archaeologists would regard as material culture. The expression, and the observer's or listener's impression of it, are multi-layered and must be dug for in the manner of Foucault's 'archaeology'. Using a better modern metaphor, Christopher Johnson says 'Derrida's model of writing . . . is in fact very close to the idea of DNA as both a conservative and a metamorphic code' (1997, 46). This metaphor can be applied to material culture too (see below). Cybernetics also provided Derrida with a metaphor, since it implies that the method by which information is transferred, and its point of arrival, are more influential than the information itself. In the age of the database, scholars have continued with this project, hoping to escape the perceived tyranny of narrative and self-interest by pre-deconstructing their findings into fragments and storing them in a dendritic form. The pre-defined information 'quanta' can now be accessed by users of the database, going in and out anywhere they please, led by keywords, creating their own ephemeral narratives. The same system now offers total access through the Internet. Thus the technology is now available to deliver the goal of the postmodernist line of thinking: a text has become something created by its reader not by its author.

'Archaeology' was used here as a metaphor for a mode of investigation. In the image applied, archaeology is adept at breaking through the polished crust and winkling out the buried assumptions beneath. When the target is the edicts of authority, academic or political, the result is a satisfying spoiling operation, diminishing the power of any proposal, even those which are ethically beneficial. The satisfaction lies in the application of the Mandy Rice-Davies principle: asked in the witness box why her married lover had denied everything, she commented, 'Well, he would, wouldn't he?' But the danger lies in the ennui which follows: having covered the play-room floor with the constituent parts of a new toy, it no longer works, even if we know now *how* it worked (when it did work).

To define what it is that we are attempting to dig out of the past, in a way that is helpful to archaeology working with texts, Barbara Little promotes the concept of 'image' as the element of expression that text, picture and material share (1992b, 219). 'Images of all kinds form the basis for Bourdieu's habitus [1984] and Giddens' structuration [1979], each of which has been adopted to structure archaeological interpretation' (ibid.). Within the repertoire of images which are 'embedded in social and political contexts and, in turn, influence those contexts', text and artefact can be dressed up in each other's clothes but their differences offer greater potential than pretending they are the same: 'Text can be interpreted as material culture, but its primary force comes from acting in its own terms, as text. Similarly, material culture may be interpreted as text, but its primary force is understood when it is interpreted in its own terms, not as text but as material culture' (ibid., 220). 'The use of text as a metaphor for material institutions and behaviours may be useful in some of the ways analogy tends to be useful, not as an end in itself, but as a way to begin' (ibid., 217).

Christopher Tilley, while agreeing that there are important differences to be conserved between text and material culture, invites us to institutionalize the word
'metaphor' as a description of what they both do (1999). The composition of a material
object is generated from numerous invisible sources or seeds (I suppose this is what
'polysemy' must mean), and then accrues additional layers of metaphorical meaning
'like the rings of an onion' (1999, 266). An observer thereafter can observe 'mixed
metaphors' which are ripe for deconstruction (1999, 266, 271). Better analogies than
'mixed metaphors' or the onion might be DNA, which expresses both the deep sourcing before birth and the life of influence and exploitation experienced thereafter, which
might apply to people, animals, objects and indeed everything in some measure. The
use of metaphor in describing a particular imagined past has had a long and useful
career, as Tilley implies: 'The abiding significance of the work of Lévi-Strauss, for the
study of material culture, is not the trappings of a structuralist mode of analysis isolating behavioural oppositions, but that he is a master of metaphor'; he is thus able to
assemble a comprehensible vision of a community from the most refractory materials
(1999, 272). It is tacitly acknowledged here that, *pace* Foucault and Derrida, creativity
does after all exist, and does have a role in making a believable image of the past, independent of, or at the least detached from, the creator's personal agenda.

So far so good; much theorizing is a game of metaphors, and there is much stimulation to be had from it. Provided that imagination is allowed its share of respect, many
recent archaeological ideas are meat and drink to those that work in multi-disciplinary
groups, since all can share the pleasant burden of dealing with the testimony of shifty,
guileful, ingenious, but dead human beings. The problem for historical archaeologists,
on both sides of the Atlantic, is when archaeology attempts to construct and impose its
own framework, and insists that it govern archaeological inquiry. Ian Hodder, a senior
champion of archaeological theory, appears to believe that a theoretical framework, special to archaeology, is needed to build archaeology a platform with a global vista. 'The
archaeologist is enabled to act in the world from a position of disciplinary authority . . .
Social praxis depends on the construction of a coherent theoretical framework' (Hodder 1992, 170). But such an idea is unlikely to cut much ice in the twenty-first century,
either with non-westerners wishing to develop their own world view, or, as a matter of
fact, with western students of historic periods. In the first place social praxis (here presumably meaning the acceptance of archaeology by the rest of society) does not in the
least depend on the construction of a coherent theoretical framework, any more than it
does in any other art or science. It depends rather on negotiation, in which archaeologists seek not to rule each other, or impress other academics, but to bargain with other
citizens and users of land for an outlet for their ideas in the public forum. The archaeological weapon in the value competition is certainly not a 'theoretical framework' which
would be rightly greeted with suspicion or boredom, but a new vision of the past based
on new discoveries. Naturally such a vision should be critically aware, and the first

message of the critically aware is that a 'coherent theoretical framework' is an impossibly ambitious aspiration.

In reaching for a coherent framework, Hodder draws an old distinction: 'On the one hand an objective, natural science position must be limited to the non-arbitrary and universal and must therefore disregard so much of what makes us human. On the other hand a commitment to culture creativity, meaning and action apparently loses claims to scientific rigour so that all we can do is tell "stories" and become fiction writers' (ibid., 169). This is an artificial distinction, since all the great scientific advances have depended on imagination, and good fiction must be accurately observed to be believable. Hodder also dismisses relativism, meaning 'the view that ideas and values do not have a universal validity, but are valid only in relation to particular social and historical conditions' (or otherwise, their context). This is puzzling since elsewhere (e.g. 1986) he fruitfully develops the idea of context as defining and controlling interpretation, as most text-users would agree. But then a startling sub-text is revealed: 'A total commitment to relativism cannot be sustained by a discipline which seeks to retain a position of authority from which to speak and wield power' (1992, 170). If archaeology claimed to have 'ideas and values that have a universal validity' it would be the only subject on earth that did, except possibly theology. Not even Niels Bohr or Einstein would claim that: quantum theory only works at sub-atomic level and relativity only works near the speed of light.

The reason some of us working in the historic periods find this line of argument inhibiting is that it is too determinant. Archaeological theories are helpful in interpretation, and it is a pleasure to learn from them, as we have from Ian Hodder. But our colleagues in history, art history, literature have many parallel versions of the same body of theory. The only special 'framework' that they are likely to respect is that developed for field archaeology, and this in turn is the only framework that is fully transferable throughout archaeology (Carver 1999a). Somewhat reassuringly, the reality seems to be that Hodder does not really believe in a general theoretical framework either. 'In both archaeological and non-archaeological studies it is particularist studies combined with a concern for the "inside" of events which have led to the most profound and far-reaching statements on the relationships between meaning and practice' (1986, 81). And he praises Duby and LeGoff, historians much admired and emulated by medieval archaeologists: 'rather than getting bogged down in epistemological issues, these scholars were getting on with using historical data, to contribute to general debate' (1992, 173). Yes indeed, and this is what classical, medieval and historical archaeologists have been largely doing. The study of literate peoples is by no means an 'easier' approach (Hodder 1986, 141), but a constant struggle with data of enormous dynamism and complexity (Little 1994, 49). For this reason, it is probably true to say that most archaeologists who use text have been reluctant to elevate their interpretational ideas to the level of general theory, but constantly refresh them through discussions with disciplines other than their own. When processual thinking was at its most active, analytical pattern-seeking was broadly applied to texts as well as material culture (*Archaeological Review from Cambridge* 3(2) (1984)), and the same warnings were voiced about treating the data as a *tabula rasa*. Looking at the distribution of the suffix 'ki' in place-names to imply a network of fortresses, Gina Barnes noted that the meaning of the symbol varied through time; 'pattern has been indicated but it is pattern at the basic transcriptional and textual levels.' 'The difficult part is resisting jumping to conclusions or making facile equations which disregard the complicated materials bequeathed to us' (1984, 46). This is the danger in attempting to create a single theoretical or methodological umbrella for archaeologists of the historic period to shelter beneath; you can be struck insensible by the lightning of dogma.

To summarize: text and material culture are both forms of self-expression and both are susceptible to analysis through pattern-seeking and both require rigorous source criticism to ensure the pattern has not been created by later processes of manipulation or survival. Both kinds of media contain the products of human agency, so both can be interpreted by comparison and analogy. But interpretation in both cases depends most on the creative imagination, and such a thing does exist. There ought to be much gained by studying all kinds of sources together, as equal partners. But in our society, with our education, the message from texts is more easily absorbed and less ambiguous than that presented by symbols, sites, sequences, objects or architecture. So texts, where they exist, still have primacy as evidence for the past, and the urge to develop specialist methodologies or special roles for the historic periods is coming from archaeologists rather than historians. Now we must confront this trend. Is there a bespoke discipline for the archaeologist-with-texts? If so, does it comprise a community united by a common methodology, or by a common agenda?

Programmes: What is historical archaeology? And what should it be?

Curiously, although historical archaeologists are not in the least theoretically naive, the debate about how archaeology and texts should relate has seemingly continued in a separate room to the one about whether archaeology is itself analogous to a text. This has led to an exhaustive attempt to reconcile two disciplines which are seen as different because they deal predominately with different media, texts on the one hand and material culture on the other. This is not actually the root of the differences, but the debate has continued all the same, because those taking part want to be seen as belonging to a discipline in its own right. One target of the debate has been to persuade the community that historical archaeology is global in application and united by a methodology; like 'underwater archaeology' adherents see themselves as mainstream archaeologists united by the difficulty of applying procedures of archaeological inquiry within a challenging medium. Another has been to promote the study, through material culture, of the world since it became a capitalist property over the last few centuries. Charles Orser explains: 'Today's archaeologists use "historical archaeology" in two ways. In the broadest sense, they use the term to refer to the archaeology of any period for which written records exist. Under this definition, an archaeologist studying the ancient Aztecs or the dynastic Egyptians would be considered a historical archaeologist[s] because both cultures used writing and were literate. In this sense, all historical archaeologists are linked through their method of using a combination of historical and archaeological sources of information to reconstruct the past. In the second sense of the term, historical archaeology is considered to be the archaeology of post-Columbian history. The theoretical basis of this perspective is the idea that the world became a different place when colonizing Europeans began to travel across the globe, meeting and interacting with diverse indigenous peoples as they went. The hybrid cultures that were subsequently created in the Americas, the South Seas, and even in Europe are the outcomes of these dramatic cultural exchanges' (Orser 1996, 11).

As a methodological project

In the perspective of methodology, historical archaeologists are distinguishable from other kinds because they must learn to appreciate and manage texts as well as dirt. There was always some rivalry as to which of these gave the truer picture, because champions of both wanted to be seen as equally useful. In a 1982 overview, Kathleen Deagan defined texts as utterances of the contemporary subjects (emic statements) while archaeology delivered an interpretation from us who came after (etic statements). Here were complementary and contrasting contributions to be made. The intellectual targets of the subject were harder to distinguish, since they depended on whether the researcher was located in an anthropology department, like most archaeologists, or a history department, like most historians. 'If historical archaeology is a scientific discipline, it should be concerned with developing general principles that can explain regularities and variability in human culture and behaviour. If it is essentially a historical discipline, it should be concerned with studying and illuminating the attributes, events and processes of a particular time, place and society; however this does not preclude the use of scientific methods in the approach to these concerns. Finally if historical archaeology is a humanistic discipline, it should impart an aesthetic appreciation of and an empathy with the human conditions of the past' (1982, 22). She found that historical archaeology had 'a unique ability to simultaneously observe written statements about what people said they did, what observers said people did and what the archaeological record said people did', expecting the latter to be the more objective record which reported 'actual conditions in the past'. She found the question 'is historical archaeology a technique or a discipline?'

remained unanswered, but felt that a distinct discipline was nevertheless emerging (ibid., 35).

In another valuable position statement Barbara Little (1994) tracks the development of archaeology from its role as the demure 'hand-maiden' of history, to its role as (argumentative) colleague. She rightly objects to dismissive attitudes to historical archaeology (above), but still sees a desperate need for a 'theory that structures research' (Little 1994, 50). She distinguishes five attitudes towards documents by archaeologists: (1) they are contradictory, (2) they are complementary, (3) they are useful sources for hypothesis, (4) they are ripe for debunking but (5) they are needed to give archaeology context. Although historical archaeologists seem to be offering these attributes of documents to encourage archaeologists to make good use of them, it is really the archaeological position that is being defended here. This anxiety becomes more overt in Anders Andrén's courageous review of historical archaeology (1998), which he wishes to promote as a global methodology.

Andrén examines how archaeology-with-texts is practised in a number of different traditions and countries the world over. His aim is to convince us that historical archaeology is a global project and should have a general methodology. His fear is that historical archaeology might not be necessary at all: 'the crucial question is whether archaeology is at all necessary in studies of literate societies. Texts can offer interesting perspectives on the interpretation of material culture, but the presence of texts always runs the risk of making archaeology tautological' (1998, 179). The famous barbed comments of eminent historians Sawyer ('archaeology is an expensive way of telling us what we already knew') and Grierson ('It's said that the spade cannot lie, but then neither can it speak') have done much to make archaeologists of the autonomy-seeking variety feel threatened. Can archaeology say anything new about history? Of course, it does, all the time; there is no culture in which everything done was written down or vice versa. But it can fail to be appreciated by being subservient, arrogant, or speaking in riddles.

Andrén struggles with the question of whether text and artefact are essentially different or essentially the same, a dichotomy he detects in all the versions of historical archaeology he visits. He discovers that the answer to this question depends on the perspective of the different subject areas (1998, 146), but ignores the consequence (neither archaeology nor history are global projects, in the sense of dictating method and theory), and soldiers on, offering us five strategies of his own (1998, 181–2). The role of archaeology in historic periods is:

1 To act as a laboratory in which prehistorians' theory can be tested

2 To fill the gaps left by documents

3 To add to the messages from documents by examining artefacts and architecture as texts

4 To examine documents as artefacts

5   To look at the contrasts in the information drawn from texts and artefacts and treat this zone of contrast as a study area in its own right.

No-one is likely to contest these strategies with great passion, since they are more or less common practice (wherever they can be practised), but they do not really solve the perceived problem of creating a global methodology for a sub-discipline. Perhaps this was a problem that did not need solving. Andrén rightly shows that the professional-ization of archaeological activities has caused a loss of integration, an integration which, he omits to stress, was in fact there before. It is probably significant that H.M. Chadwick, Dorothy Whitelock, Rosemary Cramp, Else Roesdahl, Martin Biddle, David Wilson, Leslie Alcock, Rupert Bruce-Mitford, Brian Hope-Taylor, Brian Ward-Perkins, Chris Wickham, Gian-Pietro Brogiolo, to name but a fraction of Europe's conspicuously successful integrators of history, literature, art, monuments, artefacts and excavation sequences, are not mentioned at all in Andrén's book.

Andrén's fifth category is an interesting one since it feeds on and is fed by a driving item on the historical archaeologists' agenda, namely the rediscovery and rehabilitation of the people without history. This, as mentioned by Orser (above), is providing the motor for an inspiring and multi-disciplinary programme, which unites at least one sector of the archaeologists-with-texts.

Post-sixteenth-century programmes

Archaeologists working with the material culture of the recent period in the United States (styled 'historical archaeologists') have been highly persuasive advocates of the study of the 'people without history', a study which offers the satisfaction of curiosity, retrospective justice to the disadvantaged and direct relevance to the present day. Here is Orser (1996, 10): 'Think for a moment. What do you really know about the daily lives of your grandparents and the times in which they lived? If they were like most people, they did not write laws or build monuments to honour themselves. Nor did they lead cavalry charges or write classic works of fiction. Most men and women simply went about their daily chores, remaining fairly anonymous in the process, lost to today's history books.'

This agenda has developed into a study of capitalism, its impact on disempowered peoples, and their reactive impact on the west (Leone and Potter 1994). The study area is a world that could never be the same after the contacts of the last three centuries, although it has not been exclusively fashioned by capitalism. The goal needs an inte-grated approach, although the emphasis on material culture and texts may vary, accord-ing to their relative quantity, and quality and the focus they offer — on the grand sweep of history or on the lives of individuals. Beaudry emphasizes that it is the combined, integrated or holistic approach that delivers the goods. 'By analyzing cultural texts, written or otherwise, from "the inside out", we can begin to reconstruct meaning in the active voice, in the multiple voices of the "silent majority" whose past discourse through artifacts reveals that they were not so inarticulate after all' (Beaudry, Cook and Mrozowski 1991). Documents (like material culture) 'can be unintentionally revealing about otherwise dis-enfranchised or inarticulate members of society' (ibid., n. 19 for examples).

One of the great advantages of having texts and material culture is that they can be used, through appropriate methods of source criticism, to examine how people being studied have themselves used texts and material culture. Barbara Little sees the historic periods as offering 'many opportunities to investigate power and subtleties of ideological promotion or resistance between rulers and ruled' (1994, 59). So the impact of capitalism may often provide the context, or even the primary cause, but not the only explanation of what occurred. She shows how, under European pressure, the Cherokee established their city of New Echota in north-west Georgia, and equipped it with a constitution, Christianity, and a police force to protect property. There was a national newspaper called the *Cherokee Phoenix,* which at once proclaimed the intention of the Cherokee to survive and used a metaphor from western mythology as its title. Modern investigations, including excavations at New Echota, suggested that 'while some of the most external and visible elements of material culture, especially architecture, followed white rules, less visible elements, particularly objects used within households . . . presented traditional culture' (ibid., 61). The editor of the *Phoenix* also used his editorial columns to protect Cherokee causes using a 'white medium'. Print, like material culture, was used both to 'emulate and reject white principles', creating in the process a syncretic Cherokee-and-white civilization. In this case the strategy proved unsuccessful. New Echota was occupied only from 1826 to 1838, when President Andrew Jackson had the Cherokee people forcibly removed to Oklahoma along the 'Trail of Tears'.

In South Africa, Martin Hall (1994 lecture quoted Andrén 1998, 79) shows that resistance can be detected by deliberately looking for differences between artefacts and texts. In most cases the texts represent the self-promotion of the dominant class, while the assemblages which constitute the material culture represent the subversive sub-text. Judy Birmingham's investigations at Wybalenna in Australia (1992) followed a similar quest. The site, on a wooded promontory on the north-east coast of Flinders Island, was selected by the British Government in the early nineteenth century as a home for the native Tasmanians. The choice was made on the advice of G.A. Robinson, 'who on his remarkable missions into the Tasmanian interior between 1827 and 1832 had by force of personality and friendship persuaded virtually all the surviving indigenous population to join him and leave their traditional homelands' (Birmingham 1992, 1). The Wybalenna site, occupied from 1832 to 1847, was designed and built by Robinson, who drew maps and lithographs and kept journals of his work, which were discovered in Mitchell Library, Sydney. These journals 'give a glowing but naturally subjective account of the writer's achievements which, if correct, would ensure him a place among the major enlightened philanthropists of his century' comments Birmingham with irony. And a sample of Robinson's record seems to encourage this scepticism: 'Yesterday I visited the new cottages with the catechist and found the cottages exceedingly warm although the weather was excessively cold. The natives expressed their great satisfaction at their present comfortable habitations and speak in terms of the severest disapprobations of their old dwellings, which is their wonted practice whenever interrogated on the subject' (ibid., 137). The archaeological investigations which had to take place in 1971, and consisted of an excavation of 20 2 x 2 m squares and a survey, did not have the advantage of being designed after the content of the documents had been appreciated. Nevertheless, they showed, from the assemblages left behind in two of Robinson's cottages and the likely assemblages from several others, that the occupants had reacted in different ways to their Europeanization. Some continued to hunt and others embraced European goods which improved their standard of living. Symbolically, they were apparently more sensitive to class than race, more concerned to avoid signals (such as the wearing of yellow) which might equate them with the European convict labour responsible for building their village, than European symbols as such (ibid., 196). Birmingham had some initial ground rules for the detection of the direction taken by acculturation: more European consumer goods and behaviour patterns equals acceptance and more Tasmanian artefacts and traditional behaviour patterns equals resistance. But the study showed a more subtle picture. The quality of building claimed by Robinson had certainly been delivered, and the Tasmanians' positive reaction to it is quite believable. The old ways could continue, but out of recreation and choice as much as resistance, as long as there was choice. The use of red ochre and dancing, once discouraged by Robinson, seemed to have moved to the bush. Rather than set up a dichotomy between words and artefacts, the picture had been clarified by 'the on-flow and interchange of questions between sources: documentary, graphic, oral and archaeological, a pro-active process which activates sophisticated research enquiry' (ibid., 177–8).

Pre-sixteenth-century programmes

If it is artificial to draw a line between text and artefact, since both require the same kind and degree of source criticism, it is also artificial to draw a distinction between historical archaeology either side of the Atlantic (cf. Orser 1999, below). Gerda Lerner makes a passionate case for the study of recent history: 'Just as the healing of personal trauma depends on facing up to what actually happened and on revisioning the past in a new light, so it is with groups of people, with nations' (1997, 204). History is the new moral guide: in European society up to the beginning of the twentieth century, 'religion was a more important factor in creating personal identity and in giving life meaning than was history. In the 20th century the opposite is true' (Lerner 1997, 200). The archaeologists of the later period in Europe have been less overtly united by their mission or their method, although 'industrialization', and the transition from feudalism to capitalism in Europe have provided an agenda compatible with the study of the impact of capitalism on the world (Johnson, M. 1999).

But from the period before the sixteenth century in Europe we have countless examples of archaeology working with texts, using each of the strategies mentioned above and a good many more. Criticisms of medieval and classical archaeologists for ignoring advances in field method or theory are now out of place, if they were ever true. As Harold Mytum has commented, 'All the debates regarding the integrity and nature of textual evidence as opposed to material, the biases of each, the primacy of one over the other, the stages of analysis at which both sources should come into consideration, have all been played out within the Medieval archaeology literature' (Mytum in press). Mytum has also pointed out that there are differences: the texts of the earlier period are generally less plentiful and less specific, and offer fewer encounters with the individual. In the European early medieval period, where both texts and artefacts are almost equally enigmatic and exiguous, the interdisciplinary negotiation although often heated, is on more equal terms.

Discussing the then newly defined Anglo-Saxon village at Chalton in Hampshire, Peter Addyman (1976) put forward an interpretation of a large building as the main dwelling house of what is doubtless an economic unit, and the smaller ones as dependent buildings, perhaps byres, barns, servants' quarters or workers' quarters or separate sleeping accommodation, some fenced some not. 'The Chalton occupation unit, or economic unit, or social unit, whichever way one chooses to characterize it, seems clearly to have been a house and yard with ancillary buildings, or a farm with farm buildings, or a peasant family with an individual holding,' and he goes on: 'It is interesting to speculate how many of these deductions would have been made had the excavators not been well aware, from the historical sources, that the late-seventh century Wessex village was regarded by contemporaries as a nucleated settlement of individual homesteads held by free peasant farmers, ceorls, each farming a hide which, it might be thought, was some 60 acres in Wessex at this time. Would the excavator have been so ready to identify the AZ complex as a peasant homestead had he not been aware of the fortieth clause of the Laws of Wessex (datable to AD 688–694): "A ceorl's homestead must be fenced in winter and summer. If it is not fenced, and his neighbour's cattle get in through his own gap, he has no right to anything from that cattle; he is to drive it out and suffer the damage"?' There is no coyness here about the ulterior motives of the scribes, no nervous assumption that they were exercising power and delusion by trying to convince us that fences were built to hold out cattle. Addyman went on to consider the inspirational value of the text *Gerefa*, otherwise 'The Sagacious Reeve', which lists the responsibilities for an agent running a rural estate. It contains advice on management techniques ('If he wants to begin well he must not be too lax or over-weening'), an aide-memoire of tasks to be completed season by season ('In May, June and July . . . one may harrow, carry out manure, set up sheep-hurdles, shear sheep, build up, repair, hedge, build with timber, cut wood, weed . . . and construct a fish-weir or a mill'), and a spare list in case he thinks he has time to relax ('He can always find on the manor to improve; he need not be idle, when he is in it; he can keep the house in order, set it to rights and clean it; and set hedges along the drains, mend the breaches in the dikes, repair the hedges, root up weeds, lay planks between the houses, make tables and benches, provide horse-stalls, scour the floor, or let him think of something else that may be useful'). Phew! The sagacious reeve is as busy as a Richard Scarry character, and Addyman makes us see how relevant this information is to the 'envisioning' of Anglo-Saxon England. Complementary? Naturally. Filling gaps? Of course. Contrasting? I should hope so. A laboratory for prehistorians? They would be wise to see it that way. But the principal message is that Chalton and the *Sagacious Reeve* offer context to each other, and did so before laboured definitions of 'intertextuality' were with us.

This was a study of the seventh–tenth century in England; as the centuries lengthen the balance between text and material culture is always on the move, first one then the other holding the stage. In his study on 'Amman, Alastair Northedge defines methods of inquiry that must also vary from century to century, and require different sets of skills to evaluate. He begins by establishing its collaborative character: 'It was thought wise to invite outside specialists to make contributions to the volume, because no one archaeologist or historian can hope to offer a considered judgement on such a long history' (1992, 15). In a masterly introduction, he summarizes the range of the sources: documents which make direct or indirect references to the place in the Iron Age, Hellenistic, Roman, Byzantine and Islamic periods, variously documented excavations carried out by teams from five countries, photographs taken by the American Palestine Exploration Society in the late nineteenth century, and of course the old upstanding fabric of 'Amman's buildings. The contributions of texts and material culture swing back and forth through the centuries, depending on how far each generation invested in them, and what of this has survived. Each species of source commands equal respect, but is subjected to equally tough critique, and from this hard tempering comes a sequence of political scenes of a complexity that is entirely credible. A *polis* becomes a client kingdom, which enters a province, changes to a diocese, is adopted as caliph's headquarters and then abandoned, to be resuscitated by twelfth-century Crusaders and nineteenth-century Circassians. At each stage, it is not enough to find what the occupants promoted about themselves, or what archaeology says about their economy or belief. The occupants of towns also had a deep memory to draw on; the ghost of the previous politics lingered on, conserved in the fabric of buildings, art, or in literary memory. The name Rabboth Ammon disappeared when the town was renamed Philadelphia and the name Philadelphia disappeared equally quickly when the Umayyads redeveloped the site in the eighth century — adopting the name 'Amman which itself had been mysteriously conserved throughout Hellenistic, Roman and Byzantine governance. But after the Islamic conquest of the early eighth century, the name Philadelphia also continued in Christian circles as the name of the Bishopric, and it survived as an image as well as a name. Byzantine Philadelphia was depicted in a panel 1 x 0.5 m in a floor mosaic in the church of St Stephen at Umm al-Rasas, offering a vignette that was 'quite uninfluenced by the contemporary stylistic developments in Islamic decoration' (Northedge 1992, 52) and would no doubt have been dated to the Byzantine period if it were not for the Greek inscription which dates it unequivocally to AD 756 — well within, or even after, the Umayyad period. Other examples of the vivid power of texts and archaeology working together are the unit of measurement (a cubitt of 44.75 cm), known from the water-gauge at al-Muwaqqar and used to lay out the palace at 'Amman; and the argument for the attribution of the extensive destruction on the citadel to the earthquake of AD 747 'on 18 Jan at the fourth hour' in which 'innumerable myriads died, and churches and monasteries were ruined' in Palestine, Jordan and all Syria. The results of this catastrophe have been traced archaeologically in Jerusalem, Jericho and Pella, where camels crushed by collapsing buildings were found to be among the victims (ibid., 158). The political upheaval which put the power of Islam into the Abbasids based in Iraq followed swiftly in AD 750. It was clear that the Caliph could not afford a comprehensive restoration in 'Amman. Archaeological survey reports a decrease in the numbers of settlements in the 'Amman hinterland as power moved to Baghdad and then Cairo. And in Jordan a few years later the Byzantine community was offering its own perception of what could or should or might be the role of its lost but not forgotten Philadelphia.

Northedge is sensitive to the different types of literary and material evidence that people generate, and their different allegiance to reality or to propaganda. An earthquake and an extensive layer of destruction offer one kind of equivalence, but records claiming rates of taxation and investment represent another. According to al-Baladhuri, 'Amman was conquered by Yazid ibn Abi Sufyan in the wake of the conquest of Damascus (AD 634/5). 'Amman capitulated on similar terms to Buṣrā, where 'its people came to terms, stipulating that their lives, property and children be safe and agreeing to pay the *jizya*. This was stated as one *dinar* and one *jarib* of wheat for each adult.' Northedge comments: 'as capitulation terms formed the basis for later taxation, the 9th-century books of conquest, such as Baladhuri, should not be necessarily understood as containing the literal truth about the events of the conquest, as it was in the interests of people later to falsify the supposed terms of settlement'; and he adds sensibly: 'However this is the information that survives.'

The dialogue between text and archaeology improves in courtesy and respect the more precise the dates that each can deliver. So, dendrochronology is probably the asset that will do most to invite archaeology on to the high table of history. A recent example from Lyon (Burnouf *et al.* 1991) was special because it was an imaginative and commonsense reaction to an opportunity: research plucked from the jaws of rescue. The opportunity was provided by the construction of Line D of the Lyon *metro* which was destined to tunnel under the Rhône at the point that bridges had crossed it from at least the thirteenth century. The Episcopal, Municipal and Departmental archives at Lyon provided more than a dozen documents of specific relevance to the construction, repair and exploitation of the bridge across the Rhône from the early fourteenth century to the eighteenth. Thereafter a further suite of documents reported how the stone arches of the bridge were progressively buried through the nineteenth century and demolished in 1953 and 1984, the latter providing the occasion for archaeological intervention. Rescue excavation of an area 3500 sq m and up to 15 m deep was negotiated at La Guillotière, the bridgehead, where over 4000 timber piles were encountered. Seven hundred samples of the tree-rings showing in the cross-sections of the piles were extracted by sawing off slices of timber, and a dendrochronological sequence was composed which ran for 758 years, localized by means of comparisons with Swiss and German sequences to the period AD 964 to 1721. The cutting dates of the piles could be determined in the clusters supporting 10 of the 20 piers (the remainder being still under the Rhône). In this way the sequence of bridge-building in stone and timber could be chronicled in its major phases from a date around 1065 until 1721. Interestingly, the best documented construction, which described how in 1558–60 the Town Council had sought to rectify the deplorable appearance of the wooden sector by reconstructing it in stone, left no archaeological traces, because the stone piers were built directly on to the platform provided by the pile-heads belonging to the original timber construction of 1383–7 (1991, 94, 129). Joelle Burnouf and her team deployed archaeological, architectural, pictorial and documentary research to provide as complete a picture as possible. They were aware of the gaps: 'the combination of the different kinds of information was not something easy to do; obscurities and inconsistencies remain', and less than half of the 530-m long bridge had been seen (1991, 125). But the principal arguments for a history of the bridges at La Guillotière over eight centuries could be said to reinforce or complement each other, because neither was given an artificial primacy, both were treated with critical rigour. This 'equality' was possible thanks to accurate dating in both media: convergence of interpretation was obligatory, since the dates and places cited were so precise.

Investigation of the drowned village at Coletière, Charavines in Lac de Paladru, near Grenoble, also gave an opportunity for the interaction of documentary and archaeological histories, thanks to the tight dating provided by dendrochronology (Colardelle and Verdel 1993). Posts from the submerged buildings together with detritus sampled from the silt showed a settlement area of about 1300 sq m within which two buildings were well defined: House 1 was seen as the major dwelling of a leading family, while House 2 suggested a more modest social condition. There were open sheds and outbuildings for domestic livestock. This was a manor-like settlement which housed perhaps 60–100 persons, which profited from clearing the forest and farming it with pigs as well as fishing the lake. The dating programme gave a graceful demonstration of the different kinds of dates that different methods of dating offer (ibid., 371). Had the site been dated by pottery and metalwork alone, the stated date range would have been ninth–twelfth century. Radiocarbon dating placed it in the tenth–eleventh century. But dendrochronology showed that the settlement had actually been constructed in AD 1003–4 and that the last repairs were being made with timber cut in 1034. By 1040 it had been covered by rising waters. The written documentation here begins in earnest in the period after the Coletière settlement was abandoned. Now we learn of several mottes being established nearby during the period 1030–40, and the names of feudal families and places which endured. Name-giving and documentation are attributes of the societies which they document, just as the midden heaps are attributes which help document the lives of the villagers which ended in the rising flood of water and feudalism. Dendrochronology is to the historic period what radiocarbon has been for later prehistory. Without its precision, Coletière might have been seen as a feudal outstation rather than an earlier and less visible episode in the story of land-control. Without such precision it is hard to construct a dialogue of equals, and the negotiation of interpretation between archaeology and history remains vulnerable to the striking of attitudes. Dendrochronology, and perhaps tightly dated stratigraphic sequences in towns, as at Durham and Trondheim (Carver 1979; T. Saunders, pers. comm.), may provide some of the best future opportunities for texts and archaeology to work together in the service of medieval Europe.

Documents and archaeology without such precise dating can find themselves locked in dialogue, and struggling to get on equal terms. Roberta Frank, in her article 'Beowulf and Sutton Hoo: the odd couple', explains that the prominence that both Sutton Hoo and Beowulf inevitably enjoy has drawn them to each other and comparisons and parallels drawn between them have become ever more forced (Frank 1992). Sutton Hoo, a rich burial of the seventh century AD, has been seen as the real world on which the poet of Beowulf, an Anglo-Saxon epic written down in the eighth century or later, drew. Beowulf in return offers Sutton Hoo the red-blooded emotion of its Scandinavian actors. But in practice neither the date nor the culture demands an equation at all. 'It is far from certain that the treasures from Sutton Hoo are heirlooms, handed down from father to son like Weohstan's helmet, mailcoat and sword in Beowulf. Similarities between the East Anglian and the East Scandinavian material may have more to do with the mobility of Dark Age artisans, a shared North Sea/Baltic trade in luxury items, and the desire of two wealthy fringe groups to adopt locally all the status symbols of the Franks' (ibid., 57). She asks us to put a little space between the odd couple so that even after years of being pressed together by society something of their own distinctive character and circle can emerge.

Later interpretation of the Mound 1 ship-burial and the burial ground as a whole does invite another equation to be made, if an unexpected one. To those familiar with the variety of the early Middle Ages in Scandinavia, Britain and central Europe, the connections between the two works are neither more nor less than being statements in different media reified in different periods but drawing on a similar mind-set. Ship-burial, which so evocatively connects Beowulf to Sutton Hoo, is a feature of this mind-set, practised at moments of high political and ideological stress (Carver 1995). These moments were captured in the ground of seventh-century Britain, just as another later political conjuncture was captured in Beowulf. Pursuing the analogy of material culture as text might suggest that a high-status burial had the same kind of mental genesis as a high-status poem (Carver in press). The result is not a 'time-capsule' of the dead man's possessions, nor a standard practice of which we have yet to see many examples. It is the result of a historically unique but ritually derivative event; the grave structure and the grave goods present us with a palimpsest of allusions, just as a much-recited poem contains archaic personalities and practices. This is not a contradiction or even a con-trast, but different points of privileged entry into a complex world. Sutton Hoo is not the reality behind Beowulf, because it is itself a heroic poem in which the choice of grave goods and the burial rite were metaphors for the political anxieties and aspira-tions of the burial party at a pivotal moment (Carver 1998b). The sceptre with its form derived from the Byzantine emperors, its faces derived from Germanic ritual and its stag derived from Celtic art, is a feast of metaphors, a stage-prop in a theatre of death, a triumph of 'intertextuality', in which a seventh-century working party (assisted by a later one from the British Museum) generated a striking image to serve the politics of their day. It is easier to accept this now that we know that the Mound 1 ship-burial lies in a cemetery in use for 100 years, exhibiting a variety of demonstrative burial rites (though none approaching Mound 1 in their complexity), followed by a few centuries in which the mound cemetery was used as a place of execution. This interpretation is given added substance by documentation of quite a different kind; the reports of Frankish and Italian churchmen who were engaged in a diplomatic initiative to bring Christianity to Britain, and with it subservience to a new ideological and political align-ment. The people of East Anglia built a burial ground in which their identity, their polit-ical alignments, their anxieties and their declared resistance to take-over were variously invested and signalled through burial mounds and burial rites (Carver 1986a, 1998b). By the time Beowulf was written down, that initiative had long succeeded in Anglo-Saxon England and ship-burial was practised, for not dissimilar reasons, only in Scandinavia.

These arguments, which refine and evoke the vision gained by integrating the sparse and eccentric documentation with the sparse and heterogeneous archaeology, naturally cause suspicion because they argue from such meagre sources. Even in the rel-atively harmonious world of Anglo-Saxon archaeology, these suspicions can sometimes break out. 'What we have is not, cannot be, the result of an orderly effort to search out the graves of the powerful,' said James Campbell in 1992; 'It is a random collection of chance discoveries. Arguments based on the hopeful assumption that it [the collection presumably] may be something more must have feet of clay.' Archaeologists (or literary historians) should not apparently be permitted to argue from less than the total inheritance of the past, even if historians can. But this anxiety applies equally to both kinds of evidence; the documentary may have a temporary advantage, because its sources are better researched. To continue Roberta Frank's analogy, the modern marriage is a working partnership driven by mutual respect, not slavish admiration, economic dependence or paternal condescension. Archaeology and history and literary criticism have much to do in early medieval Britain; and we are lucky enough to see that, although the household is enlivened with the occasional sour remark, none of these parties is trying to drive the stake of a controlling theory through the heart of the other.

Is there, then, a general agenda that archaeologists of the historic periods can share, in the same way that many prehistorians believe they can share a global project? Funari *et al.* (1999b, 5) felt they were doing something new in broadening the remit of historical archaeology from its interest in the impact of capitalism: 'The story of world capitalism is the history of the dominant world order within which diverse societies exist. But there are also histories (some written, some yet to be written) of the diverse traditions and practices that once shaped peoples' lives and that cannot be reduced to ways of generating surplus or conquering or ruling others.' They (ibid., 8) want to stress the common ground underlying the archaeological study of all human societies, but recognize that studying societies with texts is 'methodologically distinctive'. David Austin (1990, 30) puts it: 'A society which documents itself is of its very nature a different form of society from one which does not.' But the argument above suggests, with Derrida, that there is no such thing as a society which does not document itself. It may document itself with rock carvings or monuments, while its writings may be nothing but tax returns. The interesting differences lie in the message, rather than the media. Every society documents itself in different ways: some write turgid histories, showing how they would like events to be remembered; some build cathedrals; some have personalized tombs constructed. The modern westerner appears on television, and is famous for fifteen minutes; or exists for ever in the global memory as an electronic image on a web-site.

In the 'historical methodology' debate, the assumption which drives many of the archaeologists is that writing is necessarily and always connected with power, and that material culture is the poor man's friend (Funari *et al.* 1999a, 57). In reality, power is often exercised through material culture, as henges or tombs or very large citadels; while writing can provide a liberating outlet for the oppressed. Matthew Johnson (1999) prefers the idea of historical archaeology as quest rather than method, its purpose, aligned with that of some American historical archaeology, to track the transition from feudalism to capitalism, or from the medieval to the 'Georgian' order in Europe (ibid., 28). He cheerfully scuttles the historical archaeology battleship, wanting neither a methodological cartel nor a single global project. He is aware that the development of the archaeological agenda is parallelled by similar developments in literature and history and that what can be said about the interpretation of material culture can and indeed has been said about the insights gained by precisely the same line of argument in literary criticism and history. There is no reason to see the two sources as independent, even where they conflict: 'Often the processes that generate the archaeological record (the increasing quantity of imported pottery) are the same processes that produce the documentary record (increasingly complex systems of colonial trade and the information and power-networks that go with these): so two apparently independent sets of data may actually be produced by the same set of processes' (ibid., 30); or one may add, 'by the same people at the same time'.

As a project, archaeology in the historic period can seek identity in methodology or in agenda, such as the study of the attempted westernization of the recent world. However, a glance at some European projects suggests that there are potentially a great many objectives, involving many kinds of dialogue between the texts and the material culture. The relative abundance and precision of each media are important factors in structuring the dialogue, and the partnerships between history, archaeology, literature and art have to be redefined and recreated for each inquiry. The inquiries are held together, not by an overarching theory or agenda, but a common interest in the people studied and a united commitment to the power of the imagination. What kind of widening debate do we envisage in the next millennium? And what kind of organizations would be most amenable to host it?

The widening debate: agenda and organization

Variables

What seems to have been most missing from discussions about both theories and programmes is an awareness of the prodigious variety of information types within both material culture and text. It is fairly obvious that a bus timetable has a different kind of message to impart than the Bible, and that a cross-slab enjoys comparable differences with a midden heap, even if both were made at the same time by the same person. In combatting the artificial 'dualities' between archaeology and history, Matthew Johnson points out that texts have different types of genesis: 'The document produced by an early medieval monk sitting in a freezing monastery in eighth-century Northumbria is likely to be different from a set of eighteenth-century building accounts in Annapolis, which in turn will be different from the diary of a South African colonist' (1999, 30). Anders Andrén is also aware that material culture exhibits similar degrees of variation: 'I would still maintain that there is a difference between a refuse pit and a cathedral' (Andrén 1998, 147). Working in ancient Egypt, Barry Kemp also makes his boundary not between document and artefact, but between the formalized (i.e. expressive) and non-formalized kinds of texts and other objects (1989). Archaeological evidence is not 'theoretically homogeneous'; so that while a midden heap is suitable for processual analysis, in order to determine the economic system through the study of discarded animal bones, a furnished grave or an illuminated manuscript is clearly expressive and demands interpretation using structuralist principles: what did the burial party or the scriptorial authority intend by what they chose to highlight? Different kinds of question draw on different kinds of evidence which may be manipulated using appropriate theoretical instruments. Naturally the same variation applies to texts, which also vary through their time, in their purpose, and thus in the intensity of their investment. The variations of both text and material culture have been crudely summarized for Anglo-Saxon England in a table (Carver 1999b, reproduced at Table 1).

Table 1.

Theory	Goal	Early Period [400–650]	Middle Period [650–850]	Later Period [850–1100]
Ecological	Ecology	pollen macrofossils field boundaries	pollen macrofossils field boundaries	pollen macrofossils mss illustrations
Processual [statistically described systems]	Economy	settlement form animal bones	settlement form animal bones	burh assemblages including animal bones sculpture
Processual [statistically described systems]	Social Structure	burial	burial settlement hierarchy	burh plans sculpture
Postprocessual	Ideology	burial	burial sculpture illuminated mss church architecture	sculpture illuminated mss church architecture clothing

Text, pictures and sites each exhibit a range of expression; and the emphasis of each medium varies in a way which we can now see as intelligent, rather than random, or a product of survival. Why are burial mounds the subject of investment in one generation while the next prefers sculpture? Is this political pressure or an altered mind-set? An enormous increase in the production of letters in twelfth-century England offers historians new levels of access to social classes and ways of thinking — about property, relationships, life and life after death (Clanchy 1993, introduction and p. 60). Material culture too knows similar alterations in the target-investments of expression: a proliferation of the sites of stone monuments in Anglo-Scandinavian Yorkshire (Lang 1991), or of churches into every village in tenth-century England (Morris 1989, ch. IV), or the decrease in burial mounds in the seventh–eighth century, or of ceremonial axes in the Bronze Age. These variations, once thought to be a product of the hazards of survival, can now be viewed as real patterns in the communication system. One might suggest that there are no great quantities of texts awaiting discovery among the Picts, because they 'said it in symbols'. By contrast, mass production has made the modern western family materially repetitive and artefact-illiterate; its individual experiences are expressed in letters and photographs.

Degrees of expressiveness can also vary within a single text/artefact, the idea evoked by 'Tilley's onion' (above). BL mss Harley 603, a copy of the Utrecht psalter made in Canterbury between about 1000 and 1030 contains a copy of the psalms, in which the writing is modified from Carolingian miniscule, and pictures are copied by a succession of artists, each with a different attitude to the images in the exemplar. Some copy slavishly (Hand IB), others add realistic touches of the artefacts and architecture of their own day (Hand IA) and others let rip with highly original, creative commentaries on the politics of the day, as in Hand IF's rendering of a brave nimble Late Saxon David, stoning a huge armoured Norman Goliath (Carver 1986b, now superseded in detail by Noel 1995). Imaging, metaphor, allusion, archae-izing are the familiar heady beverages of Anglo-Saxon archaeology; but not on offer always and not everywhere. Sometimes we look at woods and fields, deer, fish-traps and tides. We recognize that for the Anglo-Saxons life was not all labour, nor all heart, but neither was it all mind.

Groupings

We should not therefore insist on an intellectual divide between the text-user and the earth-mover. There may be a divide between the act of pattern-seeking using analysis and the act of interpretation using analogy, but it ought not to be a divide between disciplines or between theory; just two consecutive stages of the same project. So neither theory nor medium offers an obvious basis for separating the students of literate peoples into different departments. Neither does methodology or agenda suggest a special long-term grouping for historical archaeologists. Charles Orser (1999) has proposed a 'modern-world' archaeology which moves some way towards acknowledging the heterogeneous character of the evidence in historic periods. His archaeology is still to be globally focused, but is 'mutualistic', 'mulitscalar' and reflexive. Mutualistic means that the study concerns itself with human connections and relations, in the broadest sense. Multiscalar acknowledges that texts and material culture, and the social relations they imply, have connections in time as well as space, and these are susceptible of study at many different scales. Some studies encompass broad sweeps of time and general conservation or change, others concern the life of a household. Reflexivity, in this case, refers particularly to the scholar's attitude to the people being studied and using current problems in social relations as a point of departure to study the immediate past: 'the archaeologist starts with a subject that is pertinent today and then works backwards in time to understand its historical roots' (1999, 281). Much of this would do no violence to the agenda of medieval archaeology today, possibly because in Europe these roots go deep. There is little difficulty in seeing the origins of England's current angst about the European Union in the post-Roman missions of the seventh century (e.g. Carver 1986a, 99, 1993, 1998b, 134–6), or of Scotland's present discussions about autonomy in its multi-ethnic struggles of the fifth–ninth centuries (above, and see e.g. Crawford 1994, 1996). But the later European prehistorians might also claim as much. There is no clear steer here in which kind of academic department, if any, the study of a 'modern-world' archaeology should be located. The same could be said about historical and medieval archaeology. Are these historical or archaeological subjects, in terms of the organization of knowledge, and of academic sponsorship and assessment? This is a question which, I believe, is fast becoming redundant.

Investigating the past will surely make use of every type of methodology in the way well understood by a GP. A doctor will note how a patient looks, what the patient says, what his records say and what the urine sample indicates. Each of these will be significant but not necessarily connected; nor will the doctor require a general theory or method about how to credit one rather than another signal, beyond being sensitive and critical towards all. The doctor will know that that depends on the patient as a person, from whom all these signals ultimately emanate. In the same way our understanding of the past depends on the people we are studying, every one of which, it may be argued, requires their own methods and theories. The analytical agenda and the interpretative methods applied to texts and material culture are equally exacting. Dozens of ideas cross daily from one to the other. To study one discipline to the exclusion of the others, on the grounds that archaeology or history or literature or art has its own theoretical framework makes no sense. If there is a framework, it will be the same one, since all the material derives from a human agency. But the humans themselves and their communities do vary; they, not the methodologies, provide the variable. Our subjects, our patients are what gives us our tasks, not whether we are using a finger or a trowel to make a diagnosis. Disciplines are simply tools, not powers. Why then do we create these disabling divisions?

The struggle to define a special identity or methodological platform for historical archaeology seems to have been driven by the need for some kind of autonomy for the subject. Having both texts and material culture is seen as a special asset worth reconciling, banding together and promoting over rival disciplines. But this only makes sense, if at all, in the context of a competition inside archaeology, in which case it is not an intellectual project but a commercial one; not to do with making sense of the past, but surviving in the present. Andrén himself reveals a certain unease about searching for an identity as a historical archaeologist on theoretical or methodological grounds or by virtue of the material studied: 'We can see artifact and text as categories, as objects, as documents, or as [different] discursive contexts, and for each of these perspectives the relations can be defined differently. The definition of material culture and writing are thus contextual and at least some of the conflicting stances are due to the fact scholars are arguing from different perspectives' (1998, 146). He recognizes that the villain of the piece is 'professionalization', the separation of research into smaller and smaller intellectual packets, which has had the concurrent effect of making it more difficult for different archaeologists to understand each other (1998, 10, 84, passim). It was not so much professionalization itself, but the chosen groupings, based on the idea of a single discipline, that were responsible for inhibiting the far more difficult but arguably more productive inquiry which can be achieved by a number of disciplines working together. Each of these disciplines develops and is developing its own body of theories and methods for source criticism, and it will never be easy for one person or even a school to keep up with them all. But that is no reason for turning away, or attempting, by purloining the advances of each and stewing them together, to create a 'leading discipline'. Those days are gone. One needs to work at least closely enough to see the other point of view: 'a community is preserved in its full context only when both the self-recorded picture and the material realities picture are placed side by side' (Rathje 1995, 65). Neither text nor material culture has the monopoly on the 'material realities' or the rhetoric. The context is not a given, provided by the other discipline or dreamt up from elsewhere used to modify our interpretations; the context is itself an objective of research, and texts and material culture, analysed for their reality and pretension, have a better chance than most of finding it.

A multi-disciplinary and multi-theoretical approach was always the most difficult and the most susceptible to superficiality, but it is still the most productive and the one most likely to minimize the ill-effects of special pleading which underlie post-structuralist anxiety. The times are in favour of such a shift (or shift back) to relativism. Post-modernism is 'a modernism [i.e. a body of theory] that expresses itself in radical pluralism and lack of consensus, in a world where economic power is no longer bound to a place or a nation state, where encounters between different people are more intensive than ever before, and where global media communication breaks down the barriers of space' (Andrén 1998, 141). In universities, the breakdown of subject areas through modularization is only part of this process; academic achievement is also being re-assessed for its public value. Post-modernism is de-professionalizing academic subjects in the sense that the official, the expert, the authorized, and their corollaries, the regulated and the institutional are giving way to a democratization of the intellectual world through the ballot box and the market. Global communication and access to knowledge are so widespread and even, and competition to lead so intense, that the only reliable, detached index of value is seen as the numbers of readers, citations or visitors that a work attracts. The terror of being pointless has allowed the academic sector to cling to assessment by peer-review, but it seems unlikely that this method will endure. Widespread appeal is viewed as the safest method of assessment in the post-expert era. History and archaeology have known plenty of periods like this, just as they have known other periods in which a dominant ideology causes monuments to be built or inflexible mono-causal philosophies to be rigorously applied. For this reason, the pursuit of capitalism or methodological unity or a controlling theory belong to yesterday's agenda. In a post-imperial age, poetry rules.

Some multi-disciplinary groupings, such as Classics departments, have been conspicuously successful, and medieval archaeologists will always be tempted to form similar alliances which give their students and researchers access to original documents, illuminated manuscripts, sculpture, sites, sequences and assemblages, animal bones, pollen spectra, art, symbolism, ideology, economy, geography, Latin, Romance and Germanic languages and literature, music. These are rich varied worlds buzzing with images and ideas, theirs and ours. But to propose this type of interdisciplinary grouping as a general prescription would be wrong too. Professional specialization is good when you research, bad when you teach, and the reverse is true of interdisciplinary groupings. Should we expect to enhance our professional structure, so that, like medics, we have a tier of specialists, serving a tier of general practitioners? Or decrease it, do away with departmental divisions and let a thousand flowers bloom? Perhaps a bit of both. Archaeology for the next decade or so will probably work most fruitfully in temporary groupings, its research, like its teaching, modularized. In Europe, at least, the most frequent partnerships for the study of the last two millennia are likely to form between archaeologists, specialists in language and literature, historians, art historians, and architectural historians. This should result in an exchange of good plain-language observations and imaginative interpretations. A new kind of writing, neither fact nor fiction, but imaginative foot-noted reconstruction, hot science, poetic argument, a good read, is needed to propel the participants out of their epistemological bog and into the public sector, where they are most likely to be assessed.

There is no need for such groupings to be institutionalized or even located in a single university, although this has advantages in promoting collaboration. Electronic media will, already are, making potential colleagues less shy, more adventurous. The hypertext idea has changed the form and structure of research, since the initiative passes from the writer to the reader. Enduring research once depended on the power to convince with fine words and progressive argument that the conclusion of an 'authority' was the right one. Now the reader can dispense with the tedium of listening to someone trying to convince them, and insist that the whole thesis is presented to them in its deconstructed form. Here the reader can nip in and out of the structure interactively responding only to their own inquiries. Empowering the reader has its dangers: life becomes a personal campaign of special pleading for the individual. So, no change there, I hear you say; but there is in its acceptance. That is why multi-disciplinary study is good. Information can be quarried at will by individuals, and the electronic web is a good place to keep both the 'accurate descriptions' and the partial discussions that result from them. But grown-up research still needs more than one individual prepared to confront their viewpoint with others, who draw on different media, have a different world view, with no chance of running away or exiting. This mimics not the lightweight debates of closed common rooms, but the serious and widening debate which happens on the street.

In his recent Reith Lectures, an annual event sponsored by the BBC, Anthony Giddens tried to persuade us that globalization, epitomized by the Internet, was not a western project. It is possible that the movement is inspired by something more benign than the urge to increase opportunities for capitalism, but the case is at best not proven. Archaeology, as has been noted, is also seen by many as a western project, and maybe it will stay one. But to give it a chance to grow, in any direction, changes in organizational opportunities and in publication would be welcome. It should be possible to work with other disciplines and other countries without feeling that the earning power of one's own has been jeopardized. Publication could also help archaeology to globalize without commercial and linguistic imperialism, if data and theoretical discussion were made readily available on the Internet, to allow creative reading. As a complement to this dissemination of accessible professional study, contemporary interpretations could be released into the public arena by a newly encouraged burst of creative writing, in which archaeologists are invited to lay aside theory and critique, and themselves write history and write literature. In this dream, the amount of archaeological publication will be reduced to saleable, readable books, a dramatic decrease of stress on academics and trees alike. The performance of academics would need to be judged by new methods. If we accept that numerical parameters of success are a nonsense, we must abandon them. But it may be that peer-review should also be widened so as to test the utility of a piece of work in both the professional and in the public mind.

Conclusion

In sum, total integration between the study of texts and material culture is thus desirable and practical where both kinds of evidence are on equal terms of abundance and precision. Where the archaeology is rich and the texts poor, archaeology will tend to set the agenda and vice versa. In these cases, the partnership can still be fruitful, where the partners give each other adequate space and audience. In organizational terms, combined studies constructed from modules are likely to lead the learning strategies over the next few decades, and these could be adapted to research. In this event projects rather than departments or institutions would have to be assessed, as has already happened in other sectors. Interdisciplinary centres such as Classics and Medieval Studies encourage collaboration and support long-term projects, but researchers can well advance from other bases using electronic connections. Academic publication is currently stimulated well beyond its innovative capacity, and beyond the capacity of academics of other disciplines to absorb; and this inhibits movement between subject areas. The solution may be to put all data and theoretical discussion on to the Internet as hypertext, where it can be freely accessed by users at different levels. This will, I believe, allow imaginative writing about the past to emerge as the most valuable of the archaeologist's contributions to societies, east and west.

In the end, the study of the past like anything else worth doing, demands our commitment — not to the titillation of telling someone else how to do it, but to the subject itself. 'A meaningful connection to the past demands, above all, active engagement,' says Gerda Lerner; 'it demands imagination and empathy, so that we can fathom worlds unlike our own, contexts far from those we know, ways of thinking and feeling that are alien to us. We must enter past worlds with curiosity and with respect. When we do this, the rewards are considerable' (1997, 201). So good archaeology is good writing, which draws on textual, artistic and other material matter, looking for sequence, pattern, connection, image and allusion in all. Sometimes the pattern-seeking analyses are at full-steam; at other times it is the analogy, the metaphor which are put to work. Consensus about the past both inside the profession and outside it will be achieved by negotiation, not by government regulations, academic power or 'force of argument'. The discussion is democratized, so that the most numerous or most passionate sometimes prevail over the logical and scientific. I see nothing terrible and nothing new in that. Archaeology came late to the game of academic competition and has succeeded mightily well. But it is now time to stop blowing our own trumpet and find others to make music with.

Acknowledgements

Thanks to Catherine Hills, Madeleine Hummler and Felicity Riddy who helped eliminate some of the wilder ideas in an earlier draft.

References

ADDYMAN, P.V. 1976: Anglo-Saxon archaeology and society. In Sieveking, G. de G., Longworth, I.H. and Wilson, K.E. (eds.), *Problems in Economic and Social Archaeology* (London), 309–22.

ANDRÉN, A. 1998: *Between Artifacts and Texts. Historical Archaeology in Global Perspective* (New York).

ATKINSON, K. 1995: *Behind the Scenes at the Museum* (London).

AUSTIN, D. 1990: The 'proper study' of medieval archaeology. In Austin, D. and Alcock, L. (eds.), *From the Baltic to the Black Sea. Studies in Medieval Archaeology* (London), 9–42.

BARNES, G.L. 1984: Mimaki and the 'matching game'. *Archaeol. Rev. Cambridge* 3(2), 37–47.

BEAUDRY, M.C., COOK, L.J. and MROZOWSKI, S.A. 1991: Artifacts and active voices. In McGuire, R.H. and Paynter, R. (eds.), *The Archaeology of Inequality* (Oxford), 150–91.

BIRMINGHAM, J. 1992: *Wybalenna: the archaeology of Cultural Accommodation in Nineteenth Century Tasmania. A report of the Historical Investigation of the Aboriginal Establishment on Flinders Island* (The Australian Society for Historical Archaeology).

BOURDIEU, P. 1984: *Distinction. A social critique of the judgement of taste* (London).

BRADLEY, R. 1987: Time regained — the creation of continuity. *J. Brit. Archaeol. Assoc.* 140, 1–17.

BRAUDEL, F. 1972: *The Mediterranean and the Mediterranean world in the age of Philip II*, Vol. 1 (London).

BRUCE-MITFORD, R.L.S. 1969: The Art of the Codex Amiatinus. *J. Brit. Archaeol. Assoc.* 32, 1–25.

BURNOUF, J., GUILHOT, J.-O., MANDY, M.-O. and ORCEL, C. 1991: *Le Pont de la Guilotière. Franchir le Rhône à Lyon* (Lyon, Circonscription des Antiquités Historiques).

CAMPBELL, J. 1992: The Impact of the Sutton Hoo discovery on the study of Anglo-Saxon History. In Kendall, C.B. and Wells, P.S. (eds.), *Voyage to the Other World. The legacy of Sutton Hoo* (Minneapolis), 79–102.

CARVER, M.O.H. 1979: Three Saxo-Norman tenements in Durham City. *Med. Archaeol.* 23, 1–80.

CARVER, M.O.H. 1986a: Sutton Hoo in Context. *Settimane di Studio del Centro Italiano di Studi sull'Alto Medioevo* 32, 77–123.

CARVER, M.O.H. 1986b: Contemporary artifacts illustrated in late Saxon manuscripts. *Archaeologia* 108, 117–45.

CARVER, M.O.H. 1993: *Arguments in Stone. Archaeological Research and the European Town in the First Millennium* (Oxford).

CARVER, M.O.H. 1995: Boat burial in Britain: ancient custom or political signal? In Crumlin-Pedersen, O. and Munch Thye, B. (eds.), *The Ship as Symbol in prehistoric and medieval Scandinavia* (Copenhagen, National Museum of Denmark), 111–24.

CARVER, M.O.H. 1998a: Conversion and politics on the eastern seaboard of Britain: some archaeological indicators. In Crawford, B.E. (ed.), *Conversion and Christianity in the North Sea World* (St Andrews), 11–40.

CARVER, M.O.H. 1998b: *Sutton Hoo. Burial Ground of Kings?* (London).

CARVER, M.O.H. 1999a: Field Archaeology. In Barker, G. (ed.), *Companion Encyclopaedia of Archaeology* (London), 128–81.

CARVER, M.O.H. 1999b: Exploring, explaining, imagining: Anglo-Saxon Archaeology 1998. In Karkov, C. (ed.), *The Archaeology of Anglo-Saxon England: Basic Readings* (New York and London, Garland Reference Library of the Humanities), 25–52.

CARVER, M.O.H. in press: Burial as Poetry: the context of treasure in Anglo-Saxon graves. In Tyler, E. (ed.), *Anglo-Saxon Treasure* (York, Centre for Medieval Studies).

CLANCHY, M.T. 1993: *From Memory to Written Record. England 1066–1307* (Oxford, 2nd edition).

COLARDELLE, M. and VERDEL, E. (eds.) 1993: *Les Habitats du Lac de Paladru (Isère) dans leur environment. La Formation d'un terroir au XI e siècle* (Paris, Editions de la Maison des Sciences de l'Homme).

CRAWFORD, B.E. (ed.) 1994: *Scotland in Dark Age Europe* (St Andrews).

CRAWFORD, B.E. (ed.) 1996: *Scotland in Dark Age Britain* (Aberdeen).

DEAGAN, K. 1982: Avenues of Inquiry in Historical Archaeology. In *Advances in Archaeological Method and Theory* 5, 151–77 [republished in Orser 1996, 16–41].

DEETZ, J. 1967: *Invitation to Archaeology* (Natural History Press).

FOUCAULT, M. 1972: *The archaeology of knowledge* (Tavistock).

FRANK, R. 1992: Beowulf and Sutton Hoo: the odd couple. In Kendall, C.B. and Wells, P.S. (eds.), *Voyage to the Other World. The legacy of Sutton Hoo* (Minneapolis), 47–64.

FUNARI, P.P.A., HALL, M. and JONES, S. (eds.) 1999a: *Historical Archaeology: Back from the Edge* (London and New York).

FUNARI, P.P.A., HALL, M. and JONES, S. (eds.) 1999b: Introduction: archaeology into history. In Funari, P.P.A., Hall, M. and JONES, S. (eds.) 1999a, 1–20.

GIDDENS, A. 1979: *Central Problems in Social Theory* (Basingstoke).

HILLS, C. 1997: History and archaeology: do words matter more than deeds? *Archaeol. Rev. Cambridge* 14(1), 29–36.

HODDER, I. 1986: *Reading the Past* (Cambridge).

HODDER, I. 1992: *Theory and Practice in Archaeology* (London).

JOHNSON, C. 1997: *Derrida* (London).

JOHNSON, M. 1999: Rethinking historical archaeology. In Funari, P.P.A., Hall, M. and Jones, S. (eds.) 1999a, 23–36.

KEMP, B. 1984: In the shadow of text: archaeology in Egypt. *Archaeol. Rev. Cambridge* 3(2), 19–28.

KEMP, B. 1989: *Ancient Egypt: Anatomy of a Civilization* (London).

LANG, J. 1991: *York and Eastern Yorkshire. Corpus of Anglo-Saxon Stone Sculpture*, Vol. III (Oxford, British Academy).

LEONE, M.P. and POTTER, P.B., Jr. 1994: Historical archaeology of capitalism. *Bull. Soc. American Archaeol.* 12(4), 14–15.

LERNER, G. 1997: *Why History Matters* (New York and Oxford).

LE ROY LADURIE, E. 1978: *Montaillou* (London).

LEVI-STRAUSS, C. 1955: *Tristes Tropiques* (Paris).

LITTLE, B. 1992a: Text-aided archaeology. In Little, B. (ed.), *Text-Aided Archaeology* (Boca Raton, Florida), 1–8.

LITTLE, B. 1992b: Texts, images, material culture. In Little, B. (ed.), *Text-Aided Archaeology* (Boca Raton, Florida), 217–21.

LITTLE, B. 1994: People with history: an update on Historical Archaeology in the United States. *J. Archaeological Method and Theory* 1(1), 5–40 [republished in Orser 1996, 42–78].

MORRIS, R.K. 1989: *Churches in the Landscape* (London).

MYTUM, H. in press: Approaches to Historical Archaeology in Britain and Ireland: an overview. *Int. J. Historical Archaeol.*

NOEL, W. 1995: *The Harley Psalter* (Cambridge).

NORTHEDGE, A. 1992: *Studies on Roman and Islamic 'Amman. Vol. I: History, Site and Architecture* (Oxford, British Institute at 'Amman).

ORSER, C.E. 1996: Introduction: Images of the Recent Past. In Orser, C.E. (ed.), *Images of the Recent Past* (California and London), 9–13.

ORSER, C.E. 1999: Negotiating our 'familiar' pasts. In Tarlow, S. and West, S. (eds.), *The Familiar Past? Archaeologies of later historic Britain* (London and New York), 273–85.

RATHJE, W.L. 1995: The sense and dollars of preservation. In Slaton, D. and Schiffer, R.A. (eds.), *Preserving the Recent Past* (Washington, D.C., Historic Preservation Education Forum).

SHANKS, M. and TILLEY, C. 1987: *Social Theory and Archaeology* (Cambridge).

TILLEY, C. 1999: *Metaphor and Material Culture* (Oxford).

Into the *black hole*: Archaeology 2001 and beyond . . .

WILLIAM L. RATHJE, VINCENT M. LAMOTTA AND
WILLIAM A. LONGACRE

[T]he day will come when we shall find ourselves at both ends of the shovel.
(Bernard L. Fontana, historical archaeologist, 1970)

Introduction: archaeology's *black hole*

The classic film *2001, A Space Odyssey* (1968), produced and directed by Stanley Kubrick, with screenplay by Arthur C. Clarke, depicts the whole of human development as punctuated evolution accelerated to warp speed. The centrepieces of the movie are two great leaps forward — hominids using tools for the first time and an astronaut being transformed through a kaleidoscope of artefact stimuli into an otherworldly 'star child'. Kubrick's haunting celluloid images clearly imply an unbroken link between the actions we take today in our own culture's material cocoon and the first experiments our remotest ancestors conducted to turn their environment into physical extensions of their bodies and minds.

Oddly enough, archaeologists — those who take it upon themselves to study the longer-than-two million year relationship between hominids and their material creations — haven't spent much time reconstructing the last links that bridge the gap between the artefacts of older societies and the seemingly endless complexes of incessantly morphing technologies that fill the contemporary world.

One reason is clearly that much of the original fascination both archaeologists and the public enjoyed in ancient finds was the artefacts' 'otherness', their utter removal from today's daily grind by large gulfs of time. In fact, such gulfs of temporal distance are so important to many archaeologists that they have been reified by long-standing academic conventions.

For example, only 14 per cent of all substantive articles published in the US journal

Historical Archaeology between 1988 and 1998 concerned material remains dated to the twentieth century; of these, only *five* publications (2 per cent) contained any reference to material culture that was 50 years old or less at the time of publication. In the US, this bias against archaeological research on more recent remains has been validated by federal legislation, such as the Archaeological Resources Protection Act of 1979 and the Archaeological and Historical Preservation (Moss-Bennet) Act of 1974, both of which state that '[n]o item shall be treated as an archaeological resource . . . unless such item is at least 100 years of age'. State and local laws, although somewhat less restrictive, still typically maintain that an object or site must be at least 50 years of age before it will be recognized as 'archaeological'. And thus, by seeming to require that an artefact be 50-or-more-years old to be worthy of archaeological interest or study (not to mention funding), an archaeological *black hole* has been created.

Strong support for the maintenance of this *black hole* derives from both practitioners' and the lay public's cognitive mindsets of what archaeology is and what archaeologists do. Nevertheless, bit by bit the arbitrary 50-year gulf between archaeology and contemporary society is being obliterated.

Foremost among those who are disturbing the *black hole* is 'Father Time' himself, who forces it to be on the move constantly. As each day passes, another day's material remains emerge from the arbitrary abyss into the sunlight of a place in a people's hegemony.

The other disturbers of the void are intrepid, but rather iconoclastic, archaeological explorers.

Among the first to probe the *black hole* were ethnoarchaeologists, whose goal was to study non-industrialized societies to record relationships between 'traditional' living peoples and the manufacture, use, and discard of stone tools, locally manufactured pottery, do-it-yourself housing, sacred objects and places, and so on. Ethnoarchaeologists rationalized venturing into these outer reaches of archaeology's no-man's-land through the valuable insights to be gained into traditional technologies, social structures, rituals and the ways these are all intricately tied together — understandings which are meant to lead to more rigour and breadth in reconstructions of the ancient societies most directly in archaeology's time-tested spotlight.

Another set of explorers are those post-medieval archaeologists in Europe and historical archaeologists in the US, who track a technological or social issue's trajectory so close to the *black hole*'s edge that they are pulled into the breach by their desire to follow a hot trail to its conclusion.

A third crew of *black hole* explorers conduct applied archaeology (aka modern material culture studies) for the sake of better understanding contemporary society, regardless of its ties to the past. In fact, these heretics suggest that their archaeological expertise centres on understanding the human-artefact bond regardless of time or place. Further, they assert that this expertise is a critical missing component without which serious contemporary issues, such as solid waste disposal, cannot be intelligently understood. Their argument continues that without the fullest comprehension of human behaviour within its material culture matrix, today's policy planners will find themselves with few options for workable solutions to impending problems.

Most of the final gaggle of *black hole* enthusiasts are currently novices who have yet to set foot into the archaeological unknown, but their rhetoric will inevitably lead them there. Committed postprocessualists and post-modernists, together with historical archaeologists in search of a public constituency that will guarantee future funding, argue that all meaningful questions to ask of the past must originate in the present. And how can an archaeological question be formed from the present without beginning with a quantifiable archaeological understanding of the present? It can't. As this paper is being written, postprocessualists and historical archaeologists must surely be girding themselves for voyages into the *black hole*.

This centennial view of how archaeology arrived where it is today and of where it is headed in the future will focus on those archaeological explorers who have ventured into the unknown realm to identify the human and material realities of the present and of the recent past — the denizens of archaeology's *black hole*.

An *Integrated Model* for studying the *black hole*

In reality, of course, the last 50 years and present-day society are not a *black hole*. In fact, they are just the opposite. Given all of the artefacts, records of behaviour, and interview-surveys of cognition that already exist, together with the capability of researchers to record all of these variables in ongoing societies at any level of detail imaginable, recent times potentially offer the most enlightening realm for archaeological research that could possibly exist.

Naturally, the majority of archaeologists study ancient material culture remains, including written records, that have survived various tests of time. Nonetheless, however resourceful these archaeologists are, their situation allows only a partial view of the past because the kinds of observations that can be made of extinct behavioural systems are limited to those involving artefacts. The result has been that archaeologists have developed a highly sophisticated toolkit for extracting subtle, but significant, inferences from both materials and texts. But this toolkit alone cannot fully describe the material-behavioural-cognitive systems within the *black hole*.

Perhaps, archaeologists would benefit from a comprehensive model, such as presented in Figure 1 (see Rathje 2001), which divides behavioural systems into key analytical components. The rationale behind this model is not to turn archaeologists into cultural or social anthropologists, census takers, or economists. Rather, it is (1) to serve as a constant reminder of all those variables which are often not available to traditional archaeologists but are continually at play and measurable in ongoing behavioural systems, and (2) to facilitate the integration of archaeological perspectives into comprehensive descriptions and understandings of contemporary society.

An *integrated* archaeology means reconstructing at least six very distinct and separate realities that are components of all human behaviours. Such an *integrated* approach is important because the various behavioural measurement perspectives in use today are not mirrors of each other. They each have different biases. They each record different data. Thus, each adds a new and important dimension to the study of any behavioural system.

Based on the significant role of material culture in our lives today, the role of these *material traces* (Rathje 1979a) in the methodology of behavioural science should be revised — and greatly elevated in prominence. In both archaeology and the other social sciences, material traces have usually been measured as reflections of behaviour to document change. But material traces are not a simple mirror; they are critical components that play active roles in the direction of behavioural change. Are McDonald's and other fast food restaurants only a reflection of changing family eating habits and values, or were McDonald's and their ilk one primary component of the cause? To sort out roles in behavioural change, the recording and analysis of material culture and its inextricable links to behaviour and cognition must be a significant, independent perspective in any behavioural science methodology.

To be comprehensive, even a simplified model of behavioural systems must include three key domains along with specific perspectives within each domain (Fig. 1, see

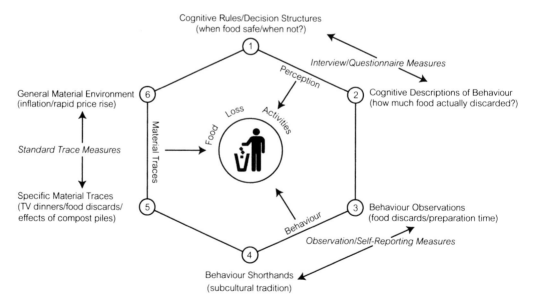

Figure 1. An *Integrated Model* of behavioural science research.

Rathje 1979b, 2001).

Cognition elements are (1) ideas, beliefs, values, and decision-making structures that can be elicited from informants and (2) informant self-reports of what behaviours, their own and the behaviours of others, actually occur as a result of these mindsets.

Behavioural elements are (3) direct observations of behaviour or informant self-report records and (4) common behavioural shorthand concepts (income level, ethnicity, demographic characteristics, education level) used to classify people in ways assumed to have significance in terms of some degree of shared behaviours. One of the primary opportunities presented by an *integrated* research approach is to test such assumptions.

Material traces elements are quantitative data in the form of standard and perceptual measures of (5) material culture and its traces in specific environmental settings and (6) the general natural, social, and economic environments in which human actions occur.

No one of these dimensions and perspectives provides a more correct or accurate view of reality than any of the others. They are, in fact, all equally informative to the researcher; however each does not inform on exactly the same phenomenon. Although individually these separate realities may give an impression of internal coherence, the most useful understanding of any behavioural system comes from comparing and integrating these independent perspectives. An example of how one might go about examining specific behaviours from all six perspectives will be presented in a later section of this paper (see below, Applied archaeology).

The opportunity to view particular behaviours from a number of independent perspectives is not usually available to archaeologists. Most archaeologists, of course, cannot study behaviour as it unfolds and cannot delve into cognitive mindsets in living humans. But where archaeologists can study these wondrous variables — in the society around us in the recent past and today — we should take full advantage of such opportunities to apply archaeological methods to better understand our position in our own material world. Moreover, we owe it to our colleagues immersed in ancient artefacts to record recent times in the fullest manner possible, the better to ferret out clues to actual behaviours and cognitive mindsets in the distant past. Documenting the fullest archaeological record of the *black hole* is the subject of the rest of this paper.

Ethnoarchaeology (aka action archaeology, living archaeology, archaeological ethnography)

In the early 1970s, at the height of the 'new' archaeology in the southwestern United States, William A. Longacre (1970) and James N. Hill (1970) published forward-looking studies that made daring inferences about prehistoric social organization and pottery design, attempting to use ceramics to reconstruct the 'immaterial' social aspects of the past that are so important to the study of culture processes (see also Deetz 1965).

Although revolutionary, Longacre's and Hill's studies soon came under scrutiny, and many of the basic assumptions of their analyses were called into question. Untested assumptions — about how pottery is made and how pottery-making techniques are passed on intergenerationally; how ceramic design and design elements carry information; how pots are used, wear out, break, and are discarded — revealed gaps that were not only specific to Longacre's and Hill's analyses, but which demonstrated a general lack of knowledge among archaeologists about how ceramic technology functioned within living communities (for exceptions see Crawford 1953; Thompson 1958).

Three decades later, archaeologists are in a much better position to make inferences about the use of ceramics in the past. Longacre's 1973 journey (and subsequent returns) to the villages of the Kalinga, a pottery-making people in the Philippines, is just one of many examples of ceramic ethnoarchaeology and experimental archaeology that has helped to fill the major voids in our knowledge of traditional ceramic technologies. Countless ethnoarchaeological and experimental research projects around the world have generated a host of correlates, relating to ceramic design and manufacture (Arnold 1975, 1983, 1989; David 1972; De Boer and Lathrap 1979; Longacre 1999; Longacre *et al.* 1988; Hardin 1970; Kramer 1982, 1997; Skibo *et al.* 1989; Schiffer and Skibo 1997), use (Hodder 1977; Neupert 1994; Schiffer 1988, 1989, 1990; Schiffer and Skibo 1987, 1989; Schiffer *et al.* 1994; Skibo 1992; Skibo *et al.* 1997), and discard (Hayden and Cannon 1983; Shott 1996; Tani 1994), that can be applied to archaeological materials to address questions about the past, both specific (e.g. When did rice cultivation reach Japan? See Kobayashi 1994, 1996) and general (e.g. How can the work of individual potters be recognized by the archaeologist? See Hill 1978; Van Keuren 1999). Ceramic ethnoarchaeology and experimental archaeology have also been used as a springboard for understanding important social and economic processes within living communities (e.g. Neupert 1999). Ceramics research, once fraught with untested assumptions, is now one of the most well studied fields of archaeological research — thanks in no small part to 'archaeologists of the present'.

* * *

Ethnoarchaeology is commonly defined as the study of variability in material culture and its relation to human behaviour and organization among living peoples — usually for the purpose of strengthening archaeological inferences about the past. The term first entered the literature in 1900, when the American anthropological archaeologist Jesse Walter Fewkes referred to himself as an 'ethno-archaeologist' (Fewkes 1900, 579). In fact, ethnoarchaeology's beginning is closely tied to the onset of anthropological and archaeological research in the United States under the aegis of the Bureau of [American] Ethnology, which saw archaeology as an extension of ethnology, inspired by the general theory of cultural evolution developed by Lewis Henry Morgan in the late 1800s. For the rest of the twentieth century, the popularity of ethnoarchaeological research closely followed the waxing and waning of 'generalizing' *versus* 'particularizing' trends in American archaeological theory.

Following a 30-year interval when American anthropology was dominated by Boasian historical particularism (Darnell 1969), a major resurgence in ethnoarchaeological research responded to calls for more generalizing approaches to archaeological research centred on structural-functional, ecological, and neo-evolutionary theory: the first wave of new ethnoarchaeological research (see Crawford 1953; Kleindienst and Watson 1956; Thompson 1958) emerged from the functionalist movement and its break from traditional culture history (Brew 1946; Steward and Setzler 1938; Kluckhohn 1940; Martin and Rinaldo 1950; Taylor 1948; Willey 1956), with a second major pulse following the advent of the 'new' or processual archaeology in the mid to late 1960s (see Binford 1976, 1978a; Yellen 1976, 1977). A third wave developed logically from methodological critiques of the new archaeology in the 1970s and '80s, and is characterized today by a greater focus on the study of behavioural traces (Skibo 1992) and the development of better material-behavioural correlates.

The face of ethnoarchaeological goals and methods has changed greatly from its humble beginnings in the American Southwest a century ago. Researchers like J.W. Fewkes (1893, 1896, 1900), F.H. Cushing (1890), Victor Mindeleff (1891) and Cosmos Mindeleff (1900), and later E.C. Parsons (1940), Julian Steward (1937, 1942), and F. Hawley Ellis (1937, 1950, 1968), for all of whom there never was a *black hole*, conceived of archaeology as a tool for pushing ethnographic studies of living Pueblo populations back in time — as 'ethnology itself carried back' (Cushing 1890, 160).

In contrast, the 'new wave' of ethnoarchaeologists in the 1950s looked to modern settings to find material-behavioural phenomena that would make archaeological methods — with their focus on artefacts and technology — relevant to answering some of the new kinds of questions emerging from cultural anthropology, such as those relating to the origins of agriculture (see Watson 1979). By the 1970s, ethnoarchaeology took on a more nomothetic character, tailored to answering processual questions dealing with broad-scale material correlates of different organization strategies among human societies; Binford's now-classic studies among the Nunamiut (1976, 1978a, 1978b, 1979, 1980), for example, examined the general effects of organizational variability on everything from subsistence practices and the trash they produced, to toolkit contents, site structure, and settlement systems. Ethnoarchaeological research of such broad scope has become less common over the past 20 years, with much current research focusing on the development of specific material-behavioural (see Longacre *et al.* 1988; Skibo 1992) or material-cognitive correlates (see papers in Hodder 1987), on better understanding archaeological formation processes (see papers in Staski and Sutro 1991 and in Cameron and Tomka 1993), or on studying and recording the last vestiges of surviving traditional technologies — such as pottery (see references above) and stone tools (see Gould 1980; Hayden 1987).

As an exemplar of the recent focus on behavioural traces and correlates, Masashi Kobayashi (1994, 1996) conducted ethnoarchaeological research among the Kalinga to identify trace patterns on vessel interiors. He found that a distinctive carbon residue permitted vessels used for cooking rice to be distinguished from other cooking vessels with a high degree of confidence (Fig. 2). Kobayashi then applied this correlate to

Figure 2. A Kalinga rice pot in use. Photo courtesy of W.A. Longacre.

answer the question, 'When did rice cultivation begin in Japan?' While most agree that rice cultivation was present by the Yayoi Period (*c*.400 BC–*c*.AD 500) (Imamura 1996, 127–34), Kobayashi was able to identify vessels used to cook rice from the earlier late Jomon Period (*c*.1000 BC), effectively pushing back the date for the earliest use of rice on the island. Residue analysis, pioneered by Skibo (1992), Kobayashi (1994, 1996) and others, holds great promise for the production of material correlates with potentially general archaeological application.

    For much of its history, the predominant theme in ethnoarchaeological research has been to study the present in order to better understand the past. Indeed, as examples above demonstrate, such research has facilitated major strides forward in our under-standings of the archaeological past, and in the next century ethnoarchaeologists should continue their important efforts in the name of building better method and the-ory. However, the disappearance of traditional technologies is clearly accelerating. For example, even when Longacre first arrived in a remote area of the Philippines in 1973 and found a potter in nearly every household in Kalinga villages, he also found chil-dren attending government-run schools, residents whose typical daily attire was indus-trially-produced clothing handed out by missionaries, and farmers raising quantities of coffee as a cash crop for shipment to the lowlands (Fig. 3). By 1987, many of the younger villagers could speak English, and pottery-making had almost completely

Figure 3. Two Kalinga males at home in western apparel in the mid-1970s. Photo courtesy of W.A. Longacre.

stopped in what had been Longacre's primary study community. Recently, a Kalinga dentist in the US produced synthetic replicas to replace human mandibles once used on ceremonial gongs in his homeland; and Longacre gets many hits on his Kalinga Ethnoarchaeology Project website from Kalinga youths living in the US who want to wear a tattoo and request inventories of traditional designs so theirs can be 'authentic' Kalinga.

In the face of such changes one must ask, 'Will the discipline of archaeology be able to sustain an ethnoarchaeology defined *exclusively* in terms of its direct analogical relevance to the interpretation of specific prehistoric archaeological records?'

The answer is 'probably not'; however, the modernization of traditional communities calls for a conceptual expansion of ethnoarchaeological research, rather than a cessation of such research altogether as 'pristine' cultures are assimilated. This expansion will have at least three components:

First, we recognize that the study of the past by means of so-called 'analogical' arguments — i.e. inferences supported by relationships observed in behavioural systems temporally and/or spatially removed from the archaeological culture under study — is a valid methodology so long as aspects of variation compared in this fashion are defined in strictly comparable material-behavioural units of analysis (see above, the *Integrated Model*; and see discussions of 'behavioral context' in LaMotta and Schiffer 2001, and in Walker *et al.* 1995).

The notion that the explanatory power of ethnoarchaeological research is limited by the *overall* comparability of the present-day society under examination to the prehistoric society in question originates from a comparative methodology in which the culture concept has been reified (Walker *et al.* 1995). We believe, instead, that one prime motive for ethnoarchaeological research is the search for, and explanation of, patterns of behavioural regularity and variability that are not defined exclusively in terms of time-space parameters (i.e. behaviours that are not culture-specific) (following Reid *et al.* 1974, 1975; Schiffer 1978; for examples, see Longacre *et al.* 1988; Walker 1995). From such a perspective, the loss of societies that are 'direct analogues' for prehistory, although regrettable, does not signal the death knell for ethnoarchaeological research, but does indicate the need to reorient such research to the study of specific behavioural processes.

For example, although household and full-time specialist potters in the Kalinga villages and in a small city in Luzon (the Philippines), respectively, have become 'modernized' to some extent in recent years, Longacre *et al.* (1988) were able to isolate a series of behavioural and material relationships that permitted these modern contexts to be compared to an archaeological record far distant in time and culture — the fourteenth-century Grasshopper Pueblo in Arizona. They found a relationship in the modern ethnoarchaeological cases between degree of ceramic specialization and metric standardization of vessels; metric variation in vessels produced by households (Kalinga) averaged about 12 per cent, whereas full-time specialists in Gubat produced vessels that varied by only about 6 per cent. Longacre and colleagues then examined metric variation in vessels from Grasshopper Pueblo in light of these data, and found that Grasshopper vessels — which varied by about 12 per cent — were probably manufactured under conditions more similar to those found among household producers in the Philippines. By isolating specific material-behavioural correlates, these researchers were able to define a behavioural context which allowed them to compare archaeological records across great distances of space and time, despite major cultural and technological differences between the societies they examined.

Second, ethnoarchaeology need not be just a tool of prehistory. Ironically, ethnoarchaeology began as an adjunct of American ethnology, and was later taken up by prehistorians who realized that cultural anthropologists would not always collect data in a fashion that was directly useful to archaeologists. As a branch of applied archaeology (see below), however, ethnoarchaeology could also serve to describe and explain material-behavioural-cognitive processes in all types of modern communities to facilitate better understandings of the operation of such communities and their relationship to the modern world system. Such research could serve as a fruitful common ground in which archaeologists and cultural/social anthropologists might collaborate, and, ultimately, produce rich understandings of human behavioural systems with both archaeological and anthropological relevance.

Although there has been, to date, little ethnoarchaeological research in this vein, a recent study by Mark Neupert (1999) serves as an apt example: Neupert's study of factionalism among potters in a small Philippine city bears relevance not only to research on the organization of ceramic production (with potential application to prehistory), but is also a contribution to the anthropology of factionalism and provides an archaeological perspective on political and economic processes in the modern-day Philippines. Studies of acculturation processes, technology transfer, or the effects of industrialization on traditional communities, are only a few of the many prominent and globally-relevant topics that beg for ethnoarchaeological study.

As another example, when ethnoarchaeologist James O'Connell studied the Alyawara of central Australia, he found a group whose mobile hunter-gatherer strategy was rapidly being replaced by a sedentary 'welfare' strategy based in more-or-less-permanent camps in the vicinity of government services and general stores. Government agencies were concerned that the European-style houses supplied by their contractors often became magnets for trash or were abandoned completely. Officials explained this behaviour by citing the 'primitiveness of the people involved', concluding that, given time and education, the Alyawara 'will eventually achieve the level of sophistication and social responsibility necessary to live in a modern house'. O'Connell's report provided a different point of view — one based on empirical data (see O'Connell 1979).

For the Alyawara, O'Connell documented that household mobility was frequently the solution to a number of recurrent problems — conflicts in obligations to family and friends, domestic quarrels, and many more. The Alyawara shelter — which may be no more than a windbreak of corrugated iron — is well-suited to such a mobile lifestyle; European-type housing is not. But O'Connell raised an even more fundamental issue. Government policies assumed that there would be a stable economic base for the Alyawara; yet, beyond welfare, there were few realistic possibilities. Under such circumstances, permanent houses were more of a problem than a solution (O'Connell 1979). As more traditional cultures are pulled inevitably into modern global society, archaeologists like O'Connell will provide information and raise issues to make that transition less cataclysmic.

Finally, ethnoarchaeology — for the purposes of understanding both the past and the present — would benefit from a greater incorporation of method and theory from experimental archaeology. Over the past three decades, experimental archaeology has experienced enormous growth in terms of sheer numbers of studies and in theoretical sophistication. Whereas experimental archaeologists were once largely concerned with replicating past technologies (see Don Crabtree's (1968) experiments with prismatic blade production), today the study of traditional technologies, their physico-chemical properties, and behavioural capabilities, in controlled laboratory settings has reached maturity as a subdiscipline, boasting dedicated research facilities such as Schiffer's Laboratory of Traditional Technology (the University of Arizona) and Nicolas Toth's Center for Research into the Anthropological Foundations of Technology (Indiana University).

The next logical step for such research would be to use experimental methods for exploring the causes of actual behavioural variability in living communities. One fruitful avenue of research involves the study of *performance characteristics*, 'the behavioral capabilities that an artifact must possess in order to fulfill its functions in a specific activity' (Schiffer and Skibo 1987). By studying the performance characteristics of artefacts recovered from living communities, for example, the ethnoarchaeologist might gain a better understanding of the determinants of decision-making processes that come into play during the manufacture, acquisition, and use of a technology (and possibly apply knowledge thus gained to the interpretation of prehistoric materials). Moreover, the controlled (and temporary) replacement of some artefacts in a real-life activity context with others possessing different (even incongruous) performance characteristics could lead to greater understandings of the complex ways in which technological change may impact human behaviour, decision-making, and activity performance.

For example, Longacre and colleagues have recently subjected a sample of pottery collected from ethnoarchaeological contexts in the Philippines to a series of experiments to measure strength and heating effectiveness. They wanted to test the belief, elicited from informants, that a certain kind of pottery produced by specialists in a small city in north-west Luzon is more durable than vessels produced by competing potters. The vessels in question possess highly distinctive visual performance characteristics — a shiny black colour produced by a combination of slipping and firing techniques — that allow consumers to identify them readily. The experiments revealed that the shiny black vessels were in fact more durable and more rapidly heated than were vessels produced by competitors, which were also tested. This research provides insights into the visual and other kinds of behavioural interactions that may come into play in consumer-oriented modes of production. Such an approach, combining ethnoarchaeology and experimental studies by way of the *Integrated Model*, holds great promise for improving our understanding of decisions made by technology-users in modern communities and in the prehistoric past.

The possibilities for ethnoarchaeological and experimental research are almost limitless. As archaeology's 'great laboratory', the living behavioural world offers the keys to understanding the processes of the past, if we are just clever enough to acquire and apply the appropriate data and techniques. As Binford wrote in 1968 (23), '[t]he practical limitations on our knowledge of the past are not inherent in the nature of the archaeological record; the limitations lie in our methodological naiveté, in our lack of development of principles for determining the relevance of archaeological remains to propositions regarding processes and events of the past.' In our fervour to develop those principles for understanding the past, however, we must not lose sight of the fact that the communities ethnoarchaeologists work in are living behavioural systems and are worthy of archaeological study in their own right.

Ethnoarchaeology is now in transition from studying present-day traditional societies to give ancient societies material-behavioural-cognitive voices[1] . . . to studying traditional societies today to give them their own clear material-behavioural-cognitive voices as they merge into the industrialized global society.

Historical archaeology

In 1973, historical archaeologist Stanley South was contracted by the US National Park Service to locate precisely the remains of the original Fort Moultrie. Most South Carolinians, like South, took pride in the fort, which had been constructed out of palmetto logs and sand fill in 1776 and was commanded by William Moultrie in a successful defence against the British fleet — in fact, that pride is symbolized by the palmetto tree at the centre of the South Carolina state flag.

Officials representing the Park Service, mindful of tourists the fort might bring, suggested that South begin by investigating a highly visible sand bastion located some distance in front of a nineteenth-century brick Fort Moultrie and within a

---

[1] The more adventurous archaeologists among us may follow the lead of Adrian Praetzellis (see Praetzellis 1998). It seems likely that in the future additional archaeologists will stand before both professional and lay audiences and give literal voice to individuals from the past by 'telling stories' about, or actually assuming the identities of, those whose possessions they have excavated. How much light these activities will shed into the *black hole* remains to be seen; but whatever kind of light is produced, it will never be boring.

stone's throw of the scenic Atlantic surf. South demurred because he had already determined that the bastion was located on top of an inland embankment of rubble erected to check erosion at the front of the brick fort. Instead, South started digging behind the brick fort, and his excavations soon uncovered a moat containing, among other artefacts, William Moultrie's Second Regiment uniform buttons, palmetto logs, refuse from meals, and black powder. To South, the locale of the Fort Moultrie of Revolutionary War renown had been fixed in space.

By the time South's official site report, poetically entitled *Palmetto Parapets* (1974), was published, the US Park Service had erected a replica of William Moultrie's fort close to the beach — not surprisingly, the reconstruction has since been removed because of water damage. As historical archaeologists have learned time and again, the past is in both the eye of the beholder and the eyes of all of those who reconstruct that which is beheld.

* * *

Somewhere between the present day and the more remote past lies a blurred region whose study is the bailiwick of historical archaeologists. South's work at Fort Moultrie is the embodiment of a significant quandary that bothers excavators to this day: Whom do historical archaeologists serve — the discipline of archaeology, historians, tourism, or the lay public's preconceptions?

Historical archaeologists typically focus on the period that begins with the appearance of written documents and ends, seemingly, at a point about 50 years before the present day. Although this definition varies somewhat by region (the term 'historical archaeology' tends to be reserved for the post-medieval period in the Old World, whereas the arrival of European colonists defines the beginning of the historical period in the Americas), the presence of written texts that are pertinent to the site(s) or region under study seems to be a necessary prerequisite for the practice of historical archaeology. The existence of textual data, which may provide the historical archaeologist with a glimpse — albeit through a glass, darkly — of artefacts, past human behaviour, and cognition, presents methodological and theoretical challenges not encountered by the prehistorian or by the applied archaeologist. Nonetheless, from their liminal vantage point, historical archaeologists hold some of the keys for spanning the *black hole* to link the material realities of the present day with the cultural processes of the distant, and not-so-distant, past.

First, let us dispel a common notion of historical archaeology that has cast a shadow over the discipline and has led to endless self-doubt and feelings of inferiority among historical archaeologists. The oft-repeated perception (e.g. as cited in Deagan 1982; Noël Hume 1964) that archaeology is simply a 'handmaiden to history' has envisioned historical archaeologists as second-class citizens in comparison to historians who maintain academic jurisdiction over the 'really significant' records of the past — written documents.

The scholarly and popular fascination with written documents from the past is understandable, given their perceived capability to transmit directly the thoughts and actions of past peoples. But textual evidence, be it from yesterday's *New York Times* ('All the News *That's Fit to Print*', emphasis added) or from stelae attributed to the eighth-century Maya ruler Great Jaguar Paw of Tikal, does not — cannot — tell the whole story. As the Garbage Project has found time and again in modern settings (see below, Applied archaeology), what people say they do, and what documentary materials vouch that they do, are often at odds with the material realities of their behaviour as measured with archaeological techniques. And, surely, so it was in the past.

Historical archaeologists should not be cast as the authors of mere footnotes to history; rather, they can exercise their expertise as material-behavioural scientists to establish a professional and theoretical voice that is complementary to that of historians and other students of textual remains.

This process has already begun along several fronts. First, archaeologists have become increasingly willing to challenge the veracity of text-based narrative histories. Yamin's (1997) recent work on the archaeology of nineteenth-century Lower Manhattan's 'mythic slum', for example, presents material evidence from a diverse working-class neighbourhood, depicting lifeways that differ significantly from documentary accounts from the period: where archaeological data provide detailed evidence regarding the mundane, proletarian economic and social lives of immigrant workers and their families, historical accounts of the area — written mainly by middle-class outsiders — are confined to lurid and stereotyped images of vice, filth, and social deterioration.

Beyond its traditional role, forensic anthropology has also made highly significant contributions to the field of historical archaeology in numerous cases (see below, Applied archaeology). Texts may record what people thought, or what they wished other people to think, but another light is cast on history when material remains themselves are carefully scrutinized. The exhumed bodies of Tsar Nicholas II and his family (Maples and Browning 1994, 238–68), or the remains of innumerable victims of Stalin's purges (Brzezinski 1989, 22–32), provide material evidence that unmasks political ideologies and exposes the sometimes-brutal behavioural realities of the past to the scrutiny of posterity. Unfortunately, this is an aspect of forensic research that will likely grow in importance in more recent contexts as forensic anthropologists are called upon by organizations such as the United Nations to recover, document, and identify human remains from mass graves resulting from state-sanctioned murder in regions of Eastern Europe, South America, Africa, Asia, and elsewhere (see Joyce and Stover 1991; Owsley *et al.* 1996; Rhine 1998, 145–7; Feder 1999, 179–93; see also Applied archaeology, below). Rogue governments that would scoff at the potential impact of such archaeological investigations need look no further than the recent collapse of the Soviet Union, stimulated in part by forensic reports that exposed the hidden violence behind long-standing state ideologies (Zbigniew Brzezinski, pers. comm. to WLR, 26 January, 1989).

Clearly, archaeological research can provide a 'check' on historical data — an alternative perspective on the past from a different vantage point which is not structured by the same biases found in the written textual record. Since the formation of some kinds of archaeological deposits is typically less of a self-conscious process than is the writing of documents, historical archaeologists can sometimes provide a more 'objective' perspective on certain aspects of the recent past.

As specified in the *Integrated Model* (see above), combining the material record, textual accounts, *and* the contradictions evident in the juxtaposition of the two, provides a perspective on history that is more complete than either line of evidence taken in isolation (see also Leone and Potter's (1988a) discussion of the use of 'middle-range theory' in historical archaeology). Handmaidens no more, archaeologists will no doubt be called upon to participate in the active construction, deconstruction, and reconstruction of history, reluctant though some may be to be cast in such a role.

Figure 4. The Peabody Museum's Awatovi Expedition delved into Hopi history by excavating the thirteenth- to seventeenth-century Pueblo of Awatovi in the 1930s and '40s. Photo used with permission of the Peabody Museum of American Archaeology and Ethnography, Harvard University.

Second, archaeological research has begun to make important forays into areas of research within the time-frame of the historic period which fall outside the capabilities of documentary studies (Fig. 4). Many social and ethnic groups within the modern world system and its historical antecedents lack major bodies of indigenous writings. Without archaeology, such people are not well known to western scholars. Archaeological techniques can pave the way for understanding the lifeways of such groups and for understanding how they articulated with the larger polities or societies in which they were (and are) embedded. The archaeology of post-contact Native Americans, Australian aborigines, or the Kalinga; of African slaves, immigrants, ethnic groups, subcultures, or of genders represent some prominent examples of such research (e.g. Deagan 1991; Lightfoot 1995; Orser 1999). In these cases, where written documentary evidence is non-existent, incomplete, or told only from the perspective of 'outsiders', archaeological data fill critical gaps in our knowledge of the identity of otherwise anonymous people. For instance, some contemporary Native American groups have turned to archaeological evidence to document their own corporate continuity into the past for the purpose of achieving federal recognition as a tribe (Kenneth L. Feder, pers. comm. to WLR, 8 October, 1999) — an example of *applied historical archaeology* (see below, Applied archaeology).

Third, by virtue of its ties with the discipline of anthropology, historical archaeology is able to articulate material evidence with non-western (i.e. non-written) forms of historical documentation (oral history) in ways that are both meaningful for anthropological research and for modern indigenous peoples (see Reid 1995).

Some of the earliest historical archaeology in the US Southwest, for example, was conducted by members of the Bureau of [American] Ethnology to examine archaeological data pertinent to oral migration histories recounted by living Pueblo groups (e.g. Fewkes 1900; Cushing 1890; see also Ethnoarchaeology, above). Southwestern archaeology today (Fig. 5) continues to generate data relevant to such research, highlighting convergences and divergences between the material record, on the one hand, and oral histories on the other (e.g. Lyons 2001). Archaeology — which is coming to be conducted more and more by Native Americans themselves in some parts of the US — is no handmaiden in this arena either. In fact, from our own personal experience (VML), we have observed instances in which some oral histories have been expanded to incorporate recent archaeological data, for example on prehistoric migrations. Clearly, this is a realm of 'historical' research which, for methodological reasons, is well beyond the purview of purely text-based history.

Today, the potential value of historical archaeological research is unquestionable for addressing historical (particular), anthropological (nomothetic), and legal questions (see below, Applied archaeology) from a material-behavioural-cognitive perspective. However, despite the fact that historical archaeology is concerned, nominally at least, with understanding the global nature of contemporary life (Orser and Fagan 1995, 14; Leone 1999), there remains one stumbling-block that has prevented this field from living up to its full potential as both an historical and behavioural science — archaeology's *black hole*! Because historical archaeologists have been preoccupied with 'the old' (for

Figure 5. Recent excavations by the Arizona State Museum at the ancestral Hopi Pueblo of Homol'ovi I continue to explore the thirteenth- and fourteenth-century archaeological record of Hopi history and culture (see Adams in press). Photo courtesy of Sarah E. Klandrud.

example, Jamestown, Martin's Hundred) or 'the significant' (for example, *The Archaeology of Shakespeare* (Wilson 1995)), there has been a dearth of archaeological research on the period of time represented by the past 50 years or so.

One creative way to fill the *black hole* would be to pursue a processual-historical archaeology; an archaeology that focuses upon the material-behavioural-cognitive processes through which contemporary societies, and the modern world system, have come to be as we find them today (for an example, see Claassen 1994). To see into the *black hole*, and to identify the processes that link the present with the past, will require the collaboration of historical archaeologists with applied archaeologists working from both ends of the gap (Majewski and Schiffer 2001).

Such an endeavour will also require more sustained attempts on the part of historical archaeologists to articulate their work with pre-existing bodies of archaeological data and theory and actively to generate new realms of material-behavioural-cognitive theory — a task so far attempted by few within the field (see papers in Leone and Potter 1988b; Leone 1999; South 1977; see also Orser 1995; Orser and Fagan 1995). From a theoretical perspective, one important area of collaboration will be in the study of the development of material-cognitive correlates, discussed above in the *Integrated Model* (see also Rathje 2001).

Historical archaeologists, working with documentary evidence, may be in a position to reconstruct some of the interactions among cognition, material culture, and behaviour. Such research topics are not new to American historical archaeologists, some of whom pioneered 'postprocessual' research questions in the 1970s: Glassie's (1975, 176–93) structural analysis of Middle Virginian domestic architecture,[2] and Deetz's (1977) examination of material culture and the eighteenth-century Georgian worldview, are two examples (see also Leone 1977, below). Through such research, archaeologists can begin to study the historical development of relationships between cognition and behaviour observed in the present, and apply material-behavioural-cognitive correlates from modern settings in a not-so-unfamiliar past.

Several thematic foci (see below, Issues of significance) will likely serve as media for collaborations among historians, historical archaeologists, and applied archaeologists. In fact, the more themes the better; historical archaeology needs to maintain a 'hybrid vigour' in the face of a modern world in a constant state of flux and with ever-changing social-science needs. Exclusionary statements to the effect that 'Historical archaeology is the study of X' — while they may attract constituents and define a much-needed audience — only serve to place unwarranted restrictions on research. To conduct research in such a fashion, in other words, exclusively from the perspective of a single political, economic, or ideological process, begins by presuming exactly that which we seek to find through historical-archaeological research: Which process or processes were instrumental in the historical development of a given aspect of modern or past life?

---

[2] From a systematic and quantitative study of the structural transformations of folk housing in Middle Virginia — one that frequently cites Claude Lévi-Strauss, Jean-Paul Sartre, and Noam Chomsky — Glassie concluded: 'The architectural design's central locus between the two ideal cognitive types would seem to accurately reflect the conflict in a society that is schizophrenically attracted at once — as American society is — to hierarchical social classification and to egalitarian activity. Middle Virginia architectural design would seem to be an exhibit of deep social tension' (Glassie 1975, 181).

Historical Archaeology is now in transition from attempting to give one material-behavioural-cognitive voice to the silent majority and the underclass in an industrializing world . . . to giving material-behavioural-cognitive depth to the wide range of silent majority and underclass voices joining today's global choir.

Applied archaeology (aka modern material culture studies)

Based on a proposition by Arthur A. Saxe (1970, 119), Lynn Goldstein (1976, 48–62) formulated the following: '[I]f a permanent, specialized bounded disposal area for the exclusive disposal of a group's dead exists, then it is likely that this represents a corporate group who has rights over the use and/or control of crucial but restricted resources.' Testing against a sample of thirty-three ethnographic cases — including hunter-gatherers, pastoralists, and small-scale agriculturalists — seemed to indicate that the hypothesis was valid.

Clearly, such an elegant relationship between social organization and material culture would be a boon to all archaeologists; and, in fact, the Saxe–Goldstein Hypothesis has been applied in a number of archaeological settings.

In the decade before Saxe or Goldstein published their findings, two popular writers, both untutored in archaeology, elected to explain to the public the form and meaning of contemporary US burial patterns. Their books, *The American Way of Death* (Mitford 1963; see also Mitford 1998) and *The High Cost of Dying* (Harmer 1963), became nationwide bestsellers and started a debate that is still simmering to this day about what is and is not an 'appropriate' burial.

Certainly, death and burial are contemporary social issues on which archaeology can provide information to an interested lay audience. And what better vehicle to use than a general hypothesis about a material-behavioural-cognitive relationship, such as the Saxe–Goldstein Hypothesis?

There is just one problem — formal cemeteries in the US are rarely related directly to a corporate group with rights to crucial but restricted resources.

Take, for example, Arlington National Cemetery, the New York African Burial Ground (La Roche and Blakey 1997), or the two Catholic cemeteries currently open in Wheaton, Illinois. All four are bounded, permanent, and exclusive disposal areas — but do these cemeteries signify the same thing in terms of social organization as, for example, the bounded clan cemeteries Saxe (1970) described among the Ashanti? Clearly not: the first receives the remains of military personnel from all over the United States; the second received the remains of African-Americans; and the last two receive the remains of members of the Catholic faith associated with a suburb of Chicago. Yet, none of these 'bounded' sets of people buried in the cemeteries was 'corporate' in any economic or kinship sense. Indeed, modern and historic landscapes in the US and many other countries worldwide are replete with similar permanent, bounded, and exclusive disposal areas which do not represent the remains of such corporate groups (rather, they represent other horizontal social groupings — be they vocational, racial, or religious).

Does this invalidate the Saxe–Goldstein Hypothesis? No. The material correlates discerned by Saxe and Goldstein are valid within a specific, yet-to-be-defined, set of boundary conditions implicit in characteristics of the societies chosen for the ethnographic test. As such, the hypothesis remains a valuable piece of research.

Nonetheless, this case exemplifies the bizarre ethnocentrism surrounding archaeology's *black hole* (for exceptions in the realm of burials see LaMotta 1998; McGuire 1988; McVicker 1972; Rathje 1985, 1986a). The failure to incorporate observations from our own societies into would-be general models of human behaviour through time (either as exemplars or as exceptions) not only prevents us from examining some of the extremes of socio-cultural variation, it also obfuscates insights into human material-behavioural-cognitive variation that can be acquired only within a living behavioural system. By not considering '**us**' worthy of study, archaeologists seem to be looking back at world history from a unique pinnacle, rather than merely from the crest of a wave that will soon sweep past us all, just as it has swept past the entire populace of ancient societies.

*   *   *

Perhaps the Saxe–Goldstein Hypothesis exemplifies the reason that archaeologists have been so loath to venture into the *black hole*. They want to wait until the dust settles, literally, before they apply their craft to the material aspects of their own society. The irony is that archaeologists have the one expertise — the ability to study material culture in order to understand how it relates to behaviour and cognition — that is largely missing in our material world.

Such opportunities have not been missed by all archaeologists, however. Take, for example, the most intrepid of archaeology's *black hole* explorers, those who must study human death and burial in a medical-legal context: forensic anthropologists.

Forensic anthropology, more than most other fields employing archaeological methods, has had a tangible impact on the day-to-day lives of people in modern societies.

Because such research is commonly conducted within a legal setting, and is often called upon as evidence in criminal proceedings, the true limits of archaeological inference are most clearly and poignantly exposed in forensic anthropology. Problems of equifinality and other limitations inherent in material correlates may be a nuisance for the prehistorian trying to reconstruct aspects of the 'Red-on-buff Culture', for example, but these problems become greatly magnified when cast in a real-world setting where justice and human lives are at stake.

To deal with these issues, forensic anthropologists have turned to observations of the modern world to create a multi-dimensional model of inference incorporating actualistic and experimental research, behavioural reconstruction through the use of material correlates and trace theory, and research into criminal psychology (e.g. see Larsen 1997; Maples and Browning 1994; Rhine 1998; Schwartz 1993; Ubelaker and Scammell 1992; Locke 2000 for recent syntheses). Forensic researchers, employing methods akin to experimental archaeology, have created an enormous body of material correlates, for example, in the fields of human skeletal taphonomy and cultural modification of human bone (i.e. through the 'nefarious application of force', to use Rhine's (1998) terminology).

Such strategies exemplify how archaeological research *could* be conducted in line with the *Integrated Model*: when the limits of inference are reached, the researcher must engage the modern world of material culture, behaviour, and cognition such that interactions among the three can be observed. For example, Maples and Browning's (1994, 75–89) discussion of the mental states and behaviours associated with the preparations for, and the act of, suicide, provides key correlates for distinguishing the material remains of such events from homicides, and especially from homicides (imperfectly) disguised to look like suicides. While such research has an important role to play within the context of our modern legal system, forensic methods and theory may also play a key role in the archaeological study of conflict, violence, and social pathology (see below). It is hoped that future collaborations among forensicists and prehistorians, historical archaeologists, ethnoarchaeologists, and researchers in modern material culture studies will stimulate the growth of such a multidisciplinary program.

Other archaeologists have pioneered the study of material culture for the benefit of modern society. Payson Sheets (1999), for example, a Mesoamericanist-*cum*-applied archaeologist, has adapted ancient obsidian blade technology for surgical uses. Sheets' obsidian scalpels (a technology first developed for surgery by Don Crabtree in 1975) are reported to be as much as 1000 times sharper than steel scalpels and promote quicker healing, reduced scarring, and less pain after surgery.

These modern forensic and surgical applications of archaeology amplify an important theme for applied archaeologists: Why wait until the people who can benefit from archaeological knowledge of their own society are dead and gone before lifting a shovel or recording data? More and more archaeologists today think that there is no good reason to wait (Rathje 1974, 1979a, 1979b; Gould and Schiffer 1981; Buchli and Lucas 2001; see also Ingersoll and Bronitsky 1987). This is especially the case when humorists (Nathan 1960; Macaulay 1979; Wiener and Tabasco 1980; see also Feder 1999, 159–76) have cultivated a large popular market by poking fun at the way archaeologists might misinterpret our society in future digs. Let archaeologists now set the record straight.

Amazingly, some of the earliest documented archaeological excavations in North America were 'applied' — carried out to settle a disagreement between the United States and Great Britain over the 1783 Treaty of Paris. The dispute hinged on *which* river surveyed earlier by Champlain was the true St Croix River, marking the boundary between US and British territory (Deagan 1982). In 1797, excavations were conducted by a group of Bostonians who located and documented the abandoned settlement of St Croix and verified the treaty boundary (Schuyler 1976).

More recently, applied archaeology has come to play a similar role in the settlement of disputes over land and resource rights among Native American groups, or between such groups and the US government. In the Navajo–Hopi land dispute in the US Southwest, for instance, archaeologists such as Harold S. Colton and Florence Hawley-Ellis were called upon to deliver testimony on historic and prehistoric land-use patterns of the disputants based on archaeological remains (Hawley Ellis and Colton 1974; Brugge 1994).

As will be shown below, these early examples of applied archaeology were amazingly indicative of the kinds of social issues, and methodological and ethical dilemmas, into which applied archaeologists of the present day would be thrust.

Any archaeologist who chooses to document the *black hole* immediately faces one mind-numbing conundrum: unlike archaeologists who study the Classic Maya or Etruscan Italy, both of which retain relatively stable places in time, the time coordinates of study for the archaeologist of contemporary society are constantly changing. In fact, no matter how quickly such archaeologists turn data observations into analyses and interpretations, the society they have just characterized will already have morphed into something else.

As unsatisfying as this basic problem may seem, the study of contemporary society also offers unlimited potentials:

1 Most other behavioural scientists who study *us* virtually ignore our material culture in favour of recording and analysing our cognitive perceptions. Pruitt Igoe, a multimillion dollar low-cost housing project for the poor in St Louis, provides an excellent example. When design flaws, combined with residents' behaviour, rendered the structures unsafe and unsanitary, Pruitt Igoe was totally demolished in 1973, just a few years after it opened. Although detailed interviews were conducted with residents to determine the causes of the fiasco, the actual design and condition of the structures *were never examined* prior to being blown to bits (see Yancey 1970).

Even when the need to focus on material culture is acknowledged, the results are often little better. Because they come from a variety of behavioural science disciplines that provide practitioners with no training in the study of artefacts, well-intentioned researchers often record, typologize and analyse our artefacts using patently simple — and ineffectual — means. The problem they often have in isolating the appropriate variability for study in material culture is illustrated in a report by two sociologists, Laumann and House (1970), on their attempt to relate living room furniture to social attributes and attitudes. For the study, the authors recorded 53 categories of artefacts, some based on design, some on function, some on frequency, and so on in a mishmash that would be largely unintelligible to any archaeologist. When evaluating their results, the authors expressed concern that their selection of measurements had masked important distinctions. Their knick-knacks category, for example, included both cheap hobnail milk glasses and extremely expensive Steuben glass sculptures. Clearly, there is a need for archaeological expertise in modern behavioural science research.

2 While 'laboratory' conditions available for the study of the past are limited to what has happened, the laboratory available for a contemporary study of what *is happening* is full of kinetic change and diversity. Consider the possibilities of archaeological studies of ethnic identity issues and ongoing warfare in dozens of countries worldwide (see Rathje 1999a) or of Y2K, the only 'disaster' whose date was known beforehand because we, ourselves, embedded it in our technologies (see Rathje 2000).

Applied archaeologists are currently exploring the opportunities for studies to define and test material-behavioural-cognitive relationships in new and innovative ways. Here we will just provide a few specific examples with which we are most familiar.

Mark P. Leone conducted a long-term study of Mormon society in America (see Leone 1973, 1977, 1979). Most intriguing were analyses of the way Mormons use material culture, such as their town plans and household fences, to make their mindset materially visible (Leone 1973). In this light, Leone's analysis of the building of the Washington Temple, begun in 1971 and completely finished within three years (Leone 1977), is especially significant.

Michael B. Schiffer has produced studies focused on the undocumented ways in which Americans buy, use, and discard large household artefacts, such as sofas and other furniture, refrigerators and other durables (Schiffer *et al.* 1981). Contrary to most expectations, a detailed interview-observation survey conducted through a transect of Tucson, Arizona, found (1) that most large household artefacts were not disposed of when they finally broke or degraded, but, instead, when similar items with new features (like ice-cube dispensers in refrigerators) were advertised and then purchased; and (2) that most large household artefacts were not discarded, but were given or sold to relatives or sold to reuse stores or given to charities.

This study was a component of a modern material culture field school for teaching archaeology developed by Rathje, Schiffer, and Wilk at the University of Arizona (Rathje 1979a; Wilk and Schiffer 1981). In its first years, literally hundreds of students tested archaeological assumptions and principles in the city where they lived. Perhaps the best known of these studies (conducted under Schiffer) led to the McKellar Principle, a general principle which states that items less than four inches (10 cm) in overall dimensions are likely to be left where they fall after use, while larger objects will be collected and disposed of elsewhere (McKellar 1983). This pattern has been affirmed through tests by both Stanley South and James O'Connell (personal communications to WLR, 1980). McKellar carried out her study in the same environment that led from two early student papers (Allen 1971; Ariza 1971) to the longest-term example of applied archaeology, the Garbage Project.

The Garbage Project was founded in 1973 at the University of Arizona to give students hands-on archaeological experience by recording and analysing the material remains of a behavioural system in which they participated — a participant-observation ethnoarchaeology of contemporary America (Rathje 1974). The first public reports of this research led to an avalanche of requests from academics, industry, government officials, various special-interest groups, and others for detailed data on the material realities of the US lifestyle as recorded from its discards. Twenty-eight years later, the requests are still pouring in (see Rathje 1984a for a ten-year summary; Rathje 1996 for a two-decade summary; Rathje and Murphy 1992 for an overall summary).

Garbage has always been a bounty for archaeology, as the pioneer garbage-archaeologist A.V. Kidder realized in 1921 when he examined stratification in the town dump of Andover, Massachusetts to test his methods of stratigraphic interpretation (see Rathje and Murphy 1992, 93–4). But garbage has never offered more than it does now and will in the coming century. That is why the subfield of *garbology*[3] — archaeological studies of contemporary refuse (see Oxford English Dictionary Editors 1995) — will certainly be 'picking up'.

At the most literal level this includes (1) characterizations of what is in fresh garbage placed out for collection in order to better plan for source reduction — 'using less stuff' — (Lilienfeld and Rathje 1995, 1998), recycling (McGuire *et al.* 1985; Rathje *et al.* 1988), and disposal (Rathje 1989; Rathje and Murphy 1992), and (2) excavation of garbage disposal sites to document actual contents (Rathje 1988, 1991; Rathje *et al.* 1992; Tani *et al.* 1992), the stages and speed of their biodegradation (Rathje 1991, 1999c), and the sources and levels of contamination (Rathje *et al.* 1992; Tani *et al.* 1992; Rathje *et al.* 1987; Rathje and Wilson 1987; and Wilson *et al.* 1994; for Mexico City, see Restrepo *et al.* 1991) (Figs. 6, 7 and 8). In terms of public policy alone, these data have been presented in testimony to the US Congress, legislatures in fifteen states, about fifty city and county government organizations, and the US Association of States' Attorneys General (for these and other impacts, see Rathje 1996, 2001).

The Garbage Project has also studied fresh garbage to compare what people say they eat and drink and waste and recycle to the material remains in their refuse. These studies have identified one basic pattern that is often repeated: *what people report that they do and the material remains of their actual behaviour are often two different realities* (Rathje and Hughes 1975; Rathje 1984a, 1984b; Rathje 1996, 2001; Rathje and Murphy 1992; for Mexico City, see Restrepo *et al.* 1982) — and these differences are not trivial.

Respondents in various government and independent diet surveys report wasting little edible or once-edible food. The Garbage Project has documented that the households of the same respondents discard about 15 per cent of the solid edible food they buy (not including peels, rinds, tops, skins, bones, etc. — see Harrison *et al.* 1975, 1983; Fung and Rathje 1982).

---

[3] Note that this definition of *garbology* in no manner relates to the practices of self-styled 'garbologist' A.J. Weberman. His 'Peeping-Tom garbology', which consists of snatching celebrities' garbage and creating von Däniken-esque exposés to display on the internet, takes archaeological looting and the violation of personal rights to a higher power.

Figure 6. A bucket auger dumps exhumed landfill contents for sampling, screening, and sorting at Fresh Kills Landfill, Staten Island, New York in 1989. Photo courtesy of the Garbage Project.

Figure 7. A sample of Fresh Kills Landfill contents excavated in 1989 are screened. Items that fell through the ½-inch screen were then wet-screened and sorted using magnifying glasses and tweezers. Photo courtesy of the Garbage Project.

Figure 8. A sort of materials exhumed in 1991 from Toronto Metroplex landfills in Canada that did not pass through the ½-inch screen. Photo courtesy of the Garbage Project.

Government and health diet surveys vary from Garbage Project food use estimates based on empty packaging and food remains in the same households by between 10 and 70 per cent (Rathje and Hughes 1975; Johnstone 1986; Dobyns and Rathje 1987; Rathje and Dobyns 1987; Rathje and Murphy 1992; and Rathje 1996; for Mexico City, see Restrepo *et al*. 1982) — the consumption of alcoholic beverages, high fibre cereals, high fat foods, and cruciferous vegetables diverge the most between reports and refuse (Johnstone and Rathje 1986; Rathje and Dobyns 1987).

To mollify recent concerns about household hazardous waste being thrown into household refuse, communities across the US have instituted household hazardous waste collections. Garbage Project studies before and after these collections have determined that if the collections are short-term, householders who are alerted to hazardous waste, but miss the collection and have no alternative disposal means, will throw such wastes in their refuse. The result, ironically, is higher hazardous wastes in household refuse after community-wide household hazardous wastes collections (Rathje and Wilson 1987; Wilson *et al*. 1994).

The variety of relevant refuse studies is immense, even including a design for a garbage census that anonymously, but with an error rate far below that of the US Census, counts residents in underclass neighbourhoods — those people most often missed by a mail-in or interview census (Rathje and Tani 1987).

In its examination of the modern world, the Garbage Project has utilized the *Integrated Model* outlined earlier in this paper. A few examples are illustrative (see Rathje 1979b, 1996). Because archaeologists start from a materialist perspective, we will relate the other perspectives to number five, specific material traces (refer to Table 1):

Table 1.

5-1: General cognitive rules — Material traces. Economists have argued that household food loss is a conscious choice that is made as a trade-off for more free time. As a result, they argue that studying actual food loss patterns would be pointless. In contrast to this argument, one survey/refuse comparison study indicates that a major correlate of food discard is the level of informant knowledge of food safety — the less knowledge, the more waste (Harrison 1976). As a result, education to a few simple rules of food safety might be useful in decreasing food waste.

5-2: Cognitive descriptions of behaviour — Material traces. First, of course, most interview-surveys indicate that respondents claim that they don't waste food. The Garbage Project has 25 years of data that refute such claims. But more to the point of truly understanding waste, Garbage Project studies indicate that people sensitive to food loss may admit more waste, but actually waste less than those who are largely unaware of their waste patterns. Consider what the Garbage Project calls the 'Fast Lane Syndrome'. Those households that buy more pre-prepared foods and less fresh food waste the highest percentage of fresh food (Rathje and Hughes 1977; Rathje 1992, 1996).

5-3: Behaviour observations and records — Material traces. It is also likely that preparation time relates to waste: the less time invested in preparing food, the more food is discarded. See above, the 'Fast Lane Syndrome'.

5-4: Behaviour shorthands — Material traces. There are lower food loss rates in Mexican-American neighbourhoods than in White neighbourhoods (Harrison *et al.* 1975; Harrison *et al.* 1983). This is likely attributable to the Mexican-American cultural background, both in terms of attitudes and values and in terms of types of foods used, preparation techniques, and ease of incorporating leftovers into other meals.

5-5: Material traces — Material traces. Rates of food loss can be recorded by types of package configurations and recorded across neighbourhoods to identify general loss/package patterns. The Garbage Project has found that food that is used regularly and comes in standard-sized packages is discarded at a much lower rate than specialty foods in odd-size packages. The best example is bread. There is very little waste associated with standard 16 oz. and 24 oz. 'sliced bread' loaves. In most households, sliced bread is used regularly at most meals. On the other hand, most wasted bread consists of specialty items, such as hamburger and hot-dog buns, muffins, biscuits, etc. These breads are used irregularly for cookouts or for other untypical meals. Specialty breads are wasted at a rate of 40 to 60 per cent (Rathje 1977a, 1986b; Wilson *et al.* 1991).

5-6: General material environments — Material traces. One early surprise in the Garbage Project's refuse studies was that during the well-publicized 'beef shortage' of 1973, the waste of edible beef was three times higher than it has been since. The increased loss of sugar products during the 1975 'sugar shortage' fits the 'crisis buying model' worked out to explain the consumer reaction to the beef shortage (Rathje 1977a, 1992).

This *integrated* approach has led to some principles of solid waste that are useful to both policy planners and householders everywhere. One primary example is the *first principle of waste*, which covers material-behavioural patterns in both food waste and household hazardous waste (Rathje 1977a, 1992; Wilson *et al.* 1991): *the more repetitive your behaviours, the less you will waste.* Thus, there is little waste recorded in commonly used foods and household cleaners. In contrast, the principle explains why beef, when it is in short supply and available erratically, specialty breads, and specialty home fix-up items — paints, stains, varnishes, and so on — are wasted at extremely high rates.

Such studies are relatively well-known (see Rathje 1984a, 1991, 1996; Rathje and Murphy 1992). What isn't well-known, but what will forge strong future directions for *garbology*, is the move from observer to participant. In other words, *garbology* will play an active part in the 'textbook ideal' of product and facility design. The first stage is providing data on what exists to those designing new products and facilities, and that process is well under way. The subsequent stage, experimentally testing new designs to determine whether they, for example, prevent waste or decompose waste in the manner designers intended, has now begun.

Over the last ten years, the Garbage Project has conducted a series of 'crushes'. This involves placing various products, including specific types of packaging, segregated by whether they were obtained from fresh refuse or landfill samples, into a confined bin and then applying increasing pressures on them from the top lid. As the known pressures increase, the volume occupied by the materials in the bin is precisely measured and graphed. This provides a record of how much space different materials will occupy under specified disposal conditions (see Wilson *et al.* 1989). Companies designing new packaging materials and configurations hire the Garbage Project to conduct comparable crushes of their prototypes to determine whether they exhibit properties that are considered more desirable in contrast to existing packaging (there are currently no published reports on prototype crushes because none of the new types of packaging are yet in full production, and the crush data are considered proprietary; results will be published when the new packaging is introduced into the market-place).

Another type of experimental *garbology* involves measuring various prototype materials' density, burying them in landfills, digging them up after specified periods of time, and testing them for both density changes and degree of degradation. Much more significant, the Garbage Project is currently testing new types of experimental landfill designs to determine the rates at which their contents both degrade and biodegrade. The first such dig was implemented to document the effectiveness of the design of a new 'bioreactor landfill' cell which pumps the fluids that collect at the bottom of the cell back into the top, in an attempt to jump-start biodegradation processes. The study compared samples from the 'bioreactor' cell and from a control cell which were both filled with similar refuse from the same community at the same time in Sandtown, DE. The analysis determined that after ten years of burial, trends towards biodegradation in the bioreactor cell were much clearer in the directions expected, but that the differences with the control cell were not yet significant (Rathje 1999c).

While much of the range of experimental *garbology* will mirror that of industry innovations that are designed to increase environmentally-friendly performance characteristics, the Garbage Project currently plans to sail untested *applied archaeology* waters — to provide immediate feedback to communities on their levels of recycling and collection of household hazardous waste and concurrently measure constituent households' response to the feedback information.

While many of the most obvious emerging foci in the applied archaeology of modern refuse have received attention, what will surely be one of the new millennium's

fastest growing specialties has not — even though it is already upon us. As Thomas
Mallon noted in an article in *Preservation* magazine (1997), when astronauts recovered
the *Surveyor 3* unmanned probe from the moon's surface on 19 November, 1969,
humans began the 'archaeology' of their presence in space, a subdiscipline that might
be called *exo-archaeology*.

And today, just as the 'Garbage Barge' returned to Long Island, New York to ignite
the 'Garbage Crisis' in the US in 1987, the garbage our extra-terrestrial missions left
behind in space has come back to haunt us. In fact, the greatest potential threat to
Earth's International Space Station is the junk we humans created. This debris includes
more than 10,000 'resident space objects' large enough to be tracked from Earth — only
5 per cent of which were functioning spacecraft in 1997. Add to that another 400,000
small space artefacts and another one million flakes of paint, all travelling at about
20,000 feet per second.

In response, military and civilian rocket scientists have usurped a subfield of archaeology that archaeologists themselves had not even envisioned! But who better to understand, explain, and provide information to prevent space garbage than archaeologists
(see Rathje 1999d)? If *exo-archaeology* seems humorous or literally too far out, ask anyone who was in the Australian outback when the 150-ton *skylab* crashed there in 1979.

If archaeologists have missed one burgeoning waste disposal field, they have not
missed another — the disposal of nuclear waste. This study is preconditioned for
archaeologists, because nuclear engineers think in archaeological time frames.

One of us (WLR) attended a US EPA workshop in Albuquerque, NM, in 1976 (Rathje
1977b). The question asked was simple: Should disposers attempt to hide nuclear wastes
from chance discoveries by archaeologists and others? The answer was just as simple: No!
Any artificial 'cover-up' would certainly be discovered by archaeologists, sooner or later
— and given the half-life of nuclear materials, just about any time would be too soon.

Since then, archaeologists have been consulted in designing markers to prevent
human disturbance of long-term nuclear waste disposal facilities. Archaeologists working with disposal engineers have examined the characteristics of ancient markers that
have survived for millennia, such as Stonehenge and the Great Wall of China, as well
as various types of pottery and other artefacts. Current design plans for nuclear waste
disposal sites include an outer ring of large stone monoliths, together with numerous
smaller buried markers of pottery. The stones would be carved and the ceramics
impressed with various symbols and languages to convey information about the site
(see Kaplan and Adams 1999). Studying the symbolic and preservation characteristics
of ancient remains is not just to benefit tourists. As our society's need to dispose of dan-
gerous wastes grows, so will its need to employ archaeologists to ensure that deposited
materials remain undisturbed over the coming millennia.

It is, in fact, applied archaeology's ability to reach from the *black hole* to the peoples
of other millennia that will be its most important asset in serving the interests and needs

of contemporary audiences. For all of the specialties and divergent theories that may lead to segmentation in archaeology, this is one aspect of its practice which can bring people together and, at the same time, bring added significance to its results. That is, bringing the results and patterns of the past directly up-to-date into the present.

If we are to learn the lessons of the past, we must see our relationship to it. Too often people see the present as removed and totally separate from the past. As the Saxe–Goldstein Hypothesis demonstrates, this is true even of archaeologists.

Only by relating something tangible in the past to something equally tangible in the present — what we will call *synthetic archaeology* — can the interrelationship and educational value of both be best communicated. A.L. Kroeber (1919), one of anthropology's stalwarts, understood this clearly when he published a paper on the repeating cycles in the lengths of women's dresses. He didn't stop 50 years before his time; instead, he explicitly linked three centuries of cycles in dress length directly to his present day.

Schiffer has followed this *synthetic* tradition by studying miniaturized radios (1991, 1992) and electric cars (Schiffer *et al.* 1994) from initial innovations all the way to the present day. His work on the techno-history of the shirt-pocket radio, for instance, demonstrates that the Japanese did *not* invent the transistor pocket radio, and, moreover, that contemporary popular and corporate accounts of the Japanese takeover of this market in the 1950s and '60s are not only inaccurate, but (as 'cryptohistory') are often tailored to suit corporate agendas regarding our government's foreign economic policy (Schiffer 1992).

Schiffer and Miller (1999) have recently presented a general theory of human behaviour and communication based on a synthetic approach. The theory lays out general principles by which a material culture medium facilitates all human interactions, including communication. Because their theory is truly general, i.e. not constrained by time-space parameters, it offers great potential for examining communicative processes from the present day into the more distant past (e.g. see LaMotta and Schiffer 2001).

A dramatic example of synthetic research in historical archaeology was provided by Deetz's work at Plymouth Plantation in Massachusetts in the late 1960s and early 1970s — one that still has stinging significance today. Deetz had excavated the trash pits of three households of known size and duration — the Edward Wilson site (1635–1650), the Joseph Howland site (1675–1725), and an unnamed site occupied by a single family (1830–1835). When he analysed the remains, the archaeologist arrived at a novel way of illustrating his ceramic serving and storage vessels: he photographed all of the ceramics he recovered on the same lab table in the same room and from the same angle (Deetz 1973). The Wilson finds comprise 14 small dabs on the table. The Howland remains fill eight rather significant piles on the table. The nineteenth-century materials — from a family of five over five years — included an almost complete eight-place table setting discernible in the piles of porcelain which cover the table to nearly overflowing (Rathje and Schiffer 1982, fig. 2–12). From 27 years of experience, one of us (WLR) can testify that all of the discarded serving materials from a family of five for five years today — mainly disposable paper and plastic plates, cups, glasses, bowls that would be preserved for centuries in today's dry landfills — would fill up the room to more than overflowing, making a picture of the table impossible! Do we really understand the material realities that we are creating today without material reference to the past?

Applied archaeology is currently documenting the differences and similarities between all of society's cognitive voices and the material-behavioural realities that surround them in today's global society.

Issues of significance for the archaeology of recent times

Together, the ethnoarchaeology, historical archaeology, and applied archaeology explorers of archaeology's *black hole* are facing a number of similar social issues. We believe that through *integrated* (material-behavioural-cognitive), *synthetic* (linking past and present), and *applied* (using archaeological techniques to study the present) approaches, archaeology can make the most significant impact on the modern world. Global realities of the present and recent past will no doubt continue to shape research goals for 'archaeologists of today'. At the date of publication, several broad themes seem to provide a common ground for many *black hole* explorers.

These themes include (but are certainly not limited to):

1 *The archaeological study of broad economic-ideological systems and their impact on global economy and society* (e.g. Capitalism, Communism — e.g. see Leone 1999; Little 1994). Such studies would focus on the way capitalist, communist, and countries following other ideologies reached their present socio-economic structure, and how they are adapting to significant social, economic, and ideological changes. One of the new emerging foci of research would be an aberration of Capitalism that is emerging full-blown in Russia and elsewhere and that might be called 'No-Holds-Barred Entrepreneurialism'. Often replete with strong underworld connections and specializing in illicit transactions, it is forming an underground network that will have important implications for above-ground transactions and social conditions.

2 *Consumerism and industrialization.* Majewski and Schiffer (2001), for example, see the development of consumer-oriented production and distribution systems, as well as their products, as a major force in the recent historical trajectories, one obviously related to Capitalism. Although their primary example, ceramic place settings, is not illustrated much beyond 1900, they suggest a comprehensive approach which draws on both historical archaeology and applied archaeology to understand the ramifications of these processes in the past and present. To continue the trajectory to the present day, the change from mass-marketed 12- and 16-place settings in the early part of the twentieth century to the 4- and 6-place settings in 'box stores', such as Walmart and Target in the US, today, clearly has significant social implications — as does the burgeoning of disposable dinnerware over the last half-century (see the reference to Deetz 1973 above).

3 *Racism, ethnicity, religions and internecine conflict.* Racial-ethnic boundaries and religious boundaries, their construction, and impact on social life and conflict are major themes of recent world history. These are issues that demand anthropological, archaeological, as well as historical, study in both the past and the present. Historical archaeologists can build on a growing body of data on ethnicity and conflict developed by archaeologists and anthropologists. We must note that the archaeological contributions currently have a long way to go to provide any material-behavioural-cognitive certainties, other than that the interrelationships are highly unpredictable, flexible, and subject to idiosyncratic manipulation (see Jones 1997).

One new archaeological focus for such research could be the periodic fluctuation between politico-economic centralization (e.g. the Roman Empire and the first several decades of the Union of Soviet Socialist Republics (USSR)) and subsequent decentralization (e.g. the Postclassic Maya and the several Soviet Union republics that are now independent or fighting for independence). Today, the trend seems to be what systems theorists identified as 'near-decomposibility'. When large-scale political systems (or any other mega-systems) collapse, they don't collapse to their most basic unit (in behavioural systems, the household or the local community); rather they condense to a more stable higher-level unit, such as the basic ethnic or religious identities recognized by their constituents. As ethnicity and religion become increasingly more important in the contemporary world as a basic common denominator and plane of cleavage, so will an archaeology which identifies it, records its history, and studies its role in the formation of new political units.

What archaeologists did in Rhodesia was valuable to appreciating the civilization in Black Africa — identifying twelfth-century Zimbabwe as a local indigenous development (Caton-Thompson 1931). But today, most colonial powers have been replaced by local rulers. The world has changed, but not always in the direction of less oppression and violence.

As we all have come to understand in the last few decades, the history of some ethnic and religious groups is a history of animosity and bloodshed. A significant problem is that the archaeology of ethnicity and religion can be used to fan the fires of hatred. Just consider Kosovo, the site of egregious turmoil in recent years, as it has been for centuries. In fact, the name 'Kosovo', or 'Black birds', comes from 'Kosovo Pulje'. This 'Field of Black Birds' is where, in AD 1389, Prince Lazar's Serbian Knights battled the Ottoman troops of Sultan Murad I. Even though by the mid-1990s, Kosovo was largely home to Albanian Muslims, most Eastern Orthodox Serbs still considered the battlefield the 'heart' of the Serbian nation. We are currently witnessing the outcome of the conflict over the differing conceptions held by the former residents of Yugoslavia (Rathje 1999a).

And most other parts of the world are no different: consider Hutu and Tutsi in Rwanda and the Congo, Muslims and Hindus in Pakistan and India, Catholics and Protestants in Northern Ireland, Christians and Muslims in East Timor, Eastern Orthodox Christians and fundamentalist Muslims in the former Soviet Union, Palestinians and Jews in the Near East. No wonder that the Yugoslavian strongman Marshal Tito de-emphasized the archaeology of ethnicity and instead built huge monuments to general human values. And the words of Heinrich Himmler, *Reichsführer*-SS and author of Nazi Germany's program of archaeo-propaganda, serve as a chilling reminder of the extremes to which archaeological data can be manipulated and distorted in the name of imperialism, ethnicity, and *Kulturkreis*:[4]

> . . . we are only interested in one thing — to project into the dim and distant past the picture of our nation as we envisage it for the future. . . . Our teaching of German origins has depended for centuries on a falsification. We are entitled to impose one of our own at any time (quoted in Arnold 1992).

In contrast, many archaeologists who are currently reconstructing the past are at the same time exposing the material realities of oppressive state ideologies and planting fertile seeds of change in the futures of present day societies — none more than forensic archaeologists in Kosovo, El Salvador, Rwanda, and the former USSR. What are the archaeological ethics of this issue?

4 *An archaeology of the uses of archaeology.* Answering the question posed above may involve studying the way archaeological data are used and misused by politicians, the media, and even teachers in schools. Postprocessualists have talked about such studies for years, and today such events are commonplace world round. What a dynamic and critical material-behavioural-cognitive arena to investigate live!

5 *Health issues.* Human health, morbidity, and disease are topics with uneven representation in the historical record. For example, in the US, the routine practice of autopsy was not common until relatively recent times. As a result, historical records on cause of death are incomplete at best. Moreover, disease, diet, and demography represent synergistic phenomena that have received inconsistent (and often inaccurate) historical documentation. Archaeologists, particularly those trained in bioarchaeology, palaeopathology, and palaeodietary and demographic reconstruction, are in a unique position to provide data relevant to these processes in the past (e.g. see references in Larsen 1997; Buikstra and Cook 1980; Larsen 1987; Swedlund and Armelagos 1976), and to collaborate with historical and applied archaeologists studying health issues in the

---

[4] *Kulturkreis*; a doctrine promulgated by Gustav Kossinna in the 1920s, 'defined as the identification of ethnic regions on the basis of excavated material culture' (Arnold 1992, 32).

present (e.g. Deagan 1991). This interest is especially relevant as one of our global society's key artefacts, the commercial jetliner, spreads diseases worldwide. At the time of this writing, the unexpected spread to North America of several pathogens, including West Nile Fever, malaria, and a drug-resistant strain of tuberculosis, is front-page news in the US.

In a related case, health officials have already begun to note that a recent *New England Journal of Medicine* report by Fuchs (*et al.* 1999), which questions the value of a high-fibre diet in protecting against colon cancer, depends entirely upon informants accurately characterizing their diet on a National Cancer Institute questionnaire. A Garbage Project study found that most respondents could not come close to accomplishing this task (Johnstone and Rathje 1986; Johnstone 1986) — don't quit eating those high-fibre cereals yet!

6 *Environmental issues.* Archaeology, more than any other discipline, can provide a truly long-term (2 million years and more) perspective on human impact on the global environment; such research should be carried through the historic and recent periods to link present situations with past processes. As the debate about the hole in the ozone and global warming heats up, the archaeology of how past societies failed to see how they were degrading their environments (see, for example, Gibson 1974; Culbert 1977) until it was far too late, and how our behaviour and material culture are transforming the environments around us in a variety of unexpected ways (see Graham 1999, in press), will provide information critical to policy planners and the public.

The archaeology of recent times — a loss of innocence

Archaeology is no longer an ivory-tower pursuit of antiquarians, but a body of knowledge that is becoming increasingly politically-charged and powerful in modern society. Archaeologists will be called upon to provide data relevant to the future fates of many people from traditional agriculturalists to suspected criminals, to write histories of combative self-interest groups, and to record information useful in planning critical actions in areas of human health and environmental conservation. An active and critical self-awareness of this use of archaeological data must be maintained to prevent archaeologists from becoming mere mouthpieces of the 'in-group'. Nonetheless, these future applications and examples discussed above highlight the central theme of this paper: archaeological methods, techniques, and interpretations are directly relevant and necessary for understanding our modern world and how the behavioural-material-cognitive processes that mark the ebb and flow of local cultural trajectories and of global history came to be. Now that we have found ourselves at both ends of the shovel, we must continue to 'excavate' ourselves in earnest.

Acknowledgements

Thanks to Marcia H. Rockman, Kenneth L. Feder, Mark P. Leone, and Michael B. Schiffer who provided references, suggestions, and/or comments on earlier drafts. Thanks also to Sarah E. Klandrud for compiling research materials for this paper.

References

ADAMS, E.C. in press: *Homol'ovi: An Ancient Hopi Settlement Cluster in Northeastern Arizona* (Tucson).

ALLEN, S. 1971: A comparison of garbage (Tucson, AZ, unpublished manuscript on file at the Arizona State Museum).

ARIZA, F. 1971: Skyline vs. a Chicano barrio garbage (Tucson, AZ, unpublished manuscript on file at the Arizona State Museum).

ARNOLD, B. 1992: The past as propaganda: how Hitler's archaeologists distorted European prehistory to justify racist and territorial goals. *Archaeology* 45(4) July/August, 30–7.

ARNOLD, D. 1975: Ceramic ecology of the Ayacucho Basin, Peru: implications for prehistory. *Curr. Anthropol.* 16(2), 183–206.

ARNOLD, D. 1983: Design structure and community organization in Quinua, Peru. In Washburn, D. (ed.), *Structure and cognition in art* (Cambridge), 56–73.

ARNOLD, D. 1989: Patterns of learning, residence, and descent among potters in Ticul, Mexico. In Shennan, S. (ed.), *Archaeological approaches to cultural identity* (London), 174–84.

BINFORD, L.R. 1968: Archaeological perspectives. In Binford, S.R. and Binford, L.R. (eds.), *New perspectives in archeology* (Chicago), 5–32.

BINFORD, L.R. 1976: Forty-seven trips: a case study in the character of some formation processes. In Hall, E.S., Jr. (ed.), *Contributions to anthropology, the interior peoples of northern Alaska* (Ottowa National Museum of Canada, National Museum of Man, Mercury Series, Paper no. 49), 299–351.

BINFORD, L.R. 1978a: *Nunamiut ethnoarchaeology* (New York).

BINFORD, L.R. 1978b: Dimensional analysis of behavior and site structure: learning from an Eskimo hunting stand. *American Antiquity* 43(3), 330–61.

BINFORD, L.R. 1979: Organization and formation processes: looking at curated technologies. *J. Anthropol. Res.* 35(3), 255–73.

BINFORD, L.R. 1980: Willow smoke and dogs' tails: hunter-gatherer settlement systems and archaeological site formation. *American Antiquity* 45(1), 4–20.

BREW, J.O. 1946: *Archaeology of Alkali Ridge, southeastern Utah* (Cambridge, MA, Papers of the Peabody Museum of American Archaeology and Ethnology, Harvard University, Vol. XXI).

BRUGGE, D.M. 1994: *The Navajo-Hopi land dispute: an American tragedy* (Albuquerque).

BRZEZINSKI, Z. 1989: *The grand failure: the birth and death of communism in the twentieth century* (New York).

BUCHLI, V. and LUCAS, G. (eds.) 2001: *The absent present: the archaeology of the contemporary past.*

BUIKSTRA, J. and COOK, D. 1980: Paleopathology: an American account. *Annu. Rev. Anthropol.* 9, 433–70.

CAMERON, C.M. and TOMKA, S.A. 1993: *Abandonment of settlements and regions: ethnoarchaeological and archaeological approaches* (Cambridge).

CATON-THOMPSON, G. 1931: *The Zimbabwe culture: ruins and reactions* (New York, reprinted in 1970).

CLAASSEN, C. 1994: Washboards, pigtoes, and muckets: historic musseling in the Mississippi watershed. *Historical Archaeol.* 28(2).

COMMITTEE ON DIET, NUTRITION, AND CANCER of the ASSEMBLY OF LIFE SCIENCES, NATIONAL RESEARCH COUNCIL 1983: *Diet, nutrition and cancer* (Washington, D.C.).

CRABTREE, D.E. 1968: Mesoamerican polyhedral cores and prismatic blades. *American Antiquity* 33, 446–78.

CRAWFORD, O.G.S. 1953: *Archaeology in the field* (New York).

CULBERT, T.P. 1977: Maya development and collapse: an economic perspective. In Hammond, N. (ed.), *Social process in Maya prehistory: studies in honor of Sir Eric Thompson* (New York), 509–30.

CUSHING, F.H. 1890: Preliminary notes on the origin, working hypothesis, and primary researches of the Hemenway Southwestern Archaeological Expedition. In *Proceedings of the 7th International Conference of Americanists* (Berlin), 151–94.

DARNELL, R. 1969: The development of American anthropology, 1879–1920: from the Bureau of American Ethnology to Franz Boas (Philadelphia, PA, Ph.D. dissertation, the University of Pennsylvania).

DAVID, N. 1972: On the life span of pottery, type frequencies, and archaeological inference. *American Antiquity* 37, 141–2.

DEAGAN, K. 1982: Avenues of inquiry in historical archaeology. In Schiffer, M.B. (ed.), *Advances in Archaeological Method and Theory*, Vol. 5 (New York), 151–77.

DEAGAN, K. 1991: Historical archaeology's contributions to our understanding of early America. In Falk, L. (ed.), *Historical archaeology in global perspective* (Washington, D.C.).

DeBOER, W. and LATHRAP, D. 1979: The making and breaking of Shipibo-Conibo ceramics. In Kramer, C. (ed.), *Ethnoarchaeology: implications of ethnography for archaeology* (New York), 102–38.

DEETZ, J.J.F. 1965: *The dynamics of stylistic change in Arikara ceramics* (Urbana, Illinois Studies in Anthropology 4).

DEETZ, J.J.F. 1973: Ceramics from Plymouth, 1635–1835: the archaeological evidence. In Quimby, I.M.G. (ed.), *Ceramics in America* (Charlottesville, VA), 15–40.

DEETZ, J.J.F. 1977: *In small things forgotten* (Garden City).

DOBYNS, S. and RATHJE, W.L. (eds.) 1987: *The NFCS report/refuse study*, 4 vols. (Washington, D.C., Consumer Nutrition Division, US Department of Agriculture).

FEDER, K.L. (ed.) 1999: *Lessons from the past: an introductory reader in archaeology* (Mountain View, CA).

FEWKES, J.W. 1893: A-WA-TO-BI: an archaeological verification of a Tusayan legend. *American Anthropologist* 64(4), 363–75.

FEWKES, J.W. 1896: The prehistoric culture of Tusayan. *American Anthropologist* 9(5), 151–74.

FEWKES, J.W. 1900: Tusayan migration traditions. *Nineteenth Annual Report of the Bureau of American Ethnology, 1897–98*, part 2 (Washington, D.C.), 577–633.

FONTANA, B.L. 1970: In search of us. *Historical Archaeol.* 6, 1–2.

FUCHS, C.S., EDWARD, M.D., GIOVANNUCCI, L., COLDITZ, G.A., HUNTER, D.J., STAMPER, M.J., ROSEN, B., SPEIZER, R.E. and WILLETT, W.C. 1999: Dietary fiber and the risk of colorectal cancer and adenoma in women. *New England J. Medicine* 340(3), 169–76.

FUNG, E.E. and RATHJE, W.L. 1982: How we waste $31 billion in food a year. In Hayes, J. (ed.), *The 1982 Yearbook of Agriculture* (Washington, D.C., US Department of Agriculture), 352–7.

GIBSON, M. 1974: Violation of fallow and engineered disaster in Mesopotamian civilization. In Downing, T.E. and Gibson, M. (eds.), *Irrigation's impact on society* (Tucson, AZ), 7–19.

GLASSIE, H. 1975: *Folk housing in Middle Virginia: a structural analysis of historic artifacts* (Knoxville, TN).

GOLDSTEIN, L.G. 1976: Spatial structure and social organization: regional manifestations of Mississippian society (Evanston, IL, Ph.D. dissertation, Northwestern University. Ann Arbor, MI, University Microfilms).

GOULD, R.A. 1980: *Living archaeology* (Cambridge).

GOULD, R.A. and SCHIFFER, M.B. (eds.) 1981: *Modern material culture: the archaeology of us* (New York).

GRAHAM, E. 1999: Metaphor and metamorphism: some thoughts on environmental metahistory. In Balee, W. (ed.), *Advances in Historical Ecology* (New York), 119–37.

GRAHAM, E. in press: Maya cities and the character of a tropical urbanism. In Sinclair, P.J. (ed.), *Urban Origins in Eastern Africa* (London).

HARDIN, M. 1970: Design structure and social interaction: archaeological implications of an ethnographic analysis. *American Antiquity* 35, 332–43.

HARMER, R.M. 1963: *The High Cost of Dying* (New York).

HARRISON, G.G. 1976: Socio-cultural correlates of food utilization and waste in a sample of urban households (Tucson, AZ, Ph.D. dissertation, the University of Arizona).

HARRISON, G.G., RATHJE, W.L. and HUGHES, W.W. 1975: Food waste behavior in an urban population. *J. Nutrition Education* 7(1), 13–16.

HARRISON, G.G., RATHJE, W.L., RITENBAUGH, C., HUGHES, W.W. and Ho, E.E. 1983: *The Food Loss Project: methodologies for estimating household level food losses* (Washington, D.C., Consumer Nutrition Division, US Department of Agriculture).

HAWLEY, F.M. 1937: Pueblo social organization as a lead to Pueblo history. *American Anthropologist* 39(3), 504–22.

HAWLEY, F.M. 1950: Big kivas, little kivas, and moiety houses in historical reconstruction. *Southwestern J. Anthropol.* 6(3), 286–302.

HAWLEY ELLIS, F.M. 1968: An interpretation of prehistoric death customs in terms of modern Southwestern parallels. In *Pap. Archaeol. Soc. New Mexico* 1 (Santa Fe), 57–68.

HAWLEY ELLIS, F.M. and COLTON, H.S. 1974: *The Hopi: their history and use of lands* (New York) (includes F.M. Hawley Ellis' report: Indian Claims Commission docket 229; H.S. Colton's report: Indian Claims Commission docket 196).

HAYDEN, B. (ed.) 1987: *Lithic studies among contemporary highland Maya* (Tucson, AZ).

HAYDEN, B. and CANNON, A. 1983: Where the garbage goes: refuse disposal in the Maya highlands. *J. Anthropol. Archaeol.* 2, 117–63.

HILL, J.N. 1970: *Broken K Pueblo: prehistoric social organization in the American Southwest* (Tucson, Anthropological Papers of the University of Arizona 18).

HILL, J.N. 1978: Individuals and their artifacts: an experimental study in archaeology. *American Antiquity* 43, 245–57.

HODDER, I. 1977: The distribution of material culture items in the Baringo district of western Kenya. *Man* n.s. 12, 239–69.

HODDER, I. (ed.) 1987: *The archaeology of contextual meanings* (Cambridge).

IMAMURA, K. 1996: *Prehistoric Japan: new perspectives on insular East Asia* (Honolulu).

INGERSOLL, D.W., Jr. and BRONITSKY, G. 1987: *Mirror and metaphor: material and social constructions of reality* (Lanham, MD).

JOHNSTONE, B.M. 1986: Alternative approaches to nutritional assessment for studies of diet and disease (Tucson, AZ, University of Arizona Ph.D. dissertation).

JOHNSTONE, B.M. and RATHJE, W.L. 1986: Building a theory of the difference between respondent reports and material realities (Dallas, TX, symposium, 'Different approaches to using food consumption data bases for evaluating dietary intake,' annual meeting of the Institute of Food Technologists).

JONES, S. 1997: *The archaeology of ethnicity: constructing identities in the past and present* (London).

JOYCE, C. and STOVER, E. 1991: *Witnesses from the grave* (Boston).

KAPLAN, M. and ADAMS, M. 1999: Using the past to protect the future: marking nuclear waste disposal sites. In Feder, K.L. (ed.) 1999, 107–12.

KLEINDIENST, M. and WATSON, P.J. 1956: Action archaeology: the archaeological inventory of a living community. *Anthropol. Tomorrow* 5, 75–8.

KLUCKHOHN, C. 1940: The conceptual structure in Middle American studies. In Hay, C.L. (ed.), *The Maya and their neighbors* (New York, reprinted 1973), 41–51.

KOBAYASHI, M. 1994: Use-alteration analysis of Kalinga pottery: interior carbon deposits of cooking pots. In Longacre, W.A. and Skibo, J.M. (eds.), *Kalinga ethnoarchaeology* (Washington, D.C.), 127–68.

KOBAYASHI, M. 1996: Ethnoarchaeological study on the relationship between vessel form and function (Tucson, AZ, Ph.D. dissertation, the University of Arizona. University Microfilms, Ann Arbor, MI).

KRAMER, C. 1982: *Village ethnoarchaeology, rural Iran in archaeological perspective* (New York).

KRAMER, C. 1997: *Pottery in Rajasthan: ethnoarchaeology in two Indian cities* (Washington, D.C.).

KROEBER, A.L. 1919: On the principle of order in civilizations as exemplified by changes of fashion. *American Anthropologist* 21(3), 235–63.

LaMOTTA, V.M. 1998: Behavioral variability in mortuary deposition (Seattle, WA, paper presented at the 63rd Annual Meeting of the Society for American Archaeology).

LaMOTTA, V.M. and SCHIFFER, M.B. 2001: Behavioral archaeology: towards a new synthesis. In Hodder, I. (ed.), *Archaeological theory today* (Cambridge), 14–64.

La ROCHE, C.J. and BLAKEY, M.L. 1997: Seizing intellectual power: the dialogue at the New York African Burial Ground. *Historical Archaeol.* 31(3), 84–106.

LARSEN, C.S. 1987: Bioarchaeological interpretations of subsistence economy and behavior from human skeletal remains. In Schiffer, M.B. (ed.), *Advances in Archaeological Method and Theory*, Vol. 10 (New York), 339–445.

LARSEN, C.S. 1997: *Bioarchaeology: interpreting behavior from the human skeleton* (Cambridge).

LAUMANN, E.O. and HOUSE, J.S. 1970: Living room styles and social attributes: the patterning of material artifacts in a modern urban community. *Sociology and Social Research* 54(3), 321–42.

LEONE, M.P. 1973: Archaeology as the science of technology: Mormon town plans and fences. In Redman, C.L. (ed.), *Research and Theory in Current Archaeology* (New York), 125–50.

LEONE, M.P. 1977: The new Mormon Temple in Washington, D.C. In Ferguson, L.G. (ed.), *Historical archaeology and the importance of material things* (Society for Historical Archaeology, Special Publication Series No. 2), 43–61.

LEONE, M.P. 1979: *Roots of modern Mormonism* (Cambridge, MA).

LEONE, M.P. 1999: *Historical archaeologies of capitalism* (New York).

LEONE, M.P. and POTTER, P.B., Jr. 1988a: Introduction: issues in historical archaeology. In Leone, M.P. and Potter, P.B., Jr. (eds.) 1988b, 1–22.

LEONE, M.P. and POTTER, P.B., Jr. (eds.) 1988b: *The recovery of meaning: historical archaeology in the eastern United States* (Washington, D.C.).

LEONE, M.P. and SILBERMAN, N.A. 1995: *Invisible America: unearthing our hidden history* (New York).

LIGHTFOOT, K.G. 1995: Culture contact studies: redefining the relationship between prehistoric and historical archaeology. *American Antiquity* 60(2), 199–217.

LILIENFELD, R. and RATHJE, W.L. 1995: Six enviro-myths. *New York Times* Op-Ed, 01/21.

LILIENFELD, R. and RATHJE, W.L. 1998: *Use less stuff: environmental solutions for who we really are* (New York).

LITTLE, B. 1994: People with history: an update on historical archaeology in the United States. *J. Archaeol. Method and Theory* 1(1), 5–40.

LOCKE, R. 2000: The body farmer: Bill Bass' studies of the dead molded forensic anthropology. *Discovering Archaeol.* 2(2), 26–9.

LONGACRE, W.A. 1970: *Archaeology as anthropology: a case study* (Tucson, Anthropological Papers of the University of Arizona 17).

LONGACRE, W.A. 1999: Standardization and specialization: what's the link? In Skibo, J.M. and Feinman, G. (eds.), *Pottery and People: Dynamic Interactions* (Salt Lake City), 44–58.

LONGACRE, W.A., KVAMME, K. and KOBAYASHI, M. 1988: Southwestern pottery standardization: an ethnoarchaeological view from the Philippines. *The Kiva* 53(2), 110–21.

LYONS, P.D. 2001: Winslow orange ware and the ancestral Hopi migration horizon (Tucson, AZ, Ph.D. dissertation, the University of Arizona).

MACAULAY, D. 1979: *Motel of the mysteries* (Boston).

McGUIRE, R.H. 1988: Dialogues with the dead: ideology and the cemetery. In Leone, M.P. and Potter, P.B., Jr. (eds.) 1988b, 435–80.

McGUIRE, R., HUGHES, W.W. and RATHJE, W.L. 1985: *The Garbage Project Report on recycling behavior* (Technical Report NSF/Cee-82145) (Springfield, VA, National Technical Information Services).

McKELLAR, J. 1983: *Correlates and the explanation of distributions* (Atlatl, Occasional Papers 4, Anthropology Club, the University of Arizona).

McVICKER, D. 1972: The cemetary seminar: exploring the research and learning potential of the 'new archaeology' (Miami, paper presented at the 37th Annual Meeting of the Society for American Archaeology).

MAJEWSKI, T. and SCHIFFER, M.B. 2001: Modern material culture studies: toward an archaeology of consumerism. In Buchli, V. and Lucas, G. (eds.) 2001, 26–50.

MALLON, T. 1997: Space junk. *Preservation* 1(2), 41–5.

MAPLES, W.R. and BROWNING, M. 1994: *Dead men do tell tales: the strange and fascinating cases of a forensic anthropologist* (New York).

MARTIN, P.S. and RINALDO, J.B. 1950: Sites of the Reserve Phase, Pine Lawn Valley, western New Mexico. *Fieldiana: Anthropology* 38(3).

MINDELEFF, C. 1900: Localization of Tusayan clans. *Nineteenth Annual Report of the Bureau of American Ethnology, 1897–98*, part 2 (Washington, D.C.), 635–53.

MINDELEFF, V. 1891: A study of Pueblo architecture in Tusayan and Cibola. *Eighth Annual Report of the Bureau of American Ethnology, 1886–87* (Washington, D.C.), 3–228.

MITFORD, J. 1963: *The American way of death* (New York).

MITFORD, J. 1998: *The American way of death revisited* (New York).

NATHAN, R. 1960: *The Weans* (New York).

NEUPERT, M. 1994: Strength testing archaeological ceramics: a new perspective. *American Antiquity* 59, 709–23.

NEUPERT, M. 1999: Potters and politics: an ethnoarchaeological study of ceramic manufacture in Paradijon, the Philippines (Tucson, AZ, Ph.D. dissertation, the University of Arizona).

NOËL HUME, I. 1964: Archaeology: handmaiden to history. *North Carolina Historical Rev.* 41(2), 215–25.

O'CONNELL, J.F. 1979: Room to move: contemporary Alyawara settlement patterns and their implications for Aboriginal housing policy. In Heppell, M. (ed.), *A black reality: aboriginal camps and housing in remote Australia* (Canberra, Australian Institute of Aboriginal Studies), 97–120.

ORSER, C.E., Jr. 1995: Is there a behavioral historical archaeology? In Skibo, J.M., Walker, W.H. and Nielsen, A.E. (eds.), *Expanding Archaeology* (Salt Lake City), 187–97.

ORSER, C.E., Jr. 1999: The challenge of race to American historical archaeology. *American Anthropologist* 100(3), 661–8.

ORSER, C.E., Jr. and FAGAN, B.M. 1995: *Historical archaeology* (New York).

OWSLEY, D.W., STRINOVIC, D., SLAUS, M., KOLLMANN, D.D. and RICHARDSON, M.L. 1996: Recovery and identification of civilian victims of the war in Croatia. *Cultural Resource Management* 19(10), 33–6.

THE OXFORD ENGLISH DICTIONARY EDITORS 1995: *Oxford Dictionary and Usage Guide to the English Language* (Oxford).

PARSONS, E.C. 1940: Relations between ethnology and archaeology in the Southwest. *American Antiquity* 5(3), 214–20.

PRAETZELLIS, A. 1998: Introduction: why every archaeologist should tell stories once in a while. *Historical Archaeol.* 32(1), 1–3.

RATHJE, W.L. 1974: The Garbage Project: a new way of looking at the problems of archaeology. *Archaeology* 27(4), 236–41.

RATHJE, W.L. 1977a: In praise of archaeology: Le Projet du Garbage. In Ferguson, L.G. (ed.), *Historic archaeology and the importance of material things* (Society for Historical Archaeology), 36–42.

RATHJE, W.L. 1977b: Radioactive wastes disposal: an archaeological perspective. Proceedings, *A workshop on policy and technical issues pertinent to the development of environmental protection criteria for radioactive wastes* (Report ORP/CsD-77-2) (Washington, D.C., Environmental Protection Agency Office of Radiation Programs).

RATHJE, W.L. 1979a: Modern material culture studies. In Schiffer, M.B. (ed.), *Advances in Archaeological Method and Theory*, Vol. 2 (New York), 1–37.

RATHJE, W.L. 1979b: Trace measures. In Sechrest, L. (ed.), *Unobtrusive measures today: new directions for methodology of behavioral science* (San Francisco), 75–91.

RATHJE, W.L. 1984a: The garbage decade. *American Behavioral Scientist* 28(1), 9–29.

RATHJE, W.L. 1984b: 'Where's the beef?': red meat and reactivity. *American Behavioral Scientist* 28(1), 71–91.

RATHJE, W.L. 1985: A decent burial. *Atlantic Monthly* 256(3), 16–18.

RATHJE, W.L. 1986a: A decent burial for the American Dream. *Missouri Rev.* 9(3), 221–2.

RATHJE, W.L. 1986b: Why we throw food away. *Atlantic Monthly* 257(4), 14–16.

RATHJE, W.L. 1988: Landfill garbage. *New York Times* Op-Ed, 01/26.

RATHJE, W.L. 1989: Rubbish! *Atlantic Monthly* 260(6), 99–109.

RATHJE, W.L. 1991: Once and future landfills. *National Geographic* 179(5), 116–34.

RATHJE, W.L. 1992: Tucson to Armenia: the first principle of waste. *Garbage* 4(1), 22–3.

RATHJE, W.L. 1996: The archaeology of us. In Ciegelski, C. (ed.), *Encyclopaedia Britannica's Yearbook of Science and the Future — 1997* (New York), 158–77.

RATHJE, W.L. 1999a: Kosovo and the archaeologists. *Discovering Archaeol.* 1(4), 92–5.

RATHJE, W.L. 1999b: *Canis familiaris*: going to the dogs again. *Discovering Archaeol.* 1(2), 108–11.

RATHJE, W.L. 1999c: Guess what? Wetter is better. *MSW-Management* 9(3), 78–83.

RATHJE, W.L. 1999d: Archaeology of space garbage. *Discovering Archaeol.* 1(5), 108–11.

RATHJE, W.L. 2000: Why we survived Y2K. *Discovering Archaeol.* 2(1), 102–4.

RATHJE, W.L. 2001: Integrated archaeology: a garbage paradigm. In Buchli, V. and Lucas, G. (eds.) 2001, 63–76.

RATHJE, W.L. and DOBYNS, S. 1987: Handbook of potential distortions in respondent diet reports, Vol. 1. In Dobyns, S. and Rathje, W.L. (eds.) 1987.

RATHJE, W.L. and HUGHES, W.W. 1975: The Garbage Project as a nonreactive approach. In Sinaiko, H.W. and Broedling, L.A. (eds.), *Perspectives on attitude assessment: surveys and their alternatives* (Washington, D.C., Smithsonian Institution Technical Report No. 2), 151–67.

RATHJE, W.L. and HUGHES, W.W. 1977: Food loss at the household level: a perspective from household residuals analysis. *Proceedings, RANN 2, the Second Symposium on Research Applied to National Needs* (Washington, D.C., National Science Foundation), 3, 32–5.

RATHJE, W.L., HUGHES, W.W., WILSON, D.C., TANI, M.K. and JONES, T.W. 1992: The archaeology of contemporary landfills. *American Antiquity* 57(3), 437–47.

RATHJE, W.L. and MURPHY, C. 1992: *Rubbish! The archaeology of garbage* (New York).

RATHJE, W.L. and TANI, M.K. 1987: *MNI triangulation final report: estimating population characteristics at the neighborhood level from household refuse*, 3 vols. (Washington, D.C., Center for Survey Methods Research of the Bureau of the Census).

RATHJE, W.L. and WILSON, D.C. 1987: Archaeological techniques applied to characterization of household discards and their potential contamination of groundwater. Paper presented at the Conference on Solid Waste Management and Materials Policy, New York City.

RATHJE, W.L., WILSON, D.C., HUGHES, W.W. and HERNDON, R. 1987: *Characterization of household hazardous waste from Marin County, California, and New Orleans, Louisiana* (Las Vegas, US EPA Environmental Monitoring Systems Laboratory Report No. EPA/600/x-87/129).

RATHJE, W.L., WILSON, D.C., HUGHES, W.W. and JONES, T.W. 1988: *The Phoenix Report: Characterization of Recyclable Materials in Residential Solid Wastes in Phoenix and Tucson, Arizona* (Phoenix, City of Phoenix Department of Public Works).

REID, J.J. 1995: Four strategies after twenty years: a return to basics. In Skibo, J.M., Walker, W.H. and Nielsen, A.E. (eds.), *Expanding Archaeology* (Salt Lake City), 15–21.

REID, J.J., RATHJE, W.L. and SCHIFFER, M.B. 1974: Expanding archaeology. *American Antiquity* 39, 125–6.

REID, J.J., SCHIFFER, M.B. and RATHJE, W.L. 1975: Behavioral archaeology: four strategies. *American Anthropologist* 77, 864–9.

RESTREPO, I., BERNACHE, G. and RATHJE, W.L. 1991: *Los demonios del consumo: basura y contaminacion* (Mexico, D.F., Centro de Ecodesarrollo).

RESTREPO, I., PHILLIPS, D.A. and REILLY, M.D. 1982: *La basura: consumo y desperdicio en El Distrito Federal* (Mexico, D.F., Instituto Nacional del Consumidor).

RHINE, S. 1998: *Bone voyage: a journey in forensic anthropology* (Albuquerque).

SAXE, A.A. 1970: Social dimensions of mortuary practices (Ann Arbor, MI, Ph.D. dissertation, the University of Michigan).

SCHIFFER, M.B. 1978: Methodological issues in ethnoarchaeology. In Gould, R.A. (ed.), *Explorations in ethnoarchaeology* (Albuquerque), 229–47.

SCHIFFER, M.B. 1988: The effects of surface treatment on permeability and evaporative cooling effectiveness of pottery. In Hancock, R.G.V., Farquhar, R.M. and Pavlish, L.A. (eds.), *Proceedings of the 26th international archaeometry symposium* (Toronto, Archaeometry Laboratory, Department of Physics, University of Toronto), 23–9.

SCHIFFER, M.B. 1989: A research design for ceramic use-wear at Grasshopper Pueblo. In Bronitsky, G. (ed.), *Pottery Technology: Ideas and Approaches* (Boulder, CO), 183–205.

SCHIFFER, M.B. 1990: The influence of surface treatment on heating effectiveness of ceramic vessels. *J. Archaeol. Sci.* 17, 373–81.

SCHIFFER, M.B. 1991: *The portable radio in American life* (Tucson, AZ).

SCHIFFER, M.B. 1992: *Technological perspectives on behavioral change* (Tucson, AZ).

SCHIFFER, M.B., BUTTS, T.C. and GRIMM, K.K. 1994: *Taking charge: the electric automobile in America* (Washington, D.C.).

SCHIFFER, M.B., DOWNING, T.E. and McCARTHY, M. 1981: Waste not, want not: an ethnoarchaeological study of refuse in Tucson, Arizona. In Gould, R.A. and Schiffer, M.B. (eds.) 1981, 67–86.

SCHIFFER, M.B., with MILLER, A.R. 1999: *The material life of human beings: artifacts, behavior, and communication* (London).

SCHIFFER, M.B. and SKIBO, J.M. 1987: Theory and experiment in the study of technological change. *Curr. Anthropol.* 28, 595–622.

SCHIFFER, M.B. and SKIBO, J.M. 1989: A provisional theory of ceramic abrasion. *American Anthropologist* 91, 101–15.

SCHIFFER, M.B. and SKIBO, J.M. 1997: The explanation of artifact variability. *American Antiquity* 62, 27–50.

SCHIFFER, M.B., SKIBO, J.M., BOELKE, T.C., NEUPERT, M.A. and ARONSON, M. 1994: New perspectives on experimental archaeology: surface treatments and thermal response of the clay cooking pot. *American Antiquity* 59, 197–217.

SCHUYLER, R. 1976: Images of America: the contribution of historical archaeology to national identity. *Southwestern Lore* 42(4), 27–39.

SCHWARTZ, J.H. 1993: *What the bones tell us* (Tucson, AZ).

SHEETS, P. 1999: Dawn of a new stone age in eye surgery. In Feder, K.L. (ed.) 1999, 104–6.

SHOTT, M.J. 1996: Mortal pots: on use life and vessel size in the formation of ceramic assemblages. *American Antiquity* 61, 463–82.

SIMON, H.A. 1965: The architecture of complexity. *General Systems* 10, 65–76.

SKIBO, J.M. 1992: *Pottery function: a use-alteration perspective* (New York).

SKIBO, J.M., BUTTS, T.C. and SCHIFFER, M.B. 1997: Ceramic surface treatment and abrasion resistance: an experimental study. *J. Archaeol. Sci.* 24, 311–17.

SKIBO, J.M., SCHIFFER, M.B. and REID, K.C. 1989: Organic tempered pottery: an experimental study. *American Antiquity* 54, 122–46.

SOUTH, S. 1974: *Palmetto parapets* (Columbia, SC, The University of South Carolina Institute of Archaeology and Anthropology Anthropological Studies no. 1).

SOUTH, S. (ed.) 1977: *Method and theory in historical archaeology* (New York).

STASKI, E. and SUTRO, L. (eds.) 1991: *The ethnoarchaeology of refuse disposal* (Phoenix, Arizona State University Anthropological Research Papers No. 42).

STEWARD, J.H. 1937: Ecological aspects of Southwestern society. *Anthropos* 32, 87–104.

STEWARD, J.H. 1942: The direct historical approach to archaeology. *American Antiquity* 7(4), 337–43.

STEWARD, J.H. and SETZLER, F.M. 1938: Function and configuration in archaeology. *American Antiquity* 4(1), 4–10.

SWEDLUND, A.C. and ARMELAGOS, G.J. 1976: *Demographic archaeology* (Dubuque, Iowa).

TANI, M.K. 1994: Why should more pots break in larger households? Mechanisms underlying population estimates from ceramics. In Longacre, W.A. and Skibo, J.M. (eds.), *Kalinga ethnoarchaeology* (Washington, D.C.), 51–70.

TANI, M.K., RATHJE, W.L., HUGHES, W.W., WILSON, D.C. and COUPLAND, G. 1992: *The Toronto Dig: Excavations at four municipal solid waste disposal sites in the greater Toronto area* (Toronto, TRC Trash Research Corporation).

TAYLOR, W.W. 1948: *A study of archaeology* (Memoirs of the American Anthropological Association 69).

THOMPSON, R.H. 1958: *Modern Yucatecan Maya pottery making* (Society for American Archaeology Memoir 15).

UBELAKER, D. and SCAMMELL, H. 1992: *Bones: a forensic detective's casebook* (New York).

VAN KEUREN, S. 1999: *Ceramic design structure and the organization of Cibola White Ware production in the Grasshopper region, Arizona* (Tucson, AZ, Arizona State Museum Archaeological Series 191).

WALKER, W.H. 1995: Ceremonial trash? In Skibo, J.M., Walker, W.H. and Nielsen, A.E. (eds.), *Expanding Archaeology* (Salt Lake City), 67–79.

WALKER, W.H., SKIBO, J.M. and NIELSEN, A.E. 1995: Introduction: expanding archaeology. In Skibo, J.M., Walker, W.H. and Nielsen, A.E. (eds.), *Expanding Archaeology* (Salt Lake City), 1–12.

WATSON, P.J. 1979: *Archaeological ethnography in western Iran* (Tucson, AZ, Viking Fund Publications in Anthropology 5).

WIENER, S. and TABASCO, E. 1980: 'Splendors of the Sohites' — an art museum exhibit (New York, O.K. Harris Gallery, and twelve other galleries in a national tour, 1980–1987).

WILK, R. and SCHIFFER, M.B. 1981: The modern material-culture field school: teaching archaeology on the university campus. In Gould, R.A. and Schiffer, M.B. (eds.) 1981, 15–30.

WILLEY, G.R. (ed.) 1956: *Prehistoric settlement patterns in the New World* (New York, Viking Fund Publications in Anthropology 23).

WILSON, D.C., RATHJE, W.L. and HUGHES, W.W. 1989: *Volume of solid wastes under differing landfill conditions: compaction experiments on fresh and landfill refuse from Tucson, Arizona* (Prairie Village, KS).

WILSON, D.C., RATHJE, W.L. and HUGHES, W.W. 1991: Household discards and modern refuse: a principle of household resource use and waste. In Staski, E. and Sutro, L. (eds.) 1991, 41–51.

WILSON, D.C., RATHJE, W.L. and TANI, M.K. 1994: *Characterization and assessment of household hazardous wastes in municipal solid wastes* (Washington, D.C., Water Quality Engineering Program of the National Science Foundation).

WILSON, J. 1995: *The archaeology of Shakespeare: the material legacy of Shakespeare's theatre* (Stroud).

YAMIN, R. 1997: New York's mythic slum: digging Lower Manhattan's infamous Five Points. *Archaeology* 50(2) March/April, 44–53.

YANCEY, W.L. 1970: Architecture, interaction, and social control: the case of a large-scale housing project. In Proshansky, H.M., Ittelson, W.H. and Rivlin, R.G. (eds.), *Environmental psychology* (New York).

YELLEN, J.E. 1976: Settlement patterns of the !Kung: an archaeological perspective. In Lee, R.B. and De Vore, I. (eds.), *Kalahari hunter-gatherers* (Cambridge), 47–72.

YELLEN, J.E. 1977: *Archaeological approaches to the present* (New York).

Archaeology, heritage and interpretation

NICK MERRIMAN

Introduction

It is an indication of how much archaeology has changed in the last generation that a paper on this subject is being included in a British Academy volume reviewing the current and future state of archaeology. A generation ago the subject of archaeology as heritage, and the communication of archaeology to the public, would not have been felt to be within the remit of academic archaeology at all. Academic archaeologists were principally interested in producing knowledge of an objective past as a general contribution to human understanding. Whilst the importance of public education was recognized, and a few academics also popularized the subject on an occasional basis, for example on radio and television programmes, it was largely the job of others (museum curators, extra-mural lecturers, journalists, television presenters, popular writers) to pass on archaeological knowledge to a wider public. This was seen to be a largely technical exercise of dissemination, and the thought that the study of the public dimensions of archaeology could be a legitimate part of academic archaeology would have been quite alien.

One of the most significant changes to occur in archaeology in recent decades has been the 'opening up' of the discipline from a relatively narrow focus on disinterested knowledge, to become a more broadly constituted field, in which the role of archaeology in wider society has become a significant element. A sub-field of 'public archaeology' has been staked out as a particular area of enquiry, examining all elements of the interaction between the public (itself comprising many different segments and interest groups) and the discipline of archaeology. These include exhibiting archaeology, archaeology and education, archaeology and politics, indigenous archaeology, popular perceptions of the past, archaeology and the law, looting and the trade in antiquities (see the new *Journal of Public Archaeology*, Schadla-Hall 1999). In this paper I shall not attempt an overview of such a broad field, but shall instead outline some of the issues that have led to this turn towards the public, and some of the consequences.

The development of a 'public archaeology'

Archaeology has always had a public dimension, from its beginnings as an antiquarian pursuit and its subsequent large-scale amateur following (Schnapp 1996; Daniel 1975), through media interest in major discoveries and 'mysteries of the past', and through its political uses in identity formation (Kohl and Fawcett 1996; Rowlands 1994). A particular aspect of this public dimension developed from the 1960s in the US and UK as a consequence of large-scale redevelopment and infrastructure projects which led to attempts to mitigate the destruction of archaeological sites through legislation and the development of contract archaeology. The term to describe this development, 'cultural resource management', also became characterized as 'public archaeology' (McGimsey 1972). This narrowly-defined public archaeology tended to concern itself with matters such as heritage values, legislation, protection, ethics, standards and funding, and its definition of archaeology as a 'resource' tended to neutralize it and make it free from the realm of politics, whose role was only rarely acknowledged at the time (e.g. Leone 1973).

In recent years, 'public archaeology' has expanded its range of topics and grown in importance through changes in thinking within the discipline itself and because of external changes in the political, economic and development spheres. Crucially, there is now a growing realisation that undertaking archaeology solely to support the interests of archaeologists is insufficient, both ethically and in terms of financial accountability, and that greater emphasis should be placed on doing archaeology to meet the public's needs for involvement, enjoyment, romance, mystery, inspiration, and meaning, as well as for the learning of facts and processes.

Theoretical developments

The impact of Marxist thought on archaeology in the early 1980s led to an explicit recognition of the importance of ideology in the regulation or transformation of past societies, including the ways in which élites in past societies appropriated the past (for example, in the form of existing monuments) as legitimation of their authority (Miller and Tilley 1984; Spriggs 1984). This inevitably led the way to an examination of ideology, domination and resistance in contemporary societies, particularly in relation to the uses of the past (Miller, Rowlands and Tilley 1995). Analyses of museum displays as examples of modern material culture by, for example, Meltzer (1981) and Leone (1981) saw the museum in Althusserian terms as an 'Ideological State Apparatus' which assisted with the economic and social reproduction of society. Institutions and practices which had formerly been seen as relatively neutral and innocent means for informing the non-specialist public about the past were now recognized as potential vehicles for 'the empirical substantiation of national mythology' (Leone 1973, 129).

The emergence of what has been broadly termed 'postprocessual' archaeology as an explicit challenge to the generalizing approach of 'new' or processual archaeology, and its consequent recognition of the role of politics and ideology in archaeology, led to a renewed interest in the public and public education (e.g. Hodder 1984; Shanks and Tilley 1987). The rejection of objectivity led to the discovery of partiality, bias and exclusion in the way in which the archaeological heritage was studied, managed and presented (Stone and MacKenzie 1990; Stone and Molyneaux 1994). The rise of the feminist critique in archaeology pointed out the neglect of the issue of gender in archaeological theorizing and in representations of the past (Conkey and Spector 1984; Gero and Conkey 1991; Sørensen 1999). Others in turn pointed to the similar lack of presence of ethnic minorities, children, and other marginalized groups in public depictions of the past. Renewed interest in the history of archaeology confirmed these absences by demonstrating, at historical distance, some of the ways in which archaeology has been used both actively to support contemporary ideologies and how it has passively reflected contemporary society (Arnold 1990; Trigger 1989). Post-modernist influences on archaeological thought also focused on the representation of the past in public, highlighting the elements of simulation, pastiche and shallowness (Walsh 1992).

New forms of archaeological thinking have thus shattered much of the consensus about the objectivity of archaeological interpretation and opened up the possibility of many different approaches to the understanding of archaeological evidence (e.g. Hodder 1992, 163–6). It is the recognition, indeed the encouragement, of diversity that is one of the factors that has led to the engagement of the public with archaeology to be embraced as a legitimate part of 'doing archaeology' (e.g. Ucko 1995).

External contestation

Another major factor in the recognition of the importance of the public aspects of archaeology has been the impact of social and political processes which have developed outside archaeology but which have targeted archaeological heritage. One of the most influential of these has been the growing assertion by indigenous and other minority peoples of their right to have a voice in the study and interpretation of their past. This has been a driving influence on the World Archaeological Congress, whose meetings and related publications since its formation in 1986 have been an important element in developing a global approach to archaeology and in highlighting the importance of the topic of archaeology and the public. Successive Congresses have highlighted 'excluded pasts' such as prehistories, or the pasts of indigenous minorities, which have been simply ignored in official accounts or educational curricula as if they had not existed (Stone and MacKenzie 1990).

The campaigning of, for example, Australian aborigines for the restitution of ancestral remains has become a potent symbol of the new assertiveness of indigenous people with regard to their past. Often archaeologists and indigenous people have co-operated well over matters of mutual interest, such as land claims (Ucko 1983), while at other times traditional guardians of heritage such as museums have been reluctant to entertain the notion of restitution for fear of losing substantial proportions of their collections (Wilson 1989, 112–17). In the USA the Native American Graves Protection and Repatriation Act of 1990 has ensured that museums have to divulge the contents of their archives and make arrangements for indigenous involvement in their curation (Isaac 1995). In Britain, voluntary examples of repatriation have occurred, most often related to human remains or items of spiritual significance of relatively recent date, such as the Lakota Ghost Dance shirt (Falconer 1998) where a clear connection can be established with a living community.

The growing involvement of local/indigenous people in the management and interpretation of their cultural heritage has forced archaeologists explicitly to acknowledge in practical terms the plurality of interpretations of archaeology which have been identified by the shifts in theory outlined above. The presentation of indigenous sites, in particular, has thrown into sharp relief the potential differences between conventional archaeological interpretation and those of indigenous peoples. For example, at the Hatzic site in Canada, a place around a natural boulder spiritually significant to the Stó:lo people, Pokotylo and Brass (1997) describe how two Stó:lo college students acted as site interpreters during the excavation, presenting both Native and academic interpretations of the site side by side when they differed.

Both the theoretical movement towards diversity of interpretations, and the challenges of the post-colonial situation, highlight something which has been very clear in a practical sense for a long time: that the archaeological past, like any other kind of past, is a highly important and contested arena in struggles between different interest groups for recognition, identity, precedence, land, and ultimately the right to exist (see Meskell 1998). This is brought out most starkly in instances of civil war and military conflict, where ancient monuments have frequently been specifically targeted in programmes of ethnic and cultural cleansing (e.g. Chapman 1994), but is also clear at the level of the everyday management of sites ranging from monuments of world-wide importance such as Stonehenge to sites of local significance where issues over access, maintenance, farming methods, restoration and interpretation can elicit strong reactions amongst a variety of interest groups (Bender 1998).

Active contestation over the significance of archaeological sites in different parts of the world has forced professional archaeologists to recognize that there are constituencies wider than their own with very definite and different views about the past and what should be done with it in the present. At Ayodhya in northern India, struggles over the primacy of occupation on this holy site have led to massacres, destruction of the existing monument, and apparent falsification of the archaeological evidence (Rao 1994). The decision by the committee of the third World Archaeological Congress in Delhi that the issue of Ayodhya could not be discussed, as the safety of the Congress participants could not be guaranteed, illustrated in a particularly powerful way the ability of present-day politics to override the concerns of academic archaeology (Colley 1995).

Commercial imperatives

A third factor that has influenced the opening up of archaeology to the public has been the huge expansion in leisure and tourism in western countries. In the UK, for example, tourism expenditure was estimated at £53 billion in 1997 in an industry with 120,000 businesses employing 1.5 million people (English Tourism Council 1999a). Cultural heritage forms one of the main components of this industry, with 80 million visits to Britain's historic properties in 1998, 78 million visits to museums and galleries, and 16 million visits to historic gardens (English Tourism Council 1999b). While there are no reliable figures for the overall number of visitors to presentations of archaeological heritage, nor for the number of people employed or the amount of revenue generated, it is clearly an important part of the cultural heritage sector. In 1998, the second most visited tourist attraction in Britain (after Blackpool Pleasure Beach) was the British Museum, and the fifth and sixth most visited historic monuments for which there is an admission charge were the Roman Baths and Pump Room in Bath (905,426 visitors) and Stonehenge (817,493 visitors). Archaeological presentations, as with museums and art galleries, can be undertaken specifically with the aim of promoting regeneration in an area. The creation of the Irish National Heritage Park, for example, was 'primarily motivated by the prospects of job creation' (Culleton 1999, 85).

As Urry (1990) has noted, the important part played by cultural heritage in Britain's tourism industry, and the role of tourism in the regeneration of many parts of Britain suffering from industrial decline, led to both continued investment, and increased visiting of the cultural heritage in the UK through the 1980s. One of the effects of this was the opening, on average, of one new museum every two weeks (Hewison 1987). The expansion of this market and the possibilities of heritage as a commercial enterprise led the Conservative government to encourage public bodies responsible for museums, archaeological monuments and historic buildings to compete in the market-place by promoting themselves more aggressively in competition with a range of commercial leisure activities that were also seeking the time and money of the public (Walsh 1992). While the development of global tourism and the apparent commercialization of the cultural heritage consequent upon it have been greeted with misgivings by many commentators, the economic power of the industry has had a direct effect on the presentation of archaeology to the public in that the introduction of business techniques has forced heritage managers to be clearer about their interpretive aims, and the need to understand audiences has led to a far more visitor-centred approach to the interpretation of the past.

In parallel with the commercialization of the archaeological heritage a strong emphasis on accountability for public funding has developed within local and national government (e.g. National Audit Office 1992). Bodies in receipt of public funds have to demonstrate not only that they are using the funds wisely and appropriately, but also that they are attempting to extend the benefits of that funding to as wide an audience as possible. In the UK, the Heritage Lottery Fund and the current Labour government both have policies which emphasize the promotion and widening of access to heritage, 'for the many, not for the few' (DCMS 1998).

The demands of public funders for increased accountability, together with the internally generated desire of the archaeological profession to make itself less élitist, have led to a much greater opening up of archaeological processes and presentations, and a greater willingness to address issues of public access and enjoyment. English Heritage, for example, has produced *Visitors Welcome*, a guide to improving visitors' experiences at heritage sites (Binks *et al.* 1988) and over the last 15 years has undertaken a major programme of improvement in the presentation and marketing of the sites under its care (Bath 1996; Chitty and Baker 1999). Gradually this improvement in presentation is taking into account the needs and opinions of visitors as revealed by visitor surveys.

The professionalization of heritage management and interpretation, together with the boom in the tourism and leisure industry, has also led to a substantial increase in the numbers of postgraduate courses dedicated to museum studies, heritage management, heritage interpretation and related fields, and the partial incorporation of these fields of study into mainstream undergraduate courses in archaeology. This in turn over the last ten years has introduced new ideas and a greater degree of professionalism into organizations concerned with the presentation and communication of archaeology to the public.

In recent years, shifts in theory, and social pressures external to the discipline, ranging from indigenous people's human rights to the rise of the heritage industry and the climate of public accountability, have thus encouraged archaeology to turn its attention on an unprecedented scale towards involving and communicating with the public. This move towards greater accessibility, however, has not been without its critics.

The 'heritage debate' of the 1980s and early 1990s (Hewison 1987; Lowenthal 1985; Shanks and Tilley 1987; Walsh 1992; Wright 1985) hinged around the apparent replacement of a productive industry (at least in Britain) by a heritage industry which marketed a sanitized version of the past for consumption by day trippers and tourists. Many of the commentators in this debate presented rather bleak assessments of the state of archaeology-in-public, in which the past was seen as a commodity to be bought and sold, depthless and devoid of meaning. The debate raised important questions in relation to archaeology and the public. What was the purpose of all of this archaeological endeavour in terms of fieldwork and synthesis if it appeared in the public domain as ideology and commodity?

Other writers (e.g. Samuel 1994) attacked the 'heritage baiters' by pointing out that their analyses ignored the fact that many of the initiatives undertaken in the post-war explosion of interest in the past were not initiated by dominant groups but by working-class and lower middle-class people, who involved themselves, for example, in industrial archaeology or re-enactment groups.

The crux of the debate is that heritage can mean many different, even contradictory things to different people. It can either be emancipatory or dominating; on the one hand it can be something which is universal, depthless and crass, while on the other hand it can denote more positive values such as belonging, identity and community (Hodder 1999, 162). The contradictions of heritage have also been compounded by the fact that commentators have often failed to distinguish between the analysis of the production of the past (for example in the form of books, displays, events and films) and the analysis of their consumption by the public. Thus, a museum presentation could be analysed by a critic (apparently endowed with a power of insight greater than that of other visitors) as an agent of the dominant ideology, with no consideration of whether that ideology was actually assimilated by the public, or re-interpreted, subverted or simply ignored.

While the idea of agency has been present in archaeological theory for some time in relation to the interpretation of past societies, it has rarely been applied to the analysis of presentations of the past. If the ideologies produced are not simply assimilated wholesale by visitors, and if indeed presentations of archaeology do not communicate a single version of the truth, what do archaeological presentations communicate to the public, and what is the role of archaeologists within the interpretive process?

Interpretation and learning

Over the last 25 years a great deal of work has been undertaken which has attempted to understand different facets of the visitor experience, especially in museums (e.g. Falk and Dierking 1992; Hooper-Greenhill 1994a, b). Perhaps because the majority of this work has taken place in science centres and science museums, which concern themselves to a large extent with communicating concepts rather than presenting tangible objects or sites, it has had relatively little impact on the presentation of archaeological sites and museums. Public archaeological initiatives have rarely been explicitly informed by recent work on informal learning, and rarely evaluated. Archaeology has too often, then, been in the position of communicating blindly, to an audience it does not understand, and with no clear idea of whether it has communicated successfully, or at all. A review of the main elements of work on the visitor experience may therefore help to point the way for the further development of the communication of archaeology.

Enough is now known from studies of visitors to museums and sites to make it clear that the model of communication within which archaeological site and museum presentation has been framed is far more complex than previously imagined. Work such as that by McManus (1987, 1989) and Dierking (1998) has established that museum and site visiting is primarily a social encounter, with family and friendship groups making up the great majority of the audience. Visitors tend to come as part of a leisure experience (for example in a family outing), because the attraction is safe, educational for children and facilitates social interaction (Falk and Dierking 1992, 35). Conversation and interaction between members of the group, often sparked off by the contents of the display, is an important and significant part of the visit.

Research work also shows that in general there is a mismatch between what visitors desire from a visit, and what is provided to them in the museum or on site. Falk and Dierking's summary of research shows visitors to be 'frequently disorientated, overwhelmed by the quantity and level of material, and desperately trying to personalize the information they are processing, all within the context of the social interaction of the group' (1992, 45). Part of the reason for this disorientation is that exhibitions (or indeed interpretive panels or trails) tend to be designed like chapters in a book, with the assumption that visitors will read all of the elements of the story, in the order prescribed. Actual observation of visitors tends, however, to show that they 'window shop', browsing some displays, missing others entirely, and paying attention in detail to a few that catch their interest (Falk *et al.* 1985). As Gurian has noted:

> try as we might, the public continually thwarts our attempts to teach incrementally in an exhibition. They come when they want, leave when they want, and look at what they want while they are there. Therefore, linear installations often feel like forced marches. (Gurian 1991, 181)

In the face of the problems inherent in the traditional didactic and linear methods of communication, based on formal educational principles, educators and museum professionals have begun to examine more closely concepts relating to lifelong and informal learning, drawing in particular on affective and non-linear approaches such as 'constructivism' (Hein 1998), which acknowledge that there are different styles of learner or learning, or what Howard Gardner (1983) calls 'multiple intelligences'.

The notion of constructivist learning is gradually growing in influence in the informal educational world of museums and sites (Ballantyne 1998). The constructivist approach acknowledges that learning requires the active participation of the learner, who constructs meaning from the objects, events and ideas that they encounter, by building on and consolidating previous knowledge:

> Meaning is not necessarily evident within the exhibition material itself. Rather it acquires meaning when visitors relate it to aspects of their own experience and reasons for being there. Learning is not only the accretion of bits of information, but the development and elaboration of a person's understanding and knowledge organisation. . .Social interaction has been found to facilitate this kind of learning, particularly when there is an opportunity to question and explore ideas and derive their implications. (Ballantyne 1998, 84)

Constructivism holds that 'the conclusions reached by the learner are not validated by whether or not they conform to some external standard of truth, but whether they "make sense" within the constructed reality of the learner' (Hein 1998, 34).

Ultimately, the position of constructivism thus comes close to the position reached by archaeological theorists in respect to claims about truth: that archaeologists, indigenous people, visitors to heritage sites and so on all construct knowledge and interpretations in a personally meaningful way. Within a shared belief system such as western rationality it might be possible to agree on certain core issues, but these themselves will be interpreted from a number of different perspectives (Thomas 1995). The constructivist exhibition is therefore likely to be non-linear, with multiple entry points, no specific route or beginning or end, to make connections with what is familiar to the visitors' everyday lives, and actively involve the visitor in the construction of knowledge (Hein 1998, 35).

Other recent studies which have examined the visiting of archaeological sites from an anthropological and sociological perspective have confirmed the personal nature of visitors' encounters with the past. Piccini (1999) shows how visitors use the sites essentially as a backdrop or 'theatre' in which to play out contemporary social relations, constantly relating what they are seeing to their present-day concerns, while Bagnall (1996) draws similar conclusions about more recent heritage sites, stressing that it is the perceived authenticity of the sites (however spurious this may seem to analysts) that visitors value about them.

Recent research has vindicated some of the now classic interpretation principles laid down over 40 years ago by Freeman Tilden. Two particularly pertinent ones are 'Information, as such, is not Interpretation. Interpretation is revelation based on information' (Tilden 1957, 9) and 'The chief aim of Interpretation is not instruction, but provocation' (ibid.), while it is noteworthy that his writing is scattered with words such as 'beauty', 'wonder', 'inspiration', 'spiritual elevation', 'discovery' and 'provocation' (Uzzell 1998, 233).

What this means is that the presentation of archaeology should not primarily be concerned with the transmission of facts about the past, but instead be more about stimulating imagination, interest, enthusiasm and enjoyment within the individual, using a variety of senses. The aim is ultimately to bring about knowledge, but this knowledge has to be personally constructed by the individual in relation to existing personal schemata. It is no doubt significant, then, that 'alternative' means of accessing the past such as 'New Age' beliefs and treasure hunting, as well as providing a nostalgic escape to an allegedly better time, or an opportunity to generate cash, may also be popular because they permit a far more personal and emotive engagement through feelings of mystery, spirituality, discovery, tangibility and excitement than many of the traditional approaches to archaeology (Shanks 1992, 114–15).

We have now reached a stage where internal and external demands have prompted a turn towards greater involvement with the public, and a framework for understanding the communication process is beginning to be developed. Whilst the majority of presentations at archaeological sites and museums are still of the traditional linear, non-active, book-chapter style, there are some encouraging signs that, in a number of areas, approaches to the interpretation of archaeology are adopting constructivist principles in involving visitors actively and in permitting the construction of knowledge through the visitors' own perspectives. As archaeology as a discipline moves through a period of critical self-reflection, it seems to be expressing this by turning itself inside out, to expose some of its inner workings to public view. Some examples of this 'opening up' may help to indicate the future direction in which archaeology may be moving.

Opening up archaeology to the public

Fieldwork and analysis

A generation ago, much archaeological fieldwork was undertaken by 'amateurs' in the absence of a developed professional framework for archaeology, and indeed it was the enthusiasm of amateur archaeologists to rescue and record sites in the 1960s and 1970s that led to the formation of professional excavation units. The ironic outcome of this has been the decline in amateur involvement in archaeology, to the extent that grass-roots support in some areas is in danger of dying out without encouragement at an official level. Stimulating local interest in archaeology can both lead to greater protection of sites and greater information sharing about archaeological finds, as well as enhancing the sense of identity of communities and giving individuals something of the sense of personal participation and direct encounter with the tangible remains of the past that facilitates personal learning. Several initiatives have attempted to recapture something of the public enthusiasm for archaeology that was evident before large-scale professionalization.

In Arizona, an Archaeology Advisory Group originally set up by the state governor in response to vandalism and looting of sites led to a major programme of public archaeology from 1986 onwards. The guiding philosophy was that greater public awareness and active participation would lead to greater valuation of sites by the public and therefore enhanced protection. Initiatives included the creation of a state archaeological park with a programme of public participation in fieldwork, classroom programmes, 'archaeology weeks' and 'archaeology months' to foster public involvement, and a site steward programme in which more than 500 volunteer stewards were trained to monitor over 600 sites in a ten-year period (Hoffman 1997).

In Leicestershire, a long-running community archaeology programme has organized groups of volunteers to take responsibility at the parish level for programmes of fieldwalking, monitoring of damage to known sites through ploughing or other actions, and in generally researching their local area (Liddle 1989). In ten years, the number of people actively engaged in fieldwork rose from six to over a hundred, and the number of sites discovered increased at least six fold. While such an approach to community archaeology is not widespread, there are indications that it is growing as local authorities look for demonstrable public outcomes for archaeological work (Holgate 1993; Schadla-Hall 1999, 150). In one example, the job of a community archaeologist in the West Midlands whose work involved both processing planning applications and educational and outreach work was saved because local people protested to their elected representatives about her forthcoming redundancy on the grounds of the importance of her work to their community (Ruth Waller, pers. comm.).

In London, the Thames Archaeological Survey was formulated explicitly to use non-professionals to 'fieldwalk' the foreshore of the tidal Thames in Greater London to establish its archaeological potential (Milne *et al.* 1997), and, equally importantly, to stimulate local interest in archaeology. Not only has the project discovered significant archaeological remains from prehistoric to post-medieval times, it has also generated a huge amount of public interest and enthusiasm, reinvigorated the formerly largely inactive local societies and received a large amount of media attention.

Archaeology in urban areas suffers from the problem that, although it has the largest potential audience, safety considerations and the pace of development schedules rarely allow public participation. The pioneering work of the Archaeological Resource Centre in Toronto, however, has shown something of what might be possible. From the outset the philosophy of the Centre was to examine what archaeology could do for the public rather than what the public could do for archaeology. The ARC therefore sought to make itself relevant and useful to the contemporary population. Imaginative ideas included using archaeological techniques to teach children about science; helping new immigrants to Toronto to settle in by teaching them about the nineteenth-century immigrant communities, and running palaeontology programmes for sick children. The most successful element of the project was probably the public excavations that ran for six months of the year and introduced some 12,000 people to archaeology by involving them, free of charge, in excavations and site tours (Smardz 1997).

Several commentators have noted some time ago that metal-detecting has increased in inverse proportion to the decline of amateur archaeology, probably because it offers the opportunity of active discovery through fieldwork largely now denied to amateurs following the professionalization of archaeology (Gregory 1986; Wright 1987). Until recently, metal-detector users were castigated by archaeologists as looters uninterested in the past. In the UK a major shift in attitudes has recently been seen, following a survey (Dobinson and Denison 1995) which showed that as many as 400,000 archaeological finds were being made by up to 30,000 metal-detectorists in England per annum, with only a tiny percentage of these being reported to archaeologists. A decision was taken by Government to initiate a pilot Portable Antiquities Recording Scheme which, instead of drawing barriers between detectorists and archaeologists, would encourage both groups to work together to record these large numbers of finds. Initially, Portable Antiquities Liaison Officers were appointed to cover six different regions of England and to develop relationships with metal-detector clubs with the aim of recording their finds. The first year of the scheme has been a great success, with 13,500 objects recorded which would not otherwise have been seen, and many new sites located (DCMS 1999). In some cases the rapprochement between archaeologists and detectorists which resulted from the work of the liaison officers led to metal-detectorists co-operating in archaeological survey projects. The scheme has made all of the finds data available on a web site with supplementary educational material in preparation, and the liaison officers' role has expanded to include giving advice to finders on the conservation of their objects, and educational work with schools and other groups.

Although it is not always possible for members of the public to undertake fieldwork themselves, strides have been made in some areas towards opening up excavation sites to the public. A pioneering example has been the excavations at Flag Fen near Peterborough where the work is undertaken as part of a public presentation on the site and its environs: visitors to Flag Fen see an ongoing research excavation where the public education aspect of the work is as important as the research: this is 'open' rather than 'closed' archaeology (Pryor 1989).

Particularly notable in North America has been the 'critical archaeology' of Leone and his colleagues at Annapolis, where the presentation of archaeology to the public was an essential element of the research project. Through guided tours, visitors were invited to examine whether the orthodox views of the past that they had received were valid, and to imagine other ways of viewing the evidence they were presented with (Potter 1994, 1997).

One of the most striking ways in which archaeology has been opened up to the public, albeit in a limited way, has been through the presentation of some of the activities that normally take place out of the public gaze. The Archaeological

Resource Centre in York was established to provide hands-on access to the raw material of archaeology, and visitors are invited to handle different archaeological finds in order to understand archaeological processes of finds identification, sorting and analysis (Jones 1995). In Liverpool, the Conservation Centre of the National Museums and Galleries on Merseyside has been established to allow public access to the behind-the-scenes activities in conservation, with a permanent exhibition on conservation including hands-on access, live video links where conservators talk about their work in the lab, tours of conservation studios, and opinion surgeries where members of the public can seek conservation advice about their own objects (Forrester 1998). At archaeological sites such as Flag Fen and the *Mary Rose* Tudor warship, viewing the conservation of ancient timbers is a significant component of any visit.

For some time, experimental archaeological research has also been held in public, to mixed opinions from researchers. For some, such as Reynolds (1999), a separate public presentation was necessary to allow the scientific research to continue undisturbed, while for others public presentation and explanation has been an essential element of the research, with the ongoing nature of the research and the continual modification of the site and its elements preventing the presentation from ever being 'complete' and 'Disneyfied' (Stone and Planel 1999, 7–8).

Sites and museums

The excitement and engagement of fieldwork can be difficult to reproduce in the more static environment of a site presentation once fieldwork has finished, or in a museum display. Recent approaches have attempted to move away from the uninterpreted archaeological site and the glass-case museum by engaging the public with a combination of innovative presentational technology, 'reconstruction' (or, better, 'construction') and more personal interactions. It is also a sign of the development of the sub-field of public archaeology that there is a burgeoning literature of critical analysis on these matters (e.g. McManus 1996; Merriman 1999; Molyneaux 1997; Stone and Planel 1999).

One of the major trends in presentation has been resolutely towards the provision of ever-greater amounts of supportive material in order to provide visitors with a fuller picture than can be gathered from the fragmentary evidence recovered by archaeology. This material can take the form of 'reconstruction' illustrations, models, dioramas, mannequins, live costumed interpreters, and full-scale 'constructions' of artefacts and buildings. These techniques can be seen at the majority of the successful museums, sites and heritage centres, and can range from those which use supporting material alongside artefacts or excavated site remains, to those which consist entirely of recent materials, such as the 'construction' sites of Butser or Lejre (Reynolds 1999; Rasmussen and Grønnow 1999).

The popularity of such 'constructions' is attested by the relatively high visitor figures for presentations using these techniques in comparison with those for traditional and largely uninterpreted presentations. Live interpretation is also clearly attractive both to the visiting public, who turn out in large numbers at sites where it is used, and to the re-enactment groups who sometimes form part of the attraction. As we have seen in relation to the heritage debate, though, the increasing — or sometimes exclusive — use of such modern 'constructions' of the past has concerned many critics, particularly when the techniques used blur the boundaries between academically rigorous presentations such as Jorvik Viking Centre and commercial enterprises such as Madame Tussaud's, the London Dungeon, and the various Disney sites.

However, as we have also seen, existing studies of visitors to museums and sites, together with recent informal learning theories, suggest that even with the best researched presentations, visitors will tend to take away messages and images that are personally meaningful rather than the ones that curators and educators intended. It is perhaps this that led Potter (1994, 219) to a certain degree of pessimism regarding the potential of archaeology to present a radical message. However, this could instead be seen as a positive indication of the resistance of visitors to *any* authoritative message, radical or conservative, and an indication of the potential of presentations to act, as some commentators have suggested, as 'dream spaces' in which individuals can come to make sense of the world (Annis 1987; Prince 1985; Silverman 1995). The implication of this is not that the actual content of presentations is meaningless — it is the raw material from which a personal engagement is constructed — but that instead of trying to force people to undertake certain tasks, whether it be to follow a prescribed route, or think about radical reinterpretations of sites, archaeological educators should accept that visitors will interpret in their own ways, and try to facilitate this personal engagement with the past to a greater extent.

This suggests that the success of an interpretive technique might be judged on the extent to which it stimulates personal engagement. Archaeological presentations and investigations have been seen as theatres (Piccini 1999; Tilley 1989) or as art installations (Pearce 1990, 168–9, 1999), where the visitors themselves form a vital component of the piece, and in the production of meaning. As with theatre and art, some presentations combine their materials to produce an emotional or thoughtful reaction, while others leave the viewer indifferent. The challenge, then, is actively to plan to stimulate affective and engaged learning at museums and sites.

In some instances, theatrical and artistic techniques themselves have been adopted to stimulate the imagination and personal engagement of visitors. In a number of museums, theatre groups already perform to visitors, as an integral part of the interpretive scheme (Alsford and Parry 1991). For example, Cannizzo and Parry (1994) have described how the theatrical presentations at the Canadian Museum of Civilisation have allowed them to involve the audiences in questioning the meaning of objects and interpretations of the past. In one example, they produced a piece of theatre to accompany a travelling exhibition on recent underwater finds from Herod's city of Caesarea. Through the use of an actor dressed as the medieval image of the diabolical tyrant Herod, and another actor playing the part of a museum security guard, the piece involved visitors in challenging stereotypes about Herod and in constructing new images of the ruler who had the city built.

The use of writers, poets and storytellers who use the collection or site as a starting point for a piece of work is also opening up new possibilities for public interpretation, and parallels calls by some academics for archaeologists themselves to relate narratives about the past rather than the dry quasi-scientific reports currently produced (Hodder 1989; Shanks 1992). Whether as part of a scripted performance or a more open-ended dialogue between an explainer or interpreter, the presence of people on site and in museums can provide a vital human link that can stimulate the visitor in a way that static presentations cannot, but can also run the risks of promoting stereotypes and misinformation when not grounded in academic research (see Sansom 1996 and Ucko 2000 for useful reviews).

At other museums, artists in residence have both produced their own installations in reaction to the 'installations' of the displays (Pearce 1999), and worked with members of the public (particularly children) to produce their own artworks stimulated by the archaeological material. In other (non-archaeological) contexts, visitors have been invited to add their own comments about displays on specially provided boards, and even make their own exhibitions using the material from the museum's collections (Martin 1996).

Other ways in which personal engagement is stimulated is through a return to physical contact with the material remains of the past rather than through the provision of narratives. Here, the hands-on approach of the Archaeological Resource Centre in York, transferring some of the interactive principles derived from science centres to the handling of real objects, has been highly influential. Increasing numbers of museums and heritage centres, including the British Museum, are now installing 'discovery centres' where members of the public can handle archaeological finds, sort sieved samples, examine them through microscopes, participate in 'experimental' activities such as spinning and weaving, flintknapping or leatherworking, undertake 'mini-excavations' in controlled conditions, and discuss the material and archaeological processes with trained 'explainers' (Southworth 1995). However, as Owen (1999) has shown, we still know very little about what visitors gain from direct contact with archaeological materials. Although the emphasis in many of these discovery centres is on understanding archaeological processes, it may be that it is the fact of handling ancient material and the stimulation of a personal encounter with the past that is most important.

Presentations have also begun to try to deal with the challenge thrown down by multi-vocal interpretations of the past, and attempt to encourage viewers to reflect that there may be many ways of interpreting the evidence that they see before them. Stone's description (1994) of the re-display of the Alexander Keiller Museum in Avebury, where for example visitors are presented with two alternative reconstructions of Neolithic people, remains one of the most useful attempts at demonstrating the partiality of interpretation in a public arena, and at stimulating visitors to think about the interpretive process itself. In the Museum of London's prehistoric gallery, visitors were asked in one of the first panels they read, 'Can You Believe What We Say?' The panel then went on to explain that views of prehistory change through time, and that the (named) curators in this particular exhibition had chosen to emphasize in particular green and gender issues. In addition, the gallery text addressed visitors directly, they were encouraged to touch some of the objects, modern equivalents of ancient artefacts were shown, and links were continually made between the prehistoric and present-day landscapes (Cotton and Wood 1996). Bender, as part of her work at Stonehenge and the multiplicity of interpretations at this contested site, worked with different interest groups (Druids, New Age travellers, archaeologists) to produce a travelling exhibition giving equal weight to all of their interpretations (Bender 1998).

The use of digital audio guides which can hold large amounts of information has been introduced across a range of sites and museums. From an interpretive point of view they are significant because they can provide information in different languages, at different levels, and the visitor can decide his or her own rate of progress or level of detail (Bath 1996). From a theoretical point of view they are also significant because they could permit the selection of a range of different interpretations of the same evidence. Whilst this has not yet apparently been used for archaeology, the potential of multiple interpretations has been shown using (static) interactive video at Birmingham Museum's ethnography gallery (Peirson Jones 1992).

Television and the Internet

Television continues to provide a major means of bringing the excitement of archaeological discovery to a wider public. Particularly successful and innovative has been the Channel 4 series *Time Team*, which has attracted audiences of 4 million to its programmes. Although its approach (a three-day excavation) has been criticized by some, its combination of professionals, an 'Everyman' presenter, high-tech surveying, technological experimentation, artistic reconstruction, and fun, has clearly proved highly popular. Some of its programmes have gone out live at intervals over the course of the three-day period, with continuous updates on its heavily used website (http://www.channel4.com/nextstep/timeteam/), which has also allowed members of the public to pose questions to the team. Now in its ninth series, *Time Team* has spawned its own club with 25,000 members, an online discussion forum (which recently focused on the controversy as to whether the 4000 year old timber circle

'Seahenge' should be left *in situ* or removed), and numerous publications. The possibility of linking up archaeological television programmes to a website which allows a degree of interactivity between archaeologists and the public may well form a major dimension of public communication in the future. Even when a dedicated television programme cannot be made, archaeologists may increasingly make their own Web broadcasts, along the lines of the JASON Project, in which an annual scientific research project is linked with host sites such as museums via satellite, allowing members of the public to view the exploration site, talk to team members and operate remote-controlled cameras (Phillips 1998). Other archaeological projects already run their own websites which report ongoing progress on excavation and analysis, and allow members of the public to pose questions or offer comments (Hodder 1998).

The Internet, by facilitating direct public interaction through comment and discussion, clearly will provide a major means of opening up archaeology to the public in the future (see Boast this volume). Initiatives such as the UK's National Grid for Learning, which will provide a national digital resource for schools, will allow archaeologists to reach a much larger constituency. The very openness of the Internet, however, also means that it provides a vast resource of spurious and unreliable information, and the challenge for archaeologists may be to make themselves heard amongst the huge variety of offerings available. Virtual archaeology offers a new kind of interpretive experience (and a new category, the virtual visitor), one which is quite different from the experience of encountering real objects and environments.

Challenges for the future

The definition of the public interest

So far in this paper it has been argued that a combination of developments, theoretical and pragmatic, have led to a general opening up of archaeology to the public, with a shift from an authoritative top-down approach to communication to a much more people-centred strategy in which the interest, involvement and relevance of the public is of prime importance. In this process, it has been recognized that the authority of public archaeological interpretations is continuously undermined, in a positive way, by the manner in which knowledge is socially constructed in the mind of the individual. However, this positive emphasis has masked a number of issues that will merit consideration in the further development of a more public-oriented archaeology.

The first of these is the continued tension within archaeology between different notions as to what constitutes the public interest. In some areas of archaeology, particularly in universities, museums and site presentations, it is becoming generally accepted that archaeological knowledge is historically contingent and multivalent. In recognition of this, it is in these areas that the turn towards involving the public has been most evident. However, in other areas, particularly archaeological heritage management, an objective and cumulative model of archaeological knowledge continues to dominate, whereby archaeology primarily serves posterity by building up a resource of information about the past for future scholars. In these circumstances, it is felt that as long as the State protects or mitigates damage to the archaeological resource according to its own priorities, then the public interest is served, because it does this 'on behalf of' the public. This creates a situation where the entire archaeological process, from the identification of priority areas, to the specification of briefs for archaeological work, the execution of that work, its publication and archiving, is, with the few exceptions outlined above, carried out by professional specialists out of the public gaze. Development-led archaeology, while allowing a great deal of fieldwork to be funded, does not at present allow for innovation with regard to public involvement and presentation (Start 1999).

This comes into particularly sharp focus in relation to archaeological archives, the products of fieldwork and analysis, which over the last 25 years have grown sufficiently large to be considered as a significant part of archaeology in their own right — the *ex situ* resource. Typically, following analysis and the (possible) production of a report, the archive is placed in a repository and rarely used, even by specialists (Swain 1998). Given the costs of long-term storage and curation of archaeological archives, and the ever-growing search for value for money for public funds, some museums have begun to question whether the public interest is really being served through this narrow and closed view of the archaeological enterprise, and have declared themselves full and unable to take further material. Here is a direct collision between the desire to preserve heritage for posterity, regardless of usage in the present, on the grounds that it forms part of the collective national heritage and has been recovered from the ground at great expense in the general public interest, and the desire to ensure that the heritage 'pays its way' today by being used and enjoyed by as many people as possible.

Clearly, a balance has to be struck between preservation for the future and use in the present. However, the influences outlined at the beginning of this paper will continue to demand public outcomes in the present in return for preservation for posterity (which after all, by definition, never comes). Contract archaeology must wrench itself away from a subservient relationship with property developers and reassert the fundamental reason for doing archaeology, which is to promote public interest and understanding. The words of Fritz and Plog remain as true today as they were 30 years ago:

> We suspect that unless archaeologists find ways of making their research increasingly relevant to the modern world, the modern world will find itself increasingly capable of getting along without archaeologists. (1970, 412)

Relevance and cultural diversity

Thinking about archaeology's relationship with the present and about ways of stimulating public engagement therefore involves thinking about audiences and relevance. For too long, often because its chronological range does not reach to the present, archaeology has failed to make connections between what it does and the needs and concerns of contemporary society. In a survey undertaken a few years ago (Merriman 1991) it was demonstrated that one of the main barriers to wider participation in archaeology was the perceived lack of relevance of archaeological pasts for many communities living today. As demands for greater public accountability grow, archaeologists will no doubt be called upon to address contemporary concerns to a greater extent than they do at present. In the UK, for example, current government policy across all areas of public life focuses on the promotion of education, the tackling of social exclusion, and the provision of access to services and information for all. An archaeology that cannot address itself to these issues may find it difficult to garner public support.

The issue of relevance comes into particularly sharp focus in relation to cultural and ethnic diversity. Despite the efforts of minority peoples across the globe to have their voices heard in official accounts of history, too often their stories remain unrecognized. In the UK, archaeology says almost nothing to the significant proportion of the population who declare themselves as belonging to an ethnic minority, despite the long history of many of the minority communities in the country. In contrast, in the USA the archaeological investigation of the Black presence has now become a major area of academic concern and allowed the incorporation of this previously largely hidden but hugely important community into archaeological narratives, including public presentations, where, for example, the slave quarters adjacent to grand houses have been excavated and interpreted (Bograd and Singleton 1997; Ferguson 1992). In South Africa, the past of the Black and 'Coloured' communities has also been recovered through archaeological investigations of the District 6 area of Cape Town which was razed to the ground in the 1970s. The presentation of this lost locality in the District 6 Museum combines photographs, testimony, maps, artefacts and archaeological finds in a moving act of collective remembrance (Uzzell and Ballantyne 1998).

In the UK, 'The Peopling of London' project at the Museum of London showed one way in which archaeology could be combined with social history to address an issue relevant to contemporary communities. The project attempted to re-tell the history of London to emphasize the time-depth to the city's cultural diversity (Merriman 1997). Rather than being primarily a post-war phenomenon, the exhibition showed that from its foundation in the Roman period London has had a cosmopolitan population and that this should be celebrated as a vital element of the city's identity. In tackling a subject that was relevant to London's current ethnic minority communities, whose long presence is usually excluded from public presentations, the museum developed a new audience, with the proportion of ethnic minority visitors rising from 4 per cent to 20 per cent for the duration of the exhibition (ibid.). Apart from this, however, archaeology in the UK continues, by implication, to be undertaken by the White community and address itself to a White audience. Archaeologists must begin to address themselves to this problem in broadening access to archaeological careers and in public presentations.

Enablers or critics?

The recognition of multiple interpretations of the past and of community involvement and empowerment raised earlier in this paper in turn raises questions about the role of professional archaeologists in relation to the public. Are they now 'hands-off' enablers who seek simply to facilitate the expression of a diversity of views by a wide variety of people, or should they exercise discretion in allowing some views official publicity while excluding others that they feel to be unacceptable? If the former course is chosen, archaeology would seem to face a future of extreme relativism, in which the engagement with actual archaeological evidence has little role to play. If the latter course is chosen, on what grounds are some versions of the past chosen as worthy of representation and others rejected? These matters are not easy ones to resolve, as some of those attempting a more open archaeology have recognized (Hodder 1999; Roth 1998). Are, for example, the beliefs of an indigenous community about the origins of a site somehow more authentic than sincerely-held beliefs of Druids or New-Agers? Just who exactly represents 'communities', and how representative are their views? How can a focus on the authenticity of community views avoid descending into an essentialist quasi-nationalism? There is a danger of naivety on the part of archaeologists who may find their well-meaning attempts at pluralism subverted by unrepresentative interest groups, a common feature of community politics at any level. Opening up archaeology may be a painful process for those reaching out for the first time, and may require a genuine loss of innocence in confronting real-world issues. It will require tact, diplomacy and firmness in working out what is academically acceptable in the name of openness, and what is not, and will require archaeologists to think carefully about how to balance the rules of scholarship, evidence and critical openness with respect for the beliefs of others.

Understanding the public

One of the major problems that hinders discussion of the public interpretation of archaeology is the dearth of studies which examine the way in which the public use archaeological materials. Apart from the few studies mentioned above, we know very little about public perceptions of archaeology and different periods of the past, or about what people derive from their visits to sites and museums, from handling objects, or from witnessing 'live' interpretation or activities. There are whole areas of popular archaeological interpretation, such as re-enactment, television, films and computer games that have received little academic consideration in terms of their use by, and impact on, the public. This means that, although archaeologists may intuitively feel that spurious, commercially-led initiatives such as a three-day Viking encampment at the Bronze Age site of Flag Fen (Sansom 1996), American Civil War re-enactments at English Heritage sites or numerous other pastiches highlighted by critics of the heritage industry are less valid than 'in-period' presentations, until more research is undertaken on how the public use the materials they are given to produce their own knowledge of the past, such views will remain assertions. A publicly-oriented archaeology requires that archaeologists understand the public more fully. This will mean undertaking studies of public consumption of the past, targeting different audiences with relevant programmes, developing clear strategies for interpretive programmes, and, crucially, evaluating every stage of interpretation and publishing the results so that others may benefit.

Conclusion

A sea-change is happening in archaeology across the globe. Popular interest in archaeology seems to be extremely high, possibly higher than it has ever been, and the recognition that archaeology is just as much about the contestation of meaning in the present as about the pursuit of disinterested knowledge of the past has made archaeology the site of lively interdisciplinary debate.

Professional archaeology has only recently begun to take the public's interaction with the discipline seriously and realise that its development raises fundamental questions. Public interest, perception and involvement in archaeology must become major areas of enquiry, alongside study of the communicative process. If archaeology does not embrace the public, a two-track system will continue to develop, with the professional archaeologists on one side pursuing their agenda, and the public on the other side pursuing theirs. One thing is in little doubt: the archaeology practised in the twenty-first century will look very different from that of the twentieth century.

References

ALSFORD, S. and PARRY, D. 1991: Interpretive Theatre — a Role in Museums. *Mus. Management and Curatorship* 10, 8–23.
ANNIS, S. 1987: The Museum as a Staging Ground for Symbolic Action. *Museum* 151, 168–71.
ARNOLD, B. 1990: The Past as Propaganda: Totalitarian Archaeology in Nazi Germany. *Antiquity* 64, 464–78.

BAGNALL, G. 1996: Consuming the Past. In Edgell, S., Hetherington, K. and Warde, A. (eds.), *Consumption Matters. The Production and Experience of Consumption* (Oxford), 227–47.

BALLANTYNE, R. 1998: Interpreting 'Visions'. Addressing Environmental Education Goals Through Interpretation. In Uzzell, D. and Ballantyne, R. (eds.), *Contemporary Issues in Heritage & Environmental Interpretation* (London, The Stationery Office), 77–97.

BATH, B. 1996: Audio Tours at Heritage Sites. In McManus, P. (ed.) 1996, 107–13.

BENDER, B. 1998: *Stonehenge: Making Space* (London).

BINKS, G., DYKE, J. and DAGNALL, P. 1988: *Visitors Welcome* (London, English Heritage).

BOGRAD, M.D. and SINGLETON, T.A. 1997: The Interpretation of Slavery: Mount Vernon, Monticello, and Colonial Williamsburg. In Jameson, J. (ed.) 1997, 193–204.

CANNIZZO, J. and PARRY, D. 1994: Museum theatre in the 1990s: trail-blazer or camp-follower? In Pearce, S. (ed.), *Museums and the Appropriation of Culture. New Research in Museum Studies* 4 (London), 43–64.

CHAPMAN, J. 1994: Destruction of a Common Heritage: the Archaeology of War in Croatia, Bosnia and Hercegovina. *Antiquity* 68, 120–6.

CHITTY, G. and BAKER, D. (eds.) 1999: *Managing Historic Sites and Buildings. Reconciling Presentation and Preservation* (London).

COLLEY, S. 1995: What Happened at WAC-3? *Antiquity* 69, 15–18.

CONKEY, M. and SPECTOR, J. (eds.) 1984: Archaeology and the Study of Gender. In Schiffer, M.B. (ed.), *Advances in Archaeological Method and Theory* 7, 1–38.

COTTON, J.F. and WOOD, B. 1996: Retrieving prehistories at the Museum of London: a gallery case-study. In McManus, P. (ed.) 1996, 53–71.

CULLETON, E. 1999: The Origin and Role of the Irish National Heritage Park. In Stone, P.G. and Planel, P. (eds.) 1999, 76–89.

DANIEL, G. 1975: *A Hundred and Fifty Years of Archaeology* (London).

DEPARTMENT FOR CULTURE, MEDIA AND SPORT 1998: *A New Cultural Framework* (London, DCMS).

DEPARTMENT FOR CULTURE, MEDIA AND SPORT 1999: *Portable Antiquities. Annual Report 1997–98* (London, DCMS).

DIERKING, L.D. 1998: Interpretation as a Social Experience. In Uzzell, D. and Ballantyne, R. (eds.), *Contemporary Issues in Heritage & Environmental Interpretation* (London, The Stationery Office), 56–76.

DOBINSON, C. and DENISON, S. 1995: *Metal Detecting and Archaeology in England* (London, English Heritage and Council for British Archaeology).

ENGLISH TOURISM COUNCIL 1999a: Website http://www.englishtourism.org.uk accessed 10/11/1999.

ENGLISH TOURISM COUNCIL 1999b: *Sightseeing in the UK 1998* (London, English Tourism Council).

FALCONER, H. 1998: Finders Keepers. *Mus. J.* 98(8), 30–1.

FALK, J.H. and DIERKING, L.D. 1992: *The Museum Experience* (Washington, D.C.).

FALK, J.H., KORAN, J.J., DIERKING, L.D. and DREBLOW, L. 1985: Predicting Visitor Behavior. *Curator* 28, 249–57.

FERGUSON, L. 1992: *Uncommon Ground: Archaeology and Early African America, 1650–1800* (Washington, D.C.).

FORRESTER, J. 1998: Opening Up. The Conservation Centre National Museums & Galleries on Merseyside. *Mus. Practice* 7, 59–61.

FRITZ, J. and PLOG, F. 1970: The Nature of Archaeological Explanation. *American Antiquity* 35, 405–12.

GARDNER, H. 1983: *Frames of Mind: the Theory of Multiple Intelligences* (New York).

GERO, J. and CONKEY, M. (eds.) 1991: *Engendering Archaeology: Women and Prehistory* (Oxford).

GREGORY, T. 1986: Whose Fault is Treasure Hunting? In Dobinson, C. and Gilchrist, R. (eds.), *Archaeology, Politics and the Public* (York), 25–7.

GURIAN, E.H. 1991: Noodling Around with Exhibition Opportunities. In Karp, I. and Lavine, S.P. (eds.), *Exhibiting Cultures: The Poetics and Politics of Museum Display* (Washington, D.C.), 176–90.

HEIN, G. 1998: *Learning in the Museum* (London).

HEWISON, R. 1987: *The Heritage Industry. Britain in a Climate of Decline* (London).

HODDER, I. 1984: Archaeology in 1984. *Antiquity* 58, 25–32.

HODDER, I. 1989: Writing Archaeology: Site Reports in Context. *Antiquity* 63, 268–74.

HODDER, I. 1992: *Theory and Practice in Archaeology* (London).

HODDER, I. 1998: The Past as Passion and Play: Çatalhöyük as a site of conflict in the construction of multiple pasts. In Meskell, L. (ed.) 1998, 124–39.

HODDER, I. 1999: *The Archaeological Process. An Introduction* (Oxford).

HOFFMAN, T. 1997: The Role of Public Participation: Arizona's Public Archaeology Program. In Jameson, J. (ed.) 1997, 73–83.

HOLGATE, R. 1993: Community Archaeology and Museums. In Southworth, E. (ed.), *'Picking Up The Pieces': Adapting to Change in Museums and Archaeology. Museum Archaeologist* 18, 36–41.

HOOPER-GREENHILL, E. 1994a: *Museums and their Visitors* (London).

HOOPER-GREENHILL, E. (ed.) 1994b: *The Educational Role of Museums* (London).

ISAAC, B. 1995: An Epimethean View of the Future of the Peabody Museum. *Federal Archaeology: Special Report: The Native American Graves Protection and Repatriation Act* Fall/Winter, 18–22.

JAMESON, J. (ed.) 1997: *Presenting Archaeology to the Public. Digging for Truths* (London).

JONES, A. 1995: Integrating School Visits, Tourists and the Community at the Archaeological Resource Centre, York, UK. In Hooper-Greenhill, E. (ed.), *Museum, Media, Message* (Leicester), 156–64.

KOHL, P. and FAWCETT, C. 1996: *Nationalism, Politics, and the Practice of Archaeology* (Cambridge).

LEONE, M. 1973: Archaeology as the Science of Technology: Mormon Town Plans and Fences. In Redman, C.L. (ed.), *Research and Theory in Contemporary Archaeology* (New York), 125–50.

LEONE, M. 1981: The Relationship Between Artifacts and the Public in Outdoor History Museums. *Annals of the New York Academy of Sciences* 376, 301–14.

LIDDLE, P. 1989: Community Archaeology in Leicestershire Museums. In Southworth, E. (ed.), *Public Service or Private Indulgence? The Museum Archaeologist* 13 (Liverpool, Society of Museum Archaeologists), 44–6.

LOWENTHAL, D. 1985: *The Past is a Foreign Country* (Cambridge).

MARTIN, D. 1996: The Open Museum. *Mus. Practice* 3, 60–3.

MCGIMSEY, C.R. III 1972: *Public Archaeology* (New York).

MCMANUS, P. 1987: It's the Company you Keep. . .The Social Determinants of Learning-Related Behaviour in a Science Museum. *Int. J. Mus. Management and Curatorship* 6, 263–70.

MCMANUS, P. 1989: What People Say and how they Think in a Science Museum. In Uzzell, D. (ed.), *Heritage Interpretation. Volume 2. The Visitor Experience* (London), 156–65.

MCMANUS P. (ed.) 1996: *Archaeological Displays and the Public: Museology and Interpretation* (London, Institute of Archaeology, University College).

MELTZER, D. 1981: Ideology and Material Culture. In Gould, R. and Schiffer, M. (eds.), *Modern Material Culture: The Archaeology of Us* (New York), 113–29.

MERRIMAN, N. 1991: *Beyond The Glass Case. The Past, the Heritage and the Public in Britain* (Leicester).

MERRIMAN, N. 1997: The Peopling of London Project. In Hooper-Greenhill, E. (ed.), *Cultural Diversity. Developing Museum Audiences in Britain* (Leicester), 119–48.

MERRIMAN, N. (ed.) 1999: *Making Early Histories in Museums* (Leicester).

MERRIMAN, N. and SWAIN, H. 1999: Archaeological Archives: Serving the Public Interest? *European J. Archaeol.* 2(2), 249–62.

MESKELL, L. (ed.) 1998: *Archaeology Under Fire. Nationalism, Politics and Heritage in the Eastern Mediterranean and Middle East* (London).

MILLER, D., ROWLANDS, M. and TILLEY, C. (eds.) 1995: *Domination and Resistance* (London).

MILLER, D. and TILLEY, C. (eds.) 1984: *Ideology, Power and Prehistory* (Cambridge).

MILNE, G., BATES, M. and WEBBER, M. 1997: Problems, Potential and Partial Solutions: an Archaeological Study of the Tidal Thames, England. *World Archaeol.* 29(1), 130–46.

MOLYNEAUX, B. (ed.) 1997: *The Cultural Life of Images. Visual Representation in Archaeology* (London).

NATIONAL AUDIT OFFICE 1992: *Protecting and Managing England's Heritage Property* (London, National Audit Office).

OWEN, J. 1999: Interaction or Tokenism? The Role of 'Hands-on Activities' in Museum Archaeology Displays. In Merriman, N. (ed.) 1999, 173–89.

PEARCE, S. 1990: *Archaeological Curatorship* (Leicester).

PEARCE, S. 1999: Presenting Archaeology. In Merriman, N. (ed.) 1999, 12–27.

PEIRSON JONES, J. 1992: The Colonial Legacy and the Community: The Gallery 33 Project. In Karp, I., Kreamer, C.M. and Lavine, S.D. (eds.), *Museums and Communities. The Politics of Public Culture* (Washington, D.C.), 221–41.

PHILLIPS, P. 1998: Developing Digital Resources. National Museums and Galleries on Merseyside. *Mus. Practice* 9, 54–6.

PICCINI, A. 1999: Wargames and Wendy Houses: Open-air Reconstructions of Prehistoric Life. In Merriman, N. (ed.) 1999, 151–72.

POKOTYLO, D. and BRASS, G. 1997: Interpreting Cultural Resources: Hatzic Site. In Jameson, J. (ed.) 1997, 156–65.

POTTER, P.B., Jr. 1994: *Public Archaeology in Annapolis: A Critical Approach to History in Maryland's 'Ancient' City* (Washington, D.C.).

POTTER, P.B., Jr. 1997: The Archaeological Site as an Interpretive Environment. In Jameson, J. (ed.) 1997, 35–53.

PRINCE, D.R. 1985: The Museum as Dreamland. *Int. J. Mus. Management and Curatorship* 4(4), 243–50.

PRYOR, F. 1989: Look What we've Found. A Case Study in Public Archaeology. *Antiquity* 63, 51–61.

RAO, N. 1994: Interpreting Silences: Symbol and History in the Case of Ram Janmabhoomi/Babri Masjid. In Bond, G.C. and Gilliam, A. (eds.), *Social Construction of the Past. Representation as Power* (London), 154–64.

RASMUSSEN, M. and GRØNNOW, B. 1999: The Historical-Archaeological Experimental Centre at Lejre, Denmark: 30 years of experimenting with the past. In Stone, P.G. and Planel, P. (eds.) 1999, 136–45.

REYNOLDS, P. 1999: Butser Ancient Farm, Hampshire, UK. In Stone, P.G. and Planel, P. (eds.) 1999, 124–35.

ROTH, A.M. 1998: Ancient Egypt in America. Claiming the Riches. In Meskell, L. (ed.) 1998, 217–29.

ROWLANDS, M. 1994: The Politics of Identity in Archaeology. In Bond, G.C. and Gilliam, A. (eds.), *Social Construction of the Past. Representation as Power* (London), 129–43.

SAMUEL, R. 1994: *Theatres of Memory* (London).

SANSOM, E. 1996: Peopling the Past: Current Practices in Archaeological Site Interpretation. In McManus, P. (ed.) 1996, 118–37.

SCHADLA-HALL, T. 1999: Editorial: Public Archaeology. *European J. Archaeol.* 2(2), 147–58.

SCHNAPP, A. 1996: *The Discovery of the Past. The Origins of Archaeology* (London).

SHANKS, M. 1992: *Experiencing the Past. On the Character of Archaeology* (London).

SHANKS, M. and TILLEY, C. 1987: *Re-constructing archaeology: theory and practice* (Cambridge).

SILVERMAN, L.H. 1995: Visitor Meaning-Making in Museums for a New Age. *Curator* 38(3), 161–70.

SMARDZ, K. 1997: The Past Through Tomorrow: Interpreting Toronto's Heritage to a Multi-cultural Public. In Jameson, J. (ed.) 1997, 101–13.

SØRENSEN, M.L.S. 1999: Archaeology, Gender and the Museum. In Merriman, N. (ed.) 1999, 136–50.

SOUTHWORTH, E. 1995: Experiments in Access to Collections in Liverpool Museum. In Southworth, E. (ed.), *'Taking Stock': Access to Archaeological Collections. Museum Archaeologist* 20, 25–31.

SPRIGGS, M. 1984: *Marxist Perspectives in Archaeology* (Cambridge).

START, D. 1999: Community Archaeology: Bringing it back to Local Communities. In Chitty, G. and Baker, D. (eds.) 1999, 49–59.

STONE, P.G. 1994: The re-display of the Alexander Keiller Museum, Avebury, and the National Curriculum in England. In Stone, P.G. and Molyneaux, B.L. (eds.) 1994, 190–205.

STONE, P. and MACKENZIE, R. (eds.) 1990: *The Excluded Past. Archaeology in Education* (London).

STONE, P.G. and MOLYNEAUX, B.L. (eds.) 1994: *The Presented Past: Heritage, Museums and Education* (London).

STONE, P.G. and PLANEL, P. (eds.) 1999: *The Constructed Past. Experimental Archaeology, Education and the Public* (London).

SWAIN, H. 1998: *A Survey of Archaeological Archives in England* (London, Museums and Galleries Commission/English Heritage).

THOMAS, J. 1995: Where are we now? Archaeological Theory in the 1990s. In Ucko, P.J. (ed.) 1995, 343–62.

TILDEN, F. 1957: *Interpreting Our Heritage* (Chapel Hill).

TILLEY, C. 1989: Excavation as Theatre. *Antiquity* 63, 275–80.

TRIGGER, B. 1989: *A History of Archaeological Thought* (Cambridge).

UCKO, P.J. 1983: Australian Academic Archaeology: Aboriginal Transformation of its Aims and Practice. *Australian Archaeol.* 16, 11–26.

UCKO, P.J. (ed.) 1995: *Theory in Archaeology: A World Perspective* (London).

UCKO, P.J. 2000: Enlivening a 'Dead' Past. *Conservation and Management of Archaeological Sites* 4.

URRY, J. 1990: *The Tourist Gaze. Leisure and Travel in Contemporary Societies* (London).

UZZELL, D. 1998: Planning for Interpretive Experiences. In Uzzell, D. and Ballantyne, B. (eds.), *Contemporary Issues in Heritage & Environmental Interpretation* (London, The Stationery Office), 232–52.

UZZELL, D. and BALLANTYNE, B. 1998: Heritage That Hurts: Interpretation in a Postmodern World. In Uzzell, D. and Ballantyne, B. (eds.), *Contemporary Issues in Heritage & Environmental Interpretation* (London, The Stationery Office), 152–71.

WALSH, K. 1992: *The Representation of the Past* (London).

WILSON, D.M. 1989: *The British Museum. Purpose and Politics* (London).
WRIGHT, P. 1985: *On Living in an Old Country* (London).
WRIGHT, P. 1987: Treasure Island. *New Society* 21 August, 14–17.

Computing futures: Visions of the past

ROBIN BOAST

There is no doubt that computers, or digital equipment, have had an impact on archae-ological work. Compared to when I started in archaeology, in the late 1970s, computers are certainly pervasive today. Then computing was a mainframe activity, where, if we used computers at all, we worked on punched cards and delegated the processing to technicians, never seeing the computer, only the reams of paper output. The develop-ment of the Personal Computer and the incorporation of *digital technology* into a variety of equipment used on site, from the EDM to the tea kettle — the use of computers for everything from project accounting to planning to GIS, and the complete domination of the word-processor — certainly seem to have justified the early claims that 'computers are going to take over'.

This prophetic claim of digital domination has been with us since the earliest electronic computers. We are constantly bombarded with endless presentations and illustrations of the digital as dominant. The Internet is soon, always soon, to be the saviour of the information society; we will soon, again soon, be performing all recording on site electronically; we will in the not too distant future, how distant is the future?, be wearing our computers. The prospect of digital field clothing is 'just on the horizon'.

But just how real is this picture of our digital future? It all seems too plausible, so possible. Aren't there prototypes available now? Haven't we seen digital technology explode in power and shrink in size? Aren't computers and digital equipment all around us, just as they said it would be, just as it was predicted? Well, yes and no.

One thing we can be sure of is that history is always written in light of the present. I can also be fairly sure that crystal-ball gazing is one of the most tenuous and myopic pursuits that one can engage in. I am reminded of a scene from the Simpsons[1] where Professor Frink, the Jerry Lewis style socially-challenged scientist, is demonstrating his first computer some time in the late 1960s. He confidently predicts for the audience of bell-bottomed students that in 50 years computers will be twice as fast, 100 times as

---

[1] Simpsons™ cartoon show (The Fox Network).

large and will be the masters of mankind. Though this is 'just a joke', it is far more accurately reminiscent of the claims I have heard over the past 30 years than the neat digital hagiographies we read today.

Computer domination has been a constituent of digital discourse since the 1940s and the advent of the first electronic computers. However, the tradition of mechanical domination, which is genealogically related to digital domination, is much older. The extensive output of H.G. Wells (Wells 1895; 1927a; 1927b) and the plethora of films that start with *Metropolis* (directed by Fritz Lang (1927)) and continue through *The Terminator* (directed by James Cameron (1984)) attest to the extensive fascination, and fear, of mechanical domination that has grown up with industrialization. The computer has fitted into this domineering, controlling, paternal role like a glove. The ease with which the computer has been able to take over the traditional, industrial, role of dominating and controlling machines seems to justify the twentieth-century postulate that machines, and then computers, will come to control and dominate us all. Who would question that computers will increasingly dominate all aspects of our lives, including all aspects of archaeological work? Whether anyone is willing, or feels it necessary, to question this postulate, perhaps we should indulge ourselves and look at just how such a postulate has managed to be built and maintained.

There is not space here to discuss in detail the history of mechanical domination as it has come to be realized in nineteenth- and twentieth-century western thought (Shapin 1996), but perhaps we could just follow a very brief resumé.

The idea of a rational society run along rational, mechanical, lines is as old as the Enlightenment, and the genealogy for the twentieth century was well formed from the eighteenth-century automatons through the nineteenth-century utilitarians (Mill 1871; Sen and Williams 1982). Many literary works in the early twentieth century presented a world controlled and ruined by machines. *Metropolis* (Fritz Lang, 1927), *The Machine Stops* (E.M. Forster, 1928), *Modern Times* (Chaplain, 1936), and *Brave New World* (Aldous Huxley, 1932) all present a rational world controlled by machines where the humans live in servitude. Though the list is potentially vast, I will, for purely arbitrary reasons, begin this resumé with H.G. Wells.

In 1936, Wells presented a paper to the Royal Institution of Great Britain on the World Encyclopaedia (Wells 1936). His premise was that 'Some favour the idea of a gradual supersession of the political forms and methods of mass democracy by government through some sort of *élite*, in which the mark of science and the technician will play a dominating part' (ibid., 11). Wells' assumption was not that there is a need for a rational, controlling *élite* — not a ruling élite. Rather, the élite would merely be the interpreters and administrators of a controlling science; 'It is *science* and not *men of science* that we want to enlighten and animate our politics and rule the world' (ibid., 11). Wells saw this World Encyclopaedia as a vast information system that would educate and determine a rational democracy:

I ask you to imagine how this World Encyclopaedia organisation would enter into his [the modern educated *man's*] life and how it would effect him. From his point of view the World Encyclopaedia would be a row of volumes in his own home or in some neighbouring house or in a convenient public library or any school or college, and in this row of volumes he would, without any great toil or difficulty, find in clear understandable language, and kept up to date, the ruling concepts of our social order, the outlines and main particulars in all the fields of knowledge, an exact and reasonably detailed picture of our universe, a general history of the world, and if by any chance he wanted to pursue a question into its ultimate detail, a trustworthy and complete system of reference to primary sources of knowledge. (ibid., 13)

In 1938, Wells published an even more demanding vision of mass control based on educational regimen. In his book *World Brain* (Wells 1938), Wells argued that 'Mental and moral adaptation is lagging dreadfully behind the change in our conditions. A great and menacing gulf opens which only an immense expansion of teaching and instruction can fill' (ibid., ix). Even more like the contemporary heroic language of the Internet, Wells continues to demand a universal system of knowledge:

The missing factor in human affairs . . . is a gigantic and many sided educational renaissance. The highly educated section, the finer minds of the human race are so dispersed, so ineffectively related to the common man, that they are powerless in the face of political and social adventurers of the coarsest sort. . . . In a universal organisation and clarification of knowledge and ideas in a closer synthesis of university and educational activities, in the evocation, that is, of what I have called a World Brain, operating by an enhanced educational system throughout the whole body of mankind, a World Brain that will replace our multitude of uncoordinated ganglia, our powerless miscellany of universities, research institutions, literatures with a purpose, national education systems and the like; . . . any hope of an adequate directive control of the present destructive drift of world affairs. (ibid., xiv)

For Wells, such an encyclopaedia 'would play the role of an undogmatic Bible to a world culture' (ibid., 14), and he dismissed the claims of the detractors of *globalization* that 'not all people think alike' as a matter of intellectual laziness:

You see how such an Encyclopaedic organisation could spread like a nervous network, a system of mental control about the globe, knitting all the intellectual workers of the world through a common interest and a common medium of expression into a more and more conscious co-operating unity and a growing sense of their own dignity, information without pressure or propaganda, directing without tyranny. It could be developed wherever conditions were favourable; it could make inessential concessions and bide its time in regions of exceptional violence, grow vigorously again with every return to liberalism and reason. (ibid., 23)

Not all saw the rational, industrialized controlling force as a democratic one. After the Second World War, in the depths of the Cold War, the fear of mechanized domination as a totalitarian force became the norm; the central, massive, electronic computer replaced the encyclopaedia as the means of rational and unerring control — a totalitarian control. Since the 1950s there has been a steady flow of prophetic claims as to when, never whether, computers would surpass humans in intelligence and, hence, control the world. In 1959, Simon and Newell stated that within the foreseeable future, thinking machines will equal humans (Newell and Simon 1972); by 1970, Martin Minsky confidently stated that 'In from three to eight years we will have a machine with the general intelligence of a human being' (Minsky 1967); and even as late as 1983, Professor Edward Fredkin predicted that:

> There is no principle of science or engineering that prevents us from making intelligent computers that are infinitely smarter than ourselves. . . . We must ask ourselves what such machines will be doing in the future. . . . They may take away some of our (nuclear) toys, they will solve weighty problems that we ourselves have been unable to solve. They will talk to us only to amuse themselves and so, in some sense, keep us as pets. (Prof. Edward Fredkin, Interview on BBC television, October 1983)

Though we may happily have our anachronistic laugh over these statements, we must remember that many of the suppositions which underlay these now seemingly absurd prophesies continue to dominate our own prophesies about the future of digital domination, especially in terms of its social impact. The forecasts about digital culture are still largely informed by assumptions of universal encyclopaedic knowledge, of self-evident technocratic efficacy, and of the necessity of globalization. One thing has changed, however, in this testimony to digital domination, that is the position of the mechanism — of the computer. Moving as it has from the dominance of knowledge (as universal information), to dominating machine, to dominating computer, it has now moved full circle back to the global encyclopaedia — to the Internet.

In this paper I will explore two areas where computers are extensively used: in the production of text and visualization. This will not be an extensive inventory of all the uses of computers, nor of the specific projects of use. Rather I will explore how computers are used and whether in the production of the products of their use, in producing texts and visualizing pasts, the computer is *necessary*.

The production of text

The single greatest use of computers in archaeology, as in all areas, is, ironically, in the production of texts. Though there are more high profile uses, such as Virtual Reality reconstructions, statistical applications, imaging, GIS, etc., there is no doubt that, if we include email, hypertext, notes as well as traditional writing, at least 80 per cent of all computer use is for the production of some sort of text. Equally ironic is the fact that much of this text production is a prelude to printing, either directly on a local printer, or for a published work in a journal or as a book. Increasingly, it is true, journal articles are produced and disseminated via the World Wide Web (WWW), so it is hoped that the volume of paper will decrease in forthcoming years. But it is equally true that since the great expansion in personal computers in offices and education, the volume of paper produced in these 'paperless offices' has skyrocketed. With the vast growth in WWW resources over the past five years there has also been an extraordinary increase in the number of published works (Tran 1998).

It seems as the ease with which text production increases, so does our ability to generate text on paper. Here I am less interested with the viability, or not, of the paperless office. The huge success of the word-processor[2] makes clear its future utility and ever-expanding use. Whether we ever manage to do the majority of our reading 'on-screen' is an unanswerable question at this stage — I find it near impossible to read more than a paragraph or two on the screen without eye-strain. I am interested, however, in the way that the use of the word-processor, email and hypertext has impacted the practice of archaeology, in particular the way archaeology is represented by text.

Despite the many heroic discussions of *electronic text* as a free and open form, textual production on computers has several distinct expressions. Though all are interrelated, they are not the same despite being lumped together. A classic example of this lumping of all electronic textual production is William Mitchell's 'on-line hypertext' *City of Bits* (Mitchell n.d.):

> . . . this same ease of cutting, copying, and otherwise manipulating texts permits different forms of scholarly composition, ones in which the researcher's notes and original data exist in experientially closer proximity to the scholarly text than ever before. According to Michael Heim, as electronic textuality frees writing from the constraints of paper-print technology, 'vast amounts of information, including further texts, will be accessible immediately below the electronic surface of a piece of writing. . . . By connecting a small computer to a phone, a profession will be able to read "books" whose footnotes can be expanded into further "books" which in turn open out onto a vast sea of data bases systemizing all of human cognition' (10–11). The manipulability of the scholarly text, which derives from the ability of computers to search databases with enormous speed, also permits full-text searches, printed and dynamic concordances, and other kinds of processing that allow scholars in the humanities to ask new kinds of questions. Moreover, as one writes, 'The text in progress becomes interconnected and linked with the entire world of information' (161). (Heim 1987; cited in Mitchell n.d.)

---

[2] One should be aware that the primary use of the word-processor, like the spreadsheet — the two most successful applications ever on computers — is tied as much to the industrialization of the office, the automation of the secretary, as it is to the utility of such computer-based applications.

Mitchell does not distinguish between word-processing, conventions of footnoting, hypertext or databasing. The ability to manipulate texts, through cutting, copying and pasting, has certainly changed the way that we go about producing texts. Even I remember, and I am not that old, having to type my essays on a manual typewriter, with carbons; then manually 'cutting and pasting' text and retyping. Using a word-processor I certainly read my text less, and less carefully, than when I had to retype it several times. I use paraphrasing less and I find it much easier to paste in quotes.

But the world described in Mitchell's paragraph takes for granted that what I do when I am writing and editing, chasing references and checking sources, somehow has a universality about it because I can now do it electronically. By simply transferring, and translating, this work from books and libraries to computer networks, this process, how we are never told, allows me to access 'a vast sea of data bases systemizing all of human cognition'. Wasn't this the same promise made for Wells' *World Brain*?

Mitchell goes on to discuss another use of electronic text as if it were all part of the greater whole:

> The keyboard is my café. Each morning I turn to some nearby machine — my modest personal computer at home, a more powerful workstation in one of the offices or laboratories that I frequent, or a laptop in a hotel room — to log into electronic mail. I click on an icon to open an 'inbox' filled with messages from round the world — replies to technical questions, queries for me to answer, drafts of papers, submissions of student work, appointments, travel and meeting arrangements, bits of business, greetings, reminders, chitchat, gossip, complaints, tips, jokes, flirtation. I type replies immediately, then drop them into an 'outbox', from which they are forwarded automatically to the appropriate destinations. . . . If I have time before I finish gulping my coffee, I also check the wire services and a couple of specialized news services to which I subscribe, then glance at the latest weather report. This ritual is repeated whenever I have a spare moment during the day. (Mitchell n.d.)

I too have a ritual, of sorts, as do most other people who more or less live the 'professional, middle-class, western' sort of life that William Mitchell and I do. I do my ritual in the office when I first arrive in the morning. I open my mail (both electronic and paper), work on drafts of papers (both electronic and paper), I go over submissions of student work (both electronic and paper), I too work out all the 'appointments, travel and meeting arrangements, bits of business, greetings, reminders, chitchat, gossip, complaints, tips, jokes, flirtation' (both electronic and paper) that I have to, or want to, deal with. I too like the speed and convenience of email for both official work and just keeping in touch, but many of my friends, especially in the developing world, do not have email, so I also have to write letters. Sometimes, with very special friends, I prefer to write, by hand, a special letter.

I am not trying to make a Luddite point here. The point that I am trying to make, as throughout this paper, is that there are a massive range of different things going on in

Mitchell's daily routine. Organizing the office, writing, editing, collaborating, teaching, gossiping, flirting have been technically mediated for millennia. The fact that Mitchell chooses to mediate most if not all of his activities electronically is a choice many of us now have. It is not necessarily better, nor worse, to mediate these social tasks electronically. The question is whether electronic mediation creates a substantially different social practice than other forms of technical mediation?

As I hope you have guessed by now, my answer is no, it does not. This is not to say that electronic mediation — the use of computers, the Internet, and email as our primary form of textual exchange — does not have any effect. It just doesn't have the effect claimed.

The claim is that electronic text, and hypertext in particular, will herald the 'death of the book' and the birth of a more 'natural', 'individualistic' and 'transparent' form of writing. The allusion is, of course, to Jacques Derrida's *Of Grammatology* and *Dissemination*. Derrida, heavily quoted by Mitchell, makes the argument at the beginning of *Of Grammatology* that 'the development of practical methods of information retrieval extends the possibilities of the "message" vastly, to the point where it is no longer the "written" translation of a language, the transporting of a signified which could remain spoken in its integrity' (Derrida 1967, 86). He goes on to declare that the purpose of *Grammatology* is to escape the encasement of the book through the end of linear writing and, hence, the end of the book. Derrida argues in *Dissemination* that 'one cannot tamper' with the book form, through writing processes that question that form, 'without disturbing everything else' (Derrida 1981).

I do hope that the irony of Derrida using the 'form of the book', twice, to make this point is not lost on him. It is certainly lost on Mitchell who declares that 'Derrida, more than any other major theorist, understands that electronic computing and other changes in media have eroded the power of the linear model and the book as related culturally dominant paradigms' (Mitchell n.d.).

We may forgive Mitchell a bit of his enthusiasm for when he was writing in 1994 the Web was yet young and seemingly democratic. The power of history is the ability to see how things turn out. In 1999 we have a clearer view of where the Web is going and what its development heralded.

In a forthcoming paper by Charles Gere on the computer and hypertext as allegory, he reminds us what should be now clear to all, that 'A map of world Internet connections showing density of net traffic could equally well serve as a map of the distribution and movement of power and capital', that largely because of the non-linearity of hypertext, the openness of the textual form and the ability to link to diverse international web-sites — but despite the fact that users cannot create links unless they set up their own site —

> . . . the Internet and the Worldwide Web are proclaimed as potentially radical and emancipatory developments in digital technology. They are characterised as potential

sites of resistance to the hegemony of the established order. However radical the Internet might appear it is fundamentally bound up with the operations of a particular phase of capitalism. The global communications network which enables the Internet to exist itself exists because of the needs of industry to communicate quickly and efficiently across national borders. Indeed the Internet is a kind of superstructural mirror image of that form of capitalism inasmuch as it reflects the distribution of computer networks across the globe. (Gere forthcoming)

Now more than ever, and even from its earliest days, the Web is a site for commerce; personal and corporate sites abound, but practically always with the same purpose, to sell something, an image, a product or a life story.[3] Identity, in many social groups, now depends on your ability to create an advertised image on the Web, and this is true whether you are a new car from Germany or a secondary student from Australia.

This may be, we could counter, a temporary setback; a momentary realignment and appropriation of a largely popular political media. The power, as Marshall McLuhan would argue, is in the media itself, not how it is used.[4] This is but a hostile invasion that must, and will, be resisted. Or, at worst, a new territory within the medium that can be ringfenced and controlled by the essentially 'fluid' and 'individualizing' nature of the Web. The Web by its nature will resist. But Gere again reminds us that:

> This is not some hostile invasion, but simply capitalism claiming its own. The Web is not a radical new phenomenon, but simply a more sophisticated development of nineteenth century technologies such as the telegraph and the typewriter. Combined with the power of the spectacle, through the monitor, it is powerful and seductive. But this should not fool us into mistaking it for something it is not. The Web exists because beneath it, and the Internet, and all the other manifestations of digital media, is the 'processed world' of millions of office workers who sit in front of terminals, word processing, data processing, or data inputting. (Gere forthcoming)

In archaeology our rhetoric of computing is almost exclusively dominated, whether Processually or Postprocessually, by an almost total ignorance of this history of such representations.

---

[3] The preliminary findings (September 1999) of the Virtual Society programme have shown that, far from being a level democratic and identityless space, it is actually a space with 'virtual power structures that mimic real space'. (http://www.brunel.ac.uk/research/virtsoc/)
[4] Hypertext creates a palimpsest of layered meaning wherein hegemonic authority defers to multilinear relativism. For McLuhan and other cyber enthusiasts, this necessarily tolerant structuration of knowledge approaches a state of spiritual nirvana more closely than any other medium to date.
(http://landow.stg.brown.edu/cpace/infotech/asg/ag25.html)

Textual representations: now and then

Now

Ian Hodder's excavations at Çatalhöyük have relied extensively on the integrative and fluid nature of computing environments to fulfil their project goal of a Postprocessual archaeological method (see the Çatalhöyük web-site at: http://catal.arch.cam.ac.uk/catal/catal.html). In his 1998 paper, '"Always momentary, fluid and flexible": towards a reflexive excavation methodology' (Hodder 1997), Hodder emphasizes the role of new information technologies in achieving his goal of moving interpretation into the context of production — of achieving integration and collaboration among all the team, specialists and diggers, on-site and fully integrating recording and interpretation.

If we look at the Çatalhöyük Home Page, we find a simple and modest outline of the contents of the web-site. Ignoring the menu for the moment, we are first told that the site is 'designed for those interested in the ongoing excavations at Çatalhöyük'. We can then follow one of the twelve links to 'Recent Additions' (three links), 'General Information' (five links) or to 'Research Materials' (four links).

Following these links, I am struck by how conventional the content and presentation are. Though the whole does not read much like a site report, it certainly reads quite conventionally as an exhibition or as a prospectus. The site as a whole would not look out of place alongside most contemporary charities' annual reports.[5]

At the beginning we have the 'Mission Statement' which tells us, among other things, that the 'ultimate aim is to provide the Turkish Ministry of Culture with a well planned heritage site'. The only allusion to the broader theoretical and IT programme is when we are told that the on-site museum will be 'enhanced by virtual reality techniques and interactive video'.

A few links do seem worthy of further investigation in this light: The 'Çatalhöyük Discussion Group' and the 'Excavation Database'. The Çatalhöyük Discussion page allows for any visitor to join a discussion of existing topics or, one assumes, start a new one. The day I logged on, in early September 1999, there were a total of 243 postings discussing around 40 topics ranging from 'the tin resources in Anatolia' (only two postings) to 'matriarchy' (with several discussions and an average of four postings each) to the most popular 'give this planet a chance; the origins question' (with 31 postings) (http://catal.arch.cam.ac.uk/discussion/cataldisc.html). Up and running since February 1999, the amount of discussion seems very impressive. The discussions range, as you would expect, is from the interesting to the banal — perhaps a bit skewed to the banal — but, as an historian, I am very pleased that such 'shop talk' is being recorded.

[5] Perhaps this is a greater indicator of Hodder's globalization than he would like to admit. The general corporate tone and presentation and the array of corporate sponsors' logos at the base of the page make certainly more than an inadvertent reference to global corporate culture.

However, what is being recorded is not so much 'shop talk' — that vital bit of interpretive discussion that takes place in all disciplines around the evening field table, in the conference pub, or at tea in the trenches — but is a 'Notes and Queries' page. Postings to a discussion page, like its published counterpart, are always argumentative essays, no matter how short, and cannot be an electronic substitution for chit-chat.

What also strikes me about the Çatalhöyük web-site, and just about every other web-site I have visited, is that there is little about the presentation of these texts that is necessarily dependent on the technology of the Web. Certainly there is a fragmentation of the narrative that is different from the standard site report or journal article, but there is much more shared between the two than is not.

Academic web-sites generally, and Çatalhöyük specifically, are largely made up of traditional textual narratives with hypertext-links rather than references or footnotes. All of the Çatalhöyük Archived Reports (http://catal.arch.cam.ac.uk/catal/archive_ reps.html) are shockingly traditional with the links only to tables and figures, presented as separate image pages, and the ubiquitous 'so-and-so this volume', linking to yet another page of traditional specialist reportage. How is the computer necessary for this? We could equally, and quite easily, argue that the traditional textual forms are better as they at least provide conventionalized textual forms whose integration of narrative, image and reference is well known.[6] As with the database and the discussion group, the texts of the site create an 'interaction' and 'flexibility' of recording and interpretation that result in little more than a rather conventional, though slightly more detailed, recording system.

The On-line Database is quite revealing in this respect. It offers the detailed and formal recorded data on features and deposits as well as skeletons — I thought that there may be more caution here, but none seemed to be considered — but also, in keeping with the project's goal to 'make visible' all aspects of recording and interpretation, the daily diaries of the excavators are also available.

This I find an enjoyable feature, with a mixture of the usual description of features, samples taken and work completed, with some lively commentary on method and site management. On 26/06/99, Craig Cessford wrote:

> I am basically treating this like an area of floor, which is what it is in terms of broad category, and this means four flotation samples which might give us west to east spatial patterning. I am also taking two archives, one from each end, as somebody might actually look at these unlike 99.9999999999999999999999999999999999999% of those we take which just waste time on site, take up lots of space while drying and then need to be stored. (Cessford n.d.)

---

[6] I am well aware of the mountain of Post-modernist critique of traditional textual forms, and do not deny many of their conclusions. The point I wish to make here is that the simple modification of the referential system and the distancing of the image from the text do not even remotely challenge the critique of the authorial status in traditional textual forms.

And on 22/08/98, Naomi Hamilton wrote:

> Some time during today, when the lab should have been locked anyway, they took away everything in my in-box in the belief that it was finished with — and didn't actually take the things from the out-box! It's going to take some work getting it all back, as it clearly wasn't all logged back into the finds lab — they only fished out 11 things, and unfortunately I know I had far more than that in my back-log. I haven't the time or energy to sort it out today, but when will I have? (Hamilton n.d.)

Though I suppose that I am meant to recognize how unique this system of recording is, and it certainly is if we only look at the past 30 years or so, I am struck by how similar these diary entries are to the many that I have read from the first 50 years of this century. In particular, I find the structure of the discussions, with their emphasis on description of work and features and the critiques of site management, to be almost identical with the site notebooks of Sir Mortimer Wheeler.

Does this mean that this programme of interaction mediated by computer systems is a mistake? Or that simply because the interaction achieved through the computer systems at Çatalhöyük or elsewhere can be achieved through other technical means that these programmes are a waste of time and money? Of course not. Simply because computers are not the only means for achieving such recording does not mean that they are not a *good* means for doing so. As Ian Hodder has reminded us so often (Hodder 1996), the work at Çatalhöyük is an experiment, and experiments are a good thing. The over-standardization of archaeological field methodology is in desperate need for alternatives, and, perhaps, the work at Çatalhöyük may offer us a few. The error here is the claim that a globalizing interaction is being achieved that is substantially different simply because it is utilizing the iconic technological mediation of global corporate culture. The impacts of the Çatalhöyük experiment, if any, will be from achieving a different mode of production and a different archaeological culture, not because it used computers, however helpful. I do not think, however, that the forms of scientific life being lived out at Çatalhöyük are anywhere radical enough to have much effect.

Then

Hypertext and the Internet are not the first settings in which the nature of the book has been challenged. All through the twentieth century the death of the book has been championed (Foucault 1977; Derrida 1976; Baudrillard 1988). Even before Derrida, Baudrillard and Foucault were questioning the authority, and accepted histories, of the book, cultural critics and social anarchists were directly challenging both the narrative and physical form of the book. We could certainly mention the work of Walter Benjamin and his *Arcades Project*,[7] or Marcel Duchamp's *Museums*, but equally, and more directly, the work of Guy Debord.

Guy Debord, of the proto-situationalist group l'Internationale Lettriste and author of *La Société du spectacle*, composed his autobiography, *Mémoires*, in 1957 as a coded history of l'Internationale Lettriste formed through collages and quotations; an 'anti-livre' that could only be fully deciphered by members of the group. Debord even had the book bound in sandpaper so that it would destroy any book it was placed with (Hussey 1999).

Despite these deliberate attempts at the destruction of the book form, the book survived. The book remains the authoritative medium for academic and official texts; it remains the primary forum for critique and political dissent despite the immediacy of both film and television; more interestingly, it remains an important medium for experimentation. The challenge, if there has been a successful one yet, is to the pre-eminence of text (Bakhtin 1984), a critique that computers cannot resolve.

In the way of an historical aside, it is useful to remind ourselves that the translation from scribal culture to printed word was not simple either. The 'printing revolution' was the effect of a long and always provisional social process in western culture that required an immense investment, in both new infrastructure and new skills. The rise of the book as an authoritative medium was neither natural nor self-evident. As Adrian Johns' book *The Nature of the Book* demonstrates, it took over 150 years and immense social and technological effort to transform the book from unauthored scribal copy, to authoritative published book (Johns 1998).

The first printing press came to London in 1476, and was kept within Westminster Abbey, printing a select series of texts for a select group. By the early seventeenth century there were 20 licensed printers in London, though it is estimated that there were several hundred unlicensed printers in London at the time. By the middle of that century, there were also presses in many other English cities printing a variety of official, but mostly unofficial, material. Though we can superficially see a great deal of similarity between this scenario and the rise of the Web, I wish to focus on the production of political pamphlets.

An enormous number of public media were available to the seventeenth-century populace. '. . . books and newspapers (relegated more to the elite), pamphlets, broadsides, oral communication, woodcut prints, paintings, stage plays, ballads, sermons, official proclamations, petitions, and riots' (Griscom n.d.) were all recognized forms of 'public communication'. Tim Harris, in his book *Propaganda and Public Opinion in Seventeenth-Century England*, sets the scene:

[7] For best discussion of Benjamin's *Arcades Project*, see S. Buck-Morse, *The Dialectics of Seeing* (Cambridge, MA, 1995).

> It is well known that from the eve of the Civil War there was a sudden and dramatic surge in the output of the press. As censorship controls broke down following the meeting of the Long Parliament in late 1640, there was a great explosion of pamphlet and other printed materials, discussing a wide range of political, constitutional, and religious topics, and it is probably not too controversial to assert that the English Revolution of the mid-seventeenth century was accompanied by a concomitant media revolution. (Harris 1987, 52)

Literacy rates were extraordinarily high[8] and, with the addition of public readings, very few members of the populace in the towns were not well informed. But the political participation did not end with the passive reading of news in its various forms. Frederick Siebert, in his *Freedom of the Press in England, 1476–1776*, gives us an astounding account of the sheer volume of print in the early 1640s:

> An analysis preserved in the Thomson collection in the British Museum shows that although only twenty-two pamphlets were published in 1640, more than 1,000 were issued in each of the succeeding four years. The record number of 1,966 appeared in 1642. (Siebert 1952, 180)

There was little financial incentive to publish a political pamphlet in the 1640s (many of which today would be viewed as at best libellous and at worst treasonable) and there was a great deal to lose. The pamphleteer was driven, so we are told, by an earnest commitment to the betterment of the state, by the direct power that could be achieved through print. Print, in the few years before the Royalists regained control over the presses in 1644, was an interactive network of common voices that was loud enough to be heard in the seats of political power in England. However, like the early Internet, this programme of 'open' publication was very difficult to control. The King and Parliament both attempted to control the presses through licensing and sanctions — neither worked. The public's prodigious desire for information had to be satiated, but, as with the Governments of today, it also had to be controlled.

The solution, as increasingly is the case today with the Internet, was the institutionalization of the newspaper and the magazine into the hands of the aristocratic and commercial authority (Griscom n.d.). The strategy of translating the public desire for information from the open unruly independent presses into an enterprise of authoritative, and regulatable, printers — the control of the citizenry through appropriation and construction of a market rather than approbation — is one of the most successful creations of modern capitalism. It worked well for printing and it is working well for the Internet.

---

[8] At an absolute minimum, 30 per cent of the male population in the countryside could read, while in London, male literacy rates were upwards of 80 per cent. Even in the lowest classes, probably over 20 per cent of husbandmen, nationally, could read.

Afterthoughts on hypertexts

In 1945 Vannevar Bush, an engineer, published what is now seen as the pioneer article on hypertext (Bush 1945). In his article, Bush defined a system that he called the 'memex', a system by which someone could follow the various pertinent books, articles and notes on any subject. Memex would allow the user not only to examine all these relevant works, but, in doing so on memex, will be building a trail of the many items. Within this memex trail the user can insert a comment or two, linking it within the path of the trail or to some item, create side trails, add a 'longhand' analysis of their own, and build up an encyclopaedia of their own on any subject.

Though Bush was not even anticipating a computer environment for his memex, his article (along with a number of other encyclopaedic utopias) is used extensively as evidence of the deeply modern and self-evident form that has now come to be known as hypertext (see Landow, http://landow.stg.brown.edu/ht/memex.html). Though the ur-article of hypertext, Bush's vision of 'hypertext' is not very much like hypertext. Bush's memex is a mechanical translation of the practice that we go through in the library; a mechanization of the card-catalogue, notepad, and manuscript on the library desk.

The hypertext of the Internet remains an authored system, where Bush's memex is an authorial system.[9] Authored systems, like the printing press, are easily appropriated; authorial systems are not. As Charles Gere reminded us above, the global capitalism that has so swiftly appropriated the WWW and has so successfully stabilized HTML as an authorial system, best suited to advertisement over research, is not a 'hostile invasion' but a claiming of what is their own. It is the application of a strategy of appropriation that is as old as modern capitalism, and it is likely to be as successful now as it was in the mid-seventeenth century.

Reconstructions

In the 1960s Robert G. Chenhall wrote in his influential paper 'The Impact of Computers on Archaeological Theory: an Appraisal and Projection', 'With this quality of perceptual data, it will then be possible to make inferential, socio-cultural statements that are also data supportable and, at least logically and statistically, replicable' (Chenhall 1968). Chenhall saw the accuracy, perceptual quality and objectivity of the computer mediating the *necessary* subjectivity of the archaeologist to produce reliable inferences about the past. The road to this golden age of understanding was limited by only four factors: (1) the speed and power of computer equipment, (2) the scale and quality of

---

[9] The only authorial system available on computer that is anything like the memex is CABINET (Boast 1997).

data (by which Chenhall meant the appropriateness of measurements for the computer), (3) training of archaeologists in programming logic and statistics, and (4) the lack of creative imagination (Chenhall 1968, 23). The first of these three are recognizable to all who have read anything on the use of computers in the arts; all identify the, temporary, limitations of computers and of the inappropriate skills of the researcher to cope with the demands of the new technology. The last needs some explanation.

Chenhall sees 'creative imagination' as a necessary skill of the researcher to open up the possibilities of testable questions. It is this 'technologically-mediated objective viewpoint from which we can see the past accurately, without the fog of our subjective selves confusing the inferences'. Clearly Chenhall felt that not only was an instrumental mediation necessary, but the mediation of a very special instrument — the computer. It was the computer, coupled with the skilled archaeologist, that could produce the perceptually accurate view of the past (Elsner 1994). Though Chenhall was not speaking of Virtual Reality, or as archaeologists prefer to label it today 'visualizing archaeology', his view was of a future where computers would act as a primary mediator through which the archaeologists could view the past.

Almost 30 years later, in his Introduction to his and Siliotti's colourful tome *Virtual Archaeology* (Forte and Siliotti 1997), Maurizio Forte would claim that:

> As progress marches on, we will be able to reconstruct 'through the use of computers' ever larger segments of our most distant past, leading to a more accurate understanding of the microcosm of the ancient world. The problem for archaeology is to retrieve the maximum possible amount of information from the material culture, so as to recapture its non-material aspects as well. (Forte 1997, 9)

Forte sees 'virtual archaeology' as a coupling of the scientifically accurate data acquisition practices of modern archaeology and the 're-presentational' accuracy of the new computer technologies. Not only is this coupling fruitful in itself, but it will lead to an 'archaeology of the third millennium [which] will very likely be a science with a strong technological element that will enhance out of all proportion our ability to explore, to interpret and to classify, bringing with it a greater and more penetrating ability to reconstruct the past' (ibid., 9). As with Chenhall, it is a coupling of an empirically rich archaeology with the presentational realism of the computer.

The stated purpose of Forte and Siliotti's book makes this clear, as we assume is the purpose of the printed computer visualizations themselves, which offer no less than 'the reader the most faithful re-presentation of the ancient world possible: highly realistic in information and with a high scientific content'. The context for computer visualization in archaeology is clear enough. As with Chenhall, the purpose is to recreate the past for the viewer: the viewer, 'Through the interaction between exact science, information technology and new research methods . . . embarks on a technological voyage into the past' (ibid., 10).

These computer presentations have moved on since Chenhall's call for deeply embedding cybernetics into archaeological practice. Forte and Siliotti remind us, however, that though the focus of application has shifted from statistics to visualization, the urgent sense of embedding this progressive medium within archaeological practice remains, and largely for the same reasons.

But the traditional roots of these reconstructions — this visualizing ambition — go back much further. During the nineteenth century, an explosion of technological innovation created whole new forms of presentation and performance. The development of then very expensive plate glass was increasingly in use in superior shops in the new Department Stores by the 1830s creating the proscenium frame that came to surround all of the various forms of *exhibition* in the nineteenth and twentieth centuries, including the computer monitor. The lighting of London's streets in 1814–20 meant that this increasing range of framed tableaux were well lit and on display throughout the day and much of the night. By the 1840s museums, increasingly public, were able to extend their openings to the night so the 'working classes' could view the edifying displays which increasingly drew on the new technologies. The developments in lighting generally[10] had a massive effect on display and the theatre. Along with the use of new materials in scenic design and costume, and the use of new pyrotechnic and chemical technologies, the ability of displays to present distant times and places advanced beyond all previous ambitions.

The advancements were not just technological, but also in the range, scale, but mostly the fidelity of the displays themselves — in the desire to create a visually 'realistic' view of the past. These technological developments helped fuel the variety of different presentations of distant lands, historical events and unique views, and in the rise of the historical theatre. In response there was a huge increase of public interest in these presentations with tens of thousands of people attending the increasing diversity of exhibitions (Mitchell 1988; Booth 1981; Stokes 1972).

My concern here is not to explore the many forms of historical representation developing from the early nineteenth century, rather with one specific setting in which the dialogue between the new technologies of accurate representation — the presentation of the new 'historical mindedness' — and the new discipline of archaeology came together to create a set of re-presentations of the past whose realism, attention to detail and engagement with the viewer were unequalled until the 'heritage' boom of the 1980s. I refer to the tradition of the Victorian Spectacular Theatre as produced and practised by Charles Kean, Beerbohm Tree, the Bancrofts, Hermann Vezin and of course William Godwin, and popularized by the paintings of Whistler and the Pre-Raphaelites and in the writings of Oscar Wilde.[11]

---

[10] Gaslight 1817, limelight 1837, electric carbon-arc 1848, incandescent carbon-filament 1881. Introduction of 'focused limelight' in Kean's *Henry VIII* (1885), first focused beam of light.

[11] See Stokes 1972 for a full discussion of the Victorian Spectacular Theatre.

By the mid-1800s, theatre had been transformed into a picture of the world. Influenced initially by the spectacle painting of C. William West, Francis Darby and John Martin, the development of which is expressed in the excessively realistic and allegorical paintings by the Pre-Raphaelites at the end of the century, theatre was increasingly considered as an artistic composition. This emphasis on composition was not as we would suspect today, an emphatically subjective presentation, but emphasized the objective and even scientific re-presentation of the objective scientific history. Painting, illustration, theatre, exhibition and the Diorama, having been stripped of their roles as the accurate recorder of the contemporary by photography, were now the definitive re-presenters of the absent, the past, the vast and the distant.

Nowhere was this preoccupation with re-presenting the objective past so apparent as in the theatre. In its ability to provide a three-dimensional, visually realistic experience of an accurately reproduced setting of the past, the theatre was unrivalled in the nineteenth century. The historical theatre of the middle and late nineteenth century in Europe, and primarily in England, was increasingly a site of collaboration between actors, artists, scenic specialists and archaeologists. This collaboration was exemplified by the productions of two men, Charles Kean and William Godwin. Both Kean and Godwin had trained as architects, published extensively on classical architecture, and both were Fellows of the Society of Antiquaries.

Kean was an avid supporter of historical reconstruction in the theatre. In his 1853 production of *Sardanapalus*, at the Princess's, Kean produced what was seen at the time as a masterful re-presentation of the Assyrian setting. Kean's purpose went well beyond performing Byron's tragedy 'to render visible to the eye . . . the costume, architecture, and customs of the ancient Assyrian people, verified by the bas-reliefs. . . . to convey to the stage an accurate portraiture and living picture of an age long since past away' (Cole 1859, 58–9).

Kean's *Sardanapalus* was a grand reconstruction of Layard's Assyrian discoveries at Nimrud and Nineveh between 1845–55, with Kean acknowledging Layard in the Programme Notes. Layard's four books on Nineveh were shown at the Great Exhibition in 1851 and then again at the Crystal Palace in 1854. The excavations, extensively covered in the *London Illustrated News* and the press generally, were hugely popular. The play opened with a massive procession with musicians, archers, spearmen, dancing-girls, nobles, officers, eunuchs, standard-bearers and Sardanapalus on an 'authentic' chariot drawn by two white horses (Booth 1981, 20). The accurate depiction of the objects and settings that most people were aware of from visits to the British Museum and the illustrated magazines was a huge success and forged a programme of further collaboration between archaeology and the historical theatre and art in the second half of the nineteenth century.[12]

[12] Art too was influenced by the effect of extreme realism. Luke Fildes constructed a life-size fisherman's cottage in his studio to complete his painting of cottages in England and Scotland. Alma Tadema, whose extensive archaeological research into his painting of Coriolanus is well known, also had a weekly shipment of roses from the French Riviera sent to him throughout the winter to produce the petals in *The Roses of*

William Godwin, born in Bristol in 1833, made his living, initially, as an architect, but wrote regularly in his early years as a theatre critic for the Bristol paper. Only after 1865, and with the help of a long-term affair with the actress Ellen Terry, did Godwin gain the contacts and associations in the West End theatres to realize his programme of extreme historical realism.

Godwin published what is seen as both his manifesto and the manifesto of the realist theatre in 32 articles on 'The Architecture and Costume of Shakespeare's Plays', published in *The Architect* (31 October 1874 to 26 June 1875).[13] These articles represented years of scholarly research by Godwin into the fifteenth-century architecture, costume and furniture, and formed the basis of his life-long critique of the London Theatre. The foundation of this critique was the lack of fidelity between the scenery, setting and costume of the productions and the 'real' past; a critique against the emphasis, as was common in the nineteenth-century theatre, on the actor and their persona to an emphasis on the play as a re-presentation of the past as it was.

> The use of scenery, dress and other accessories directly implies an intention to reproduce the original scene, and consequently an error in either of these vitiates the whole result, nor will excellence on the part of any actor atone for the inaccuracy of his personal appearance or of the scenery by which he is surrounded. I do not need to deny that a person totally ignorant of the past may feel himself satisfied in spite of the grossest anachronisms, but his satisfaction will be that of a man who is merely anxious to be amused, entirely irrespective of any desire to be instructed, whereas I maintain that we do not go to a theatre simply to hear passionate recitations and funny speeches, but to witness such a performance as will place us nearly as possible as spectators of the original scene of the thing represented, and so gain information of man, manners, customs, costumes, and countries — and this result is only obtainable where accuracy in every particular is secured. (Godwin 1864)

Through his theatrical contacts, provided largely by Ellen Terry, Godwin began working on a number of productions as scenic and costume designer including several projects with the Bancrofts at the Prince of Wales's Theatre and one at the Haymarket.[14] One of the early, and greatly successful, productions was W.G. Wills' play *Claudian*, which Godwin worked on for some time in 1876–7, with Wills and Lady Archibald Campbell.

Claudian was the story of the curse of eternal youth, put on the Byzantine emperor by a Christian Hermit; a curse that could only be broken when the rock of Byzantium was 'rent asunder'. Godwin invested a more scholarly effort and research on *Claudian*

Heliogabalus (1896). Holman Hunt brought both a goat and Dead Sea mud back with him to paint *The Scapegoat* (1854). Every object in John Poynter's *Israel in Egypt* (1867), an extensive outdoor spectacle, was recreated from intensive archaeological research.

[13] The articles were reprinted in Edward Gordon Craig's, Godwin's son, journal *The Mask* May/June 1908–April 1914.

[14] See Booth 1981, 23, for a detailed discussion of the early theatrical consultations of Godwin.

than any other project he had taken on to that time. He comprehensively reviewed the standard works on Byzantine art and architecture, read Apollonius Sidonius and Eusebius, describing his design for the first act in an open letter to his fellow architect, and producer of the play, Wilson Barrett:

> The foreground is a bit like Constantine's forum; to the left, solidly built, and of true dimensions, is the end of a Doric portico; to the right a portion of a circular Ionic portico; a low wall bounds the plateau, and over this we see the tops of dark cypresses among other trees and commemorative pillars, and, on a rising hill beyond, stately many-pillared structures, while, in the far distance, the blue waters of the Bosphorus and the hilly shore beyond, complete a picture of which Mr Walter Hann might well be proud. In the walls beneath the porticos we recognise the *opus sectile*, or large mosaics, of which Mr Godwin speaks in his pamphlet. The capitals and friezes reveal the coarse carving of the time, and the marble and gilding exhibit something of the costly splendour. Under one portico is a marble statue of Venus with gilded drapery and in the centre of the stage is another statue similarly treated. (Godwin 1883, 277)

The extreme archaeological realism of the scenic design drew a number of criticisms. The scenic spectacle was described as an 'archaeological tyranny' that could go no further and the play was subjected to parodies in *Punch* (Anonymous 1883).

A view from the Gods

If anyone has seen a virtual archaeological reconstruction, or any VR reconstruction for that matter, you almost always start with the same initial view. It is an angelic view, a view taken from the optimal position for the detached objective eye: the position taken is always about 200 metres up in the air, 300 metres distant, and always at a slight angle to the main orientation of the structure to be viewed. As a view it has a very long pedigree, it can be seen in the 'antiquarian' and architectural etchings of the eighteenth century, in the popular panoramic paintings, in the panoramas themselves and in the 'scenic' photography from the nineteenth century.[15] It is also the view of the stage from the upper balcony of a European theatre, better known as the 'Gods'.

The perspective is a necessary one, one that sets the viewer up as a subject; a subject that can view in a detached and internal way. Just as the theatre sets us in a dark and comfortable environment to detach our bodies, but not our vision, from the action on the stage, so the angelic perspective, the view from the Gods, is appropriated for the entry into the framed performance of the computer representation. As Damisch put it:

---

[15] The 'Angelic View' was first seen on William Sherwin's engraving of 'The Royal Exchange' (1674) (BM 1880-11-13-3679). Such engravings were not used as architectural drawings but as limited edition gifts to benefactors and sponsors of the construction.

Perspective is not a code; but it has in common with language the fact that, in it and by it, is instituted or constituted, by means of a point, an instance analogous to that of the 'subject' in language, of the 'person', always placed in relation to a 'here' or a 'there', with all the possibilities of passing from one position to the other which derive from that. (Damisch, quoted in Bann 1995, 116)

This view portrays the historicity of the activity at hand, that of the production and use of the virtual archaeological reconstruction. From the early days of the 1980s, archaeologists have claimed that their primary interest in this technology is as an exploratory tool; as a means of investigating the past (Reilly 1992; Miller and Richards 1995; Huggett 1995; Wood and Chapman 1992; Eiteljorg 1988; Burridge *et al.* 1989). This investigation is through a realist reconstruction of the past — an archaeological investigation that returns the archaeologist to the stage. As an interpretive statement of current research, the computer representation offers a contemporary stage on which the realist agenda of William Godwin is again played out. As with Godwin's productions, they are not *the* past, but an authoritative, archaeologically valid, replica, where the key issue is getting the view of the archaeology right.

Paul Reilly recognizes that the models created are surrogates when he defines the *virtual* as 'an allusion to a model, a replica, the notion that something can act as a surrogate or replacement for an original. In other words, it refers to a description of an archaeological formation or to a simulated archaeological formation' (Reilly 1992, 162). Reilly defines a *virtual archaeology* as the construction of a rich variety of metaphorical data on the computer and sees *these* data as the evidence for archaeological discussion. He argues that by 'enhancing and enriching the quality of this metaphorical data we hope to stimulate more and new archaeological discussions' (Reilly 1992, 166–7). Forte, Siliotti and Reilly recognize that the computer reconstruction is a 'picture' of the past. The contemporary 'virtual' status of the reconstruction is recognized by all as a 'model' or 'replica' that can stand for the original. A statement, more sympathetic to that made by Reilly 100 years later, is found in Godwin's article of 10 October 1885 in *The Dramatic Review*:

> The Archaeologist or antiquary, however much Mr. Whistler may think the contrary, is something more than a frequenter of museums and a patron of pigeon-holes. His method or mental attitude is of special significance; and you can no more make his off hand than you can make an artist: indeed he must have some of the artist's qualities, or, at least, be able to imagine in his mind's eye the features of the past and interpret its records and memorials.[16] (Godwin 1885, 113)

---

[16] The Mr. Whistler he is referring to is the painter, and Godwin's good friend James Whistler. Despite the snipe at Whistler's comments on Archaeologists, Whistler remained Godwin's friend and champion, even marrying Godwin's widow and defending his honour in a brawl with Augustus Moore at the Drury Lane Theatre in 1890.

Here Godwin is arguing for a situation far more similar to that attributed to virtual archaeology by Reilly; that there is a special kind of an artistic eye that can recreate the vision of the past. Godwin does not mean by 'artist's qualities' what we might mean today; he means the ability to represent the subject accurately, as it is or was. The *art* for Godwin, and his friends such as Wilde and Whistler, is not an interpretive endeavour, but a representational craft: it is not the art of the impressionists, but the scholarly art of the Pre-Raphaelites and nineteenth-century realists.

In both of these settings, that of the archaeological computer representation and the historically realist stage of Godwin, what matters is not the objects from the past, the 'raw material' or 'thing in itself', but the idealized space of the reconstruction. It is through this reconstructed frame that the analyst, or viewer, is provided with 'a powerful analytical aid in allowing computer representation of primary data. . . . Unlike the raw material from which the recorded data was drawn, this metaphorical data can be dissected and explored repeatedly in an almost limitless number of ways' (Reilly 1992, 166–7).

Just as Forte informs us that as 'progress marches on, we will be able to reconstruct ever larger segments of our most distant past, leading to a more accurate understanding of the microcosm of the ancient world' (Forte 1997, 9), so Godwin tells us that 'to witness such a performance [of a realist play] as will place us as nearly as possible as spectators of the original scene or of the thing represented, and this result is only possible where accuracy in every particular is assured' (Godwin 1864). Accuracy in both cases was, and is, the paramount concern; necessary to produce the effect of realism in staging the past.

Most important is authenticity. This is not just a measure of the correspondence of the *presented* to the *real*, but a matter of determining the authority of this correspondence. In his foreword to Forte's book, Lord Renfrew claims for the validity of such reconstructions, he argues that it is necessary that:

> In every case it is the archaeologist who has to supply the data. If the aim is to reconstruct a ruined site to show how it originally looked, then ultimately the archaeologist is responsible for providing the missing elements. If there is guess-work involved, the archaeologist does the guessing. But now 'because he is using a computer' he has to do it in a logical and structured and ultimately more fruitful way. The very task of setting up a computer reconstruction obliges the archaeologist to pose the right questions, and then answer them. This whole procedure makes the computer reconstruction a valuable research tool. (Renfrew 1997, 7)

The emphasis on both valid expertise and the computer as a rational setting for exploration emphasizes the importance of the computer in archaeology. It is not just an instrument, no matter how useful; it is not just a more efficient representational device, the time, expense and effort put into computer reconstructions deny any such claim; it is a necessary archaeological site upon which the expert archaeologist, the archaeological evidence and the viewer come together to confirm the 'valid' past.

Stephen Bann argues that this effect, the desire for the real which began in the nineteenth century, of which photography was only an unambiguous sign, made the 'staging of the past' an inadequate goal by the end of the nineteenth century. In staging the past, the historical objects were given heightened identity through representation. Coupled with the recreated historical settings that were becoming commonplace, it became possible to 'live the past' (Bann 1995, 130–1). He was speaking of the nineteenth- and twentieth-century pastime of 're-enactment', but the reality effect of the computer reconstruction, with the requirement of interactivity, creates a stage where it is both possible to maintain the *objectivity* of 'staging the past' and the romanticism of 'living the past'. In the interactive computer model, the stage can be set for the viewer as a detached observer, the angelic eye, the view from the Gods, but it can also be set for the viewer as re-enactor. The voyeuristic viewer, empirical to some, can follow any number of historical narratives within the reconstructed space as either detached observer or engaged re-enactor.

The computer has become a *scientific* stage on which archaeologists can finally re-enact the past 'accurately', 'authoritatively', and without the annoying subjectivity of human actors. Archaeologists, like the nineteenth-century theatre-goer, 'register the image not only as an accurate record, designed to satisfy antiquarian interest, but as a "shifter" (to use the linguist Jakobson's term) between present and past' (Bann 1995, 120). It does not matter that much if the contemporary archaeologist uses the computer-generated stage as Godwin intended, as an objective detached view of a scene from the past, or as an engaged Postprocessualist interpreter; the game is the same:

> The computer program requires the archaeologist to make decisions about the original texture and colour of all the surfaces of the buildings. Decisions have to be taken, or alternative possibilities formulated, about the destroyed upper parts of buildings. The computer reconstruction also brings to the surface interesting questions about the original lighting of each room and house. The resulting 3-D experience has to be seen to be believed: that is what virtual reality is about. (Renfrew 1997, 7)

Indeed it is. It is a spectacular performance, one that again demands that we suspend our belief that the object we are engaging with is a contemporary computer with a keyboard and mouse, as the theatre-goer of the mid-nineteenth century was to suspend their belief that they were looking at a contemporary stage, to convince ourselves that we are looking at the *real* past.

Computing futures

Where does this leave us? What is the hope for computing in archaeology if all it really is is the continuation of traditional representations by other means? What happens to computing in archaeology if it is stripped of its pre-eminent position as a unique modernizing force? What happens to archaeology's 'brave new world'?

The answer, as far as I am concerned, is 'not much'. If we look to computing as a valuable tool, at least in some contexts, rather than uncritically converting to the corporate hype, then there is little to be worried about. If I may remind us again of Charles Gere's declaration that computers — whether denoting the Internet or the box — are the natural instruments of modern global capitalism, then it is less surprising that they should occupy, mythologically, the position of Colonizer. How similar the discourse of computers is to that of the 'improving' colonizers of the nineteenth century. We continue blindly to accept this global colonizer into our discipline as an unquestionable civilizing force. The evidential connotations of power, efficiency, technological superiority and universality are constantly mobilized to paint the computer as such a force for all places, all times and all genres.

But we must remember, in these post-colonial times, that we now know a thing or two about such imperialistic claims. We know from the post-colonial experience of the past 50 years that far from swamping and destroying the colonized culture,[17] as many early anthropologists believed, we now find that western imperialistic culture was simply assimilated. Just as nineteenth- and twentieth-century European culture is characterized by the assimilation and translation of diverse colonized cultures, so the colonized cultures were assimilating useful bits from us.

Just as there is not one universal cinema, or photography, or literature, so there is not one universal computing. The question should not be what the future of computing in archaeology will be, but what archaeologies may choose to do with computers in the future? Far more interesting questions may be asked such as: What can we show, and learn, from a computer reconstruction that we cannot from a model?; What opportunities for archaeological writing arise when we can move records, descriptions, notes and other 'data' exclusively onto interactive databases?; What happens to our use of objects when they move from the collection to diverse representations on a computer?; and, most importantly, What can't we do with computers?

I have said before that this is not a Luddite text. I used a word-processor to write it and many of the references are intentionally from on-line sources. I use computers daily in my work and will continue to do so. My problem has been with the idea that there is this *thing* called Archaeological Computing that has some identifiable future, as though the prophetic identity is attached and determined by the instrument. Of course there are *things* called computers — and many associated things called applications, networks, digital images, etc. — and they will continue to be used in archaeology as elsewhere. These things will also have a *future* in that they will change in form and purpose. But the question of the futures addressed here is

---

[17] This of course precludes the most effective colonial tactic for destroying a colonized culture, genocide.

a matter of changing practice. We can easily imagine a future for archaeology where there is no computer use at all. We can equally imagine a future for archaeology where the only instrument used is the computer. The choice between these extreme, and all intervening, futures is up to us, not a capitalist mythology about a single instrumental domination.

References

ANONYMOUS 1883: *The Daily News* 7 December 1883 and *Punch* December 1883 (cited in Stokes 1972, 44).

BAKHTIN, M. 1984: *Problems of Dostoevsky's Poetics* (edited and translated by C. Emerson) (Minneapolis).

BANN, S. 1995: *Romanticism and the Rise of History* (New York).

BAUDRILLARD, J. 1988: *The Ecstasy of Communication* (translated by B. and C. Schutze; edited by S. Lotringer) (New York).

BOAST, R. 1997: Virtual Collections. In Denford, G. (ed.), Representing Archaeology in Museums. *Museum Archaeologist* 22, 94–100.

BOOTH, M. 1981: *Victorian Spectacular Theatre: 1850–1910* (London).

BURRIDGE, J., COLLINS, B.M., GALTIN, B.N., HALBERT, A.R. and HEYWOOD, T.R. 1989: The WINSOM solid modeller and its application to data visualization. *IBM Systems J.* 28(4), 548–78.

BUSH, V. 1945: As We May Think. *Atlantic Monthly* 176 (July), 101–8.

CESSFORD, C. n.d.:
http://catal.arch.cam.ac.uk/catal/database/scripts/diary/diary98.idc?

CHENHALL, R. 1968: The Impact of Computers on Archaeological Theory: an Appraisal and Projection. *Computers and the Humanities* 3(1), 15–24.

COLE, J.W. 1859: *The Life and Theatrical Times of Charles Kean Vol. II* (2nd edition), 58–9 (cited in Booth 1981, 57–9).

DERRIDA, J. 1967: *De la Grammatologie* (Paris).

DERRIDA, J. 1976: *Of Grammatology* (translated by G. Chakravorty Spivak) (Baltimore).

DERRIDA, J. 1981: *Dissemination* (translated, with an introduction and additional notes, by B. Johnson) (London).

EITELJORG, H. 1988: *Computing Assisted Drafting and Design: new technologies for old problems* (Bryn Mawr, Centre for the Study of Architecture).

ELSNER, J. 1994: A Collector's Model of Desire: The House and Museum of Sir John Soane. In Elsner, J. and Cardinal, R. (eds.), *The cultures of collecting* (London).

FORSTER, E.M. 1928: *The eternal moment, and other stories* (London).

FORTE, M. 1997: Introduction. In Forte, M. and Siliotti, A. (eds.) 1997, 9–13.

FORTE, M. and SILIOTTI, A. (eds.) 1997: *Virtual archaeology: great discoveries brought to life through virtual reality* (London).

FOUCAULT, M. 1977: What is an Author? In *Language, Counter-Memory, Practice: Selected Essays and Interviews* (translated by D.F. Bouchard and S. Simon) (Ithaca, N.Y.), 113–38.

GERE, C. forthcoming: The personal computer as an allegory of the information age. In Boast, R. and Gere, C. (eds.), *Allegories of the Information Age*.

GODWIN, W. 1864: *Western Daily Press* 11 October (cited in Stokes 1972, 37).

GODWIN, W. 1883: *The British Architect* 14 December (cited in Stokes 1972, 43).

GODWIN, W. 1885: Archaeology on Stage. *The Dramatic Review* 24 October.

GRISCOM, A. n.d.: *Trends in Anarchy and Hierarchy: Comparing the Cultural Repercussions of Print and Digital Media.*
http://landow.stg.brown.edu/cpace/infotech/asg/contents.html

HAMILTON, N. n.d.:
http://catal.arch.cam.ac.uk/catal/database/scripts/diary/diary98.idc?

HARRIS, T. 1987: *London crowds in the reign of Charles II: propaganda and politics from the restoration until the exclusion crisis* (Cambridge).

HEIM, M. 1987: *Electric Language: A Philosophical Study of Word Processing* (New Haven) (quoted in W. Mitchell, *City of Bits.* http://mitpress.mit.edu/e-books/City_of_Bits/Pulling_Glass/index.html).

HODDER, I. 1996: *TAG 1996 — Intro Talk: Globalising Catal: towards postprocessual methodology.* Notes on-line at:
http://catal.arch.cam.ac.uk/catal/TAG_papers/ian.htm

HODDER, I. 1997: 'Always momentary, fluid and flexible': towards a reflexive excavation methodology. *Antiquity* 71, 691–700.

HUGGETT, J. 1995: Democracy, data and archaeological knowledge. In Huggett, J. and Ryan, N. (eds.), *Computer Applications and Quantitative Methods in Archaeology, 1994* (Oxford, BAR Int. Ser. 600), 23–6.

HUSSEY, A. 1999: The self-concealing situation. *Times Literary Supplement* 27 August, 29.

JOHNS, A. 1998: *The Nature of the Book* (Chicago).

LANDOW, G. n.d.: http://landow.stg.brown.edu/ht/memex.html

MILL, J.S. 1871: *Utilitarianism* (4th edition, London).

MILLER, P. and RICHARDS, J. 1995: The Good, the Bad, and the Downright Misleading: Archaeological Adoption of Computer Visualization. In Huggett, J. and Ryan, N. (eds.), *Computer Applications and Quantitative Methods in Archaeology, 1994* (Oxford, BAR Int. Ser. 600), 19–22.

MINSKY, M. 1967: *Computation: finite and infinite machines* (New Jersey).

MITCHELL, T. 1988: *Colonizing Egypt* (Berkeley, California).

MITCHELL, W.J. n.d.: *City of Bits.*
http://mitpress.mit.edu/e-books/City_of_Bits/Pulling_Glass/index.html

NEWELL, A. and SIMON, H.A. 1972: *Human problem solving* (New Jersey).

REILLY, P. 1992: Three-dimensional modelling and primary archaeological data. In Reilly, P. (ed.), *Archaeology and the Information Age: A global perspective* (London), 147–73.

RENFREW, A.C. 1997: Foreword. In Forte, M. and Siliotti, A. (eds.) 1997, 7.

SEN, A. and WILLIAMS, B. (eds.) 1982: *Utilitarianism and beyond* (Cambridge).

SHAPIN, S. 1996: *The Scientific Revolution* (Chicago).

SIEBERT, F. 1952: *Freedom of the Press in England, 1476–1776* (Urbana).

STOKES, J. 1972: *Resistible Theatres: Enterprise and Experiment in the Late Nineteenth Century* (London).

TRAN, M. 1998: Couch-potato Americans emerge as culture vultures. *The Guardian* Friday, 18 September.

WELLS, H.G. 1895: *The time machine* (London).

WELLS, H.G. 1927a: *The Island of Doctor Moreau* (Essex edition, vol. 14) (London).

WELLS, H.G. 1927b: *The war of the worlds* (Essex edition, vol. 13) (London).

WELLS, H.G. 1936: *World Encyclopaedia* (lecture given at the Royal Institution of Great Britain, 20 November).

WELLS, H.G. 1938: *World Brain* (London).

WOOD, J. and CHAPMAN, G. 1992: Three-dimensional computer visualization of historic buildings — with particular reference to reconstruction modelling. In Reilly, P. and Rahtz, S.P.Q. (eds.), *Archaeology and the Information Age: a global perspective* (London), 123–46.

Abstracts

ROBERT FOLEY

Parallel tracks in time: Human evolution and archaeology

Although much of the early work on human evolution took place in the context of archaeological discoveries, the two disciplines have diverged over the course of the twentieth century, especially as archaeologists have turned to non-evolutionary models and theories. However, the growth of evolutionary genetics and evolutionary approaches to behaviour have led to a resurgence of common interests. This paper explores a number of issues where both archaeology and biological anthropology can contribute to an understanding of human prehistory, namely 1) the patterns of hominid evolution over the last five million years; 2) the adaptive approach, and the question of how the evolution of behaviour is rooted in biology; 3) the relationship between phylogeny and technological change; 4) the evolution of modern humans; and 5) the evidence for the evolution of cognition and behaviour that can be approached from beyond the ethnographic record and archaeological inference. Evolutionary theory is a growing and dynamic field, and it is likely to have an effect on archaeological thought beyond the study of the remote past.

COLIN RENFREW

Genetics and language in contemporary archaeology

The techniques of genetics, and especially DNA studies, applied to living human populations as well as to ancient human remains, are proving so informative that it has been possible to define a new research field: *archaeogenetics*, the study of the human past using the techniques of molecular genetics. The study of mitochondrial DNA (passed on in the female line) and of the non-recombining portion of the Y chromosome (passed on down the male line) in particular are making impressive contributions to human population history, confirming the Out-of-Africa origins of our species, and throwing new light on the first peopling of Europe and other continents.

Systematic attempts are also currently being made to relate the findings of historical linguistics to those of archaeology, with the hope of reconstructing the histories of language families and of casting light upon the origins of world linguistic diversity. There are however methodological problems in equating the findings of the two disciplines. They are not yet resolved when data from molecular genetics are brought to bear, but the pace of research is rapid and there are hopes that a new synthesis is beginning to emerge.

IAN HODDER

Archaeological theory

This paper begins with a recognition of the current diversity of archaeological theory. It tries to classify this diversity in a number of ways (e.g. analytic, hermeneutic and critical; or in terms of level such as low, middle range and high level). The paper then describes the main historical developments of archaeological theory in the twentieth century, paying special attention to the conditions of production of archaeological knowledge. The account includes non-Western traditions of archaeological theoretical scholarship. The widening and diversification of debate in archaeology is linked to post-colonialism and to the globalization of economies, societies, and information systems at the end of the twentieth century. A shift from 'pure theory' to 'ethical practices' is identified.

WILLIAM W. FITZHUGH

Yamal to Greenland: Global connections in circumpolar archaeology

Once thought to be a region of low cultural achievement and homogeneity, recent archaeological discoveries are revealing the circumpolar region as a region of surprising complexity and diversity. Early circumpolar theorists saw the circumpolar region as a single culture area dominated by the spread of Eskimo-like cultures derived from Upper Palaeolithic peoples in north-western Eurasia. New research is revealing the history of arctic and subarctic peoples unfolding as a response to local adaptation and innovation, circumpolar migration and diffusion, and interactions with southern cultures. This presentation highlights themes and new discoveries in the prehistory of northern peoples spanning the region from Western Siberia to Greenland, during the past 15,000 years.

GEORGE L. COWGILL, MICHELLE HEGMON AND GEORGE R. MILNER

North America and Mesoamerica

Problems of data accessibility and comparability are pervasive in all parts of North America and Mesoamerica and better databases and knowledge repositories, aided by new electronic technology, are needed everywhere. Basic time-space frameworks are well developed in much of North America; in Mesoamerica they are adequate in some regions but other regions are still nearly unknown. Everywhere, finer time-space resolution is needed in order to deal with issues of process and agency. In North America more extensive survey coverages have given us a better view of human occupation and this work indicates that demographic and political landscapes were more dynamic than previously recognized. Perhaps the biggest challenge now is harnessing a wealth of new information to increasingly sophisticated theoretical questions. Issues include relations between religion/ritual and power/leadership, the nature and impact of violence and warfare, and better concepts relating agency and structure.

GUSTAVO G. POLITIS

South America: In the Garden of Forking Paths

The archaeology of South America is rich and diverse. Its theoretical foundations have varied origins while its praxis has strong regional variations. As a result, the archaeological output and the social use to which this knowledge is put show great disparities within the region. Some subjects of perennial interest will be discussed in this chapter: the early peopling of the sub-continent; the adaptation of humans to the Amazon rainforest; and the emergence of complex societies and the production of food in the Andes. It also summarizes the status of the development of sub-disciplines of archaeology which have had a significant impact in the region, among which taphonomy and ethnoarchaeology are pre-eminent. Moreover it will also explore some recent methods of the discipline which expand its range of interests and applications to include forensic anthropology and also historical archaeology, focusing on Afro-American groups. Finally the possible future directions are discussed with regard to the potential of local archaeologists to develop distinct ways of approaching the past.

RHYS JONES AND MATTHEW SPRIGGS

Theatrum Oceani: Themes and arguments concerning the prehistory of Australia and the Pacific

Archaeology is a very young discipline in the Pacific region. We are still much concerned with the 'when' of prehistory and still working out the implications of this for the 'why' which justifies its study. It is thus the 'when' we stress here in an overview of the settlement of the region, and the difficulties involved in establishing acceptable chronologies. There are difficulties of techniques of dating beyond the 'radiocarbon barrier' of about 40,000 years and difficulties of interpretation of stratigraphy at major sites in Southeast Asia and Near Oceania. At the other end of the chronological and geographical spectrum in East Polynesia, with a less than 2000 year prehistoric archaeological record, the problems are those of the interpretation of the radiocarbon dates themselves. Problems of old wood, natural or cultural burning and proper calibration of marine shell samples loom large in sometimes spirited discussion.

K. PADDAYYA AND PETER BELLWOOD

South and Southeast Asia

This chapter has two separate sections. Firstly, the archaeology of South Asia is discussed from both descriptive and interpretative perspectives by one of India's leading archaeologists. This is an account from 'within' the South Asian archaeological tradition, written by an author who is highly aware of the aspirations of his peers at the turn of the twenty-first century. The archaeology of Southeast Asia is not so amenable to such an approach, being divided into a much greater number of national traditions. This region is therefore described in the second part of the chapter from an 'outside' perspective, with a focus more on outstanding issues of cultural history than on issues of interpretative theory. Archaeology in the twenty-first century will doubtless have room for both approaches, indeed it will probably demand that both go hand-in-hand if wisdom and the search for truth are not to be overwhelmed by political expediency.

Both regions share many significant elements of history, especially from Neolithic times onwards into the Classical Period of Hindu and Buddhist tradition. They also share archaeological traditions which are today being internalized from colonial period foundations. Both have similar problems with protection of their heritage in an increasingly commercialized world. Most importantly perhaps, both regions have a lively new generation of indigenous archaeologists who will carry the search for our common heritage into the new century with vigour.

C.F.W. HIGHAM

Eurasia east of the Urals

Eurasia to the east of the Urals incorporates arid deserts and sub-tropical rainforests, arctic tundra and coastal mangroves. It witnessed the spread of *Homo erectus* and anatomically modern humans, the domestication of millet and rice, the widespread adoption of bronze and iron, and the development of the world's most durable civilization. Until very recently, this vast area has been excluded from the vital fertilization of ideas and approaches, which comes with cooperation between scholars from different backgrounds. We are now, however, entering a new and dynamic period, in which east meets west in cooperative research. So the expansion of people who spoke Indo-European languages east along what was to become the Silk Route is under intense scrutiny. The past decade has seen the Yangzi Valley join the Chinese nuclear area as one seminal in the development of agriculture and civilization. Yet the overall impression remains that we are still only in the exploratory stage of understanding the human past there: much remains to be discovered.

A.F. HARDING

Western Eurasia

Archaeology in Western Eurasia (essentially Europe) has changed dramatically in recent years, as contextual, phenomenological and ideological approaches have tended to replace the positivist ones of previous decades, and fieldwork is concentrated in the hands of contract workers rather than academic researchers. This has greatly influenced the types of activity that archaeologists engage in. Specific debates that now occupy the attention of scholars include ethnogenesis (particularly the identity of specific 'peoples' such as the Celts, and the origin and arrival date of Indo-European speakers in Europe), the question of personal or group identity in archaeological sources, the organization of ancient societies (particularly the relevance of the chiefdom model), and the relevance of 'World Systems Theory' or core-periphery interactions. The task for archaeology in the coming decades is to widen the debate about the past in terms of approachability without lessening the rigour with which it proceeds.

NICHOLAS POSTGATE

The first civilizations in the Middle East

The future of archaeology in the Tigris and Euphrates and Nile valleys will always be dictated by conditions in the modern Middle East. The increasing costs of responsible fieldwork will combine with the insistent demand posed by economic development to shift the balance of excavation and survey to rescue archaeology initiated by the host countries. The challenge will be to find research enterprises which address the legitimate expectations of the host countries at the same time as the current research agenda.

Other kinds of collaborative venture are much needed. The ancient Near East especially requires better information flow between the philologists who control the documentary sources and the archaeologists. Both need to reach out to the less specialist audience if they are to hold at bay the forces of sensationalism and trivialization. As for advances in the application of science to archaeology, we need a change of ethos, whereby these early urban societies are seen as the preferred forum for experimentation, rather than being at the back of the queue for the application of techniques.

ANNA MARIA BIETTI SESTIERI, ALBERTO CAZZELLA AND ALAIN SCHNAPP

The Mediterranean

Recent trends in Mediterranean archaeology are marked by the transition from the *ex Oriente lux* paradigm, wherein any development in the central and western regions was seen as a result of an oriental or Greek influence, to the adoption of a broadly anthropological perspective, with a distinct shift in focus toward local contexts and processes.

For the Neolithic and the Copper Age, Alberto Cazzella outlines the complex interplay between long-term selective approaches and influences from the east in crucial fields (agriculture, metallurgy and the emergence of social complexity) and regional developments throughout the Mediterranean. These developments differ widely in relation to both the specific cultural features and the relative speed of evolutionary trends.

For the Bronze and Early Iron Ages, Anna Maria Bietti Sestieri focuses on the strategic role of the major islands in the intensified Mediterranean interaction which characterizes this period. Mycenaean integration in the Sicilian culture and communities was the basic requirement for the establishment of systematic trade between the Aegean and the central Mediterranean in the fifteenth to thirteenth century BC; in the subsequent period Phoenician voyages, which included the northern coast of Africa and Iberia, depended on an equally strong connection with Sardinia and western Sicily.

For the historical period (Orientalizing to the Roman age), Alain Schnapp underlines the dramatic change which classical archaeology has undergone in the last few decades. Due to the growing role of anthropology, history and contextual studies, the academic pre-eminence of this discipline, as well as its own self-perception, have been greatly influenced by a more balanced consideration of Greece and Rome among the contemporary peoples and cultures. Moreover, the widespread adoption of modern field techniques and methods is changing our perception and knowledge of rural and urban life in the classical world, and even the classicist Altertumswissenschaft is now the subject of a fresh, more secular approach.

MARTIN HALL

Timeless time: Africa and the world

This chapter explores ideas about Africa, a continent which has been an object of exploration since the earliest years of colonial settlement. Early ideas stressed the timeless nature of this continent 'without history'. Africa could be a place of darkness or a spur to romantic fantasy, but its people were depicted as frozen in an endless present. Such concepts shaped archaeology in the discipline's early years, and continue to have an influence today. Following independence in the mid twentieth century, many countries developed a distinctly African approach to reading the evidence of material culture (although the apartheid south continued to cling to European ideas about history). Very often, though, these historiographies have been starved through lack of resources. As we enter the third millennium, archaeology in Africa faces many challenges. The ways in which these challenges are addressed will determine the future of the discipline in this part of the world.

MARTIN CARVER

Marriages of true minds: Archaeology with texts

Is archaeology-with-texts different from other kinds of archaeology? Since material culture and text are both types of human expression, their analysis and interpretation have much in common, and the differences between text and material culture as media are less significant than the differences in expression found in each. The study of literate societies, in which both media are manifest, is especially rewarding due to the context that each gives the other. But examples of recent work (mainly from medieval Europe) suggest that there is no useful theoretical or methodological framework, or a unifying agenda, for a historical archaeology and there probably should not be. It seems more useful to risk being 'particularist' and 'relativist', and design each inquiry in terms of the kind of question being asked and the kinds of evidence available, using theories of interpretation liberally and eclectically. In the next millennium, multi-disciplinary study-groups should also become more flexible and less institutional, adapting the modular system to research as well as teaching. As to our output, it should develop interactive electronics for the airing and sharing of data and theory, reserving publication for imaginative, graphical and poetical versions of the past.

WILLIAM L. RATHJE, VINCENT M. LAMOTTA AND WILLIAM A. LONGACRE

Into the *black hole*: Archaeology 2001 and beyond . . .

Relatively little archaeological research has been devoted to the study of material, behavioural, and cognitive realities in modern, living communities and their recent antecedents. In essence, the material record of the past 50–100 years is an archaeological *black hole*. Ethnoarchaeologists, experimental archaeologists, and historical archaeologists have begun to explore this *black hole* — but mainly to apply the knowledge gained to understanding the more distant past. In this paper, we provide examples of how archaeological techniques, methods, and theories can be applied to understanding the present as well as the past. Archaeological studies of the present and recent past will become increasingly important in issues with global significance. We argue that through *integrated* (material-behavioural-cognitive), *synthetic* (linking past and present), and *applied* (using archaeological techniques to understand the present) approaches, archaeology can make a significant impact on the modern world.

NICK MERRIMAN

Archaeology, heritage and interpretation

A combination of theoretical and pragmatic factors have led in recent years to a greater 'opening up' of archaeology to the public. Popular interest in archaeology is extremely high, and the recognition that archaeology is just as much about the contestation of meaning in the present as about the pursuit of disinterested knowledge of the past has made archaeology the site of lively debate. Recent work on interpretation in museums and sites suggests that members of the public continually reinterpret the materials provided to them in ways that are personally meaningful. It is suggested as a consequence that the 'constructivist' learning theory will provide a fruitful framework for the conceptualization of archaeological presentations, with its stress on active engagement, relevance to the individual, and the personal construction of knowledge. Examples are given of recent initiatives in this vein, and challenges for the future arising from them are offered.

ROBIN BOAST

Computing futures: Visions of the past

Computers have become pervasive in archaeology — they dominate almost all aspects of archaeological work from writing to calculation, from measurement to presentation, from project management to complex visualization. With a multitude of prophetic claims, computers are even beginning to infest the theoretical. Computers, or more precisely visualization and the Internet, are being appropriated by both the archaeological Right and the archaeological Left as a pre-eminent revelatory medium. For both sides, it is legitimate because it is dominant. But this idea of mechanical revelation has a long history, both in Modernism and in archaeology. This paper explores the range of claims about computing in archaeology and situates those within their progenitors as a way of predicting the future. By comparing claims about the usefulness, applicability or value of computing with similar claims made for other information technologies in the late nineteenth and early twentieth centuries, the question 'What is the future of archaeological computing?' becomes too limited, and we end by asking 'Is there any non-trivial future for archaeological computing?'

Index

Illustrations are denoted by page numbers in *italics*.

Chengtoushan (China), 354, 355
Chengzi (China), 347
Cherokee, 477
Chertov Ovrag (Siberia), 109
Chichén Itzá (Mexico), 149, 156
chiefdoms
    Americas
        Amazonia, 215–16
        Andes, 218–19
        Mesoamerica, 151, 157
        North American Eastern Woodlands, 175–8
        US Southwest, 158
    Europe, 372–5, 378–9, 411, 418, 422
    South Asia, 302
Childe, V.G., 64, 196, 372, 399
Chile
    archaeological theory, 195, 197, 198
    forensic anthropology, 227
    see also Andes; Easter Island; Monte Verde;
        Patagonia
chimpanzees, 6–7, 8, 16, 61
China
    agriculture, 323, 328, 337–43, 346–7, 353, 358
    bronze technology, 336, 337, 352–5, 356, 357–8
    civilization, 322, 336, 352–8
    environment, 337
    Homo erectus, 14
    languages, 328
    trade, 330
Chopani Mando (India), 301
Choris culture, 118, 124
chronologies
    Americas
        Mesoamerica, 149
        North American Eastern Woodlands, 171–3
        US Southwest, 160, 161–6
    Australia, 247, 255–62, 263–6
    DNA chronology, 53
    human evolution, 5–18
    Pacific region, 247, 270–3
Chuck Lake (Canada), 114
Chukchi, 93, 111, 118, 121, 122
    reindeer camp, 119
Chukotka (Siberia), 94, 111, 118, 121
circumpolar archaeology
    archaeological record, 132–4
        Beringia, 111–13
        Canada and Labrador, 122–9
        coastal migration hypothesis, 113–16
        eskimo origins, 116–18
        Neolithic revolution, 118–22
        site preservation, 104
        Viking settlement, 129–32
        Wrangel Island, 108–11
        Zhokhov, 104, 105, 106–8
    arctic stereotypes, 92–5
    circumpolar theory, 98–103
    geography and environment, 95–8
Cishan (China), 342
city-states, Mediterranean, 372, 373, 411, 421

civilization
    China, 336, 352–8
    Europe, 372, 376, 411
    Middle East, 385–409
    South Asia, 301, 302
    Southeast Asia, 330
    see also states
cladistics, 25, 26–30, 38
Clark, Desmond, 448
Clark, Grahame, 25–7
Clarke, David, 82
classical archaeology
    a future for, 429–33
    texts, 479
    theory, 411, 412, 413
Claudian, 584–5
climatic change
    China, 338–42
    circumpolar region, 93, 116, 124–7, 128–9, 132
    human evolution, role in, 15, 33, 34
Cloggs Cave (Australia), 267
clothing
    circumpolar region, 91, 94, 102
    Europe, 371
    Tarim Basin, 350, 351
    see also dress length study
Clovis culture, 58, 112–13, 147, 199–200, 208
Co Loa (Vietnam), 330
cognitive-processual archaeology, 84
Cohenim, 59–60
Coletière (France), 482–3
Colima (Mexico), 157
Collins, Henry, 116, 118
Colombia
    ethnoarchaeology, 211, 212, 213–14
    forensic anthropology, 227
    pre-Clovis site, 200
    Sierras del Tairona, chiefdoms, 218
colonial archaeology
    Africa, 440–8
    Middle East, 388–9, 444
    South Asia, 297–9, 309–10
    theory, 82, 85
colonialism, archaeology of, 228, 231
colonization, human
    Americas, 33, 34, 92, 147
        Beringia, 111–16
        genetic studies, 57–9
        South America, 198–209, 231
    Australia, 32, 33, 34, 263–6
    Eurasia, east, 32, 33, 34
    Europe
        fossil record, 14, 26–7, 29, 31, 32–4, 36
        genetic study, 53–6
    Pacific region, 32, 56–7, 270–3, 280
    South Asia, 32, 33
    Southeast Asia, 33, 34, 321, 326
    see also migration theories; seafaring
Columba, St, 465
communism, 528

migration theories (*cont.*)
circumpolar region, 113–16
Eurasia, east, 343
Europe, 67–8, 366, 368
Southeast Asia/Pacific region, 56–7, 67, 281, 322, 327–8, 331
see also colonization; seafaring
Milena (Sicily), 427
Miletus (Turkey), 390
military sites
circumpolar region, 118, 133
New Zealand, 272
North America, 509–10
South America, 228
millet, domestic
China, 342, 346, 351, 352, 357, 358
Japan, 345
Korea, 345
Mimbres (USA), 161, 162, 163, 164
pottery, *163*
Mindanao (Philippines), 254
mining
Africa, 445, 446
Eurasia, east, 350
Mediterranean, 417, 425
Minoan culture, 424
Miocene, 6, 7
Mississippian societies, 174, 175–8
Mitchell, W., 571–3
Mitza Purdia (Sardinia), 424
Mixe, 58
Mixtecs, 58
modern material culture studies, 516–28
Mogollon area (USA), 158, *159*, 161, 162
Mojokerto (Java), 252
molecular biology, 6–7
molecular genetics *see* genetic studies
Moluccas (Indonesia), *319*, 320, 321, 326, 327, 330
Mommsen, Theodor, 411
Mon, 322, 328
Mongolia, 353
monoliths, contemporary, 526
Montaillou (France), 468
Monte Albán (Mexico), 149, 155
Monte Alegre (Pedra Pintada) (Brazil), 200, 207–8, 215
Monte d'Accoddi (Sardinia), 418
Monte Grande (Sicily), 422
Monte Verde (Chile), 147, 171, 200, *202*, 203–4
Montenegro, 418
Montoro (Spain), 424
Morgan, Lewis Henry, 372, 502
Mormon society, 520
Moseley, C.W.R.D., 442–3
Moundville (USA), 175, 177
Mount Carmel (Israel), 29
Mousterian debate, 24, 25
Mozambique, 444, 450, 458, 461
Muller, Professor, 446

mummies
Egypt, 60, 400
Eurasia, east, 351
South America, 230
Murray Springs (USA), 199
museums
ideology, 461, 542, 547
increase in numbers, 85–6, 545, 546
interpretation, 547–50, 553–6, 559–60
museum studies, 546
repatriation of artefacts, 544
by region
Africa, 449, 450–1, 458, 459, 460, 461
Europe
African collections, 444; display, 19th century, 582; Middle East collections, 388, 393
Middle East, 390, *391*, 393
South Asia, 311, 312
mushroom people, *110*, 111
Mushroom Rock (Australia), 263
Musonda, Francis, 457
Mycenaean culture, 368, 421–2, 424–5, 429
Mytum, Harold, 479

Na-Dene languages, 57, 58, 68
Nagarjunakonda (India), 302, 310
Nahuatl, 156
Nairobi (Kenya), 447
Nambikwara, 469
Namibia, 444
Namu (Canada), 114
Nanchoc Valley (Peru), 220
Napoleon, 388, 440, 444
Nariokotome (Kenya), 20, 22
nationalism, archaeological, 81
Africa, 449–51, 459, 460
Middle East, 386–7
Native American Graves Protection and Repatriation Act, 146, 160, 544
Nauwalabila (Australia), 258
Navajo, 57, 519
Navdatoli (India), 305
Nayarit (Mexico), 157
Nechtan, King, 465, 466
Negau (Austria), 368
Negrito, 327
Negritude movement, 449–50
Nenana culture, 112
Nenet, 120, 121
Neoeskimo cultures, 123, 126
Neolithic period
circumpolar region, 118–22, 123, 133
Eurasia, east, 337–43, 346–7
Europe, 53–5, 69–70, 368–9, 374, 376
Mediterranean, 414–17
Mesoamerica, 150–1
Pacific region, 270–1, 276–82
South Asia, *301*, 302, 305, 307, 308